The Thomas Cook Guide to

GREEK ISLAND HOPPING

1995

Written and researched by
Frewin Poffley

With additional field research by
Andy Dunham

Thomas
Cook

Published by Thomas Cook Publishing
The Thomas Cook Group Ltd
PO Box 36, Thorpe Wood, Peterborough PE3 6SB, United Kingdom

Text & Artwork
© 1995 Frewin Poffley

ISBN   0 906273 59 5

Published annually
ISSN   0968-8226

Whilst every care has been taken in compiling this
publication using the most up-to-date information
available at the time of going to press, neither the author
nor the Thomas Cook Group Limited as publishers can
accept any liability arising from errors or omissions in the
text or maps, however caused. Readers should note
especially that timings and fares of many Mediterranean
ferry services are fixed only shortly before the beginning
of the season and are often subject to change without
notice. It is therefore strongly advised that all such
information should be checked before beginning any
journey on one of the services listed in this publication.
The views and opinions expressed in this book are not
necessarily those of the Thomas Cook Group Ltd.

Typesetting processed by Riverhead Typesetters Limited, Grimsby

Printed and bound in Great Britain by Bell & Bain Ltd, Glasgow

Drawn   & typeset by Frewin Poffley/Thingumajigolo Productions

Contents

1

Overview
& Itinerary

The initial — 'Where can I go to?' — section of each chapter is
intended to give you a clear idea of the geographical area covered
by the chapter and the best means of tackling the islands and ports
within it. On the title page itself you will find a map showing the
main ferry route linking the islands, along with approximate
sailing times between them and the island name in Greek (in the
form — usually accusative — that you are most likely to encounter
it on ship destination boards and timetables). This is followed by
a brief description of the characteristics of the group, a map of the
area covered, and a model itinerary showing a practical way of
tackling the islands in the chain. The itinerary also identifies the
best 'base' port in the group should you wish to use one island as
a springboard to viewing the rest.

2

Ferry
Services

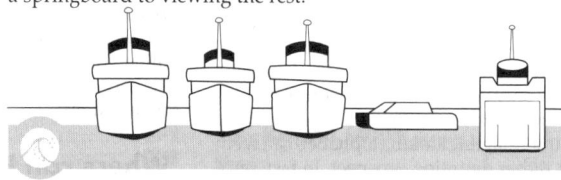

The second — 'How can I get there?' — section is devoted to the
ferries that link the islands within each group. (Where a ferry
covers the geographical area of several chapters it is described in
the chapter in which it plays the most important role.) Each boat's
previous High Season route is mapped along with comments on
its history, reliability and likely changes in 1995. This will give
you the means to interpret local advertising and assess the merits
or otherwise of the individual boats. You should find that all
ferries are covered bar the 4 or 5 last-minute arrivals that turn up
out of the blue each year. Usually these boats are not too much of
a problem since they tend to either line up in competition with
an existing service or simply replace it.

3

Islands
& Ports

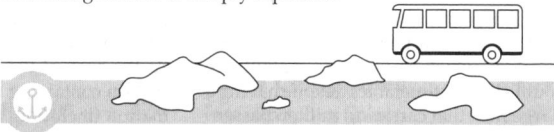

The third — 'What will I find there?' — section consists of a mini
A—Z of the Islands and Ports found within the chapter area. All
islands, mainland ports and the major sights are briefly described.

Build in a 2-day 'delay' into your itinerary

One of the great attractions of Greek island hopping is that every island is different and sooner or later you will be washed up on the shores of the one the Gods made just for you; tempting you to linger for longer than intended. Build this into your calculations before you start. It will also provide you with an extra safety net should thunderous weather or a lightning ferry strike disrupt your plans.

Allow plenty of time to catch your return flight

Always arrange an easily accessible final / return port of call and *allow at least one clear day spare* to ensure that you don't miss your return ferry or flight away from civilisation. If you are starting from a poorly connected airport give yourself two clear days. If you are moving between chains (e.g. starting from the Dodecanese and moving into one the Cycladic Lines) save the visits to islands near your return destination for the end of your holiday so that your final hops are both short and easy.

When you've used this book ...

... help us update

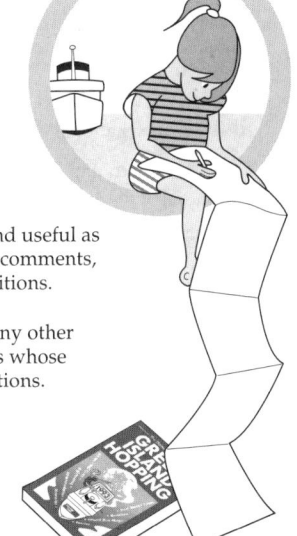

The Thomas Cook Guide to Greek Island Hopping is field researched each year before being updated. Nevertheless, there will always be instances where up-to-date information was not obtainable at the time of research and we welcome reports and comments from users of the Guide.

Similarly, we aim to make the Guide as practical and useful as possible to island hoppers and are grateful for any comments, criticisms and suggestions for improving future editions.

A free copy of the next edition of the Guide, or of any other Thomas Cook publication will be sent to all readers whose information or ideas are incorporated in future editions. Please address all contributions to:

The Editor, Greek Island Hopping,
Thomas Cook Publishing,
PO Box 227,
Peterborough, PE3 8BQ.
United Kingdom.

Symbols, Maps & Tables

Symbols

	Car Ferry		Accommodation
	Landing-craft Car Ferry		Hotel / Pension (category unknown)
	Passenger Ferry	**A**	A-class Hotel / Pension
	Taxi Boat	**B**	B-class Hotel / Pension
	Catamaran	**C**	C-class Hotel / Pension
	Hydrofoil	**D**	D-class Hotel
	Aircraft	**E**	E-class Hotel
	Helicopter	**P**	Pension (unlisted)
	Train	**Y**	Youth Hostel
	Metro	**R**	Rooms
	Cable-car	**A**	Campsite
	Bus Link		Luggage Deposit
	Train Link		Port Police
	International Link		Post Office
	Island Map = Airport Town Map = Ticket Agent		Town Map = OTE Text = Phone Number
	High Season		Beach
	Low Season		Archaeological Site
	Annual Service		Theatre / Odeon
	Tourist Sight		Church / Monastery
	Port		Rom. Cath. / Anglican
	Island Summit		Mosque
	Volcano		Synagogue

Times

12.00	Midday
24.00	Midnight
00.00	Time Unknown
x	Frequency / times per …
♦	Return Time
◊	Time of last service
ex	Except on the Day/s Stated

①	Monday
②	Tuesday
③	Wednesday
④	Thursday
⑤	Friday
⑥	Saturday
⑦	Sunday
Ⓐ	Alternate Days
Ⓝ	Next Day
Ⓓ	Daily
Ⓦ	Weekly
Ⓗ	Hourly
○	Day Unknown / Irregular
①-②	Duration of Service (Example = 'Monday to Tuesday')

Street Maps

┠┼┼┼┼┼┨	Railway
┨☐┠	Railway Station
─○─	Metro Station
	Street / Path
┉┉┉	Staircase / Muletrack
	Building
	Open Ground
	Park / Woodland
	Beach
	Sports Field / Playground
○	Fountain / Pool

	Cliff / Steep Slope
	Map Cross-Section
	Waterlogged Land
	Riverbed
	City / Castle Wall
	Ruins
	Ruins (roofed over)
	Cemetery
	Windmills

Ferry Route Maps

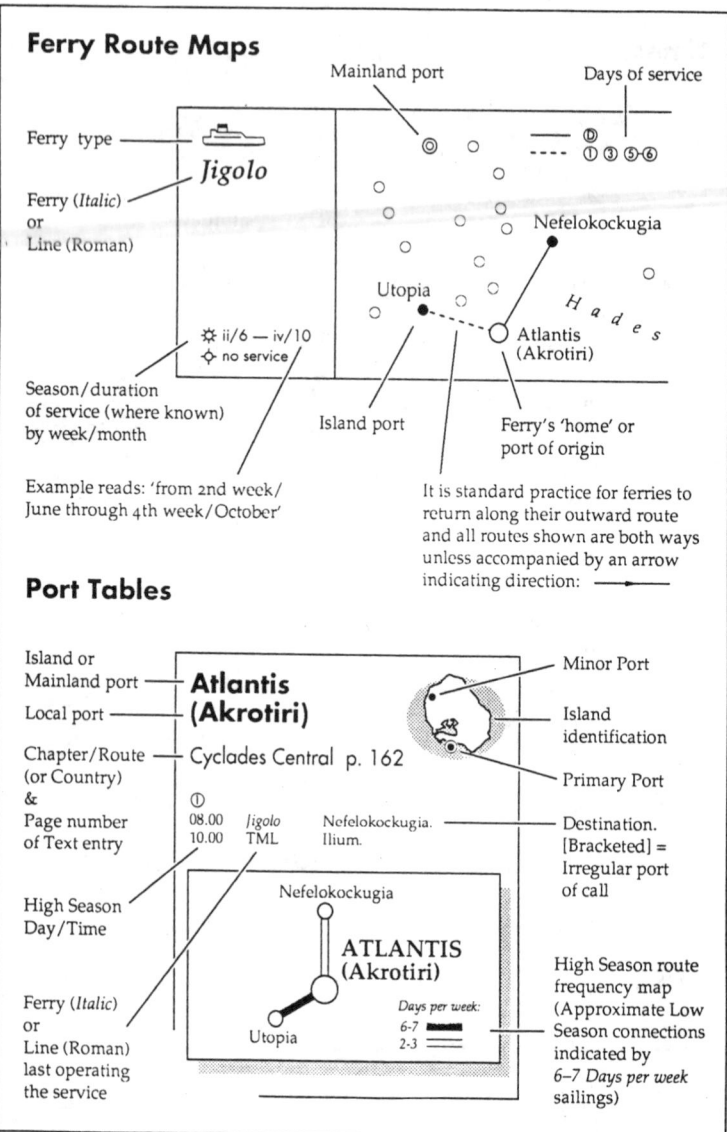

Mainland port

Days of service

Ferry type

Jigolo

Ferry (*Italic*)
or
Line (Roman)

Nefelokockugia

Utopia

$H_a d_e s$

Atlantis
(Akrotiri)

☀ ii/6 — iv/10
◇ no service

Season/duration
of service (where known)
by week/month

Island port

Ferry's 'home' or
port of origin

Example reads: 'from 2nd week/
June through 4th week/October'

It is standard practice for ferries to
return along their outward route
and all routes shown are both ways
unless accompanied by an arrow
indicating direction: ——▶

Port Tables

Island or
Mainland port

Local port

Chapter/Route
(or Country)
&
Page number
of Text entry

High Season
Day/Time

Ferry (*Italic*)
or
Line (Roman)
last operating
the service

Atlantis
(Akrotiri)

Cyclades Central p. 162

①		
08.00	*Jigolo*	Nefelokockugia.
10.00	TML	Ilium.

Nefelokockugia

ATLANTIS
(Akrotiri)

Utopia

Days per week:
6-7 ▬▬▬
2-3 ═══

Minor Port

Island
identification

Primary Port

Destination.
[Bracketed] =
Irregular port
of call

High Season route
frequency map
(Approximate Low
Season connections
indicated by
6–7 Days per week
sailings)

Island Bus & Beach Boat Maps

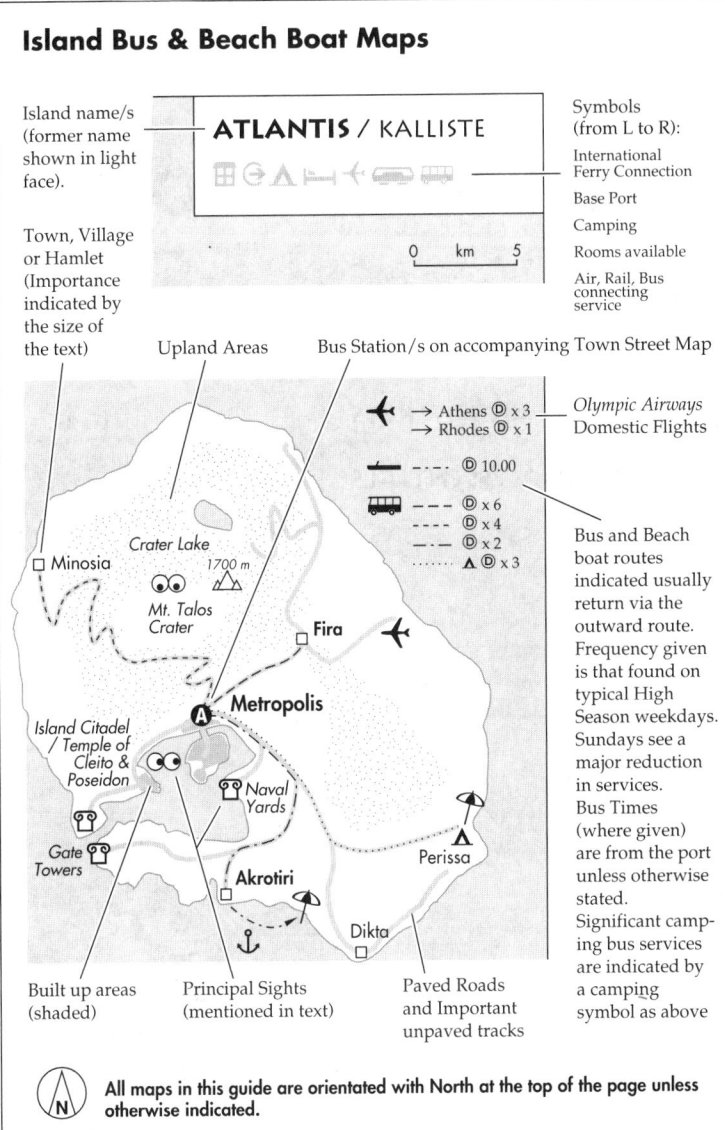

Island name/s (former name shown in light face).

ATLANTIS / KALLISTE

Town, Village or Hamlet (Importance indicated by the size of the text)

0   km   5

Symbols (from L to R):

International Ferry Connection

Base Port

Camping

Rooms available

Air, Rail, Bus connecting service

Upland Areas

Bus Station/s on accompanying Town Street Map

→ Athens Ⓓ x 3
→ Rhodes Ⓓ x 1

Olympic Airways Domestic Flights

Ⓓ 10.00

Ⓓ x 6
Ⓓ x 4
Ⓓ x 2
Δ Ⓓ x 3

□ Minosia

Crater Lake

1700 m

Mt. Talos Crater

□ Fira

Metropolis

Bus and Beach boat routes indicated usually return via the outward route. Frequency given is that found on typical High Season weekdays. Sundays see a major reduction in services. Bus Times (where given) are from the port unless otherwise stated. Significant camping bus services are indicated by a camping symbol as above

Island Citadel / Temple of Cleito & Poseidon

Naval Yards

Gate Towers

Perissa

Akrotiri

Dikta

Built up areas (shaded)

Principal Sights (mentioned in text)

Paved Roads and Important unpaved tracks

All maps in this guide are orientated with North at the top of the page unless otherwise indicated.

INTRODUCTION

- THE GREEK ISLANDS
- FERRIES AND TICKETS
- HOLIDAY ESSENTIALS

SIGHTSEEING ISLES

CYCLADES NORTH	DELOS
CYCLADES CENTRAL	SANTORINI NAXOS ANTIPAROS
CRETE	IRAKLION
DODEC-ANESE	RHODES KOS PATMOS
ARGO-SARONIC	AEGINA
NORTH AEGEAN	THESSALONIKA KAVALA CHIOS SAMOS SAMOTHRACE
EASTERN LINES	CHIOS SAMOS (PITHAGORIO)
IONIAN	CORFU

NIGHTLIFE ISLES

CYCLADES NORTH	MYKONOS
CYCLADES CENTRAL	IOS SANTORINI PAROS
CYCLADES WEST	SIFNOS
NORTH AEGEAN	SKIATHOS THASSOS
IONIAN	CORFU LEFKADA ZAKINTHOS
DODEC-ANESE	KOS RHODES
EASTERN LINES	SAMOS (PITHAGORIO)
ARGO-SARONIC	SPETSES

BEACH ISLANDS

CYCLADES NORTH	MYKONOS ANDROS
CYCLADES CENTRAL	IOS NAXOS PAROS SANTORINI
CYCLADES WEST	SIFNOS
NORTH AEGEAN	SKIATHOS SKOPELOS SKYROS THASSOS LIMNOS
IONIAN	CORFU ZAKINTHOS LEFKADA
DODEC-ANESE	KOS KARPATHOS RHODES LIPSI PATMOS
EASTERN LINES	LESBOS
ARGO-SARONIC	SPETSES KITHERA AEGINA

WINDMILL ISLES

CYCLADES NORTH	MYKONOS
CYCLADES CENTRAL	IOS SANTORINI PAROS ANITPAROS
CYCLADES WEST	SERIFOS
DODEC-ANESE	RHODES
CRETE & EASTERN CYCLADES	ASTIPALEA

QUIET ISLANDS

CYCLADES WEST	FOLEGANDROS SERIFOS SIFNOS
CYCLADES NORTH	KEA ANDROS KYTHNOS
CYCLADES CENTRAL	ANTIPAROS
NORTH AEGEAN	LIMNOS SKYROS SAMOTHRACE ALONISSOS
DODEC-ANESE	NISSIROS TILOS
IONIAN	ITHACA MEGANISI
EASTERN LINES	IKARIA PSARA
ARGO-SARONIC	KITHERA

PICTURESQUE 'CHORA' ISLANDS

CYCLADES NORTH	MYKONOS	NORTH AEGEAN	SKYROS
CYCLADES CENTRAL	IOS SANTORINI PAROS	CYCLADES WEST	SERIFOS SIKINOS FOLEGANDROS
EASTERN LINES	LESBOS	CRETE & EASTERN CYCLADES	ASTIPALEA AMORGOS

IDEAL ISLANDS
FOR MAROONING YOUR PARTNER ON WHEN THEY ARE BEING PARTICULARLY IRRITATING

CYCLADES CENTRAL	ANAFI
NORTH AEGEAN	AGIOS EFSTRATIOS
CRETE & EASTERN CYCLADES	GAVDOS
ARGO-SARONIC	ANTIKITHERA

The Greek Islands

Guidebooks to Greece are apt to intimidate any would-be island-hopper by observing that the country has some 1,425 islands of which 166 are inhabited. In practice, life is much simpler: Greece has 78 islands connected by regular ferry or hydrofoil, with another 40-odd islets

ISLAND GROUPS

CYCLADES

DODECANESE

EASTERN

NORTHERN AEGEAN

IONIAN

SARONIC

CRETE

visited by tour or beach boats (the remaining 48 'inhabited' islands being occupied by odd monks, goat-herds and the occasional shipping billionaire). You can therefore get to some 120 islands by using commercial boats. Of course, apart from the growing number of island hopping fans devoting holidays toward the goal of doing them all, in the eyes of most tourists not all these islands are *worth* a visit; but which you add to, or cross off, your list rather depends on your vision of the ideal Greek island. Herein lies the fascination of the islands, for the mix of history and geography is different on every one. It is almost as if the Olympian Gods had taken turns at trying their hands at different combinations and then laid the results down side by side to compare each in their turn. Any temptation to linger is tempered by curiosity as to what one is likely to find at the next island down the line.

If you are new to island hopping, the first decision that you need to make is which group of islands to visit. They fall into six groups. The most popular are the Cyclades. With 26 ferry-linked small islands this is the chain that naturally comes to mind when thinking of island hopping. Following close on behind are the 17 ferry-linked Dodecanese islands running down the coast of Turkey. The other groups have less mass appeal, but are growing in popularity. The widely scattered Eastern and Northern Aegean islands have much to offer if you have more than a fortnight at your disposal, while the closely bunched Saronic Gulf islands provide a complete contrast as all can be 'done' by day-trippers from Athens. The Ionian islands, distinguished by being the only group to lie outside the Aegean, are poorly connected with the rest of the ferry system but also have many fans.

Primary Islands & Ferry Routes

ALBANIA

Corfu/
Kerkyra

GREECE

Sporades

Skopelos

Skiathos

Chapter

Paxi

Lefkada

Evia

Ithaca

1. **Trans-Med Lines**
   International services.

2. **Adriatic Lines**
   Corfu & Adriatic services.

3. **Athens & Piraeus**
   including *Lavrion* and *Rafina*.

ATHENS
(Piraeus)

Kefalonia

4. **Cyclades Central Line**
   Paros. Naxos. Ios. Santorini. Anafi.

Peloponnese

Aegina

5. **Cyclades North**
   Syros. Mykonos. Delos. Tinos. Andros.

Zante/
Zakinthos

Poros

6. **Cyclades West**
   Kea. Kythnos. Serifos. Sifnos. Milos. Folegandros.

Hydra

Spetses

7. **Crete and the Eastern Cyclades**
   Cretan Ports. *Amorgos. Astipalea.*

8. **Dodecanese Lines**
   Patmos. Leros. Kalimnos. Kos. Nissiros. Symi. Rhodes. Karpathos. Kassos.

9. **Eastern Lines**
   a. Ikaria. Samos (Vathi).   b. Chios. Lesbos (Mytilini).

Kithera

10. **Northern Aegean**
    Limnos. Thassos. Samothrace. Skyros and the Sporades *(Skiathos. Skopelos).*

Antikithera

11. **Argo-Saronic Lines**
    Aegina. Poros. Hydra. Spetses. Peloponnese ports and *Kithera.*

Argo-Saronic

12. **Ionic Islands**
    Kefalonia. Lefkada. Paxi. Zakinthos/Zante.

13. **Turkish Lines**
    Including Greek Island—Turkey links.

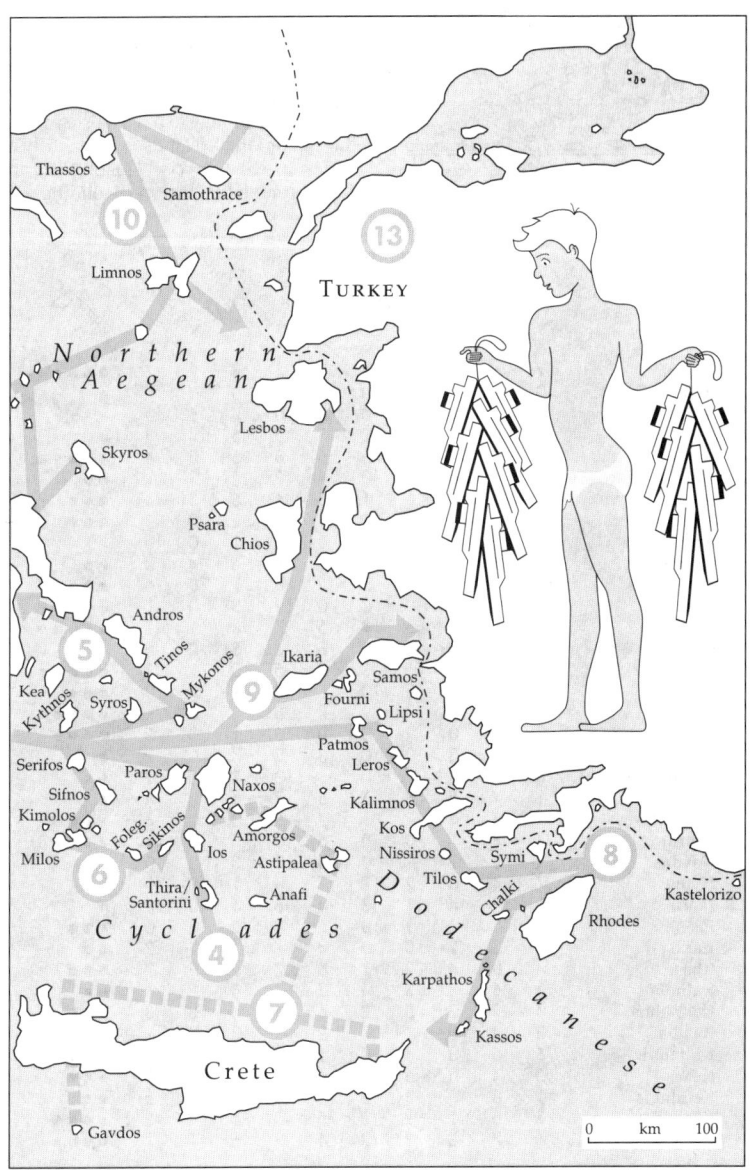

Thassos

Samothrace

10

13

Limnos

TURKEY

Northern Aegean

Lesbos

Skyros

Psara

Chios

Andros

5

Tinos

Mykonos

Ikaria

9

Samos

Kea

Syros

Fourni

Kythnos

Lipsi

Serifos

Patmos

Leros

Sifnos

Paros

Naxos

Kimolos

Kalimnos

Milos

Foleg.

Sikinos

Amorgos

Kos

Ios

6

Astipalea

Nissiros

Symi

8

Thira/
Santorini

Anafi

Tilos

Chalki

Kastelorizo

Cyclades

4

Dodecanese

Rhodes

Karpathos

7

Kassos

Crete

Gavdos

0   km   100

Island Ratings

Having established which island group you want to visit, the next question you need to address is which islands within the group are likely to have most appeal. Rating the Greek islands is necessarily a very subjective exercise. Not only are an island's merits (or otherwise) conditioned

ISLAND RATINGS

	Main Town	Landscape	Tree Cover	Sightseeing	Nightlife	Eating	Peace & Quiet	Beaches	Nudism	Tourism Level	Summary (out of 5)
Aegina	7	4	4	8	7	7	4	4	2	7	●●●●
Agathonisi	0	1	0	0	0	2	10	0	0	1	●
Agios Efstratios	1	3	0	0	0	0	10	4	6	0	
Alonissos	3	6	8	1	2	5	5	5	4	3	●●●●
Amorgos	8	9	3	6	3	6	8	5	5	4	●●●●●●
Anafi	4	4	0	2	0	2	8	5	3	1	●●
Andros	4	6	4	1	1	5	6	6	3	3	●●●
Angistri	2	3	7	0	1	3	4	2	0	5	●●
Antikithera	0	2	3	0	0	0	10	1	0	0	
Antipaxi	2	4	4	0	0	3	6	6	4	3	●●
Antiparos	6	4	2	4	5	5	6	7	10	6	●●●●
Arki	0	2	1	0	0	0	10	3	0	1	
Astipalea	8	5	2	6	4	5	7	4	1	2	●●●●●●
Chalki	7	3	0	1	2	6	6	3	0	5	●●●
Chios	4	7	6	5	3	7	5	3	2	3	●●●
Corfu	6	6	6	8	10	6	2	9	4	10	●●●
Crete	5	10	6	10	9	7	8	8	5	9	●●●●
Delos	0	4	0	9	0	0	6	1	0	5	●●●●
Donoussa	2	5	2	0	0	3	8	4	0	2	●
Elafonissos	6	5	1	0	0	6	10	7	5	2	●●
Evia	1	7	5	3	1	5	7	4	0	4	●
Folegandros	9	5	1	2	1	7	8	3	2	4	●●●●●●
Fourni	4	4	1	0	0	6	10	5	0	1	●●●●
Gavdos	1	5	2	1	0	0	10	3	0	0	●
Hydra	7	4	0	2	7	7	4	1	0	10	●●
Ikaria	2	9	4	1	3	4	6	5	3	3	●
Ios	7	5	1	1	10	2	3	9	8	10	●●●
Iraklia	2	3	2	0	0	4	7	4	1	2	●●
Ithaca	4	8	4	2	1	6	7	2	0	2	●●●
Kalimnos	3	6	3	3	4	5	3	6	2	6	●●
Karpathos	4	9	3	5	2	6	6	6	3	3	●●●
Kassos	2	4	0	1	0	2	9	3	0	1	●
Kastelorizo	6	5	3	4	0	5	9	0	0	2	●●●●
Kea	5	4	3	6	2	6	6	4	1	5	●●●
Kefalonia	1	8	5	3	2	7	6	7	3	5	●●
Kimolos	5	5	1	2	2	5	10	5	2	2	●●●●
Kithera	6	7	3	3	2	6	9	6	1	1	●●●●

by whether your priorities are beaches and nightlife or peace and quiet, but many islands are apt to leave very different impressions at different times of the year. Ios is a classic example of this; quiet and dreamy in the Low Season, it becomes *the* party island in August, thus usually attracting very unfavourable reviews in consequence. Nevertheless, it is possible to give some indication of an island's likely appeal, and the table below should help in this respect. Ratings are given out of ten (*the* place to go if you want this), with '0' representing 'forget it'. Summaries are given out of five. Those islands rating less than one are better avoided.

THE TOP 14	Main Town	Landscape	Tree Cover	Sightseeing	Nightlife	Eating	Peace & Quiet	Beaches	Nudism	Tourism Level	Summary (out of 5)
Kos	6	3	2	8	10	3	1	8	4	10	●●●
Koufonissia	3	4	0	1	1	6	10	6	0	2	●●●
Kythnos	2	3	1	1	0	1	8	4	0	1	●
Lefkada / Lefkas	7	7	4	4	5	4	4	6	2	6	●●●
Leros	5	5	2	1	2	5	6	4	0	3	●●●
Lesbos	5	7	3	4	3	7	6	7	3	3	●●
Limnos	6	6	2	6	3	4	8	7	2	1	●●●●
Lipsi	4	2	1	1	0	5	9	5	3	3	●●
Milos	5	4	2	4	2	6	6	4	1	3	●●●
Mykonos	10	4	0	6	10	8	2	10	10	10	●●●●●
Naxos	7	8	6	6	7	7	5	9	7	6	●●●●
Nissiros	6	9	4	6	1	4	8	2	0	3	●●●
Oinousses	1	2	3	0	0	2	9	4	0	1	●
Paros	6	5	3	4	9	4	2	8	6	10	●●●
Patmos	8	6	1	6	4	5	7	5	2	7	●●●●●
Paxi / Paxos	5	6	5	2	6	5	6	2	0	8	●●●
Poros	4	4	5	2	6	5	3	2	0	8	●
Psara	3	5	0	1	0	4	10	4	0	1	●
Rhodes	8	7	4	10	10	6	1	8	3	10	●●●
Salamina / Salamis	0	2	0	1	0	0	2	0	0	0	
Samos	3	7	7	6	4	5	5	8	2	6	●●●●
Samothrace	4	8	5	4	0	6	9	3	1	2	●●
Santorini / Thira	10	10	0	10	8	5	2	4	1	10	●●●●●
Schinoussa	1	3	1	0	1	5	9	5	0	2	●
Serifos	6	6	1	1	2	5	9	7	2	4	●●●
Sifnos	7	7	3	5	5	7	6	6	0	6	●●●
Sikinos	5	4	2	2	0	3	10	3	0	1	●●●
Skiathos	7	6	8	5	8	6	3	9	10	9	●●●●
Skopelos	7	7	7	3	5	5	3	5	8	6	●●●
Skyros	8	5	5	2	1	4	9	4	3	3	●●●●
Spetses	3	4	6	1	7	4	4	3	0	8	●●
Symi	8	5	1	4	5	6	5	4	1	6	●●●●
Syros	5	1	2	2	3	4	4	3	0	4	●●
Thassos	8	9	8	7	6	7	7	10	7	5	●●●●●
Tilos	4	7	2	3	3	5	9	5	0	2	●●●●
Tinos	6	7	6	5	3	4	4	3	0	8	●●●
Zakinthos / Zante	3	8	7	3	10	5	3	9	3	8	●●●

Historical Background

Scattered like confetti on Homer's 'wine dark' Aegean Sea, the Greek islands lie on one of the crossroads of world culture. Almost every Mediterranean civilization has left some mark, resulting in plenty of sightseeing and adding a fascinating dimension to the ubiquitous sun and sand of an island hopping holiday. Island histories vary, but each has been influenced by the major periods of Greek history:

Early Cycladic
4500—2000 BC

The first evidence of human activity in Greece dates from around 8500 BC. The islands appear to have been quickly populated thereafter. Most being wooded, within sight of each other, and of an ideal size for easy defence by small fishing and agrarian communities they were natural centres of population. The Cyclades in particular flourished during the latter part of this period (3200—2000 BC). Removed from the outside influences of mainland cultures, they developed a distinct and unique sub-culture of their own. Now known mainly through small figurines, this prehistoric Cycladic culture remains tantalizingly elusive. Even the idols carved out of white marble remain a mystery, as their function is far from clear (in this respect, echoes with the massive Easter island figures extend beyond looks). Most have been recovered from graves (though they have also been found in settlements) and depict naked women — usually in a highly stylised form (see p. 225) — standing with arms folded (left above right) and sometimes pregnant. Their 'modernist' appearance has also made them very popular around the world, with high prices and a large number of fakes typifying the market today. All this is a long way removed from the culture that created them. In the absence of evidence of political or military facets to this society, in retrospect, it looks to have existed in something like the garden of Eden. But clearly it was not all apples and Eves if the depressed, introspective posture of the occasional carved Adam is anything to go by.

Minoan
2000—1500 BC

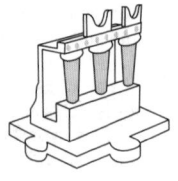

Around 2000 BC the first major power emerged in the Aegean. Named after a king whose name passed down through legend, the non-Greek Minoans were only rediscovered in the early years of this century thanks to archaeology. Based on a commercial hegemony, the Minoan civilisation, with its huge palaces, brilliant frescos, intricate jewellery, baths, drainage systems, and above all the first writing, marked a cultural high point that was not to be regained for over a thousand years. Known only through their artifacts, the Minoans never recovered from the economically distructive volcanic eruption of Santorini c. 1500 BC. Taken over by the first Greeks, they disappeared and were forgotten even by the ancient Greeks themselves. They hovered on the edge of memory in dark legends of the sea-king Minos and his labyrinth palace, built to house his half-man, half-bull son (the Minotaur) who lived on a healthy diet of Athenian maidens, and the story of Atlantis — an island of bull-worshipping affluent people who angered their god, who then sank their island into the sea by way of retribution.

Mycenaean & Dark Ages
1500—776 BC

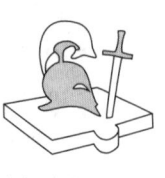

The successors to the Minoans were the Mycenaeans. Already established on mainland Greece, they were able to rapidly take over the remnants of Minoan power when it collapsed. They also inherited the Minoans' Linear alphabet but wrote in their own language — Greek. Much more militaristic than their predecessors, these Ionian Greeks rapidly built a trading empire across the Eastern Mediterranean (the odd little 10-year local difficulty over Troy aside). In later archaic times this period was mythologised into the 'heroic' age given life by the Homeric poems, but latterly the clumsy fortified town walls surviving from this period have been dubbed 'Cyclopic' as they look to have been built by the one-eyed giants that the ancients believed lived on the earth before mankind arrived. Mycenaean power diminished with the arrival of invading Dorian Greeks (c. 1100 BC): trade and communications fell away, leaving the islands in the thrall of a mini dark age. Painting and writing were forgotten, and, left to their own devices, communities reorganised themselves on a city state basis. This, combined with the arrival of the Phoenicians reopening the trade routes, proved to be the catalyst for change that led to a resurgence in Greek culture. Cities expanded (and established colony daughter cities as far afield as France), painting and writing (this time using a variation of the Phoenician alphabet) reappeared, and in 776 BC the Olympic Games were established; an event now regarded as marking Greece's coming of age.

Archaic
776—490 BC

During the Archaic period Greek art and architecture developed from Egyptian models of heavy pillared buildings and votive statues into the more elegant Greek forms that we know today. Very much an age of transition, these early examples of Archaic painting and statuary — with limbs and features all misproportioned — look to the modern eye like something 'done' by an exhibitor at the Royal Academy's summer exhibition; but the artists of this period increasingly acquired a mastery of basic technique and moved steadily towards a more realistic rendering of their subject matter. The islands were particularly prominent during this period as their easily defended boundaries produced a number of powerful island city states; with the result that from Aegina to Samos the remains of Archaic structures and statuary (the Delian Lions among them) can be found. This greater artistic and cultural cohesion was bolstered towards the end of the period by a succession of invasions by the dominant East Mediterranean power of the time — Persia. The first of these attacks came against the Cyclades in 499 and 490 BC. However, the victory by the Athenian-led Greek army at Marathon later in 490 BC and then the Athenian naval victory over the Persians at Salamis in 480 BC saw the emergence of a Greek political supremacy in the region and this brought with it a renewed political and artistic confidence that became the hallmark of the 'Classical' era.

Classical & Hellenistic
490—180 BC

The great winner in the Persian wars was the leading Greek participant, Athens. The Aegean islands, weakened by the Persian invasion, agreed to contribute to a fund to maintain a fleet under Athenian leadership to protect them from further aggression. Known as the Delian League, this alliance was used by Athens to exert de facto political control over the islands and prompted leading Greek city states (principally Sparta and Corinth) to fight the Peloponnesian War (431–404 BC) to prevent Athens emerging as the master of Greece. The islands were reduced to minor players in the larger Greek scene with local art and architecture being neglected in consequnce. The islands became more important as sources of revenue and marble than centres in their own right. Islands that dared to oppose Athens (notably Aegina and Milos) also suffered greatly.

Athens, meantime, having been sacked during the Persian invasion, was ripe for redevelopment and under the leadership of Pericles spent (without consent) much of the Delian League contributions on rebuilding the temples on the Acropolis. Accompanied by an equally spectacular literary, theatrical and philosophical cultural explosion this was the golden age of Greek civilisation. However, Sparta's eventual defeat of Athens prevented Greek domination by one city and the states (none of whom was powerful enough to take control of all of Greece) bickered on until Alexander the Great succeeded to the throne of Macedonia (336 BC). This event marked the tansition from the Classical to the Hellenistic periods, for Alexander unified Greece at the start of a wave of conquest that was to extend to the borders of India. With the death of Alexander his empire collapsed and the weakened city states and islands rapidly reasserted their quarrelsome independence.

The Hellenistic period also left a major mark on Greek culture, though this was more of a natural progression from the symitary of the classical period than a radical or sudden change. Buildings and artwork generally became far more decorative and ornamental, while literature and schools of

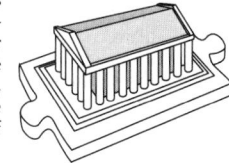

learning grew from the classical foundations. Some of the islands benefitted greatly from this, with Rhodes, Kos and Samos exerting greater influence in part as a result of their emergence as major centres of learning.

Roman
180 BC—395 AD

As Greek power waned, neighbouring Rome gradually came to exercise influence over the divided city states and islands, initially as an arbiter in inter-city disputes but then as a force in her own right. Having entered Greece in response to an attack by King Mithridates in 88 BC she never really managed to leave and by 31 BC the whole of Greece had been incorporated into the Roman Empire: the islands divided between five provinces (the Adriatic islands were part of Epirus, the Dodecanese and Eastern Line islands were in Asia, Thassos was in Macedonia, Crete was joined with Libya in Cyrenica–Creta, and the remainder formed part of Achaea along with the Peloponnese, Evia, and the Greek mainland north of the Gulf of Corinth).

Despite the four centuries of stability that followed the islands went into a very slow but marked decline. Reduced to the edges of even provincial centres of power they saw comparatively little new monumental building (a feature of Roman rule in other parts of the empire) and were increasingly prone to pirate attack. Athens and the islands also saw their first tourists during this period — notably the Roman writer Pausanias (fl. c. 150 AD) who wrote an important guide (beloved by archaeologists wanting to know what specific buildings were called, looked like, and where they stood) to Greece describing the cities and their mon-uments. Other tourists were more mercenary, and the Roman epoch also saw denudation in local art as many ancient treasures were carted off to embellish the cities and villas of Italy (the occasional shipwrecks that turn up filled with bronze statues are a legacy of this trade). The Greek cities suffered in another important respect; losing all sense of a separate political identity they were subsumed into Rome's urban culture, and were never again able to emerge as major centres of political or cultural power.

Byzantine
395—1453

By 395 AD the Roman empire had grown so large that it became unmanageable. Thus the practically-minded Emperor Constantine divided it into two. Greece came under the control of the Eastern empire and was ruled from Byzantium (later named Constantinople): a city still viewed by many Greeks as a capital under occupation. The islands now began the descent from a period of gradual decline to one of almost total anarchy, suffering considerably in the Slavic and Saracen invasions of the 7th and 9th centuries before becoming embroiled in the general stagnation of the Byzantine empire. Considerable depopulation followed with the further destruction wrought by the misguided Crusaders of the 1204 crusade who chose to sack Constantinople rather than retake the holy land. The Greek islands were part of the spoils and were divided up among the plunderers with the Venetians taking control of Crete, the Genoese of Chios, Lesbos and Astipalea among others. Thus when Constantinople finally fell to the Turks in 1453 many of the islands remained in Christian hands with widespread castle building going on — courtesy of ancient temple demolition.

Venetian & Ottoman
1453—1832

During the succeeding centuries the Aegean islands gradually fell to Ottoman Turk rule. Some — such as Rhodes — were lost early (1522) but others under Venetian control held out until the last (Tinos) went in 1715. For the most part Turkish rule was benign. The new landlords were content to appoint island governors and collect taxes. But even as the Turks were completing their conquest of the Aegean their power had begun to wane. The islands became famous either for being the

victims of pirates or for becoming their haunts; for the islands were natural strongholds from which they could attack other islands and the rapidly increasing trade between Europe and the Levant.

The years between 1450 and 1750 marked the nadir of the islands' fortunes, with many being abandoned altogether after their populations were massacred or sold into slavery. With Christian, Turkish, Barbary Coast, and local pirates all preying on the islands the role call of horrors is a long one. The 1500's saw the worst of it, with Ios being devastated in 1528, and the notorious Barbarossa starting his many depredations in the Aegean by attacking Aegina in 1537; killing all the men and taking 6000 women and children into slavery. In 1570 the Barbary pirate Kemal Reis went on a little slave-gathering expedition and removed the entire populations of Kithera, Skiathos and Skopelos to North Africa.

In the face of these attacks island communities did their best to protect themselves by abandoning coastal settlements in favour of defendable villages (or choras) inland. On a number of Cycladic islands these were built as stockade-like 'kastro's with the houses built on the inside of a defensive wall (these still survive on Folegandros, Kimolos and Antiparos — though in the case of the latter, it didn't prevent the islanders being massacred in 1794). Gradually, however, the more successful 'pirate' islands began to gain a degree of control via their fleets of ships which also took advantage of the growing trade opportunities to enhance their status still further by building impressively mansioned towns (e.g. Hydra, Spetses, and Chios). The arrival of foreign powers (notably the Russians who held control over a dozen islands during the 1770–4 Turkish war) also helped to stabilise the region. By the 19th century Greek nationalism was becoming a potent force: the islands coming to the fore as natural bastions from which insurgents could operate against weak Turkish rule. Less powerful islands demonstrated defiance of Turkish rule by the painting of island houses (heretofore kept an inconspicuous mud brick brown) in the Greek national colours of white and blue (now the hallmark of the typical Cycladic town), while the more powerful islands, via their fleets, gained a notable place in Greek history in the independence struggle; being more than a match for the Turks. This, however, led to reprisals (notably the massacre of 25,000 islanders on Chios in 1822).

Modern

1832—

Independence in 1832 did not see all of modern-day Greece gain its freedom. The Cyclades aside, the islands remained in foreign hands, only gradually being gathered into the protective arms of the Greek state. Corfu and the Ionian islands were transferred from British control in the 1860s. The First World War saw the islands of the Northern Aegean come under Greek rule, while the Italians took the Dodecanese from Turkey and attempted an unsuccessful Italianisation programme; only to see the islands handed over to Greece at the end of the Second World War.

Since independence Greece has been engaged in sporadic conflicts with Turkey; notably the war of 1920–23, when Greek armies attempted to gain control of the ancient Greek cities on Turkey's Aegean seaboard, as well as the former capital of the Byzantine empire — Constantinople (now İstanbul). The war ended disastrously for Greece, culminating with the sack of Smyrna (now İzmir) and a territorial settlement that resulted in 1½ million ethnic-Greeks leaving Turkey for Greece, and some 400,000 ethnic Turks (mainly from the islands) going the other way. Relations between the two countries remain tense. Turkey has failed to recognise Greek sovereignty over the Aegean sea-bed (with its oil deposits) and the Turkish invasion of Cyprus in 1974 has done nothing to heal old wounds. But as both are members of NATO and have economies dependent on tourism they have a vested interest in avoiding outright hostilities. Greece's position has also been bolstered by its emergence as a democracy and membership of the EU (European Union): you can expect to see election posters and EU flags everywhere.

Politically, Greece is now relatively stable after a torrid post-Second World War period which saw a civil war (1945–49) between the government and communist forces, the military dictatorship of the colonels (1967–74) and the formal abolition of the monarchy (an institution acquired by modern Greece after the Great Powers that had championed her independence installed Prince Otto of Bavaria as King in 1833 after the assassination of the country's first president) in 1975.

Ferries & Tickets

The Greek Ferry scene has everything from large ex-Scandinavian train ferries to local fishing cum taxi-boats known as *caïques*. The evolution of this ferry network has been, and continues to be, largely dictated by two features: the economic pull of the capital Athens (home to one third of Greece's population), and the disparate nature of the Greek island chains (or more to the point, the uneconomic sailing distances between them). Together they combine to produce a 'hub and spoke' ferry network radiating from the Athenian ports of Piraeus and Rafina. Ferries operate down these spokes regardless of the tourist season. The amount of traffic is, however, very tourist-dependent with over 10 million passenger journeys a year. The daily sailing between the popular islands and the capital either side of the High Season can mushroom up to six or more once the summer crowds start arriving. The smaller, less touristed islands tend to retain an annual twice-weekly subsidised lifeline with the capital regardless of season. Travel is therefore easy on the large ferries operating between islands up and down chains, but cross-chain connections are far less frequent. The pattern of scheduling remains poor, with operators able to pretty much choose when they want to run a service. Most opt for the popular times, with the result that the London bus syndrome is often in evidence: you wait hours for a boat until the three scheduled to call at the next island arrive within half an hour of one another. All departures are coordinated by smart white-uniformed officers of the Port Police service. Their port office will have a list of the day's arrivals/departures and the officers (armed with whistles) supervise the quay side disembarkation and loading of all ferries.

HIGH SEASON
Late June—Late
September

The summer tourist influx is substantial but the High Season period is, in fact, surprisingly short (lasting only 12—14 weeks, from late June through to late September), one result being that the accompanying high level of ferry services is a relatively short-term phenomenon. Unfortunately, as Greek ferry operators do not arrange their schedules until just before the season starts it is impossible to provide definitive timetables in advance of the summer season. That said, the majority of summer services either remain the same or undergo only minor modification, so that despite the almost total lack of availability of even the scantiest pre-season information, it is possible to give a reasonable report of probable activity. Given previous years' experience you can expect to find between 75—90% of the High Season sailings or an equivalent running in 1995 (this varies greatly depending on the location). In some instances names of boats or days they run specific itineraries will have changed as companies swap boats around in fleet reorganisations, and sailing times might have been brought forward or put back an hour or two. Daily services are least likely to be altered, as too are the services heading for the remoter islands; since these ferries are usually the island's only connections with the wider world. If ferries in either of these categories are out of action other vessels are taken off their routes to cover. Odd-ball boats running one-off or very wide-ranging services are more vulnerable to change. Amidst this sea of probability one consolation is that *routes* remain constant each year while the number of ferries increases.

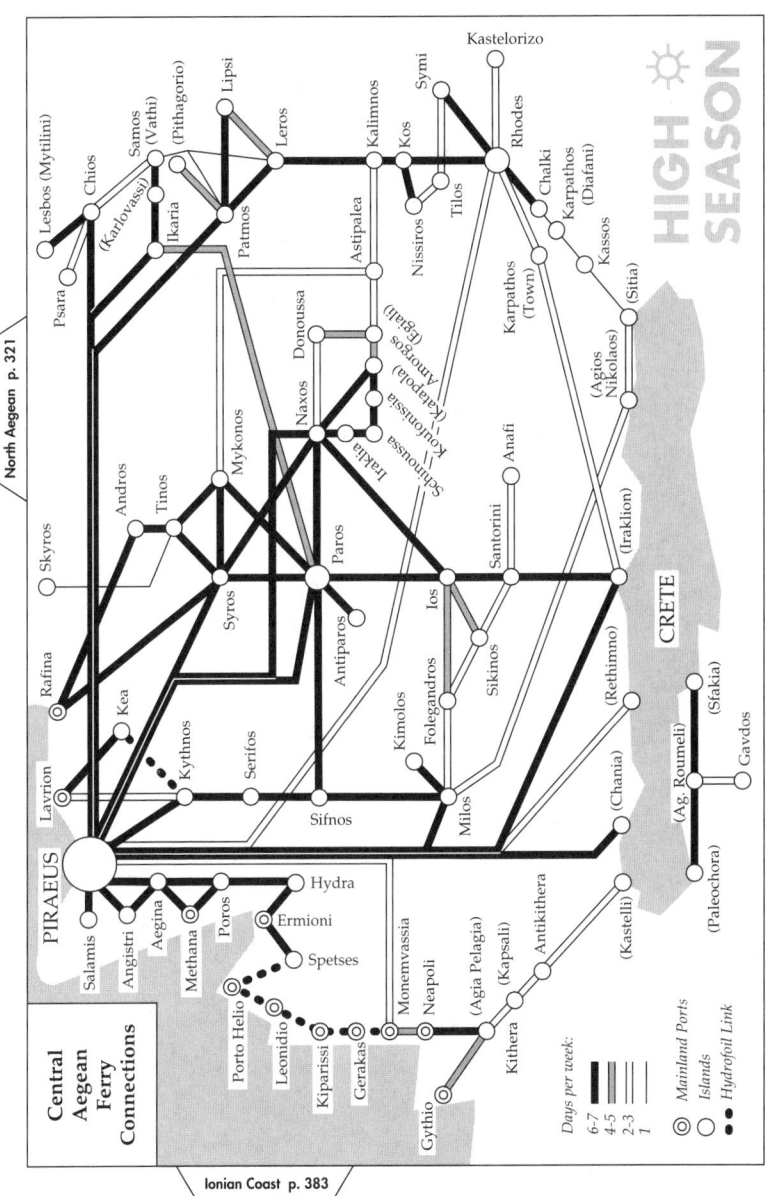

North Aegean p. 321

HIGH SEASON

CRETE

Central Aegean Ferry Connections

Days per week:
6-7
4-5
2-3
1

◎ Mainland Ports
○ Islands
••• Hydrofoil Link

Ionian Coast p. 383

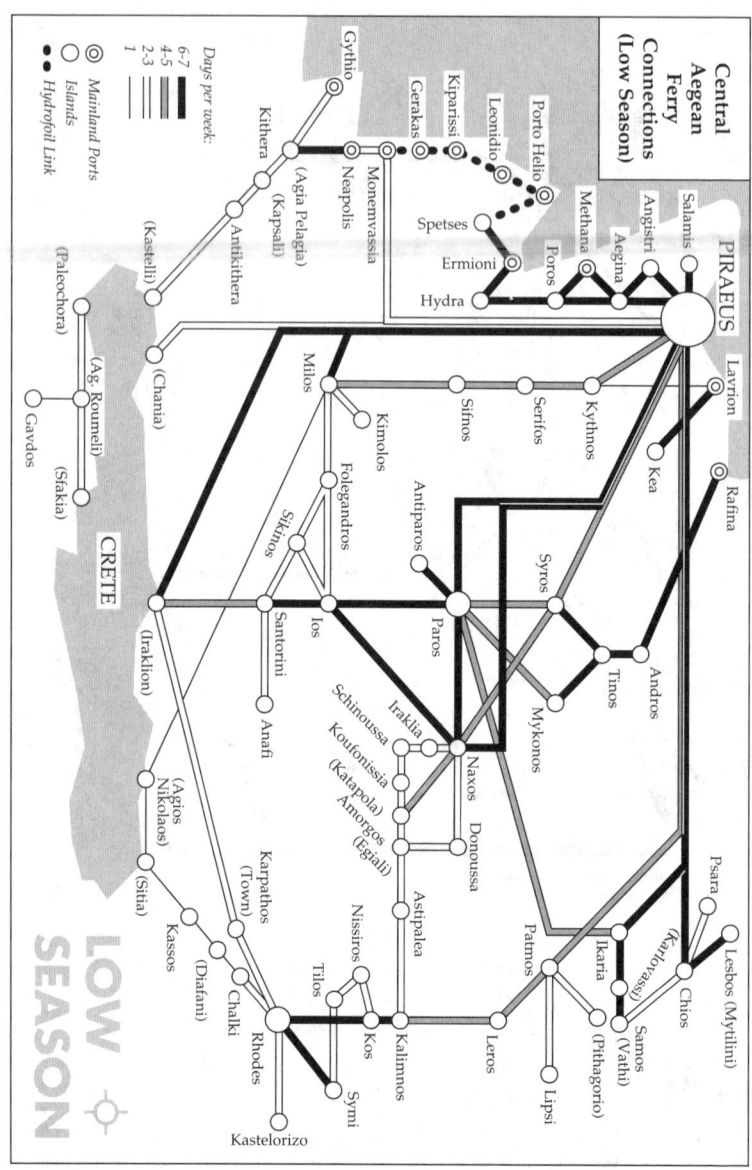

LOW SEASON
October—Early June
There is a lot to be said for travelling out of the popular High Season period, particularly during the months immediately either side of it (the spring is the nicest time for sightseeing in Greece), but there is a penalty to be paid. Although the number of boats operating annual services is increasing, ferry activity is at a greatly reduced level, with considerable fluctuations in the times of services — and indeed the ferries running them. Low Season Port Tables are not provided simply because in most instances travelling between the islands is merely a matter of catching the single boat every 24/48 hours running up or down the major chains (a rough guide to the likely links available is to take the Port Table Connections Maps and ignore all but the 6—7 days per week links). Times are very dependent on sea conditions, as is the likelihood of any of the smaller boats running — with hydrofoil and catamaran services at a minimum (if extant at all). June and October are particularly awkward months to describe simply because services are either expanding during the former, or running down in the latter.

During the Low Season reliability also declines. This is partly due to poorer sea conditions (as late as the end of May you can encounter storms that will leave ships port-bound for 24 hours), but economic factors also come into play. Ferry companies are granted licences by the Greek government provided they (i) operate on an annual basis, (ii) regularly visit the less popular islands. The result is that boats run very profitably for four months of the year and at a loss for the remainder. Even though the operator is able to minimise his losses by running a reduced winter service it is very tempting to have a ferry suffer a 'mechanical' failure from time to time, thereby reducing them further.

Car Ferries
Of the 100-odd larger car ferries licensed to operate in Greek waters, some 50 are engaged on international routes, with the rest operating around the islands. International ferries are on a par with those operating cross-Channel services a few years ago and are slightly better than their domestic counterparts with duty-free shops, swimming pools (filled), and the all important deck-class shower. Accommodation options range from cabins (prices vary according to the number of berths and their position in the ship), lounges with aircraft-style seats (Pullman class) and basic deck-class facilities (i.e. saloons and open decks).

Most of the large Greek domestic ferries operate out of Piraeus, providing either a daily service (returning overnight) or (if venturing further afield) running a thrice-weekly service. These services tend to be reliable (this means to within 2—3 hours of their scheduled arrival time); the most likely cause of disruption coming from the annual one day strike each summer. Even so, this is normally confined to the daily Piraeus departures/arrivals rather than ferries already at sea. Normally there are a few days' warning of a strike, though unless you hear of it on the grapevine the chances are that you will only find out when you go to buy your ticket.

Conditions on domestic ships vary widely. You can take it for granted that pools will be empty, deck-class showers locked, and that the vessel will have its name in English on the bow and in Greek on the stern. Otherwise anything goes. Class distinctions are somewhat arbitrary, with facilities classed as 'deck' on the better ships classified as 2nd or 'tourist' on the less good. Classes are segregated pretty strictly on board most vessels via a combination of locked doors and barred gates. Unfortunately, there is no similar distinction made between smoking and non-smoking areas (the latter being totally unknown). With a 'deck' ticket you can expect the seating to be divided pretty equally between interior saloons (complete with TVs) and the outside upper decks (where plastic-moulded park bench style seats welded to the deck are the norm). For those who choose to go by 2nd class, cabin accommodation is also on offer on all large boats (prices are comparable to C-class hotel rates); and can be booked when you buy your ticket. Food and drink facilities are always on offer, though this will vary from self-service cafeterias to a hatch providing (along with the all-pervasive smell of burnt cheese) soft drinks, beer, biscuits, toasted sandwiches and microwaved floppy things the locals call pizzas. All foodstuffs are more expensive than those ashore.

If you want more ferry information (previous names, capacity, lengths etc.) you will find most listed in Geoffrey Hamer's excellent *Trip Out in Southern Europe* — available from 'Trip Out', PO Box 1287, London, W4 3LW: £3.80.

Landing Craft Ferries
In sheltered coastal waters where car ferries are needed on short haul routes (usually mainland to island links) small 'Landing Craft' type vessels predominate. The large ferry operators don't have an interest in these locally operated craft, which can carry anything from four to forty vehicles. Passengers are accommodated in the cabin decks at the stern of the ship. These vessels usually only offer deck-class facilities: the bigger boats have a bar. Usually running all year round,

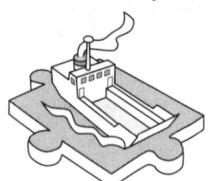

High Season sees occasional fights among motorists over the limited space available. Tickets are normally bought on board.

Hydrofoils
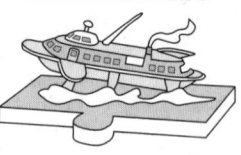

Known throughout Greece as 'Dolphins' (i.e. *Delphini*), there are now some 60 of these craft operating in Greek waters. Travelling at twice the speed of the average ferry, they each carry around 140 passengers. Very much fair weather craft, they require reasonably calm sea conditions and so tend to confine visits to islands in more sheltered waters. Consequently services are greatly reduced out of High Season. Rarely operating in the winter or out of daylight hours (their hulls are not strong enough to cope with chance collisions with large pieces of flotsam), they are a fast (if noisy) way of rattling around the Aegean.

All these boats are fitted-out with aircraft-style seats divided between bow, central and rear cabins. The rear cabins (complete with WCs) sometimes have a bar where the crew socialize. As a rule, the further back you go the less bumpy the ride: an important consideration given that these boats often bring out the worst among those inclined to sea-sickness. Between the central and rear cabins there is usually a small open deck over the engine. Here you can stand and admire the view — provided you can cope with the noise, the petrol fumes and (when underway) the 'riding a kicking mule' sensation and occasional cascades of surf. Easily the best seats on a hydrofoil lie at the stern: here there is a small open deck complete with a popular seat offering the smoothest ride and panoramic views.

With tickets (always bought in advance from agencies: they are not on sale on the quayside) costing the equivalent of a 2nd class ferry ticket, it is rare for hydrofoil companies to compete against each other: the market just isn't strong enough. As a result, apart from a few local operations, the hydrofoil scene is dominated by two companies; CERES and ILIO, each with

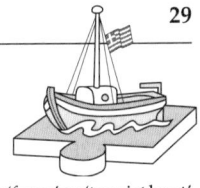

their own zone of operations. CERES are the better established and run the better operation with timetables published for the year and a good record for reliability and continuity of services between years. ILIO operate in less hospitable areas and are less consistent: timetables are only available for the month in hand, if at all, and there are major variations in the itineraries and schedules each year. In short, you can assume boats run by the former will be operating, while regard Port Table entries for the latter as 'optimistic' projections of what might be around!

Catamarans

The last decade has seen half a dozen of these vessels arrive in the Aegean; so far without much success. Offering a fast ride in flat seas and a slow, stomach-churning roll in anything else, they are very much summer boats. As such, they are not viewed with much favour by the Greek government as they are seen to siphon off ferry profits during the High Season and don't operate during the loss making Low Season period when ferries are still contracted to run. Fares are normally on a par with hydrofoils (except for excursion catamarans which are very expensive). The larger catamarans have superior aircraft-style seating and TVs. Numbered seat tickets are usually bought from agencies, though in a pinch you can buy one on board.

Passenger Boats

Increasingly operated as purely tourist boats, these craft range from small car ferry-sized vessels to converted fishing boats known as caïques. Less strike-prone than the large ferries, their main bane are the seas whipped-up by the *meltemi* wind in the summer months and the generally more volatile conditions during the rest of the year. They do, however, provide a useful adjunct to the larger boats though you will encounter wide disparities in fares depending on their 'ferry' or 'tourist boat' status (the latter can be used for one-way island hopping if you are prepared to pay for a return ticket). Some larger 'passenger' boats can also accommodate 2 or 3 cars, or more commonly, motorbikes.

Ticket Agents

In the absence of any central ferry ticket issuing or information authority, ticket agents are to be found at every port in the Eastern Med. Usually occupying offices in buildings near the quay or along the seafront they also frequently offer exchange facilities (albeit at a higher rate of commission) and room finding services as well. Hours are variable (an attractive feature if you need to change money or cheques out of banking hours) and are often determined by the arrival times of the boats. In Greece most agencies will open up for a short time to sell tickets during the night if a boat is due in. They sometimes also offer luggage deposit facilities to ticket purchasers. Ticket agents are the only people who seem to thrive on the apparent chaos of the ferry system. Many would argue that they are largely responsible for it. Inevitably they are very keen to relieve you of your money and you should enter an agency with eyes open. The vast majority of passengers do, however, use them without any difficulty, for although you can buy tickets on the boats (if you do then expect to surrender your passport between the ferry door and buying your ticket at the ship's purser's office), when large numbers of passengers are involved it is more diplomatic to buy in advance. When dealing with an agent bear in mind that:

1. It is rare for a ticket agent to sell tickets for all the vessels calling at a port. The schedules they advertise are therefore incomplete and many will lie blatantly in order to get custom by telling you that their boat is the fastest, next, or the only available. A common dodge is to advertise arrival rather than departure times if this will put 'their' boat ahead of a rival agent's.

2. As fares are regulated by the government there is no difference in the prices ticket agents are able to charge. Any agent's claim that their tickets are cheaper is rubbish. Another dodge is to advertise prices omitting the port tax and VAT to entice the unwary inside.

3. Some agents have been known to claim that tickets can't be bought on board. This latter assertion is *usually* false — but it is worth noting that for some of the small passenger ferries in High Season buying a ticket in advance is a necessity.

4. Outright attempts to sell tourists something they don't want are rare, but they do occur; either by selling a higher class ticket than the basic 'deck' fare, or selling a ticket for a boat other than the one wanted, without telling the customer (usually because they don't act for that boat). You can prevent this by checking that the class, ferry's name, and departure time are on the ticket.

5. The separate billing of the fare, port taxes, harbour dues and VAT on tickets can sometimes lead to some interesting exercises in addition — invariably in the agency's favour.

International Tickets

International ferry travel in the Eastern Mediterranean is comparatively expensive. This is due to the longer distances involved, the much higher port taxes international boats attract (currently around £5 per person and also per vehicle), and partly because in some instances you are obliged to buy a bunk or aircraft-type seating as a minimum rather than a deck ticket. It is normal to buy international tickets in advance. Various discounts are available, depending on the operator. These range from a Student discount (20%), Return ticket discount (5%) — usually advertised as a 10% discount, but in fact only given on the cost of the return part of the ticket — Group concessions (usually 15% for nine or more), as well as reduced Low Season fares. In addition a number of lines operating to Greece offer 'Stop-over' tickets allowing you to break the journey along the way (though they are quick to point out that during the High Season re-embarkation on a particular boat cannot be guaranteed). One problem you could encounter: it is rare for you to be able to travel between two ports in the same country using international boats except as a designated 'stop over' on an international ticket. Fares also tend to be structured on a country to country basis so, for example, if you travel from Greece to Cyprus the ticket will usually cost the same if you start from Piraeus or a port en route such as Rhodes.

Typical International High Season 'Deck' Fares	
Long Haul:	**£**
Iraklion—Alexandria	224.24
Limassol—Haifa	56.70
Limassol—Rhodes	33.30
Piraeus—Haifa	60.60
Piraeus—Limassol	42.50
Italy—Greece:	
Ancona—Corfu	42.50
Ancona—Iraklion	72.12
Ancona—Patras	42.50
Bari—Corfu	21.90
Bari—Patras	30.30
Brindisi—Corfu	34.90
Brindisi—Patras	37.90
Trieste—Patras	53.35

Greek Domestic Tickets

Tickets can be bought on the boat itself or via the agencies to be found near every quayside. There are usually three classes on the larger vessels; 1st (Luxury), 2nd, and 3rd (Deck). Deck tickets are the norm and unless you state otherwise you can expect to be sold one if you buy from a ticket agency. However, if you buy your ticket on board a ferry, you should be aware of the existence of an ill-defined 'Tourist' class. This is used by a small (but increasing) number of ferry companies to get round government price-setting and enables them to charge roughly 20% extra for a 'Deck' ticket. Class numbers are indicated on the ticket using a letter and apostrophe numbering system derived from the classical Greek alphabet. The 'class' (ΘΕΣΙΣ/ΘΕΣΗ) is thus written accordingly: A'= 1st, B'= 2nd, and Γ'= 3rd. Signs on ships all use this system. It is standard practice to issue one-way rather than return tickets; though the latter are

Inter-Island 'Deck' Fares

£8.30	£9.90	£10.30	£12.00	£14.60	•	£17.10	£19.00	£20.50	£28.00	**Rhodes**
Kos	£3.60	£5.00	£6.10	£7.70	•	£12.70	£15.50	£17.25	£26.50	**Kos**
	Kalimnos	£3.20	£4.70	£6.50	•	£11.10	£12.15	£15.00	£24.00	**Kalimnos**
		Leros	£5.20	£8.15	£8.10	£12.60	£14.40	£19.60	£22.30	**Leros**
			Patmos	£5.00	£5.00	£10.80	£11.90	£17.60	£20.00	**Patmos**
	Thessalonika		**Samos**		£4.80	£5.30	£8.00	£9.70	£16.80	**Samos**
Skiathos	£8.60	**Skiathos**		**Ikaria**	£7.20	•	•	•		**Ikaria**
Skyros	£13.75	£9.40	**Skyros**		**Chios**	£7.20	£11.70	£14.50		**Chios**
Tinos	£14.15	£11.10	£9.50	**Tinos**		**Lesbos**	£7.70	£12.35		**Lesbos**
Mykonos	£16.90	£11.10	£11.10	£2.70	**Mykonos**		**Limnos**	£7.90		**Limnos**
Syros	•	•	•	£2.60	£2.90	**Syros**		**Kavala**		
Naxos	•	•	•	£3.10	£3.00	£3.30	**Naxos**			
Paros	£16.40	£12.50	£11.65	£3.85	£4.30	£2.75	£2.90	**Paros**		
Ios	•	•	•	£7.35	£6.90	£6.30	£6.00	£5.80	**Ios**	
Santorini /Thira	£18.50	£17.15	£15.55	£7.90	£7.30	£7.00	£5.60	£6.30	£3.05	**Thira**
Crete (Iraklion)	£22.20	£21.00	£18.80	£12.25	£12.25	£11.40	£11.40	£10.90	£7.10	£6.05

Piraeus–Island Fares		
(Excluding £1.15 port taxes and 8% VAT)		
PIRAEUS to:	Deck £	2nd Class £
Aegina	2.50	3.90
Amorgos	7.70	8.00
Anafi	11.10	14.40
Antikithera	9.30	11.50
Astipalea	10.30	13.20
Chalki	16.00	21.60
Chios	8.00	10.85
Crete (Agios Nikolaos)	13.40	17.85
Crete (Chania)	9.30	12.80
Crete (Iraklion)	10.00	13.60
Crete (Sitia)	15.00	19.85
Donoussa	7.70	8.00
Folegandros	8.90	11.40
Fourni	8.00	10.15
Gythio	9.60	11.35
Hydra	5.00	9.25
Ikaria	7.22	9.50
Ios	8.90	10.70
Iraklia	7.70	8.00
Kalimnos	10.30	13.00
Karpathos	12.50	16.40
Kassos	12.50	16.40
Kastelorizo	15.00	18.15
Kimolos	7.20	8.70
Kithera	8.50	11.35
Kos	12.50	16.45
Koufonissia	7.70	8.00
Kythnos	4.65	5.95
Leros	10.30	13.00
Lesbos (Mytilini)	10.10	12.60
Milos	7.20	8.70
Monemvassia	7.00	8.80
Mykonos	6.90	8.40
Naxos	7.20	8.55
Neapoli	8.70	10.50
Nissiros	12.50	16.45
Paros	6.25	7.45
Patmos	10.30	13.20
Poros	3.75	7.20
Rhodes	13.90	18.20
Samos (Karlovassi)	9.00	11.90
Samos (Vathi)	9.65	12.60
Santorini / Thira	8.90	10.70
Schinoussa	7.70	8.05
Serifos	5.30	6.80
Sifnos	6.50	7.70
Sikinos	10.50	13.55
Spetses	6.05	10.20
Symi	12.50	16.45
Syros	6.20	7.20
Tilos	12.50	16.45
Tinos	6.90	8.00

available (at a saving of 10–15% of the cost of two single fares) provided you don't mind the inconvenience of being locked into using the same company's boats for your return. Groups of 10 or more can get a similar discount on single tickets. Past years have seen a number of failed attempts by operators to introduce 'Greek island passes'. None has lasted long as the unreliability of boats and the limitations of travel when confined to one line have conspired against the idea.

In Greece it is expected that you will pay for passenger ferry tickets in cash: credit cards are usually only accepted when buying international tickets. The tickets are not transferable to other lines and are only refundable if a ferry fails to arrive. In such instances, standing inside the office of the agent who sold you the ticket until they refund your money is the most effective way of getting it back. Prices are preset for each island, though local port taxes differ. These are a matter of a few pence on domestic services. 6% VAT is also levied on all tickets in Greece. The average 3rd-class fare, when hopping to the next island down the line, is about £7. 2nd-class tickets cost 50–60% more than deck. 1st-class tickets are not bound by government regulation so operators can charge what the market can bear. You can expect to pay at least double the 3rd-class fare. Children between 4 and 10 travel half-fare. Car rates average 4 or 6 times the cost of a deck ticket, depending on whether the length of the vehicle exceeds 4.5 m. Motorcycle rates also go according to size. For a sub-250cc machine the fare is similar to a deck ticket, larger machines double. Bicycles are usually free. Excursion boats are not bound by government price regulation and are apt to charge about twice what you would expect to pay if travelling by ferry. Catamaran and hydrofoil ticket prices are government regulated, with fares something around 2nd-class ferry rates.

Sources of Information

Current information on most international services can be gleaned from the *Thomas Cook European Timetable* and the *Thomas Cook Overseas Timetable*. Finding valid information on Greek domestic services is, however, another matter. Greece is an awkward country when it comes to obtaining reliable information in advance. In order to get the maximum information you will need to consult a number of sources:

(1) **The National Tourist Organisation of Greece** (4 Conduit Street, London, W1R 0DJ; ☎ 071 734 5997) can give you (along with excellent free maps of Greece and Athens) photocopies of the monthly timetables produced in a Greek trade publication: the *Greek Travel Pages*. Produced in English, these timetables are well worth obtaining before you go. However, they are by no means comprehensive and are less than easy to consult as individual ferries are identified by a code rather than by name and their routes to given destinations are not indicated.

(2) **In Greece** you will find all ticket agents will have a copy of the *Greek Travel Pages*, and most will let you have a look if you ask. You could also find that they have copies of a second, similar, publication called *Hellenic Travelling*. Also listing island ferry times it is less comprehensive, but is on sale in some Athens bookshops.

(3) **In Athens** there are additional sources of information. Foremost among these are the National Tourist Organisation of Greece (known locally as the EOT) ferry departure sheets (available from the Syntagma Square tourist information centre — see p. 103). These contain a list (in English) of the main domestic ferry departures from Piraeus to the islands (excluding hydrofoils and Saronic Gulf boats). Issued on a weekly basis they run from Thursdays through to the following Wednesday. (Note: if you ask for ferry information in the latter half of this period

you will only be given the 'back-half' of these photocopied pages instead of the full list.)

If you don't want to venture into central Athens or want information on other mainland port departures you can always do what the locals (and many Piraeus ticket agents) do and resort to the city newspapers. The best of these is a bland business daily:

Η ΝΑΥΤΕΜΠΟΡΙΚΗ

which always has Piraeus departures for the following week (usually around p. 27) as well as limited information about departures from other mainland ports. If you are prepared to struggle with the Greek alphabet it is worth the 150 GDR (£0.40) price and is on sale at the newspaper kiosk in the Piraeus Metro station among other places. Finally, several agents in the central ticket agency block at Piraeus display full departure lists in English (along with fares minus every extra you can think of) inside their 'showrooms'. You are free to take a look without buying. If you can ignore agent hassle and go a wandering, you will also find a number will have ferry company timetables that you can take away.

(4) **On the islands** available information is usually confined to departure times for the island you are on. Occasionally company timetables are available and EOT offices (see individual island entries) also distribute lists of ferry times. Some agents make up (incomplete) photocopy ferry timetables to augment the billboards to be found outside all agencies advertising boats and current times. These are usually in both English and Greek — except on remote islands where Greek only (usually in capitals) is the norm. In the last resort you can always try the local Port Police, who are guaranteed to have a complete list of the day's sailings as well as someone who can't speak English.

Ferry Safety

In the wake of the *Estonia* ferry disaster in the Baltic in October 1994 the safety record of ro-ro (roll-on, roll-off) ferries has become an issue of considerable concern. As island hoppers largely depend on such vessels, some comments on the safety record of Greek ferries in general, and the pitfalls you could encounter using them are worth making here:

1. Operating Habits & Safety Record

The most encouraging thing one can say regarding Greek ferries is that the way local operators use ro-ro ferries, combined with the local climate, conspire against a major disaster occurring from similar reasons. The argument that ro-ro ferries are inherently unsafe because of their liability to capsize if only a small amount of water reaches the car-deck is a formidable one, but against this must be set the fact that the use of ro-ro ferries in Greece make this sort of event a less likely prospect than in other parts of the world.

Both the *Herald of Free Enterprise* and the *Estonia* sank because of water entering via open front car doors. It is virtually unheard of for a Greek ro-ro ferry to use the front car door. The standard practice employed by all ro-ro ferries of backing, stern first, up to a quay and then unloading and loading cars and passengers via the rear door means that bow doors are rarely opened (except on occasions at Piraeus harbour in order to ventilate car decks when a ferry is idle for a day).

In the *Estonia* disaster heavy seas played a critical part in the sinking; causing the front car door to fall off. The landlocked Mediterranean (with a tide rise of only 50 cm) is relatively calm most of the year, so door fittings designed for much harsher sea conditions (most large ferries are ex-North European or Japanese boats) are not subjected to the same sort of strains.

In view of the above, the greatest danger of a Greek ferry capsize comes from a collision, but even here the loss of life would probably be a lot less than elsewhere, as passengers are mostly located on the upper decks (rather than in cabins) and are thus more likely to be able to avoid being trapped below. Moreover, the close proximity of land and the large number of ferries, tour and beach boats operating in Greek waters means that help would arrive relatively quickly (though it would be foolish to pretend that if an overcrowded ferry was involved in a major collision that there wouldn't be a high probability of some loss of life). Collision combined with fire poses a greater risk, and this lethal combination accounts for both the worst ferry disaster in the Mediterranean (in 1991, when the Italian *Moby Prince* collided with a tanker outside Livorno while the crew were watching a TV soccer game, with the loss of 140 passengers and crew) and the world (in 1987 when the Philippineo *Dona Paz* collided with a tanker with the loss of all 4386 on board). Fortunately, in the case of Greece, collisions of any kind are a rarity as seamanship is generally good (compulsory national service ensures a regular supply of trained manpower emerging from the Greek navy) and the dexterity with which ferries are manoeuvred in and out of some of the tiny island harbours is doubly reassuring.

This is not to say that Greek ferries are wholly without problems. Age does take its toll (the *Estonia* — built in 1980 — has been described as a ferry 'well into middle age'; yet, with one or two exceptions, every large ferry in the Greek fleet is older), and the last few years have seen several evacuations at sea due to engine room fires. This is the most common problem encountered with Greek boats (roughly one a year). This might seem a lot, but given the fact that Greece has the largest ferry fleet of any country in Europe (over 40% of the EU total), coupled with the age of many of the boats, the country has a good safety record. There are now over 10 million untroubled domestic ferry passenger journeys in Greece each year.

Of course, there is always room for improvement. It is regrettable that Greece, along with other Mediterranean nations, has opposed the proposed EU adoption of the safety recommendations following on from the *Herald of Free Enterprise* disaster because of the cost of modifying their elderly ferry fleets: a significant number of the large ferries now in Greece are boats replaced by West European operators — in part because they do not conform to the safety standards imposed on ferries using UK ports after the *Herald of Free Enterprise* disaster. Another area of concern is the haphazard nature of ticket sales. While a system that allows island hoppers to treat ferries as if they were buses (i.e. just buy a ticket and board) is very convenient, it also means that it is difficult to know to the nearest hundred how many passengers are on a ferry, never mind who they are. Finally, the rigorously enforced class system on some boats means that locked through doors, and iron-gate sun-deck partitions (neither featuring in the original design for the ships in question) could hamper quick evacuations and should be relaxed.

2. Taking Precautions

Without going overboard about safety it is worthwhile taking a moment to consider what you would do if you have to go overboard in a hurry. After all, once you have found a seat it only takes a couple of minutes to ascertain where the nearest life-jacket is, and, if you are inside, where the nearest exit points are. Those contemplating taking an overnight cabin should also take on board the fact that the chances of surviving a ferry capsize will be greatly reduced. Statistically, the chances of being involved in such an incident are minuscule and on a day-to-day basis you are safe enough; though a number of — albeit

mundane — dangers unlikely to be encountered on a typical cross-Channel ferry do remain:

1. In order to facilitate rapid ferry turnaround, passenger embarkation/disembarkation is normally via the stern car door. Passengers are often 'invited' down on to the car deck before the ferry has docked, and are usually left standing among the vehicles while the mooring lines are secured. Vehicles are rarely secured to the car-deck — if the ferry was to collide with the quay or another boat, things could get very unpleasant.

2. The time of greatest danger for the foot passenger is when boarding or disembarking. Once mooring ropes are secured, and the stern door lowered, ferries keep their vulnerable stern away from the quay by maintaining sufficient 'slow forward' propulsion to keep their mooring ropes taut. This means that the lowered door is apt to slide along the surface of the quay while passengers are stepping on or off — occasionally trapping feet in the process. When you are caught in a pushing crowd of locals and backpackers (the concept of 'queuing' is unknown in this part of the world) this can become a major hazard, particularly as vehicles load and disembark along with the foot passengers.

3. The lowering/raising cables on the door should also be treated with considerable caution. Get a backpack snagged on one of those in a pushing crowd and as likely as not you'll end up in the water next to those turning propellers.

4. At the height of the summer ferry crews will try to cram everyone on board — even if it means opening up areas of the ship you would not normally expect to find passenger access. The bow deck (complete with anchor chains, capstans, winches and other dangerous equipment) is a favourite alternative passenger deck. Anyone with children should check that areas containing kiddie-crushing contraptions are inaccessible before they are allowed to run free.

Holiday Essentials

Accommodation

Arguably the most challenging part of island hopping is finding accommodation once you arrive. But then this is part of the challenge of this sort of independent holiday. Generalisations on room availability and price are difficult to make since much depends on when and where you arrive. But in High Season, whatever you are planning to do, it doesn't hurt to take a sleeping bag along so you can decamp to the local campsite should your luck be really out. That said, it is *very* rare to find island hoppers *forced* to resort to roughing it in one of the local beaches.

All types of accommodation are graded by the Greek government (via the NTOG / EOT). Unfortunately, an increasing number of establishments are operating without a licence, or doing their best to evade regulation by understating the number of rooms on offer, or proclaiming themselves to have a higher grade listing than their official one (thus enabling them to charge higher prices). A survey of 25 hotels on Santorini in 1994 showed that all had unlisted rooms and three no operating licence. Other islands produced similar statistics. As a result, some of the hotels mapped in this guide are shown without a class rating, and all those that are shown are given their listed class. Prices also vary greatly between accommodation in the same class group: a reflection of the hoteliers ability to levy additional charges and supplements (e.g. if you stay under three nights you can be charged an extra 10%). Breakfast sometimes must be paid for whether wanted or not. Regardless of where you stay, you should therefore try to ascertain exactly what your total bill will be when you check in. It also never hurts to ask to see a room before you agree to take it. If you encounter any problems don't hesitate to call in the tourist police (usually the threat is enough to resolve disputes!). It is standard practice for all types of accommodation to hold on to your passport while you are in residence (see 'Scams' p. 54).

The accommodation options in Greece are divided between hotels, pensions, rooms in private houses, the odd youth hostel and numerous campsites.

Hotels:

These are categorised by the Greek government into six classes ranging from 'L' (Luxury), followed by 'A' through to 'E' (Eugh!). Prices are very good value by West European standards. Island hoppers usually find that most A to C category hotels are booked en block by package tour operators (though if you go in and ask they often have booked but untaken rooms available). D and E category hotels rely much more on independent clientele.

A-Class:

Singles: 15,000 – 22,000 GDR
Doubles: 20,000 – 28,000 GDR
Top quality rooms with prices to match. You can be virtually certain of finding air conditioning, en suite bathrooms with unlimited hot water, TVs in all rooms and full restaurant facilities within the building. On the down side, A-class hotels are comparatively rare on all but the major tourist islands and are usually inconveniently placed out of town so that they can take advantage of a nearby beach.

B-Class:

Singles: 10,000 – 18,000 GDR
Doubles: 13,000 – 22,000 GDR
Basically cut-down A-class hotels, B-class establishments are more common on the islands. They usually have en suite bathrooms and hot

water but TVs and air-conditioning are less common. Prices are often as high as A-class hotels. Former government-run quality hotels known as 'Xenias' usually fall into this category.

C-Class:

Singles: 7,000 – 13,000 GDR

Doubles: 9,000 – 18,000 GDR

Mid-range hotels offering reasonable rooms. Fairly common all over Greece, they are often the top dollar hotels of twenty years ago. En suite bath-rooms are uncommon. No air-conditioning or restaurant facilities.

D-Class:

Singles: 3,000 – 5,000 GDR

Doubles: 4,500 – 6,500 GDR

Once you reach this level then shared bathrooms become the norm (most bedrooms have a sink — minus plug of course). Buildings tend to be much older; usually being converted turn-of-the-century mansions. Popular with backpackers and local Greeks, they offer good basic accommodation, usually close to town centres and ports.

E-Class:

Singles: 3,000 – 4,000 GDR

Doubles: 4,000 – 6,000 GDR

Bottom of the range. Don't expect too much. At their best E-class hotels offer spartan, clean rooms, at their very, very worst you will find saucers of rat poison on the landings. Hot water is unheard of and the other plumbing is usually of the hole-in-the-floor type. Room keys will usually open half the doors in the building. In popular locations in High Season hoteliers offer backpackers roof space for a small sum.

Pensions:

Now the popular choice with island hoppers, pensions offer quality rooms at a reasonable price. Like hotels they are graded, but confusingly the grades are A to C and are rated one grade lower than the hotel equivalent (i.e. a B-class pension offers comparable rooms to a C-class hotel). Clean rooms, usually sharing a bathroom, and with a refrigerator thrown in. Hot water is usually solar-generated; so is only available in the evenings. Friendly and helpful pension owners usually live in the building.

Rooms (Domatia):

Mainly on offer in High Season, rooms in private houses sup-up the thousands of independent travellers who haven't hotel accommodation and who don't want to camp. Morning ferries at most islands will be met by eager householders thrusting placards at you as you disembark, adorned with photographs of the room on offer and a price that makes a good starting point for negotiation. Conditions will vary greatly — despite government regulation (officially checked out domatia are slightly more expensive and have an EOT plaque on the door):

Establish exactly what you are getting while haggling over the price (e.g. Where is the room? Is this sum (get them to write it down to avoid future arguments) for one or two people? Has the room a private bathroom, shower, hot water? — important points as you could be sharing amenities with a family). Many ticket agencies also have lists of rooms (and hotels) and will push you in the direction of a bed. As with hotel accommodation, room availability does tend to dry up during the day and evening arrivals could have problems.

Youth Hostels:

Facilities are basic (i.e. grimy) but usually adequate for the needs of the night. Unlike the rest of Europe, Youth Hostels are something of a rarity in Greece outside the big mainland cities. YHA cards are rarely necessary but are worth taking if you already have one to hand. Only three islands have hostels: Crete (7), Santorini (2) and Corfu (2). All offer the cheapest, and therefore popular, 'roofed' option.

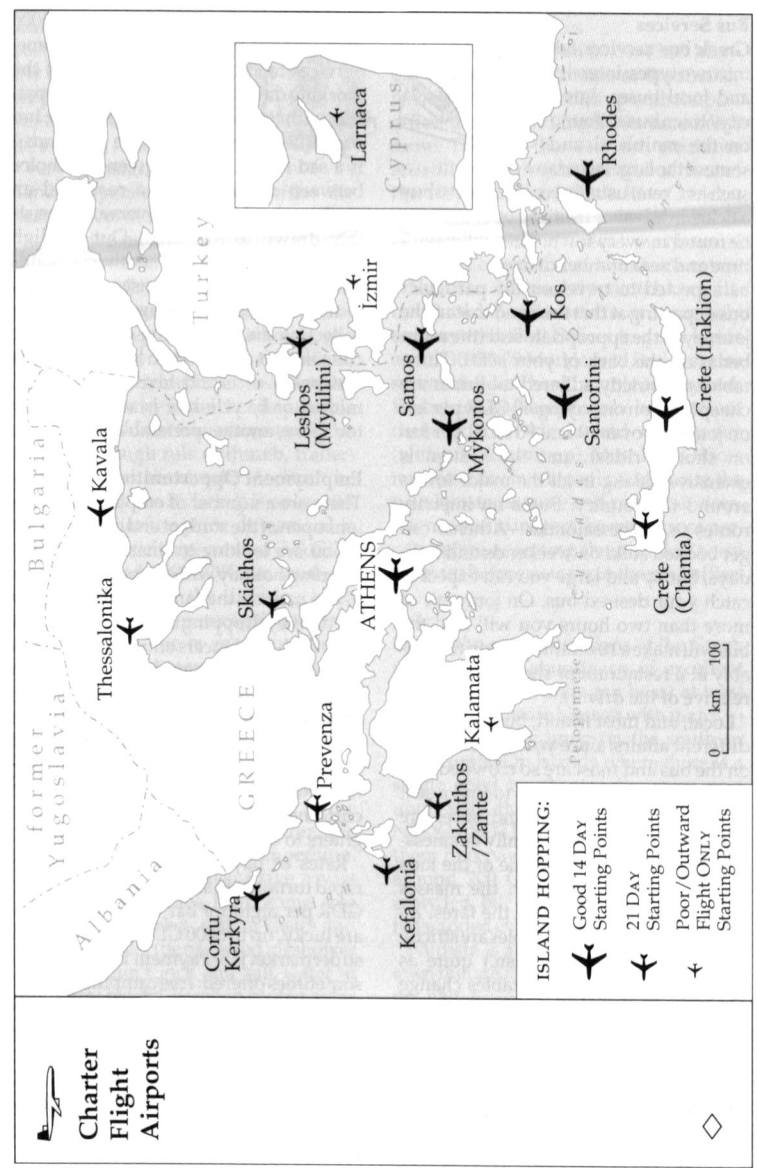

Charter Flight Airports

ISLAND HOPPING:

✈ Good 14 Day Starting Points

⊥ 21 Day Starting Points

+ Poor/Outward Flight Only Starting Points

Larnaca
Cyprus

Turkey

izmir

Rhodes

Kos

Crete (Iraklion)

Santorini

Samos

Mykonos

Lesbos (Mytilini)

Cyclades

Crete (Chania)

Kavala

Bulgaria

Skiathos

ATHENS

Thessalonika

former Yugoslavia

GREECE

Prevenza

Kalamata

Peloponnese

Zakinthos /Zante

Kefalonia

Corfu/ Kerkyra

Albania

0   100 km

◇

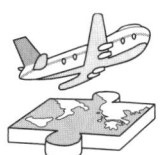

Flights to Greece

Despite the recent cutbacks in charter holidays, even in High Season it is possible to visit a Thomas Cook Flight Centre or other travel agent and pick up a last minute return charter flight ticket from around £150. At other times of the year you can do even better with some tickets costing under £120.

Apart from flights to Athens there are UK connections to 17 Greek airports. However, most are of limited use to the would-be ferry user. The arrival/departure point is an important consideration since you will have to plan your movements with a view to getting back there. Of the various destinations available, **Athens** remains the safest in this respect, since its port of Piraeus is accessible on a daily basis from most islands in the Aegean. The Cycladic islands of **Mykonos** and **Santorini** are also good starting points (though flights to both are apt to be more expensive than elsewhere) and Crete has a useful airport at **Iraklion** (and to a lesser extent **Chania**) as well. Other regional airports tend to restrict the wider island hopping options available. The Dodecanese island chain is well served with frequent flights to **Kos** and **Rhodes**. Other destinations are often better avoided since they do not connect well into the ferry system. **Samos** and **Skiathos** are perhaps the best placed of these, but **Kavala (Keramoti)** and **Thessalonika** can be hard to return to quickly and shouldn't be considered unless you are planning to pick up a return flight elsewhere. The isolated Ionian group is better served by aircraft than ferries with charter flights to **Corfu**, **Kefalonia**, **Lefkada (Preveza)** and **Zante**. Finally, a small number of charter flights also operate to Patras (Araxos) and the poorly connected islands of Karpathos and Limnos, but these are not served by all tour operators.

One way Student/Youth Charter Flights also operate from the UK. These offer the possibility of staying in Greece over the one month regular charter flight limit since you can buy a one way return ticket (ferry ticket agencies also widely advertise these flights) at your leisure — though you should take care to buy early or avoid the popular end-of-August flights when seat availability declines dramatically. If you are holidaying on a 2-week charter flight ticket it cannot be emphasised enough that you should always plan to be back at your arrival point at least one clear day before your return flight, otherwise a ferry strike, bad weather or missing a boat could result in your having to buy an expensive regular flight home via one of the three airports with scheduled flights to the UK (Athens, Thessalonika and Corfu). You should also be aware that charter tickets are cheap concessionary tickets aimed at encouraging tourism. A usual condition of issue is a requirement that you do not stay overnight out of the destination country. This is particularly relevant should you be tempted to take one of the ferry boats to Turkey. You are likely to be denied your flight home should you stay there.

Flights Within Greece

Greece has a very well-developed internal air service operated by Olympic Airways and its associated company Olympic Aviation. This state airline has a monopoly of services within Greece. In the past this has served the islands well, with fares kept down to attractive levels (approximately five times the ferry fare) and a reasonable number of flights on offer; most running direct to or from Athens. This is now beginning to change as the financial difficulties encountered by the airline are beginning to make an impact. Courtesy buses from

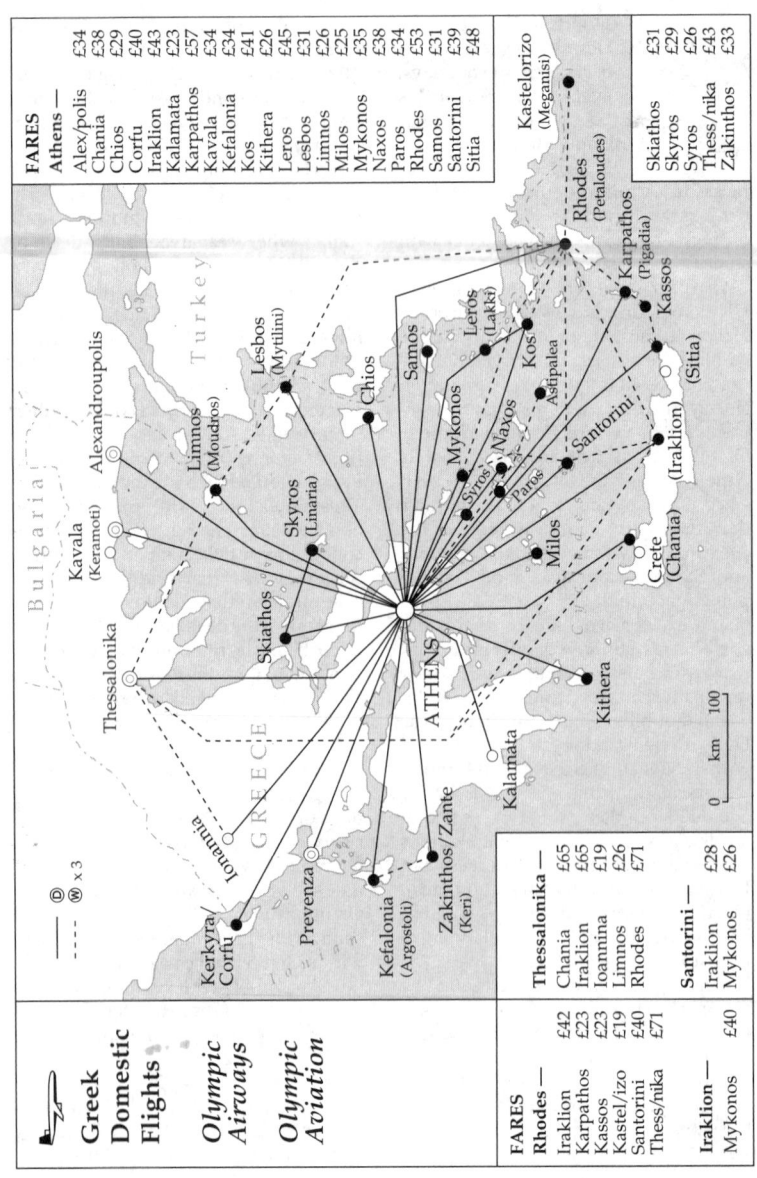

Greek Domestic Flights

Olympic Airways

Olympic Aviation

Legend: ⑩ —— ⑩ × 3 (dashed)

FARES

Athens —	
Alex/polis	£34
Chania	£38
Chios	£29
Corfu	£40
Iraklion	£43
Kalamata	£23
Karpathos	£57
Kavala	£34
Kefalonia	£34
Kos	£41
Kithera	£26
Leros	£45
Lesbos	£31
Limnos	£26
Milos	£25
Mykonos	£35
Naxos	£38
Paros	£34
Rhodes	£53
Samos	£31
Santorini	£39
Sitia	£48

Skiathos	£31
Skyros	£29
Syros	£26
Thess/nika	£43
Zakinthos	£33

FARES

Rhodes —	
Iraklion	£42
Karpathos	£23
Kassos	£23
Kastel/izo	£19
Santorini	£40
Thess/nika	£71

Iraklion —	
Mykonos	£40

Thessalonika —	
Chania	£65
Iraklion	£65
Ioannina	£19
Limnos	£26
Rhodes	£71

Santorini —	
Iraklion	£28
Mykonos	£26

Map labels: Kastelorizo (Meganisi), Rhodes (Petaloudes), Karpathos (Pigadia), Kassos, Samos, Leros (Lakki), Kos, Astipalea, (Sitia), Lesbos (Mytilini), Chios, Mykonos, Naxos, Santorini, Iraklion (Iraklion), Limnos (Moudros), Skyros (Linaria), Syros, Paros, Milos, Crete (Chania), Alexandroupolis, Kavala (Keramoti), Thessalonika, Skiathos, ATHENS, Kithera, Ioannina, Prevenza, Kerkyra/Corfu, Kefalonia (Argostoli), Zakinthos/Zante (Keri), Kalamata

Region labels: Turkey, Bulgaria, GREECE, Ionian

Scale: 0 —— km 100

main towns to island airports have now mostly gone, and fares are predicted to rise sharply over the next few years (though given their relatively low starting level they still represent good value). The only consolation to be found in this is that the traditional problem of poor avail-ability of aircraft seats on all the popular islands is likely to ease. This could work ·to the benefit of the island hopper, as in the past one has often had to book flights at least a week in advance via the Olympic offices to be found amidst the plethora of island ticket agents. If you are trying to pack a lot of islands in to a holiday then these flights do offer the option of a quick transfer to the islands, and of course, they offer a potentially invaluable lifeline if you need to return to the capital in a hurry. Much of the domestic fleet consists of light aircraft so you have to take care not to exceed the 15 kilo baggage allow-ance. All the seats are non-smoking. Prices given opposite were announced at the start of 1995. Timetables and bookings for Olympic Airways can be obtained from the company office at 11 Conduit Street, London, W1R 0LP (☎ 071 409 2400).

Food & Drink

The demands of tourists have, if anything, added to an uninspiring cul-inary scene. You can't get far these days from a corner supermarket selling all the essentials. However, since you can get a reasonable meal and beer in a restaurant for around £5, there is little incentive for island hoppers to come armed with camping stoves and few do. Greek menus tend to be rather limited (chicken, grilled steak and fish dishes predominating). It is standard practice in Greece to do the cooking well before eat-ing; the theory being that luke-warm food is better for the digestion. Large quantities

of olive oil are also added to 'lube the tubes'. As a result, foreign food outlets have sprung up on many of the popular islands. Thanks in part to the large US Greek community providing a steady stream of holidaying ex-patriots, pizzer-ias now exist on most islands and, increas-ingly exotic establishments are adding colour to the scene. Ios now has a Chinese restaurant, Mykonos a Thai; both looking somewhat incongruous amidst their whitewashed Greek chora surroundings.

Despite its poor reputation Greek food is by no means all bad. Common to all islands is the much underrated local **fast food**. Sold from small street shops and bars it consists of an Arabic bread-style roll (known as *Pita*) filled either with *Gyros* (spit-cooked layers of meat — usually pork) or *Souvlaki* (kebab), with tomatoes, onions and yoghurt. For a hungry island hopper a plateful of Souv-laki Pita is positively divine, but when choosing which shop to patronise it pays to look to see where the locals are congre-gating for they are the ones who really know which is the best outlet in town. Sadly, in many tourist areas fast food shops have taken to adding french fries to the mélange (thus saving on the amount of meat in the pita).

The other great mainstay of the island culinary scene is the ubiqitous **Greek salad**. Known as *choriatiki* it is made up of sliced tomatoes, onions, peppers and cucumbers topped with *feta* (goat's cheese) and the odd decorative olive. It is often produced as a side dish to the main course in tavernas. **Main courses** tend to be uninspiring. The most common offerings are spiced meat-balls (*keftedes*), mousaka, and roast chicken.

Seafood is naturally abundant in the islands; though the more popular fish are surprisingly pricey as a result of over-fishing depleting stocks: the strings of *chtapodi* (octopus) hung out to dry on washing lines outside island tavernas being one of the more photogenic culinary

sights. Somewhat less attractive is the sight of the little critters fresh from the sea being clobbered until their pips squeak in order to soften them up to the point of being nicely chewy when chopped up and boiled in vinegar. If this doesn't appeal, you can always eat tender-fried baby squid (*kalamarakia*) instead. **Shellfish** is also very popular. Crayfish (*astakos*) and Lobster (*kalogeros*) are commonly found on taverna menus. Of the fish proper, the most sought after dishes are grilled mullet (*bouni*) and bream (*lithrini*).

Alongside the fast food outlets, tavernas and full blown restaurants, are an increasing number of outlets offering snack foods. Most of the more chic islands now sport waterfront patisseries offering a selection of fancy cakes and pastries. These include traditional Greek fare; notably **cheese pies** (*tiropitta*) served piping hot. Island bakeries also get in on the act by selling these, and breakfast **doughnuts**, alongside freshly baked bread during the tourist season. Many also now stock soft canned drinks, ice cream and refrigerated chocolate bars (forget about buying chocolate that isn't) as well.

The usual brands of **soft drinks** are all widely available in the Eastern Mediterranean though you will find shop prices are half what you are charged elsewhere. Still **mineral water** (available in blue plastic bottles that litter some beaches) is the staple backpacker day-time drink. On many of the islands it is claimed that you can drink the tap water, but this isn't to be recommended given that summer fresh water shortages often result in supplies being heavily adulterated with sea water. Many of the islands also produce wines; with heavy reds predominating, along with another Greek island speciality: *retsina* — a dubious pine barrel 'wine' that doubles up wondrously as turpentine in a pinch.

Greek

One of the most immediate (and often intimidating) problems new visitors to Greece expect to encounter is the apparently strange Greek language with its alien-looking alphabet. Such worries are all but groundless these days. Greece has been on the tourist map for so long that Greek phrase books are now to be numbered among the 'non-essential' items (though they are widely on sale in Greece). In fact, you can be sure of finding someone who can speak English in all the tourist facilities, if only because the language is compulsory in Greek schools, and each summer the country is full of Greek-expatriate families from the USA, Canada and Australia (it isn't usually even necessary to ask the locals if they can speak English). Reading the Greek alphabet on signs and maps is a different matter. Fortunately most road and other tourist-related signs are in both Greek and English, as are most ferry timetables outside ticket agencies. The only exceptions to this are the less touristed islands of the Northern Aegean and the Turkish coast, where German is now the de facto lingua franca; reflecting the nationality of the majority of visitors. Even though you don't need any Greek, any efforts to speak it are appreciated, and a few basic phrases are given on p. 501 along with a summary of the letters and their English equivalents.

Precise transliteration between Greek and English letter forms is difficult as in some instances equivalents are lacking. For example: the Greek for 'Saint' Agiou can be variously transcribed as Agiou, Ag., Ayios, or Aghios. It is also not uncommon to find non-Greek names used alongside their older Greek counterparts. Hence the Cretan town of Agios Nikolaos is known by island bus drivers as 'San' Nikolaos (a hangover from the days of Venetian control of the island). 'Santorini' is another example of a later Venetian name co-existing with an earlier one: 'Thira'. Both are commonly used but refer to the same island. Just to make life really interesting 'Thira' can also be transcribed as 'Phira' or even 'Fira' and like a lot of Greek islands both the island and its principal town have the same name. This all sounds horribly confusing but it isn't really a major problem provided you look at any unfamiliar name with an eye to the possibility that it could be a variation on the name you are looking for. Thus: Cos = Kos, Lesbos = Lesvos, Siros = Syros, etc. Where an island is commonly known by two names or in the UK by a name in a form which does not correspond particularly closely to the form used in Greece (e.g. Rhodes is always referred to locally as 'Rodos', Crete = 'Kriti') both names are given on island maps.

To help aid recognition on each chapter title page you will find the names of the major ports covered by the chapter in Greek. For the most part they are shown in the accusative form as they appear on ticket agency timetables and ship destination boards. E.g. Paros = ΠΑΡΟΣ (nominative) is shown in its more commonly encountered accusative form: ΠΑΡΟ. As a further aid to the language you will find below an old school rhyme (even though it doesn't) used to drum the Greek alphabet into the minds of countless poor kids:

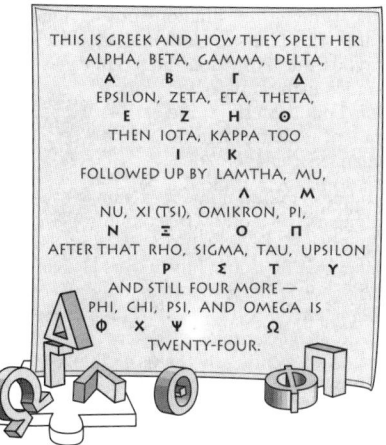

THIS IS GREEK AND HOW THEY SPELT HER
ALPHA, BETA, GAMMA, DELTA,
Α   Β   Γ   Δ
EPSILON, ZETA, ETA, THETA,
Ε   Ζ   Η   Θ
THEN IOTA, KAPPA TOO
Ι   Κ
FOLLOWED UP BY LAMTHA, MU,
Λ   Μ
NU, XI (TSI), OMIKRON, PI,
Ν   Ξ   Ο   Π
AFTER THAT RHO, SIGMA, TAU, UPSILON
Ρ   Σ   Τ   Υ
AND STILL FOUR MORE —
PHI, CHI, PSI, AND OMEGA IS
Φ   Χ   Ψ   Ω
TWENTY-FOUR.

Health & Insurance

The countries along the northern shore of the Mediterranean maintain reasonable levels of sanitation and no inoculations are mandatory. However, vaccination against tetanus, typhoid, hepatitis A and polio is a good idea. Minor ailments are often treated by chemists, who have a wider remit than in the UK. All the large islands have 'cottage' hospitals, though most are primitive by West European standards (you should get all injuries treated checked by your own doctor as soon as you get home). These are backed up with at least one doctor on all the islands served by regular ferry and an emergency air service. Reciprocal arrangements for NHS patients exist with most countries but the widely mentioned E111 form is of limited value and no substitute for proper insurance. Full medical insurance (including emergency flight home) is strongly recommended. Amongst the easiest to obtain is the Thomas Cook Travel Insurance Package. This offers comprehensive medical insurance (including the all-important cover for accidents on mopeds 125cc and under) and is available from all Thomas Cook Retail travel shops.

Luggage Deposits

The large number of island-hoppers has encouraged a growth in outlets offering luggage deposit facilities. Most charge between 200 and 400 GDR a day and staple a numbered ticket to each bag (to redeem it you produce the counterfoil). Ticket agents have also got into the act by offering to look after bags if you buy a ticket from them. These are often useful but should be treated with some caution: look to see if any check is being made on who is removing bags as they rarely ticket them. You should be aware that if your bag goes missing from such an establishment there is a possibility that your insurer will not be willing to recognise any claim for 'unsecured' baggage.

**Maps &
Guides**

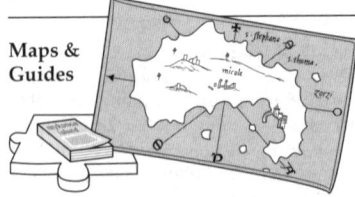

Greece has attracted guide-writers ever since Pausanias put stylus to scroll in Roman times — so much so, that there are few series that don't include the country. If you want to take an additional volume along with you, you will be spoilt for choice. However most are re-research-ed every second or third year. This tends to be the great weakness of most guidebooks as the Greek islands are changing rapidly: it therefore pays to look at the edition date (not the reprint date) and reckon that the information therein dates from at least a year earlier. Inside Greece it is difficult to obtain West European published guidebooks outside of Athens, and those that are on sale have at least a 25% mark up on their published prices. Individual island guides (in a form of English) are on sale on most islands.

The Greek islands also have a place in the history of cartography; featuring pro-minently in one of the earliest printed atlases: the *Isolario* of Benedetto Bordone. Published in 1528, it carried woodcut maps based on old books of sailing direct-ions known as 'island books'. The exam-ple above is of Mykonos (orientated with Jerusalem at the top) and its accuracy helps to explain the large number of ship-wrecks in medieval times. Almost all Greek islands have more modern island maps on sale (often with a town plan of sorts on the reverse) — most are under £1. Unfortunately, the quality of these maps varies greatly. Some of them are excellent, but there are a number that are at best vague, at worst fiction (i.e. with minor tracks shown as major highways), and it is only by trial and error that you can determine the good from the bad.

Money
While it is desirable to have some hard cash always to hand the safest way of hanging on to your money is to take the bulk in Travellers Cheques (Thomas Cook MasterCard Travellers Cheque 24-hour emergency number: ☎ 00 44 1733 502 995). American Express (emergency number: ☎ 00 44 273 696933) are also well represented in the islands, with a Travel Centre in central Athens (see p. 103). Travellers Cheques, along with Eurocheques, are accepted by banks in Greece (Eurocheques, despite their name, are also accepted in Cyprus, Israel and Turkey). Outside banking hours currency and cheques can be exchanged at many ticket agencies (albeit at a slightly worse rate of exchange). Every year sees tourists arriving armed with plastic cash cards only to discover that cash dispensing machines are a rarity except on the very popular islands. You are strongly advised to ensure that you have access to your cash via other means (Travellers Cheques remain the most versatile way of carrying money). Banknotes come in 5,000, 1,000, 500, 100 and 50 Drachma denominations; the latter two now being replaced by over-heavy coins.

All the nations of the Eastern Med. are 'blessed' with relatively high inflation and running devaluations in exchange rates. This tends to work in the tourist's favour, and even after the recent depre-ciation in the value of the GB Pound Sterling, the rate of exchange is little changed from 1992. Tour-ist exchange rates to the GB Pound Sterling (US$ 1.56, DM 2.38) at the start of 1995 were:

Cyprus [Pound]	CY£	0.736
Egypt [Lira]	EG£	5.2951
Greece [Drachma]	GRD	372.56
Italy [Lira]	ITL	2519.13
Israel [Shekel]	NIS	4.7121
Turkey [Lira]	TKL	64226.90

Moped & Car Hire

In recent years the islands have seen a dramatic increase in the numbers of moped and car hire outlets. The numbers renting mopeds in particular ensures that any town with a significant tourist presence will have at least one. Prices are surprisingly low (reckon on £5–6 for a day's rental for a low powered machine). Unfortunately, with the rise in the numbers of machines has come a large rise in the numbers of moped-related tourist deaths and serious injuries. The former are now running at over 100 a year and the latter are almost too numerous to count. Many of these are the result of inexperienced and ill-equipped riders attempting too much on poor roads using often poorly maintained machines. Before you succumb to the temptation to mount one and go roaring off into the sunset you should consider the possibility that — unless you are an experienced moped handler — that sunset could be more final than picturesque.

Even if you are an experienced moped rider, there are a number of points and pitfalls worth noting. First, insurance: does your holiday insurance cover all the potential risks you run riding a moped or motorbike without a helmet (these can't be hired along with the moped as no-one bothers with them in Greece)? Secondly, before you hand over your day's rental money and your passport (a guarantee that you will bring the machine back) you should: (1) check the condition of the machine you are hiring, (2) ascertain who is liable for what if it brakes down, (3) check how much fuel you are getting with the machine (more reputable outlets can often be distinguished by the amount of fuel in the tank). Once you have your machine, accept its limitations; most are not powerful enough to negotiate steeper

hills and many island roads are more pot-holes than Tarmac. All the above points also apply to car hire. This is fairly expensive in the islands: reckon on paying £40 per day in High Season for a Jeep or beach buggy. In order to hire one you will need to produce a current driving licence. A Green Card insurance warranty is also strongly recommended.

Newspapers & Books

Most UK and major European papers are available on all but the remotest of the Greek islands — usually via a newspaper and book-cum-stationery shop or street kiosk. On the majority of islands they appear a day after publication, though in central Athens they are usually available on the evening of the day they are published. In High Season it pays to arrive early if you want the more popular titles. The difficulty is determining when 'early' is, for it varies according to an island's links with Athens or the nearest island with a direct airport link to Western Europe. On Paros, for example, it is mid-afternoon as the newspapers are carried on the early morning ferries from Piraeus. Prices are quite high: expect to pay at least double the home country published price. Most of these newsagents also have a pricey supply of pulp fiction (along with volumes 2 and 3 of Tolkien's *Lord of the Rings*) as well as locally produced island maps and guides.

Nightlife

One of the most charming aspects of Greek islands life is the traditional evening promenade around the centre of town. Nights in Greece are the time for the locals to bask in the cooler temperatures and catch up with the gossip. As a result, even the most uninspiring

of towns can, for a few hours, exude an air of companionable bustle. Normally this lasts from dusk to 10 or 11 pm. Thereafter, the tavernas take in the lingerers who want to chat (those near the ports also serve as a temporary home for those waiting for night ferries). Most island towns also now boast at least one disco where you can touch a few more hands in the dance of life. Discos and bars usually stay open until around 3 in the morning. Thereafter the streets are often filled for a hour or so with slowly dispersing crowds of the slightly inebriated. This can be a problem time in some parts as a lack of manpower means that there is very little by way of a police presence on the streets to curb the excesses of the more exuberant foreign revellers.

Passports and Visas
No visa required for EU nationals or nationals of Australia, Canada, New Zealand, and the USA for visits to any of the countries below for up to three months unless stated. As of January 1993 EU nationals carrying ID cards are not requ- ired to carry passports within the EU. As the UK has no ID card scheme, UK nation- als must continue to travel with a passport. All nationals are recommended to continue carrying passports as they are often required when cashing travell- er's cheques or exchanging money within Greece. Passports are also required when taking day excursions to Turkey.

Greece:
UK Embassy – 1 Ploutarchou Street, 106 75 Athens (☎ 72 36211).
UK Consulates –
Corfu: 2 Alexandras Avenue, 491 00 (☎ 0661 30055, 37995).
Patras: 2 Votsi Street, 262 21 (☎ 061 227329).
Rhodes: 25th Martiou Street, No 23 (PO Box 47), 851 00 (☎ 0241 27247, 27306).
Thessalonika: 8, Venizelou Street, Eleftheria Square, PO Box 10332, 541 10 (☎ 031 278006, 269984).

Other Mediterranean Countries:

Cyprus:
Turkish Cypriot stamp in passport could hinder entry. UK High Commission – Alexander Palis Street, **Nicosia.** (☎ (0) 2 473131/7).

Egypt:
Visa required for EU and English language nationals. Fees vary according to nationality. UK single entry visa costs £15.
UK Embassy – Ahmed Ragheb Street, Garden City, **Cairo** (☎ 354 0850, 354 0852/9).
UK Consulates –
Alexandria: 3 Mina Street, Roushdi, 21529 (☎ 5467001/2, 5467171).
Port Said: Hilton Compound Complex, 6 Room 623 (☎ 231155).
Israel:
UK Embassy – 192 Rechov Street, Tel Aviv 63405 (☎ 249171/8).
UK Consulate – 198 Hayarkon Street, Tel Aviv 63405 (☎ 242105/6, 230776).

Italy:
UK Embassy – Via XX Settembre 80A, 00187 Roma (☎ 4755441, 4755551).
UK Consulate – (Postal address) PO Box 679, 1-30100
Venice: (Callers) Accademia 1051, Dorsoduro (☎ (041) 5227207, 5227408).

Syria:
Visa required for EU and most other nationals. Tourist visas require accompanying travel agent letter giving proposed itinerary. Israeli stamp in passport invalidates visa.
UK Embassy – Quarter Malki, 11 Mohammed Kurd Ali St. Imm Kotob, Damascus (☎ 11 7125 61/62/63).

Turkey:
Entry visa charge (£5) for UK, British Hong Kong and Irish nationals. US$5 for Italian, US$10 for Portuguese and Spanish nationals.
UK Embassy – Sehit Ersan Caddesi 46/A Çankaya, Ankara (☎ 127 43 10/15).
UK Consulates –
Istanbul: Mesrutiyet Caddesi 34, Tepebasi, Beyoglu, PK 33 (☎ 1447540, 1447545/9).
Marmaris: Haci Imam Sokak No 17, Tepe Mahallesi (☎ 2289, 1838, 4932).

popular islands have extra officials drafted in to help cope with the tourist season. Islands with

Photography

Popular makes of film are available on all but the smallest Greek islands. However, if your requirements are in anyway exotic (e.g. brands like Kodachrome 64) you can be certain of encountering considerable difficulty replenishing supplies. The cost of film (generally around 25% more than UK prices) also varies wildly from centre to centre. An extreme example of this is the fact that it is actually cheaper to buy a return ticket to Aegina to buy some brands than it is to buy them at Piraeus. If you want to view the results of your endeavours sooner rather than later you will find that all the popular islands now have at least one 1-hour film processing outlet in the centre of town.

If you want something more than the usual holiday snaps then you should consider using a polarizing filter to combat the brilliant sunlight that bathes the islands. A second constraint on a photographer's prowess are the signs prohibiting photography in military areas. This is particularly true on parts of Kos (and other islands and ports along the Turkish coast) and Crete (home to a major NATO base). Given local sensibilities on this subject it is best to work on the assumption that it is unwise to snap naval craft or personnel no matter where you are.

Police

Greece has three types of police in addition to the usual customs and traffic officials: the regular police, the tourist police and the port police. The islands have a varying number of each depending on their population size. Small or very

a population of under 400 usually only have one permanent official who wears all three hats.

The regular **Police** (identified by a regular police-style blue uniform and peaked cap) have a station on most islands. For the greater part of the year they don't have a lot to do given the very low crime rate among islanders (it is difficult to get away with crime on an island where everyone knows everyone else). For this reason they are relatively few in number and have little opportunity to practice and develop such detection skills as they may possess. Things of course change in the summer when they are faced with a procession of foreigners who have had a couple of dozen beers too many, their possessions stolen (usually by other holiday makers), or worse (see p. 59). Sad to say it, but the reaction to tourists beating at their doors is often one of polite indifference. If you are reporting a crime, the chances are it will be solely for insurance purposes; the probability of the police recovering lost items is very low. It therefore pays to be extra vigilant when it comes to looking after your property. If you are one of the very few who hit serious trouble, then it is advisable to contact your nearest consulate before the police if practicable.

The **Tourist Police** are not to be confused with the regular police (despite having an all but identical uniform: this makes it easier for small island officials to do a quick change act). As their name implies, their function is to look after tourists and ensure that outlets serving them (i.e. hotels, pensions, restaurants, shops, taxis, etc.) are conforming to official regulations. In common with the NTOG / EOT and occasional island tourist offices they also provide maps, island information, travel, and accommodation details. If you ever have difficulty finding a bed or end up embroiled in an argument with a local over a bill, then the tourist police should be your first port of call (often the mere threat of bringing them in is enough to resolve arguments): they are generally very helpful, can speak some English (of a sorts) and are disposed to be on the tourist's 'side' if there is a just cause for complaint. They can also perform a valuable liaison role if you need to visit the regular police (their offices are often to be found in the same building); so much so, that it is worth taking most problems to them first. Unfortunately, they generally only have officials on islands with a large summer tourist population.

The third — and most visible — police are the **Port Police**. Decked out in a natty all-white naval officer-like uniform, their sole responsibility is the supervision of the island and mainland ports. Armed with whistles (that are blown constantly) they attempt to keep tourists and locals alike from boarding ferries before those passengers that wish to disembark have done so, as well as keeping both out of the road of cars and lorries attempting to use the same exit/boarding door. They tend to be a fairly frustrated lot as no-one takes a blind bit of notice of them as a rule. On the busier islands quayside passenger sheds have been installed to make the port police's job easier as they enable foot passengers to be corraled behind a locked gate at the end of the shed until the port police deign to release them with a key. On smaller islands they don't bother resorting to such stratagems and just roll up (often on a moped) 20 minutes before the ferry turns up; armed with ship-to-shore radios, they *know* exactly when a ferry is going to arrive. If you have been waiting several hours for an overdue ferry

a port policeman is a very welcome sight.

The port police are usually stationed in a separate building from the regular police. More often than not it is within a couple of hundred metres of the ferry quay and sometimes has a board outside listing the day's ferry departures. As a rule, port policemen are not interested in helping you to find a room or anything else for that matter — though they are approachable enough if you want ferry information.

Public Holidays

As a rule public holidays tend to have much more impact on bus rather than ferry services within Greece. Plans to travel on religious holidays should allow for the possibility that services will be reduced or suspended. The Greek Orthodox church still exerts a powerful influence and ferries are sometimes diverted to carry pilgrims to the shrine of the moment. Greek public holidays in 1995 are:

January 1, 6;
March 6, 25 (Independence Day);
April 21, 23, 24 (Easter);
May 1;
June 12 (Day of the Holy Spirit);
August 15 (The Feast of the Assumption of the Virgin Mary);
October 28 (Ohi Day);
December 25, 26.

Rail Links — Aegean

The Greek railway system (known by the initials OSE) offers the cheapest way of getting around the country as well as (mules or walking excepted) the slowest. The network has suffered from a chronic lack of investment and this is all too evident in the condition of much of the rolling stock (broken windows are a local speciality) and the interminable delays to be encountered when travelling. Most of the system is single track; so trains have to keep stopping to allow oncoming trains to clear the line. Timetables are often as

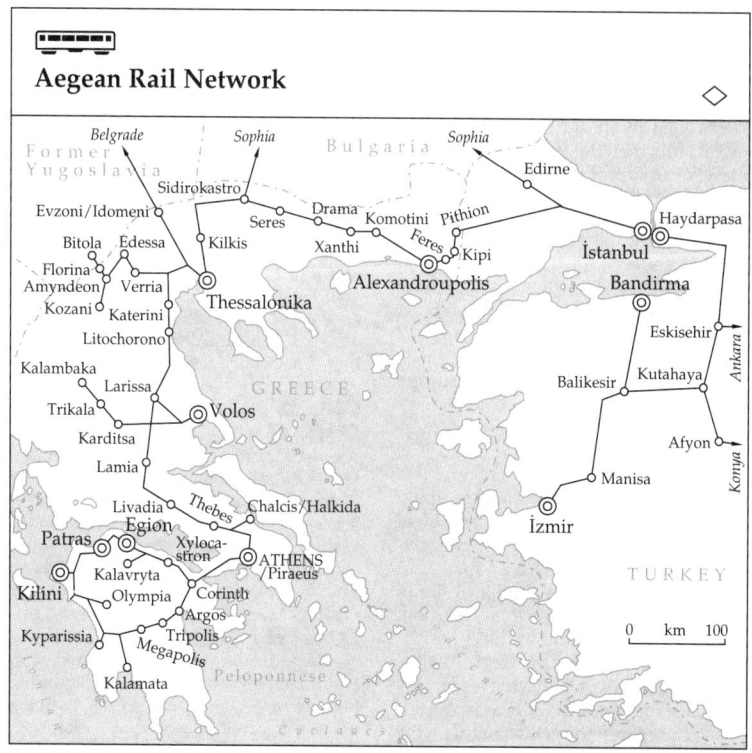

🚃
Aegean Rail Network

◇

much theoretical as factual (the Thessalonika—Perissa/Volos service (£4.70) has a habit of leaving up to an hour before its stated departure time) and are invariably crowded. Inter-city trains are somewhat better, but fewer in number. As a result, the recently launched rail pass — the Vergina Flexipass — includes other features to increase its appeal (these include accommodation and a city tour of Athens and a one day cruise to Aegina, Poros and Hydra). If you are on a wide-ranging island hopping holiday then the pass is worth considering. In any event the rail system, for all its faults, is useful, providing an invaluable back-up to

missing ferries when travelling in the Northern Aegean, or in moving between ports on the Peloponnese. Likewise the equally antiquated Turkish rail link up to İstanbul offers a back-up option to the limited ferries running up the Turkish Aegean coast.

Rail Links — International
There are two traditional rail routes into Greece: the first (and most popular) is via ferry from Italy, the second, through Eastern Europe and the Balkans.

1: London—Milan—Ancona/Brindisi: ferry to Patras, and train to Athens. Offers the option of visiting additional islands by stopping in the Ionian chain. Two lines — HML Ferries and Adriatica — offer free 'Deck' accommodation to Inter/Eurail ticket holders on their Brindisi—Patras ferries. You just turn up at the boat; but given the limited space available, you should arrive *very* early.

2: London overland to Athens.

The civil war in what was Yugoslavia has made the traditional route via Venice and Belgrade impracticable. In order to avoid the areas of conflict travellers now have to change in Budapest and Belgrade.

One Stop Island Hopping

The appeal of travelling across Europe and hopping on to a Greek island is seemingly very great if the numbers of Inter-Rail and Eurail card users doing this is anything to go by. However, time is a problem since days spent island hopping are wasted rail ticket days. The ideal island is therefore one with good connections to the mainland. Many mainland holiday makers have a similar desire to 'do' a Greek island. Unfortunately, both groups tend to fall foul of the rip-off '3-Island' cruises from Piraeus to Aegina, Hydra and Poros; islands that are largely devoid of the Greek island atmosphere. If you are prepared to spend a night on the island of your choice a more attractive range of possibilities are open to you:

Option 1

1) **2** +) **4** ?

Rail travellers arriving in Greece via Eastern Europe tend to head straight for Athens and then worry about finding a boat once there. Escape the crowds by abandoning your train corridor at Larissa. Frequent connections to Volos will see you a mere three hours from Skiathos — one of the most attractive Greek islands. Daily sea links with Thessalonika mean that you can jump from there as well or return to Eastern Europe without retracing your rail journey. Day trips from Athens are another way to do Skiathos; but the island deserves more time than this. Save a day for hops to neighbouring Skopelos and Alonissos.

Option 2

3) **5**) **7**

As everybody stops off at Athens it is inevitable that most island-hoppers tend to start from Piraeus and that means a wide choice of possible destinations. Paros is the easiest island to get to. A second day can be spent on Santorini before hopping back to Piraeus overnight.

Option 3

5) **6**) **7**

For those in a real hurry; Athens then on to Patras stopping over on Corfu for a day before heading on to Italy. Again a popular stopping point with travellers in either direction.

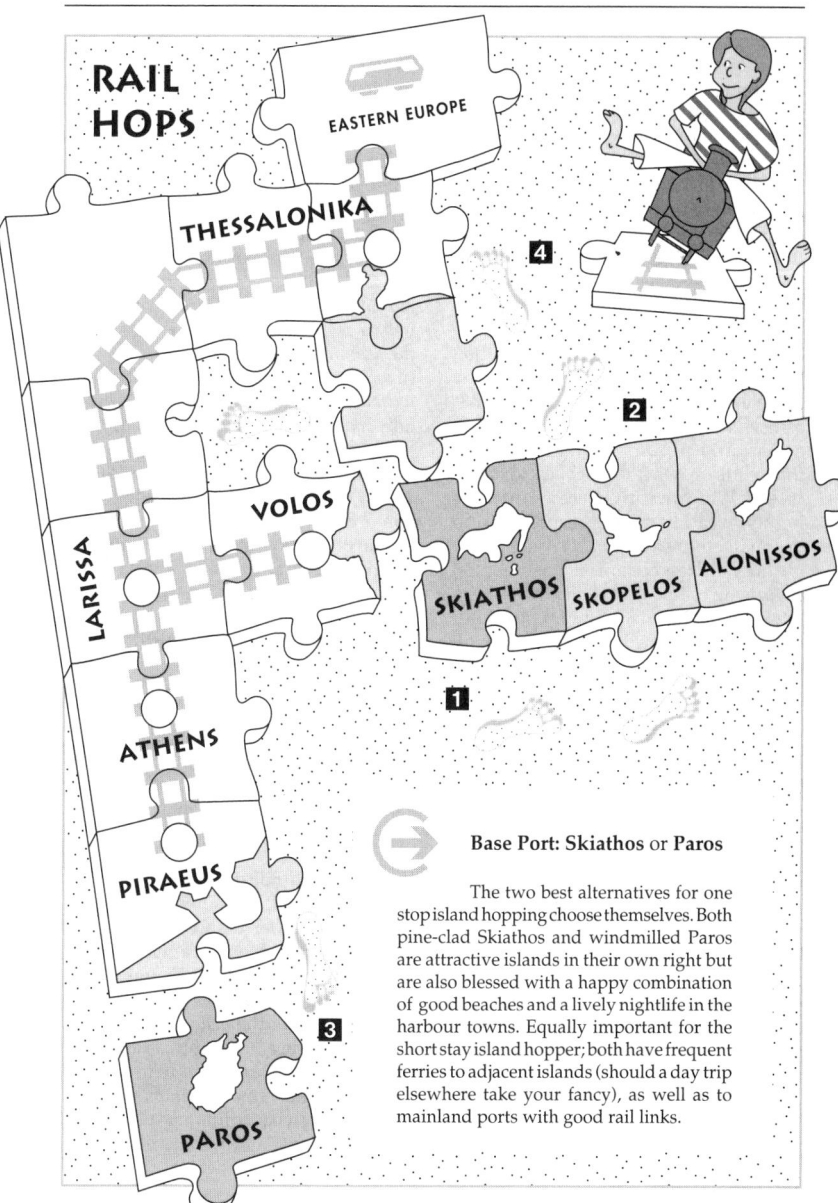

RAIL HOPS

EASTERN EUROPE

THESSALONIKA

4

2

VOLOS

LARISSA

SKIATHOS SKOPELOS ALONISSOS

1

ATHENS

PIRAEUS

Base Port: Skiathos or Paros

The two best alternatives for one stop island hopping choose themselves. Both pine-clad Skiathos and windmilled Paros are attractive islands in their own right but are also blessed with a happy combination of good beaches and a lively nightlife in the harbour towns. Equally important for the short stay island hopper; both have frequent ferries to adjacent islands (should a day trip elsewhere take your fancy), as well as to mainland ports with good rail links.

3

PAROS

Religion

Thanks to the Greek Orthodox church religion continues to play an important part in Greek society. The result is a profusion of churches and a veneration of things religious no longer seen in Western Europe. This even extends to little old ladies giving up their bus seats to priests just out of theological college — something which might not seem so surprising until you try to get on a ferry along side them, for the little old ladies in black — the notorious black widows — are the original Hell's Grannies of Monty Python fame: kicking and shoving their way aboard with grim determination that refuses to admit defeat. Much of their anger can be put down to the convention that requires them to wear black for years on end. Widowers in Greece get off more lightly, wearing a black armband for a year. Given this strict observance of the traditional dress code, it isn't perhaps too surprising to find that islanders get very upset when tourists attempt to enter churches in shorts or beachwear. Properly dressed (i.e. with torso and legs covered) tourists are made to feel very welcome.

Thanks to a tradition which expects every family to build its own chapel, small room-sized chapels abound on the Greek Islands. Roman Catholic communities are also to be found on some — a remnant from the days of Venetian or Italian rule. Thanks to the population exchanges that followed the Helleno-Turkish war of 1919–22 Islam has all but disappeared from the islands. Athens and a number of island towns still contain mosques sporting minarets, but without exception they have been taken out of use as places of worship and converted into

museums or warehouses. This process has been reversed in the former Greek towns along the Turkish coast.

Scams

The large number of tourists (particularly to Athens) has, sad to say it, produced some sharp practices by an unscrupulous few. These are the most common scams:

1. The 500 Drachma Note Trick

The tourist pays a taxi-driver (airport taxis love this one) or waiter with a 5000 Drachma note and by a slight of hand it is handed back with the protest that it is only a 500 Drachma note. *Always* check the size of notes when paying a bill. You can avoid the problem arising by holding it up before handing it over and saying 'I only have a 5000 Drachma note'. If, however, you do get done, stand your ground and suggest a visit to the Tourist Police.

2. The Passport Trick

Some hotel and room owners charge tourists who have checked-in, found the room unsatisfactory and checked-out again, a fee for the return of their passport. You can avoid this by keeping your passport until you have checked the room. If you do get caught don't hand over any cash: instead call in the tourist police.

3. The Meths Trick

It is not unknown for meths or some other tasteless additive to be added to spirits in resort bars. If in doubt, sound out fellow tourists for tried and tested nightspots.

Sea Sickness

If you are apt to fall victim it is more likely as not that it will be thanks to the vessel you are on rather than changes in sea conditions. The Mediterranean is calm compared to the English Channel. Obviously it can get rough — particularly in the Aegean when the *meltemi* wind rushes down from the north — but as a rule on most ferries you are hard put to distinguish any sea movement. Catamarans and hydrofoils can be a different matter. Sea sickness is caused by the inability of the brain to correlate conflicting information from the eye and ear. The eye perceives the vessel as being a static object while the balance mechanism of the ear is telling the brain that the body is travelling up and down, and all over the place. The easiest way of resolving this cerebral conflict is to (1) go up on deck where you can keep the horizon rather than the ship as the static point of reference, thus allowing the brain to more accurately interpret the balance information received from the ear, and (2) take up a position in the centre of the vessel about two-thirds the length of the ship from the bow. This will be the optimum point of least vertical and horizontal movement (akin to the top — rather than the bottom — of a pendulum) and (3), eat before you sail and keep nibbling on something during the journey to keep the stomach occupied.

A number of over-the-counter drugs can be obtained locally in Greece. *Dramamine* is the most widely available but like many of these drugs it is apt to cause drowsiness; for this reason alone it is better to get motion sickness drugs before you travel so that you can be advis-ed as to possible reactions. Alternatives such as adhesive patches, Ginger Root Capsules (the herbalist remedy) and Sea Bands (wrist-bands that rely on Nei-Kuan acupressure point techniques) aren't available in this part of the world anyway.

Shopping

Regular shopping hours in Greece are 08.00–13.30/15.00 Monday to Saturday and 17.30–20.30 on Tuesday, Thursday and Friday. In lucrative tourist towns an open-all-hours (even Sundays) regime is adopted in High Season. Pharmacies in the towns open in the evenings on a rota basis: a sign in Greek on the door would tell you which one if you could read it. Street kiosks are usually open from 08.00–23.00 — so liquid refreshments, snacks and English language newspapers (one day late) are always readily available.

Each island chain has its own specialities (the Cyclades have reproduction Cycladic idols, the Dodecanese duty-free liquor). Leather goods, reproduction statuary, bronzes and ceramics by the score and sponges are common to all. Other islands are noted for individual goods; e.g. the pistachio nuts of Aegina. The more popular islands are 'blessed' with pricey gold and clothing boutiques. A rather incongruous (given the temperatures) and less attractive feature of the more up-market islands are the fur shops now driven to extinction elsewhere.

Sightseeing

Most archeological sites and museums in Greece are regulated by the NTOG / EOT. Opening hours vary, but most operate something akin to a 08.30–15.00 timetable, Tuesdays to Sundays, and are closed on Mondays. Major archaeological sites in Athens and elsewhere usually stay open until at least 18.00 in High Season. You can expect to pay to enter all archaeological sites and museums in Greece (except on Sundays, when free admission is standard for both museums and all sites). Ticket prices are around £2 to enter the average town museum, £3–4 for any of the major sites. ISIC-carrying students usually get a 50% discount. For the most part, ruins and exhibits are usually labelled in Greek and English.

On archaeological sites tourists are increasingly being prohibited from entering important individual buildings or standing on mosaics left in situ (to prevent wear and tear): each usually has a warden armed with a whistle to bring those who step beyond the boundary ropes back into line; as a result a visit to the Athenian Acropolis or Olympia is apt to sound like a school sports day.

Taxis

Island taxis perform a valuable back-up role to the buses; on some islands (e.g. Leros) they have all but replaced them. All are metered, but it is not uncommon for the driver to forget to switch the meter on. In view of this, you should always ask how much the journey will cost before you get going. Also, don't be too surprised to find locals grabbing a lift if they know your driver. Athenian taxi drivers are a far less friendly lot. In Athens get into a taxi before stating your desired destination: most have their own patch and aren't interested in going anywhere else (anywhere else being where you want to go).

Telephones

The Greek telephone system has seen a radical change over the last couple of years thanks to the widespread introduction of the telephone card. As many homes in Greece have yet to be linked to the world by phone, phonecards have become the way to make both domestic and international calls. Phonecards are on sale from street kiosks and the communal telephone offices to be found in every port and town. Easily spotted by the grey satellite dish that adorns the roof, they are advertised by the initials OTE (ask for the 'Otay'). Usually open from 07.00—23.00 most contain 6 to 8 booths equipped with meters. You make your call and pay afterwards at the supervisor's desk. Until the arrival of the phonecards the OTE was one of the hubs of island life. These days it is usually empty apart from the staff gloomily contemplating the prospect of impending unemployment in-between selling the odd phonecard (1994 prices were 4500 GDR for a 500 unit card, 6000 GDR for 750, and 8000 GDR for 1000).

Phonecards aside, the Greek telephone system is pretty antiquated (on average it takes five years to have a domestic phone installed). Connections are often hard to make within Greece as most go via under-sea cable and you can spend a happy 20 minutes re-dialling. International calls (via the satellite) are far less of a problem. Prefix the UK number (after removing the initial '0' of the area code) with: 0044 in Cyprus, Greece, Israel and Italy, and 9944 in Turkey and Yugoslavia. Telephone calls can also be made from the confectionery and tobacco kiosks found in main town streets and from some ticket agencies (in both instances you will have to pay roughly 10% more for your call).

Time

Greece and the Eastern Mediterranean countries are — apart from a few days during the change-over period to and from summer time — 1 hour ahead of Italy and most European countries, 2 hours ahead of UK GMT/Summer Time.

What to take

When Phileas Fogg went around the world in 79 days he packed only 2 shirts and 3 pairs of stock-ings. Admittedly this was backed up with a manservant complete with a carpet bag containing £20,000, but this item aside you could do worse than follow his example and pack as little as you can get away with: the big disadvantage of island hopping is that you have to carry all your luggage with you. Luckily, Greece in the summertime is warm and dry enough for most people to comfortably get by with their beach-wear and a couple of changes of clothes. Add to this sundry items determined by your interests in life (those keen on monasteries or churches tend to take more formal clothing, while most male Italians go for tortoise-shell sunglasses and five bottles of aftershave lotion) and this is quite enough to be going on with. Some other ideas that are worth considering:

A good **novel**: all island-hopping holidays involve a certain amount of waiting around for boats — a novel will do a lot to reduce any tedium. **Backgammon** is also a popular ferry-waiting pastime. Card games, however, are far less successful thanks to the wind.

A **pullover** or **windjammer**: ferries are a good way of keeping cool during the day but a poor way of keeping warm at night. Deck-class passengers travelling on outside decks will soon regret not having some kind of protective clothing.

Sleeping bags are also commonly seen accoutrements and the nights (ashore) are so mild that it is often only the more amorous (and moany) campers who bother bringing a tent.

Foam mats and **airbeds** are also very popular with deck-class passengers wanting to sleep or lie out on deck. Both are available in Greece at a price, along with the cheap straw roll-up beach mats used by almost everyone.

Earplugs are occasionally desirable on some campsites and if you want to stand on the noisy outside decks of hydrofoils.

A **can opener** is invaluable if you are eating out of local supermarkets (even small grocery shops carry odd tins from the Heinz range and Kellogg's cereals).

Student Cards: if you have one, take it, as it will get you significant discounts on tours and site entry charges.

Luxury items are better brought with you than in Greece. Cosmetics, contact lens solutions (the choice is limited outside Athens) and medicines are all notably more expensive than in the UK. Unusual makes of **film** should be brought with you. Regular film is often more expensive than in the UK, but as keeping your luggage weight down is a priority, this sort of item can be bought as you travel. You should also assume that you will need to carry **mosquito repellent** (there are more mossies than tourists in Greece) and a **sink plug** wherever you go. 'Befores, durings, and afters' (tampax, condoms and nappies) are available almost everywhere.

When to go

The Eastern Mediterranean has a similar climate to California: hot dry summers, warm wet winters and around 3250 hours of sunshine a year. August is the hottest month, with average daytime temperatures around 26° C. July follows a degree behind but boasts a higher sea temperature. It rains roughly one day per month between early June and mid September in the Northern Aegean, rarely in July and August south of Athens. More of a problem are the occasional heat waves that leave birds dropping from the trees with heat exhaustion. Fortunately among the islands the worst excesses are offset by the July and August *meltemi* wind (caused by summer low pressure over Asia) and sea breezes, though islands that see little of these can get oppressively hot. The nicest time to visit Greece is in

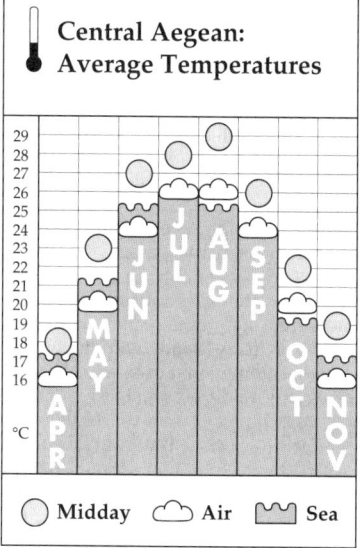

Central Aegean: Average Temperatures

°C		
29		
28		
27		
26		
25		
24		
23		
22		
21		
20		
19		
18		
17		
16		

⭕ Midday   ☁ Air   〰 Sea

April and May when the wild flowers are out, but — sad to say it — many of the ferries don't run until the summer crowds come hopping. September and October also have their fans, but are characterised by a gradual running down of ferry services, jaded hoteliers and taverna owners, and the first of the Autumn storms (when the weather first breaks these can be positively vicious).

Within the Aegean there are also significant climatic variations, with the north being a couple of degrees cooler than average, Rhodes and Crete a degree above the average and the centre and west being appreciable drier than the east. This latter feature is in part due to the Cyclades which form a rain 'shadow' thanks to a ring of hilly islands (notably Kea, Kythnos, Serifos, Santorini, Ios, Sikinos, Folegandros, Anafi and Amorgos) obscuring rain-bearing clouds. Though there has been little apparent change in climate since prehistoric times, extensive deforestation has also contributed to the dryness of the region.

Wildlife

Sad to say it, the most visible wildlife to be found in Greece these days is human rather than animal, for the country is remarkably free of potential pests to tourists. **Insects** pose the biggest problem; particularly the large mosquito population that feed along every island promenade on the tourists passing by. Other threats are something of a non-event. A small scorpion exists but possesses a very indifferent sting. Snakes play an important part in many island traditions, but are very uncommon in tourist areas besides being only mildly poisonous (this doesn't

 stop the locals going hysterical whenever they see one). Rabies is also known, but isn't a significant threat to tourists. The

rockier island coasts are home to some painful **Sea Urchins** that regularly inflict minor damage; likewise the **Dragon Fish** (or 'Drakena'), which has poisonous spikes on its spine and gills. It is to be found in the summer months hidden off sandy beaches where it burrows under the surface awaiting its prey. Most injuries are incurred while paddling. The symptoms are sharp pain followed by numbness: local doctors are equipped with a serum for immediate relief. Conger eels also inhabit rocky areas and can inflict a nasty, non-poisonous bite.

Greece is also home to a number of attractive species now in decline. Most notable of these is the small colony of **Monk Seals**. One of the 12 most endangered species in the world (estimates as to its numbers range from 750 to 300), this poor creature hangs on in its reduced breeding grounds around the small islets east of Alonissos island. **Loggerhead Turtles** on Zakinthos are rapidly going the same way thanks to tourism (see p. 402) and government neglect. In a more enlightened action the Greek government has moved to protect the magnificently horned **Kri-kri** mountain goats of Crete. Sanctuaries have been established on a number of deserted islets around the Cretan coast (notably on the island of Dia just north of Iraklion). **Dolphins** are also common in Greek waters. If half the passengers on a ferry sun deck suddenly rush over to one side of the ship as sure as eggs is eggs the cause will be a school of dolphins swimming alongside. All is not carefree abandon, however, for the dolphin population has declined by two thirds in the last decade thanks to a morbillivirus borne out of the increased levels of pollution that are causing Mediterranean watchers considerable concern (over 80% of the coastal settlements do not treat sewerage before discharging it into the sea: the worst offenders are Italy and France, but the effects on animal populations extend over a far greater area).

Women Travellers

There is an old Chinese saying that runs something like 'Ying chu you yong chee choo yee' which roughly translated means 'the difference between a dream and a nightmare is no more than the thickness of the wing of a butterfly'. The Greek islands are often deemed dream country thanks to their all-pervasive laid-back atmosphere. However, this appealing feature is a disadvantage when it encourages one to drop one's guard too much. Greece has long taken pride in its long-merited reputation as a 'safe' destination for women travellers, and solo women island hoppers are not uncommon — particularly from Scandinavian countries. However, there appears to be a small, but growing problem of assaults on women.

A recent *World in Action* TV programme reported the alarming statistic that rapes reported by British women in Greece rose by 112% between 1992 and 1993. Even allowing for the fact that the increased number only totalled 34 (a tiny figure when one considers that over two million Brits visit Greece each year) it is still a worrying trend, given that many assaults undoubtedly go unreported. Part of the trouble is that the past treatment of rape victims by Greek police officers has left a lot to be desired. Even the Foreign Office has been moved to complain that victims have been treated unsympathetically. This is not because officials are indifferent, but more the combination of a lack of language, training and experience in dealing with victims (rape is very rare within Greek society), combined with a conservative outlook that leads them to regard scantily clad young women who party day and night with crowds of young men, both downing alcohol as fast as they can open the bottles, as asking for trouble: it is noticeable that young Greek women have yet to gain a similar degree of freedom. A further unpalatable fact that local officials are loath to recognise is that a large proportion of reported attacks

are by Greek youths or men. This doesn't fit readily with the undoubted fact that, once tourists are taken out of the equation, most islands are crime free zones. The problem is, of course, the old Mediterranean male one of seeing Western girls as (1) loose, and (2) available. Add to this the chaste nature of most of the local girls and it is inevitable that the unattached Greek male is going to turn the charm on when holidaying alongside zillions of foreign tourists. With a new lot of 'pinkies' arriving every fortnight they have plenty of opportunity to practise their lines.

In view of all this the best advice must be to enjoy yourself but take care to avoid potentially dangerous situations. Most attacks appear to take place at the big resorts and party islands. Women walking home alone in the early hours or accepting lifts from locals are particularly vulnerable. Obviously on holiday one wants a night or two on the town; on these occasions consider splashing out on a reasonable hotel bed near the centre, and don't hang around until closing time when the streets are suddenly awash with inebriated men looking for a good time.

If you are attacked there are a number of things you can subsequently do:
1. Get medical help or, if that isn't available, seek help from women locally who may lend emotional support.
2. Inform your embassy or consulate (both are very sympathetic) before you talk to the police as they can liaise on your behalf.
3. If you can't be represented by an embassy or consular official, try to go to the police with a companion — preferably someone who can speak Greek.
4. Don't be afraid to curtail your holiday: embassy officials or tour reps can arrange your early return.
5. If you haven't felt up to reporting the attack in Greece, do so when you get back home: inquires can still be pursued.

1
TRANS-MED LINES

CYPRUS · EGYPT · GREECE · ISRAEL · ITALY
LEBANON · TURKEY

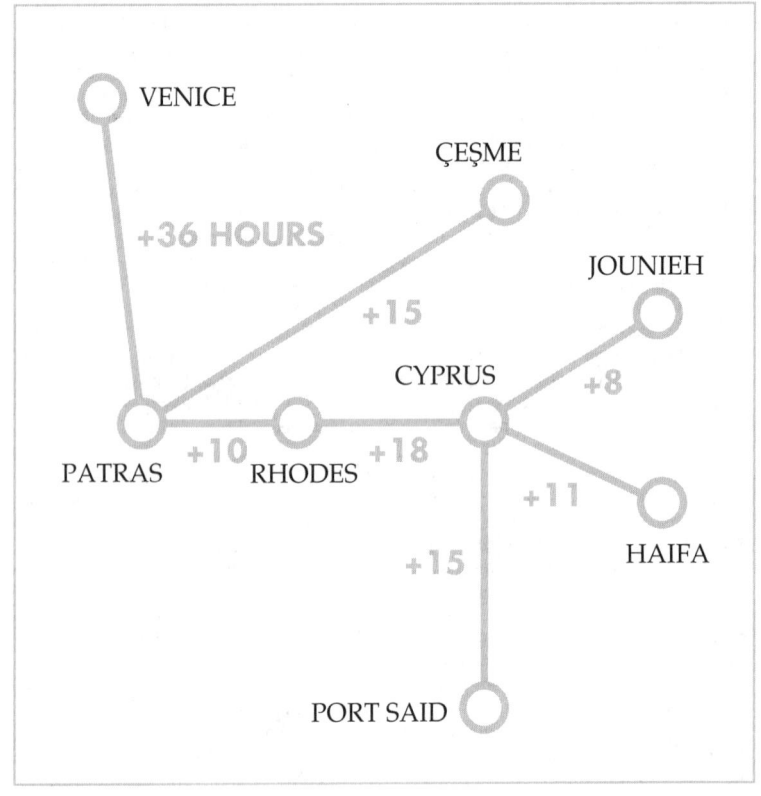

General Features

The Eastern Mediterranean is rather lop-sided in the distribution of ferry services. Beyond the extensive Greek and Croatian domestic systems there is little traffic other than international lines, and the bulk of these are confined to the Adriatic (Chapter 2). Long-haul services are more constricted, with services largely confined to running along a Venice—Alexandria axis, with services thus tending to exclude Albania, Syria, Lebanon, and Libya. The number of 'true' long-haul ferries is very small — for given the journey times and the subsequent level of fares, few routes can compete with the relative cheapness of air travel. Some of the ferries, thanks to six to eight hour stop-overs in each port, are advertised as cruise ship operations. They are cheaper in all respects than true cruise liners but have the saving grace of allowing you more flexibility in planning your itinerary. The lack of Trans-Adriatic style competition on these longer routes also makes itself felt: many of the ferries, while being marginally better than their Greek domestic counterparts, are not that much better considering the amount of time one has to spend aboard. Most have been operating in the region in various company guises for the last decade.

Suggested Itinerary [4 Weeks]

Although the international ferry network is limited it is possible (provided you are not bound by the constraining time limit of a return charter flight ticket) to devise an alluring itinerary linking some of the most famous places on the map. One good example is to attempt to see the sites of the Seven Wonders of the World:

1 Athens [5 Days]

A natural starting point; plenty of things to see and daily buses to the Temple of Zeus at **Olympia**; site of Wonder 1: *The Statue of Zeus*. The 12 m gold and ivory masterpiece of the great Athenian sculptor Phidias, it stood in the temple for 700 years before being removed

to Constantinople (now İstanbul) and lost in a fire (475 AD), leaving you the floor on which it stood to gawp at instead.

2 3 Greek Islands [6 Days]

From Piraeus you then take a ferry to **Samos** (home of the 8th of the 7 Wonders: *The Heraion* — which made the lists Babylon didn't). Here you can also take a day trip to Turkey and visit Ephesus and Wonder 2: *The Temple of Artemis*. Four times the size of the Parthenon in Athens, only one column survives: most being used in the construction of Agia Sophia in İstanbul.

Hopping via Patmos to **Kos** you can take a second day trip to Bodrum and visit Wonder 3: *The Mausoleum*. The tomb of the Hellenistic king Mausolus; again the foundations are intact, along with a good museum model.

4 Rhodes [3 Days]

On your return to Kos you can pick up a daily ferry down to Rhodes harbour; the site of Wonder 4: *The Colossus*. Here you can wonder along with everyone else as to where this 27 m high bronze statue of the Sun-god Helios stood between 290–225 BC and lay (after an earthquake) from 225 BC to 653 AD (when it was carted off to Syria as scrap), and whether it had its legs spread or (probably) not.

5 Limassol [3 Days]

At Rhodes you join the international ferry system and take a boat to Cyprus; from where you can get a connecting ferry on to Egypt.

6 Egypt [7 Days]

Ideally, you'd find a boat to **Alexandria**; site of Wonder 5: *The Pharos* (the famous lighthouse now reduced to a few marble blocks), but more likely you will have to ferry to Port Said and then take a bus to Cairo. From here you can get easily to both the above as well as Wonder 6: *The Pyramids*.

7 Haifa [7 Days]

The final Wonder: *The Hanging Gardens of Babylon* are currently inaccessible by ferry as the rivers of Babylon have long since dried up. Rather than sitting down and weeping, catch a bus to Zion. The Sinai road and Jerusalem are more than adequate compensation, and when you are ready to return to Athens, ferries are on hand from the nearby port of Haifa.

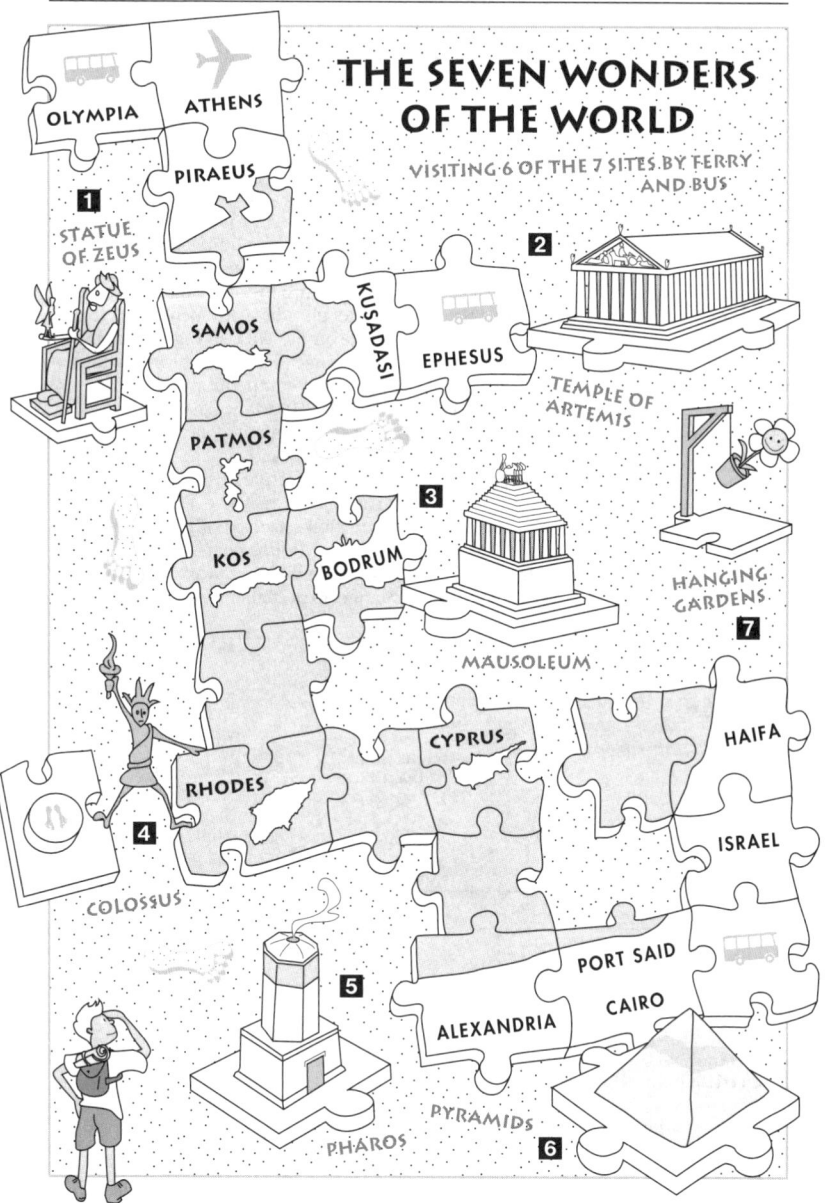

THE SEVEN WONDERS OF THE WORLD

VISITING 6 OF THE 7 SITES BY FERRY AND BUS

OLYMPIA ATHENS

PIRAEUS

1 STATUE OF ZEUS

SAMOS

KUSADASI

EPHESUS

2 TEMPLE OF ARTEMIS

PATMOS

KOS BODRUM

3 MAUSOLEUM

HANGING GARDENS

7

RHODES CYPRUS HAIFA

ISRAEL

4 COLOSSUS

PORT SAID

ALEXANDRIA CAIRO

5 PHAROS

PYRAMIDS

6

Long-Haul Ferry Services

C/F Festos
Minoan Lines; 1966; 7978 GRT.

Long-haul ferry services in the Eastern Med. are characterised by frequent changes to both ferry and itineraries. After two years of running an Ancona—Turkey service via the Corinth Canal, Piraeus, Paros and Samos, Minoan Lines disappointed many by abandoning this route in favour of a less attractive run via Crete. Last year saw the first step towards the return of the former run with the resurrection of Kefalonia (Sami) as one of the ports of call. On the down side, the final destination switched from Kuşadası to Çeşme. Small, but well-kitted-out, the *Festos* (or a successor; for her size is not one of her assets and new boats are due to join the Minoan fleet) could see further changes in 1995 given that the Italy—Turkey run has become very competitive.

C/F Baroness M - C/F Crown M
Marlines

Baroness M; 1967; 3987 GRT.
Crown M; 1966; 9499 GRT.

After a number of years confined to the Adriatic, the *Baroness M* (see p. 76) returned to her traditional Italy—Turkey route last year; running out of Bari (an unusual port to play host to such a service) to Çeşme on the Turkish coast. In doing so she took over from the *Crown M*, which in 1993 ran in competition to the *Festos* by sailing to Kuşadası. Last Summer however, she terminated her runs at Crete (Iraklion), presumably hoping to pick off the most lucrative section of the route by virtue of her larger size. When not engaged on this service, both boats augment the other Marline boats. Given this company's on-going history of chop and change, expect alterations in 1995.

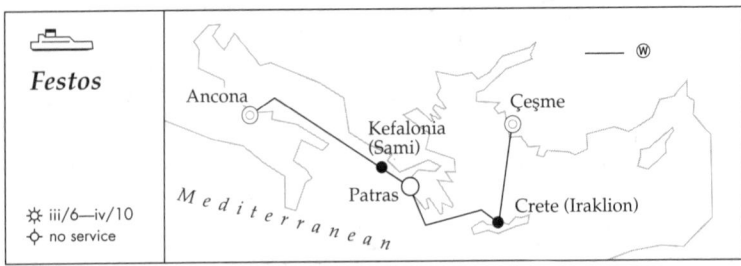

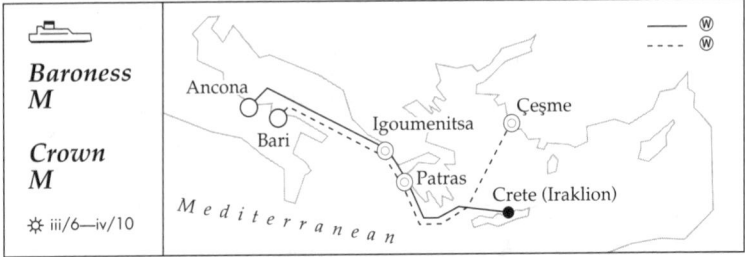

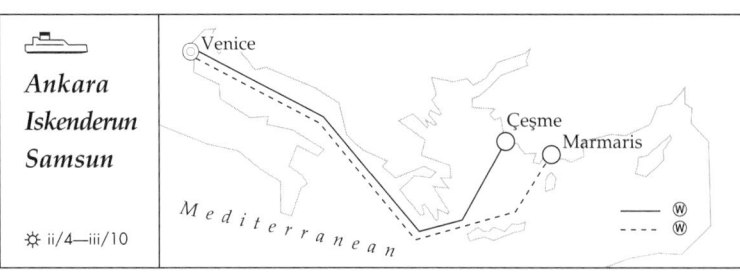

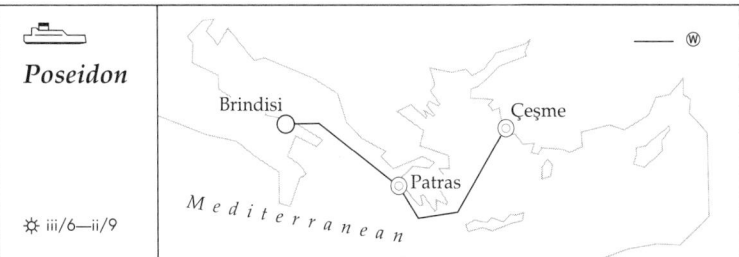

C/F *Ankara* - C/F *Iskenderun*
C/F *Samsun*
Turkish Maritime Lines
Ankara; 1983; 10,552 GRT.
Iskenderun; 1991; 10,583 GRT.
Samsun; 1985; 10,583 GRT.
Thanks to the large number of Turkish nationals now guest-working in Europe, Turkey's national ferry company now provides ferry services between Venice and ports on the Turkish coast to cater for this burgeoning travel market. The Venice—Çeşme (nearby İzmir formerly being the end destination) link is the most popular of the two routes, and is usually run by the C/F *Ankara*. Like most of the Turkish Maritime fleet she is a reasonably well equipped vessel, but with deck-class seating being something of a scarce commodity. The Venice—Marmaris (formerly Antalya) link is usually run by the *Samsun*. As with most of these long-haul boats, on-board prices reflect the captive market and it pays to bring your fodder and water with you.

C/F *Poseidon*
Med Link Lines; 1971; 8980 GRT.
The large 'new' addition to the small but expanding Med Link Lines fleet comes in the form of the *Poseidon*. Twice the size of her companion ferry — the *Afrodite II* (see p. 80)— she has extended the company's operation into the Aegean with a Brindisi—Çeşme service. This completed the very unusual feature of 1994 long-haul sailings: i.e. the appearance of a ferry link from every major Italian port on the Adriatic coast to the Turkish port of Çeşme (there were none in 1993). For no apparent reason, all the ferry operators have taken it into their heads to run competing services to a relatively small port on the Turkish coast: this does not bode well for 1995 for there must surely be major changes. The *Poseidon* could well be one of the casualties given that she was only able to offer limited support to the *Afrodite II*, and most of this out of High Season when she added stops at Igoumenitsa to those at Patras.

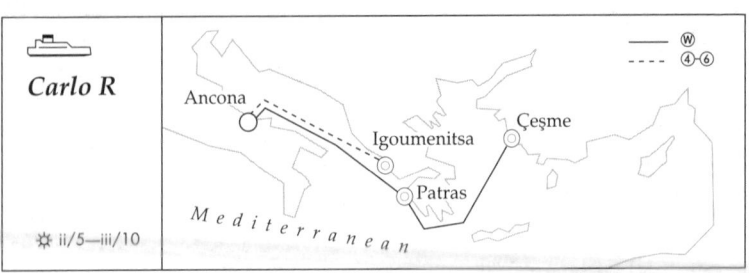

Carlo R

Ancona   Çeşme
Igoumenitsa
Patras
M e d i t e r r a n e a n

☼ ii/5—iii/10

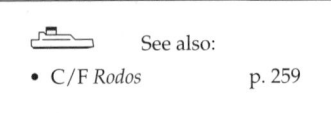

See also:
• C/F *Rodos*   p. 259

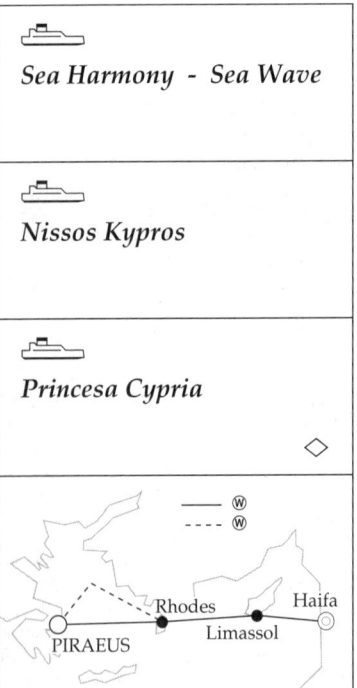

Sea Harmony - Sea Wave

Nissos Kypros

Princesa Cypria

◇

Rhodes   Haifa
PIRAEUS   Limassol

C/F *Carlo R*
Horizon Sea Lines
A new arrival on the Eastern Med. ferry
scene, the *Carlo R* is a big boat with a thin,
wispy smokestack and a large number of
lifeboats along her sides. In 1994 her 5-
day run to Turkey and back was augmented by a quick trip to Igoumenitsa;
presumably this was deemed to be a greater source of revenue than adding stops to
her main run. Given that this is a new
service, changes are probable in 1995.

C/F *Sea Harmony* - C/F *Sea Wave*
Poseidon Lines
Sea Harmony; 1977; 5477 GRT.
Sea Wave; 1961; 1996 GRT.
This company maintains an annual
service between Piraeus and Haifa via
two ferries. The main boat on the route is
the *Sea Harmony* (formerly the *Lasithi*) —
the largest vessel in the company's dilapidated looking fleet (her interior isn't as
bad as her rusty hull implies). For most of
the year she runs the no-frills standard
route via Rhodes and Limassol, but in
High Season she mimics the *Princesa
Cypria* by running an island 'drop off'
schedule: Piraeus—Patmos—Rhodes—
Limassol—Haifa—Limassol—Rhodes—
Santorini—Tinos—Piraeus (sadly, you
must have an international ticket to take
advantage of these boats for island
hopping). The diminutive *Sea Wave* runs
several days after the *Sea Harmony* and
invariably does the 'direct' route. Pokey
and old, her days are surely numbered.

C/F *Nissos Kypros*
Salamis Lines; 1958; 6103 GRT.
A Scandinavian-built train ferry that still has the railway lines extant on her car deck, the *Nissos Kypros* was the new arrival on the route in 1993. Long familiar to island hoppers (she is the old *Homeros*, a former NEL ferry that has furrowed the Aegean since the late 70s), she is now freshly painted in the livery of an equally fresh ferry company, and on the last leg of her Mediterranean career, running a straightforward Piraeus —Rhodes— Limassol—Haifa service. Spacious, but reflecting her age, on-board facilities are not really in the international ferry league.

C/F *Princesa Cypria*
Louis Cruise Lines; 1968; 8669 GRT.
The Piraeus—Limassol—Haifa route is well established and an area of intense competition by the (mainly elderly) boats that run along it. These tend to change quite frequently, but the *Princesa Cypria* has been a familiar part of the Eastern Mediterranean scene for a good few years. Ranked at the cruise ship end of the scale, she regularly includes assorted calls at Greek islands on her itinerary. Of late this has run: Piraeus—Patmos— Limassol—Haifa—Limassol—Rhodes— Lesbos (Mytilini)—Tinos—Piraeus. Facilities are better than on some other boats, no deck-class tickets are available, aircraft seating being the minimum.

C/F *Vergina Sky*
Stability Line; 1971; 3624 GRT.
Stability Line have long run a Piraeus— Limassol—Haifa service via a series of elderly ferries that change almost with every passing year. Most of these vessels have been worthy of recognition as floating archaeological exhibits, but that said, the current vessel — the *Vergina Sky* — is marginally better than most. Itineraries change almost as often as the boats. Bar the starting port of Thessalonika (a very unusual base port for international

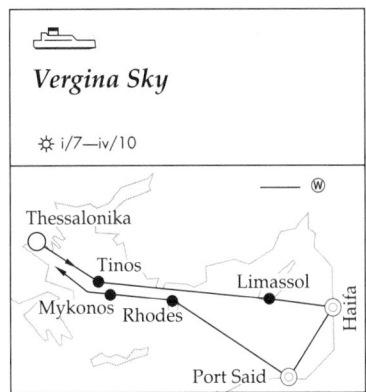

boats), this weekly one-way trip reflects previous extended itineraries.

C/F *Princesa Marissa*
Louis Cruise Lines; 1966; 9491 GRT.
The *Princesa Marissa* combines with the P/S *Princesa Victoria* to offer 2/3 day or weekly 'cruises' out of Limassol to Egypt and Israel. Irregular schedules tend to see minor alterations each year, but as the only competition is another cruise type boat — the P/S *Romantica* — there is little incentive for radical change.

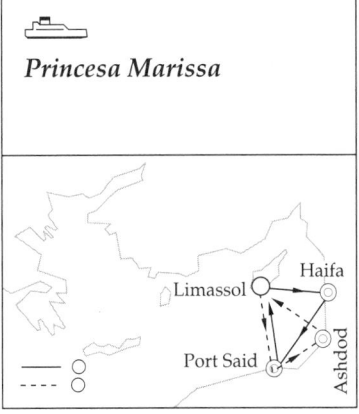

Trans-Med Ports (Non-Adriatic)

Alexandria

Egypt is too far removed from the rest of the ferry network to figure widely on schedules. Services that do exist are rather irregular with most operating via the Cypriot port of Limassol. Alexandria is an attractive neo-colonial city with good bus and rail links to the capital Cairo, some three hours drive to the south. The port area is very extensive, though ferry traffic has declined with the re-opening of the Suez Canal and Port Said.

Ashdod

Very much Israel's second port, lying just north of the Gaza Strip, Ashdod very occasionally appears on cruise/ferry schedules. Links are very erratic. Given the troubled state of the Gaza Strip an increase in ferry activity is unlikely.

Cyprus

Offering an interesting mix of sun, sand, and antiquities — to say nothing of Greek and British military cultural lifestyles happily co-existing side by side — Cyprus offers a worthy stop-over should you be hopping between Greece and Israel or Egypt. Since the 1974 Turkish invasion the Cypriot Republic has been confined to the southern 60% of the island. Despite this the south has prospered while the isolated Turkish-occupied north (set up as an unrecognised Turkish Cypriot republic) remains stagnant. The UN-monitored Green Line between the two sides of the island cannot be crossed at any point. A peace process of sorts (aimed at reunion of the island along federal lines) has been crawling along for years, but is now so bogged down it would be unrealistic to expect the situation to improve in the foreseeable future. Given that northern Cyprus can only be accessed via Turkish ports, those services are covered in Chapter 13. You should also note the potential pitfall of having a Turkish-Cypriot stamp in your passport. This can cause difficulties when entering Greece, since you will be deemed to have inevitably been in receipt of 'stolen property' (e.g. by staying in a hotel owned by a displaced Greek Cypriot), your new 'criminal' status will go down even less well if attempting to enter Greek Cyprus: you could well be denied entry.

With the division of the island has come a shift in the focus of Cypriot life, from the divided capital of Nicosia, to the south coast ports. **Limassol** (a seemingly unplanned concrete town) has became the de facto centre of Greek Cyprus as well as the ferry hub of the Eastern Med. beyond Greece. The centre is quite pleasant in a garrison town sort of way; the nearby British forces base at Akrotiri dominating the local economy. Helpful tourist offices at both new ferry terminus building (linked to the centre by city bus #1) and Limassol waterfront have free maps showing all hotels and guest houses.

The island's second port is at **Larnaca**. A prosperous resort that has grown up since the invasion thanks to the new international airport and the need to replace lost Famagusta. The Costa del Sol atmosphere of the seafront (complete with an awful beach) contrasts greatly with the ghost town ferry terminus (Larnaca is one of the quietest international ferry ports in the Med.) 2 km east of the centre. **Λ**

Geroskipou Camping: Only island site, on the beach 3 km to the east of Paphos.
🏕️

Tourist offices carry information on all the easily accessible sights from Limassol. These are the ruined cities at Kourion and Paphos and the Troodos mountains: a cool retreat from the heat of the coast.

Haifa

Haifa is a large (and not particularly attractive) port on the northern edge of Israel's Mediterranean seaboard. Conflict with her neighbours means that the country has no land route to Europe, and this is reflected in the relatively high level of ferry traffic linking Haifa with Limassol, Rhodes and Piraeus. This link operates three days a week in High Season and is maintained at twice-weekly level throughout the rest of the year. Since the peace treaty with Egypt irregular services to Alexandria and Port Said are also on offer, but most are tourist/cruise ship vessels with prices to match. Most casual non-vehicle traffic on both these routes is gleaned from the ranks of the backpacker and Kibbutz brigade. Security problems within the country are reflected on ferries that include Israel in their itineraries. This is tighter than on other boats (particularly since the terrorist attack on the Greek tourist ship *City of Poros* in 1988) and even if your destination is not Israel you can expect rigorous questioning on boarding.

Jounieh

A small port set safely in the Christian enclave of the Lebanon in a wide bay 20 km north of Beirut. A ferry link was established on the outbreak of the civil war that left Beirut port in ruins. For the bulk of the last 20 years operating a 'rat' run to Larnaca on Cyprus. Services were suspended in 1994.

Port Said

Lying on the north-eastern entrance to the Suez canal Port Said has regained its role among Egypt's premier commercial ports following the re-opening of the canal. Good bus links with Cairo, which is just as well since — canal excepted — there is little of interest here. Fortunately the Cairo road follows the bank of the canal (free sightseeing) so that arrival here has some advantages. That said, if you are arriving as an independent traveller outside a cruise/tour visit, you should allow 3–4 hours to negotiate the tortuous local immigration and customs processing operation.

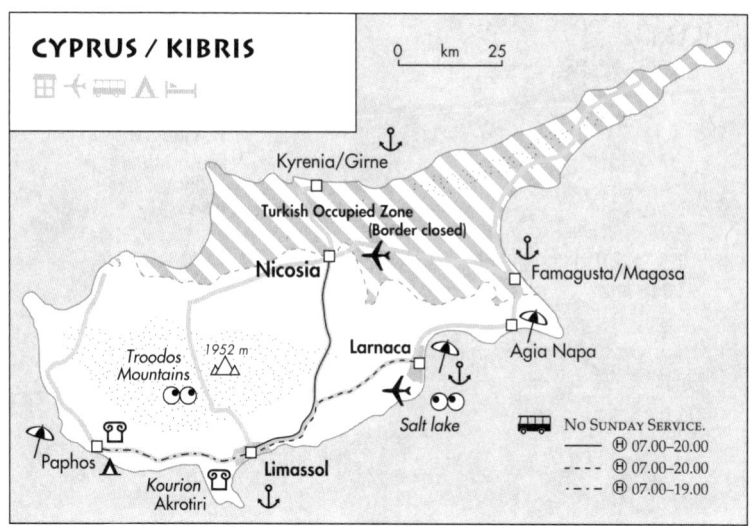

2
ADRIATIC LINES

**ANCONA · BARI · BRINDISI · CORFU / KERKYRA
IGOUMENITSA · OTRANTO · SPLIT · ZADAR**

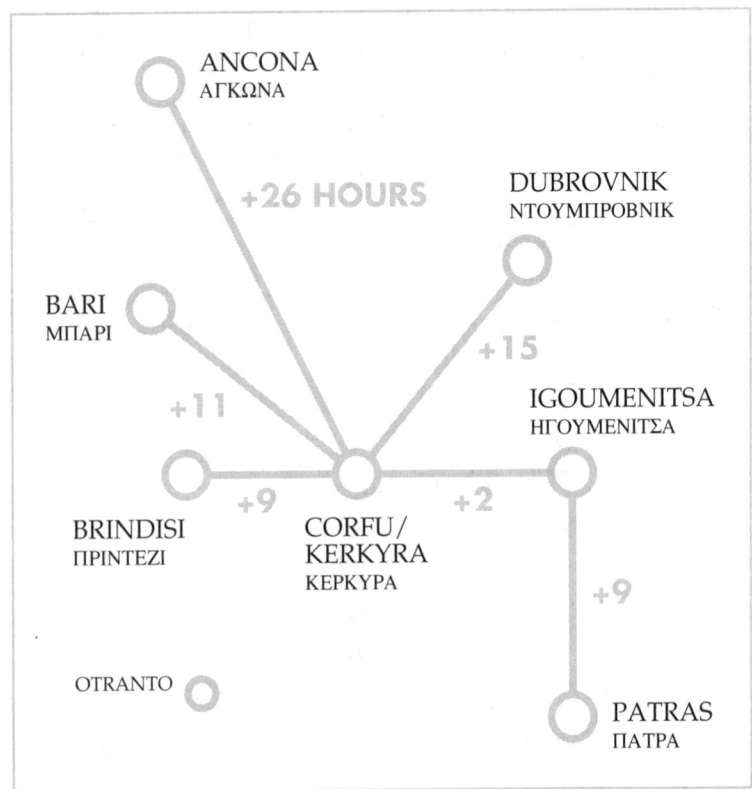

ANCONA
ΑΓΚΩΝΑ

+26 HOURS

DUBROVNIK
ΝΤΟΥΜΠΡΟΒΝΙΚ

BARI
ΜΠΑΡΙ

+15

+11

IGOUMENITSA
ΗΓΟΥΜΕΝΙΤΣΑ

+9

+2

BRINDISI
ΠΡΙΝΤΕΖΙ

CORFU /
KERKYRA
ΚΕΡΚΥΡΑ

+9

OTRANTO

PATRAS
ΠΑΤΡΑ

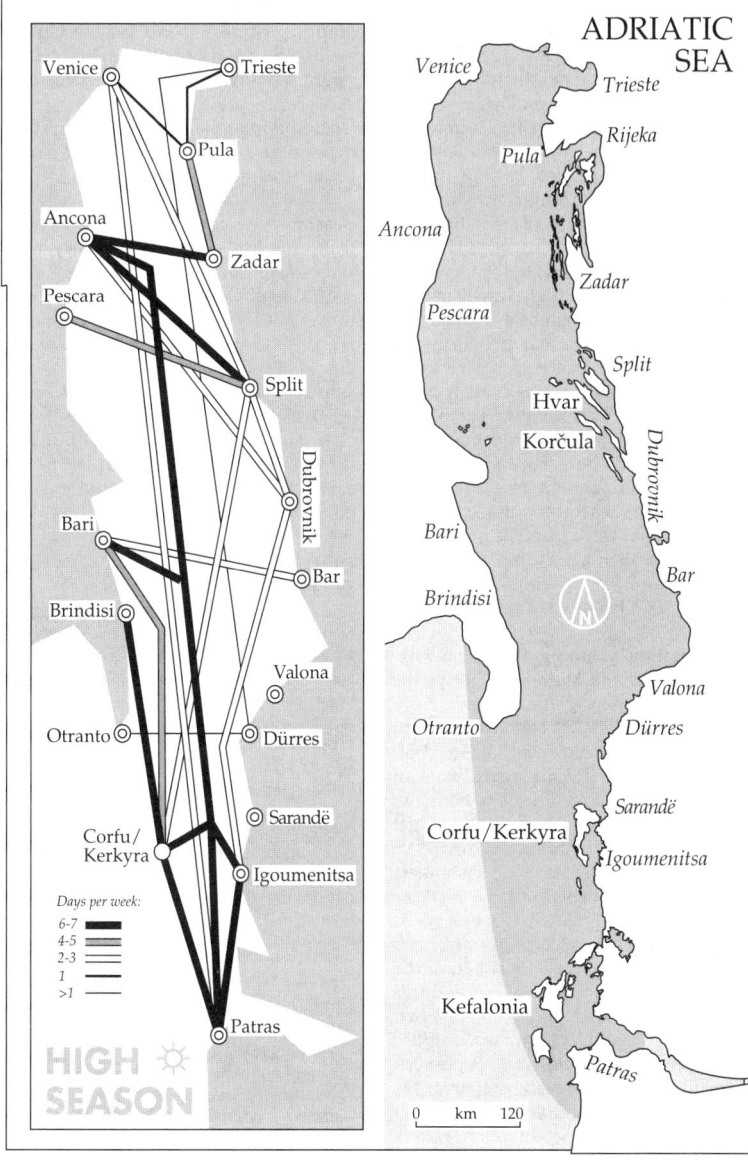

ADRIATIC SEA

Venice
Trieste
Rijeka
Pula

Ancona

Pescara

Zadar

Split

Hvar
Korčula

Dubrovnik

Bari

Bar

Brindisi

Valona

Otranto

Dürres

Sarandë

Corfu/Kerkyra

Igoumenitsa

Kefalonia

Patras

Venice
Trieste
Pula
Ancona
Zadar
Pescara
Split
Dubrovnik
Bari
Bar
Brindisi
Valona
Otranto
Dürres
Sarandë
Corfu/Kerkyra
Igoumenitsa
Patras

Days per week:
6-7
4-5
2-3
1
>1

HIGH ☀ SEASON

0   km   120

General Features

The Adriatic is very much part of Italy's back yard and is treated as something akin to the English Channel, with the coastal resort towns of her rather bland east coast serving as jumping-off points. Almost all of the larger ferries run down the Adriatic to Greece, encouraged by the tourist hordes who pass through each summer as well as the freight trade generated by Greece's membership of the EU (now greatly enlarged thanks to the closure of the land route through the war-torn countries of former Yugoslavia). This is a potent combination that produces the most competitive international ferry services in the Mediterranean: even deck-class passengers are almost treated with respect. Boats tend to be larger than those on other routes but you do have to be wary of maverick companies; the profits are such that the temptation to chuck on a clapped-out ferry to make a few easy drachma is often irresistible. Every year you will see at least one boat Nero would happily send his mother to sea in.

Embarkation & Immigration Controls

As with much of Continental Europe the countries bordering the Adriatic have adopted a rather low-key approach to border controls. However, their 'abolition' within the EU has yet to have an appreciable effect in Greece (where you still have to show your passport and get an associated ferry boarding card), but all EU countries greet arriving passengers with the minimum of fuss anyway. Passport control is now usually done on board ship in the self-service restaurant, so it pays to find out where it is before the queue tells you. Customs procedures (where they exist) take place ashore. Embarking tends to be more complex; you are usually required to report for boarding 2—3 hours before departure so you have time to get your passport or boarding card stamped by immigration.

Suggested Itinerary

Hopping across the Adriatic to Greece needn't be the chore that at first sight it might seem. With judicious choice you can add an additional dimension to an island hopping holiday. Some variants to one of the various direct Italy—Patras routes are offered below:

Season

Daily services operate from early June through to late September. Thereafter, most lines offer a reduced (alternate day/thrice-weekly) service. Weekend boats are the most crowded, as are Greece-bound ferries at the beginning of the summer and Italy-bound boats from mid-August. If you are planning to 'Stop-over' it is best to do so against the popular flow — that is on the return leg in the early part of the season and on the outward leg from mid-July.

Option A [4 Days]
1) **2**) **3**) **4**) **5**

Several ferry companies have boats running via Kefalonia, offering the possibility of a little-known stop en route. Once at Patras you'll have to take a bus to Athens and Piraeus before setting out for the Aegean.

Option B [4 Days]
6) **7**) **4**

Perhaps the most popular route, Corfu is an attractive stop-over point and the number of boats (running to both Ancona, Brindisi and Bari) calling ensures that it is easy to get to, and escape from. Most companies seem reluctant to offer stop-overs on the Greece—Italy leg, so Corfu is best visited en route to mainland Greece.

Option C [3 Days]
6) **8**

The most expensive option, but the most direct — running from Italy to the Aegean (usually stopping at Igoumenitsa or Patras en route). If you are buying a return ticket, then you needn't return to Crete, but can pick up the boat at one of these ports on your way home.

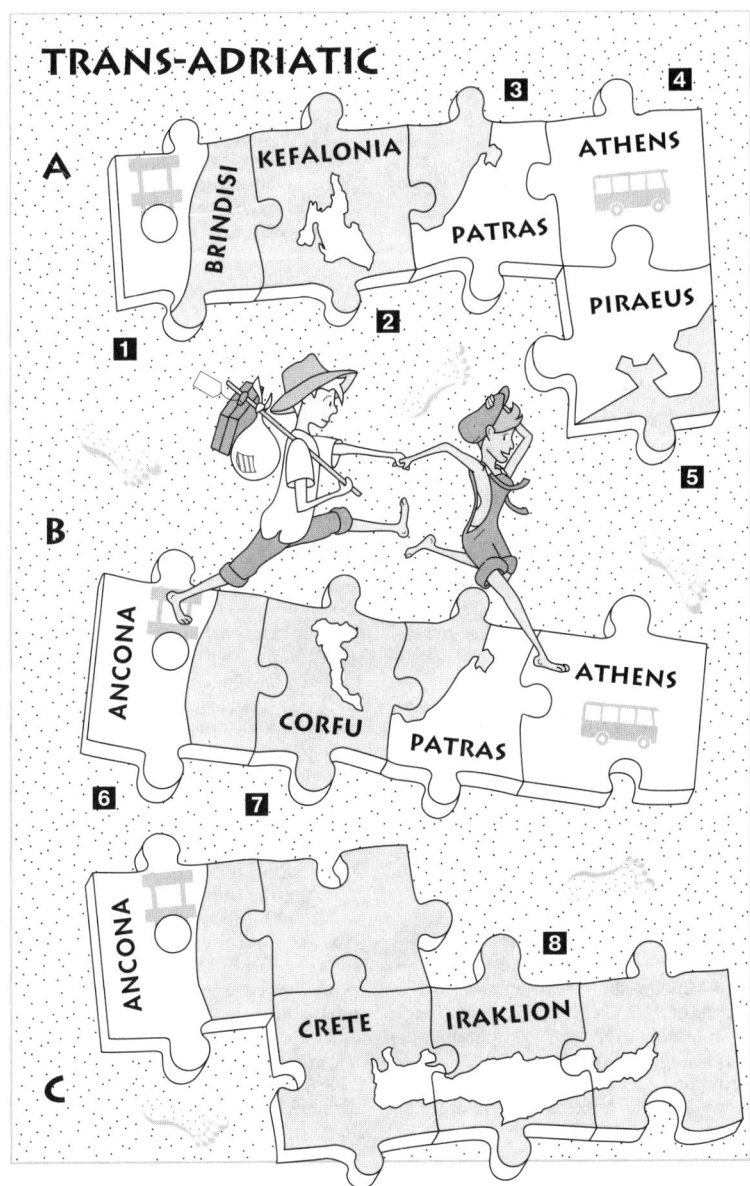

Adriatic Ferry Services

Ancona—Greece Links

C/F *Aretousa* - C/F *Ariadne*
C/F *Daedalus* - C/F *Fedra* - C/F *El Greco*
Minoan Lines
Aretousa; 1995; 31,000 GRT.
Ariadne; 1967; 7748 GRT.
Daedalus; 1973; 7323 GRT.
Fedra; 1974; 12,527 GRT.
El Greco; 1972; 9562 GRT.

One of the two big names on this crossing, Minoan Lines are able to offer a daily boat on this very competitive route. Boats, however, could well change in 1995 when two new super-ferries make an appearance. Quality of facilities is extremely good — reflecting the high level of competition, but also a recognition that this is where the real money is made — this prompts changes each year. In addition to the lucrative international travellers, Minoan also pick up additional revenue by selling domestic inter-Greece tickets (e.g. Patras to Corfu). International tickets cost the same from both ports, so passengers get 'stung' as they have to pay extra when buying a domestic ticket (you can't buy 'stop-over' tickets when heading north). You should also note one quirk peculiar to Minoan boats: a tendency to call at Corfu before Igoumenitsa when heading north (and at Igoumenitsa before Corfu on their return south). All boats run to time and are very reliable.

C/F *Erotokritos*
Minoan Lines; 1974; 12,888 GRT.
The Minoan short-term answer to the arrival of ANEK's *El. Venizelos*, this longer, but smaller, ferry runs a less ambitious service three times every eight days, providing a 24-hour direct ferry service from Patras to Ancona. In an attempt to drum up custom 'Camping Aboard' is her advertising slogan: though one is apt to wonder as to the safety implications of allowing passengers to live (and cook all meals) during the voyage in their trailers and caravans on an open car deck. Those looking for more conventional shipboard facilities will find them aplenty (including a sauna) and up to Minoan's usual very high standard.

C/F *El. Venizelos* - C/F *Kydon* - C/F *Lato*
ANEK Lines
El. Venizelos; 1992; 23,000 GRT.
Kydon; 1975; 6135 GRT.
Lato; 1975; 12,798 GRT.

The main rival of Minoan Lines on Piraeus —Crete routes, ANEK also provides a first-class service on this one. This received a major boost in 1992 with the introduction of the 3000-passenger *El. Venizelos*: running thrice-weekly to Ancona. The biggest and best boat on the route, she is almost too big for comfort, since — apart from the very height of the season — she seems all but empty even with a regular complement of passengers aboard. The ghost ship atmosphere almost justifies a change of name (not so much *Flying Dutchman* as *Flying Greek*): she can usually be reckoned to out-steam all rivals, despite often starting after scheduled departure time.

Her companions are equally reliable, running slightly eccentric itineraries; the *Kydon* often omitting Corfu from her itinerary, the *Lato* making an usual midweek run to Trieste instead of Ancona. This Trieste service has been complemented in the past by the *El. Venizelos* calling in after Ancona on one of her northerly runs. If you are travelling at something other than deck-class, then check-out respective company fares. In past years ANEK's have tended to be slightly higher than Minoan Lines. When heading north boats call at Igoumenitsa before Corfu (on the return south, vice versa).

C/F *Ionian Galaxy* - C/F *Ionian Island*
C/F *Ionian Star*
Strintzis Lines
Ionian Galaxy; 1972; 9964 GRT.
Ionian Island; 1973; 9547 GRT.
Ionian Star; 1992; 14,398 GRT.
Strintzis Lines have run the *Ionian Galaxy* and *Ionian Island* on the Ancona—Patras route for a number of years. Both chunky affairs with distinctive red and white striped ski-slope shaped funnels, they offer facilities only outdone by the best of the competition on the Ancona run. There is little to choose between them, though the *Ionian Galaxy* has the edge with sundeck sloanes. They have now been joined by the much larger *Ionian Star*: their joint efforts combining to provide an almost daily service throughout the year.

C/F *Crown M* - C/F *Countess M*
C/F *Dame M* - C/F *Vicountess M*
Marlines
Countess M; 1968; 6013 GRT.
Crown M; 1966; 9499 GRT.
Dame M; 1972; 6987 GRT.
Vicountess M; 1967; 5776 GRT.
The increased commercial opportunities brought about by the closing of the Yugoslav land link between Greece and the rest of the EU seems to have prompted Marlines back into trans-Adriatic services in a big way after several years of running a single token boat on the route. The three boats above combine to offer a service five days a week; with some services running on to Crete (Iraklion) — see p. 64. All older boats, they are a bit long in the tooth but have undergone 'rebuilding': as a result, facilities are reasonable all things considered, even if they wouldn't figure in the top half-dozen. Out of High Season, sees services greatly reduced.

C/F *Superfast I* - C/F *Superfast II*
Both; 1995; 24,000 GRT.
Due on stream in 1995 are two large, new boats to look out for offering a fast direct Patras—Ancona sailing (24 hours?).

Aretousa - Ariadne
Daedalus - Fedra
El Greco - Erotokritos

El. Venizelos - Kydon - Lato

Ionian Galaxy
Ionian Island - Ionian Star

Crown M - Countess M
Dame M - Vicountess M

Superfast I - Superfast II ◇

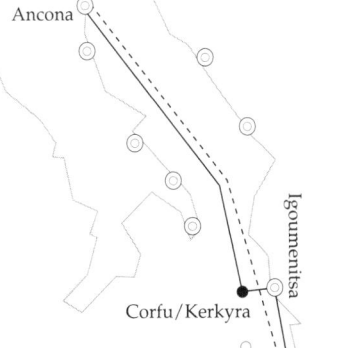

Bari—Greece Links

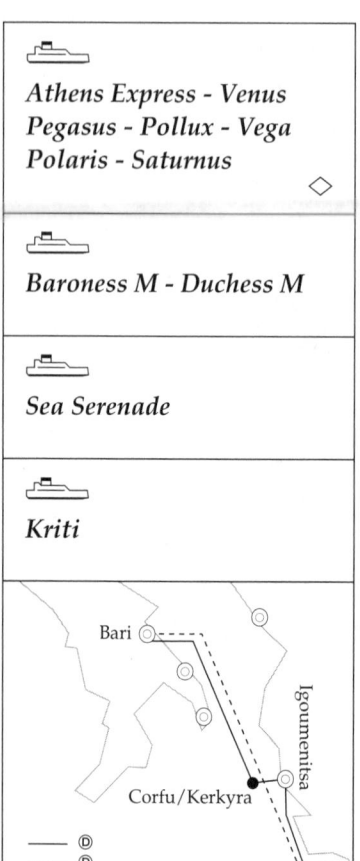

Athens Express - Venus
Pegasus - Pollux - Vega
Polaris - Saturnus

Baroness M - Duchess M

Sea Serenade

Kriti

Bari

Igoumenitsa

Corfu/Kerkyra

Patras

Ventouris have managed to carve out a nice little position for themselves in recent years by concentrating all their resources on the Bari—Patras run and then packing it with boats to discourage competition. The result being a daily sailing between Brindisi and Patras, as well as via Igoumenitsa and Corfu. Quality of the boats varies greatly. The *Athens Express* being a good example of the pokey end of the scale — being topped with a funnel so weedy that if it had been afloat in Victorian times, photographs of it would have been furtively circulated amongst the members of London clubs as a warning on the dangers of excessively cold baths. The other boats are better, particularly the modern *Venus* which runs the Patras—Kefalonia (Sami)—Bari route in tandem with the above. The *Saturnus* is also unmissable: its porthole and windowless sides giving way to a prefab-like super-structure. She combines with the *Polaris* to provide a direct Patras—Bari daily service. Finally, the *Pollux* and *Vega* run to Brindisi out of Corfu and Igoumenitsa.

C/F *Baroness M* - C/F *Duchess M*
Marlines
Baroness M; 1967; 3987 GRT.
Duchess M; 1970; 2786 GRT.
Marlines joined the Bari ferry throng in 1994 when they transferred the *Baroness M* and *Duchess M* from their traditional Brindisi route: this, and their previous attempts to increase custom by adding Ithaca and then Kefalonia to their itineraries strongly suggests that these boats are finding it difficult to compete effectively. Both elderly ferries, they have all undergone extensive 'rebuilding', but this has been more practical than sympathetic and detracts somewhat from their now built-on-top appearance. The *Baroness M* is easily the better of the two boats, and briefly steamed to fame a few years back when she was shelled off the Lebanese coast with the deaths of a couple of the passengers.

C/F *Athens Express* - C/F *Venus*
C/F *Pegasus* - C/F *Pollux* - C/F *Vega*
C/F *Polaris* - C/F *Saturnus*
Ventouris Ferries
Athens Express; 1969; 6416 GRT.
Venus; 1976; 14,540 GRT. *Pegasus*; 1977; 4810
GRT. *Pollux*; 1975; 19,212 GRT.   .
Vega; 1975; 2308 GRT. *Polaris*; 1975; 20,326
GRT. *Saturnus*; 1974; 1953 GRT.

C/F *Sea Serenade*
Poseidon Lines; 1976; 4123 GRT.
Apart from a change of name from *Lady Terry* to the above, this vessel has operated an unchanged schedule for the last four summers and is one of the bigger boats on the route: running Patras—Igoumenitsa—Corfu—Bari. Out of the August / September High Season peak she excludes Corfu from her itinerary, and during previous Low Seasons has helped out on the Piraeus—Haifa route (see p. 66).

C/F *Kriti*
ANEK Lines; 1972; 6843 GRT.
Something of a wanderer on the ferry scene, the *Kriti* has ventured from the Adriatic to the Piraeus—Crete run, before returning last year to the Adriatic, taking on the Patras—Bari service. History would suggest that there will be changes in 1995: though it is difficult to see where she could go now that she is numbered among the older trans-Adriatic ferries.

C/F *Dimitrios Express*
C/F *Silver Paloma*
Arkadia Lines
Dimitrios Express; 1973; 5284 GRT.
Silver Paloma; 1959; 6530 GRT.
The last four years have seen Igoumenitsa emerge as an alternative starting point to Patras for Bari-bound ferries. Arkadia Lines have made the most impact on this route via two large ferries that combine to provide a daily overnight service from mid-June to mid-September. The newest is the *Dimitrios Express*; lately refurbished, she is easily the best boat on the route. Her only weak point is her layout; built for colder climes she is all cabins and not a lot else. As a result, public rooms are small and awkwardly placed, while her limited exterior deck space restricts the numbers moonbathing to a select few. Her companion ferry, the *Silver Paloma*, is a very different beast: much older and distinctly frayed around the edges, having operated a Piraeus—Cyprus service for

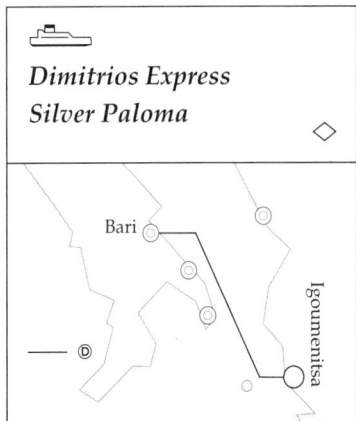

Dimitrios Express
Silver Paloma

years. Arkadia Lines brochures are emblazoned with the slogan 'There is no substitute to perfection'. A piece of hyperbole that this boat proves in a way the company surely didn't intend.

C/M *La Vikinga*
Pantheon AS
An irregular catamaran service since 1993; it worth looking out for on the off-chance it is running again in 1995.

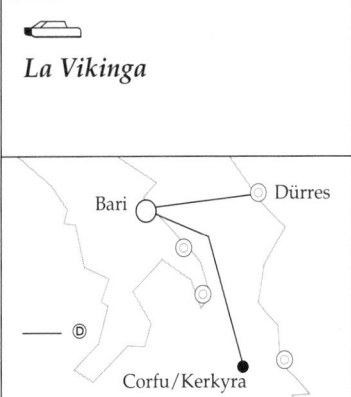

La Vikinga

Brindisi—Greece Links

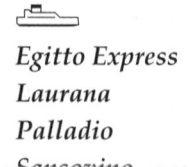

Egitto Express
Laurana
Palladio
Sansovino

Eolos
Ouranos

Apollonia II
Lydia

Kapetan Alexandros

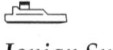

Ionian Sun

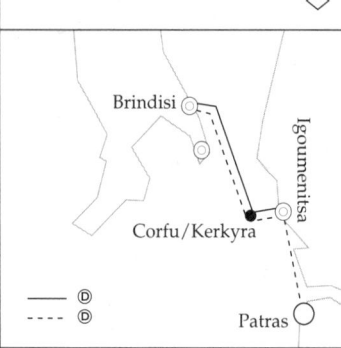

C/F *Egitto Express* - C/F *Laurana*
C/F *Palladio* - C/F *Sansovino*
Adriatica
Egitto Express; 1973; 8957 GRT.
Laurana; 1992; 10,000 GRT.
Palladio / Sansovino; 1989; 10,000 GRT.
Adriatica run several medium-sized annual ferries on the Brindisi—Patras route as part of their more wide-ranging Italian Adriatic seaboard operation. Packed to bursting with backpackers (taking advantage of Inter/Eurail concessionary rates) and Italian holiday-makers using a national carrier, deck passengers not in one of these categories will probably do better with one of the rival lines. All boats in the fleet have reasonable on-board facilities that are very well-maintained. Only problem is that they interchange with each other, and, occasionally the route itself changes, according to the season. In 1994 they were joined by the *Egitto Express*. This ferry normally runs a Venice—Bari—Piraeus—Crete (Iraklion)—Alexandria service every 10 days, but was moved off the route as tourists have all but given up visiting Egypt thanks to the terrorist threat.

C/F *Eolos* - C/F *Ouranos*
Fragline
Eolos; 1962; 2977 GRT.
Ouranos; 1969; 3777 GRT.
Two small and totally mis-matched ferries that provide a daily service each way between Brindisi and Igoumenitsa, these boats have been running across the Adriatic for as long as most ferry watchers can remember. The *Ouranos* is the larger of the two and just about holds its own with the competition (often running an extended itinerary south to Patras), while the feeble *Eolos* is another of those boats too poor to be able to make a go of it on any of the Greek domestic routes. With both boats nearing the end of their working lives changes are now long overdue, but the probability is that both will be running much as usual in 1995.

C/F *Apollonia II* - C/F *Lydia*
Hellenic Mediterranean Lines
Apollonia II; 1964; 2736 GRT.
Lydia; 1962; 3676 GRT.

These two ferries usually combine to run a twice daily Brindisi—Corfu—Igoumenitsa service (both being fast enough to make the round trip on a daily basis). Both are old even by Mediterranean standards. However, they — like all the HML Ferries fleet — are reliable, but have comparatively poor on-board facilities (none of the bow to stern carpeting and discos to be found on the Ancona ferries). Ferry buffs will find the *Lydia* (the ex Belgium cross-Channel *Koningin Fabiola*) particularly appealing, with a delightful unchanged 1960s atmosphere that puts the anodyne modern 'super ferry' to shame. However, the attraction can wear a bit thin on longer voyages given the absence of anything to do.

C/F *Kapetan Alexandros*
Agoudimos Lines; 1962; 3250 GRT.
Formerly the Rafina-based *Alekos*, this ferry moved into the Adriatic in 1992. She has continued crossing the Adriatic, though schedules have been erratic. During the High Season she usually runs a simple, daily one-way Igoumenitsa—Corfu—Brindisi service, while the rest of the year she operates a thrice-weekly Patras—Igoumenitsa—Corfu—Brindisi extended run. Although not as large as some of the other boats on either route, she is a well appointed craft with a very glitzy, if small, deck-class lounge.

C/F *Ionian Sun*
Strintzis Lines
Ionian Sun; 1978; 11,179 GRT.
One of those ferries that have had a turn doing everything from Trans-Adriatic runs to a Rafina—Rhodes service in recent years, the *Ionian Sun* has never managed to find a regular niche of her own since leaving the Irish Sea. How long she survives running an Igoumenitsa—

Brindisi service is problematic given the fact that she is a middle of the range boat, both in size and on-board facilities. In previous years she has run a wide ranging itinerary across the Adriatic — in tandem with the *Ionian Sea* (which replaced her after a year's gap in the Aegean in 1994) — but will probably be operating solo to Brindisi again in 1995.

C/F *Egnatia* - C/F *Media II*
C/F *Poseidonia*
Hellenic Mediterranean Lines
Egnatia; 1960; 4459 GRT.
Media II; 1964; 3680 GRT.
Poseidonia; 1967; 4479 GRT.

HML Ferries, one of the mainstays of the Brindisi—Patras route, in past years have offered services that take in a number of Ionian islands via three equally dated ferries. Period on-board facilities are more than compensated for by innovative itineraries that include useful calls at Kefalonia (Sami) and Paxi — otherwise ignored by ferry operators. Only quibble is the swapping around of boats in annual fleet reshuffles that means you should check the name of your boat when buying your ticket.

Egnatia - Media II
Poseidonia

Brindisi

Corfu/
Kerkyra

Paxi
Ithaca

Ⓓ
Ⓓ   Kefalonia (Sami)
Ⓓ
Patras

Afrodite II
Poseidon

Anna V - Agia Methodia
Igoumenitsa Express

Raffaello - Valentino
Queen Vergina

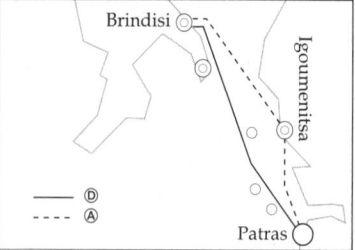

C/F *Afrodite II* - C/F *Poseidon*
Med Link Lines
Afrodite II; 1967; 4190 GRT.
Poseidon; 1971; 8980 GRT.
A relatively new company to the Adriatic scene, Med Link run two elderly, but reasonable boats on the Patras —Brindisi route from April to September. In 1994 they extended some of the runs on to Turkey (see p. 65).

C/F *Anna V* - C/F *Agia Methodia*
C/F *Igoumenitsa Express*
AK Ventouris
Anna V; 1969; 4061 GRT.
Agia Methodia; 1976; 4376 GRT.
Igoumenitsa Express; 1961; 2455 GRT.

A new arrival in 1993, the *Anna V* is a dour-looking ferry that isn't too bad once you are aboard. Last year she was paired with the similar *Agia Methodia*. In 1995 they will be joined by an old Aegean ferry, the *Igoumenitsa Express* (formerly the *Sifnos Express*). Not the fastest of boats, she has a good deck-class saloon.

C/F *Raffaello* - C/F *Valentino*
C/F *Queen Vergina*
Mediterranean Lines
Raffaello; 1968; 5169 GRT.
Valentino; 1972; 4469 GRT.
Queen Vergina; 1967; 9934 GRT.
These two ferries offer an annual direct Patras—Brindisi service (though schedules include Igoumenitsa at the height of the summer). Their main source of income is derived from the transportation of commercial vehicles rather than foot passengers. The *Raffaello* is the better of the two (having formerly served in the Aegean as the *Ierapetra*). The romantically named *Valentino* is singularly ill-named, looking something like a floating municipal car-park with funnels attached. Recently the pair were joined by the elderly *Queen Vergina*.

European Pride
European Spirit

C/F *European Pride* - C/F *European Spirit*
C/F *European Glory*
European Seaways
European Pride; 1967; 4390 GRT.
European Spirit; 1956; 3807 GRT.
European Glory; 1961; 2125 GRT.

One of those companies that buys ferries at the end of their working life and then reaps the rewards gained from the fact that most tourists buy tickets for international boats without checking them out first, European Seaways can hardly be described as one of the best ferry operators. All three vessels in the fleet are old and small, and look as if they've been put on the route to make easy money rather than provide a good service. Unless you are a travel writer looking for colourful subject matter, all three boats are better avoided. The *European Spirit* is the best of the fleet, while the *European Glory* (the 'retired' ancient Greek domestic *Ikaros*) is now so uncompetitive she runs a Corfu—Albania—Brindisi service.

C/M *Misano*
Misano Alta Velocità
A swish Italian operated catamaran, the *Misano* appeared in 1992 offering a quick (3½ hours) crossing between Brindisi—Igoumenitsa—Corfu, at a price (in 1993 this came to £50 with port taxes).

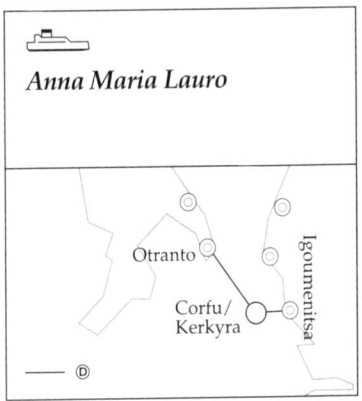

C/F *Anna Maria Lauro*
The shortest crossing across the Adriatic is not popular. As a result the 9-hour Otranto link only has one ferry — most recently the *Anna Maria Lauro* — running an irregular service. The probability is that this service will not change in 1995.

T/B *Petrakis* - T/B *Sotirakis*
Tourist boats make day trips to the Albanian port of Sarandë, making the 90-minute run four days a week (the days are apt to change each year). Must be pre-booked several days in advance; see p. 89.

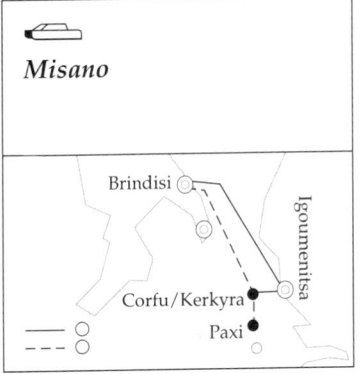

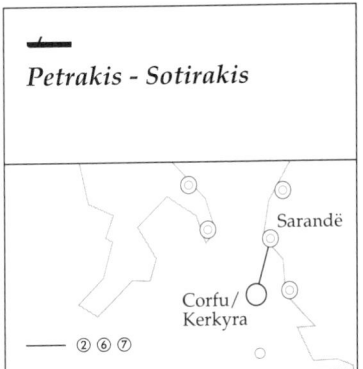

Adriatic Line Islands & Ports

Ancona

The number two destination for north-bound Patras ferries, Ancona is a substantial — but thanks to its commercial activities not particularly attractive — city on the upper Italian Adriatic coast. It sees considerable ferry traffic thanks to good road connections north (and hence is a natural departure point for holidaying Italians from the northern cities) and trans-European rail links (daily departures for Frankfurt and Munich). Nearby Rimini also has a daily overnight express train to Milan, Bonn and Amsterdam.

Those mad enough to want to stay will find several cheap hotels opposite the railway station, which is home to a tourist information kiosk that issues free city maps along with accommodation information.

Bari

An attractive — if unspectacular — city, Bari is too far south down the Italian boot to be an appealing port of call for travellers heading on to Northern Europe, nor is it sufficiently north to appeal to holidaying Italians either. As a result, it is very much the number three west-Adriatic ferry port. On the same rail line as Brindisi, but a longer journey by ferry, your chances of finding a train seat in summer are likely to be limited.

Brindisi

This pleasant city is the destination for the majority of the Patras—Italy ferries. This is due to the easy turn-around time (22 hours); thus allowing two ferries to combine and offer a daily service in each direction. This is the best arrival point if Rome or southern Italy is your next port of call. However, if you are passing through Italy you will still be faced with a long drive or rail journey north.

Accommodation could be a problem thanks to the unwelcome arrival of boat people from Albania (most of whom are temporarily housed in local hotels).

Corfu / Kerkyra

ΚΕΡΚΥΡΑ; 592 km²; pop. 89,600.

Long considered the most beautiful of Greek islands thanks to the abundant rainfall and vegetation, Corfu (or Kerkyra as it is known locally) is now among the most package-touristy parts of Greece. This being so, you have to venture quite far to escape the crowds, but on the plus side the island doesn't attract millions each year without good reason: it is beautiful, people and all. Ruled by the British between 1815 and 1864, the island retains a colonial feel — thanks in part to it being wetter than other islands out of High Season, and the large number of holiday homes scattered around. As with the other large Ionian islands, the main settlement — **Corfu Town** — lies on the east coast along with most of the tourist development (patronised largely by Brits). On Corfu this is particularly heavy, with a hotel strip running from **Pirgi** down to **Benitses** (the booze and snooze resort of Greece) that contrives to place Corfu close to the top of the 'expensive island' rankings. Luckily, both island and capital are sufficiently attractive to overcome this handicap; with even the worst resorts having the kernel of a former fishing village at their heart.

Unless nightlife is a priority, the overcrowding to be found in Corfu Town and the east coast villages will soon tempt you into venturing further afield. The north and west coasts of the island have most to offer. Along the north coast Kassiopi (the centre of Corfu in Roman times) is an attractive fishing village resort

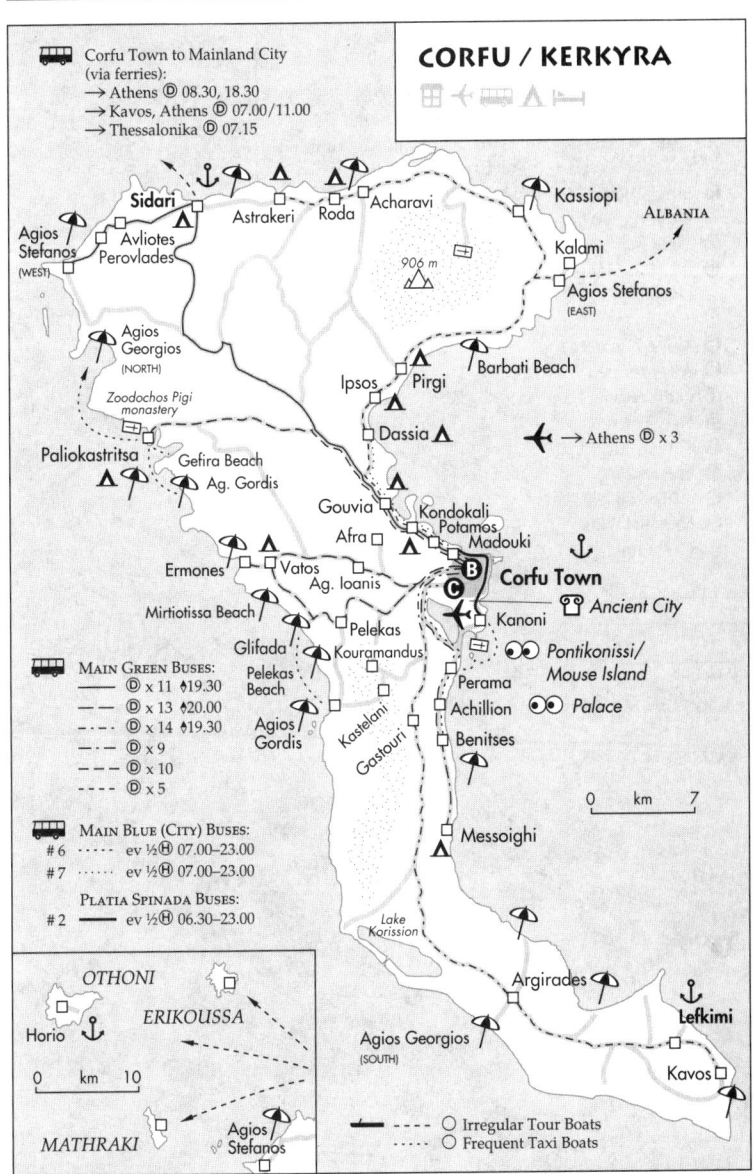

CORFU / KERKYRA

Corfu Town to Mainland City
(via ferries):
→ Athens Ⓓ 08.30, 18.30
→ Kavos, Athens Ⓓ 07.00/11.00
→ Thessalonika Ⓓ 07.15

Sidari
Astrakeri Roda Acharavi   Kassiopi
Agios   ALBANIA
Stefanos   Avliotes   Kalami
(WEST)   Perovlades   906 m
                                                    Agios Stefanos
         Agios   (EAST)
         Georgios
         (NORTH)
    Zoodochos Pigi
    monastery   Ipsos Pirgi Barbati Beach
Paliokastritsa   Dassia   → Athens Ⓓ x 3
         Gefira Beach
         Ag. Gordis   Gouvia   Kondokali
                                 Afra   Potamos
                                          Madouki
Ermones Vatos   B Corfu Town
         Ag. Ioanis   C   Ancient City
Mirtiotissa Beach   Kanoni
                                 Pelekas   Pontikonissi/
         Glifada   Kouramandus   Mouse Island
MAIN GREEN BUSES: Pelekas   Perama
—— Ⓓ x 11 ⬧19.30   Beach   Achillion Palace
— — Ⓓ x 13 ⬧20.00 Agios
–·–· Ⓓ x 14 ⬧19.30 Gordis   Benitses
–··– Ⓓ x 9
– – – Ⓓ x 10
···· Ⓓ x 5   0   km   7

MAIN BLUE (CITY) BUSES: Messoighi
#6 ····· ev ½Ⓗ 07.00–23.00
#7 ····· ev ½Ⓗ 07.00–23.00
PLATIA SPINADA BUSES:
#2 —— ev ½Ⓗ 06.30–23.00
                                 Lake
                                 Korission
OTHONI   Argirades
       ERIKOUSSA   Lefkimi
Horio
                                            Kavos
0   km   10

MATHRAKI   Agios   – – – ○ Irregular Tour Boats
                Stefanos   ····· ○ Frequent Taxi Boats

CORFU
TOWN CENTRE

Key

A International Ferry Building / WCs
B Main Bus Station
C City Bus Station / Hospital (200 m)
D Tourist Information
E Moped Rental
F Airport Road
G Old Venetian Fortress
H New Fortress
I Town Hall
J Esplanade
K Cathedral
L National Bank / Cathedral

M Archaeological Museum
N Byzantine Museum
O UK Consulate (100m)
P Old Palace
Q Cricket Pitch / Kanoni Bus Stop
R WCs / Showers

1 International Ferries
2 Igoumenitsa Ferries
3 Paxi Ferries
4 Othoni Ferries

0   m   150

New Port

Old Port

Europa

Ionian

Ipsilantou Stratigou

Aramiou

Leof. Georgiou Theitoki

Vraila

Mantzarou

Corfu Palace

Platia Georgiou II

Spilia

Cyprus

Constantinoupolis

RC

Acropolis

Criti

Nea Yorki

Metropolis

Voulgareos

Zambelli

RC

Kapodhistriou

Arcadion   Suisse

Platia Spinada

Dousmani

Arseniou

N

over-looked by the remains of a 12 c. castle built on the site of a Temple of Zeus. **Sidari**, backed by rich farmland, is a less picturesque but equally lively village offering excursion boats to the islets north of Corfu as well as several reasonable beaches. However, the west coast has by far the best of Corfu's beaches, including Agios Georgios (both north and south), Glifada, Agios Gordis, Pelekas and **Mirtiotissa** (arguably the best beach: its isolation ensures it gets the thumbs — among other things — up from nudists). The cliffs around **Paliokastritsa** are also a great draw·— particularly at sunset.

The southern limb of Corfu is quieter than the rest of the island with the exception of the large resort at **Messoighi** and the youth dominated **Kavos**: a beach and disco village — now the 'Ios Town' of Corfu. Nearby **Lefkimi** sees a limited number of ferry services, though the bulk of these operate to Corfu Town. Most ferries that call are international boats, and the island sees an irritating stacking of services with most ferries departing in the same direction within a couple of hours of each other and then nothing for the rest of the day.

⊨

The NTOG / EOT (☎ 37520) and Tourist Police offices are normally housed in the Governor's House on Spinada Square in Corfu Town but have moved (while the building is refurbished) to a site near the main bus station. Free maps are on offer as well as hotel, room and campsite information. Most ticket agents also have lists of rooms and are worth a try. Hotel beds are adequate in number for the bulk of the year; but try to find a budget hotel bed by noon in High Season. Near the New Port are the *Europa* (☎ 39304) and the reasonable *Ionian* (☎ 39915), while the Old Port has the over-popular budget *Constantinoupolis* (☎ 39826) and *Acropolis* (☎ 39569). Nearer the top end of the market is the delightfully placed (and thus pricey) *Arcadion* (☎ 37670) overlooking the cricket pitch. Finally, and at different ends of the spectrum, there is a poor *IYHF Hostel* (☎ 91292) at Konto-kali, and the luxury class, ultra expensive *Corfu Palace* (☎ 39485) near the town museum.

A

Nearest camping to Corfu Town is *Camping Kontokali* (☎ 91 170) 5 km to the north: a rather basic site, it scores on convenience rather than the facilities on offer. There are many better sites around the island: mini-buses lay siege to the ferry terminal when the morning boats come in and are thereafter conspicuous by their absence. The best of these sites lie away from the tourist strip: *Vatos Camping* (☎ 94393) and *Paliokastritsa Camping* (☎ 0663 41204) on the west coast are both attractive, along with the clutch of sites abutting the northern beaches. Nightlife lovers will do better sticking to the sites on the tourist strip north of Corfu Town. These include Dassis's *Kada Beach Camping* (☎ 93595) and *Corfu Camping* (☎ 93246) near Ipsos. Those seeking quiet days and loud nights could do worse than try *Ippokambos (Sea Horse) Camping* (☎ 55364) at Messoighi.

👓

Corfu Town is the premier tourist attraction thanks to a delightful mix of Venetian, French and British Georgian buildings straddled by a couple of fortresses partially demolished by the British when they left the islands in the 1860s. The focus of the town is park-like **Spinada** Square or Esplanade and is the site of its famous cricket pitch now used early Saturday mornings as a practice marching ground by the local High School band. The square is bounded on the western side by the **Liston**: a row of tall arcaded houses-cum-cafés built during the brief period of French rule (1807–14), and on the east side by the moated Old **Fortress** — built on the Corfu·('two hills') promontory, and once the site of a Temple of Hera. North of the cricket pitch lies the **Royal Palace**, looking like a Georgian English country house, it was built in 1819 to house a series of British High Commissioners who considered themselves sufficiently high to require a throne room of the regal rather than the convenience variety. These days the building (if re-opened to tourists) is home to a display of Chinese and Japanese porcelain and bronzes (the collection of a former Greek ambassador in the Far East).

Some 50 m south of the square lies Corfu's **Archaeological Museum**: home to the famous pedimental sculptures (dominated by a primitive figure of a Gorgon — considered to be among the greatest Archaic-period sculptures) from the Temple of Artemis (580 BC) in the ancient town. The museum is also home to an assorted collection of classical and Roman sculpture recovered from various sites on the island. The best of these lies just south of Corfu Town: the ancient city of Kerkyra (now little more than foundations — including the Temple of Artemis). Beyond the ruins lies Kanoni; jumping-off point for a couple of monastery topped islets. The first — **Vlakerani** — is linked to Corfu by a picture-postcard causeway, while **Pontikonissi** (or Mouse Island) is reached by regular caïque and is said to be the boat of Odysseus turned into stone by the wrathful Poseidon.

Further afield, Corfu has a disparate collection of other sights. Nearest to Corfu Town is the 1891-built **Royal Palace** (now a casino) at Achillion; the summer home of Kaiser Wilhelm II from 1908–14, it was the birthplace of Prince Phillip. Far prettier is the cliff and beach beauty spot of **Paliokastritsa**, home to a castle (c. 1200 AD) and a monastery (1228) replete with icons (Icon fans should also check out the **Byzantine Museum** in Corfu Town).

To the north-east of Corfu lie three islets also open to island hoppers. Regular ferries leave from Corfu Town (see p. 390), but given that each can be 'done' in a couple of hours it is better to visit by excursion boat from Sidari. Arid and hilly **Othoni** is the largest of them, and the only one with a resident summer tourist population. Even so, it is very quiet with nothing to do except lounge on the beach and make the dusty walk to the inland Horio. **Erikoussa** is the main objective for the Sidari excursion boats thanks to a good sand beach at the island port village. **Mathraki**, the smallest of the three, sees few tourists and her beaches are home to nesting Loggerhead Turtles each summer. Rooms are available on all three islets. Erikoussa has the only hotel.

☎

TOWN CODE 0661, EMERGENCY 100, NTOG/TOURIST POLICE 30265.

Dürres

The principal port of Albania and its nearby capital of Tirana, ugly Dürres is not a leading candidate for an increase in ferry activity in the near future. Until the recent wave of liberalisation the thrice-monthly ferry link to Trieste was one of the principal means of entering the country.

Igoumenitsa
ΗΓΟΥΜΕΝΙΤΣΑ

Set within the inner recesses of a deep and steamy calm bay, this is one of those places which always prompt the question 'Where are we?' from puzzled ferry passengers. In fact, Igoumenitsa is Greece's major western port north of the Gulf of Corinth and thus on the itineraries of many ferries (though in practice few foot passengers choose to set down here). The waterfront is fairly pleasant — given its commercial role — with a park of sorts (filled with bushes used for highly dubious purposes) and a frontier town air, but walk a street inland and you will find a dusty collection of drab Greek streets of the kind that bedevils many an otherwise pretty town. Igoumenitsa is, in fact, a rather small place and there is nothing to do here except catch the ferry to Corfu or bus to other Greek destinations. Buses run (from the bus station one block in from the waterfront) direct to Athens (⊕ 08.30, 11.00, 13.30, 19.45), Thessalonika (⊕ 11.45) and also to Prevenza (⊕ 11.45, 15.30) — with its short ferry hop to Aktion and the bus link to Lefkada (last bus 16.10).

🛏

Most folks head for Corfu Town rather than stay in the dozen odd hotels. In a pinch try the D-class *Egnatias* (☎ 23648) or the C-class *Epirus* (☎ 22504). Ticket agents offer some Rooms.

Λ

Kalami Beach Camping (☎ 71245); 2 km south of the town. Quite awful — avoid it.

☎

CODE 0665, POLICE 22100, WATERFRONT GNTO/EOT 22227.

Otranto

Cornered on the heel of Italy, Otranto is too remote to attract ferry traffic bar the odd maverick boat, and even then only because it offers the shortest (a beguiling advertising point) Adriatic crossing from Corfu and Igoumenitsa. Poor road and rail connections with the rest of Italy.

Patras
ΠΑΤΡΑ
The busiest international port in Greece after Piraeus, Patras is (thanks to its position on the northwest coast of the Peloponnese and its motorway link with Athens) a popular port of call not only for ferries running down the length of the Adriatic or south from Italy, but also for ferries continuing into the Eastern Mediterranean. However, the presence of thousands of holidaymakers passing through daily brings out the worst rip-off merchants in Greece; the practical upshot being that if you want either a top-class meal or bed in this city you have to look pretty hard to find it.

The third largest city in Greece, Patras's fate was sealed with the decision to re-build the centre (following its destruction by the Turks during the war of independence) using an uninteresting grid pattern. The grime laden buildings, relieved only by occasional attractive park-like squares, offer little incentive to hang around, and few tourists do. Fortunately, all facilities and means of escape are on or near the waterfront. The down side of this is that, alongside the ferry terminus and the railway and bus stations, the quayside road is loaded with the worst 'restaurants' in Greece (offering warmed-up greasy — rather than Grecian — cuisine) and the usual collection of ticket agents. Given this, the best advice has to be to feed and change money before you arrive in the port area of town (the streets near the Acropolis have a number of reasonable restaurants and fewer hawks); that way you can still enjoy your holiday without being ripped off. Take care too, if you are getting your currency converted: in this town ticket agents are to be avoided as they will convert your currency — at a price (the National Bank of Greece and the Thomas Cook *Bureau de Change* — both just south of the bus station at ❸ — excepted). Most ticket agencies are only interested in selling international tickets,

so (tickets to Corfu aside) you will find tickets for domestic ferries and hydrofoils on sale from kiosks at ❶.

A recent change at Patras has been the introduction of sign-post 'Gates' along the waterfront. Your ticket agent should be able to indicate from which your boat will depart, but all international travellers still have to clear passport control in the International Ferry Terminal (❹) to get their boarding pass stamped (this is checked on boarding).

Patras is naturally a major destination for both trains and buses. The former depart from a quayside station every couple of hours and then crawl to Athens or the Peloponnese, the latter are based at a waterfront bus station (complete with a pricey, but popular, snack and drink shop) and offer a far wider variety of destinations. The most important of these are: to Athens (⊕ 05.00–21.00), Thessalonika (⊕ 08.30, 15.00) and Kilini (⊕ 08.00, 14.45). Buses running between Athens and Zakinthos also make a WC stop at ❶ and are manned by drivers open to minor bribery (seats permitting). Finally, most of the big Adriatic ferry lines run their own ultra-smooth air-conditioned buses to and from the centre of Athens. Seats can be booked along with your ticket.

🚭

The friendly NTOG office (☎ 42 3866) located in the ferry terminal provides good town maps and can point you in the direction of a room or one of the budget hotels. The port area of town has the greatest concentration, with the waterfront D-class *Splendid* (☎ 27 6521) along with the C-class *Acropole* (☎ 27 9809) offering tolerable rooms at better than most prices. Near the bus station you will find the noisy C-class *Adonis* (☎ 22 4213), and another C-class establishment — the *Mediterranee* (☎ 27 9602) is located on Ag. Nikolaou, the main shopping street. The up market *Rannia* (☎ 22 0114) lies on the next block east. Patras also has a couple of good pensions at the southern end of the port; the *Marie* (☎ 33 1302) and the *Nicos* (☎ 27 6183). There is also an IYHF *Youth Hostel* (☎ 42 7278) 2 km north at 68 Iroon Polytechniou.

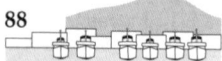

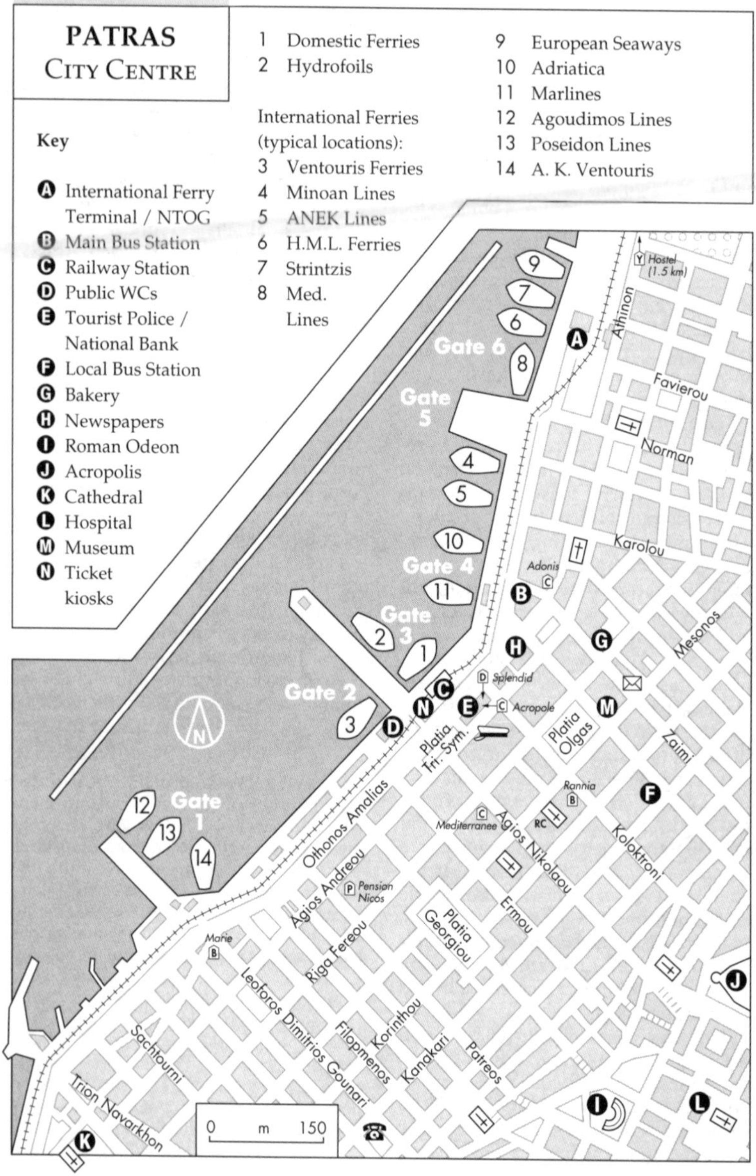

PATRAS
City Centre

Key

Ⓐ International Ferry
   Terminal / NTOG
Ⓑ Main Bus Station
Ⓒ Railway Station
Ⓓ Public WCs
Ⓔ Tourist Police /
   National Bank
Ⓕ Local Bus Station
Ⓖ Bakery
Ⓗ Newspapers
Ⓘ Roman Odeon
Ⓙ Acropolis
Ⓚ Cathedral
Ⓛ Hospital
Ⓜ Museum
Ⓝ Ticket
   kiosks

1 Domestic Ferries
2 Hydrofoils

International Ferries
(typical locations):
3 Ventouris Ferries
4 Minoan Lines
5 ANEK Lines
6 H.M.L. Ferries
7 Strintzis
8 Med.
   Lines

9   European Seaways
10 Adriatica
11 Marlines
12 Agoudimos Lines
13 Poseidon Lines
14 A. K. Ventouris

Athinon

Ⓨ Hostel
  (1.5 km)

Gate 6

Gate 5

Gate 4

Gate 3

Gate 2

Gate 1

Ⓐ

Favierou

Norman

Karolou

Adonis Ⓒ

Ⓑ

Ⓗ

Ⓖ

Mesonos

Ⓝ Ⓒ

Ⓓ Splendid

Ⓔ Ⓒ Acropole

Ⓜ

Platia
Olgas

Zaimi

Platia
Tri-Sym.

Rannia
Ⓑ

Ⓕ

Mediterranee Ⓒ
RC

Agios Nikolaou

Kolokironi

Othonos Amalias

Ⓟ Pension
   Nicos

Agios Andreou

Ermou

Platia
Georgiou

Ⓙ

Marie
Ⓑ

Riga Fereou

Leoforos Dimitrios Gounari

Filopmenos

Korinthou

Kanakari

Patreos

Sachourni

Trion Navarkhon

0   m   150

☎

Ⓘ

Ⓛ

Ⓚ

Λ

Kavouri Camping (☎ 42 8066): 2 km east of the port and crowded. Better by far is *Camping Rhion* (☎ 99 1585): on the beach 7 km north.

◐◑

Patras has just enough sights to keep you occupied while you await your ferry. None are in the top league of Greek sightseeing, but they are more attractive than the port area of town. Locals tend to head first in the direction of **St. Andrew's Cathedral**. The largest in Greece, it lies to the south of the port and is a major shrine thanks to its role as the repository of **St. Andrew's head**. Being a local (he lived and died in Patras) he is one of the most revered saints in Greece, after being crucified at his own request the wrong way round (i.e. on an X–shaped cross) so that no one could confuse him with Jesus Christ. A sad case of excessive humility going to the head, the poor saint started off with his in the clouds and has ended up with it in a gem-encrusted gold casket.

Foreign nationals will find more of interest in the remains of a **Venetian Castle** on the site of the city's ancient **Acropolis**. Hardly in the top ten kastros, some compensation is to be found in the views it offers of Ithaca and Kefalonia. Classical and Roman remains are confined to a few temple fragments and a heavily restored **Odeon** still used for occasional performances. Patras also has a small **Archaeological Museum** (② to ⑦ 08.30–15.00) filled with minor finds from the ancient city.

☎

CODE 061, TOURIST POLICE 22 0902, NTOG OFFICE 65 3368, FIRST AID 150.

Sarandë

This shop and restaurant-free town on Albania's southern coastline is now visited by Corfu tour boats four days a week. Passengers must pre-book at least four days in advance: this is to enable visas to be prepared. When booking you will be asked to provide your surname, forenames, father's name, place of birth, date of birth, nationality, and occupation. Fares are quite high: 6000 GDR one way, 11,000 GDR return (plus a £22 visa). A one-way ticket out of Albania to Corfu sees the price rise to US$ 40 (it never hurts to have the odd dollar in your pocket when venturing off the tourist trail). Given the current shortages in Albania you are also advised to take absolutely everything bar drinking water with you.

Trieste

Argued over by Yugoslavia and Italy after the last war, Trieste voted to join the latter in a UN plebiscite. Despite this, it retains strong connections with the Slovenian Istrian peninsula and is awkwardly linked with the rest of Italy (by rail — via a branch line out of Venice). A gateway to the northern countries of former Yugoslavia, the city remains a ferry backwater tucked away at the head of the Adriatic and unlikely to see an increase in traffic in 1994.

Valona

Albania's third, and most northerly port, it saw its first regular ferry service in 1993. A town with few facilities, it is unlikely to develop in the future. Conditions of passage as for Sarandë above.

Venice

Considering how great an impact Venice has had over the history and culture of the Mediterranean it is surprising how little it figures on ferry schedules. To some extent this is due to the geographical difficulty that affects Trieste: being at the head of the Adriatic the city does not figure prominently on road or rail routes. Since motoring around Venice is somewhat handicapped by the canal system, and the fact that Yugoslavia (only a couple of hours away by road) is no longer on the tourist map, it is inevitable that the *Stazione marittima* is underutilised. This is a pity, as arriving by boat is one of the best ferry landfalls going. It is almost worth waiting for one of the few ferries that visit simply to enjoy this experience. In practice, however, Venice remains the preserve of long-haul travellers, with the majority of boats voyaging to Turkey by way of Greece.

3
ATHENS & PIRAEUS

ATHENS · PIRAEUS (GREAT HARBOUR) · (ZEA)
LAVRION · RAFINA · SALAMIS

RAFINA
ΡΑΦΗΝΑ

ATHENS
ΑΘΗΝΑ

LAVRION
ΛΑΒΡΙΟ

PIRAEUS (GREAT HARBOUR)
ΠΕΙΡΑΙΑ (ΚΕΝΤΡΙΚΟ ΛΙΜΑΝΙ)

ZEA
ΛΙΜΑΝΙ ΖΕΑΣ

ANAVISSOS
ΑΝΑΒΙΣΣΟ

SALAMIS
ΣΑΛΑΜΙΝΑ

General Features

Lying at the centre of the Eastern Mediterranean ferry web, and still the most popular charter flight entry point into Greece, Athens sees more tourists passing through than any other port of call. Unfortunately, the rise in the city's population from 12,000 in 1820 to over 4 million today has done nothing for one of the greatest cities in the world. The ancient heart is now lost amidst a grimy concrete urban sprawl. Athens is a Betty Davis-at-80 sort of city; looking like an ugly spider, but graced with the remains of a pair of wondrously beautiful eyes. Consequently, most visitors profitably fill a couple of days doing the Acropolis and the National Museum and then get out fast. This chapter can thus be said to cover the 'damaged' area of Greece. Like most tourists, its gaze is firmly directed on the ancient city centre and the Athenian ports of Piraeus, Rafina and Lavrion, as well as mentioning in passing the ugly suburb island of Salamis. If sightseeing is not your thing (or if you want to retain the relaxed frame of mind that idling around the islands has wrought), a final day or two in or around Athens waiting for your flight home can come as something of a shock to the system and it is worthwhile considering the alternative of flying to one of the island airports and then island hopping to the city for a long weekend from there.

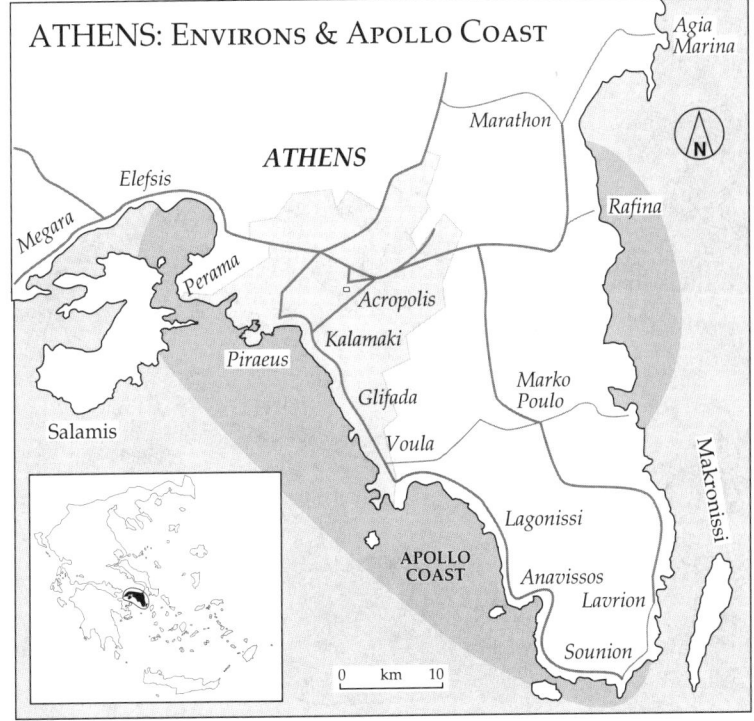

ATHENS: Environs & Apollo Coast

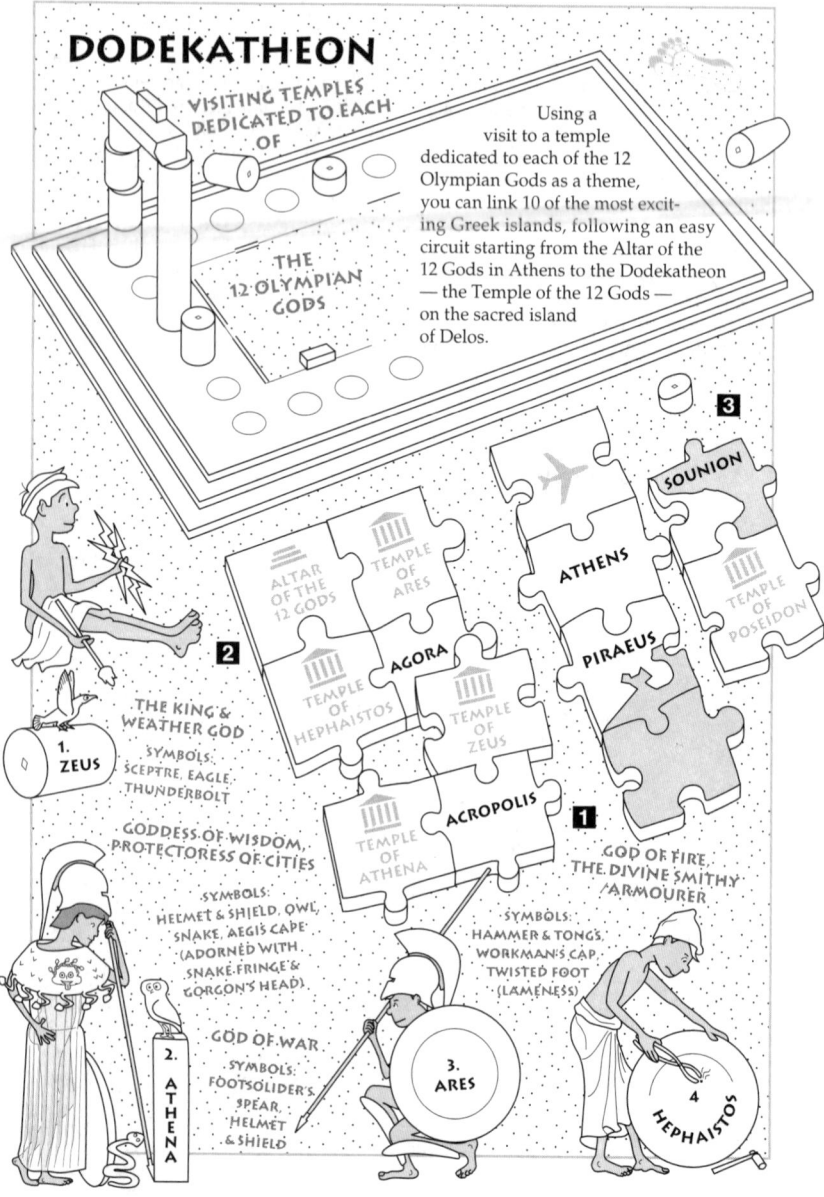

DODEKATHEON

VISITING TEMPLES DEDICATED TO EACH OF

THE 12 OLYMPIAN GODS

Using a visit to a temple dedicated to each of the 12 Olympian Gods as a theme, you can link 10 of the most exciting Greek islands, following an easy circuit starting from the Altar of the 12 Gods in Athens to the Dodekatheon — the Temple of the 12 Gods — on the sacred island of Delos.

ALTAR OF THE 12 GODS

TEMPLE OF ARES

AGORA

TEMPLE OF HEPHAISTOS

TEMPLE OF ZEUS

ACROPOLIS

TEMPLE OF ATHENA

ATHENS

PIRAEUS

SOUNION

TEMPLE OF POSEIDON

THE KING & WEATHER GOD

SYMBOLS: SCEPTRE, EAGLE, THUNDERBOLT

1. ZEUS

GODDESS OF WISDOM, PROTECTORESS OF CITIES

SYMBOLS: HELMET & SHIELD, OWL, SNAKE, AEGIS CAPE (ADORNED WITH SNAKE-FRINGE & GORGON'S HEAD)

2. ATHENA

GOD OF WAR

SYMBOLS: FOOTSOLDIER'S SPEAR, HELMET & SHIELD

3. ARES

GOD OF FIRE, THE DIVINE SMITHY, ARMOURER

SYMBOLS: HAMMER & TONGS, WORKMAN'S CAP, TWISTED FOOT (LAMENESS)

4 HEPHAISTOS

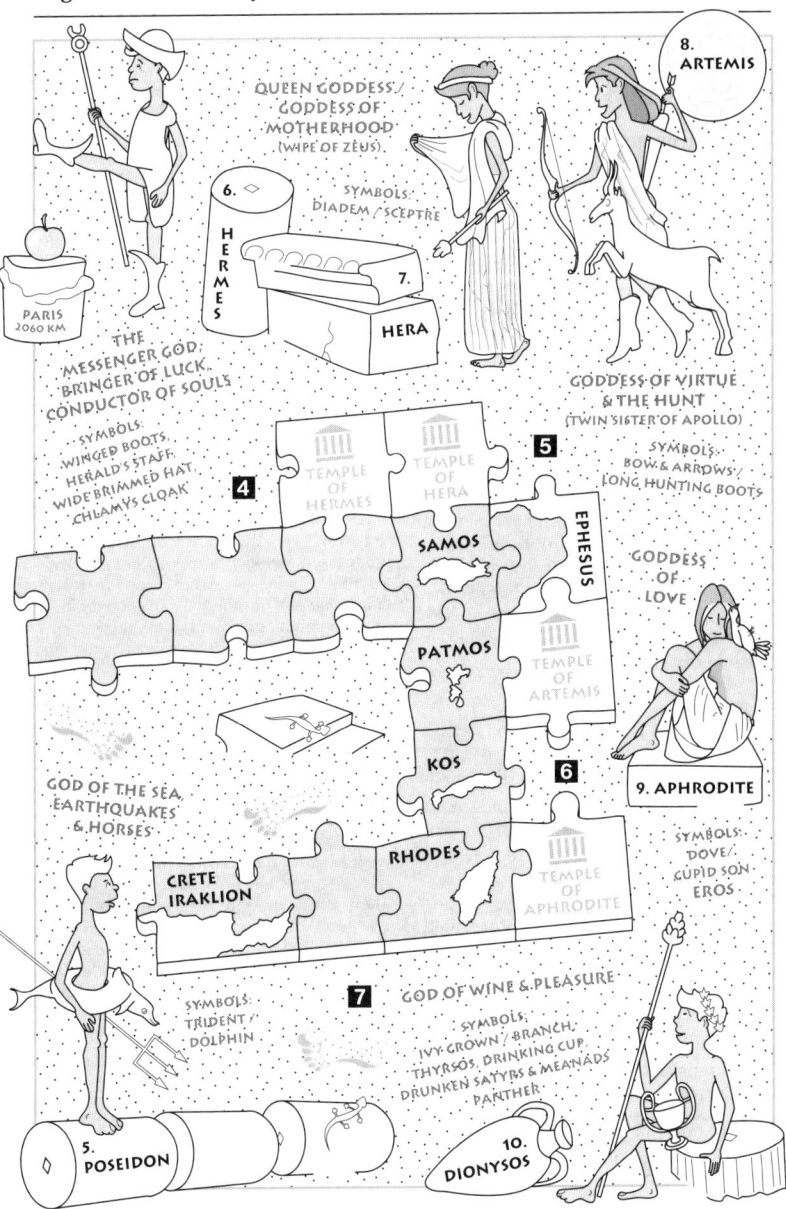

PARIS
2060 KM

6. HERMES

7. HERA

QUEEN GODDESS/
GODDESS OF
MOTHERHOOD
(WIFE OF ZEUS).

SYMBOLS:
DIADEM / SCEPTRE

8. ARTEMIS

THE
MESSENGER GOD,
BRINGER OF LUCK,
CONDUCTOR OF SOULS

SYMBOLS:
WINGED BOOTS,
HERALD'S STAFF,
WIDE BRIMMED HAT,
CHLAMYS CLOAK

GODDESS OF VIRTUE
& THE HUNT
(TWIN SISTER OF APOLLO)

SYMBOLS:
BOW & ARROWS /
LONG HUNTING BOOTS

4

TEMPLE OF HERMES

TEMPLE OF HERA

5

SAMOS

EPHESUS

GODDESS
OF
LOVE

PATMOS

TEMPLE OF ARTEMIS

KOS

6

9. APHRODITE

GOD OF THE SEA,
EARTHQUAKES
& HORSES

CRETE
IRAKLION

RHODES

TEMPLE OF APHRODITE

SYMBOLS:
DOVE /
CUPID SON
EROS

SYMBOLS:
TRIDENT /
DOLPHIN

7 GOD OF WINE & PLEASURE

SYMBOLS:
IVY-GROWN / BRANCH,
THYRSOS, DRINKING CUP,
DRUNKEN SATYRS & MEANADS
PANTHER

5. POSEIDON

10. DIONYSOS

The Dodekatheon
Suggested Itinerary [3 Weeks]

In the Greco-Roman world many deities were worshipped but only the 12 Gods with thrones in the palace above Mt. Olympus (and therefore known as the 'Olympians') had temples built to them on a wide scale. They were the national gods; transcending the political boundaries of the city states. The later Romans (whose capacity for original ideas didn't extend much beyond roads, concrete and killing people in circuses) adopted the Olympians wholesale, contenting themselves with giving them new names (with the exception of Apollo). Widely depicted in all forms of ancient art, each of the 12 Olympians had their own symbol/s to aid recognition (a fortunate circumstance as 'god spotting' will enliven many a vase-filled museum visit today). The remains of their temples also offer a light-hearted excuse for some excellent island hopping. The following itinerary offers an easy circuit around the Aegean islands seeking out the ghosts of the gods.

Arrival/Departure Point
Athens is the best starting point because you will encounter the only weak link in the itinerary (Samos to Patmos) early in the loop. But you can also join the circuit at Kos, Rhodes, Crete (Iraklion), Santorini or Mykonos should you so choose.

Season
This itinerary can be successfully executed at any time from June to September as it runs down the two most popular lines in the Greek ferry system — the Dodecanese and Cyclades Central lines.

1 Athens: The Acropolis
The centre of Athens offers an easy way to notch up a handful of the twelve temples without difficulty. If you join the circuit at the Thissio Metro station and walk to the north entrance of the Agora you will pass the site of the **Altar of the Twelve Gods**. It is now not clear if these included all the Olympians but the altar served as the *omphalos* (navel) of the city. The milestone for measuring distances throughout Attica, it is the logical starting point for the itinerary. Walking east around the north and east sides of the Acropolis you will come to the largest temple ever built in Greece; the Olympieion or **Temple of Zeus**.

Zeus (Roman **Jupiter**), the king of the Olympian gods, was also the god of the sky, or weather god. He walked around with a handful of thunderbolts and was wont to give any passing nymphs a quick flash if his wife Hera was out of sight. He passed the rest of his time upon a throne of black marble set upon a pedestal of the seven rainbow colour steps keeping a moody eye on the affairs of gods and men.

Turning west, a walk along the south side of the Acropolis will bring you to the western entrance. The Acropolis includes the Parthenon among several **Temples of Athena**.

Athena (Roman **Minerva**), the goddess of wisdom, was the most popular of the goddesses (thanks to her role as the protectress of cities). She also enjoyed a secondary role as a patroness of the feminine arts and crafts — notably spinning and weaving. She frequently appears in ancient art, usually wearing the distinctive Aegis cape (made out of snake's scales, fringed with snake's heads and sporting a Gorgon's head) showing her association with the hero Perseus who killed the Gorgon Medusa with the goddess's help.

2 Athens: The Agora
Assuming you haven't broken your leg on the slippery marble of the Acropolis then you next head for the nearby south-east entrance of the Agora site. Walking across the Agora to the northern entrance, turn west to the mound that is all that remains of the **Temple of Ares**. Believed to be almost identical to the nearby complete temple of Hephaistos, it originally stood elsewhere only to be re-erected here during the Roman infilling of the Agora.

Ares (Roman **Mars**) was the god of war and thus not the most popular of deities. Feared rather than revered, worshippers sacrificed dogs to him. Nauseatingly handsome and usually naked, he was the paramour of Aphrodite, possibly siring her son Eros.

On the hillside to the west lies the complete **Temple of Hephaistos**. Once surrounded by artisan and craftsmen's workshops it is the most complete temple surviving in Greece.

Hephaistos (Roman **Vulcan**), the workman's god, was arguably the unhappiest deity. Not only was he once thrown (literally) out of Olympus by Hera (laming himself when he landed on the island of Limnos), he was also married to Aphrodite and thus forever hopping mad with her hopping into bed with just about everybody and then coming up with all sorts of lame excuses. He is easily identified by his tools and is often riding a mule.

3 Sounion

Athens sightseeing can be wound up with a day trip to Cape **Sounion** and the impressive **Temple of Poseidon** on the hillside overlooking the Aegean Sea.

Poseidon (Roman **Neptune**) was another moody god, swimming around with a chip on his shoulder because he lost out to his younger brother Zeus when the three brothers divided the universe between them by lot after defeating their father **Kronos** (Roman **Saturn**). Poseidon got the sea, Zeus the heavens, and Pluto the underworld (they shared the earth). The god of the sea, earthquakes and horses, he is often only distinguishable from Zeus by his trident and dolphin.

4 Piraeus to Samos

Returning to Athens, head on to Piraeus and your first island hop to the ugliest island port on the itinerary — Samos (Vathi). Buses here will take you on to Samos (Pithagorio) and the nearby Heraion — the largest Greek-built temple in Greece. Just to the east of it lie the foundations of two tiny **Temples of Hermes**.

Hermes (Roman **Mercury**) always managed to come in as 12th man when listing the Olympians in order of importance. His natty winged boots and traveller's hat hardly encouraged respect. Temples to him were thus thin on the ground, and although he was revered as the conductor of souls to the underworld, his reputation as a trickster and cheat confined his following to the ranks of merchants, traders and thieves. Easily identified by his herald's staff he is frequently pictured taking Hera, Athena and Aphrodite to the first ever Miss Universe contest; the judgement of Paris.

The **Temple of Hera**, although only one column remains standing, is a much more

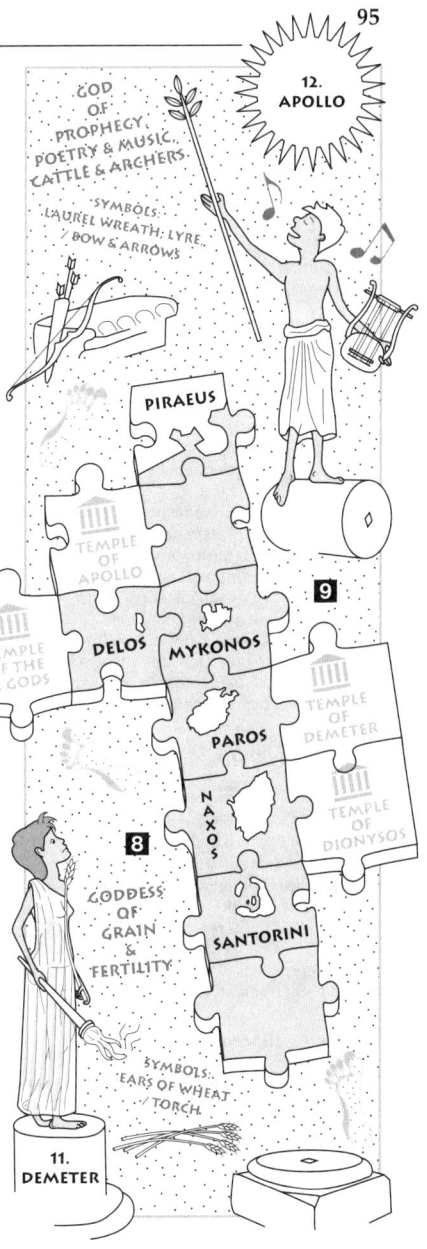

12. APOLLO

GOD OF PROPHECY, POETRY & MUSIC, CATTLE & ARCHERS.

SYMBOLS: LAUREL WREATH; LYRE, BOW & ARROWS

PIRAEUS

TEMPLE OF APOLLO

TEMPLE OF THE 12 GODS

DELOS

MYKONOS

9

TEMPLE OF DEMETER

PAROS

N A X O S

8

TEMPLE OF DIONYSOS

SANTORINI

GODDESS OF GRAIN & FERTILITY

SYMBOLS: EARS OF WHEAT, TORCH

11. DEMETER

substantial affair: this being one of the major shrines to the goddess in Greece.

Hera (Roman **Juno**), the queen goddess, was both the sister and wife of Zeus. They never got on, thanks to his constant attempts to ravish passing nymphs. Their life together was a litany of attempts by Hera to catch him in the act. This thwarted voyeur's symbol was a heifer but she is usually depicted with Zeus and adorned with a diadem and sceptre.

5 Turkey & Patmos

Samos (Vathi) is also the jumping-off point for day trips to Ephesus in Turkey and its **Temple of Artemis**. With one column standing it looks pretty similar to the Heraion. If you don't fancy visiting Turkey then pick up one of the few ferries or a tourist boat and hop down to Patmos. The monastery here was also built on the site of a temple to the goddess.

Artemis (Roman **Diana**), the beautiful virgin huntress, was goddess of all wild places, with a secondary role as the moon goddess. Having no time for the opposite sex she spent her hours protecting female chastity—along with mopping up when that failed (she was also the goddess of childbirth). Often pictured with Apollo, she used her bow and arrows to put suffering animals painlessly out of their misery—thereby acting as a sort of anti-cupid figure.

6 Kos & Rhodes

From Patmos you have very easy hops down to Kos and Rhodes. Both were home to a **Temple of Aphrodite** — though only the foundations of the Rhodes Town example are identifiable today.

Aphrodite (Roman **Venus**), the goddess of love, beauty, fertility and the sea, was very popular for obvious reasons. Usually depicted with either a dove or her winged son Eros (often depicted as a fully grown man rather than a baby-blobs style cupid).

7 Crete & Santorini

Alongside the Rhodian Temple of Aphrodite stood a temple of Dionysos. However, little of this building survives. For a better example of a temple to this god you have to do some serious island hopping on to Naxos. Easiest way is to bounce off Crete, taking one of the regular ferries from Rhodes to Crete (Iraklion). Crete was the birth-place of Zeus so there is

some logic in the hop. After touring Knossos, from Iraklion you can then pick up a Cyclades Central Line ferry stopping off at Santorini for more sightseeing before hopping on to Naxos.

8 Naxos & Paros

Naxos is home to a large Archaic temple on the small islet of Palatia just north of the ferry port. Thought to have been dedicated to either Apollo or Dionysos, visit it on the probability that it is a **Temple of Dionysos**, since Naxos was this god's island and where he married the abandoned Ariadne.

Dionysos (Roman **Bacchus**) was the god of fun; inventing wine and orgies. Often shown accompanied by Satyrs (naked bald men with horse's tails and large what-nots), nymphs or maenads (frenzied women dressed in fawn and panther skins) he started out as the god of the fruit of the trees. He was not originally one of the Olympians but gained admission when **Hestia** (Roman **Vesta**)—the old maid goddess of the hearth — stepped down in his favour.

From Naxos you have an easy hop on to Paros: the Kastro at Parikia being built on the site of a **Temple of Demeter.** Its surviving wall is made up of stones from the building.

Demeter (Roman **Ceres**) was famous for not smiling. The goddess of fertility, she was particularly associated with the crops of the soil such as grain and corn. She is often depicted holding the torch carried when she went down into the underworld (Hades) to recover her daughter Persephone whom Zeus had ordered to be married to their brother Pluto.

9 Mykonos & Delos

From Paros you have another easy hop on to Mykonos: the starting point for excursion boats to the island of Delos — home to the foundations of an important **Temple of Apollo**.

Apollo the god of poetry, music and prophecy, was the most popular of the Olympian gods. He was also thought by some to be the sun god Helios. His popularity ensured that plenty of temples were erected in his name. He is often pictured as a naked and beardless youth holding a lyre.

Delos is also home to smaller temples to Aphrodite, Artemis, Demeter, and Hera as well as the **Dodekatheon** itself. Having visited Delos and returned to Mykonos you can complete the island circuit by taking a ferry back to Piraeus for your return flight home.

Athens: City Links

Getting Around

Athens has a large and overcrowded public transport system made up of buses, trolley-buses, a single line metro and 1000 of the most uncooperative taxi drivers in Europe. The metro offers the cheapest and quickest means of moving around — unless you want to get to either of Athens' airports or intercity bus stations. For these you will have to take either an expensive taxi or resort to the great Athenian bus system. The NTOG/EOT office in Syntagma Square provides the timetables and route summary sheets on request. Athens' buses come in two colours: Blue, the city buses running from the centre to the suburbs (books of 75 GDR tickets bought in advance from street kiosks), and Orange, running further afield within the local province of Attica.

Airport Buses & Taxis:

Athens has two airports 9 km south-east of the centre. Always check with the bus driver that you are going to the right one:

Express Buses A & B: run between the **East Airport** (for all foreign airlines and charter flights) and the centre of Athens (Syntagma Square and/or Omonia Square — see the map on p. 102). The blue and yellow double-decker service runs every 30 minutes from 06.00–01.30, and hourly during the night. The journey time is 30 minutes; the fare is 160 GDR.

Express Buses A & B: run between the **West Airport** (Olympic Airways International and Domestic Flights only) and central Athens (from the same bus stops as the above) every half hour 06.00–01.00.

Those seeking a direct bus between Piraeus and the airports will find that city bus **#19** runs between **Piraeus** (see map on p. 123) and the **East Airport** (via the **West Airport**) roughly every fifty minutes 06.00–22.00, then hourly to 01.00. Journey time 40 minutes; the fare is 160 GDR.

Taxis also prey on the unsuspecting at the airport. They will rook you if they can (see p. 54), so be sure to establish the fare before you use one — the 'official' 1993 fare between the centre of Athens and the East Airport was listed as 1500 GDR (double fare at night): expect to pay significantly more, but not too much more!

Buses to Intercity Bus Stations:

City buses run from the centre to the two main bus stations:

#024: Runs between the Intercity Bus Station serving Evia and Northern Greece (**Terminal B**) at Liossion St. and Amalias Ave. (entrance to the National Gardens).

#051: Runs between the Intercity Bus Station serving Patras and the Peloponnese (**Terminal A**) at 100 Kifissou Street and Omonia Square.

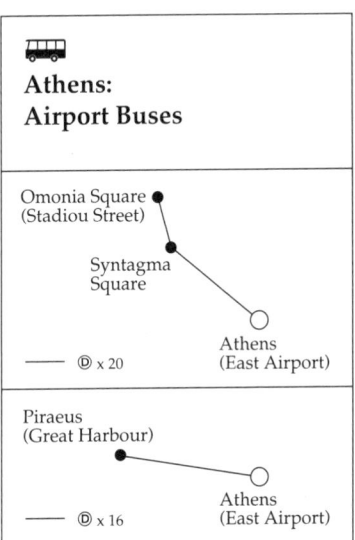

Athens Metro

The easiest way of moving between the centre of Athens and Piraeus is via the metro system. Largely above ground, the single line is efficient, if somewhat crowded (it is better avoided in the rush hours). The only minor problem you are likely to encounter is finding the station entrances, since they are not signposted, you therefore have to look for suitably wide doorways at the station sites. Tickets are obtained from ticket machines or manned kiosks. However, you have to remember to insert your ticket in one of the date-punching machines sited at platform entrances. The fare from the centre of Athens to Piraeus is 75 GDR. Trains run roughly every 20 minutes from 05.00–24.00 and each one invariably has its own resident busker.

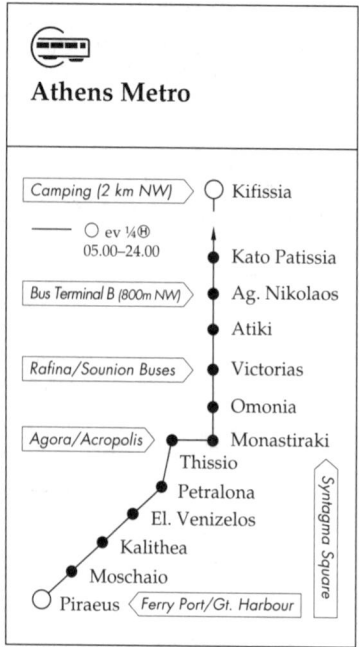

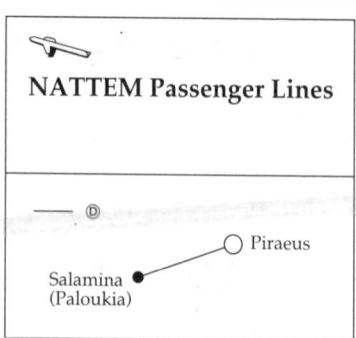

Piraeus—Salamina / Salamis Links

The island of Salamina lies so close to Piraeus that its links are viewed as merely an extension of the suburban traffic system. Two boats chug regularly from Piraeus to ports on the island's east coast. All are commuter services and tourists are a rarity. One look at the tiny T/Bs *Aias* and *Demokritas* is enough to explain why; for they are no more substantial than tourist caïques painted in the usual white and orange colour scheme. In 1993 a hydrofoil joined them on the most lucrative of the routes. Times change every other month: summer examples are given in the port table section.

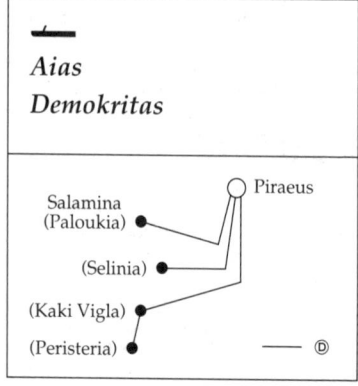

Athens—Mainland Port Bus Links

Athens: Terminal A
(100 Kifissou St.)

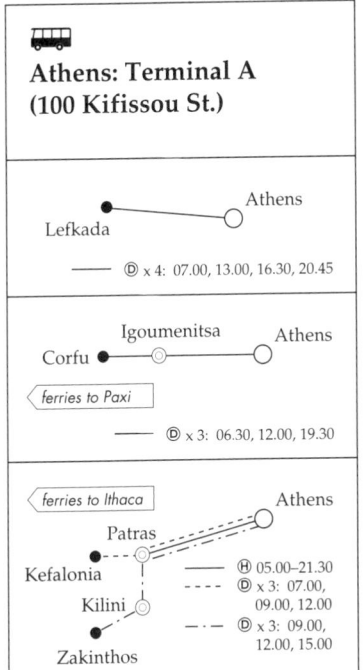

Lying at the centre of the Greek bus system, Athens has a number of wider-ranging bus services of value to the island hopper. These bus routes link the capital with ports not served by Piraeus or Rafina-based ferries but which have ferry links of their own to adjacent islands. For the most part, important centres in their own right, a few bus services are actually timed to connect with ferry services so that buses can take passengers on to the island capitals (you buy a ferry ticket along with your bus ticket). Some ferry companies also run private Athens—mainland port buses for the benefit of their passengers.

The largest bus station in Athens (Terminal A) at 100 Kifissou St., lies an inconvenient 4 km from the centre of the city, buried behind a block of semi-derelict buildings on the east side of one of the city's freeways (home to innumerable run-down scrap-yards and warehouses). From the road it would be impossible to spot were it not for the constant procession of buses mysteriously disappearing down adjacent side-streets. The terminal is in fact a warehouse-like building filled with numbered bus bays and lined with confectionery stalls. Only the ticket hall

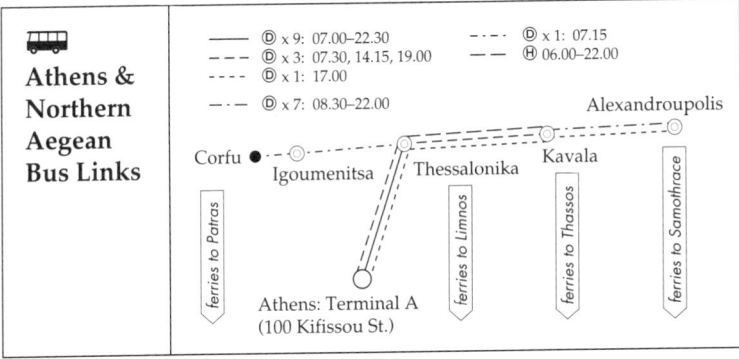

is new: contrasting vividly with the surrounding decrepitude. The terminal serves most intercity buses (including buses to Thessalonika) as well as the west coast ports (Patras and Igoumenitsa), the Ionian islands and the Peloponnese.

Terminal B at 260 Liossion St. is a much smaller and altogether friendlier affair 800 m NW of Ag. Nikolaos metro station. A similar distance out from the centre as Terminal A, it is equally badly signposted; both are best reached via taxi. Connections from Terminal B are much more limited with port/island links confined to Evia and the Sporades. Buses from both these stations usually stop in one or two of the larger towns en route but are otherwise difficult to board from the roadside (the notable exception being the popular Patras buses — which are flagged down just north of the Corinth Canal bridge as they do not enter Corinth itself). All the important bus times are listed in the *Greek Travel Pages* and similar publications.

The third terminus of note in Athens is near Areos Park north of the National Archaeological Museum at the junction of Platia Egyptou and Mavromateon St. (running down the west side of the park). There is no terminal building here, just a small bus park with bus stops. Buses departing from here are orange suburban buses. These provide a frequent service between central Athens and the ports of Rafina and Lavrion.

Most of the companies running boats out of Patras lay on air-conditioned coaches for passengers between Athens and the port. More expensive than regular buses (you book when buying your ferry ticket), they are worth considering since you make the 3½ hour journey in comfort without the hassle of getting to the bus station (most start from Syntagma Square or the National Gardens and run via Piraeus). Hydrofoil companies serving the Sporades also offer buses between Athens and Agios Konstantinos.

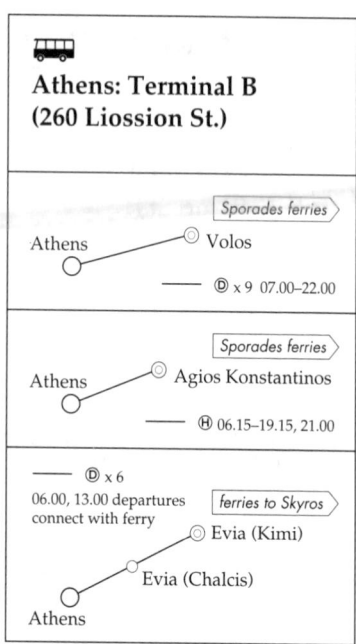

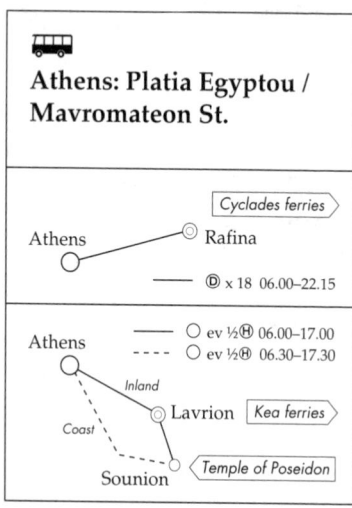

Athens: Centre & Ports

Athens

Given her pedigree, Athens is apt to disappoint. The transition from quaint Turkish town to a city housing a quarter of Greece's population has been an ugly one, producing a glorious (if very touristy) city centre surrounded by a sea of grime. Air pollution is also a serious problem. The Athenian conurbation is home to half of Greece's cars and 90% of the country's industry, and while the beauty of the Acropolis buildings can go to your head, so do the smog clouds (the *nephos*) that periodically force the government to ban motorists from the streets. In High Season Athens is also very hot and steamy, protected by the surrounding hills from the cooling winds that bathe the islands. However, for all this, the city offers a couple of days of fantastic sightseeing and has excellent links with the islands.

When visiting Athens priority should be given to an early visit to an NTOG/EOT office. This excellent tourist service provides free street maps along with information sheets on hotels, buses and ferry departure times for the main ferry port at Piraeus. There are several offices in the city. The easiest to find is housed in the National Bank on Syntagma Square, but there are also airport desks. Athens airport has two terminals (see p. 97).

Most visitors negotiate Athens without problems but you should be aware that the impact of 4 million tourists a year has had an unfortunate effect on a minority of the locals. There have always been two types of Athenian: the hospitable and charming individuals on a par with most of the Greek islanders and the other kind — who in days past ordered the death of Socrates, amongst others. Sadly, most of the descendents of the latter class have become waiters or taxi drivers. It pays to keep your eyes open (see: 'Scams' p. 54).

Historical Background

The city of Athens was once the most powerful of all the Greek city states, yet, for all this, it is best known for the work of a mere three generations in the 5 c. BC when it first stood alone as a bulwark against the massed forces of the Persian Empire (see p. 21) and then, under the leadership of Pericles and his successors, played host to the sudden flowering of the Greek genius that gave the western world its first theatre, greatest art and architecture, and first true history and philosophy. However, the dynamic that had set the city apart soon faded, and Athens had to settle for becoming, in turn, a major learning centre during the Hellenistic and Roman periods, then a fortified minor town under the Ottoman Turks, before emerging as the capital of the Greek state in the 19 c.

Thanks to the protection offered by the Acropolis, Athens has been occupied since Neolithic times. During the Mycenaean period the Acropolis was fortified, and this served the city well during the dark ages that followed as it was able to repulse the waves of Doric Greeks pouring into Greece. A stable centre in an unstable age, by the 8 c. BC Athens had gained control of the surrounding province of Attica and emerged as one of the major art centres in Greece. This developed into a leading cultural role in the 6 c. BC under the patronage of Pisistratus who initiated the Great Dionysia as part of the annual Panathenaic festival that gave the world the first established texts of Homer and later produced the birth of drama; for it was in Athens that all the great plays of Greek tragedy and comedy were conceived and first performed. A succession of leaders — Draco, Solon and Cleisthenes — also instituted constitutional reforms that led to Athens emerging as the champion of democracy in Greece (her power largely financed by the silver mines at Lavrion). This in turn prompted debate and enquiry into words and ideas with the result that the city developed as the centre for philosophical debate; attracting the great philosophers — Socrates, Plato and Aristotle among them — and their schools.

Athenian victories over the Persians gave her the role of leading protector of the Greeks and on this basis the islands contributed to the

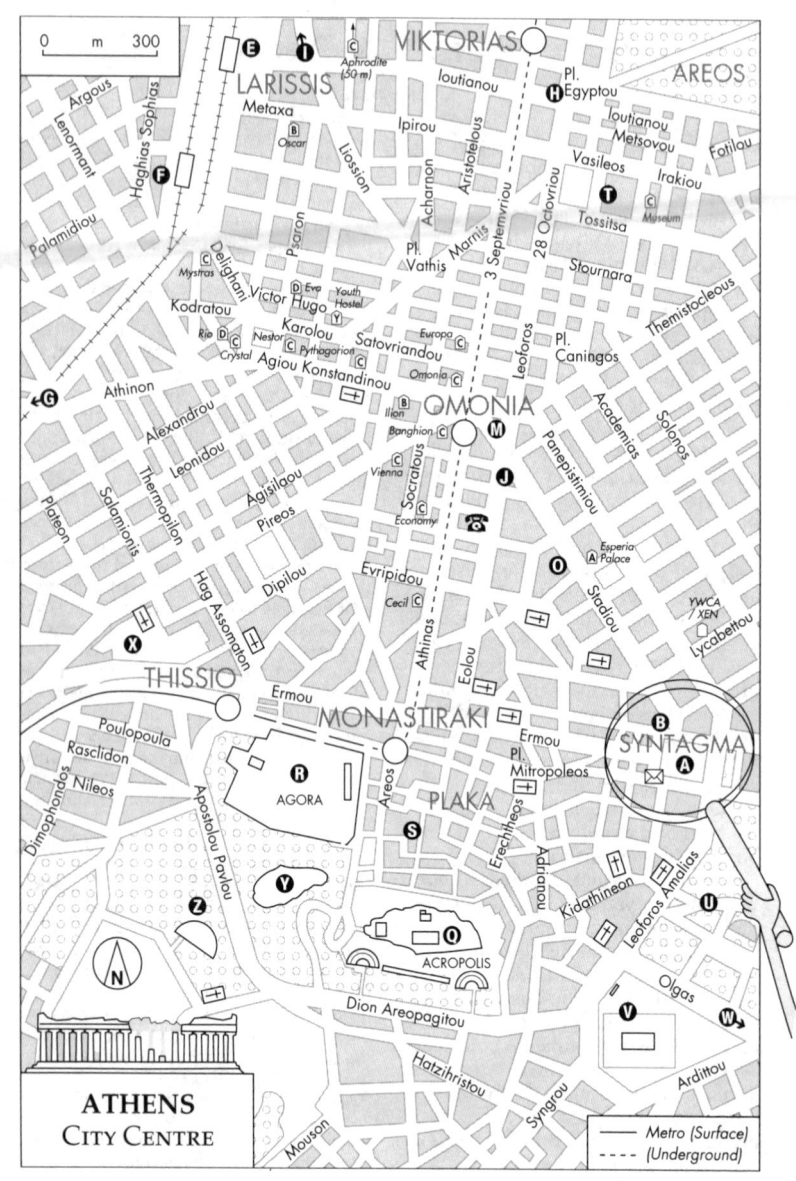

0 m 300

E **I** **C** Aphrodite (50 m) **MIKTORIAS** **AREOS**

LARISSIS Ioutianou **H** Pl. Egyptou

Argous Metaxa Ipirou Ioutianou Metsovou Fotilau

Lenormant **C** Oscar Vasileos Irakiou

Haghias Sophias Liosion Acharnon Aristotelous Tossitsa **T** **C** Museum

F Paron 3 Septemvriou 28 Oktovriou Stournara

Polamidiou Pl. Vathis Marnis Themistocleous

Mystras **C** Delighani Victor Hugo **D** Evo Youth Hostel **Y** Europa **C** Stournara

Kodratou Karolou Satovriandou Leoforos Pl. Caningos

Rio **D** **C** Nestor **C** Pythagorion **C** Omonia **C** Academias Solonos

Crystal Agiou Konstandinou **C** **OMONIA**

G Athinon **H** Ilion **C** **M**

Alexandrou Banghion **C** **J**

Leonidou Vienna **C** Panepistimiou

Thermopilon Agisilaou Socratous **C** Esperia **A** Palace

Plateon Salaminis Pireos Economy **C** **O** YWCA / XEN

Hag Assomaton Dipilou Evripidou Stadiou Lycabettou

Cecil **C** Athinas

X Eolou

THISSIO Ermou

Poulopoula MONASTIRAKI **B** SYNTAGMA

Rasclidon Ermou **A**

Dimophondos Nileos Areos Pl. Mitropoleos PLAKA

Apostolou Pavlou **R** AGORA **S** Erechtheos Kidathineon **U**

Z **Y** Adrianou Leoforos Amalias

N **Q** ACROPOLIS Olgas **W**

Dion Areopagitou **V**

Hatzihristou Arditou

ATHENS
CITY CENTRE

Mousan Syngrou

—— Metro (Surface)
----- (Underground)

Key

Ⓐ Syntagma Square
Ⓑ National Bank & NTOG/EOT Office
Ⓒ Thomas Cook *Bureau de Change*
Ⓓ American Express Travel Centre
Ⓔ Railway Station (Eastern Europe)
Ⓕ Railway Station (Corinth/Patras)
Ⓖ Bus Terminal A (Main Bus Station)
    (100 Kifissou St: 2 km W.)
Ⓗ Bus Stop (Rafina/Lavrion/Sounion)
Ⓘ Bus Terminal B (Evia/Kimi)
    (260 Liossion St: 1.5 km NW.)
Ⓙ Airport Bus Stop (Omonia)
Ⓚ Airport Bus Stop (Syntagma)
    / International Press
Ⓛ MacDonald's (Syntagma Sq.)
Ⓜ MacDonald's (Omonia Sq.)
Ⓝ Bookshop
Ⓞ Delicatessen
Ⓟ Parliament Building
Ⓠ Acropolis (map: p. 109)
Ⓡ Agora (map: p. 115)
Ⓢ Roman Agora (map: p. 118)
    / Plaka District (map: p. 105)
Ⓣ National Archaeological Museum
Ⓤ National Gardens
Ⓥ Olympieion & Arch of Hadrian
Ⓦ Stadium (50 m)
Ⓧ Kerameikos (Ancient City Cemetery)
Ⓨ Areopagus (Ancient 'Senate' Hill)
Ⓩ Pynx (Ancient 'Parliament' Hill)

maintance of the Athenian trireme fleet. Unfortunately, Athens rapidly turned these contributions into a tribute, and the islands into a de facto empire, and used the excess funds to build the Acropolis temples. Fearful of Athenian domination, the cities of Sparta and Corinth were soon embroiled in the Peloponnesian war with Athens, which the latter lost after 30 years of struggle in 404 BC. Never regaining her military pre-eminence, Athens fell to Phillip of Macadon in 338 BC. and came under Roman control in the 2 C. BC. The city was sacked by Sulla in 86 BC, briefly saw a renaissance — thanks to the patronage of Hadrian, and finally faded from the scene when it was sacked by the Herulian Goths in 267 AD. A minor town in the Byzantine Empire, it was ruled by the Franks and the Venetians before the Ottoman Turks gave it four quiet centuries (their rule being only briefly interrupted by the disastrous Venetian conquest of the city in 1687) prior to Greek independence in 1833.

Modern Centre

The centre of Athens is now split between the old town (now known as the Plaka district) with archaeological sectors and the new city to the north. When Athens became the capital of Greece it was little more than a minor town. The new Bavarian-born king took advantage of the opportunity to construct a fitting capital of wide boulevards outside the old town (which was intended to become an archaeological park). All went well with this grand scheme until the disastrous Turkish war of 1920–22 which resulted in a flood of refugees into Athens. As a result, the new city has its wide boulevards (graced with turn-of-the-century blocks up to a dozen storeys high) defiantly ignoring the hilly terrain, but beyond this commercial centre chaos reigns.

Often jammed with traffic, the new city (the map opposite only shows the major roads) isn't the perfect tourist destination, and has little appeal beyond the large numbers of hotels, the National Archaeological Museum and the pleasant National Gardens to the east. Its one saving grace is that the grid-iron street system at least makes it easy to walk between the major points via the main streets without getting lost. The most important of these, Stadiou St., runs between the two main squares: Syntagma (Constitution) Square — the tourist 'hub' of the city, and Omonia Square — the very grimy traffic hub that sits spider-like in the centre of the web of new city streets. Adopted as a meeting point for the men of Athens, it is an even less attractive spot at night. It is not surprising therefore, that most tourists prefer to stick to Syntagma Square and the charming rabbit-warren of old town streets nestling around the base of the Acropolis that make up the Plaka district.

Plaka District / Old Town
Plaka is the last remnant of pre-Greek-independence Athens. The old town extended over the Agora but the buildings there were demolished between the two world wars. The 'archaeological park' plan envisaged the total demolition of the Plaka district as there are thought to be important sites obscured under the current buildings, but their merit has now been recognised. The only area now scheduled for demolition lies to the north of the Agora. Very dilapidated, this area (unlike the rest of Plaka) is best avoided at night. During the day it is home to a flea market that includes a shop selling detritus from scrapped ships and an outlet offering a million and one different type of beads. The bulk of the old town — although throbbing with tourist shops, restaurants, hotels and everything else — is very appealing; with a maze of streets lined with old red tile-roofed Turkish mansions that give way to leafy archaeological sites. Towering over all is the Acropolis, which, floodlit at night, casts a golden glow over the crowds that wander in numbers into the small hours. Fortunately, all the principal sights are within easy walking distance of each other, and the Acropolis provides a ready point of reference should you lose your way.

Syntagma Square lies to the north-east of the old town and is another easily located point of reference. If you are in Athens any length of time you may wish to invest in a definitive street map. The *Historical Map of Athens* (1000 GDR), on sale at the Agora and newspaper kiosks around town, sounds stuffy, but is much better (for both old and new parts of the centre) than any of the other maps on sale in Athens. Its coverage of Plaka is particularly good, with all the buildings colour-coded according to age.

Key

Ⓐ Syntagma Square (map: p. 103)
Ⓑ MacDonald's / American Express
Ⓒ English Bookshops
Ⓓ Cathedral
Ⓔ Kapnikarea Church
Ⓕ Monastiraki Square
Ⓖ National Gardens
Ⓗ Old Bazaar Street
Ⓘ Flea Market
Ⓙ Restaurant Area
Ⓚ Agora Ticket Kiosks (map: p. 115)
Ⓛ Library of Hadrian (map: p. 118)
Ⓜ Roman Agora
Ⓝ Tower of the Winds
Ⓞ Roman Baths (Two sites)
Ⓟ Monument of Lysicrates
Ⓠ Arch of Hadrian
Ⓡ Propylion to Olympieion
Ⓢ Olympieion
Ⓣ Temples to Kronos & Rhea, Apollo, Hera, and Zeus
Ⓤ Agora Viewing Mount (with lethal, slippery marble steps)
Ⓥ Acropolis Ticket Kiosks (50 m) (map: p. 109)
Ⓦ Parthenon
Ⓧ Propylaia to the Acropolis
Ⓨ Erechtheion
Ⓩ Acropolis Museum

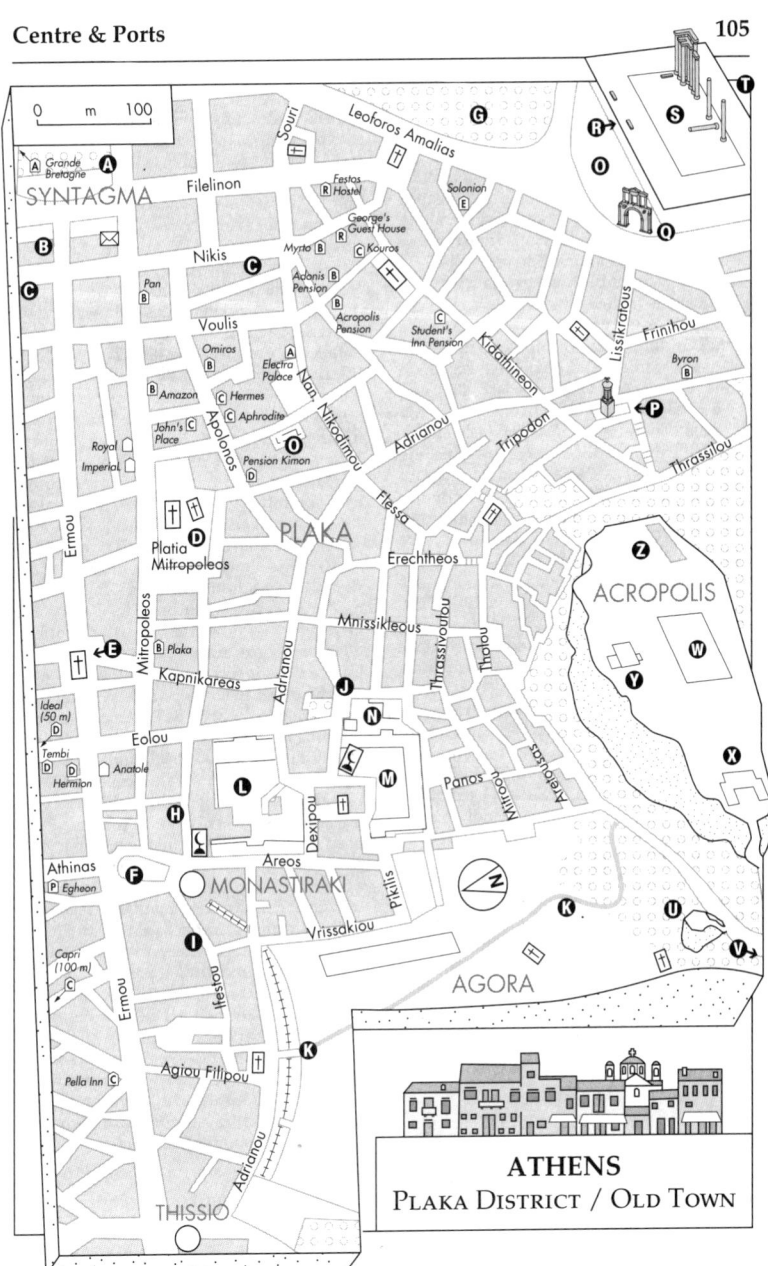

0 m 100

SYNTAGMA

Grande Bretagne **A**   **A**

Filelinon

Souri

Leoforos Amalias **G**

R Festos Hostel

Solonion **E**

George's Guest House **R**

Myrto **B**   Kouros **C**

B

Nikis **C**

Pan **B**

Aidanis Pension **B**

C Student's Inn Pension

C

Voulis

Omiros **B**

Electra Palace **A**

Amazon **B**

Hermes **C**

John's Place **C**

Aphrodite **C**

Royal **Imperial**

Apollonos

Pension Kimon **D**

O

Nan. Nikodimou

Adrianou

Kidathineon

Acropolis Pension **A**

Frinihou

Lissikratous

Byron **B**

P

Tripodon

Thrassilou

Flessa

PLAKA

Platia Mitropoleas **D**

Erechtheos

ACROPOLIS

Z

W

Y

Mnissikleous

Ermou

Mitropoleos

E

Plaka **B**

Kapnikareas

Thrassivoulou

Tholou

Ideal (50 m) **D**

Eolou

Tembi **D**   **D**

Hermion

Anatole

L

J

N

C

M

Dexipou

Panos

Nikis

Areopas

X

H

Athinas

Egheon **P**

F

MONASTIRAKI

Areos

Pikilis

N

U

K

V

Capri (100 m) **C**

I

Ifestou

Vrissakiou

AGORA

Pella Inn **C**

Agiou Filipou

K

Ermou

Adrianou

THISSIO

ATHENS
PLAKA DISTRICT / OLD TOWN

▣

It is not much of an exaggeration to say that every street in central Athens boasts a hotel. Accommodation is not hard to find, though, as always, it pays to find a bed before mid-afternoon. Hotels are found in the greatest numbers in the western Plaka district, along Ermou St. (which divides Plaka from the new city) and west of Omonia Square.

As **Plaka** has the bulk of the restaurants and is conveniently close to all the sights it is the obvious place to try and find a bed. The nature of the buildings mean that top-end hotels are relatively scarce: with the notable exception of the A-class *Electra Palace* (☎ 324 1401), and the B-class *Plaka* (☎ 322 2096) and *Amazon* (☎ 323 4002). There are a number of B-class pensions in the middle price range. These include the nice *Adonis* (☎ 324 9737) and *Acropolis* (☎ 322 2344) along with the small and popular *Byron* (☎ 325 3554). If you are looking for a reasonable C-class hotel, then the *Hermes* (☎ 323 5514) and the *Aphrodite* (☎ 323 4357) are good bets. At the budget end of the range are the C-class pension *John's Place* (☎ 322 9719), the E-class *Solonion* (☎ 322 0008) along with several places offering rooms south of Syntagma Square. Plaka also has a number of dubious unclassified establishments.

The streets running north from **Ermou St.** also have a number of D-class hotels that are adequate for a night or two. The best are along Eolou St., notably the *Tembi* (☎ 321 3175). The nearby *Hermion* (☎ 321 2753) — tucked down a blind alley — is also a very friendly place.

Omonia Square also has a fair number of budget establishments tucked away in the backstreets. Most in the immediate area of the square are pretty ropy and contrast greatly with the large number of excellent mid-range hotels that line the streets to the north-west. Agiou Konstandinou St. is one of the most fertile hunting grounds, with the C-class *Pythagorion* (☎ 524 2811), and *Nestor* (☎ 523 5575). Two blocks to the north, along Victor Hugo St., there is also the D-class *Eva* (☎ 522 3079) and a new *Youth Hostel* (☎ 524 1708).

Λ

Athens has several poor trailer sites in the outer environs that are better avoided. The best sites are a longish bus ride away along the Apollo coast near Cape Sounion, including the popular *Camping Sounio Beach* (☎ 0292 39358) and *Camping Varkiza* (☎ 01 8974329).

◎

Athens has 40 museums or historic sites, but the main ones can be covered in a couple of days — the big four being: 1. The Acropolis, 2. The Agora, 3. The Plaka District / Old Town, and 4. The National Archaeological Museum. As a book for island hoppers, this guide assumes that the reader won't be spending more than a couple of days in the capital and therefore only these major sights are described in detail in the following pages. If, however, you are staying longer you might care to consult a detailed city guide — the *Blue Guide to Athens* (Black/Norton) is easily the best, but adequate alternatives are on sale from local bookshops.

In addition to the 'big four' there are a number of other sites of interest. East of the Acropolis, and just inside the Plaka district is the **Monument of Lysicrates** (335 BC) erected to display the tripod won at the Dionysia festival of that year by Lysicrates. The skimpy **Arch of Hadrian** (2 C. AD) stands nearby. Built to mark the old city from the Emperor Hadrian's Roman additions, it provides a gateway to the largest temple built in Greece: the **Olympieion** (515 BC–132 AD) — the Temple of Olympian Zeus. An archaic work completed by Hadrian, it was built near the site of the plug hole opened when Deukalion's (the Greek Noah) flood was abated. To the east of these buildings lies the **Stadium** (143 AD), rebuilt in 1870 for the first modern Olympiad in 1896.

West of the Acropolis are a couple of lesser hills. The oddly named **Pynx** is the best: offering stunning views of the Acropolis, it was used during the Athenian democracy for citizen's meetings. The nearby **Areopagus** has a good view over the Agora, and was reputedly used by the Amazon women, the Persians and St. Paul during their attacks on the city. Finally, **Kerameikos**, the cemetery of Ancient Athens, is now a monument-filled park.

Outside Athens is one major site within easy reach. Few regret taking the 2-hour bus ride to **Sounion**, the cape on the southern tip of Attica that is home to the photogenic **Temple of Poseidon**. Built in 444–440 BC, the columns are unusually tall for its size: it functioned as a landmark, guiding sailors towards Athens (it lies about 90-minutes from Piraeus).

☎

CODE 01, TOURIST POLICE 9699523, NTOG INFORMATION DESK 322 25 45.

The Acropolis

The great attraction in Athens, the Acropolis (literally 'the city on the rock') is open ⓓ 08.30–18.30. Standing some 90 m above the surrounding plain, it proved easily defendable, later becoming the focus of religious activity before its defensive value again came to the fore. The buildings constructed on the rock add up to one of the most important archaeological sites in the world. Even in their ruined state, the Parthenon, and the Erechtheum, remain architectural wonders, forming the nucleus of an ensemble of buildings that led the Roman writer Plutarch to say of them that 'they were created in a short time for all time … a perpetual newness blooms upon them untouched by the years, as if they held within them some everlasting breath of life and an ageless spirit intermingled in their composition'. These days this effect is somewhat diminished by the presence of three million visitors a year, but if you arrive early you can avoid the worst of the crowds. Tickets cost 1500 GDR (entry is free on Sundays). Coach tour guides have the right to push to the head of the queues. Tourists not allowed to venture inside the Acropolis buildings.

The Acropolis has evidence of occupation dating back to Neolithic times, though later building has destroyed most traces. It is known that in the Mycenaean period it had a palace and saw its first major fortifications. In the Archaic period the Acropolis emerged as the religious centre of the city with a succession of temples erected on the rock before the Persians fired them in their invasion of Greece in 480 BC. Calamitous at the time, this event proved to have a happy outcome as it cleared the way for the massive rebuilding programme inspired by the Athenian leader Pericles some 30 years later — just as the flower of Greek culture was busting into full bloom: it is the ruins of these buildings that remain today.

Through the Hellenistic and Roman periods the Acropolis saw little further building (apart from on its outer slopes), and it was only from the 7 C. on that the area around the temples was in-filled with other buildings, as the rock was again used as a fortress. This state of affairs continued through the period of Turkish rule (one of the early European visitors describing the Acropolis mentions that there were two streets of whitewashed houses between the Parthenon and the Erechtheum).

Once Athens became the capital of an independent Greek state the Acropolis was rapidly converted from a fortress-town to a museum. In 1833 work began in stripping away the detritus of 2000 years to reveal the ancient buildings in all their ruined glory. However, this did result in unwitting damage due to poor restoration techniques. The worst of these was the use of iron staples in rebuilding that rusted and caused many marble blocks to split (the ancients coated the staples with bronze to prevent this process occurring). This has resulted in all the buildings on the Acropolis requiring major attention in the last few years, and quite a lot of new marble is visible. The degree to which restoration should be undertaken is a subject of much controversy. Current rebuilding is limited to work needed to ensure the structural integrity of the monuments and all new blocks are dated to ensure there is no confusion between old and new material. Previous restoration has been more substantial; notably the rebuilding of the centre columns on the north facade of the Parthenon in 1933. It has been suggested that the south side be similarly 'repaired' but this remains a contentious idea and has been put to one side while other worries — notably the growing threat of atmospheric pollution — are resolved.

Acropolis Entrance / West Side

Modern visitors approach the Acropolis from the same side as the ancients: though the first building encountered is a late construction. ❶ the **Beulé Gate** (named after its excavator) formed part of the inner defensive wall constructed in the 3 C. AD. It replaced a large processional stairway constructed by the Emperor Claudius in 52 AD. Today the path winds up to the Acropolis much as it did in classical times. After the Beulé Gate you are confronted by two bastions projecting out from the Acropolis proper. On the northern one is ❷ the distinctive 'Tower' of Agrippa (C. 178 BC). A Hellenistic plinth 8.8 m high, it bore a number of statues (including a chariot carrying Antony and Cleopatra), and takes its name from a statue of Marcus Agrippa erected on it in 27 BC.

The south bastion is more appealing, being home to ❸ the lovely small **Athena Nike Temple** (427–424 BC). Designed by Kallikrates, it was dismantled in 1686 by the Turks so that the bastion could be used to house cannon. Fortunately, all the stones were preserved on site and it was re-erected in 1836–42. The building has a freeze running right around it, and contained a statue of Athena with a Nike (victory). Unfortunately, the lack of retaining walls on the bastion means that it is inaccessible: the steps to the Acropolis offer the best view you can get of it. Like all the Acropolis buildings it is carved out of pentallic marble. Thanks to small deposits of iron in the marble, the colour has gradually mellowed from white to a creamy yellow as the iron has gradually oxidized over the millennia.

Extending out onto the bastions are the wings of ❿ the **Propylaea** (438–432 BC): the ceremonial gateway to the Acropolis. Deemed to be the best of its kind by the ancients, it was never fully completed. The outbreak of the Peloponnesian war and Athenian defeat ensured that its decoration was never finished. Designed by Mnesikles, the building was famous for its five massive doors and painted ceiling. The north wing was also a noted picture gallery. The building was used as a bishop's palace in the 13 C. , and in the 17 C. became a magazine for the Turkish garrison; suffering severe damage when a passing lightning bolt struck. The Venetian bombardment of 1687 finished the job of demolition by putting paid to the famous ceiling. South-east of the Propylaea and now represented only by scattered stones are the foundations of a double-winged stoa; ❸ a votive shrine to **Artemis Brauronia** (the bear goddess), and nearer the Parthenon, the **Chalkotheke** or magazine of the bronzes.

The North Side

Surprisingly, the magnificent Parthenon was not the holy of holies on the Acropolis. It was more of a glorious anti-chamber to the true religious centre — the Erechtheum — which was located on the north side, on the probable site of the Mycenaean palace. This complex of shrines was guarded by a large bronze statue that stood at ❻ facing the Propylaea. Known as the **Athena Promachos**, this famous figure is long lost, but part of the stone base has been identified. The path takes you past the site where it stood and then divides. One branch takes you along the north side of the Parthenon (the traditional approach route to this temple), the other runs northward past some foundations at ❻. This is the site of the Parthenon's predecessors, the melodiously named **Hekatompedon** — meaning 'one hundred footer'

— (c. 556 BC) which was replaced by the Archaic **Pre-Parthenon** (530–528 BC) destroyed by the Persians. After this event, the Athenians swore never to rebuild the temples as a memorial to the sacking of the city. They later got around this vow by constructing the Parthenon to the south of the old temple site, and having made a gesture in this direction proceeded to rebuild their holy of holies on its original site.

Now known as the **Erechtheum** (c. 421–405 BC), the Athenian holy of holies is a four-chambered building (❿) that conformed to an ancient and irregular shrine plan. It was home to several ancient and venerated wooden figures — notably a statue of Athena Polias — that were removed (along with the population of Athens) to the island of Salamis and spared the ravages of the Persian capture of the city. The path approaches the building running past ❶ the site of the **Sacred Grove**, which was home to a sacred olive tree (that the Persians used as fire-wood), and then turns east at the **North Portico** (fronting a shrine to Poseidon). Designed by Kallikrates, the Erechtheum is graced with delicate Ionic columns. It became a church in the 6 C. and later the harem for the Turkish commander — an idea no doubt inspired by ❿, the **Caryatids** — the famous maiden-column porch. All the figures are now copies: the originals being on show in the Acropolis Museum (barring the one in the British Museum). The east portico fronted the main shine to Athena Polias and now has a **Restored Column** (❿) at the north end. Added in 1981 (most postcard photos are still without it), it has attracted criticism thanks to its pristine, white marble. In fact, it is an accurate copy of the original, now in the British Museum.

To the south east of the Erechtheum stood a large stepped altar at ❿ dedicated to **Zeus Polieus**, of which little remains. Instead the path runs east of the site past a deep well in the floor of the rock at ❿. Known as the **Mycenaean Stairway** it was one of two stairways up the north side of the rock that were covered over or destroyed in the classical period (the Persians gained access to Acropolis via the lost staircase north of the Erechtheum). From here the path then runs east to the flag bastion and its views of the city. On its way it passes the scanty remains of ❿ the tiny, round tholos **Temple of Rome and Augustus**; a late and clumsy addition (27 BC) to the Acropolis monuments, all but ignored by ancient writers.

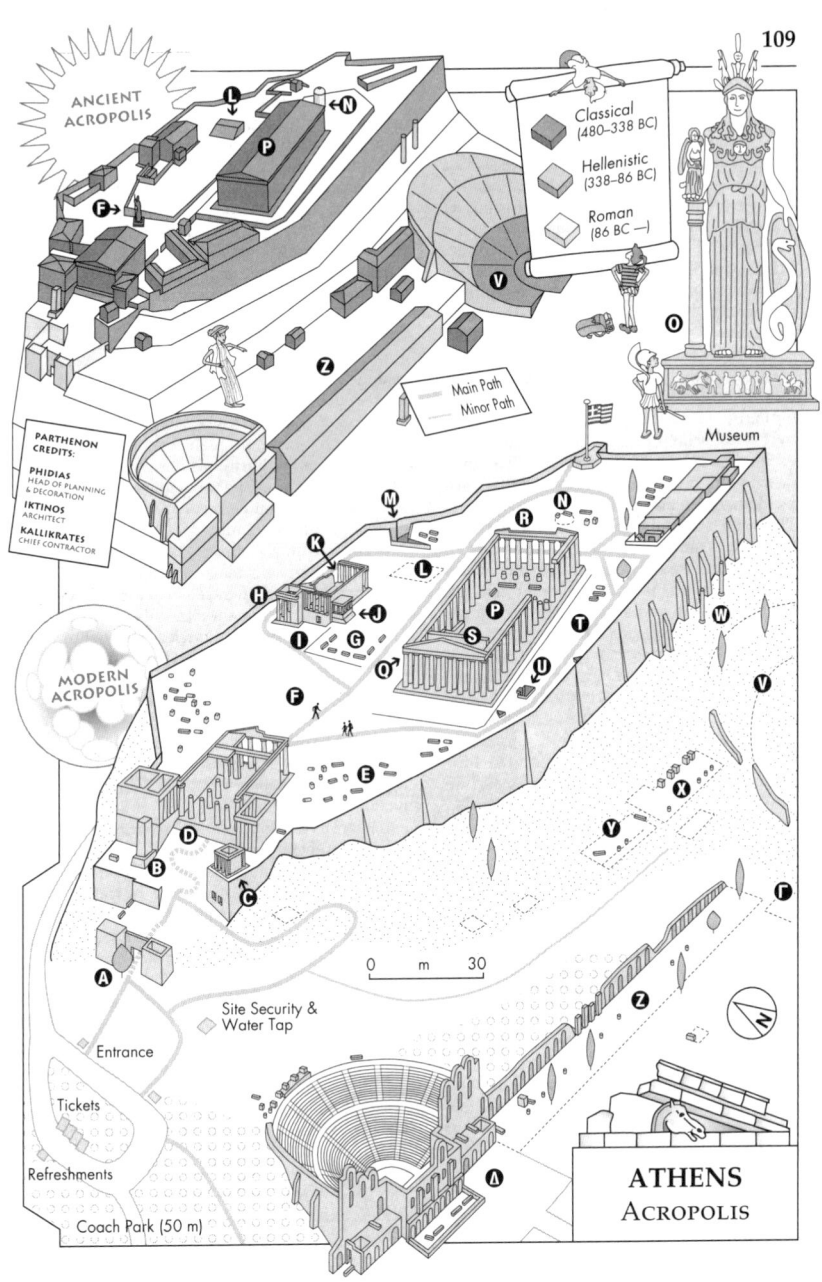

ANCIENT ACROPOLIS

Classical
(480–338 BC)

Hellenistic
(338–86 BC)

Roman
(86 BC —)

Main Path
Minor Path

PARTHENON
CREDITS:

PHIDIAS
HEAD OF PLANNING
& DECORATION

IKTINOS
ARCHITECT

KALLIKRATES
CHIEF CONTRACTOR

MODERN
ACROPOLIS

Museum

Site Security &
Water Tap

Entrance

Tickets

Refreshments

0   m   30

Coach Park (50 m)

ATHENS
ACROPOLIS

The Parthenon

The main temple cum city treasury dedicated to Athena Parthenos (the Virgin Athena), the Parthenon (**Ⓟ**) dominates the Acropolis. Built between 447–432 BC, the building is remarkable for not having a straight line in it (both columns and the platform are deliberately convex); a feature designed (by its designer and architect Phidias and Iktinos) to correct the optical illusion that makes straight columns appear thinner in the middle. The simple Doric columns are also abnormally tall and placed closer together than was traditional. Tradition was also defied in the size of the building; most temples were built 6 columns wide — the Parthenon has 8. Its length was determined by a standard formula (2 x the number of width columns + 1) producing 17 columns down the sides: thus retaining regular proportions yet making it appear unusually long. The result is a building that makes other Greek temples look small and clumsy by comparison.

Intact for over 2000 years, the Parthenon has had a chequered history. Highlights include a couple of passing rulers using it to put a finger (among other things) up at the city population by using it as a brothel. In the 6 c. it was converted into the church of St. Sophia: a change which inflicted major structural damage as the orientation of the building had to be turned 180 degrees (the main entrance was originally on the east side to allow the rising sun to shine in upon the statue of the goddess), and an apse was added to the east end. In the Ottoman period the Parthenon became a mosque, with a minaret poking through the roof on the south-west corner. It met its end in 1687 when a Venetian army besieged the city. On hearing that the Turks were using the Parthenon as a hiding place for their arsenal (they assumed their attackers would never bombard a former church) the Venetian commander Morosini did just that. A shell landed on the building, blowing it apart, and leaving fragments of the roof, cella and the 300 women and children sheltering inside, all over the Acropolis.

In its ruined state, the Parthenon continued to suffer. Reduced to two unconnected gable ends, it was used as a quarry for a mosque that was built in the shell (described by one visitor as looking like 'an ugly cork in a beautiful bottle'). Its remaining sculptures were removed by Elgin (see p. 113), and poor restoration and pollution have taken their toll since.

In its prime the Parthenon was ornately decorated, with sculpture and other decorative features brightly painted in gaudy 'Mickey Mouse' colours. As much a statement of civic pride as a temple, it housed a treasury in the smaller room in its west end, but its main function was to house the 12 m high chryselephantine (gold and ivory) statue of **Athena Parthenos** (**Ⓞ**). This remarkable figure cost more than the Parthenon itself, and its designer, Phidias, his reputation and almost his life. Known now through small copies bought by ancient tourists, it stood 12 m high and represented the goddess holding a shield in her left hand and a man-sized winged victory in her right. Her helmet was topped by a sphinx and two griffins and her shield was decorated with scenes from the mythical battle between the Athenians and the Amazon women. It was this shield that brought about Phidias's downfall. His pre-eminent position as the supervisor of the Acropolis rebuilding programme brought him many enemies who took advantage of a perceived likeness in the faces of two of the figures on Athena's shield to himself and his mentor Pericles to have him charged with sacrilege. Forced to flee the city, he took sanctuary at Olympia and there created one of the seven wonders of the world — his chryselephantine statue of Zeus. The Athena was deemed to be the inferior of the two, though she was impressive enough; with clothing was made of sheets of gold tacked onto a wooden frame. Her flesh was sculpted ivory and her eyes precious gems. The figure stood, facing east, before a pool of sea-water in the middle of the room. In its prime it must have been overwhelming. To the ancients, walking into the chamber, lit only by the light from the doorway and oil lamps, it must have seemed as if the goddess was actually standing before them, glinting in the half-light. It survived in until c. 400 AD when it was removed to Constantinople and destroyed by fire.

The Parthenon also boasted other major art treasures that survive in part. The **Pediment Sculptures**, noted for their beauty, are the most obvious of these. Now reduced to fragments in museums, by great luck, they were drawn in 1674 by Jacques Carrey, a French painter, a few years before they were damaged. **Ⓞ** the **West Pediment**, was the best preserved until 1687. Its theme was the contest between Athena and Poseidon (tradition had

it that the two fought for the right to be the city's patron). Unfortunately, once the Venetians captured Athens, Morosini decided to remove the central figures as war trophies, but they fell and were smashed in the attempt to take them down. The central **East Pediment** (**R**) figures were lost in the 4 C. AD when the Parthenon was converted into a church. According to Pausanias the theme was the birth of Athena, but he gives no further details. Traditionally this subject was represented with Athena sitting on Zeus's lap (legend had it that she sprang from his brow) but a 1–2 C. AD altar from Spain, thought to be based on this pediment, shows the two side by side in much the same pose as the main figures on the west pediment. The third great art treasure on the Parthenon is the **Frieze**. Over 159 m long, it is one of the high points of Greek Art. It ran around the outer wall of **S** the **Cella** (the 'building' inside the ring of columns) and depicted the annual procession to the Acropolis in honour of the goddess. Just over half of the surviving panels were recovered by Elgin and are now in the British Museum with the majority of the surviving pedimental figures.

The South Side

The area to the south of the Parthenon contains a couple of oddities. Now unmarked, is the site of **T** **Phidias's Workshop**, used for the construction of the gold and ivory statue. Fragments of the materials used have been found in this area. Walking along to the west end of the Parthenon you will come to **U** the **Pre-Classical Wall trenches**. These pits were natural fissures in the rock inside the Acropolis walls. In the classical period they were used as 'graves' for the damaged sculptures from the temples destroyed by the Persians and now in the Acropolis museum. Left open, with low skirting walls, they form a minor hazard. The Acropolis wall is also dangerously low, but looking over it you are able to take in

the layout of the buildings lining the southern slope better than you can at street level.

Looking down from left to right, the first, and largest of the south slope structures is **V** the **Theatre of Dionysos** (C. 330 BC). Marking the spot where most of the great plays of Greek tragedy and comedy were first performed, the site now has a separate entrance on the south-east corner of the Acropolis area. In the classical period the stage and seating occupied the lower tiers and were made of wood. With the rebuilding, the seating was extended right up the acropolis slope, though most of this has now gone. Above the theatre and close under the Acropolis walls stand **W** the **Thrasyllos Monument**, (320–310 BC) consisting of two **Corinthian columns**. To the right of the theatre are the foundations of two small healing sanctuaries sited on a couple of springs; **X** the **Old Asklepieion** (C. 420 BC), and **Y** the **New Asklepieion** (C. 300 BC). A number of minor shrines lay between these buildings and the west acropolis slope. Running east of the theatre is **Z** the **Stoa of Eumenes II** (C. 197–159 BC), the back wall of which has survived as part of the later city wall. At its eastern end lie the foundations of **1** the **Nikias Monument** (320–319 BC). Finally, **2** the **Odeon of Herodes Atticus**, is the best preserved of the ancient structures on the Acropolis slopes. Built in 160–174 AD, the inner section of its façade survived by being incorporated into the later city wall that ran around the acropolis. The interior seating was lost thanks to the same reason, but has since been replaced to allow performances in the theatre during the summer. The rooms behind the stage have also been rebuilt from the foundations.

Marbles in Athens

Elgin Marbles (removed 1801)

Marbles lost (1674–1801)

Acropolis Museum & Elgin Marbles

After looking at the buildings on the Acropolis, the museum cut into the rock behind the Parthenon is apt to be something of an anticlimax. A small building, repeatedly enlarged, it is due to be replaced by a more substantial affair (though this ambition is unlikely to get beyond the intention stage unless the Elgin marbles are returned to Greece — an equally unlikely event). With the best exhibits now in the British Museum in London (thanks to Lord Elgin), and the more interesting smaller Acropolis-related pieces (notably the marble copy of the statue of Athena Parthenos, and most of the bronze work) housed in the National Archaeological Museum, the Acropolis Museum has to make do with the residue — principally the remains of the pre-classical sculpture from the buildings destroyed in the Persian sack of the Acropolis and the handful of sculptures and reliefs that escaped Elgin and other collectors. This said, the museum does merit a visit (if only to see close up the original Caryatids — now housed behind protective glass). The more archaeologically minded, might also consider buying a detailed Acropolis guide as, unusually, few of the museum exhibits are labelled, and are spread over nine rooms:

Rooms I–III: Persian Rubble Rooms

These rooms are devoted to the sculptures damaged by the Persians in 480 BC and later ceremonially buried by the Athenians. These include: **A** the **Lioness and Calf**, the latter creature is being torn to flesh (6 C. BC); **B** a **Gorgon's Head** (550 BC); **C** part of a pedimental sculpture depicting **Herakles fighting the Triton**; **D** the **Calf Bearer**, one of the most influential and important Archaic works of art; and **E** the **Lion Group**, also from the pediment of an Archaic temple (570-560 BC).

Room IV: Phaidimos Room

Devoted to sculptures (not all from the Acropolis) by this artist. Primary exhibits are **F** the **Equestrian Statue**: the torso of the first European equestrian statue known, and **G** the **Peplos Kore**: a woman named after her clothing with traces of her original paint (530 BC).

Room V: Gigantomachia Room

Lined on one side by **H** the **Showcases**. Behind the glass, running from left to right are ceramics from south slope buildings, archaic marble fragments from the Acropolis, small masonry and clay sculptures and wooden blocks from the holes of the Parthenon column drums. This room also contains **I**, the **Gigantomachia**. The battle between the Olympian Gods and the giants was a popular theme in Ancient Greek art. This example shows Athena fighting a giant and comes from the Archaic temple that proceeded the Parthenon.

Room VI: Late Archaic Works

This room contains a mixed collection of items, notably **J**, the **Mourning Athena,** C. 460 BC,

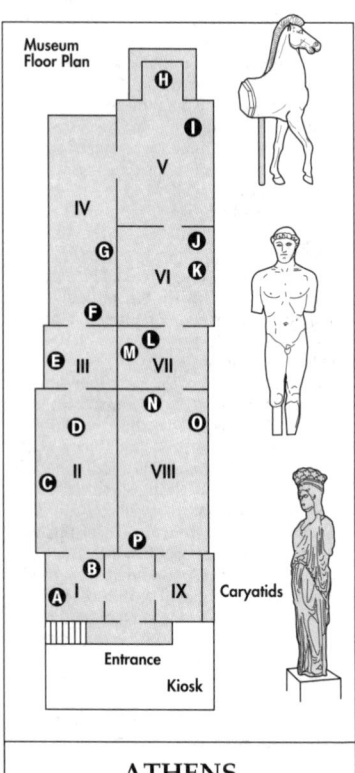

Museum Floor Plan

Caryatids

Entrance

Kiosk

ATHENS
ACROPOLIS MUSEUM

(see p. 92), a famous relief, it was discovered in 1888 south of the Parthenon; and **O** the **Kritios Boy**; 480 BC, (illustrated opposite) an early statue of a youth in Parian marble.

Room VII: Parthenon Fragments
This rather thin collection is dominated by **O** the **West Pediment figure**; a male figure — possibly the river god Ilissos, and **O** the **East Gable figure**; the torso of a woman — thought to be the moon goddess Selene driving her chariot toward the sunset.

Room VIII: Parthenon Frieze fragments
Most of the surviving frieze is now in the British Museum, but several weathered slabs are here: **O** the **East Frieze** depicts the sacred procession with sacrificial animals and athletes, and **O**, which shows **Youths with Amphorae**. This room also contains **O**, the **Nike Relief**, from the Temple of Nike, showing Athena undoing a sandal (409–406 BC).

Room IX: The Caryatids
Five of the six maidens-cum-pillars are preserved here along with a copy of the one in the British Museum.

The Elgin Marbles
The best preserved Parthenon sculptures, along with fragments from other Acropolis buildings, are now in the British Museum thanks to Lord Elgin who removed them in 1801–4. The Greek government has sought their return over the last two decades via a high profile campaign — without success. As a result, you will find that Elgin is vilified in most local guides and (taking their lead from these) not a few international ones. Over-the-top phrases like 'looter Elgin' abound, but are hardly appropriate given the facts.

Elgin was one of a number of individuals (inspired by the revival of interest in the classical tradition that swept Europe in the 18th and early 19 C.) who dared to enter the mysterious Ottoman Empire in search of the past. Travellers' tales of collapsing temples thanks to neglect by the 'infidel Turk' (in 1813 John Cam Hobhouse wrote that 'there will, in a few years, be not one marble standing upon another on the site of the Parthenon') led to a general perception that an important part of European heritage was being lost, and prompted these individuals into action. They

sketched, copied via plaster casts, or removed what they could (almost all the most important sculpture and artifacts discovered in Greece and Turkey prior to the 20 C. are now in European museums). Elgin, the British ambassador in Constantinople, sought out the authorities who had been ruling Athens for over 350 years and gained written permission to remove 'inscriptions and sculptures' from the derelict Acropolis buildings. He was not alone in doing this — only narrowly beating his French counterpart to the marbles, and indeed, other Parthenon sculptures are now in the Louvre and Vatican museums. The Greeks have never accepted the legitimacy of Turkish rule, and perceive these agreements as being akin to one thief passing on stolen goods to another.

Given the uniqueness of the Parthenon and its universal recognition as *the* symbol of Greece, a strong case can be made for the return of the marbles. However, Elgin bashers hardly help their cause by failing to acknowledge that his motives in removing parts of deteriorating ruins were hardly on a par with a looter (the perception at the time was that this sort of action was more akin to pulling art treasures out of a burning building), or that plaster casts made by him of sculptures he didn't remove show that they deteriorated significantly before their importance was recognised. In this respect, Elgin's claim that he was 'saving' the marbles was borne out by subsequent events.

The impact the sculptures had in London is also not readily acknowledged (beyond the fact that they helped bankrupt Elgin). Widely admired (the poet Keats gazed at them for hours at a time like a 'sick eagle looking at the sky'), they have been very influential; occasionally in quite bizarre ways. Most important was their contribution to the pro-Greek romanticism sweeping Europe that led to the Great Powers supporting Greek nationalism and the foundation of the Greek state. At the other end of the scale, fashionable London dandies made total fools of themselves adopting a posture known as the 'Grecian bend' based on the figures. However, the most delightful fallout from Elgin's acquisitions came with the horse's head removed from the north corner of the Parthenon's east pediment. Subsequently used as the model for what has become the standard international chess-set knight, it has acquired an unassailable status as the most copied piece of sculpture in human history.

The Athenian Agora

Within easy walking distance of the Acropolis lie a number of important archaeological sites. The most important of these is the **Agora**, the ancient marketplace, to the north-west. An open square during classical times, bounded by all the major administrative buildings in the city, it was in-filled with buildings in the Hellenistic and Roman periods. Add to this 3000 years of continuous occupation and the result is the confused jumble of foundations that one sees today. The Roman travel writer Pausanias described all the major buildings; so most of those unearthed have been identified. Problems, however, do remain. The north side of the Agora still lies under the modern city (the buildings here are dilapidated, with the sword of demolition hanging over them) hindering a comprehensive assessment of the site's history. Moreover, two important buildings — the **Theseion**, the major shrine of the city's founder, and the **Stoa of Herms** — are known to have been in the vicinity of the Agora, but remain undiscovered.

The area so far exposed has been excavated since the 1930s when the Turkish buildings covering the Agora were demolished. The metro line cutting off the northern third of the site is a legacy of the last century (1891) when its importance was unrecognised. Today the Agora is heavily planted with trees; offering a shady retreat from the hot city streets.

The North and East Sides

There are two entrances to the Agora; one on the Acropolis side, and the main entrance, sited on a bridge over the metro line. The street leading to the latter (Adrianou) offers you a glimpse of several inaccessible buildings. Most notable of these is the corner of **❹**, the **Painted Stoa** or **Stoa Poikile** (C. 460 BC), currently being excavated by students from the American School of Archaeology. Once the most famous secular building in Athens it was a natural meeting place for the city intelligentsia. Its reputation was based on the paintings that adorned its walls (it was the Louvre of the ancient city) and the bronze shields hung about it (captured from the Spartans at the battle of Sphakteria in 425 BC — one is now in the museum). As a result of the chattering crowds that gathered here, it became the only building to give its name to a school of philosophy; as those that followed

the philosopher Zeno regularly met in the building and thus became known as 'Stoics'.

Turning to the other side of the road you can look down on the foundations of the small, winged **Royal Stoa** (C. 500 BC) at **❽**, where the city magistrates took their oath of office. Hereafter, the road runs to the railway bridge. From the ticket kiosk on the bridge the main path descends onto **❾** the **Panathenaic Way**. Running south-east to the Acropolis, this was the most important road in the city. It was the ceremonial route for the annual procession depicted on the Parthenon frieze. Nowadays it runs to the south end of **❿** the **Stoa of Attalos**. Rebuilt between 1953–56 by the American excavators, it is now the **Agora Museum**. The original was a gift from the king of Pergamum c. 145 BC. It replaced an earlier row of shops and is a typical example of this type of building, with two storeys and 21 square rooms at the back that functioned as shops. A pillar with a statue of Attalos in a chariot stood in front of the stoa, with **❺** a **Bema** (a speaker's platform), directly in front of that. Nearby are the circular remains of **❻** a Roman **Fountain**. To the north stood the classical law courts, but the surviving foundations (straddled by the railway line) are a later **Hadrianic Basilica** (**❼**) with an **Augustan Colonnade** (**❽**) running west from it.

The Central Area

The centre of the Agora was an open square during the classical period. Now it is dominated by **❶**, the **Odeon of Agrippa** c. 15 BC. Rebuilt several times (largely on account of the massive vaulted roof that collapsed now and again) it was later rebuilt as a vast gymnasium c. 400 AD. The most prominent feature today are the three colossal statues of tritons and giants that formed part of the entrance of the original building. The triton heads are of particular significance as ancient sources say that they were modelled on the (now lost) pedimental sculpture of Poseidon on the Parthenon. To the north of the Odeon lies the remains of **❷** the **Altar of Ares** (C. 420 BC). It was here that dogs were sacrificed in honour of the god. To the west was **❸** the **Temple of Ares** (C. 435 BC). Now no more than a low mound, it was originally very similar in design to the Hephesteion on the hill to the west (it is thought to possibly be the work of the same architect). The building wasn't originally

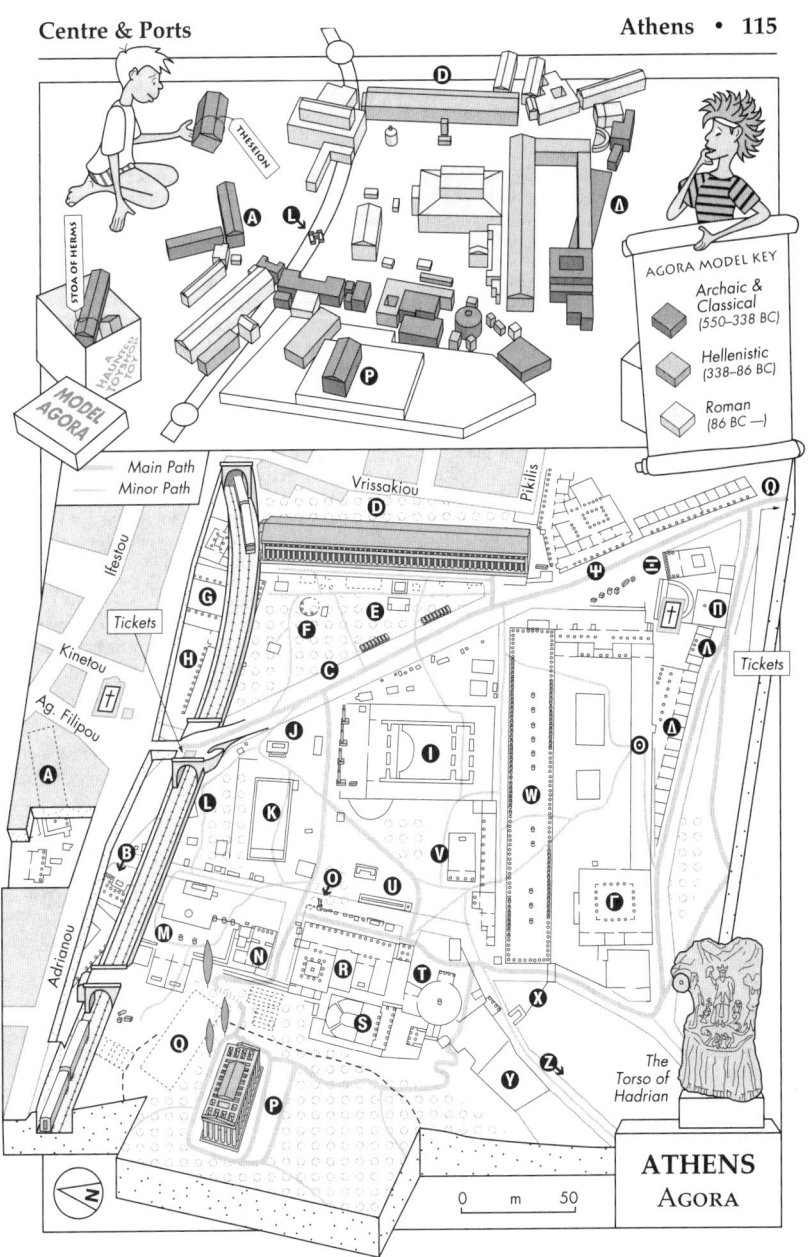

AGORA MODEL KEY

Archaic & Classical
(550–338 BC)

Hellenistic
(338–86 BC)

Roman
(86 BC —)

Main Path
Minor Path

Vrissakiou

Ifestou

Tickets

Kinetou

Ag. Filipou

Adrianou

Pikilis

Tickets

The Torso of Hadrian

ATHENS
AGORA

0   m   50

N

located here. All the surviving stones are numbered (indicating it was moved from a different site); the foundations are Roman, and some of the guttering seems to have come from the Temple of Poseidon at Sounion. The original location of the temple isn't known (suggestions range from the Roman Agora to Acharnai outside the city), but this sort of movement wasn't uncommon in the Roman period when many outlying shrines were abandoned due to urbanisation.

North of the Temple of Ares, and now tucked against the metro line wall, lies a corner of the boundary wall that surrounded the small ❶ **Altar of the Twelve Gods** (6 C. BC). Now all but lost under the railway, this was one of the most important monuments in Athens. The altar was not only venerated as a place of sanctuary (particularly for the destitute) but had a more important role as the *Omphalos* or navel of both the city and the surrounding province of Attica. In short, it was the point from which all distances were measured.

The West Side

Travelling west the path then emerges at ❿, the **Stoa of Zeus Eleutherios** C. 430 BC, which was an early (and therefore small) stoa with projecting wings. Ornately decorated, it was the base for the official in charge of religious ceremonies and trials for murder or impiety. It is better known in literature as the favourite stoa of the philosopher Socrates. It was in this building that he was wont to argue with his fellows, taking the line that he knew nothing and then proceeding to demonstrate that those who claimed to know something 'didn't know nuffin' either. Showing up large numbers of people who thought that they were intelligent didn't exactly endear Socrates to those in power and he was tried and executed.

South of the stoa of Zeus lies the foundations of ❶ the **Temple of Apollo Patroös** (4 C. BC). One of the oldest temple sites in Athens, it was destroyed and rebuilt several times. The colossal statue of Apollo (now in the Agora museum) once stood in it. On a somewhat smaller scale, on the other side of the path, and to the south, stands a replica of the torso of a **Statue of Hadrian (❶)**; notable for the breastplate adorned with the delightful mix of Athena (accompanied by a snake and owl) standing on the back of a wolf suckling Romulus and Remus.

Behind the buildings on the west side of the Agora and overlooking all is ❶ the **Hephaisteion** (449–444 BC). The best preserved temple in Greece, it is the only temple to retain its roof substructure substantially intact (the inner cella now has a medieval roof over it). Built just before the Parthenon (but not with island money: this temple hadn't a predecessor to be destroyed by the Persians), for many years it was thought to be another important temple — the Theseion (hence the metro station of that name nearby) — but this notion has now been discredited. Inside it still contains the bronze cult statues of Hephaistos and Athena. Around it are trees planted in their classical positions; the original pots were unearthed when the site was excavated. This excavation also revealed that to the north of the Hephaisteion stood ❶ the **Arsenal** of ancient Athens; now known only through post holes.

The steps leading up to the Hephaisteion also marked the boundary between the religious and secular buildings on this side of the agora. To the south stood ❶, the **Metroön** (430 BC); theoretically a temple dedicated to the mother of the gods, it became the repository for the government archives. It was built on the original site of ❶, the **Bouleuterion** (5 C. BC). This was the council chamber for the city senate house, and was rebuilt a number of times during its working life, gradually increasing in size, and each time further back from the main line of buildings. This allowed the Metroön to be expanded south to ❶ the circular **Tholos** (C. 470 BC). One of the most important buildings in Athens (being the headquarters for those charged with the running of the city) it was manned 24 hours a day (and had its own kitchen). It is a controversial structure, with widely differing reconstructions being put forward (in part because it was rebuilt several times). In its last incarnation it had a conical roof with diamond-shaped tiles. Opposite this collection of buildings was ❶, the long narrow monument of the **Eponymonus Heroes**. Adorned with the statues of the founders of the political tribes of Athens, it was used to display public notices.

The South Side

The southern boundary of the Agora was dominated by a series of stoas that gradually encroached north to the point where they added to the in-filling of the classical Agora square. Temples were also added at this later stage. They included the small **South-West Temple** at **❼**, with an altar (of Zeus Agoraios) 30 m to the north, and a small stoa-like building to the south (used by the Athenian civil service). Behind these lies the foundations of **❿** the **Middle Stoa** (2 C. BC). The largest stoa to be built in Athens, it took the form of a double-aisled hall open on both sides. It was later incorporated into the 4 C. AD gymnasium along with the nearby Odeon. Abutting it to the west was **❽**: a block of **Small Buildings** that included a cobbler's shop and a latrine, and **❾** the **Stratagion**. Only tentatively identified, this building was perhaps the Pentagon of ancient Athens, and used as both the military headquarters and home of the supreme commander. Conveniently located near the city prison, its incumbents tended to move from one to the other with alarming regularity — particularly during the Peloponnesian war when the 30 year stalemate between Athens and Sparta lead to a succession of commanders being executed for failing to win the war. The **Prison** (**❷**) lies 50 m down the path and was where Socrates was executed (a small figure of the philosopher was found on the site).

South of the Middle Stoa lie the foundations of the classical south Agora buildings. These include **❼** the **Heliaia** (C. 470 BC), the original city courthouse, and **❹** the **South Stoa I** (5 C. BC). Now overlain by **❺** the **South Stoa II** (2 C. BC), the former is of greater interest as the surviving fragment contains the foundations of the small dining rooms (the walls being no more than a dining couch and a doorway wide) that stood at the back of this stoa.

Beyond this the remains are largely Roman, consisting of: **❻** the **South-East Fountain House** (C. 470 BC); now partly overlain by a Byzantine church. The back walls also survive from **❿** the **Athens Mint** (C. 400 BC) where the famous City owl coins were struck. To the east lies **❽** the **South-East Temple** (1 C. BC). This was another Roman import; the materials being taken from a classical temple of Aphrodite at Sounion. The other side of the Panathenaic way was also embellished in the Roman period with **❹** the **Library of Pantainos** (102 AD) and **❿** the **South-East Stoa** (1 C. AD): yet another shopping mall on the path to the later **Wall of Valerian**, which was constructed out of the remains of Agora buildings following the Herulian sack of the city in 269 AD.

The Roman Agora

(Map overleaf.) Sandwiched between 18 C. mansions in the Plaka district are the remains of several important ancient structures: notably the **Roman Agora**, the adjacent **Library of Hadrian** and the Hellenistic **Tower of the Winds**. Unfortunately, an unsympathetic medieval street plan makes interpretation of the remains difficult, running as it does across the lines of the ancient ground plan.

The **Library of Hadrian** (2 C. AD) is usually the first building encountered thanks to the nearby Monastiraki metro station. Sadly, the library is still undergoing excavation and tourists have to make do with peering through the iron railings of the fence surrounding the site. The most prominent feature of the extant remains is the north side of the front façade. This was abnormally high to counter the fact that the library is lower down the Acropolis slope than the adjacent market: the library was therefore made to appear the same height. The façade consists of seven columns, each of which would have been surmounted with a statue. The main peristyle court behind was, according to the Roman travel writer Pausanias, graced with a 'hundred splendid columns' — none of which have survived. The quad had an ornamental pool in the centre (later replaced with a 6 C. basilica, several columns from which still stand) with lecture rooms down the sides. Books took up a relatively small part of the library's space and were housed in a scroll room at the back of the building; by lucky chance the surviving wall has the storage niches extant.

The **Roman Agora** (1 C. BC) is known to stand on the site of the classical commercial market, but of earlier structures there is no trace. In the Roman period it was linked to the classical Agora via a couple of stoas running east behind the Stoa of Attalos. The surviving remains are equally diverse as those of the library; in this case consisting of a reasonable number of columns arranged as picturesquely as possible around the two surviving sides of the peristyle court. Behind them lie the foundations of a number of stoa style shops. The gateways have survived; the main entrance now reduced to an arch standing in glorious isolation (now fenced off; access to the site is from the rear: tickets 400 GDR). The rear gate only exists as a series of square columns bounded by a drain on the outer side.

ATHENS
Roman Agora Area

Key

- **A** Monastiraki Metro Station
- **B** Mosque of the Bazaar
- **C** Library of Hadrian
- **D** Front Façade
- **E** Late Roman Wall
- **F** Book Room with Scroll Niches
- **G** Pillars of Byzantine church
- **H** Fethiye Djami (Victory) Mosque
- **I** Roman Agora
- **J** Arch of Athena Archegetis
- **K** Agora Site Ticket Kiosk
- **L** Roman Latrines

- **M** Pillared Gateway (Propylon)
- **N** Unidentified 1 c. AD Building

- **O** The Tower of the Winds (also called the Horologion of Andronikos Cyrrhestes)
- **P** Entrance Portico
- **Q** Sundial Lines
- **R** The Lost Triton Weathervane

The Winds:
- **S** NW: **Skiron** (holds bronze cauldron)
- **T** W: **Zephyros** (showers lap of flowers)
- **U** SW: **Lips** (holds stern of trireme-like ship)
- **V** S: **Notos** (emptying an ern of rain showers)
- **W** SE: **Euros** (mantled, with arm cloaked)
- **X** E: **Apeliotes** (showers lap of fruit)
- **Y** NE: **Kaikias** (holds shield of hailstones)
- **Z** N: **Boreas** (mantled, and holding a conch)

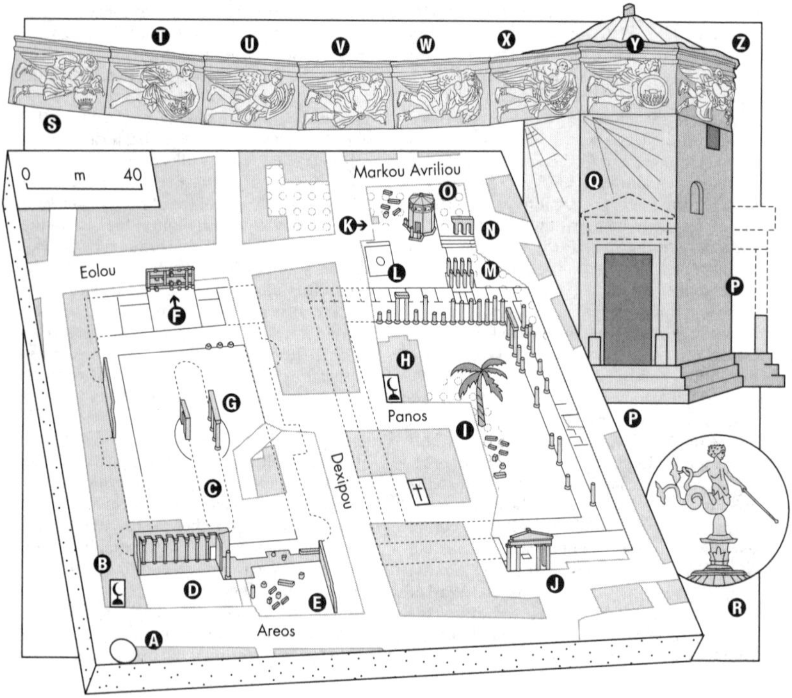

Markou Avriliou

Eolou

Panos

Dexipou

Areos

0   m   40

As you enter the Roman Agora site you are confronted by two contrasting structures. On your right are the remains of a 1 C. AD **Roman Latrine**; built to seat the masses in comfort, it offered a secluded spot to sit and chat while getting on with the business of the day. To the east stands the wonderfully preserved 2 C. BC **Tower of the Winds**. A remarkable building, cute and approachable in size, it has survived against all the odds in various guises (not least as a dervish clubhouse during the years of Turkish rule). A marble octagon, the tower was a waterclock, sundial, and weather-vane combined, and possibly the city planetarium. On the north-west and north-east sides were porticoed doors, while up the south side climbs the remains of the clock mechanism in the form of a semicircular turret. Quite how this worked is still not understood. Given that the ancients measured time by dividing the daylight hours into 12 (so an 'hour' was never the same length on any consecutive day) it, presumably, caused its designers a headache and a half too. The 8 cardinal winds are aligned to their respective points of the compass. Favourable winds are shown as youths; hostile winds as bearded, older figures. Each holds an appropriate object. Most are self explanatory, with the exception of Lips (responsible for blowing an enemy fleet ashore: hence the ship's stern), and Skiron (the charcoal cauldron symbolised drought). The Roman writer Vitruvius records that the tower was topped with a bronze triton weather-vane holding a wand which pointed to the prevailing wind.

Hellenistic (200–100 BC)

Augustinian (50 BC–14 AD)

Hadrianic (117 AD —)

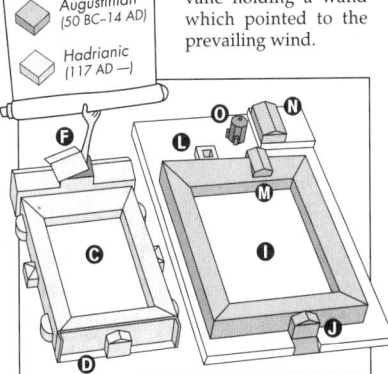

National Archaeological Museum
One of the great cultural treasure houses of the world, this is one attraction that should figure prominently on the itinerary of every visitor to Athens. Among the principal exhibits are the **Minoan Frescos** from the excavations on Santorini, the **Mask of Agamemnon** and other gold work uncovered by Schiliemann at Mycenae, and **Sculpture** from all the important sites in Greece. Supposedly open ① 12.30–19.00, ②–④ 08.00–19.00, ⑥, ⑦ 08.30–15.00 times do vary a bit depending on the numbers of attendants who turn up (no room is left without a guard). Some rooms (usually the less important ones) are occasionally closed off for an hour or two if they can't be manned. If you really want to get the most out of a visit then you should consider buying a copy of the detailed museum guide (these are on sale in Room 3, which contains the ticket kiosk, sales desk and cloakroom, where bags and cameras must be deposited).

Room 4 is the first visitors enter and one of the most dramatic in the museum. Known as the **Mycenaean Hall**, it contains the magnificent **Mask of Agamemnon** among its impressive gold collection culled from the graves at the palace of Mycenae in the Peloponnese.

Room 5 contains Neolithic and Pre-Mycenaean artifacts, though island hoppers will find **Room 6** of more interest — known as the **Cycladic Room** as all the exhibits have been recovered from the Cyclades. The haul adds up to a pretty disparate collection. At the main entrance end are the early Cycladic figures — including the largest figurine yet discovered (see p. 233) and the better known **Harpist** (see p. 239) and **Flautist** (illustrated overleaf). At the other end of the gallery you will find the **Flying-Fish Fresco** fragments recovered from Milos: though the described 'blue cloth' on the display label is now thought to be a net.

Rooms 7–8 and **11–12** are devoted to **Archaic Sculpture** (**Rooms 9–10** being devoted to smaller works). Room 9 has a number of pieces from Delos and a very Egyptianesque-looking kouros from Milos. **Room 13** contains more such figures including the **Aristodikos** figure that gives the room its name. Used to mark graves, it is logical to find next door, in **Room 14**, a collection of **Early Classical Gravestones**.

Room 15 is known as the **Poseidon Room** thanks to the large bronze of the God that dominates it. Some believe the figure to be the

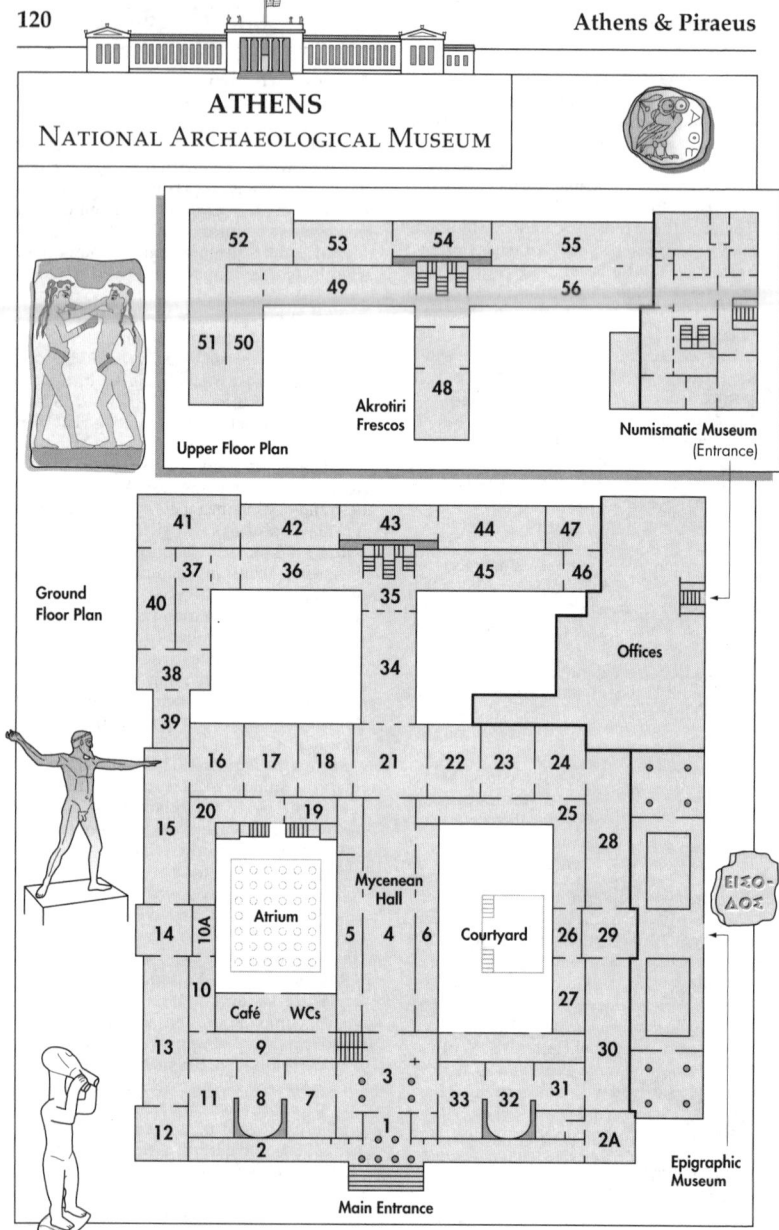

ATHENS
NATIONAL ARCHAEOLOGICAL MUSEUM

Upper Floor Plan

52   53   54   55
49   56
51 50
48

Akrotiri
Frescos

Numismatic Museum
(Entrance)

Ground Floor Plan

41   42   43   44   47
37   36   45   46
40   35
34
38
39

Offices

16 17 18   21   22 23 24
20   19   25
15   28
        10A Atrium   Mycenean
14   Hall   Courtyard   26 29
10   5 4 6   27
        Café   WCs
13   9   30
                    3
11   8   7   33 32   31
12   2   2A

Main Entrance

Epigraphic
Museum

ΕΙΣΟ-
ΔΟΣ

god Zeus, but without knowing what he held in his right hand (it could have been either a trident or a thunderbolt depending on the god) we will never be sure. The figure lacks its eyeballs but otherwise has all its attributes. For this reason it is usually surrounded by packs of French schoolgirls gazing intently at the god's tackle (a pretty convincing argument for the pro-Poseidon lobby). This is one of many similar hazards you will encounter if you visit this museum with children; for not only does the National Archaeological Museum not have the Elgin marbles, it also hasn't got a 'willie box' either (all the statues in the British Museum were defaced by a Victorian curator worried about visiting young ladies' morals: the results are now kept out of sight in a large cardboard box).

Rooms 16 and **18** are devoted to **Classical Gravestones**, and **Room 17** to **Classical Votive Reliefs. Rooms 19–20** display **Small Classical Works**. The most interesting exhibit in Room 20 is the best preserved miniature of the famous figure of **Athena Parthenos** that stood inside the Parthenon. Hardly of great artistic merit in itself (the figure is leaning to one side and the detail is very crudely reproduced), it has nonetheless been of great value in determining the form of the original statue. A doorway from Room 20 leads to a staircase decending to the **Courtyard** adorned with marbles recovered from a wreck off Antikithera — especially a young athlete, half-corroded by the sea, half-preserved by the mud.

Room 21 has one of the most impressive of the museum's exhibits; the bronze **Horse and jockey of Artemision**. Fished out of the sea off the north coast of Evia it captures the movement of boy and horse wonderfully.

Room 22 is devoted to sculpture from the sanctuary at **Epidavros**. **Rooms 23–24** and **28** contain 4 c. BC Gravestones (including in Room 28, the Youth from Antikithera), **Rooms 25–27** to Votive Reliefs. **Room 29** is known as the Themis Room thanks to a statue of the goddess. **Room 30** contains further **Hellenistic Sculpture**. Including the large **Poseidon of Milos** and an ugly little cloaked child known as the 'little refugee' recovered from Turkey. More fun is a statue of Aphrodite about to spank a cupid with a slipper. **Rooms 31–33** contain yet more Hellenistic Sculpture, and **Room 34** remnants of an Altar and reliefs and sculptures from other sanctuaries.

Room 36 is the first housing the museum's impressive collection of bronzes. Devoted to the smaller items, the room includes a well endowed dwarf and a grizzly collection of dismembered fingers and thumbs, and a collection of tiny animals (from Deukalion's ark?). **Rooms 37–39** contain a mix of bronze figures including some early figurines from the Acropolis, and a collection of bronze mirrors.

What you will find in the remaining ground floor rooms is less certain as they are being renovated. **Room 40** is supposed to house the Stathatos Collection and Gold Objects; **Room 41** Clay Figurines. **Rooms 42–47** are used for **Temporary Exhibitions** (in 1994 some were devoted to an Egyptian Display).

The upper floor occupies only a fraction of the ground floor area, yet they include one room that is the highlight of the museum; **Room 48**, home of the **Thira Frescos** (see p. 162), it has all the famous ones lining the walls of partially reconstructed houses. The outer section of this room has a number of artifacts discovered within the houses at Akrotiri, including a bed reconstructed from a plaster cast made by pouring plaster into the holes left in the ash by the long disintegrated original. The other upper floor rooms are of less interest. Home to the greatest collection of ancient Greek pottery in the world, the sheer number of artifacts makes it very difficult to give the individual pieces their just attention. The collection is divided by date and style between the various rooms: **Room 49–50:** Geometric Vases, **Room 51:** Vari Vases, **Room 52:** Heraeum of Argos and Sophilos, **Room 53:** Black-figure Vases, **Room 54:** Red-figure Vases, **Room 55:** White Background Vases, **Room 56:** 4 c. BC Vases.

Along the south side of the National Archaeological Museum are two related museums that attract fewer visitors. Nearest the main entrance to the former is the **Epigraphic Museum**. Home to a large collection of monumental inscriptions it is an important archive of ancient literary material. Unfortunately, unreadable letters on stones don't have much mass appeal so this museum is always quiet. Somewhat busier is the **Numismatic Museum**; one of the best coin collections in the world, it is housed on the first floor of the Archaeological Museum, but has its own staircase entrance on the south side of the building and has recently been refurbished.

Piraeus
ΠΕΙΡΑΙΑΣ
The main port of Athens for some 2800 years, Piraeus is the hub of the modern Greek ferry system. Lying 8 km south-west of the Acropolis, it was once a town in its own right, but in the years since Greek independence it has been reduced to a suburb by the capital's urban sprawl, and a frenetic, less than pleasant place at that. In fact, it is difficult to conceive of a spot more removed from the dreamy idyllic island most tourists are in search of. This is one port of call where it pays to know in advance roughly what you are trying to do and where you are going. Once an island itself, Piraeus is a hilly peninsula decked with anonymous, tall apartment blocks laid out in a strict grid fashion, and with harbours on each side. This is where the fun starts; for Piraeus has three harbours of note. By far the largest is the **Great Harbour**; situated on the western side, it is departure point for all car and passenger ferries as well as the Aegina hydrofoils. **Zea**, the second harbour (500 m over the hill on the eastern side), is primarily a yacht marina, but the quay (Zea Marina) near the entrance is also the departure point for the hydrofoils and catamarans running to the Saronic Gulf islands. The third, **Flisvos** is an excursion-boat port 7 km to the east of Zea: vessels departing from here are sure to be expensive and to be avoided.

The Great Harbour
Regardless of how you get to Piraeus you are likely to find yourself dumped at the north-east section of the Great Harbour; home to the bus, metro and railway stations. The waterfront consists of a wide quay, separated by a hedge-cum-wall from the six-lane streets (so clogged with traffic that in the rush hour motorbikes resort to the pavements) behind. Piraeus is primarily a commercial town and this is reflected in the buildings on the waterfront: most of these are shipping offices or branches of banks with maritime interests. Food shops, tourist facilities and hotels are thin on the ground. For these reasons Piraeus is not a place to arrive at the last minute or in the small hours. Plans are now being implemented to turn the Great Harbour exclusively into a passenger terminal (all cargo vessels now berthing at a new container port) with improved passenger and transit facilities. Tourists arriving this side of 2004 will thus find building and roadworks adding a definite something to the melée.

The focal point for ferry travellers is the square housing the bus station just south of the railway and metro stations (Platia Karaiskaki). In the billboard encrusted, dilapidated block next to the Port Police building you will find the nucleus of the ticket agents. Most are sharks. Step within hailing distance of an agency door and you'll get hassle. A chorus of 'Where are you going?' rings out from the moment the agencies open at 05.00. So it helps to be both prepared (the NTOG ferry information sheets are invaluable in this respect) and not over trusting. Likewise, you should note that although ticket agents in the islands can be very useful for changing money out of banking hours, if you use the Piraeus agencies you can be sure of being ripped off. The only plus is that an increasing number of them are offering baggage storage facilities if you buy a ferry ticket. The 'see a tourist and double the price' snack and produce shops along the waterfront should also be treated with caution.

Boats are (very) loosely grouped according to destination. The harbour has destination indicator boards at some of the quay entrances, but unfortunately these face the road so the ferries don't see them. To be on the safe side you should allow yourself thirty minutes to find a ferry. The easiest way of doing this is to look for the funnel or hull logo as most companies only have three or four boats. (It also pays to be aware that ferries might not arrive

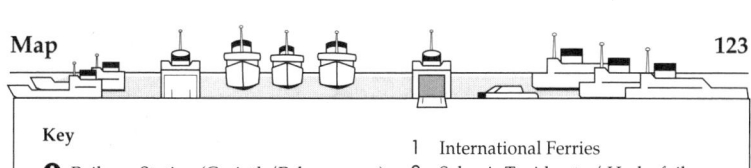

Map 123

Key

Ⓐ Railway Station (Corinth/Peloponnese)
Ⓑ Railway Station (Northern Greece)
Ⓒ Metro Station / WCs
Ⓓ Bus Station
Ⓔ Ticket Agency Block
Ⓕ Domestic Passenger Terminal & WCs
Ⓖ Athens Airport Bus Stop /
　Hydrofoil Ticket Kiosk
Ⓗ Post Office (cashes Eurocheques)
Ⓘ International Ferry Terminals

1　International Ferries
2　Salamis Taxi-boats / Hydrofoils
3　Saronic Gulf Ferries
4　Cyclades Central & West Ferries
5　Cyclades North Ferries
6　Dodecanese Ferries
7　Crete Ferries (ANEK & Minoan)
8　Cyclades West Ferries
9　Eastern Line / N. Aegean Ferries
H　Flying Dolphin Hydrofoils
　(hourly to Aegina only)

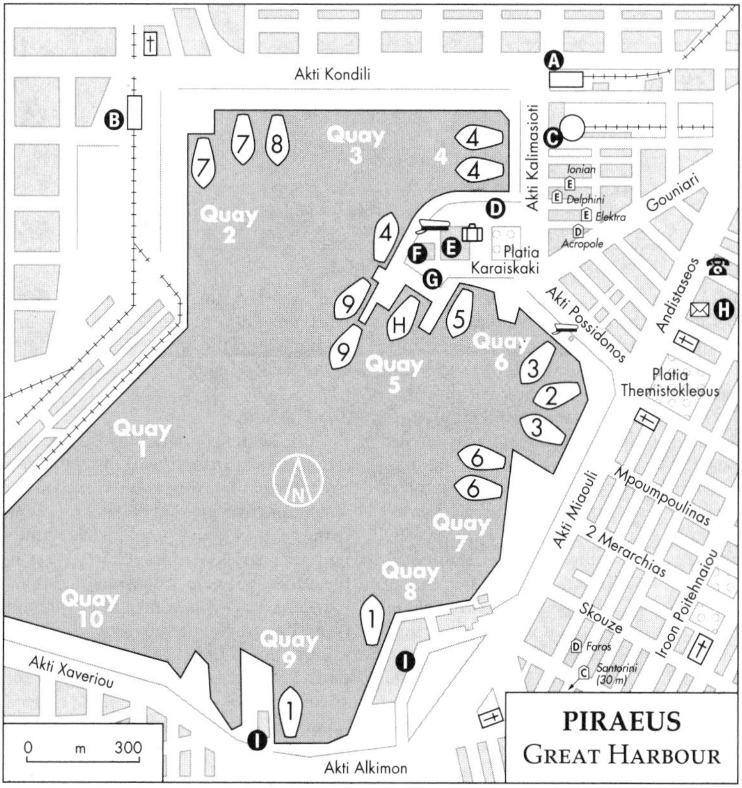

Akti Kondili

Ⓐ

Ⓑ

Akti Kalimasioti

7　**8**

Quay 3

4
4

Ionian

Ⓔ Delphini

Ⓓ

Gouniari

7

Quay 2

Ⓔ Elektra

Ⓓ Acropole

4

Ⓕ Ⓔ

Platia
Karaiskaki

Ⓖ

Akti Possidonos

Andistaseos

☎

⊠ Ⓗ

9

H

5

Quay 6

3

Platia
Themistokleous

9

Quay 5

2

3

Mpoumpoulinas

Quay 1

6

6

Akti Miaouli

2 Merarchias

Quay 7

Quay 8

Skouze

Iroon Poitehniou

Quay 10

1

Ⓓ Faros

Quay 9

1

Ⓘ

Ⓒ Santorini
(30 m)

Akti Xaveriou

1

Ⓘ

PIRAEUS
GREAT HARBOUR

0　m　300

Akti Alkimon

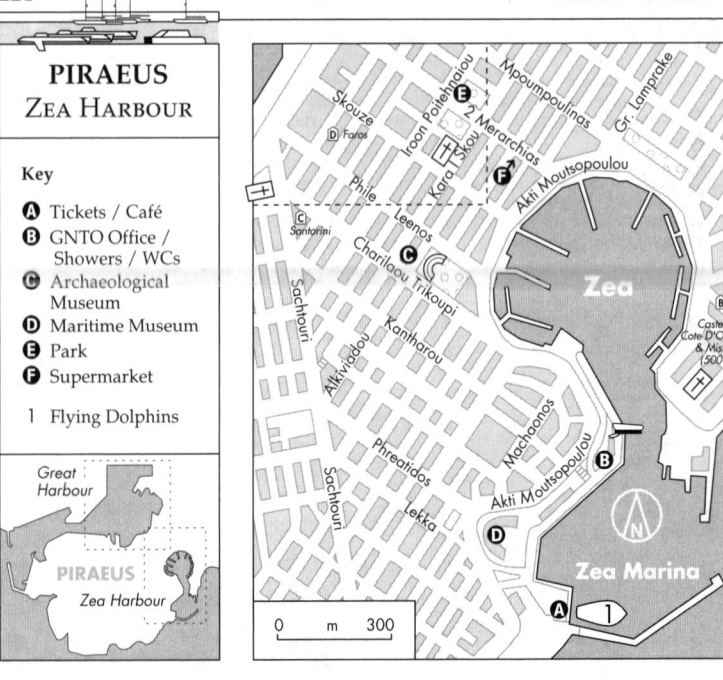

PIRAEUS
ZEA HARBOUR

Key

A Tickets / Café

B GNTO Office /
Showers / WCs

C Archaeological
Museum

D Maritime Museum

E Park

F Supermarket

1   Flying Dolphins

Great
Harbour

PIRAEUS
Zea Harbour

0   m   300

back from their previous excursion much before their listed Piraeus departure time.) Given the limited number of access points in the wall-cum-hedge it pays to walk inside this barrier when ferry hunting; for boats can be berthed anything up to a kilometre along the dock. Most ferries have ticket stalls alongside so if you find a suitable boat before you've visited the agencies you can spare yourself a walk by buying a ticket at the quayside or — in the last resort from the purser's office on board. If you do buy from an agent (and most tourists happily do), ensure that the service is as direct as possible: in High Season rooms disappear fast and arriving even half an hour ahead of the other boats often makes all the difference to what's on offer and how much you'll have to pay. International boat tickets must be bought from a ticket agent. All international boats

dock on the south side of the Great Harbour. There are several customs and immigration buildings — the dilapidated Quay 9 shed being the most used.

Zea Harbour

Zea (the ancient trireme war-fleet base) is much more attractive than the Great Harbour, with seats on the rampart-like waterfront overlooking the shoal of yachts in the basin below. The waterfront buildings are also less commercial and there is the added bonus of a reasonable super-market not too far from the waterfront. Near Zea Marina itself you will find a minuscule EOT / NTOG office (note: they don't have ferry departure information) sited at the posh end of the yacht marina. Catering for the yachtsmen it is something of a boon, since the back of the block contains public showers and WCs.

ⱶ◄

Few tourists attempt to stay in Piraeus as the available accommodation is either downright horrible or inconveniently located. The most obvious clutch of hotels are near the Great Harbour in the backstreets south of the metro station. For the most part they are to be avoided as most are more like sailor's dosshouses, lacking even a modicum of comfort (of either mattress or maid variety). If desperate however, try the *Electra* (☎ 417 7057) just off Gouniari Street. Those who are prepared to walk should find a better bed at the *Santorini* (☎ 452 2147) just off the south-east end of the Great Harbour. Meanwhile, plush establishments shun the Great Harbour altogether, and lie on and behind the up-market waterfront to the east of Zea Harbour. These include the expensive *Kastella* (☎ 411 4735), *Cote D'Oro* (☎ 411 3744), and *Mistral* (☎ 411 7094).

👓

Amidst today's grime one is apt to forget that Piraeus was an important historical centre in its own right. In fact, during the 5—4 c. BC it was seen as substantially more than just the Athenian harbour-cum-naval base, becoming as a sort of sister city in all but name. The historian Thucydides wrote that the Athenian leader 'Themistokles thought Piraeus more useful than the upper city' (the upper city being Athens), and this comment reflected Piraeus's growing role as a business and commercial centre. Unbelievably (when one looks around today), ancient Piraeus was also regarded as a very beautiful city — and given the proximity of Athens with all its splendours for comparison, the modern town has obviously lost a great deal. Part of this reputation was due to town planning; for unlike Athens, it was designed by one of the greatest of Greek city planners, Hippodamos, and boasted a grid-like street system of the kind now usually associated with North American cities (the modern streets between the Great Harbour and Zea still follow the ancient pattern).

In addition to all the regular accoutrements of an ancient city (i.e. important temples, major public buildings and even two agoras) Piraeus was very heavily fortified; with skirting walls protecting both the city and harbours. Athens likewise boasted a circular city wall, and it and Piraeus were connected by two walls running parallel to each other several hundred metres apart known as the 'Long Walls'. This added up to a formidable defensive system that from the air must have looked like a giant dumbbell. Unfortunately, following the Athenian defeat in the Peloponnesian War in 404 BC, the Long Walls were demolished. Thereafter, weaker defences made Piraeus a less attractive centre than Athens and after the Roman era it went into a period of prolonged decline — so much so, that by 1833 Piraeus had a recorded population of only 22.

Time and 19 c. building has obscured most traces of the ancient city. Current knowledge is very sketchy, with few of the buildings described by Pausanias located to date. Visible remains are scanty: the best being the fragments of a small Hellenistic odeon west of Zea. The famous trireme sheds have been found, but are locked away in the basements of buildings around Zea harbour. The **Maritime Museum** (on the waterfront of Zea) ② to ⑥ 08.30–12.30. has one on view. Archaeological finds (including bronzes fished out of the harbour) are currently housed in the **Archaeological Museum** ② to ⑦ 08.30–15.00.

☎

CODE 01, TOURIST OFFICE 4135 716, PORT POLICE 4511 311, 4172 657.

Lavrion
ΛΑΡΙΟ

A small, sun-touched commercial port that in classical times was famed for its silver mines Lavrion (or Lavrio) offers little today apart from a few fishing boats, a blackened pier, and a close up view of the sad island of **Makronissi**: used to detain political prisoners for much of this century. Lavrion is now the main ferry port for the island of Kea. Occasional services head further south to Kythnos, but this is far more easily reached by ferries operating out of Piraeus. A town of wide and dusty streets, the most important thing you need to know in Lavrion is that the bus stop lies on the roadside of the square next to the fishing quay. Buses do the 1½ hour Athens run hourly as well as heading south to Cape Sounion and the nearest campsite (8 km).

☎

CODE 0292, PORT POLICE 25249.

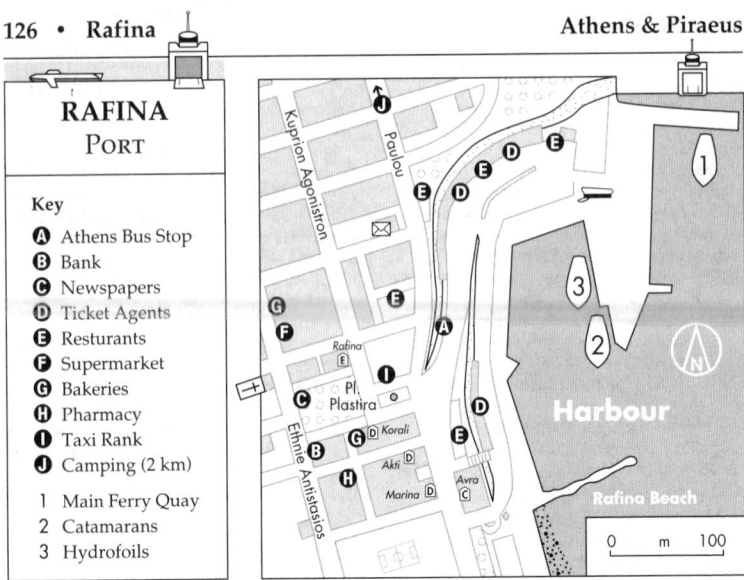

RAFINA PORT

Key

A Athens Bus Stop
B Bank
C Newspapers
D Ticket Agents
E Resturants
F Supermarket
G Bakeries
H Pharmacy
I Taxi Rank
J Camping (2 km)

1 Main Ferry Quay
2 Catamarans
3 Hydrofoils

Rafina

ΡΑΦΗΝΑ

Some 27 km from the centre of Athens, Rafina is a pleasant leafy suburb town on the west coast of Attica with a reputation for good fish restaurants (courtesy of its role as the main fishing port for the capital). The port also has another — and growing — role as the second departure point from the capital to the islands: notably destinations on the Cyclades North Line (some island agencies even go so far as to list Rafina as 'Athens' on their schedules). Now being enlarged, the port lies below the town's main square cum park, and offers a much more attractive starting point for island hopping than Piraeus. Instead of grime and hustling ticket touts you wade through fresh fish stalls (at their busiest in the evenings) to reach the boats. Furthermore, boat fares to and from Rafina are 20% cheaper than Piraeus, and although the bus fare into Athens erodes most of this saving on short hops, there are gains to be made on longer journeys. Connections with Athens

are good, with hourly buses departing from the port slip road. The catch to all this is that the number of ferries is far fewer and travellers are often forced to repair to the scruffy, but popular, beach just south of the port while they wait for an evening sailing. Rafina departure times are also not listed on NTOG sheets, but Athenian papers (see p. 33) and other printed sources list them after a fashion.

Most tourists are in transit so there are no rooms. Of the hotels, the *Korali* (☎ 22477) in the main square is reasonable and inexpensive, if not inspiring, as is the *Rafina* (☎ 23460). More pokey is the *Atki* (☎ 24776), while the large *Avra* (☎ 22781/3), above the port, offers the nearest you will find to the high life.

A well-signed beach site 2 km north of the port (though the walk seems longer). Excellent facilities, but usually empty: the Balkan war has depleted the numbers motoring from central Europe. A second site on the Athens road isn't worth the hassle of finding it.

☎
CODE 0294, PORT POLICE 228 88.

Salamina / Salamis

ΣΑΛΑΜΙΝΑ; 93.5 km², pop. 23,000.

Cowering behind the shipyards and rows of rusting ships anchored west of Piraeus lies the famous, but lamentably ugly, island of Salamis (known these days as Salamina). Its great claim to fame comes via the battle between the Greek and Persian trireme fleets in 480 BC which took place in the narrow straits between the north-east side of the island and the mainland. This encounter, one of the great naval battles in history, prevented the Persian conquest of Greece and in so doing altered the destiny of European civilisation. Unfortunately, Salamis has been in decline from this high point ever since and after 2500 years this means that things are pretty bad. The close proximity of Athens has resulted in it becoming little more than a smoggy suburb of the capital. Not the cleanest water to swim in either (this is one of the few places in the Aegean where bathing is a health hazard), so unless you are clocking-up islands, ferry hops, or are a student of military history, then sadly, it is worth giving a miss. None of the settlements has much to offer; the capital, Salamina, is dusty and lacking even a modicum of town planning, while Selinia (the nearest thing Salamis has on offer to a 'resort') is rather scruffy. Nicer, in a very quiet way, are the villages of Eantio and Peristeria.

Bus services are good along the limited routes run, but the south of the island (easily the nicest part with even the odd patch of forest cover on the hillsides) is not served. The main ferry link runs from the mainland suburb of **Perama** to **Paloukia** on the east coast, while a second operates from **Steno** to **Nea Peramos**. In addition, commuter boats run frequently to Piraeus Great Harbour (see p. 98).

⊨

No rooms. Budget hotels at Selinia and Eantio.

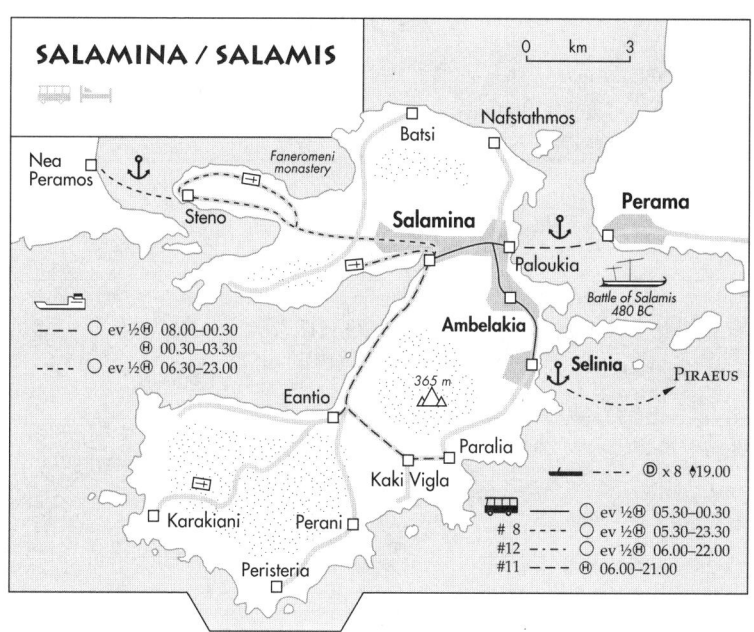

4
CYCLADES CENTRAL

ANAFI · IOS · NAXOS · PAROS · SANTORINI / THIRA

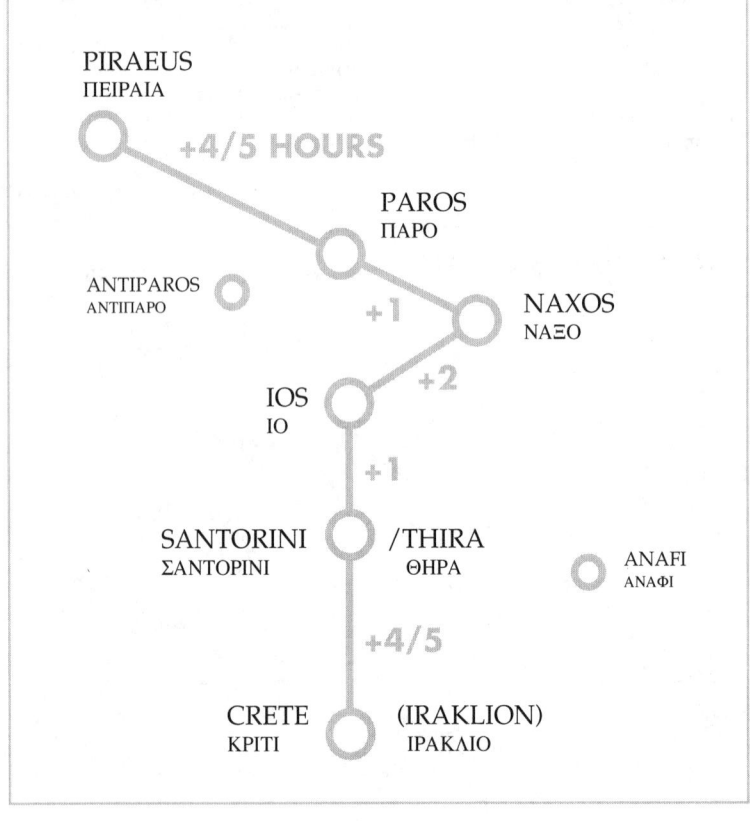

PIRAEUS
ΠΕΙΡΑΙΑ

+4/5 HOURS

PAROS
ΠΑΡΟ

ANTIPAROS
ΑΝΤΙΠΑΡΟ

+1

NAXOS
ΝΑΞΟ

IOS
ΙΟ

+2

+1

SANTORINI
ΣΑΝΤΟΡΙΝΙ

/THIRA
ΘΗΡΑ

ANAFI
ΑΝΑΦΙ

+4/5

CRETE
ΚΡΙΤΙ

(IRAKLION)
ΙΡΑΚΛΙΟ

General Features

The Cyclades derive their name from being said to 'circle' the island of Delos. In practice, Paros and the Central Cyclades line islands are the true centre of the group. The Central Cyclades consist of a number of islands that are known by name to most travellers to Greece. Among these, Santorini/Thira is deservedly the most popular, being identified with the legend of Atlantis, disco-laden Ios is known by repute to every student under the sun, and Paros has a happy mix of almost everything. Given that most newcomers to Greece start from Piraeus

and make for an island that they've at least heard of, and that the bulk of these better known islands lie in a line running north to south (ending conveniently at the Cretan capital of Iraklion), it is inevitable that this should form a natural artery in the Greek ferry system. Most of the ferry traffic is tourist-orientated and therefore seasonal; but enough tourist activity exists outside the summer months for this line to be the best supported out of season. Ironically, also on the Cyclades Central Line lies the small island of Anafi: the worst supported of all the Greek islands served by regular car ferries.

CYCLADES

Andros
Gavrion
Kea
Tinos
Kythnos
Syros
Mykonos
DELOS
Naxos
Serifos
Paros
Donoussa
Antiparos
Koufonissia
Sifnos
Egiali
Schinoussa
Katapola
Kimolos
Iraklia
Amorgos
Sikinos
Ios
Milos
Astipalea
Folegandros
Santorini / Thira
Anafi

0   km   30

N

Suggested Itinerary [2 Weeks]

A justifiably popular group of islands forming the backbone of the Greek ferry system. High Season connections are so frequent that it makes for extremely relaxed island hopping. With ferries almost as frequent as red buses down Oxford Street even the most timid of travellers can wander without fear. The main islands can be done in any order since there are boats up and down the line at all times of the day. You won't be short on company either. Even so, with a little effort you can escape the worst of the crowds almost whenever you choose.

Arrival/Departure Point

With good ferry links to Athens/Piraeus, Santorini, Mykonos and Crete (Iraklion); — all ports with charter flight connections — you are spoilt for choice. Athens and Santorini (with several connecting boats daily in High Season) remain the safest options should you find yourself in a rush to get back for your return flight. Crete and Mykonos are a little less easy since you are often dependent on a single boat each day.

Season

Daily boats operate up and down the line through most of the year, though out of High Season it will be just the one boat rather than the daily dozen.

1 **Athens [1 Day]**

Unless you are really unlucky with your flight arrival time you should be able to ship out of Piraeus the day you fly in. With boats to the Cyclades Central line mornings and evenings in the High Season you are not going to be obliged to spend a night in the capital. Grab some drachma, a meal and, of course, the NTOG ferry departure sheets and go.

2 **Paros [3 Days]**

Paros is a genial stopping point for your first few days as you wind down and acclimatise.

Plenty of beaches, nightlife and that all important Greek island atmosphere, and, when you want to avoid the worst of the sun, the cave on Antiparos makes an interesting excursion easily to hand.

3 **Naxos [2 Days]**

More relaxing and sleepy than Paros, Naxos is the next stop down the line. If you don't want to stay you can always visit as a day trip from Paros; a morning boat will set you down in time for lunch and you can then pick up one of the Paros-bound evening Santorini—Piraeus boats. If you visit on one of the days that the small *Skopelitis* (p. 229) heads to Amorgos you can take her as far as Paros (Piso Livadi) and then a bus over the island back to Paros Town.

4 **Santorini [4 Days]**

Although Ios is the next in the chain, time spent there is unlikely to leave you in a fit state to explore Santorini. Pick up one of the ferries running down the line in the early hours when heading on to Santorini (this way you don't waste a day of your holiday looking for a room). You can always make up lost sleep on the nearest black sand beach. This is one island that shouldn't be missed. Realistically you will need three days to explore the sights.

5 **Ios [2 Nights]**

Ios doesn't wake up much before 23.00 hours. The mixture of sun, 'slammers' and sand is so over the top that most island hoppers can't stand it for more than a day or two.

1 **Athens [2 Days]**

Get a boat back to Athens and spend your flight 'safety' day in hand touring the city.

Alternative 1

Rather than spend two days on Naxos, advance your schedule and return to Piraeus via Paros and **Mykonos**. You can glean the latest Paros departure times on your way south.

Alternative 2

Another option is to head further south to **Crete (Iraklion)** and take in the Minoan palace at Knossos. Ferry links are more tenuous this far south so allow 3 days to do the round trip.

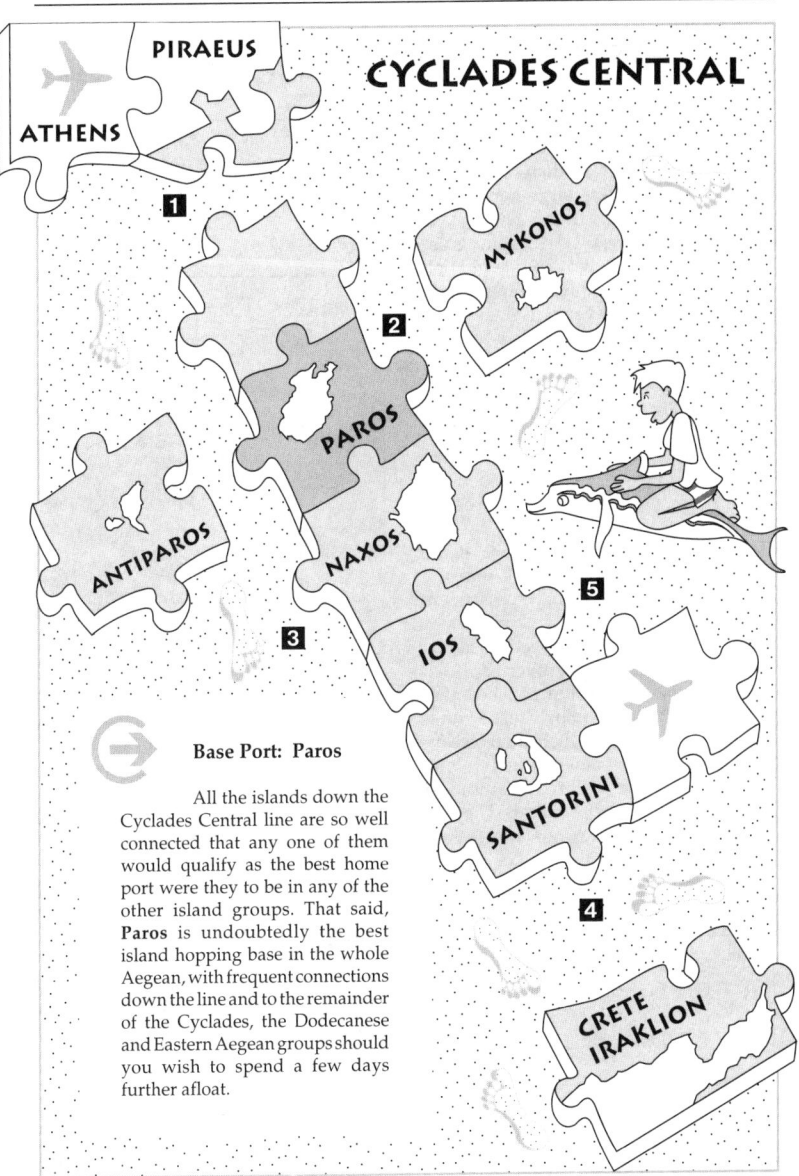

PIRAEUS

ATHENS

CYCLADES CENTRAL

1

MYKONOS

2

PAROS

ANTIPAROS

NAXOS

3

IOS

5

SANTORINI

4

CRETE
IRAKLION

Base Port: Paros

All the islands down the Cyclades Central line are so well connected that any one of them would qualify as the best home port were they to be in any of the other island groups. That said, **Paros** is undoubtedly the best island hopping base in the whole Aegean, with frequent connections down the line and to the remainder of the Cyclades, the Dodecanese and Eastern Aegean groups should you wish to spend a few days further afloat.

Cyclades Central Ferry Services

Main Car Ferries

Because most of the islands on this line are popular tourist destinations, ferries are geared to moving large numbers of passengers on to the next island — fast. The rich pickings result in a dozen regular ferries operating down the line in High Season, with departures from Piraeus both mornings and evenings. Even out of High Season there are usually two boats a day in each direction. The emphasis on passenger traffic means that the usually longer port turnaround times of the larger boats does not exist as vehicle traffic is often all but non existent and this helps to foster a healthy amount of competition on this line. On the Piraeus—Paros leg relative ferry speed is a factor as it affects the arrival order at Paros. Once at the islands, the only way a ferry can jump the queue is to land and embark passengers faster than an adjacently docking rival as the distances between respective islands are insufficient for ships to over-haul each other. Complementing the main boats are ferries heading on to Samos, Crete, Rhodes and the Dodecanese, which often pick up extra drachma by making stops along this line (it is these boats that are the most vulnerable to change each year). They are described in the chapter most appropriate to their route.

⌂ See also:	
• C/F *Anemos*	p. 326
• C/F *Ergina*	p. 229
• C/F *Golden Vergina*	p. 298
• C/F *Ionian Sea*	p. 228
	p. 258
• C/M *Catamaran II*	p. 173
• T/B *Margarita*	p. 202
• ILIO Hydrofoils	p. 174

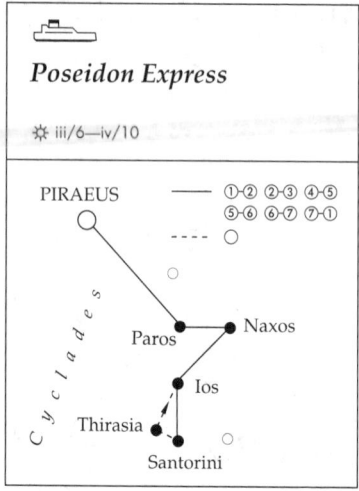

Poseidon Express

☼ iii/6—iv/10

PIRAEUS —— ①-② ②-③ ④-⑤
                    ⑤-⑥ ⑥-⑦ ⑦-①
            - - - - ○

Naxos
Paros
Ios
Thirasia
Santorini

Cyclades

C/F *Poseidon Express*

Arkadia Lines; 1974; 7824 GRT.

Formerly the Marseilles-based *Provence*, this ferry is the largest and fastest in the Aegean (Piraeus—Paros in four hours). She was the big surprise of the 1989 season, turning up out of the blue in early July and causing chaos as existing services juggled their timetables in response. Despite the handicap of operating without a companion, she has established herself as the premier boat on the line; as, for once, biggest is best. Schedules undergo regular 'tweaking' but have not changed drastically since. One feature of note are the August calls at Thirasia (otherwise unvisited by a Piraeus ferry). Conditions on board are better than most, though you can forget the advertised swimming pool; this has now been converted into the largest ash tray in the Aegean. A very good overnight boat as there is plenty of exterior deck space and seating.

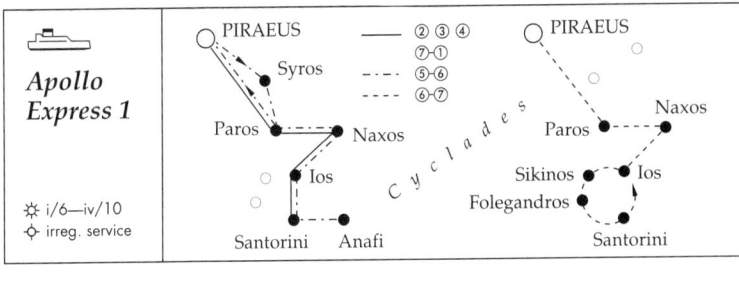

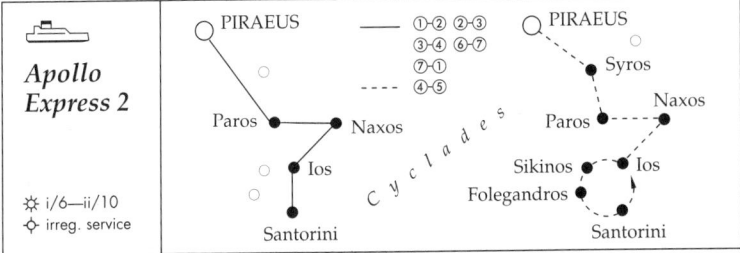

C/F *Apollo Express 1*

Ventouris Sea Lines; 1973; 5101 GRT.
Formerly the cross-Channel ferry *Senlac* (named after the hill on which the Battle of Hastings was fought) her new Greek owners renamed her after the god of archery. This is surely one in the eye for all those who — even after using a local timetable — maintain that ferry operators have no sense of humour. Despite being displaced as the largest ferry on the route she remains competitive, with summer schedules seeing only minor changes in the last five years. The arrival of the *Apollo Express 2* means that Ventouris are able to advertise standard morning and evening 'Apollo Express' departure times at all ports down the line. Changes to High Season schedules in 1995 are therefore likely to be minimal, with regular runs down the Cyclades Central line and a weekly call at Sikinos and Folegandros. Anafi is also visited on occasions. Conditions on board are adequate, but somewhat utilitarian.

C/F *Apollo Express 2*

Ventouris Sea Lines; 1972; 5590 GRT.
All but identical in external appearance to the *Apollo Express 1*, this reliable ferry was one of the new arrivals on the Cyclades Central Line in 1993. Formerly the cross-Channel *Hengist*, she operated briefly in Greece as the G.A Ferries' *Romilda* before being replaced by another vessel with the same name. Now steaming in Ventouris Sea Lines colours, her itinerary is very similar to her sister's (albeit somewhat streamlined) and unlikely to change much, if at all, in 1995 (1994 saw no change to her summer schedules). After a grubby start, on-board facilities are now marginally better than those on the *Apollo Express 1*: her extra tonnage reflecting later interior rebuilding. As a result she boasts features (e.g. an Arcade Game room) not found on most other Greek ferries, though it doesn't pay to expect too much in the way of splendour: she is more shabby than chic.

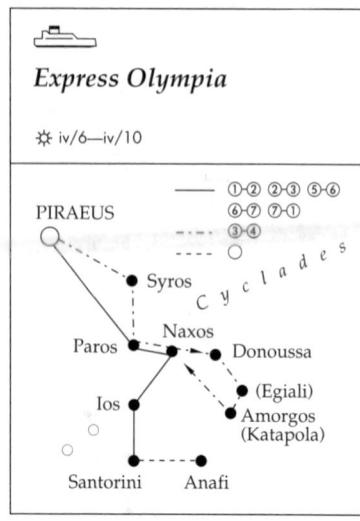

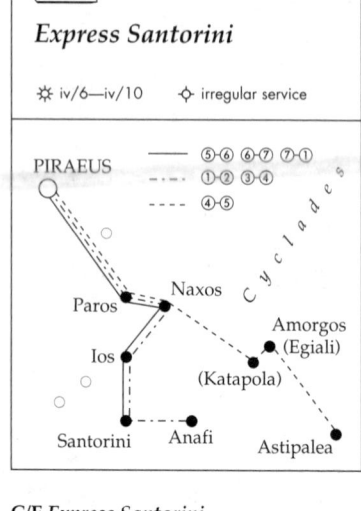

C/F *Express Olympia*

Agapitos Express Ferries; 1973; 4657 GRT.
The 'new' ferry down the line in 1991, this vessel is not the glamorous boat her stern neon destination board suggests. Within a couple of months of entering the Aegean she was reduced to a grime bucket with bannister rails hanging loose et al. Some improvement has been noticable since, but in High Season she still offers a definite 'something' to any island hopper's holiday. In part this is due to her chronic lack of deck-class sun-deck space. If you board early enough to collar one of the reasonable interior seats (or are travelling out of High Season), life is pleasant enough, but for many passengers it is a case of camping in the aisles. This is *not* a good overnight boat, though she often performs that role, running a night service to Piraeus several times a week. Her saloon also conspires to add a touch of the bizarre to the Greek island hopping experience; decorated with murals of the white cliffs of Dover, it is an incongruous hangover from her days as the cross-Channel *Earl Granville*.

C/F *Express Santorini*

Agapitos Express Ferries; 1974; 4590 GRT.
Introduced into the Aegean in 1994, the *Express Santorini* replaced the elderly *Aegeon* which had run on this line over the previous five years. Operating in tandem with the *Express Olympia* she takes on the bulk of the Piraeus evening departures, running five nights a week to the islands in High Season. Decidedly the better of the two boats, she thus ensures that passengers come away with a good impression of the line, with the result that they then buy a passage on the *Express Olympia* (passage usually being the operative term) for their return to Piraeus. Schedules of both boats are unlikely to change much in 1995; though the Anafi calls by the *Express Santorini* could be transferred to another line. The mid-week Astipalea run should also be treated with caution: new in 1994, it is vulnerable to change. Previous years have seen this line offering Island Ferry passes via ticket agents at Piraeus. If you are on a tight budget it might be worth asking around.

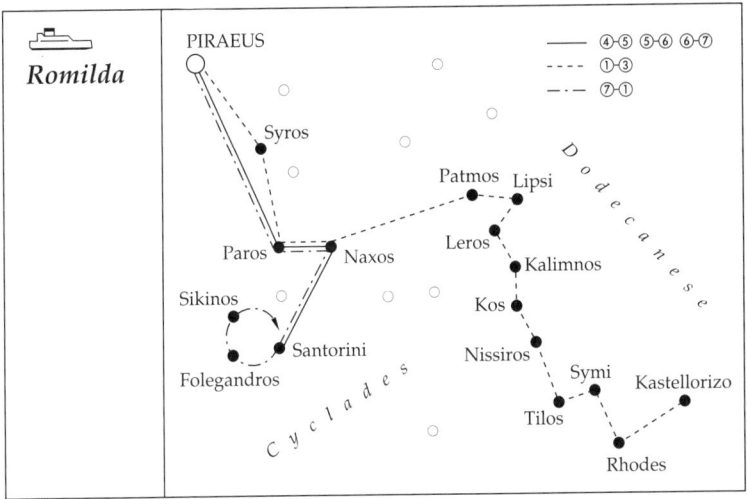

C/F *Romilda*

G.A. Ferries; 1974; 5169 GRT.

Another of the new arrivals in the Aegean in 1994, the *Romilda* is one of the best ferries running down the Central Cyclades Line. Until recently she was the cross-Channel *Pride of Canterbury* and has facilities to match, with an excellent deck-class interior. Her only minor weakness is the limited amount of sun-deck space. The history of boats with her name is a good example of the vagaries of the Greek ferry scene. For several years G.A. Ferries offered an impressive and reliable service via four boats — including one called the *Romilda*. In 1993, however, she was sold to Ventouris at the start of the High Season (see *Apollo Express* 2), and a replacement *Romilda* appeared, but running across the Adriatic — leaving ticket agents everywhere issuing tickets for a boat that wasn't in the Aegean. Last year she was transferred to the Adriatic running mainly down the Cyclades Central Line with a token sojourn down the Dodecanese. All other things being equal she should be running a similar schedule again in 1995.

Ventouris Sea Lines

Over the last five summers this company has operated a regular service down this line via a now discontinued ferry — the C/F *Sifnos Express*. It is possible that the service will be maintained in 1995 — perhaps via the C/F *Artemis* (see p. 201)?

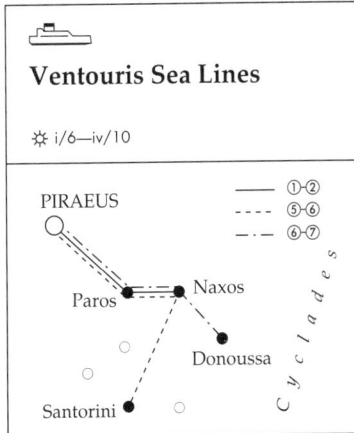

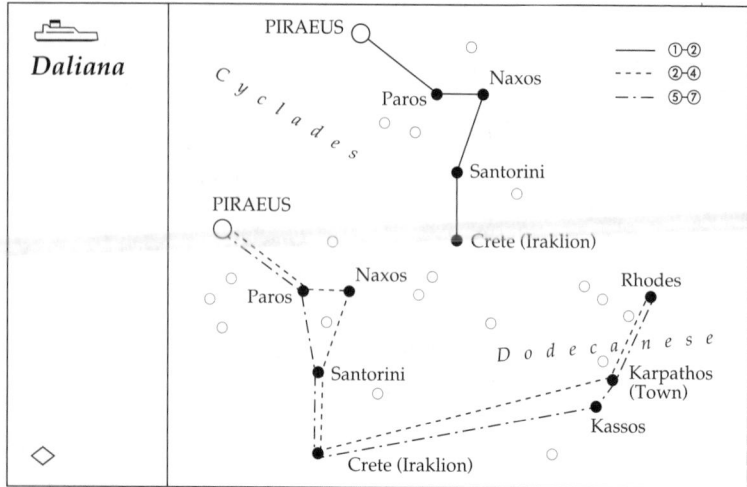

C/F *Daliana*

G.A. Ferries; 1970; 5528 GRT.

A popular ferry, the *Daliana* has run this Cyclades Central—Crete—Rhodes route since 1990. Now offering an annual service, the last couple of years have seen adjustments to her schedule, but these have been confined to the Karpathos and Kassos calls on her itinerary (Kassos was an addition in 1994). Cyclades Central services have remained largely unchanged since they were inaugurated, as too have been her Piraeus departures; a feature that ensures her Crete arrivals/

departures are usually in the small hours. A large ex-Japanese boat (and almost identical to her sister boat: the *Milena*) with small smokestacks astern, she has comfortable interior deck-class facilities and plenty of outside bench seating for sleeping bags; making her a good overnight ferry. One feature that could irritate: as in other vessels in the G.A. Ferries fleet, Greek music is piped through the overhead loudspeakers during the day. Atmospheric at first, it can get a bit wearisome after a few hours. Major changes to this service unlikely in 1995.

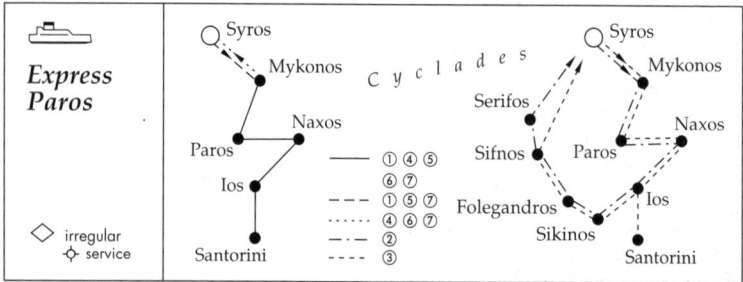

C/F *Express Paros*
Local; 1965; 1365 GRT.
Formerly the Ionian island *Kefallinia*, this small car ferry replaced the *Paros Express* (the ex *Elli*, ex *Schinoussa* — that had run around the Cyclades since the late 60s) in 1994. Far too small to cope with the summer crowds and too slow to run her predecessor's itinerary to time, she made a lot of people very late last year and surely cannot survive long on the route before a replacement is found. Her only redeeming feature is that she is a character ferry, conspicuous by the absence of a funnel. Her Greek architect also had a passion for narrow stairwells and low doorways which means that she is difficult to board and disembark from. Schedules tend to change every other month, but her main role is to provide a morning Mykonos to Santorini service (daily in High Season). Several nights a week she stops overnight at Syros. Low Season sees services operating when sea conditions permit, often with a more wide-ranging itinerary.

P/S *Mykonos Express*
Local; 1962; 292 GRT.
A small rust-bucket ferry that has run an unchanged route (Santorini to Mykonos) for years (formerly as the *Ios Express*). Out of High Season she often returns on following days rather than doing the round trip daily. In High Season she suffers in strong winds due to her size. On such occasions she is forced to stay in port or curtail her run; so if the sea looks rough the chances are she won't go. When she does, she is crowded to the point where it gets like one of those 'How to fit 39 people into a Mini' demonstrations. It doesn't pay to think as to what would happen if she ever went down. She briefly steamed to fame with a 5-second appearance in *Shirley Valentine*; a strange film in which the heroine flies to Mykonos and then takes this ferry to the same island.

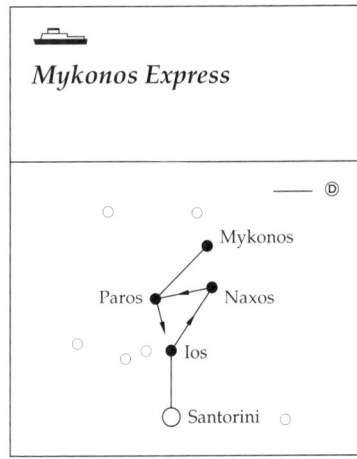

Mykonos Express

P/S *Delfini Express*
A rather swish, but tiny, passenger boat (that replaced an earlier vessel of the same name made out of old biscuit tins); the *Delfini Express* operates a 'daily' service to Sikinos and Folegandros. Unfortunately, she doesn't run if bookings on Ios fail to reach a reasonable level; so in practice she only runs three times a week in High Season (not very helpful if you want a boat off Sikinos or Folegandros on one of the other days). She is *very* irregular during the rest of the year.

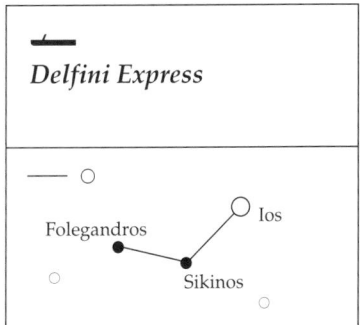

Delfini Express

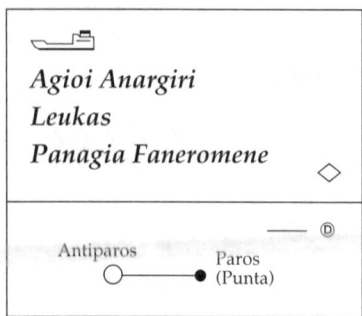

Agioi Anargiri
Leukas
Panagia Faneromene

C/F *Agioi Anargiri*

Several small ferries make hourly 10-minute crossings across the straits between Antiparos Town and the landing quay at Paros (Punta). Their great redeeming feature is the fare: at 130 GDR it is much cheaper than the Paros town boats even allowing for the Punta—Paros Town/Parikias bus fare (160 GDR).

Paros—Antiparos Taxi boats

The *Kasos Express* and odd tourist boats roll wildly from Paros to Antiparos Town providing the 40-minute 'tourist' link between the two. In High Season don't be surprised if you have to take the Punta ferries back due to choppy seas. Fare was 400 GDR one way in 1994.

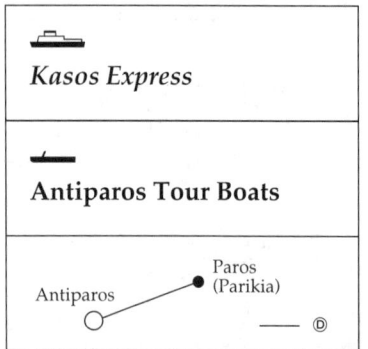

Kasos Express

Antiparos Tour Boats

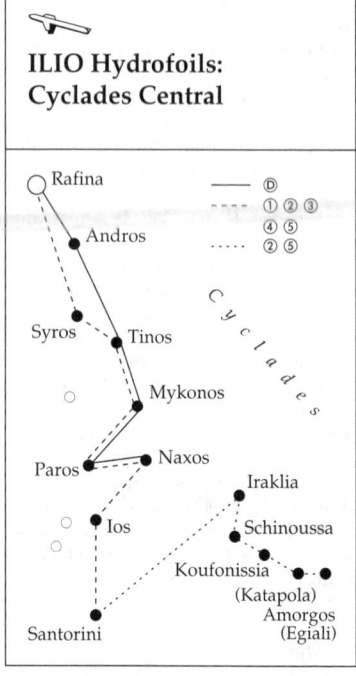

ILIO Hydrofoils: Cyclades Central

ILIO Hydrofoils

After a failed attempt by CERES to run a *Flying Dolphin* hydrofoil service around the Cyclades a few years ago, ILIO are now attempting to provide a Cycladic service out of the port of Rafina (see also p. 174) and Santorini with their *Delphini* fleet. Now into its fourth year it is obviously here to stay, though reliability has been a bit problematic to date. As ever with small boats in the Cyclades in summer, the *meltemi* wind plays havoc with schedules, so it is a case of seeing what is going on the day you want to travel. Eastern Cyclades calls were new to schedules in 1993, and further adjustments to itineraries are highly probable in 1995. Services are also greatly reduced out of High Season.

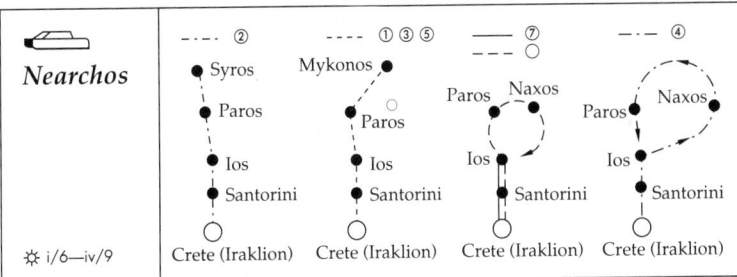

C/M *Nearchos*

Given the choppy nature of the southern Aegean, this small, and increasingly tatty catamaran seems to be singularly mislocated with frequent cancellations in High Season. That said, when she does run, she provides a quick and invaluable morning service from Crete (Iraklion) to the Central Cyclades — she is twice as fast as a ferry and three times as expensive. However, if things are going badly (due to rough seas) it could take you a stomach-churning 4½ hours to make the '165-minute' journey to Santorini: you'll either arrive in time for an early lunch or end up with your breakfast in one of the little blue bags distributed by crew at 15-minute intervals. Her main clientele are Santorini-bound day-trippers from Iraklion. The incentive to continue north is thus rather small and any further progress is seemingly regarded by her captain as an unlooked-for bonus. The chances of her arriving at Mykonos, for example, are poor unless seas are totally flat — so it pays to plan accordingly. Her 'timetable' has changed little in the last four years with services running from April to October (three times weekly out of High Season). Those listed in the port tables are for the June—September period.

C/F *Theoskepasti*

This boat operates a 'life-line' ferry service to Thirasia disguised as a Santorini caldera tour. Tickets are bought from a one-off agent housed just north of the Port Police office in Fira town. Those who want to use her as a tour boat rather than as a regular ferry should note that a connecting return tour bus exists to whisk you from Riva port to the main town.

Tour Boats

Two light-weight tourist boats (the *Aphrodite Express* and the *Agios Nektarios*) also operate in the Central Cyclades. Not for sea-sickies and very expensive, their great redeeming feature is their propensity to make hops rarely impossible by regular ferry: in 1994 this included Paros to Delos (7000 GDR) and Paros to Serifos three times a week (6000 GDR).

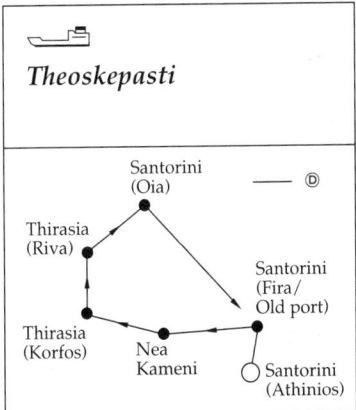

Cyclades Central Islands & Ports

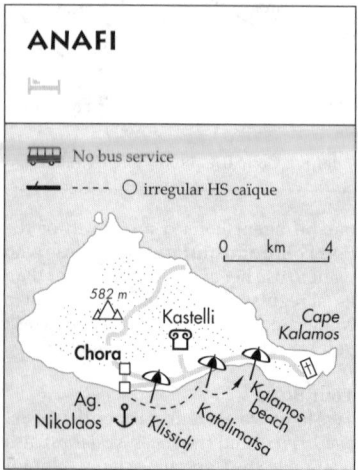

ANAFI

🛏

🚌 No bus service

⚓ - - - - ○ irregular HS caïque

582 m
Kastelli   Cape Kalamos
Chora
Ag.
Nikolaos ⚓ Klissidi
Kalamos beach
Katalimatsa

Anafi

ΑΝΑΦΙ; 38 km²; pop. 340.

One hour's sailing east of Santorini, at first sight it seems something of a paradox that Anafi is one of the least accessible islands in the Aegean: so much so, that 'Anafi' is the Greek word for 'Timbuktu'. Tradition has it that the island sprang up out of the sea by order of Apollo when the legendary Argonauts were in need of a berth. This was as near as the island has ever got to a spring; apparently the Argonauts didn't need water as the island isn't furnished with any. Covered by a 25 m thick blanket of pumice from the eruption of Santorini, it has never been a prosperous place. Those who are washed up on Anafi's mountainous shores will find a barren island with one small chora village 1 km up a steep track from the diminutive port. The Chora can lay claim to be the last truly unspoilt Cycladic chora in the world, and is a pretty little place in a downbeat sort of way. Needless to say

there is no island bank; but there is a small post office and a couple of tiny shops. Twice weekly ferry links remain consistent through the year; though days and times of the few boats that call change every summer — so establish how you are going to leave prior to your arrival: unless you can afford to wait 3—4 days to get off again this is an island to be avoided.

🛏

No hotels, but rooms at both port and chora.

👓

Unless you are a fan of wild, abandoned places, the best sight on Anafi is apt to be the ferry arriving to pick you up. However, those with several days on their hands waiting will find a ruined **Venetian Kastro** at Kastelli, a deserted monastery (built on the supposed site of a **Temple of Apollo** set up by the Argonauts) on the eastern tip of the island, and several deserted beaches along the south coast.

Antiparos

ΑΝΤΙΠΑΡΟΣ; 55 km²; pop. 540.

One of those less well-known islands that have more going for them than their larger and more popular neighbours, Antiparos is a veritable gem. If your idea of the perfect Greek island includes excellent sand beaches, a cosy atmosphere, a picturesque port filled with prune-faced fishermen mending their nets, and plenty of discrete nightlife (the local disco is housed in the inland town windmill) then Antiparos is it.

In many ways the island is a strange place, having been severed from Paros as the result of an earthquake. The straits between it and Paros are both shallow and narrow with the fields on the northern side of the island rolling into the sea. The only settlement — **Antiparos Town** — straddles the northern tip, with a fortress at its centre and the irregular main street forming the focus of island life. Enough of the old town survives to give it plenty of atmosphere; though the environs are dominated by establishments offering accommodation. Apart from the sleepy tavernas and boutiques lining the High Street, the town's great attraction lies in its beaches. Within easy walking distance you will find one guaranteed to suit your tastes. Families head for the shallow and sheltered town beach to the north of the port; the beach opposite **Diplo** island (to get to it take the track to the campsite and then follow the 100 m path to the right) is excellent and the preserve of windsurfers (boards can be hired by the hour) and nudists (this is one of the few official nudist beaches in Greece). More hardy types in search of solitude head for sunset beach on the west side of the town; wind-swept and with an abandoned air it is a great place for contemplating the meaning of life and what one is doing with it.

The rest of the island is relatively un-developed. A decent road is only now be-ing constructed. Nonetheless, dusty buses run south to the island cave, and occasion-ally to Agios Georgios on the south-west coast. There is a comfortable scatter of holiday homes along the coast road as well as a quiet beach at **Glyfa**.

The beach at **St. Georgios** is remote, but if you hire a car or moped it is worth the effort of getting to. The hills behind are nothing to look at, but are nonetheless notable. Home to a major early Cycladic settlement — the first to have ever been explored, they have yielded up a large collection of Cycladic figures (excavated by James Theodore Bent in 1833–34, they now form the nucleus of the British Museum's impressive collection). Most notable are the early highly stylised 'violin' figurines (see p. 225).

⊢⊣

There is plenty of hotel accommodation in Antiparos Town; though it is on the pricy side. Top of the range is the C-class *Artemis* (☎ 61460) with good views over the harbour. Equally good, but rather less well-placed, is the inland *Galini* (☎ 61420). The remainder of

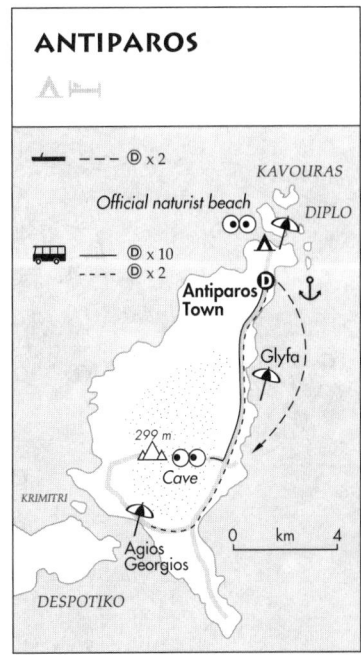

ANTIPAROS

KAVOURAS

Official naturist beach

DIPLO

Ⓓ × 10
Ⓓ × 2

Antiparos Town

Glyfa

299 m

Cave

KRIMITRI

Agios Georgios

0   km   4

DESPOTIKO

the hotel accommodation is cheaper. This includes the waterfront D-class *Mantalena* (☎ 61206), and a collection of E-class establish-ments in the backstreets between the tourist and ferry quays — the *Korali* (☎ 61236), *Antiparos* (☎ 61358) and *Chrisoula* (☎ 61224). Budget travellers should note that the E-class *Begleri* (☎ 61378) is more expensive than the C-class establishments! Room availability in town is also good, but many are booked on a long-stay basis so arrive early in High Season.

Å

Camping Antiparos (☎ 61221): a nice site (bar a poor site store) — with trees and a series of bamboo compounds — 1 km along a dirt track north of the town. A disco hums nearby.

◠◠

Nudist beaches aside, Antiparos has two sights of note. The first is a small medieval **Kastro** (c. 1440) at the heart of Antiparos town: though until one is inside it one is hard put to recognise it at all. Sited at the end of the high street, it is

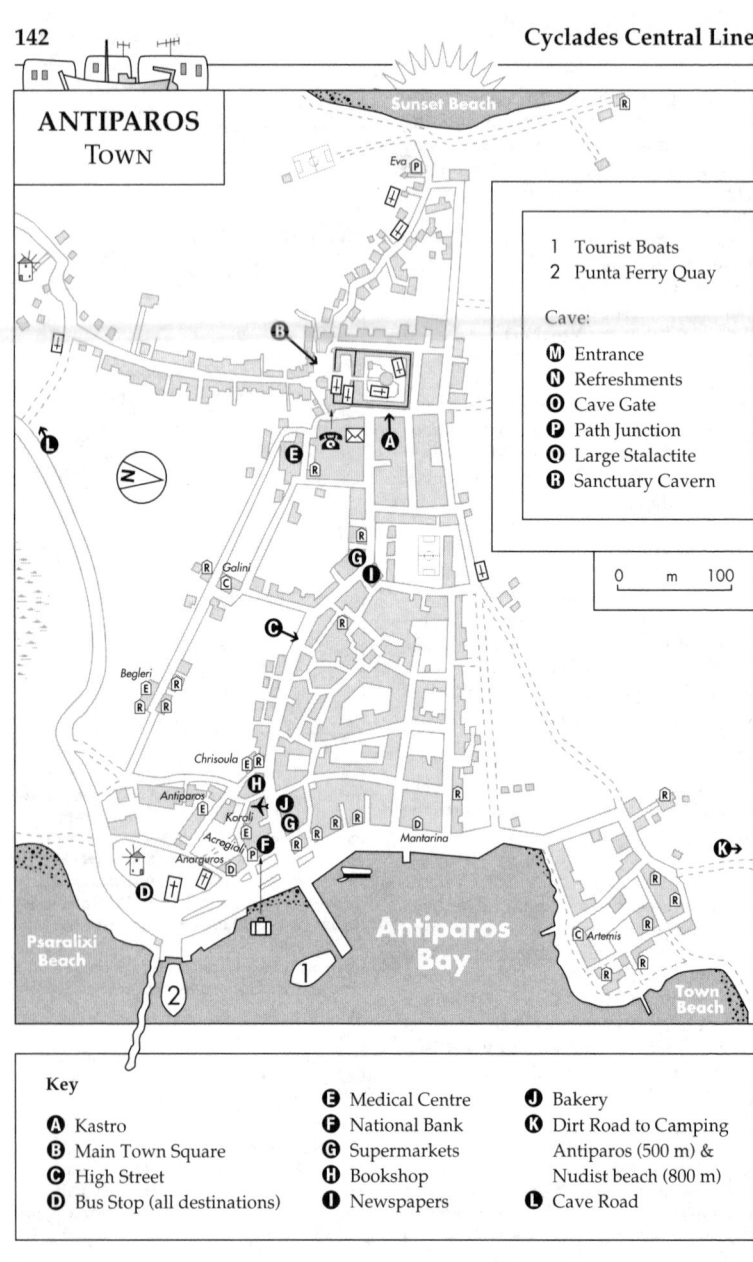

ANTIPAROS
TOWN

1   Tourist Boats
2   Punta Ferry Quay

Cave:

M   Entrance
N   Refreshments
O   Cave Gate
P   Path Junction
Q   Large Stalactite
R   Sanctuary Cavern

0   m   100

Sunset Beach

Eva

Galini

Begleri

Chrisoula

Antiparos

Karoli

Acregio

Anargiros

Mantarina

Artemis

Antiparos
Bay

Psaralixi
Beach

Town
Beach

Key

A   Kastro
B   Main Town Square
C   High Street
D   Bus Stop (all destinations)

E   Medical Centre
F   National Bank
G   Supermarkets
H   Bookshop
I   Newspapers

J   Bakery
K   Dirt Road to Camping
     Antiparos (500 m) &
     Nudist beach (800 m)
L   Cave Road

a rectangular structure that in its hay-day looked akin to a three-storeyed Alamo-like stockade, with houses lining the inside walls. In the years since it has been painted white, the top storey has gone, and windows and doors have been let into the outside wall. As a result, from the outside, the walls now look like any typical white cubist Cycladic row of buildings. On the south side, however, you will find a small un-painted Gothic archway — the original single doorway in the walls. Even today it is the only way you can gain access to the courtyard of the stockade-cum-castle without going through one of the houses.

The second (and well hyped) sight on Antiparos is the **Antiparos Cave**. Once lauded as one of the best caves in Greece, it now suffers in comparison with some of the other accessible caverns. However, even allowing that discriminating troglodytes are likely to be disappointed, for most the cave is a gentle and rewarding introduction to the underworld. Certainly there are enough buses and agency tours hell bent on getting you there (and making an equally big hole in your pocket). For this reason you should exercise caution; for if you are not careful the cave is not the only pitfall that you could encounter. You should be aware of the following:

(1). In the summer of 1994 the round bus trip to the cave was 1000 GDR. One-way tickets cost 500 GDR. Several agency buses and the island bus run to the cave but tickets are not interchangeable; it therefore pays to buy single tickets so that you can return on the first available bus back.

(2). Tours and bus tickets do not include the cave ticket price of 400 GDR.

(3). All buses decant passengers on a bend of a dirt track half-way up an apparently isolated mountain-side. Here you will be met by mules with touting owners. Those taking up the offer to be taken for a ride are apt to feel bigger asses than their mounts when they find that the cave entrance is only 150 m up the path.

(4). Low Season sees buses reduced to a trickle; so expect delays when both departing and returning. In addition, the cave is often locked, prompting further delays.

Once inside Mt. Agios Gianni you will find yourself in a cave that has been on the tourist map almost as long as the Parthenon, and unfortunately, it is as badly damaged. Many of the stalagmites and stalactites (sexist

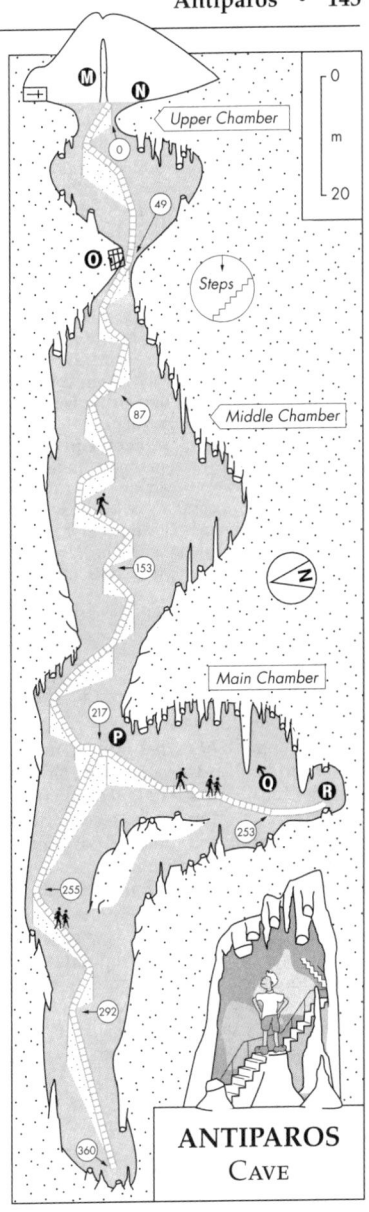

ANTIPAROS
CAVE

mnemonic: tights come down) are broken. In times past the cave's fame was such that stalagmites were carried off by the Russian navy to the Kremlin. More recent damage was inflicted during the last war when German soldiers used the stalactites for rifle practice. The walls are also covered with graffiti dating back 300 years. This is less of a problem today as movement in the cave is restricted to a narrow stairway barely wide enough for two people to pass (in High Season rotund visitors have been known to commit mass murder simply trying to pass by on the other side). Handrails for midgets are provided but at several points the stairs are built onto stalagmites and taller vertigo suffers could be in for a heady time (for these reasons photography in the cave is forbidden).

Pottery has been found in the cave indicating occupation back to ancient times, though the nearest it has ever come to fame was in 1673 when a potty Frenchman (one M. de Nointel) organised a Christmas Day mass in the main chamber — complete with the bemused population of Paros and fireworks.

☎

CODE 0284, POLICE 61202, FIRST AID 61219.

Ios

ΙΟΣ; 108 km²; pop. 1200.

Ios (pronounced *EE*os) has gained a reputation and a half as *the* party island since it emerged as a popular student destination in the 60s, offering a heady cocktail of sun, sand and sex. The reality is a little more complicated, for a lot depends on when you go and which part of the island you visit. From mid July to the end of August the crowds pour in, and Ios attempts to live up to its reputation — those looking for a traditional, unspoilt Greek island would do better to avoid it, but for the rest of the year, even if partying isn't your thing, it is worth paying a call for Ios has a lot going for it. In many ways Ios is an ideal *holiday* island; it has two of the best beaches to be found anywhere in Greece, a picturesque old Chora, good connections for day trips to other islands, and — most importantly of all — a buzz about it that you just don't find anywhere else. It is difficult not to get caught up by the atmosphere, and, as you don't have to join the all-night party, it is possible to turn a blind eye to the excesses of those that do and simply embrace those aspects of the island that appeal to you. In some respects the island's reputation is rather overblown, for although the days of the youthful hanger-out are not exactly over, a growth in the number of families visiting (thanks to the thirty-somethings returning to the haunts of their giddy youth) is beginning to restore the balance a bit. The telling fact that Parikia on Paros and Fira Town on Santorini both now have more night-spots is also rarely acknowledged.

Not all is sweetness and light, however, and Ios does have a less appealing side that the island's more passionate fans are loath to accept. The height of the season sees it ludicrously over-crowded, with the attendant problems of noise, poor sanitation, alcohol abuse and theft — all of which are more evident than on other Greek islands. In one respect the locals have got in on the act as well, with some of the bars adding god-knows-what to spirits and cocktails; invariably with dire consequences for the drinker a few hours later (you will be particularly vulnerable to this ploy if you are perceived to have had a few). Violence is also a problem: the rumour mill was putting it about that there were a dozen rapes during the summer of 1994.

Describing Ios is easy enough for there are only three main points of reference with a bare 4 km between them: the Port, the chora set up on the hill behind (known as the Village), and the Beach (Milopotas) on the other side of the chora hill. At first sight the island seems innocuous enough for the port of **Gialos** is quite sleepy. Indeed, it is positively quiet compared to its counterparts on Paros and Santorini. For this reason it attracts those who want to be able to escape the island's nightlife, and has a good supply of hotels, along

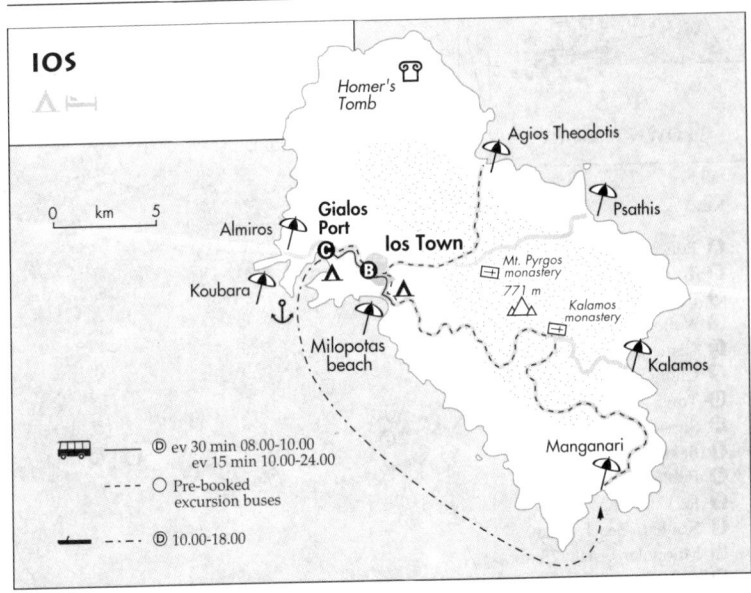

IOS

Homer's Tomb

Agios Theodotis

Psathis

Gialos Port

Almiros

Ios Town

Koubara

Mt. Pyrgos monastery
771 m

Kalamos monastery

Milopotas beach

Kalamos

Manganari

0   km   5

ⓓ ev 30 min 08.00-10.00
   ev 15 min 10.00-24.00

O Pre-booked
  excursion buses

ⓓ 10.00-18.00

with an excellent bakery and several restaurants. It is only when you step inside one of the two supermarkets and discover that the check-out sweet racks are filled with Durex that you first get a hint that something, somewhere, could be up. A second oddity is to be found at the waterfront Acteon Travel agency: this takes the form of the island's annual 'Time Out'; a free booklet worth collecting as it gives a run down on the latest night-spots.

Behind the port climbs the old mule stairway up to the chora. This offers an appealing alternative to the new road, but thanks to slippery, sloping steps that are awkward enough when you are sober (never mind when one is totally sozzled and in the dark) it accounts for the fact that there is always someone hopping around with a leg in plaster. **Ios Town**, (alias the Village) at the top is a real contradiction: the islanders have made a far better job of combining a pretty chora village with a heavy bar and disco scene

than their counterparts on the other popular islands. During daylight hours it retains much of its former small village atmosphere, and at first sight you would be hard put to know that it was anything more. This has been achieved by separating the old part of town (running up the side of the northern hill) from the new tourist inspired buildings which are confined to the quarter south of the port—beach road. The majority of the bars and discos, however, are in the old quarter, but even here they are confined to a distinct circuit, and it is easy enough to slip into backstreets made up of family homes, with the occasional donkey tethered outside.

The two island buses run from the port to the chora and then down (past yet more nightspots) to the island's best beach at **Milopotas**. A long stretch of golden sand, it is large enough to accommodate even the High Season crowds and is backed by a scatter of bars and tavernas.

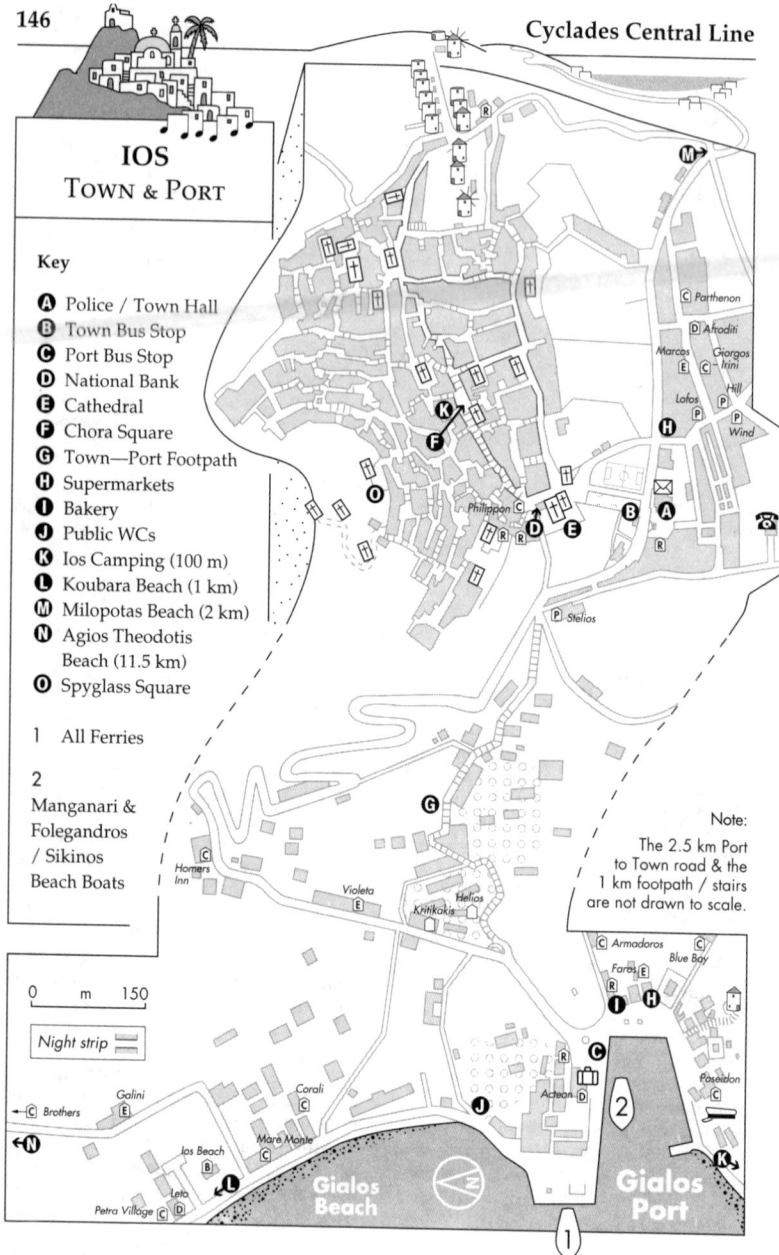

Cyclades Central Line

IOS
TOWN & PORT

Key

Ⓐ Police / Town Hall
Ⓑ Town Bus Stop
Ⓒ Port Bus Stop
Ⓓ National Bank
Ⓔ Cathedral
Ⓕ Chora Square
Ⓖ Town—Port Footpath
Ⓗ Supermarkets
Ⓘ Bakery
Ⓙ Public WCs
Ⓚ Ios Camping (100 m)
Ⓛ Koubara Beach (1 km)
Ⓜ Milopotas Beach (2 km)
Ⓝ Agios Theodotis
   Beach (11.5 km)
Ⓞ Spyglass Square

1   All Ferries

2
Manganari &
Folegandros
/ Sikinos
Beach Boats

0   m   150

Night strip

Note:

The 2.5 km Port
to Town road & the
1 km footpath / stairs
are not drawn to scale.

Parthenon

Afroditi

Marcos   Giorgos
         Irini

Lofos   Hill

Wind

Philippon

Stelios

Homers
Inn

Violeta

Krihkakis   Helios

Armadoros   Blue Bay

Faros

Poseidon

Galini

Corali

← Brothers

Acteon

Ios Beach

Mare Monte

← N

Leto

Petra Village

Gialos
Beach

Gialos
Port

The rest of the island — being arid and hilly, with poor dirt roads — is quiet, though regular tour buses (starting at the port) ferry people to the main beaches. The best of these is the superb stretch of sand taking in several bays at **Manganari** on the south coast (beach boats also visit). **Agios Theodotis**, on the east coast, is almost as good, with the ruins of a Venetian kastro in lieu of the former's disco / taverna and windsurfing school. Both have their nude ends, unlike Milopotas and oily **Koubara** (reached via a path from the port) which have become more restrained of late.

⊨

Rooms are plentiful on Ios; though the usual caveat about arriving early in the day applies to Ios as well. If you are staying more than a fortnight (it is not unknown for people to get off a ferry and then ask in the nearest ticket agency where they can stay for three months!) it is worth trying to negotiate a reduced rate. If you are staying for several weeks you will be expected to pay your bill on a weekly basis (this applies on campsites as well).

The **Port** is well equipped with several good mid-range hotels (though the noise from the ferries can be a problem). These include the C-class *Armadoros* (☎ 91201), *Blue Bay* (☎ 91533) and the *Poseidon* (☎ 91091). There is also the somewhat noisy D-class *Acteon* (☎ 91207) over the ticket agency, and the E-class *Faros* (☎ 91569). Nearby **Gialos Beach** offers some of the most relaxed (and quietest) rooms on Ios. These include the beach-side C-class *Corali* (☎ 91272) and *Mare Monte* (☎ 91564), the expensive *Petra Village* (☎ 91409) and B-class *Ios Beach* and the D-class *Leto* (☎ 91279).

The **Chora** has a plentiful supply of rooms — mostly in the old part of town — and, a number of reasonable hotels. Best among these are the D-class *Afroditi* (☎ 91546) and the C-class *Parthenon* (☎ 91275). The C-class *Giorgos —Irini* (☎ 91527) is also very popular, as is the *Philippou* (☎ 91290) near the Cathedral, and the E-class *Marcos* (☎ 91060).

The road to and behind **Milopotas Beach** also has a large number of pensions and hotels perched along it. These include the C-class *Far Out* (☎ 91446), *Delfini* (☎ 91340), and *Nissos Ios* (☎ 91306), and the E-class *Aegeon* (☎ 91392).

Milopotas is also home to the expensive B-class *Ios Palace* (☎ 91269).

Λ

Thanks to the high student numbers, Ios is well equipped with four campsites, but even this is not enough at the height of the season when you will find tents pitched peg to peg by the early evening. The rest of the year there is space aplenty. Regardless of when you visit you should take pains to secure all valuables as petty theft is more of a problem here than anywhere else. Thanks to the number of long stay (i.e. a couple of months or more) visitors — many of whom are strapped to find the funds to party *and* pay their camping bills — it is all but impossible to stay a week at a campsite on Ios without hearing of someone losing their travellers' cheques or cash from their tent. Of the sites, *Ios Camping* (☎ 91329) opposite the ferry quay is the cheapest (with no tent charge). Most campers however, like to be near the beach and head for one of the three sites behind Milopotas. *Camping Stars* (☎ 91302) nearest the village road, is a well-established, if smallish, site. *Milopotas Camping* (☎ 91554) further along the beach is the poorest, and suitably named *Far Out Camping* (☎ 91468) at the end of Milopotas is both the newest and the best when it comes to facilities. Mini-buses from all three scramble desperately for the masses streaming off the boats.

👓

The official and oft-quoted sight: **Homer's Tomb** — or rather the alleged stones of, is all but impossible to get to and not worth the effort. As a result most visitors prefer to get stoned in the bars and discos of Ios Town instead. However, one sight not to be missed is the view from the top of the **Chora hill**. Finding your way up through the warren of streets is, admittedly, half the fun of it (a couple of stairways that disintegrate into steep tracks on the western side of the Chora will eventually get you there), but there is usually a steady trail of sunset watchers heading in the same direction to help you. The top, adorned with several chapels and a scree slope of pebbles, offers fantastic views of the port framed with the island of Sikinos behind in one direction, and the Chora and distant Santorini in another.

☎

CODE 0286, PORT POLICE 91264, POLICE 91222, FIRST AID 91227.

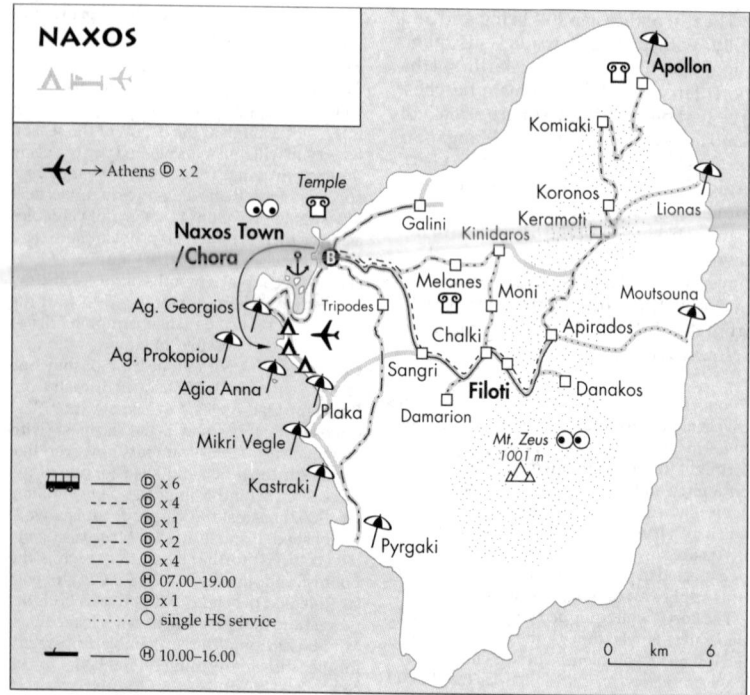

Naxos

ΝΑΞΟΣ; 448 km²; pop. 14,000.

Considered by writers ancient and modern to be the most beautiful of the Cyclades (thanks to a landscape of lush valleys and ruin-topped skylines), mountainous Naxos is not only the largest island in the group, but is a popular day-trip destination and is a significant ferry junction in its own right; being the primary jumping off point for Amorgos and the Little Cyclades. Thanks to a prosperous agricultural economy the island has long been able to ignore the tourist market, but this is now changing. The last five years have seen the opening of an airport and a large increase in the number of tourists. Fortunately, the impact on the island has been relatively benign as the tourist area is largely confined to the main port and capital of Naxos Town and its environs, and even here it is hardly oppressive. At the moment the island thus enjoys just enough tourism to make the 'typical' tourist feel comfortable, but not so much that the island's character is irredeemably damaged.

Naxos Town is the arrival point for all but air visitors. Hardly representative of the island as a whole, it is a mass of contradictions, offering a mix of a brash, touristy waterfront, a warren of lovely little backstreets winding up to a Venetian Kastro, and one of the most dramatic harbours in the Aegean — thanks to the romantic skyline arch of a ruined temple

on the causeway-linked islet at the edge
of the town (Naxos is one island where it
is difficult not to know that you have
arrived at the right island). The temple-
topped rock provides a beguiling pro-
mise to arriving ferry passengers of things
to come. The 'rock' disco cowering beneath it is equally apposite in its own way.

Surprisingly, as far as most tourists are
concerned, Naxos is still something of a
one town island: most are content to
divide their time between Naxos Town
(or Chora) and the miles of fine sandy
beaches that run down the coast to the
south where freelance camping and
nudity abound. First impressions of the
town can be rather mixed as the enchant-
ment of the temple is somewhat offset by
an increasingly glitzy waterfront; the cute
old hardware shops of just a few years
ago have now given way to tourist shops
and cash dispensing machines. Most of
the town's amenities are to be found here,
including a good bookshop and a bus
station complete with timetables for the
island. The municipal authorities have
also woken up to the tourists' occasionally
more pressing needs and have just opened
a WC and shower house on the main
street behind the promenade. Once you
step into the streets behind the main street
and wander into the chora you will
discover the older and far more attractive
face of Naxos Town. The combination of
13 c. castle, Greek chora and Venetian
houses (some still adorned with the crumbling escutcheons of the noble families
who lived here during three centuries of
rule) combine to make for shady, and
interesting, wandering, and near the
castle walls you will find several good
restaurants to augment the collection
running the length of the promenade.

The town centre aside, the tourist strip
is confined to the excellent series of sandy
beaches to the south. The nearest, Agios
Georgios, is an excellent family beach,
shallow and very close to the town.
Further south lie Ag. Prokopiou and Agia

Anna beaches, equally sandy and home
to the island's campsites. Taxi boats run
down from Naxos Town to the latter.
Plaka beach to the south is possibly the
best of the lot; a long and empty stretch of
white sand running for over a mile.

In spite of its beaches Naxos's fame has
always rested on its verdant hinterland
where an attractive rural Greek atmosphere pervades (making the island particularly popular with those who enjoy
walking holidays). Farming is still an
important feature of the island economy
(the island is noted for its wines and
cheeses), and indeed, is so good that it is
only now that Naxos is really taking to
tourists in a big way. Sadly, roads have
yet to catch up with this trend and are in
a positively lethal condition in parts (this
is one island where it is better to stick to
buses rather than resort to mopeds). Most
tourists tend to compromise and see the
interior via a daily tour bus that heads
along the meandering mountain roads to
the small developing northern resort of
Apollon. Few people stay here, however,
and the village subsists on the buses that
decant tourists taking in the local sight
(see overleaf) and lunch before heading
back to civilization. Two villages en route
also attract attention. **Filoti**, starting point
for the 2-hour trek to the summit of **Mt.
Zeus** (the highest in the Cyclades), to
marvel at the view of the archipelago,
and the cave half-way up (where the god
was supposed to have been born), and
Apirados (home to a small museum of
Early Cycladic figures). The east coast of
Naxos is very quiet with tourists something of a rarity. This is in part due to the
large open-cast mine south of Lionas.
⊨
The self-styled 'Tourist Information Center'
on the waterfront is a good starting point
when bed hunting (assuming you escape the
room owners besieging the ferries). **Naxos
Town** is home to the bulk of the island
accommodation, with an easily located batch
of hotels in the northern town. Nearest the
ferry quay is the D-class *Oceanis* (☎ 22436),

with the E-class *Anna* (☎ 22475) and *Savvas* (☎ 22213) down the street behind. There is also a nice hotel in the C-class *Grotta* (☎ 22215) beyond the *Apollon* (☎ 22468). In addition to several places offering rooms, the promenade has a cluster of C-class hotels at its southern end: the *Hermes* (☎ 22220), the *Aegeon* (☎ 22852), and the *Coronis* (☎22626). The warren of streets around the castle is also home to a number of hotels. At the top of the range is the C-class *Renetta* (☎ 22952) to the south; the maze of streets to the north containing the *Panorama* (☎ 22330) and the pricey *Chateau Zevgoli* (☎22993), along with the D-class *Anixis* (☎ 22112) and a youth hostel/pension, the *Dionysos* (☎ 22331).

The **Agios Georgios Beach** area is also well endowed with hotels and pensions including the E-class *Soula* (☎ 23637) and the C-class *Asteria* (☎ 23866). On the town road to the beach stands the C-class *Helmos* (☎ 22455), with the E-class *Folia* (☎22210) opposite. Two other hotels of note are nearby: the E-class *Korali* (☎ 23092) by the beach, and, hidden three blocks behind, the C-class *Zeus* (☎22912).

Δ

There is fierce competition between the three sites that lie on the beaches south of Naxos Town, though there is little to choose between them. *Naxos Camping* (☎ 23501) is the nearest (2 km), just south of Agios Georgios Beach. *Apollon Camping* (☎ 24117), 4 km from the town, lies near Ag. Prokopios Beach to the south and Agia Anna Beach has *Maragas Camping* (☎ 24552), 7 km from the town. An air-conditioned coach and mini-buses meet all boats, and students are employed on ferries handing out promotional flyers as well.

◯◯

Naxos Town offers the best sightseeing options. First of these is the **Archaic Temple** (6 c. BC) and its remarkably well-preserved cella doorway. Reached via a surf-kissed causeway, it is now expected of most visitors that they will come away with at least one photograph of themselves standing astride the base stones inside the arch (this isn't quite as famous a being photographed holding up the leaning tower of Pizza, but it runs it pretty close). The arch was initially believed by antiquarians to be the doorway of Ariadne's palace, for tradition has it that Naxos was the home of Dionysos, the God of wine and pleasure. It was on Patatia that he is supposed to have ravished

Ariadne, the beautiful maiden dumped here by Theseus after their escape from the Labyrinth at Knossos on Crete. Having loved her and built her a home she (being a mere mortal) went and died on him; whereupon the God got the hump, threw her bridal crown of seven stars into the night sky (these now form the constellation Corona Borealis) and went off and invented orgies. The temple is something of an enigma as no surviving literature from antiquity mentions it. With no inscriptions from the site recovered either, debate rages as to whom it was dedicated; the main candidates being Dionysos or Apollo. Sentiment favours the former, but its age and the particular affinity that the Archaic Naxians enjoyed with Delos and its Apollo cult suggests the latter.

The **Old Town** (largely a product of the period of Venetian rule between 1207−1566 when members of the Sonudi family set up shop as the Dukes of Naxos) runs around the kastro walls and is filled with geraniums and — particularly on the northern side — a lovely warren of little streets to get lost in. The **Kastro**, built on the site of the ancient acropolis, contains a Roman Catholic cathedral and a **Museum** (one of the few where you can see some of the Early Cycladic marble figurines so sought after by art thieves). It is well preserved, though its heart has a somewhat antiseptic feel to it. Finally, the northern shoreline of the town, known as **Grotta**, is of interest thanks to a couple of caves and the submerged remains of an Early Cycladic town just off the beach.

Around Naxos are a number of minor archaeological sites; notably at **Melanes** and **Apollon** where the remains of large marble stylised male statues known as **Kouroi** were abandoned half-completed in the Archaic period due to faults in the marble. Naxian marble was popular in the ancient world (the famous Lions on Delos were carved from it), but as with Paros, export rather than local construction was the order of the day. Fragmentary remains of earlier ancient structures are to be found within the buildings of the kastro, and a temple to Demeter existed on the road from Naxos Town to the beach hamlet at Pyrgaki, but little survives to be seen today. There is also a well-preserved **Medieval Castle** one hour's walk inland from **Kastraki** beach.

☎

CODE 0285, PORT POLICE 22300, POLICE 22100, FIRST AID 23333.

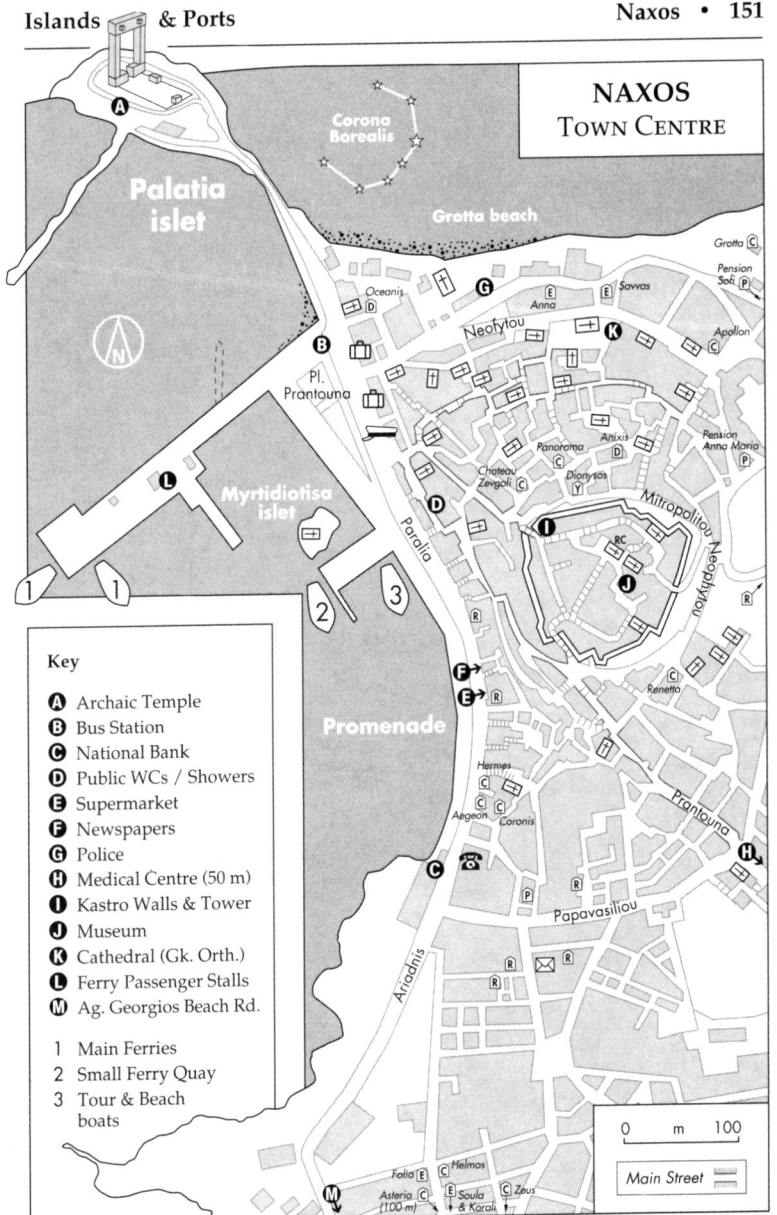

NAXOS
TOWN CENTRE

Corona
Borealis

Grotta beach

Grotta C

Pension
Sofi P

Palatia
islet

Oceanis
D

G

E
Anna

E Savvas

Neofytou

K

Apollon

B

Pl.
Prantouna

Panorama

Anixis
D

Pension
Anna Maria

Myrtidiotisa
islet

Chateau
Zevgoli C

Dionysos
Y

Mitropolitou Neofytou

L

D

Paralia

I

RC

1

1

2

3

J

R

Promenade

F

E

R

C
Renetta

Prantouna

Hermes
C

Key

C
C

H

Ⓐ Archaic Temple

Aegeon Coronis

Ⓑ Bus Station

Ⓒ National Bank

Ⓓ Public WCs / Showers

P

Ⓔ Supermarket

C ☎

R

Ⓕ Newspapers

Ⓖ Police

Papavasiliou

Ⓗ Medical Centre (50 m)

R

Ⓘ Kastro Walls & Tower

Ⓙ Museum

Ⓚ Cathedral (Gk. Orth.)

R

✉

Ⓛ Ferry Passenger Stalls

Ⓜ Ag. Georgios Beach Rd.

R

1 Main Ferries

2 Small Ferry Quay

3 Tour & Beach
boats

Ariadnis

0   m   100

Folia E C Helmos

M

Asteria C E Soula C Zeus
(100 m) ↓ & Korali

Main Street

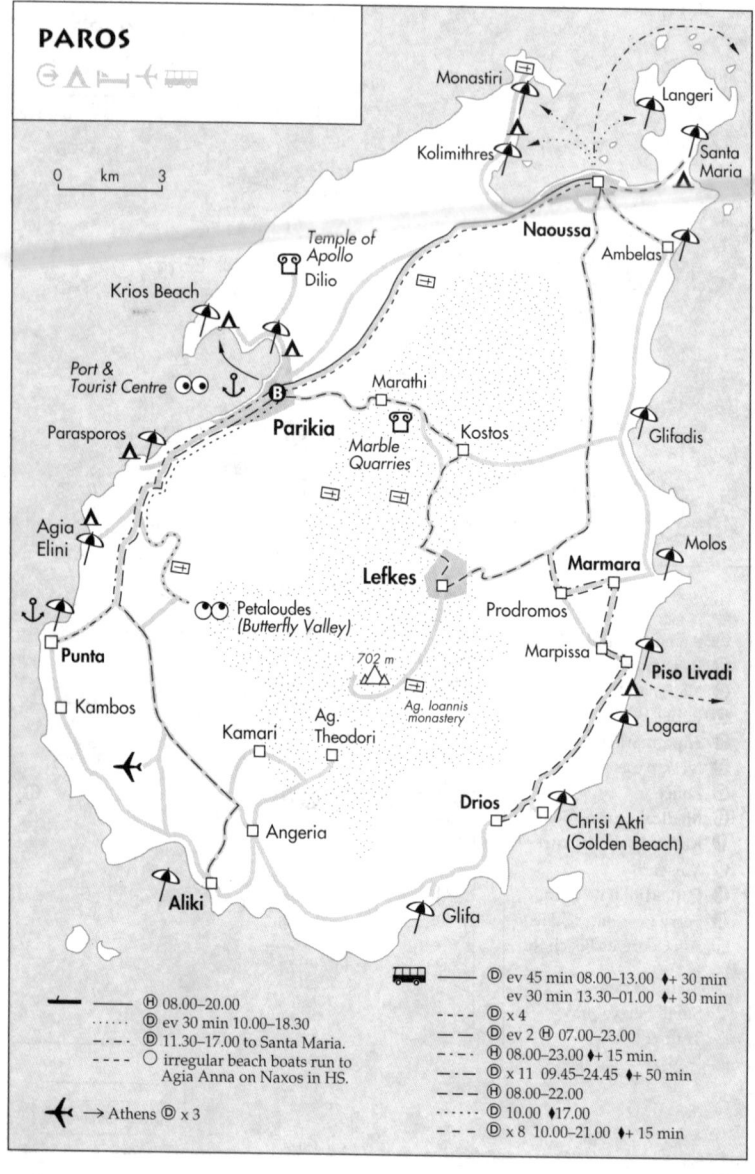

PAROS

0   km   3

Monastiri

Langeri

Kolimithres

Santa Maria

Temple of Apollo
Dilio

Naoussa

Ambelas

Krios Beach

Port & Tourist Centre

Marathi

Parikia

Parasporos

Marble Quarries

Kostos

Glifadis

Agia Elini

Lefkes

Molos

Marmara

Petaloudes
(Butterfly Valley)

Prodromos

Punta

702 m

Marpissa

Piso Livadi

Kambos

Ag. Ioannis monastery

Logara

Kamari

Ag. Theodori

Drios

Chrisi Akti
(Golden Beach)

Angeria

Aliki

Glifa

⊢—⊣ Ⓗ 08.00–20.00
.... Ⓓ ev 30 min 10.00–18.30
–·–·– Ⓓ 11.30–17.00 to Santa Maria.
– – – ○ irregular beach boats run to
Agia Anna on Naxos in HS.

✈ →Athens Ⓓ x 3

──── Ⓓ ev 45 min 08.00–13.00 ♦+ 30 min
      ev 30 min 13.30–01.00 ♦+ 30 min
– – – Ⓓ x 4
— — — Ⓓ ev 2 Ⓗ 07.00–23.00
–·–·– Ⓗ 08.00–23.00 ♦+ 15 min.
–··–··– Ⓓ x 11 09.45–24.45 ♦+ 50 min
– – – Ⓗ 08.00–22.00
.... Ⓓ 10.00 ♦17.00
– – – Ⓓ x 8 10.00–21.00 ♦+ 15 min

Paros

ΠΑΡΟΣ; 194 km²; pop. 7900.

A large and well-placed island, Paros has become the de facto hub of the Greek ferry system in recent years and it is now difficult for Cycladic island hoppers to avoid calling at some point during their holiday. As a result Paros is apt to get horribly over-crowded in High Season. In part this is due to the charms of the island itself, for it is ringed with good sandy beaches, is fertile inland (in a dusty sort of way), and now has more nightlife than neighbouring Ios into the bargain.

Paros' main port and tourist centre is at **Parikia** (though you find that except on the island itself all ticket agents and schedules simply refer to it as 'Paros'). Occupying a sheltered bay on the west coast, it has been the main island centre since the bronze age when an early Cycladic village existed on the site. It briefly lost its role as the island capital during the Ottoman period when inland Lefkes took over (being far less vulnerable to pirate attack). Today the port town has re-emerged as the undisputed centre on the island; ribboning ever further along the shore. At its heart lies a typical Cycladic chora complete with the odd wall of a Venetian kastro built on the site of the ancient acropolis in 1207. Neither are the best examples of their type (though the chora manages to retain a surprising amount of charm even when it is swarming with tourists); but are suitable symbols, in their way, of Paros as a whole.

Very much tied to the shoreline, Parikia does not extend inland to any great extent, and is neatly divided by the road running south from the recently extended ferry quay (Prombona St.). To the west lies the old part of town, to the east the modern hotel and beach strip. Between the two lies the church of Ekatontapilani discretely tucked out of sight behind a park cum wood of pine trees. All the essential facilities are within easy distance of the quay, with a tourist office open in the windmill during office hours. The buildings near the quay are devoted en masse to ticket agents. Behind them is the main town square; though it has more the feel of a quiet crossroads between the quarters of the town and the ferry quay; for the waterfront is the real centre of activity in the town. Apart from the section composed of the whitewashed kastro walls it is lined with restaurants, bars, shops and hotels; though it has to be said that it isn't the most photogenic waterfront in the Aegean by a long way. The best thing it has going for it is its orientation; for it ideally positioned for sitting back and admiring the sunset over a drink or two. At night it is very lively, with the bulk of the nightlife located along the western end of the promenade (the more 'wild' bars — the Irish bar included — being behind the west beach), while the waterfront on the eastern side of town is quieter and home to the better restaurants in town. Up one of the backstreets behind lies the open air town cinema which offers current release films in English served up with pop-corn and all the trimmings in someone's back yard.

Parikia also has a number of beaches within easy reach. The most popular being the main town beach opposite the tourist hotel and restaurant strip east of the ferry quay. In addition, there is another — albeit more skimpy — beach on the east side of the bay that is also crowded, and a less attractive strand on the west end of the town promenade. All are adequate for the odd day of sunbathing but only rate from three to five out of ten compared to some of the other beaches on Paros. One of these, a collection of coves a boat ride across the bay at Krios, is easily accessible from Parikia, and has many fans thanks to the opportunity it offers to remove more beach-wear than is acceptable nearer the town. Buses from Parikia are also geared to moving tourists to beaches further afield. Both bus station (in the form of a dinky little kiosk) and

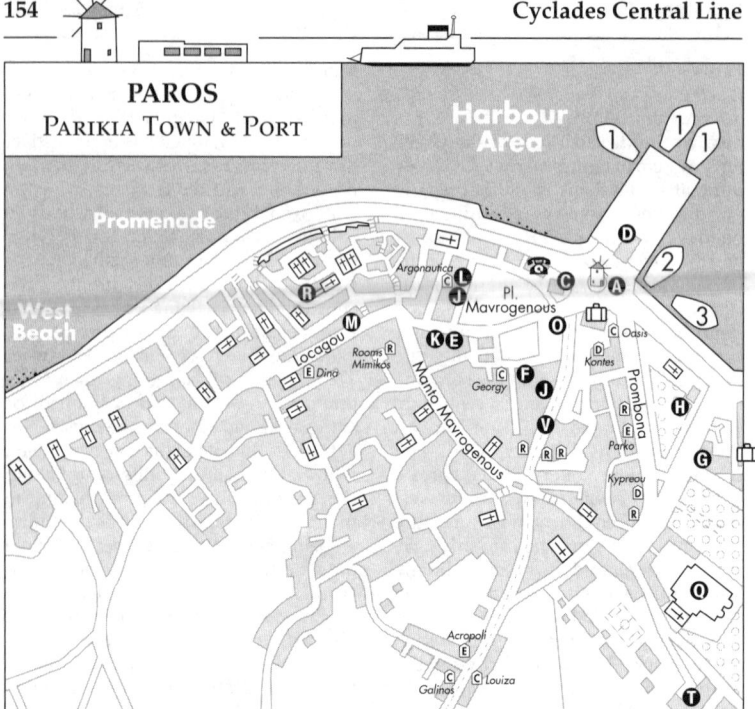

PAROS
PARIKIA TOWN & PORT

Key

A Windmill /
  Paros Tourist Office
B Bus Station (all destinations)
C Hotel Information Office
D Ferry Passenger Stalls
  (Signs posted up for the next three
  ferries due to call)
E National Bank of Greece
F Police / Tourist Police
G Hospital / Clinic
H Public WCs
I Large Supermarket
J Supermarkets
K Bakery

L Pharmacy
M Bookshops & International Press
N Moped Rental
O Taxi Rank
P Cinema
Q Ekatontapiliani Cathedral
R Old Kastro & Temple Walls
S Classical & Hellenistic Graveyard
T Archaeological Museum
U Pine Wood Park
V Street / River Bed (dry in summer)

1 Ferries (All destinations)
2 Antiparos Town & Cave Tour Boats
3 Krios Beach & Camping Taxi Boats

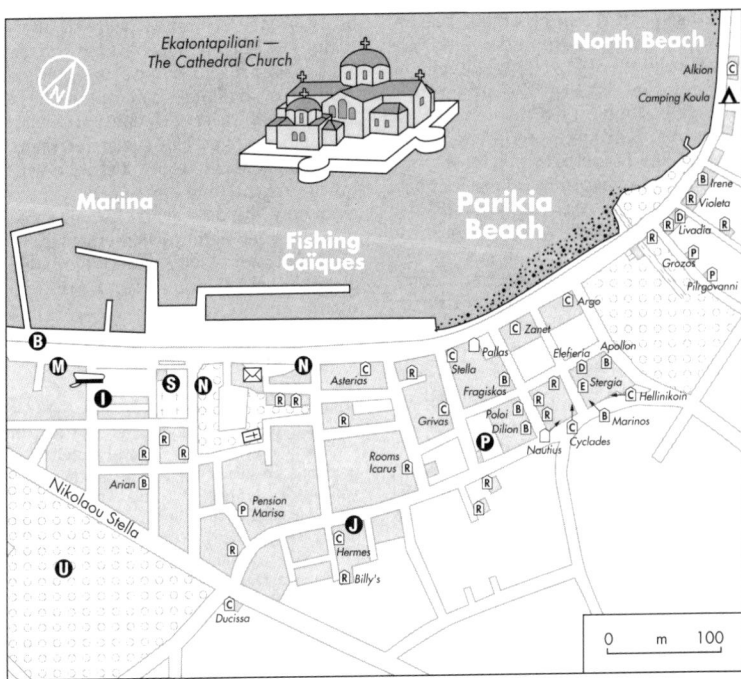

the beach boats operate from points just to the east of the ferry quay.

The ferry quay is one of the largest in the Cyclades. Passengers are not allowed to wait on it where they will as is the practice elsewhere. Instead, you have to gather in one of the three passenger stalls located on the town side of the quay. At the ferry end of each is a gate that is unlocked when the ferry calls: it therefore pays to be in the correct stall! When arriving at Paros you should also note that the quay exit gate is on the west/old town side of the passenger stall block. Midday and midnight see the large ferries queuing up to take turns docking. On Paros the sheer number of tourists also dictate that it is politic to have a ticket in your hand when you board. Certainly given the popularity of some of the small-

er boats, it is advisable to buy your ticket in advance. Apart from the crowds the only real problem you are likely to encounter is the choice of connections available. During the Low Season Paros remains the best served island in the Aegean, though this is relative, with departures rarely in double figures.

Around Paros there are a number of tourist resorts and beaches that are easily accessible thanks to the good (but invariably very crowded) bus service. The picturesque chora town of **Naoussa**, set in a bay on the northern coast and dominated by a tall orthodox church, has rapidly expanded to become the island's second major tourist centre. Smaller and prettier than Parikia, it shares one thing in common in as much as it is also bursting at the seams with tourists during the summer months. At the height of the season numbers get quite oppressive. At the centre of the town is a whitewashed chora. Laid out in an almost grid-like pattern, it is more boutique filled than its Parikia counterpart. In spite of this, it is the taverna-lined waterfront that is the great draw, with a charming caïque harbour protected on the seaward harbour wall side by the remains of a Venetian kastro-cum-tower now reduced to a surf-topped breakwater. Running through and dominating the centre of town is a dry (in summer) river bed that is home to the town bus stop. The chora lies to the east, gradually ascending the hillside to the dominating church and a handful of derelict windmills to the north. West of the river bed the town is reduced to a ribbon of houses running a mere two or three blocks deep along the coast. This coast road is home to the OTE and Police station as well as the best Naoussa can offer by way of a beach: be warned, this isn't a lot. As a result, boats run from the waterfront to beaches around the bay and round the headland to the beach at Santa Maria (also reached via a daily bus from Parikia or a local bus from Naoussa).

The number three resort town, **Piso Livadi**, is a quaint village gathered around a cute little harbour on the east side of the island with a thrice-weekly link to Amorgos, besides being a nice place to stay if you want to escape the worst of the crowds. It is also conveniently close to the island's best beach (all the best beaches on Paros are to be found along this stretch of coast) at **Chrisi Akti** (Golden Beach). As the name suggests, this is an excellent stretch of sandy coast and is popular with wind-surfers (despite the pretensions of less attractive Santa Maria beach to the north). Nearby lies the village of **Drios**; now rapidly being spoilt by ugly hotel development, it is the destination of Parikia buses.

The forth centre of note is at **Aliki** on the south coast. Little more than a quiet

beach village it offers a peaceful alternative to the main resorts. In High Season it also has an irregular taxi boat service to Antiparos (sometimes continuing east to a beach on the islet of **Despotiko**). Other destinations have less going for them. The inland chora village of **Lefkes** is very quiet, unspoilt and an appealing hangover from the days when pirates ruled the shores preventing development there. No doubt one casualty of this is the lonely quay at **Punta.** Landing place for the regular Antiparos ferry, it is linked via a short bus ride to Parikia (times are posted up on the chapel wall near the quay).

🛏

Hotel accommodation is easy to find on Paros thanks to the Accommodation Office just off the ferry quay. All the island hotels and pensions are listed on boards on the office walls along with their prices. The staff will phone around for you. Plentiful offers of rooms also greet the early boats but prices rise in High Season when the morning ferries from Piraeus start arriving after midday. From then on you will have to be prepared to pay up or look further afield. Naoussa is the best bet as the town is plastered with 'Rooms' signs. Piso Livadi also has a reasonable supply.

Well-endowed **Parikia** is home to the greatest number of the island's hotels. These are divided between the old part of town (mostly smaller, budget establishments) and the new tourist dominated suburb to the east (which is home to the bulk of the package tour hotels). Other hotels lie around the town environs — including the pricey *Xenia* (☎ 21394) located 100 m west of the town's west beach behind a couple of windmills.

Mid-range hotels mostly cater for package tourists, but they are quick to snap up island hoppers to fill any empty beds. Some even have signs outside indicating vacancies. The waterfront east of the ferry quay includes the C-class *Asterias* (☎ 21797), *Stella* (☎ 21502) and the *Argo* (☎ 21367). Quieter hotels lie in the streets behind, including the *Cyclades* (☎ 22048). If you want to splash out at the middle end of the range, the C-class *Argonautica* (☎ 21440) is conveniently placed behind the main town square with attractive, if pricey, rooms. Near the ferry quay are a couple of reasonable

D-class establishments that are also easy to find: the *Kontes* (☎ 21096) and the *Kypreou* (☎ 21383). The latter is the cheaper of the two.

Another popular group of hotels lie along the river bed cum road: the C-class *Galinos* (☎ 21480), *Louiza* (☎ 22122) and E-class *Acropoli* (☎ 21521). Other E-class hotels in town include the *Dina* (☎ 21325) and the *Parko* (☎ 22213). At the budget end of the market are a number of establishments offering rooms (these are effectively backpackers' pensions), notably *Rooms Icarus* (☎ 21695) in the new strip and the better *Rooms Mimikos* (☎ 21437) in the chora part of town.

Other towns also have hotels on offer (again details from the Accommodation Office in Parikia). **Naoussa** is the best equipped, with the B-class Naoussa (☎ 51207) overlooking the waterfront standing out from the rest. Another town with a good hotel named after it is **Piso Livadi** which has the C-class *Piso Livadi* (☎ 41309) near the town bus stop.

Λ

On Paros there are a number of sites of varying quality: *Camping Koula* (☎ 22081), the nearest to the port, is the second worst site in Greece; cashing in on its convenient location with high prices, poor facilities and 03.00 ferry arrivals. *Camping Krios* (☎ 21705) is a newer site on the beach opposite the port. Not much better, and the taxi-boat link to Parikia is not conducive to nightlife or catching an early morning ferry. *Parasporos Camping* (☎ 21394), is a better site 3 km south of the town with mini-buses meeting ferry arrivals. *Camping Agia Elini* is an indifferent site on one of the best island beaches. The same can be said of *Camping Surfing Beach* (☎ 51013), nestling in the scrub behind Santa Maria beach. *Camping Naousa* (☎ 51398) is arguably the best site on Paros; again mini-buses meet boats. Finally, if you prefer a quiet life try *Captain Kafkis Camping* (☎ 41392),1 km outside Piso Livadi.

∞

Considering that Paros was famed in antiquity for the quality of its marble (Parian marble is more translucent than other types in Greece — that is to say, light penetrates further through it, giving it a sparkling white, light-absorbent appearance) it is sad that the island boasts no classical archaeological site of importance (though there is the scanty remains of a temple at Dilio). The **Marble Quarries** do

survive just outside Marathi, though few visitors venture beyond the cave-like entrance.

The **Venetian Kastro** at **Parikia** was largely constructed from the remains of archaic **Temples of Demeter & Apollo**, remnants of which can be seen in the form of the circular column drums now embedded in the surviving kastro walls. The town does, however, have one notable architectural monument: the 6 c. AD cathedral church of **Ekatontapiliani**. This rather odd name (thought to be a corruption of 'in the lower town') now means 'Our lady of the 100 doors' — for the building was supposed to have had as many. Truth to tell you would be hard put to know it today; though a number of students of architecture have managed to trace a dozen on their first attempt and 99 after a few ouzos. The 100th is widely believed to have been carried off by the Turks (a delightful notion as it suggests in a subtle way that the old enemy is completely unhinged along with it). Tradition also claims that the church was designed by Isidore of Miletus; with the construction carried out by his pupil Ignatius. When it was completed, Isidore is said to have been so jealous of the church's beauty that he attacked his pupil on the roof with the result that both fell to their deaths in the ensuing struggle. Given that Isidore was one of the architects responsible for the infinitely more wondrous Agia Sofia in İstanbul/Constantinople one suspects this is local hyperbole. The oldest part of the building is Roman anyway. The **Archaeological Museum** behind the church and its adjoining baptistry has part of the Roman pavement uncovered in the church on display amongst other island exhibits.

The final tourist destination of note is to the **Valley of the Butterflies** (alias tiger moths) at **Petaloudes** (from May to July). These gather before dying to mate in this quiet spot. Unfortunately, the poor creatures are now subjected to clapping and shouting exhibitions by tourists — thus alarming them into flight: the clouds of butterflies are, after all, what they have come to see. This is very debilitating for animals nearing the end of their lives and trying to conserve energy, and is producing dire consequences; as every jump means one less hump their numbers are now declining.

☎

CODE 0284, PORT POLICE 21240, POLICE 21221, FIRST AID 22500.

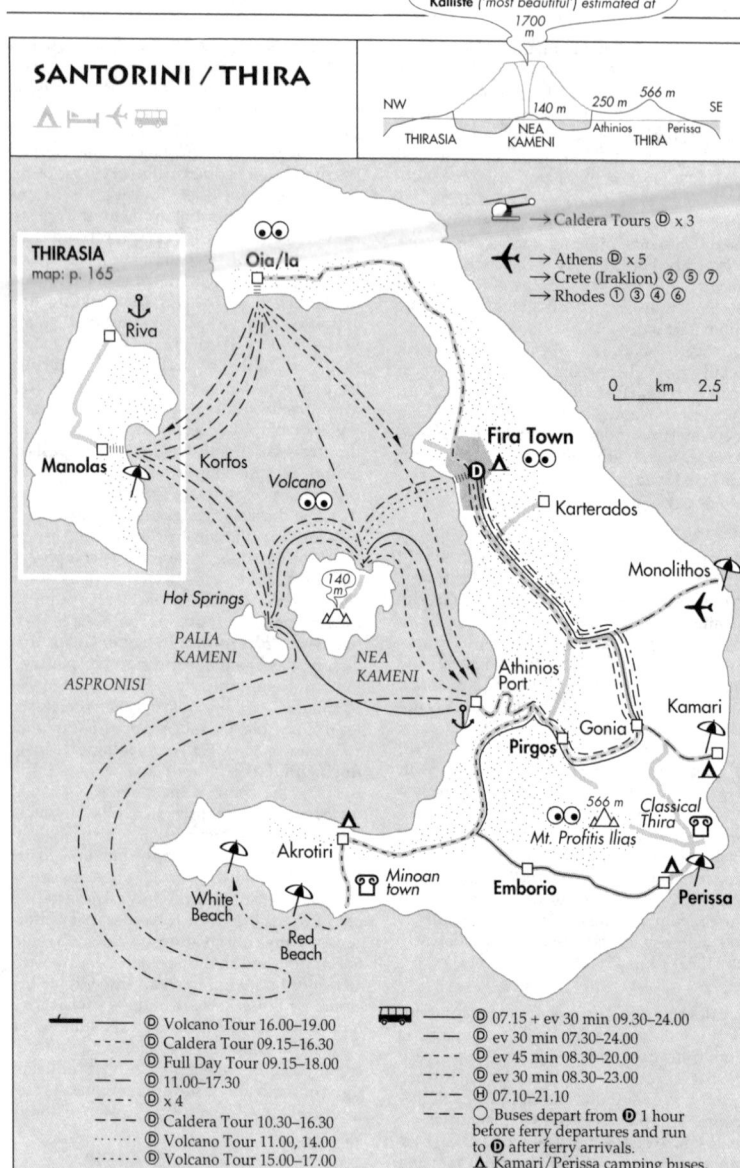

SANTORINI / THIRA

Summit of the pre-eruption island of **Kalliste** ('most beautiful') estimated at 1700 m

NW   140 m   250 m   566 m   SE

THIRASIA   NEA KAMENI   Athinios Perissa
             THIRA

→ Caldera Tours Ⓓ x 3

→ Athens Ⓓ x 5
→ Crete (Iraklion) ② ⑤ ⑦
→ Rhodes ① ③ ④ ⑥

THIRASIA
map: p. 165

Riva

Manolas   Korfos

Oia/Ia

Volcano

Hot Springs

PALIA KAMENI

ASPRONISI

NEA KAMENI

140 m

0   km   2.5

Fira Town

Ⓓ

Karterados

Monolithos

Athinios Port

Gonia   Kamari

Pirgos

566 m   Classical Thira

Mt. Profitis Ilias

Akrotiri

White Beach

Red Beach

Minoan town

Emborio

Perissa

— Ⓓ Volcano Tour 16.00–19.00
--- Ⓓ Caldera Tour 09.15–16.30
-·- Ⓓ Full Day Tour 09.15–18.00
— — Ⓓ 11.00–17.30
-··- Ⓓ x 4
- - - Ⓓ Caldera Tour 10.30–16.30
······ Ⓓ Volcano Tour 11.00, 14.00
······ Ⓓ Volcano Tour 15.00–17.00

— Ⓓ 07.15 + ev 30 min 09.30–24.00
— — Ⓓ ev 30 min 07.30–24.00
- - - Ⓓ ev 45 min 08.30–20.00
···· Ⓓ ev 30 min 08.30–23.00
-·- Ⓗ 07.10–21.10
- - - Ο Buses depart from Ⓓ 1 hour before ferry departures and run to Ⓓ after ferry arrivals.
Δ Kamari/Perissa camping buses.

Santorini / Thira

ΣΑΝΤΟΡΙΝΙ / ΘΙΡΑ; 73 km²; pop. 7100.

The most spectacular of all the Greek islands, Santorini is subject to ever increasing waves of tourists drawn by the landscape, the archaeological discoveries at Akrotiri, and the legend of Atlantis. The island is commonly known by two names: the Venetian 'Santorini' (after the 3 c. AD St. Irene who died in exile hereabouts) or its Classical name of 'Thira' (now reinstated as its official name). 'Santorini' is more popular with tourists. Ferry operators prefer 'Thira' in the interests of brevity on ship destination boards. The island is the largest fragment of a volcanic archipelago made up of the broken remnants of the largest caldera on earth and now thought by many to be the origin of the Atlantis legend; when the inpouring of the sea into the caldera during a massive eruption circa 1500 BC gave the impression that the greater part of the island had sunk. Within the caldera subsequent volcanic eruptions (the last in 1925–26) have spawned new islets of razor-sharp lava. The volcano is now quietly simmering with sulphur emissions and hot springs. If this wasn't enough by way of icing the tourist cake, the caldera rim is frosted with scenic white cubist towns and villages that take a tumble every time an earthquake hits and the island also has a reputation as a home for vampires. All this ensures that Santorini is on the itinerary of every passing cruise ship and casual tourist within range, and usually full to overflowing regardless of the time of year.

The centre of island activity is **Fira Town** (or Thira/Phira) perched precariously on the edge of the caldera rim and complete with a switchback staircase carpeted with donkey droppings down the crater wall (negotiable via cable car or donkey if you don't care for the 587 awkward steps) to the old island port of Skala Fira. Now unashamedly a tourist town, Fira has preserved enough of its charm to make a visit enjoyable. This might not seem to be the case if you arrive in the early hours when the main town square is thronged with nightlife fans and literally ankle deep in litter, but once the efficient town sweeps have done their stuff a vague semblance of the Greek island idyll is restored. The great attraction in town is the view over the caldera (principally from Ipapantis St.), along with the cable-car and staircase down to the old port (now reduced to serving tour boats). There is also an Archaeological Museum (with virtually no Minoan artifacts) that is just about worth a visit, and a Municipal Museum that isn't (a repository for odds and ends, its most interesting exhibits are the — sadly unlabelled — photos of pre-1956 earthquake Fira). Along the rim you will find a number of ruined buildings damaged beyond repair by the 1956 earthquake which struck the island on the 9th of July, killing 53 people and destroying 2400 homes. If losing its most impressive buildings wasn't bad enough, Fira has suffered further disfigurement thanks to the large pumice quarry at the southern edge of the town. This has been excavated down to the pre-eruption ground level, revealing the stumps of petrified trees.

The island ferry terminus is at **Athinios** (the only one of Santorini's three ports with a road link) 4 km south of Fira. Little more than a long quay inside the caldera topped with ticket agencies and tavernas, it exists here solely because it was at this point that it was possible to cut a switchback road down the cliff-side. In High Season the number of vehicles and buses attempting to reach the quay can result in major traffic jams and it is not unknown for bus passengers to have to walk down the cliff to join their boats. Santorini's popularity is reflected in the ferry schedules. Some 8—9 hours sailing time from Piraeus, the island forms an obvious terminus for those ferries doing a regular daily round trip. A number of ferries continue south to Crete (Iraklion).

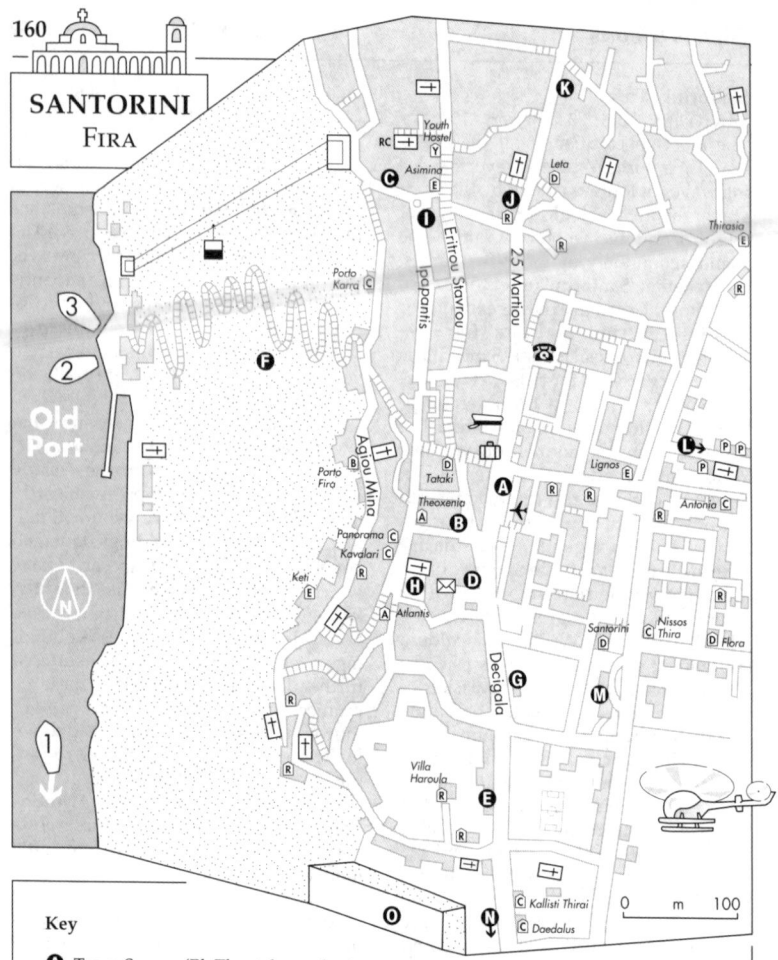

SANTORINI
FIRA

Old Port

3

2

1

Porto Karra

Porto Fira

Panorama

Keti

Atlantis

Villa Haroula

Tataki

Theoxenia

Kavalari

Youth Hostel

Asimina

Leta

Thirasia

Lignas

Antonia

Santorini Thira

Nissos Thira

Flora

Kallisti Thirai

Daedalus

Eritrou Stavrou

Ipopantis

25 Martiou

Agiou Mina

Decigala

RC

0   m   100

Key

A Town Square (Pl. Theotokopoulou)
B National Bank of Greece
C Cable Car Ticket Office
D Bus Station (all destinations)
E Police
F Stairway / Mule track to Old Port
G Public WCs
H Cathedral
I Archaeological Museum
J Municipal Museum
K Old Style (unwhitewashed) Street
L Camping Santorini (200 m)
M Medical Centre
N Road to Port (4 km) & Heliport (2 km)
O Pumice Quarry

1 Athinios Port / Ferry Terminus (4 km)
2 Old Port Tour Boats & Thirasia ferry
3 Cruise Ship taxi boat arrival point

The pretty northern town of **Oia** (otherwise known as Ia) was also badly damaged by the 1956 earthquake. Now rebuilt, it is promoted locally as the 'Paris of the Aegean' for no apparent reason other than its photogenic nature (most of the best picture postcard caldera rim views are of Oia). It has fewer crowds than Fira, a similar staircase down the caldera wall, a reconstructed windmill, and an excellent Naval Museum for good measure. The tiny port below the town has seen occasional ferries stop to deposit passengers into taxi boats in past years.

Being a volcano, Santorini suffers from both a lack of water (most is tankered in and then piped up the cliff face) and brilliant beaches. The black volcanic sand that predominates along the island's coast lacks sparkle and gets painfully hot, leaving sun worshippers looking like rows of pink sausages in a teflon frying pan. The biggest and best resort beach is at **Perissa** with a smaller centre at **Kamari**. Both get very crowded in High Season.

The bulk of the island is dry and treeless; the land being given over to producing tomatoes and the heavy red wine for which Santorini is famous. Dotted around the landscape are a number of villages, which these days serve to mop up the tourists who can't find beds elsewhere. The largest of these such as **Pirgos**, **Emborio** and **Gonia** have become minor centres in their own right. Others, such as **Akrotiri**, still retain much of their traditional character, though in this case things are changing thanks to the nearby Minoan town excavation which provides the substance to the connection of the Atlantis myth with the island.

🛏

Supply of beds dries up early in High Season on Santorini. Even if you arrive on the first of the Piraeus morning boats (berthing around 15.00) you could have to settle for a night in a campsite or hostel before finding something more to your taste. The more expensive hotels tend to lie on the caldera rim (if you choose to stay in one it pays to forget both your bank

balance and the fact that when the last earthquake struck most of the rim-side buildings ended up a lot nearer sea level than they were before). Top of the range, and a landmark in its own right, is the chunky A-class *Atlantis* (☎ 22232). It is followed by B-class *Porto Fira* (☎ 22849). To the north of this hotel is the C-class *Porto Karra* (☎22979), while two more C-class hotels occupy the block up the slope: the *Panorama* (☎ 22481) and *Kavalari* (☎ 22455).

The east side of Fira Town offers the best prospect of finding a bed in High Season, with a number of 'cheaper' hotels. These include the C-class *Nissos Thira* (☎ 23252) and *Antonia* (☎ 22879), the D-class *Santorini* (☎ 22593) and *Flora* (☎ 81524), and the E-class *Lignos* (☎ 23 101) and *Thirasia* (☎ 22546). The road to the campsite is also worth trying as it is lined with pensions. Other hotels lie to the south of the town, including the C-class *Kallisti Thirai* (☎ 22317) and the *Daedalus* (☎ 22834). More hotels are being built to the south, overlooking the ugly old pumice quarry — pretty desperate stuff. The cable-car area of town also has a number of cheaper establishments. These include a good *Youth Hostel* (☎22722) and the E-class *Asimina* (☎ 22034). Inland the D-class *Leta* (☎ 22540) stands near the main road. A final option is to head for the village of **Karterados** which sups up the tourist overspill at the cost of a thirty minute walk into town.

Perissa Beach is also popular with two large hostels — the *Perissa Youth Hostel* and *Youth Hostel Anna*. There are also plenty of pensions and small hotels. Other towns with hotels and rooms include **Oia** — complete with a good *Youth Hostel Oia* (☎ 71465) — and **Pirgos** on the road to the port.

Λ

There are four campsites on Santorini, with mini-buses meeting ferries. *Camping Santorini* (☎ 22944) is the most convenient and with its own swimming-pool lies on the eastern outskirts of Fira town. It is, however, rather pricy: those on a tight budget will do better staying at the youth hostel. Massive *Perissa Beach Camping* (☎ 81343) is an expensive and crowded site behind the beach. *Kamari Camping* (☎ 31453) is less popular since it lies 1 km from its namesake beach and has the nearby airport noise to contend with. Finally, a new site, *Caldera Rim Camping* has recently opened outside the village of Akrotiri. Complete with swimming pool, it is clean but lacks tree cover.

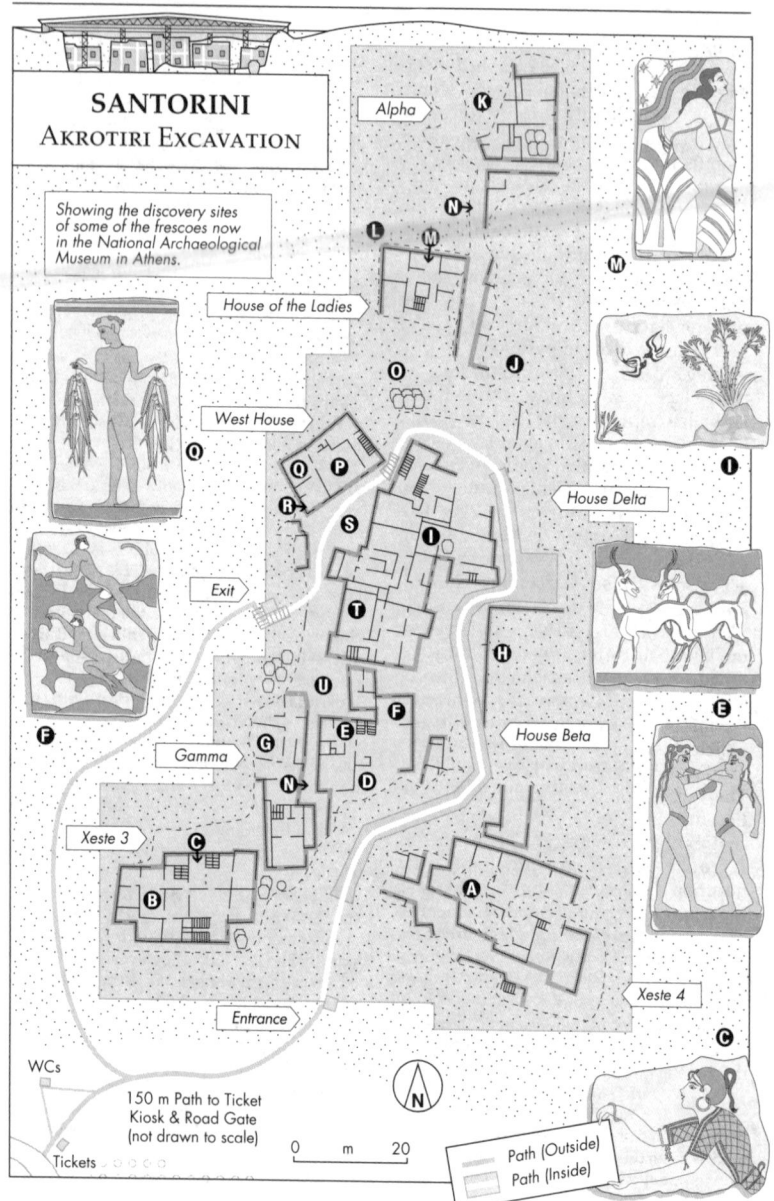

SANTORINI
AKROTIRI EXCAVATION

*Showing the discovery sites
of some of the frescoes now
in the National Archaeological
Museum in Athens.*

Alpha

House of the Ladies

West House

House Delta

Exit

House Beta

Gamma

Xeste 3

Entrance

Xeste 4

WCs

150 m Path to Ticket
Kiosk & Road Gate
(not drawn to scale)

Tickets

N

0   m   20

Path (Outside)
Path (Inside)

∞
The whole 'Thira' archipelago is one vast tourist attraction but there are 3 major sights:
Akrotiri
On the south coast lies the Pompeiian-like Minoan village at Akrotiri adding flesh to the Atlantian atmosphere of Santorini. The 35-century old site was discovered in 1967 and is still under excavation, protected by a tin roof that makes for a stuffy atmosphere. Tourists are confined to a predetermined route. Some 10,000 m² of the site has now been excavated. Estimates as to the town's size range from 30,000 to 200,000 m². Neither the harbour (thought to lie in a now pumice filled inlet west of the current excavation) nor any public buildings (if they exist) have been unearthed. Sadly, the much admired frescos that adorned the buildings' walls and brought international fame have been removed to the National Archaeological Museum in Athens. Buses run direct to the site gate. The entrance fee is 1000 GDR. A good guide to Akrotiri (complete with reconstructions of the fresco rooms) is available on the island. Entitled *Art and Religion in Thera* it is worth reading before you visit.

In the years following the discovery of the Minoan civilization (with the excavation of the palaces on Crete) archaeologists were increasingly wont to ask why they were finding palaces and villas but nothing resembling towns or commercial centres. Their absence implied that they must have existed elsewhere in the Aegean and attention turned to possible sites; notably to Santorini where, in 1867, a fresco-filled house had been uncovered and then subsequently lost. The site near Akrotiri came to light thanks to its location in a ravine: the stream that formed it eroded the layers of pumice to reveal evidence of buildings beneath. Once a prospering 16 c. BC town that — if the street plan revealed to date is typical — looked similar to Greek island *choras* today, it was abandoned by its inhabitants a year or two prior to the eruption that ripped the heart out of the island. Covered by layers of volcanic ash, the quake-damaged buildings, some several stories high, have been preserved.

On entering the site shed you arrive on a ramp running down to the ancient street level. On either side you can see the remains of two major buildings. Both are examples of the first of three types of structure on the site, being large mansions with ashlar block façades. On

the right lies ❹ **Xeste 4**; still yet to be fully explored, it has yielded up only odd fresco fragments from the central staircase region. The building to the left of the path; ❺ **Xeste 3**, has provided much richer finds (though the frescoes have yet to be reassembled from the fragments recovered), with the discovery of the **Monkey Musician fresco** (depicting blue monkeys — a sacred animal in Minoan art — playing lyres and pipes) and ❻ **The Crocus Gatherers** fresco (showing young girls picking blooms). These buildings are the largest single habitations on the site and clearly reserved for the higher ranks of Akrotiri society. They are notable for possessing removable interior wooden panel walls in the major rooms along with 'lustral basins' (which appear to have had some religious use).

At the bottom of the ramp to the right of the path stands ❼ **House Beta**. This is an example of the second type of building, being a large structure filled with small rooms. Their layout and the lack of kitchen facilities (there is usually only one per block) suggests that the inhabitants lived in a communal, rather than family, unit. These houses represent the lowest housing rank. They did, however, have a fresco room like the others, and House Beta has provided us with ❽ the **Boxing Children and Antelope Frescos**, along with ❾ the **Blue Monkey Fresco** (though the latter has been badly damaged by the stream that ran down the site through this room).

Behind House Beta lies a similar type of building: ❿ **House Gamma**. Still only partly excavated, the fresco rooms have yet to come to light. To the right of the tourist path lies the wall of the, as yet unexcavated, ⓫ **Xeste 2**: the third of the mansion type of buildings.

The central part of the excavation is dominated by **House Delta**. Another of the communal living type buildings, it contained the almost complete ⓬ **Lilies (or Spring) Fresco**, depicting a landscape of lilies and swallows. The swallows provide a poignant insight into the changed conditions on the island; for Santorini is now one of the few Aegean islands not to see swallows nesting in the summer (the dry volcanic ash isn't adhesive enough for them to build their mud nests).

The path turns west at this point taking you past the northern section of the site. Currently under excavation, it is inaccessible to tourists. It includes ⓭ an **Unexcavated house** that has one wall exposed, **③** a **Pithoi jar Storehouse** that is several storeys high and where digging commenced in 1967, **④** the **House of the Ladies**; a partially excavated building that has yielded up **⑩** (the **Fresco of the Ladies**) depicting some well-endowed women robing a lost figure, and the **Papyrus Fresco**. Running down the middle of this northern section of the site is **⑪** the **Torrent Bed** and the **Telchines' Road**. The two divide where they join the tourist path; the former running down the east side of the main block, the latter down the west. On top of this main street now stands **⑫** a rather contrived **Pithoi Jar Display**.

Turning south-west at the jar display the path leads on to **⑬** the **West House**. Along with the House of the Ladies, this is an example of the third type of building on the site: being a large independent house for the middle rank of Akrotiri society. Smaller than the mansion type it is nonetheless well adorned with frescos; yielding up **⑩** the **Fisherboy, River** and **Naval Festival Frescos** (the latter being of particular importance as it shows ships and houses of the period). The house also possessed an upstairs bathroom — **⑭** (complete with a latrine connected to a pipe running down inside the external wall). This led to a mains drain under **⑮** the **Triangular Square**. The tourist path runs through this square and then out of the excavation. You can, however, catch a glimpse (through the windows of House Delta) of **⑯** the **Burial Site of Prof. Marinatos** (the site's discoverer) who has been repeatedly buried here; first by a fatal wall collapse in 1974, then — very controversially, on the site — an action that has caused many a grave look from less sentimental archaeologists. If you too, find the wreaths and candles distracting you can always look instead down the **Telchines' Road** to **⑰** the **Mill-House Square**; another of the tiny squares that appear to have played an important part in the town's life.

Ancient Thira

A few centuries after eruption that destroyed the Minoan settlement on Santorini, the fertile volcanic soils brought colonising Doric Greeks to the island. The new centre emerged on the east coast on the high headland north of Perissa and the largely Late Hellenistic and Roman remains of the town can be explored. Consisting mainly of building foundations (including a temple of Dionysos) and a poorly preserved theatre, the site is more of scenic rather than archaeological merit. Its main attractions are a number of faint carvings of an erotic nature on some of the buildings. It is thus a popular destination for island walkers along with Mt. Profitis Ilias, which offers an interesting hike to the radar station and monastery at the top.

Kameni Islands

Since the eruption circa 1500 BC new islands (known as the 'Burnt Islands') have risen out of the caldera in subsequent eruptions. The largest, the volcano islet of **Nea Kameni** (Great Kameni), is a popular sight on the itineraries of all the caldera boat tours; though the sun-baked 20-minute walk to the rather disappointing George I crater that does nothing more than give off a bad smell is not the idyll that it seems from Santorini. Most tour boats also make a call to the hot springs found off the smaller and older island of **Palia Kameni**. This was the first island to emerge from the caldera during an eruption in 196 BC. A second briefly put in an appearance in 46 AD before Mikra Kameni emerged in 1573. Nea Kameni appeared in 1711, was enlarged in the great eruption of 1866–8 when the St. George I crater appeared, and was finally joined with Mikra Kameni in the 1925–26 eruption. As Santorini must be due for another one sooner or later island hoppers should note that before the last two eruptions the waters around the islands have turned a milky colour thanks to the increase in underwater sulphur emissions. If this were to re-occur, catching the next ferry to anywhere is probably a very good idea. For the time being, however, the popularity of the offshore sights is such that Santorini boasts a fleet of small orange and white tourist boats in the employ of various agencies. These craft run various tours; all include visits to Nea Kameni and the hot springs off Palia Kameni. There are three basic tours on offer: the daily Full Day Tour (09.00–18.30) costs £10.50 and takes in the works, including the hot springs at Cape Akrotiri. The Caldera Round Trip (09.00–16.30) is slightly better value at £7.50, and the half-day burnt islands trip (three times daily) is a rather rushed £5. Students receive a 20% reduction on all trips.

☎

CODE 0286, PORT POLICE 22239, TOURIST POLICE 22649, HOSPITAL 22237.

Thirasia

ΘΙΡΑΣΙΑ; 9 km²; pop. 300.

The second largest fragment of the pre-eruption island, Thirasia offers a blissfully quiet alternative to Santorini's crowds. The island — and particularly the chora — is a miniature version of Santorini before mass tourism swamped all. An earlier swamping saved Thirasia from sharing Santorini's fate; for the island was joined to northern Santorini until an eruption in 236 BC collapsed the land bridge between them. Without it, Thirasia remains a relatively quiet island. The main town is perched high on the caldera rim at **Manolas**. Far smaller than Fira (of which it has good views), it is a more irregular and stringy affair, ribboning along the rim without a maze of back-streets behind. In many ways this makes it more attractive; with a windmill adding to its charm (Fira lost all its mills in the 1956 earthquake). Most tourists visit via the caldera rim staircase (boasting 300-steps and the usual donkey transport).

Caldera tour boats (and the weekly High Season Piraeus ferry) stop at the main island port of **Korfos** tucked inside the caldera below Manolas. Surprisingly, it is more substantial than Fira's Old Port and has a pebble beach as well. It is also home to excursion boats running to the volcano and hot springs. Thirasia's second port is located in the isolated northern bay at **Riva**. This is the main stopping point for the daily landing-craft ferry from Santorini. It has a reasonable (and delightfully quiet) beach and a taverna. To the west of the bay lies the church of Agia Irini: a structure of no great architectural distinction, in singular Greek fashion it is notable for giving neighbouring Santorini (literally 'Saint Irene') its name.

The rest of the Thirasia shows considerable scarring thanks to years of heavy pumice quarrying. In fact, much of the island is now lining the banks of the Suez Canal as it was a principal source of both materials and manpower. This activity

also exposed the first 'Minoan' remains to be discovered in the archipelago (in 1869); alerting later archaeologists to its potential. Unfortunately, the site is lost; so there is nothing in the way of sightseeing on the island. Tour buses try to make up for this by stopping at the inland hamlets of **Potamos** (home to an ugly multi-coloured campaniled church) and **Agrilia**, but are unable to reach the more interesting southern tip of Thirasia which has the 1851-built Kimisis monastery. This is accessed via a caldera rim path from Manolas (which passes through an abandoned and catacombed village of Kera).

⊨

There are no hotels on Thirasia, but quayside tavernas at Korfos offer rooms, as do tavernas in the town above (near the top of the staircase).

☎

CODE 0286.

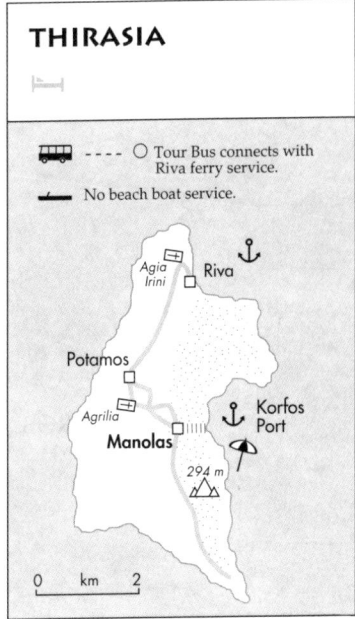

THIRASIA

⊨

🚌 - - - - ○ Tour Bus connects with Riva ferry service.

⚓ No beach boat service.

Agia Irini   Riva ⚓

Potamos

Agrilia   Korfos Port ⚓

Manolas

294 m ⛰

0   km   2

5
CYCLADES NORTH

ANDROS · DELOS · EVIA · MYKONOS · SYROS · TINOS

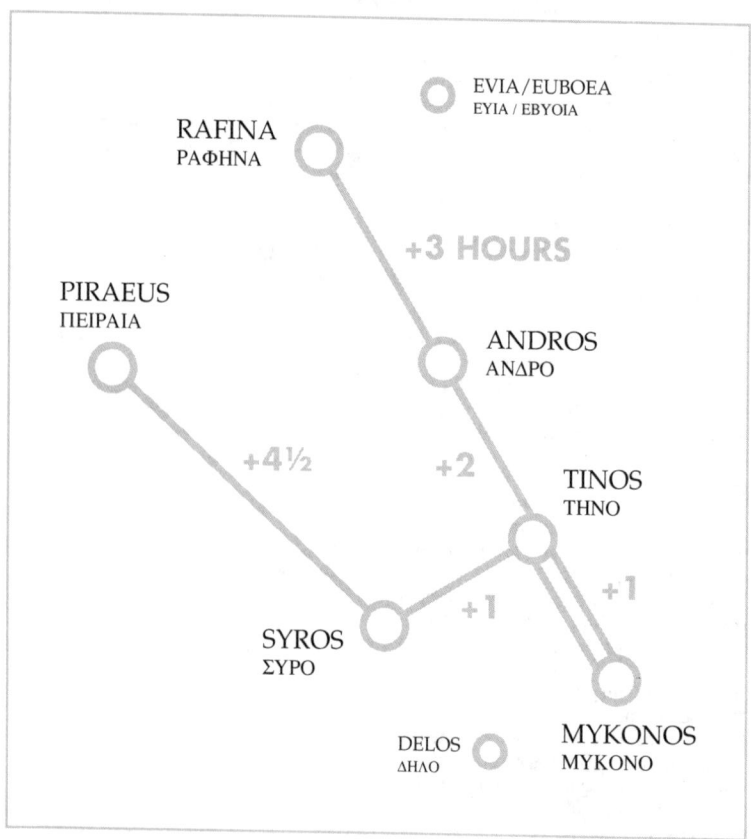

EVIA/EUBOEA
EYIA / EBYOIA

RAFINA
ΡΑΦΗΝΑ

+3 HOURS

PIRAEUS
ΠΕΙΡΑΙΑ

ANDROS
ΑΝΔΡΟ

+4½

+2

TINOS
THNO

+1

+1

SYROS
ΣΥΡΟ

DELOS
ΔΗΛΟ

MYKONOS
MYKONO

General Features

The Northern Cyclades Line covers those Cycladic islands to the east of Piraeus and the 'Athenian' port of Rafina and is served by daily boats from both. The islands lying along this line include the former Mecca of the Greek World — the sacred island of Delos (birthplace of the God Apollo) and its modern equivalent; the island of Tinos (home to the most important shrine of the Orthodox church in Greece). Delos, lies in theory if not in fact, at the centre of the Cyclades. While all the islands vary greatly in their characteristics, the one feature common to all is a tendency to be extremely windy. The *meltemi* 'hits' these Greek islands the hardest and they form something of a buffer for the rest of the Cyclades. Cosmopolitan Mykonos and its satellite Delos remain the best known islands on this line, the former being numbered among the most popular of all the Greek

islands. Syros is often mentioned in older guide books as being the hub of the Cycladic ferry network as its 19 c. commercial port of Ermoupolis is the formal capital of the group; however, the island has faded into relative obscurity and can now only boast half the number of ferry sailings of its southern neighbour Paros. The remaining islands are very much orientated to Greek rather than international tourism. Andros and Evia (now little more than an extension of the Greek mainland) remain well off the beaten track. Tinos is less so, thanks to the constant stream of locals enjoying a spot of religious pilgrimage and has hordes of little old ladies descending upon it to join the — mainly package — tourists at the height of the season for the feast of the Assumption of the Virgin Mary. As for little Giaros, it does not figure on ferry schedules as it is now an assault course for the military, with access prohibited.

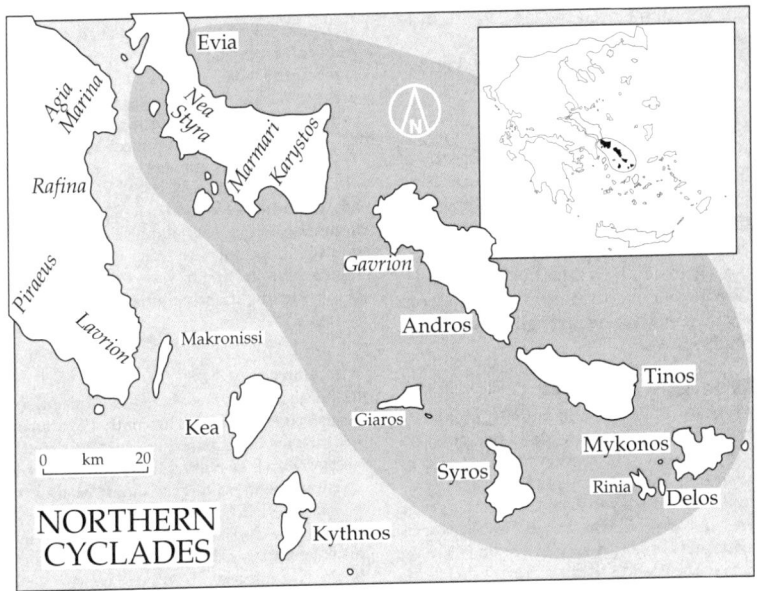

Suggested Itinerary
[2 Weeks]

The two ferry routes running out of Piraeus and Rafina that meet at Mykonos combine to provide a nice island hopping circuit that is both easy and for the inexperienced reasonably safe. Boats are sufficiently frequent down both lines for you to be sure of a daily boat up and down at least one of the lines even out of High Season.

Arrival/Departure Point

Two easy alternatives: Athens and Mykonos. Athens is usually the cheaper of the two and with far more frequent flights into the bargain. You can do the loop easily from either base. Mykonos is chosen here as it offers a more relaxed start and end to a holiday and a pleasant alternative to arrive at and rushing back to Athens. The other ports on the route are well worth visiting for a few hours but you don't need to stay overnight to see such as there is to see; the loop to Athens can effectively be undertaken as a long weekend excursion.

Season

As Mykonos is served by boats out of both Piraeus and Rafina, ferry links tend to be better either end of the High Season than elsewhere. The result is that from early June to the end of October coverage is very good down the line. During the Low Season a single ferry service from Piraeus and Rafina normally operates on alternate days.

1 Mykonos [4 Days]

Mykonos offers the opportunity for a very relaxed start to a Greek Island holiday. You can happily idle away the first few days of your stay with day trips to Delos and Paros and even Tinos if you want to cut corners later on. In-between you can tilt at Mykonos windmills and start an all-over body tan on one of the island's many naturist beaches.

2 3 Tinos/Andros [1 Day]

If you take the daily 08.00 Mykonos—Rafina ferry to Tinos you'll arrive in time for a late breakfast. An interesting day stop, you can either stay overnight or have the option of picking up the afternoon boat to Andros (note; accommodation is thin on the ground there) or on to Rafina where you can take an evening bus into Athens.

4 5 Rafina/Athens [4 Days]

If you are not tied to budget accommodation it will be to your advantage to pre-book your Athens hotel accommodation while on Mykonos via one of the ticket agents. It will be hard not to arrive in the capital at any other time than the evenings (hardly an ideal time to start hunting for your bed). Thereafter you will be free to explore at your own pace and adjust the length of your stay as your fancy takes you.

6 Syros [1 Day]

On the schedule of Piraeus—Mykonos ferries, Syros offers an interesting day out. The difficulty comes in getting off the island since the Mykonos link is usually only once daily. If you don't fancy staying here you might have to repair to Tinos or Paros for the night. After Athens you could find Syros something of an anti-climax; but the island does ensure that you appreciate how much nicer Mykonos is during the rest of your stay.

1 Mykonos [4 Days]

Returning with plenty of days to spare gives you the scope for a relaxing finish to your holiday. Not having to worry about missing your return flight is something not to be under-estimated.

Alternative

Rather than returning via Syros, **Paros** offers an attractive alternative (or for that matter an addition to your itinerary). A stop here could necessitate a stay overnight — though if you arrive in the morning you should be able to pick up the C/F *Express Paros* on her evening run back to Mykonos. A Paros stop would also open up possible calls to Naxos, Ios and Santorini for those with time to hand.

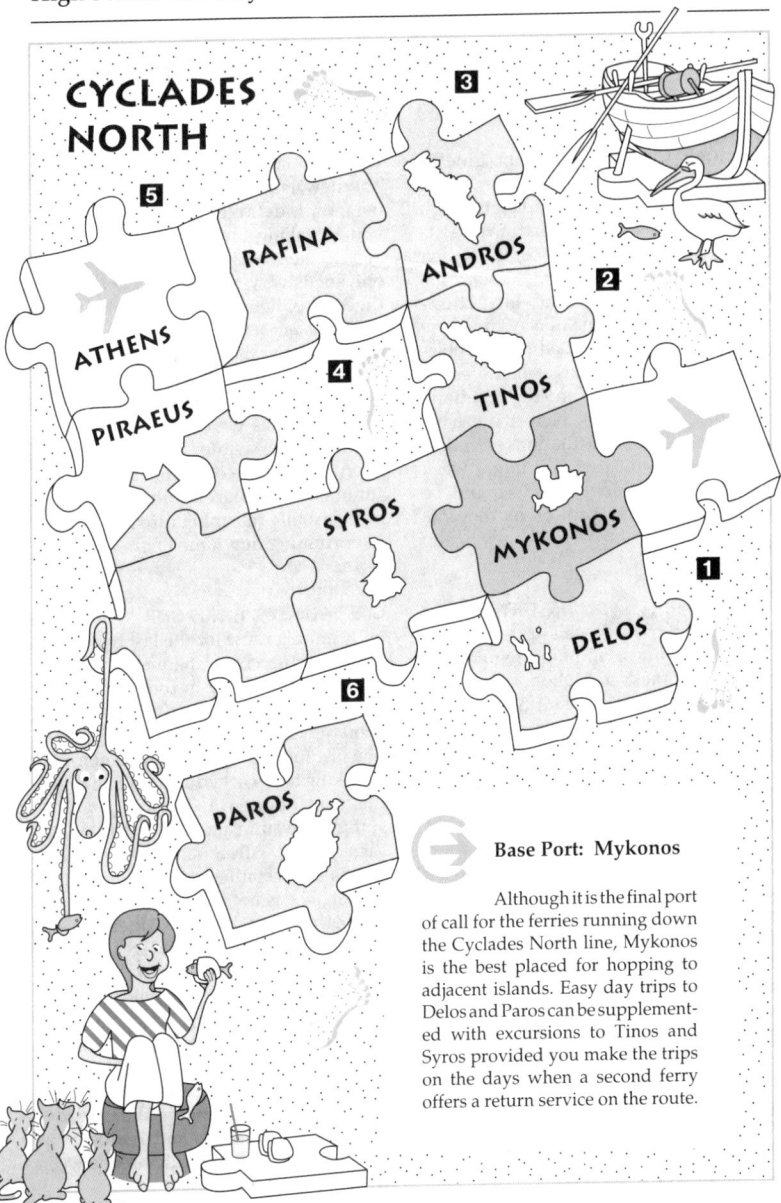

CYCLADES NORTH

5

3

RAFINA

ANDROS

ATHENS

PIRAEUS

2

4

TINOS

SYROS

MYKONOS

DELOS

1

6

PAROS

Base Port: Mykonos

Although it is the final port of call for the ferries running down the Cyclades North line, Mykonos is the best placed for hopping to adjacent islands. Easy day trips to Delos and Paros can be supplemented with excursions to Tinos and Syros provided you make the trips on the days when a second ferry offers a return service on the route.

Cyclades North Ferry Services

Main Car Ferries

Although the Cyclades East Line is defined within this section as a single line, in practice it is not a complete through route. Daily ferries run both from Piraeus (to Syros, Tinos and Mykonos) and Rafina (to Andros, Tinos, and Mykonos); the combination of the two sub-lines effectively forming the 'line'. Ferry times are reasonably well established. More problematic are the fewer longer-haul vessels that run down the line and then continue on into other groups. Here there have been considerable fluctuations in the last few seasons, and the 2—3 day a week island-direct linkings listed should be treated with some caution as they are dependent on comparatively few boats.

C/F Naias II

Agapitos Ferries; 1966; 4555 GRT.

The first of two vessels (operated by 'competing' lines) running a regular service from Piraeus to Mykonos, the *Naias II* has been on the route for many years, first as an independent ferry, and latterly as part of the Agapitos Line fleet. Her sister is the notoriously awful *Golden Vergina* and this tells you all that you need to know about this boat too; for she is slow and grimy and is, for many tourists, a less than happy introduction to the Greek ferry scene. This is a boat that gets you where you want to go but offers nothing more: so much so that it is to be hoped that her days are numbered. On the plus side her day-time schedule has seen little change over the years (and is odd insofar as she calls at Syros only on alternate days). The recent provision of High Season overnight services — often running via islands down the chain before returning direct to Piraeus — has been less consistent, with some changes to itineraries and days each year.

C/F Panagia Tinou 2

Ventouris Sea Lines; 1973; 5071 GRT.

The 'new' boat on the line, this slick-looking ferry is definitely the vessel to take if you are taking a morning boat from Piraeus to the islands. Easily the best kitted out, she is very reliable, taking over the itinerary of her predecessor on the route — the *Panagia Tinou* (which has latterly been roaming the Aegean in search of a new billet). Unlike her rival, the *Panagia Tinou 2* calls at Syros every day during the summer as well as taking the four-times-weekly winter service running down this section of the line. During the summer she makes additional evening runs (usually returning direct to Piraeus after running down the line).

C/F Dimitra

G.A. Ferries; 1971; 3715 GRT.

Now on this route for the last five years, the *Dimitra* (ex cross-Channel *Earl Harold*) is the smallest ferry in the G.A. Ferries fleet. She is nonetheless a comfortable enough boat even if she isn't the fastest. The last four summers have seen minor tweaking to her schedules, and no doubt this will happen again in 1995. Last summer saw unusual calls at Patmos and Lipsi, along with an additional visit to Astipalea to her itinerary. Reliable in High Season, she is not so consistent over the rest of the year, when she is often missing for no obvious reason. Her departure times for outward runs from Piraeus are poorly advertised on Tinos and Mykonos (where agents prefer to promote her as an Athens-bound boat) so don't be misled into believing she isn't running to islands further afield. In this respect she plays a very useful role in linking the Cyclades East line to Amorgos and Astipalea as well as providing a weekly link between Mykonos and Samos.

Naias II

☼ i/6—iv/10

Panagia Tinou 2

◇

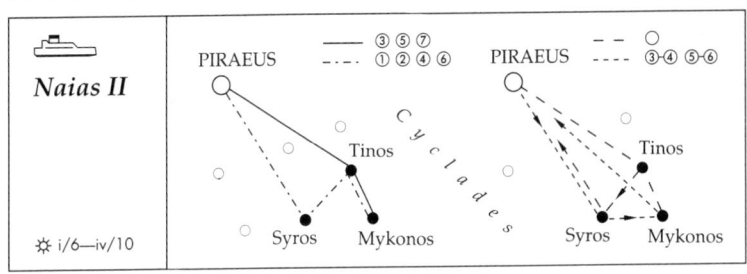

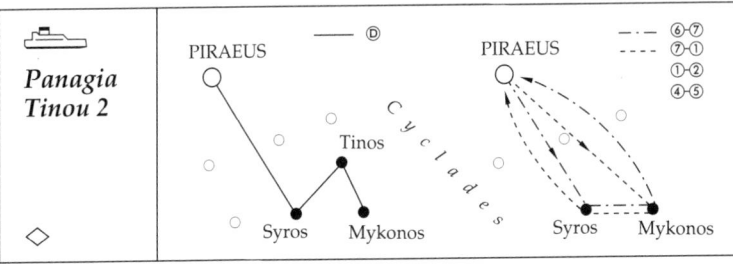

Dimitra

☼ i/7—iv/9

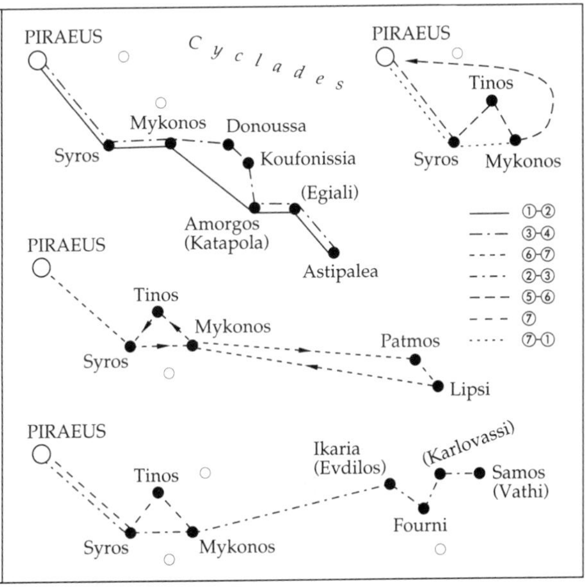

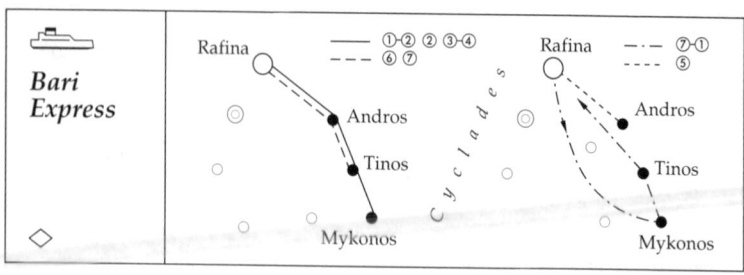

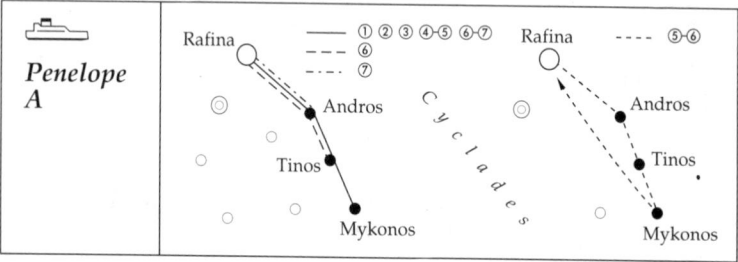

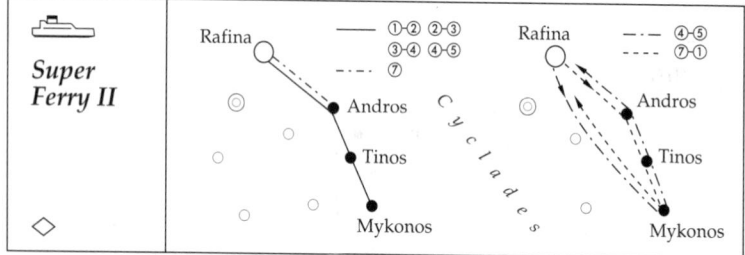

C/F *Bari Express*

Ventouris Ferries; 1968; 3397 GRT.

In recent years the Rafina—Mykonos branch of the Cyclades North line has seen some quite vicious competition between the three main ferry players. This involved ferries literally racing each other down the line, with local TV interviewing ferry captains et al. This all changed in 1994 with the introduction of a joint timetable. The *Bari Express*, now the oldest boat operating down the line,

lost her lucrative Mykonos morning departure, but has gained in as much as she isn't forced to compete directly with her better fitted out former rivals. This said, although she is now rather long in the tooth, she is very reliable and onboard facilities are adequate (though they have a utilitarian feel). As her name implies, she formerly operated across the Adriatic. Rumours that she is to be replaced have circulated for several years without coming to anything to date.

C/F *Penelope A*
Agoudimos Lines; 1972; 5109 GRT.

Over the last few years a small company — Agoudimos Lines — have operated a single vessel out of Rafina. Schedules have been inconsistent since this boat appeared in 1992 (though this should not be a problem as long as joint operations down the line continue). Formerly the cross-Channel *Horsa*, the *Penelope A* is the same class of vessel as the two *Apollo Express* boats now in the Ventouris fleet, and company insignia aside, she looks identical. On-board facilities however, are a touch above her former stable-mates: the competition on this route forced Agoudimos to fit her up in style.

C/F *Super Ferry II*
Strintzis Lines; 1974; 5052 GRT.

Now undoubtedly the premier boat on the line, the well-equipped *Super Ferry II* is an escalator and a patisserie ahead of her rivals. Her open-deck plan is also far in advance of the competition and she feels ten years newer than the *Penelope A* although she is barely two. Distinctly 'chunky' in appearance, this large and unwieldy boat initially encountered docking problems in the small island ports (enabling her rivals to consistently nip in ahead of her on runs down the line). However she has got her manoeuvring down to a fine art and is quite zippy even in Mykonos's tiny harbour. A good overnight boat thanks to the space available, her sole drawback is that backpackers are 'encouraged' to leave packs in the tiny luggage room at the top of the escalator.

	See also:

- C/F *Anemos* — p. 326
- C/F *Express Paros* — p. 136
- P/S *Mykonos Express* — p. 137
- P/S *Skopelitis* — p. 229

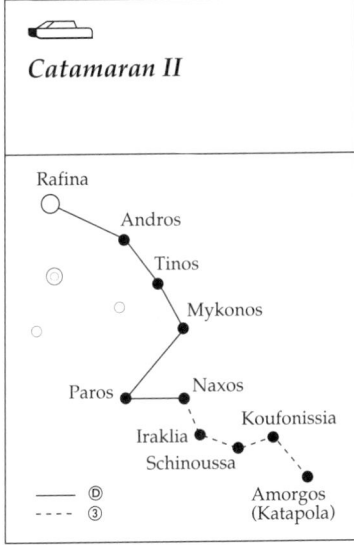

Catamaran II

C/M *Catamaran II*
For the last few years catamarans have provided a popular and fast way of negotiating the islands of the Central and Northern Cyclades. Unfortunately, the service was severely curtailed in 1993 when the *Catamaran I* demolished her port side in collision (she now sits forlornly on Quay 11 of Piraeus (Great Harbour). Her companion has been struggling to make a go of things ever since. Times and starting port seem to be in a constant state of change (she has now operated out of Piraeus (Flisvos), Piraeus (Great Harbour) and most recently Rafina; all in the space of four summers). Expect further changes in 1995. On board conditions are good, though in choppy seas you will get thrown about a bit (particularly in the unsheltered waters off Amorgos) and be anything up to two hours late. Note: seats at the bow take the biggest bumps; with a succession of second-rate on-board video films doing nothing to make viewers feel less queasy.

ILIO Hydrofoils

Among the ILIO services running out of Rafina (for the others see p. 138 and 203) are a number specific to the Northern Cyclades. Growing in popularity, they have increased in 1992 and 1993 only to be cut back somewhat in the summer of 1994. Schedules are thus still very erratic, and ILIO do themselves no favours by their inability to publish monthly timetables before they come into effect. As a result, these are craft to look out for but never to rely on. The only consistent feature to date has been a daily service down the Rafina branch of the Cyclades North line to Mykonos (often continuing on to Paros and Naxos). These runs include occasional calls at the otherwise unconnected Tinos village of Isternia (or more accurately, Ag. Nikitas beach nearby). Hydrofoils visiting Andros have also taken to calling at Batsi rather than the ferry port of Gavrion of late. Irregular, but frequent hydrofoils also operate to an odd assortment of ports on the Evian coast as well as the mainland up to Chalcis (where they invariably stop overnight). Out of High Season all routes see a great reduction in services.

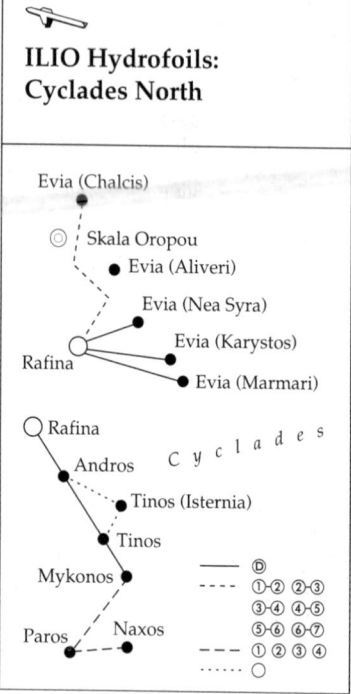

ILIO Hydrofoils: Cyclades North

H/F *Hermes*

Looking more like a jet-boat than a conventional hydrofoil, this new orange and blue vessel was proudly tied up in Rafina in the summer of 1994. Despite the fact that she was quite widely advertised as running a daily service (to Syros, Paros, Naxos, the Little Cyclades and Amorgos), she never seemed to go anywhere: a boat to look out for — perhaps?

C/F *Karistos*

Goutos Lines; 1968; 830 GRT.

A small Greek-built ferry that rattles daily between Rafina and the port of Karystos on Evia. Her hull, painted (uniquely among Goutos Lines boats) in a snappy racing green, is the only thing fast about her. If she wasn't providing an 'essential'

link service she would be a top candidate in the 'next tub for the scrap-yard' stakes, as it is she is set to crawl and crawl. As with the *Marmari I* below, timetables see minor changes every other month.

C/F *Marmari I*

Goutos Lines; 1961; 1492 GRT.

A venerable ferry well into old age, this boat makes the Rafina—Evia (Marmaris) run several times daily. Slightly larger than the *Karistos*, she occasionally puts in at Karystos. Painted in a natty blue, she operates out of (Evia) Marmaris. On-board facilities are distinctly utilitarian, but ferry buffs will love her; she is such a period piece: a ferry relic that even *looks* like something from the steam train era.

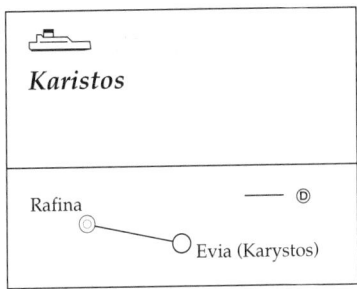

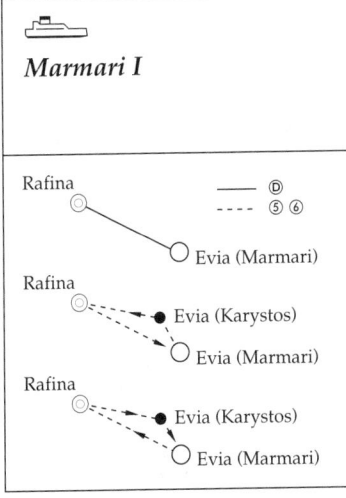

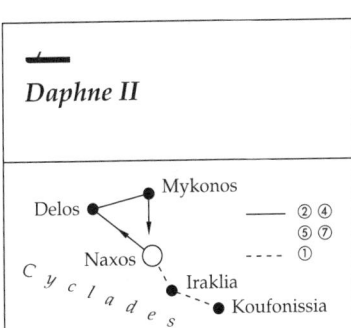

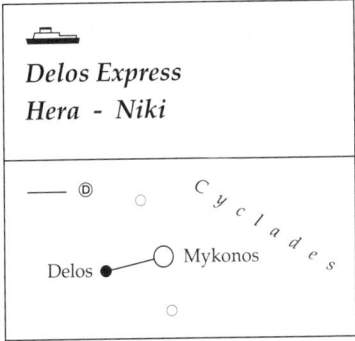

Delos Tour Boats
The island of Delos is only accessible via tourist boats. The best run direct from Mykonos each morning giving you about three hours on Delos. The P/S *Hera* is the largest and most comfortable of the three, the P/S *Niki* and P/S *Delos Express* run more frequently but being smaller, roll about much more. Tour boats from Tinos, Naxos and Paros also visit Delos, but as they include a stop at Mykonos tend to divide their time roughly 1½ to 3 hours in favour of the latter. The Naxian *Daphni II* is the best of these boats. The P/S *Megalochari* is a 1959-built rust bucket. Top-side seating gives tourists a 'hole' new experience; those carrying planks of wood will find themselves at a distinct advantage.

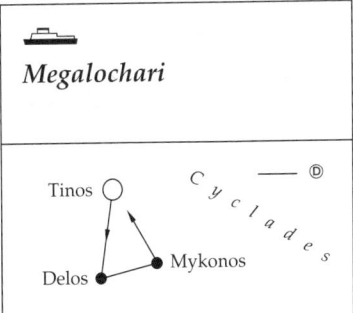

⚓ Cyclades North Islands & Ports

Andros

ΑΝΔΡΟΣ; 380 km², pop. 9020.

Despite being the second largest and most northerly of the Cyclades, Andros is only slowly edging its way onto the tourist map. A combination of rich vegetation and mountains have failed to bring the crowds. The only obvious reason for such a paradox is the lack of any notable population centre; for Andros really has a lot going for it if a downbeat understated beach holiday is your kind of thing. The locals of course have long been in the know, and like Kea, Andros has thus been the preserve of Greek, rather than foreign, tourists with many of the better-off Athenians having villas on this minor

gem among islands. The great majority of tourists spend their time on the south coast, split between the ferry port of Gavrion, and the tourist village of Batsi to the east. Relatively few venture across the island to the capital of Andros Town.

Most visitors arrive by ferry and thus find themselves deposited at the port of **Gavrion**. Set in a deep inlet it consists of an intimidatingly large ferry quay backed by a little port village strung along the waterfront behind. All the usual facilities (including a tourist information office housed in an old dovecote) lie along the shore: Gavrion is one of those 'what you can't see isn't there' sort of places, besides usually being very windy. Island buses

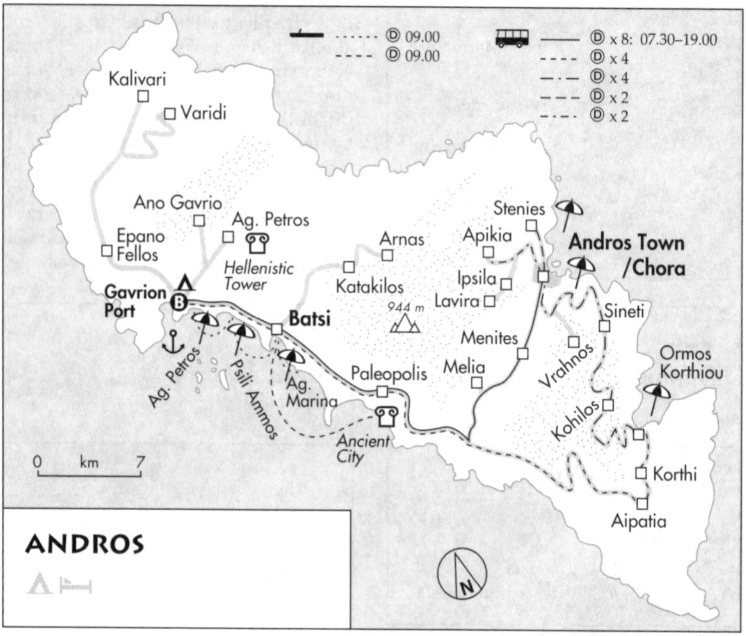

Map legend:
- ●···· ⓓ 09.00
- ---- ⓓ 09.00
- 🚌 —— ⓓ x 8: 07.30–19.00
- ---- ⓓ x 4
- —·— ⓓ x 4
- --- ⓓ x 2
- ─··─ ⓓ x 2

Map labels:
Kalivari
Varidi
Ano Gavrio
Epano Fellos
Ag. Petros
Hellenistic Tower
Gavrion Port
Batsi
Ag. Petros
Psili Ammos
Ag. Marina
Paleopolis
Ancient City
Arnas
Katakilos
944 m
Lavira
Melia
Stenies
Apikia
Ipsila
Menites
Vrahnos
Sineti
Kohilos
Andros Town /Chora
Ormos Korthiou
Korthi
Aipatia

0 km 7

ANDROS

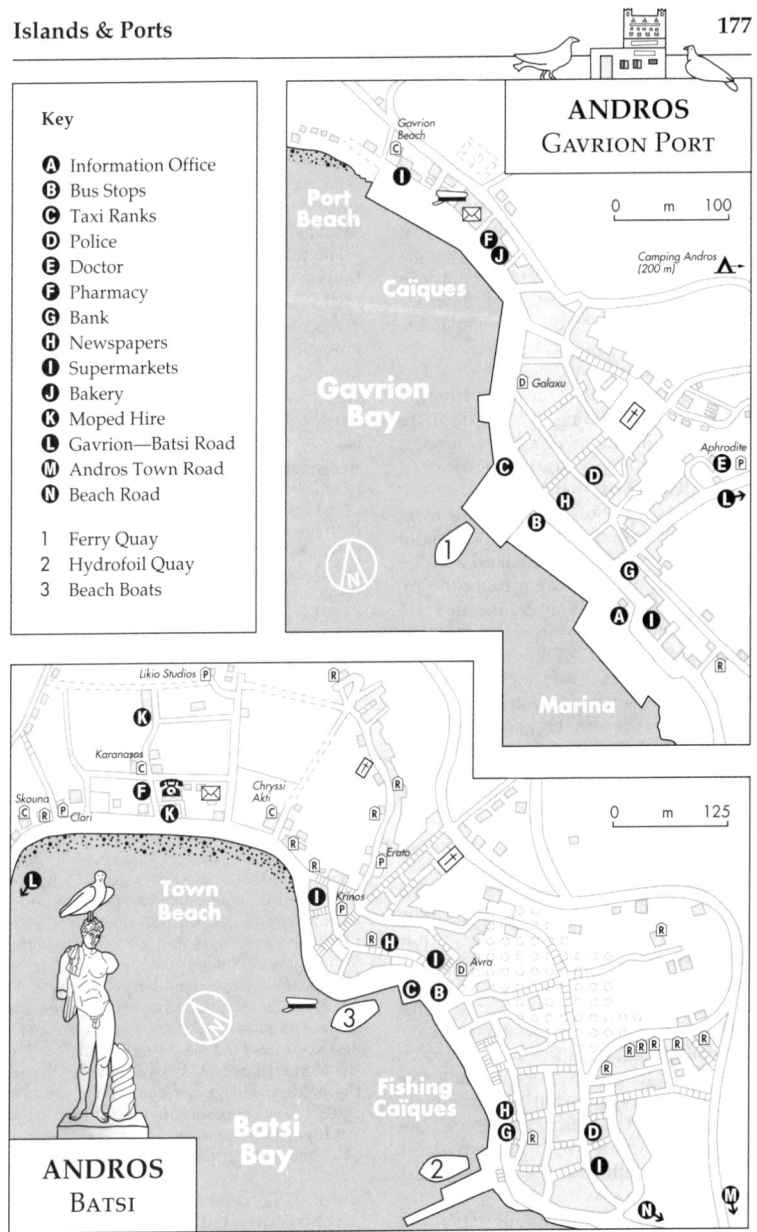

Key

Ⓐ Information Office
Ⓑ Bus Stops
Ⓒ Taxi Ranks
Ⓓ Police
Ⓔ Doctor
Ⓕ Pharmacy
Ⓖ Bank
Ⓗ Newspapers
Ⓘ Supermarkets
Ⓙ Bakery
Ⓚ Moped Hire
Ⓛ Gavrion—Batsi Road
Ⓜ Andros Town Road
Ⓝ Beach Road

1 Ferry Quay
2 Hydrofoil Quay
3 Beach Boats

ANDROS
GAVRION PORT

Gavrion Beach

Port Beach

Caïques

Gavrion Bay

0   m   100

Camping Andros
(200 m)

Galaxu

Aphrodite

Marina

ANDROS
BATSI

Likio Studios

Karanasos

Skouna

Clari

Town Beach

Chryssi Akti

Erato

Krinos

Avra

0   m   125

Batsi Bay

Fishing Caïques

(centred on Andros Town; Gavrion times are posted up in some shops and ticket agents) turn around by the ferry quay before running back along the coast to the capital.

The island capital, **Andros Town** (also known as Chora), is something of a disappointment and just about deserves inclusion in a 'island capitals one can afford to miss' list. Sited on a wind-buffeted, finger-narrow peninsula, the majority of the buildings are typical neo-classical 19 c. piles of the uglier kind. The main street dominates the town, running its length, and ending in a small square adorned with an ugly bronze of a sailor waving out to sea across the remains of a long abandoned Venetian kastro. The lovely bus ride (just over an hour from Gavrion — it is one of the cheapest island tours around) across the island and the better than average town museum are the only reasons to venture this far.

The main tourist resort on Andros is at **Batsi** (in Greek ΜΠΑΤΣΙ) some 8 km east of Gavrion. Unashamedly a tourist town, it has developed from a tiny hamlet since the last war to become the island's premier resort. Given that it is so new, the town has managed to acquire a surprising amount of character with an attractive and lively waterfront (it is easy to see why some tourists return regularly). Thereafter it is divided into two halves by a tree-filled valley, with the east (and older side of the town) clambering rapidly up a stair-case cluttered hillside, while the western 'hotel strip' end lies along the plain behind the beach. However, there is little to see beyond the sea and the usual collection of tourist tavernas and bars.

Batsi's importance to tourists has grown of late as it has taken over Gavrion's role as the island's hydrofoil and catamaran port; no doubt because these vessels offer the only means by which the town's large tourist population can go day-tripping to other islands. It is also the base for the island's beach boats with daily departures

to a number of good sand beaches in the coves and bays either side of the town. Most are accessible from the well made main road, and Andros is one island where moped hire can be an advantage since you can thus guarantee a stretch of sand beach all for your very own.

The rest of the island remains virtually tourist free: Andros is a good island to visit if unspoilt hill villages filled with dovecots (a legacy of the period of Venetian rule) appeals. For a detailed assessment of each (along with suggested island walks) you should seek out *A Practical Guide to Andros*, which is on sale locally.

⊨

Accommodation is thinly spread around the island. In **Gavrion** the waterfront *Galexu* (☎ 71228) offers rooms for the desperate along with the better *Gavrion Beach* (☎ 71312). **Batsi** is host to the bulk of the island's accommodation, with the *Chryssi Akti* (☎ 41236), *Skouna* (☎ 41240) and *Karanasos* (☎ 41480) — complete with restaurant — being augmented by several pensions and plenty of hillside rooms. In **Andros Town** options are fewer. Best bet is the C-class *Egli* (☎ 22303), just off the High St.

Λ

Camping Andros (☎ 71444): reasonable site just behind Gavrion, complete with pool.

👓

Sightseeing is limited on Andros as the major archaeological sites have yet to be explored. The most accessible object of interest is a 20 m high **Hellenistic Tower**: a 3 km hour long hike inland from Gavrion. Known as the 'Tower of Agios Petros', conjecture varies wildly as to its purpose and age, with Mycenaean to Byzantine dates being suggested. The remains of the ancient city of **Paleopolis** offer an attractive boat excursion from Batsi. Largely unexcavated, the ancient capital (from 600 BC to 500 AD) is sited down a steep path off the town road and also under the sea. Tourists visit to enjoy the pretty valley walk between the beach and the modern village. Of ruins there are few signs; the most notable discovery being in the **Andros Town Museum**: a 2 c. BC marble copy of a bronze statue of Hermes by Praxiteles.

☎

CODE 0282, GAVRION POLICE 71220, ANDROS TOWN POLICE 22300.

Delos

ΔΗΛΟΣ; 3.6 km², pop. 20.

In an effort to escape the amorous attentions of the god Zeus, a wench named Asteria ignored the maxim that no man is an island and in desperation contrived to metamorphosise into one, drifting where tide and current would take her, sometimes above the surface, sometimes submerged. Not unnaturally, this did nothing for ancient ferry schedules and Poseidon finally intervened and anchored Asteria to the sea-floor off Mykonos: the island becoming known as Delos (visible). Leto, another of Zeus's lovers, landed here and gave birth to the twin deities Apollo (the most popular of all the Greek gods) and his sister Artemis. Not unnaturally with a background of sex and religion Delos became the leading spiritual centre in Ancient Greece. This role was bolstered by a quadrennial games festival on a par with the Olympics and an important subsidiary role as the trade centre of the Aegean. The ruined complex of temples and markets (abandoned in the Middle Ages; so uncluttered by the accretion of later building) is now one of the premier archaeological sites in Greece. That said, the extant structures are mostly confined to foundations and mosaics thanks to a history of gradual demolition.

The initial spate of building developed around a Temple of Apollo built when the sanctuary emerged as an important site in the early 7 c. BC (largely under Naxian patronage). In 540 BC this sanctification process went a stage further when Delos underwent a form of ritual purification with the removal of all graves to neighbouring Rinia island. In 426 BC it was made illegal to give birth or die on the island. This policy is still maintained today via a ban on overnight stays. If that was not discouragement enough, the only hotel has been in ruins for 1600 years.

Acting as a neutral mini-Switzerland between the warring Greek city states, Delos became the nominal centre of the

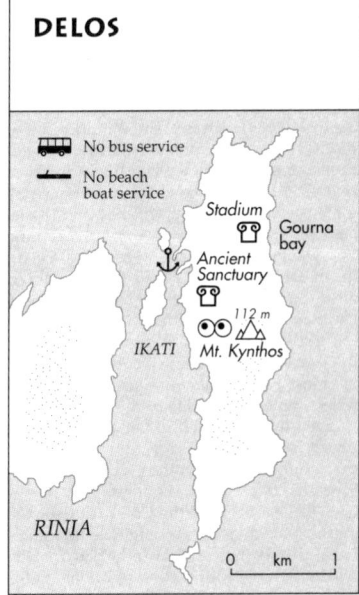

anti-Persian alliance following the repulsed Persian invasion of Greece. The Delian League (as the alliance was known) was soon dominated by Athens; and this led to effective political control of Delos passing to Athens. Thereafter, under Athenian patronage, the commercial aspect of Delos became ascendant, with the island becoming the largest slave market in the Med. Strabo estimated that on a typical day 10,000 slaves would change masters. The wealth that came with this trade brought about the island's downfall. Sacked in 88 and 69 BC, Delos never recovered. Abandoned by her rich patrons, and her trade functions recentred elsewhere, she was all but abandoned once Christianity destroyed her religious role. Thereafter the tiny population did a brisk trade in masonry before being driven away when Delos became a pirate base in the Middle Ages.

👓

Visitors to Delos should bring a sunhat, good shoes and beverages. Most tour boats operate out of Mykonos arriving at 1; a mole built out of the debris from the excavations. In poor sea conditions they occasionally berth at 2 in Gourna Bay. There is a site entrance fee of 1000 GDR (this is included in the price of *some* agency tours — check when buying) which also includes entrance to the museum. Also establish how long you will have on the island; different tours stay from 1½ to 3½ hours. You will need 2—3 hours in order to visit all the major features on the site (all are marked with stones inscribed in English and Greek). Delos was already off the tourist trail when the 2 C. AD writer Pausanias wrote his guide to Greece: so the names of buildings are, for the most part, unknown. Their current titles reflect contents, function or the excavators.

Given the summer heat, an anti-clockwise circuit is recommended as you can attempt the summit of Mt. Kynthos while still fresh. From the ticket kiosk the main path moves onto **Ⓐ** The **Agora of the Competialists**; the marketplace dividing the religious and commercial areas of the site. Taking the path into the residential area you will find secondary paths leading off to **Ⓑ** the **House of Cleopatra**; (named after a statue to be seen within) and the first of the 'mosaic' houses, **Ⓒ** the **House of the Trident**. The path eventually emerges in the theatre area. Behind the stage is a roofless **Ⓓ** Cistern. This stored rainwater running off the now badly preserved **Theatre Ⓔ**. From here the main path ascends steeply east to the mosaic **Ⓕ** House of the Masks and **Ⓖ** House of the Dolphins. Above these it divides, with one branch stepping up to the summit of **Mt. Kynthos** on which lie a few slippery foundation stones of **Ⓗ** the **Sanctuary of Kynthian Zeus & Athena** and a superb view. Many take one look at the irregular steps and take the other branch of the path instead; running past **Ⓘ** the foundations of a small **Heraion** (a temple to the goddess Hera). North of this is a well preserved arched **Temple of Isis Ⓙ** with **Ⓚ** the **Sanctuaries of the Foreign Gods** clustered around a small religious amphitheatre.

The main path now descends to the museum, with a small path branching off to the west. Along it lies one of the few buildings to have survived beyond the foundations; **Ⓛ** the two-storey **House of Hermes**, as well as a **Temple**

of **Aphrodite** and an early basilica. Returning to the main path, head onto the **Museum** with a model of the site as well as some of the more interesting finds — mainly sculpture, mosaics and wall paintings. The path north of the museum divides into a track running over the site of the (now lost) **Hippodrome** to **Ⓜ** the **Gymnasium & Stadium.** (Set aside from the rest of the site you really need to be on a 3 hour trip in order to take them in along with everything else.) The other path runs over the old city wall past the birthplace of Apollo: **Ⓝ** the **Sacred Lake**. Dry since 1925, it is surrounded by a modern stone wall and contains a commemorative palm tree (Leto gave birth hanging from one) and various shady shrubs. To the north lies **Ⓞ** the **Palaestra** and **Ⓟ** the **House of the Comedians & Poseidoniasts of Berytos**. To the east of these is **Ⓠ** the famous **Terrace of the Lions**. Thought to have once been up to 16 strong, only 5 survive (a 6th is now outside the Arsenal in Venice: the Greek government has lately requested its return). South of the Lake is **Ⓡ** the large **Agora of the Italians**. West of this lies the foundations of **Ⓢ** the **Dodekatheon**. Behind which lies **Ⓣ** the **Stoa of Poseidon** (the absence of columns amid the capitals is a clear sign of deliberate demolition). To the south lies **Ⓤ** the **Agora of Theophrastos** bounded by a **Temple to Demeter** and **Ⓥ** the **Artemision** (a temple to Artemis) to the east. Near the north-west corner of this temple lies the divided torso of a 6 C. BC monumental **Kouroi** of the god Apollo. Four times life-size, it was known as the **Colossal Statue of the Naxians** and was drawn in 1673; complete with its now missing head. It originally stood just to the south-west of the great temple of Apollo.

Beyond the Artemision is the main sanctuary area (now a confused mass of rubble). Along the north side (toward the museum) runs **Ⓦ** the **Stoa of Antigonos**. At the museum end is a **Sanctuary of Dionysos** (adorned with two broken giant phalli on pillars). South of the Stoa are the remains of a group of **4 Treasuries** running east to west, and south of these are the foundations of three temples to Apollo the most southerly being **Ⓧ** the **Great Temple of Apollo**, built on the founding of the Delian League in 478 BC. Running south the main path enters the **Sacred Way**: the processional road to the sanctuary, bounded by **Ⓨ** the **Stoa of Phillip** and **Ⓩ** the **Agora of the Delians**.

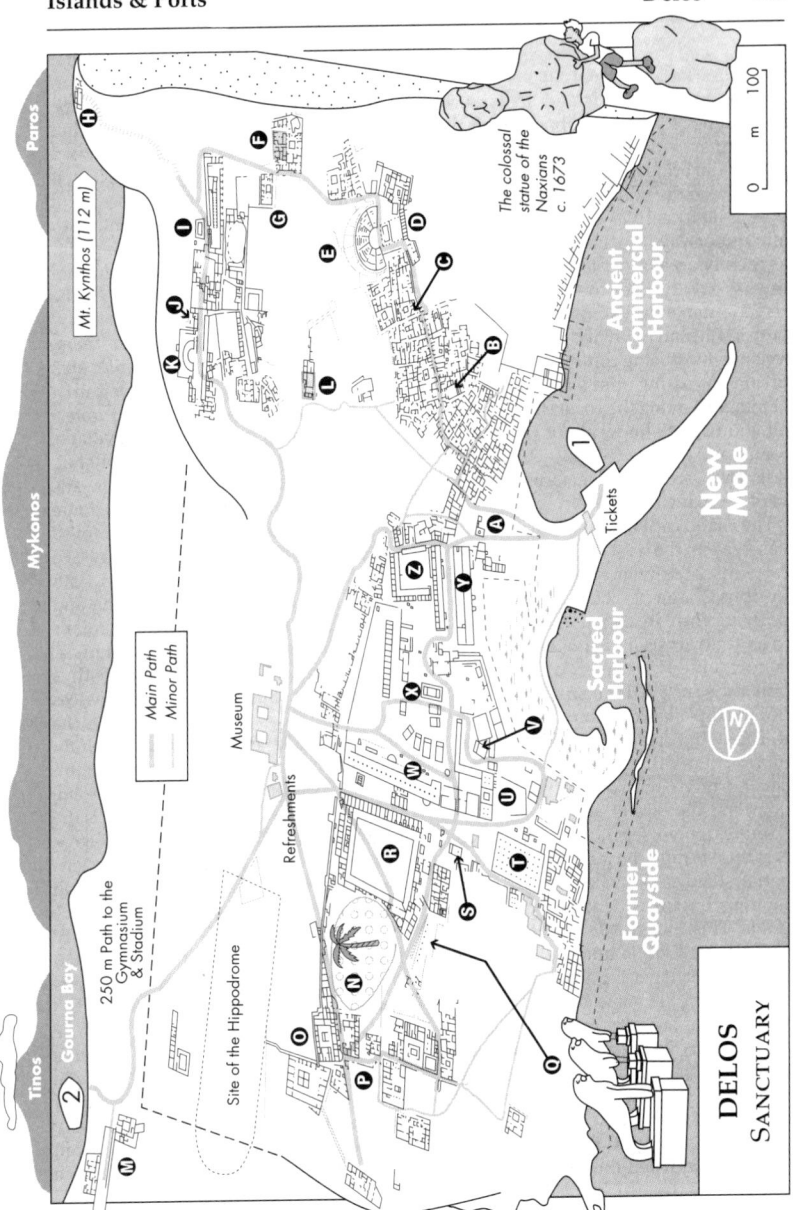

Evia

EBIA; 3580 km², pop. 165,000.

The second largest island in Greece, mountainous Evia (or Euboea) is off the tourist map; lacking the beaches or sights that would bring the crowds. The island's position on the north-east coast of Attica does little to help as linked by a bridge and motorway to Athens it is often seen as merely an adjunct to the mainland it hugs so closely. Even the main town can't seem to make up its mind and clings to both island and mainland. Ferry connections are poor; being confined to a number of minor crossing points to the mainland at intervals along the coast (this tells you all you need to know about the island's roads) and the main Skyros—'mainland' link. These are all local services and times vary little during the year.

The island capital is at **Chalcis**, located half-way up the west coast at the narrowest point of the Evian Strait (known as the Euripus Channel). The town was an important centre in ancient Greece, thanks to its strategic position on the straits, but is now an ugly commercial centre with only a distinctive Turkish quarter, and a popular up-market waterfront to redeem it. The swing bridge that straddles the 30 m strait marks the boundary between the chic northern and southern commercial quarters: the straits are too narrow to admit cargo vessels north of the bridge. Not unnaturally the town is also the hub of the island bus services. These are wide ranging, but infrequent, and on difficult roads. This, and the distances involved, means that Evia is not really a moped island either. If getting around is not very easy, getting to Evia is: bus and rail links with Athens are very good.

Around Evia are a number of towns or villages with little in common. **Eretria** is easily the best of them and now emerging as a tourist resort. Like Chalcis, it was a major ancient city in the 6 C. BC, before Athens dominated the region and it fell into decline. Indeed, by the beginning of the 19 C. the population was so small that the town was used to re-house those inhabitants of Psara that managed to escape the 1824 Turkish devastation of that island. As a result Eretria is also known as **Nea Psara**. Set on a dry dusty plain, it is a garden of Eden short of beautiful thanks to the half-empty grid layout of the incomplete new town, but the plentiful archaeological remains of the ancient city are some compensation, as is the good beach east of the harbour.

Other centres have less going for them. **Loutra Edipsos** is Greece's premier spa; though it has yet to emerge as a tourist resort and retains the air of a faded watering hole. **Limni** is a pretty coastal village, as is **Pefki** on the northern coast, but neither are worth flying to Greece for. The latter does, however, receive occasional visits from Sporades-bound hydrofoils.

The south of Evia is dominated by two port villages **Karystos** and **Marmari**. Both have direct ferry links with Rafina and tend to clog up with escaping Athenians during the weekends. Karystos is the nicer of the two; set in a wide bay with a Venetian-built harbour. Marmari has less charm but does offer boat trips to the small wooded Petali Islands (**Megalo Petali** & **Xero**) one kilometre to the south.

Kimi Port (as distinct from Kimi town; a cute hillside village 4 km inland), is the principal jumping off point for Skyros and its links with the other Northern Aegean destinations. It is tucked beneath the mountain range that makes up the backbone of Evia and is a very pretty little place with an excellent beach just below the harbour. Unfortunately, beds are thin on the ground. Thanks to Evia's motorway link with Athens, Kimi is a de facto mainland port with regular buses and most visitors pass straight through. The link with Skyros is the mainstay of ferry activity. Other departures (usually a twice weekly to the Sporades in High Season) are poorly advertised and remain easier to arrive than depart on.

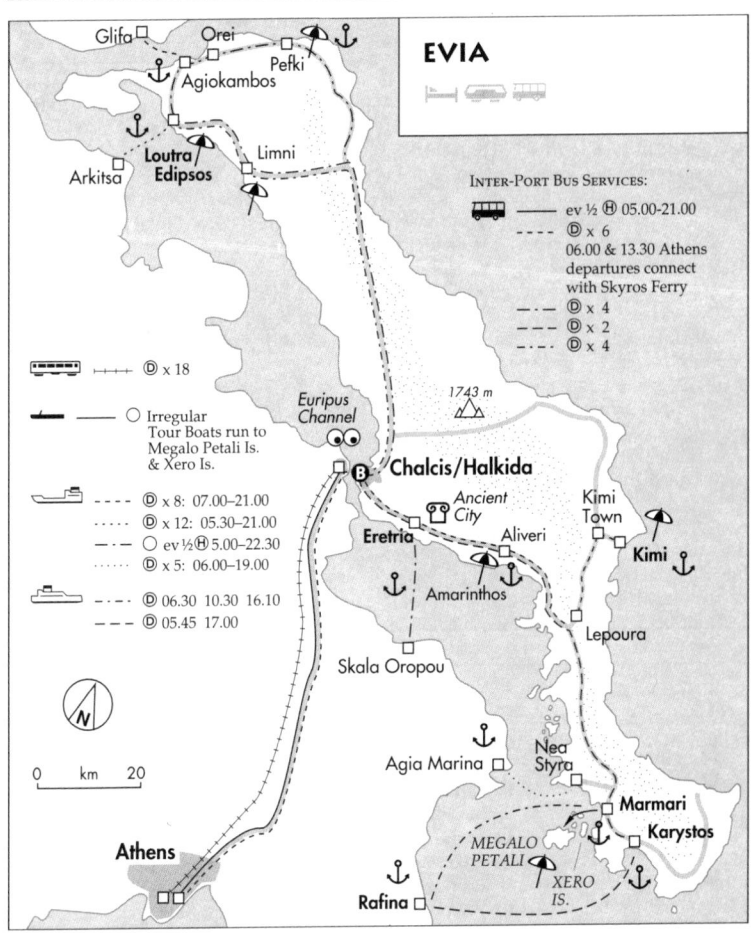

Glifa Orei
Pefki
Agiokambos
Arkitsa Loutra Limni
Edipsos

INTER-PORT BUS SERVICES:

ev ½ Ⓗ 05.00-21.00
Ⓓ x 6
06.00 & 13.30 Athens
departures connect
with Skyros Ferry
Ⓓ x 4
Ⓓ x 2
Ⓓ x 4

Ⓓ x 18

Euripus
Channel

1743 m

Chalcis/Halkida

Ancient
City

Kimi
Town

Eretria Aliveri Kimi

Amarinthos

Irregular
Tour Boats run to
Megalo Petali Is.
& Xero Is.

Ⓓ x 8: 07.00-21.00
Ⓓ x 12: 05.30-21.00
○ ev ½ 5.00-22.30
Ⓓ x 5: 06.00-19.00

Lepoura

Ⓓ 06.30 10.30 16.10
Ⓓ 05.45 17.00

Skala Oropou

N

0   km   20

Agia Marina Nea
Styra

Marmari

Karystos

Athens

MEGALO
PETALI

XERO
IS.

Rafina

Considering its size, Evia is poorly equipped
with hotels, and rooms are a rarity. **Chalcis**
offers the greatest choice of beds thanks to its
hotel littered waterfront. Unfortunately, the
majority are pricey, top end of the market,
establishments. Top of the range is the A-class
Lucy (☎ 23831). Budget hotels lie nearer the
bridge. These include the *Kentrikon* (☎ 71525)
and the very noisy (and somewhat primitive)

Kymata (☎ 21317) and *Iris* (☎ 22246). Meantime, on the mainland side you will find the
quieter *Hara* (☎ 25541) is very reasonable.

Eretria has several mid-range hotels including the good C-class *Xenia* (☎ 61202). As it
stands alone on a causeway-linked islet on the
east side of the town (recently re-named **Dream
Island**) noise is not a problem. **Kimi Port** has
rooms and two hotels; the best being the C-
class *Beis* (☎ 22604).

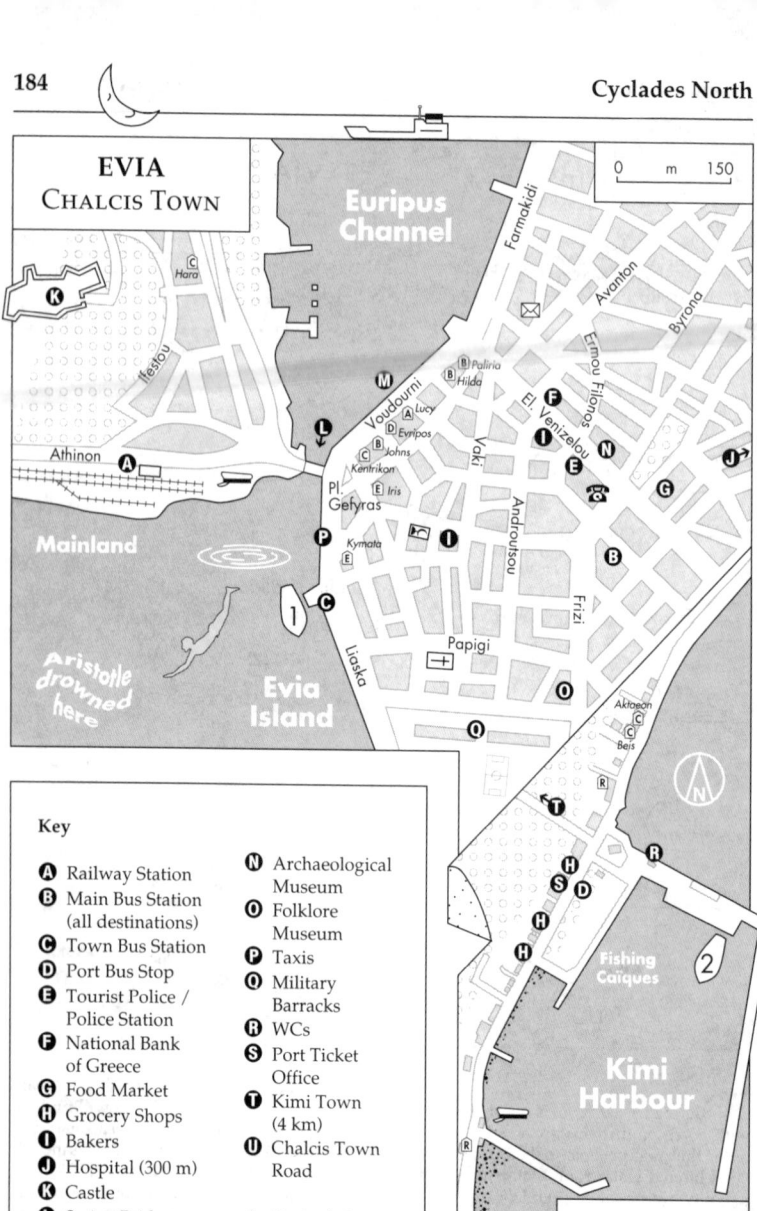

EVIA
CHALCIS TOWN

Euripus Channel

Farmakidi

Avanton

Byrona

0　　m　　150

Ifestiou

K
C Hara

Athinon

A

Mainland

Aristotle drowned here

Evia Island

M
Voudourni

L

B Paliria
B Hilda

D Lucy
D Evripos
C Johns
C Kentrikon
E Iris

Pl Gefyras

P

E Kymata

I

C

1

Liaska

Papigi

+

Q

Ermou Filonos

El Venizelou

F
I
E

N

D

G

B

Vaki

Androutsou

Frizi

O

Aktaeon
C
C Beis

R

T

S D

H

R

H

H

Fishing Caïques

2

Kimi Harbour

EVIA
KIMI PORT

U Beach

R

Key

Ⓐ Railway Station
Ⓑ Main Bus Station (all destinations)
Ⓒ Town Bus Station
Ⓓ Port Bus Stop
Ⓔ Tourist Police / Police Station
Ⓕ National Bank of Greece
Ⓖ Food Market
Ⓗ Grocery Shops
Ⓘ Bakers
Ⓙ Hospital (300 m)
Ⓚ Castle
Ⓛ Swing Bridge
Ⓜ Promenade

Ⓝ Archaeological Museum
Ⓞ Folklore Museum
Ⓟ Taxis
Ⓠ Military Barracks
Ⓡ WCs
Ⓢ Port Ticket Office
Ⓣ Kimi Town (4 km)
Ⓤ Chalcis Town Road

1 Hydrofoil Berth
2 Ferry Quay

Λ

There is camping on Evia, but the sites (5 km north-west of Eretria and near Pefki) are poorly placed and geared to motor-campers.

◎◎

If you discount the attractive mountain scenery, the **Euripus Channel** is Evia's most noteworthy sight and boasts a 2500 year pedigree as a tourist attraction thanks to the odd combination of land and currents which make the tide change eight times a day. Aristotle is reputed to have drowned when he threw himself into the sea in exasperation at his inability to explain the phenomena. His successors still haven't come up with the answer but, given the state of the water, have generally opted for cleaner forms of suicide.

☎

CHALCIS: CODE 0221, POLICE 22100, KIMI: CODE 0222, FIRST AID 22322, POLICE 22555.

Mykonos

ΜΥΚΟΝΟΣ; 88 km², pop. 5,700.
Now among the most heavily touristed of all the Greek islands, Mykonos has long been on the tourist map courtesy of one of the most scenic harbours in the Mediterranean and a profusion of good sand beaches tolerating nudism. Formerly a preserve of the world's jet-setters, Mykonos town still exhibits inflated prices, expensive boutiques and night clubs where French and the male gay scene thrive. A procession of cruise ships calling does nothing to reduce local prices. Not withstanding the cost of living, backpackers also swarm over the island each summer in increasing numbers; their sole redeeming function being to make the island much safer for the single male who, in years past, was apt to find out what the fairer sex have to put up with.

The only large settlement on a small island, **Mykonos Town** is the hub of all this activity. Centred on the famous crescent-shaped harbour bay, it is an attractive maze of whitewashed cubic houses riddled with alleyways designed to distract both would-be pirates (to say

nothing of tourists) and the *meltemi* wind that attacks Mykonos hard each summer. The harbour, naturally the focal point of the town, is among the prettiest in Greece at night, but is revealed as rather tacky in the dazzling light of day. The heavy waterfront mix of tavernas, souvenir and expensive gold and silver shops, backed by bars, nightclubs and restaurants galore quickly dispels any pretence that this is an unspoilt island town. This is not to say that Mykonos Town doesn't exude Greek island charm, for it does — almost to excess. But it is somewhat contrived and done purely for the tourists' benefit. This can be seen in the spate of windmill rebuilding on the hills around the town (leaving town postcards struggling to keep pace) and the famous (very photogenic) Mykonos Pelican that is allowed to flap the streets at will. Once night falls however, if it's got any sense, it keeps its feathers well down, for Mykonos Town after dark is something else. At the height of the season the whole town literally throbs. Unfortunately, of late the island has attracted more than its fair share of yobs who throb too much; particularly when confronted by an unattached female and there have been problems. Those who find all this difficult to square with the fact that Mykonos was the island on which *Shirley Valentine* was filmed, should take note that it was produced well out of season when the pretence of a dreamy, idyllic Greek island could be maintained (courtesy of some pretty obscure beaches).

The beaches are the island's other big draw — particularly those on the south coast; which is a very appealing mix of windy headlands and bays decorated with long strands of sand. These start at **Plati Yialos** to the west, from where a couple of beach boats shuttle along the coast to Paradise, Super Paradise and Elia Beaches. All bar Plati Yialos itself have their nudist end (Elia being predominately so). Super Paradise has a long-standing international reputation as

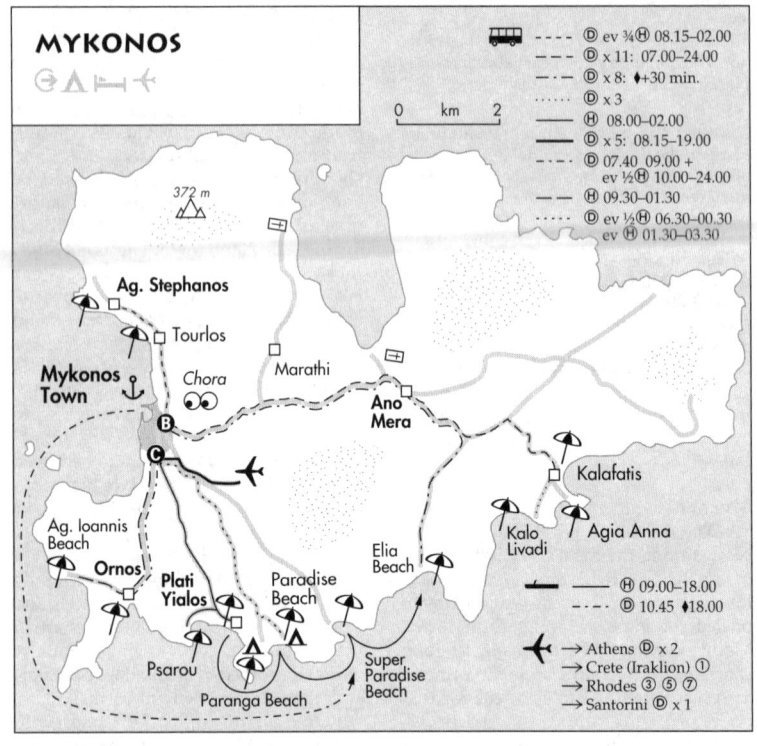

MYKONOS

🚌	---- Ⓓ ev ¾Ⓗ 08.15–02.00
	--- Ⓓ x 11: 07.00–24.00
	–·– Ⓓ x 8: ♦+30 min.
	······ Ⓓ x 3
	—— Ⓗ 08.00–02.00
	—— Ⓓ x 5: 08.15–19.00
	–··– Ⓓ 07.40_09.00 + ev ½Ⓗ 10.00–24.00
	—— Ⓗ 09.30–01.30
	····· Ⓓ ev ½Ⓗ 06.30–00.30 ev Ⓗ 01.30–03.30

0 ___ km ___ 2

372 m

Ag. Stephanos

Tourlos

Mykonos Town

Chora

Marathi

Ⓑ

Ano Mera

Ⓒ

Kalafatis

Ag. Ioannis Beach

Ornos

Plati Yialos

Paradise Beach

Elia Beach

Kalo Livadi

Agia Anna

Psarou

Super Paradise Beach

Paranga Beach

—— Ⓗ 09.00–18.00
–·– Ⓓ 10.45 ♦18.00

→ Athens Ⓓ x 2
→ Crete (Iraklion) ①
→ Rhodes ③ ⑤ ⑦
→ Santorini Ⓓ x 1

Key

- Ⓐ Accommodation Office / Tourist Police / Camping Bus pick-up point
- Ⓑ Bus Station (N. & Central Mykonos)
- Ⓒ Bus Station (Pl. Plati Yialos)
- Ⓓ Police
- Ⓔ Tourist Police
- Ⓕ National Bank of Greece
- Ⓖ Supermarket
- Ⓗ Newspapers / Bookshop
- Ⓘ Ferry Passenger Stalls
- Ⓙ Public WCs
- Ⓚ Moped Rental

- Ⓛ Paraportiani Church
- Ⓜ Archaeological Museum
- Ⓝ Maritime Museum of the Aegean
- Ⓞ Folklore Museum
- Ⓟ Windmill Museum
- Ⓠ Little Venice
- Ⓡ School of Fine Arts
- Ⓢ Cathedral

1 Ferry Quay
2 Delos Tour Boats
3 Excursion Boat Berth
4 Cruise Ship mooring point

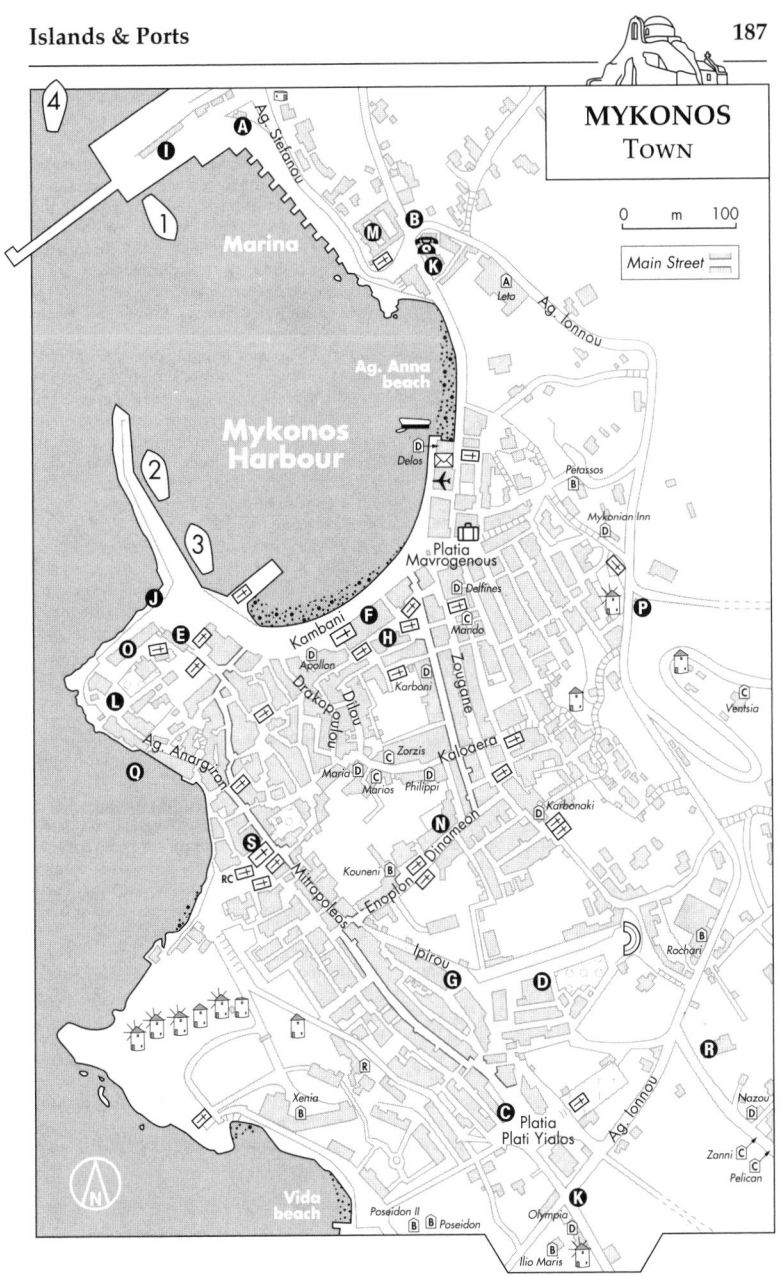

MYKONOS TOWN

0 m 100

Main Street

Marina

I

A Ag. Stefanou

M **B**
K

Leto **A** Ag. Ioannou

Ag. Anna beach

Mykonos Harbour

1

2

3

Delos **D**

Petassos **B**

Platia Mavrogenous

Mykonian Inn **D**

J

E **O**

Kambani
Apollon **D**

F **H**
Mardo **D** **C**
Delfines **D**

Karbani **D**

P

Ventsia **C**

Drakopoulou Dilou

Zougane Kalogera

L

Ag. Anargiron

Q

Zorzis **C**
Maria **D** **C**
Marios Philippi **D**

Karbonaki **D**

S
RC

Mitropoleas

N
Kouneni **B** Dinameon
Enoplon

Rochari **B**

Ipirou

G **D**

R

Xenia

R

Nazou **D**

C Platia Plati Yialos

K

Zanni **C** **C**
Pelican

Vida beach

Poseidon II **B** **B** Poseidon

Olympia **D**
Ilio Maris **B**

N

the gay beach; though it is now pretty mixed with only a small 'beach boy' end.

The interior of Mykonos is hilly and barren with surprisingly few villages. However, farms and holiday homes leave the landscape cluttered with Cycladic cubic architecture in abundance. Other centres are small: the most visited being **Agios Stephanos**, which has a sub-standard (for Mykonos) beach that is nonetheless popular because it is easy to get to.

Buses run frequently between the town and all the popular beaches — unusually for a Greek island — operating into the small hours during the summer months. Ferry links are good, for Mykonos is an important bridging port for those wanting to travel onto or from the Cyclades Central line. Sailings to Rafina (usually labelled 'Athens') are widely advertised without mention of the stops at Tinos and Andros.

⊢

The number of visitors to Mykonos has prompted the construction of a hotel and room information office near the ferry quay: this makes life relatively easy, but not that easy as hotels and rooms fill up early in High Season. More than with any other island, it pays to arrive before noon. Mykonos is also noted for having very expensive accommodation.

The town has a number of C and D 'standard' (one hesitates to say 'priced') hotels including the waterfront *Apollon* (☎ 22223) and a varied collection on Kaloaera St. including the C-class *Zorzis* (☎ 22167) and *Marios* (☎ 22704) and the D-class *Maria* (☎ 24212) and *Philippi* (☎ 22294). The hills behind the town are another fertile hunting ground and include the noisy *Olympia* (☎ 22964) and the better placed *Nazou* (☎ 22626) and C-class *Zanni* (☎ 22486) and *Pelican* (☎ 23454). *Paradise Beach Camping* also offers popular chalets. Those who can afford the luxury should try the A-class *Leto* (☎ 22207).

A

Mykonos has two pricey sites close by each other and engaged in cut-throat competition. Rival mini-buses meet all ferries. Expensive *Paradise Beach Camping* (☎ 22508) is justifiably the most popular (Note: Mykonos has the distinction of being one of the few places where you go *down* to Paradise) and sees a steady trickle of converts from *Camping Mykonos* (☎ 24578): a cheaper site at nearby Paranga beach.

∞

Mykonos lacks archaeological or historical sites (the proximity of neighbouring Delos did little to encourage building during the classical period), but **Mykonos Town** offers plenty by way of compensation. Although the Venetian kastro that once adorned the western promontory of the town is long gone, a row of wooden galleried houses known as 'Little Venice' remain from the period; the multi-coloured balconies hanging over the sea providing one of the town's picture-postcard views. On the site of the kastro now stands the **Paraportiani**, a group of picturesque chapels plastered together in the traditional 'melting ice cream' fashion. The rest of the town also lends itself to exploration, though most only dates from the 18–19 c. There are also a clutch of museums with visiting:

A working **Windmill Museum** is open to tourists on the hillside east of the harbour: admission is free and you should take the opportunity to have a look (this is the only working example you can visit in the islands).

The **Archaeological Museum** contains finds from excavated Delian graves on the nearby island of Rinia (when Delos was sanctified all burials were re-interred on Rinia). Commanding pride of place among the exhibits is a 7 c. BC vase painted with the earliest known depiction of the wooden horse of Troy.

Hidden away in an old town house is the **Maritime Museum of the Aegean**: not quite up to the standard of its Santorini (Oia) counterpart, but it still offers a rewarding hour's browsing. The exhibits consist of a pretty varied collection of nautical odds and ends spread over three rooms and a lawned back garden (the latter being home to assorted gravestones and the top 20 feet of a late 19 c. lighthouse). Maps and models on an Aegean theme make up the bulk of the collection (including the *Endeavour:* the ship made famous by the explorer Captain Cook; who apparently discovered the Aegean by way of Australia).

Finally, the **Craft and Folklore Museum** takes the form of a restored 19 c. house complete with contemporary artifacts: an attractive display of pre-tourist island life.

☎

CODE 0289, PORT POLICE 22218, POLICE 22482, FIRST AID 23994.

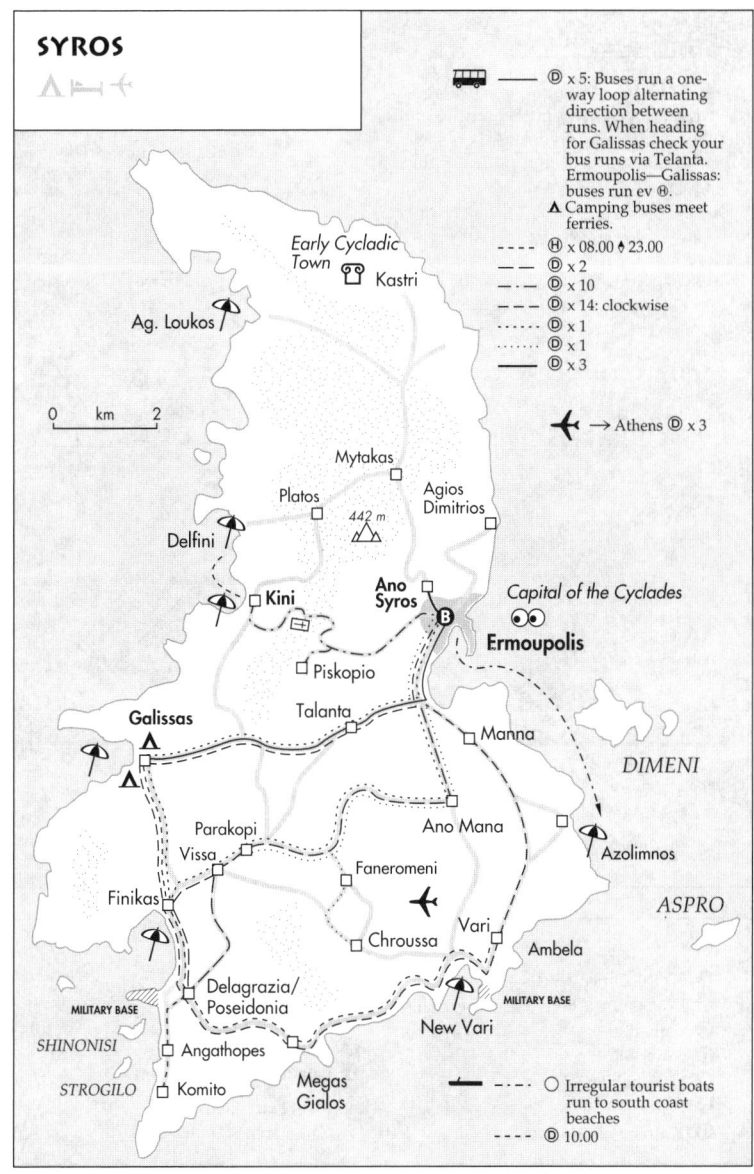

SYROS

⊞ x 5: Buses run a one-way loop alternating direction between runs. When heading for Galissas check your bus runs via Telanta. Ermoupolis—Galissas: buses run ev ⊕.
▲ Camping buses meet ferries.

---- ⊕ x 08.00 ⬧ 23.00
— ⓓ x 2
—·— ⓓ x 10
— — ⓓ x 14: clockwise
······· ⓓ x 1
······· ⓓ x 1
—— ⓓ x 3

✈ → Athens ⓓ x 3

Early Cycladic Town Kastri

Ag. Loukos

0 km 2

Mytakas

Platos

442 m

Agios Dimitrios

Delfini

Kini

Ano Syros

B

Capital of the Cyclades

Ermoupolis

Piskopio

Talanta

Manna

DIMENI

Galissas

Parakopi

Ano Mana

Azolimnos

Vissa

ASPRO

Faneromeni

Finikas

Chroussa

Vari

Ambela

MILITARY BASE

Delagrazia/ Poseidonia

New Vari

MILITARY BASE

SHINONISI

Angathopes

STROGILO

Komito

Megas Gialos

○ Irregular tourist boats run to south coast beaches
---- ⓓ 10.00

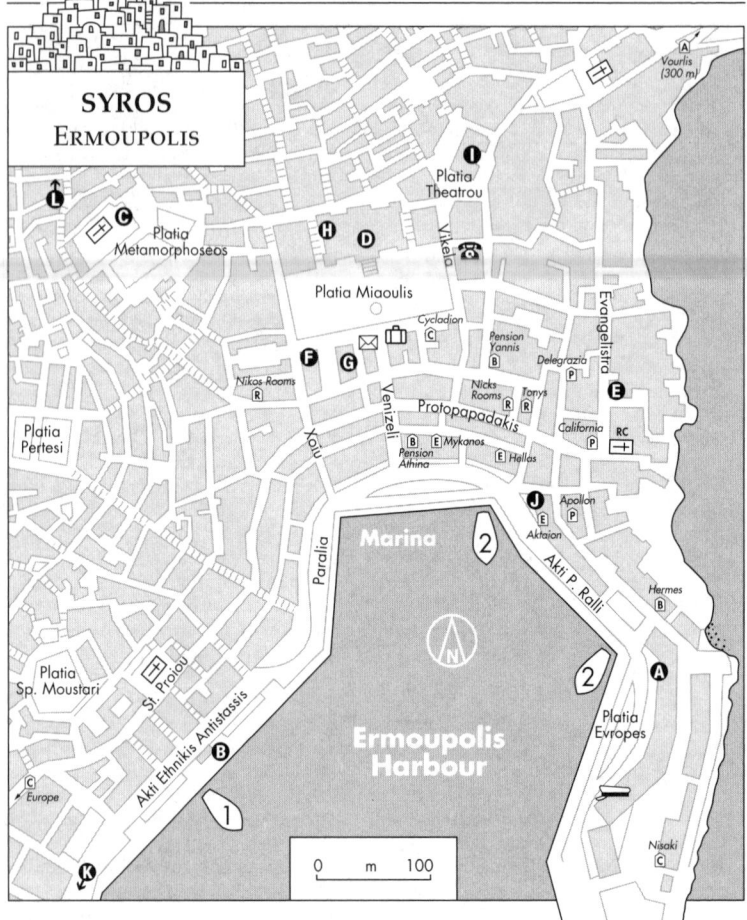

SYROS
ERMOUPOLIS

Vourlis
(300 m)

Platia
Theatrou

Platia
Metamorphoseos

Platia Miaoulis

Cycladion

Pension
Yannis

Delegrazia

Protopapadakis

Nikos Rooms

Nicks
Rooms

Tonys

California

Mykanos

Pension
Athina

Hellas

Platia
Pertesi

Apollon

Aktaion

Marina

Hermes

Platia
Sp. Moustari

Ermoupolis
Harbour

Platia
Evropes

Europe

Nisaki

0   m   100

Venizeli

Xoiu

Paralia

Vikela

Evangelistra

Akti P. Ralli

Akti Ethnikis Antistassis

St. Proiou

Key

A NTOG Office / WCs & Showers
B Bus Station / Ferry Passenger Stalls
C Cathedral
D City Hall
E National Bank
F Police
G Tourist Police

H Museum
I Theatre
J Newspapers
K Main Road
L Path to Ano Syros (2 km)

1   Main Ferry Quay
2   Catamaran / Hydrofoil Berth

Syros
ΣΥΡΟΣ; 86 km², pop. 21,000.

Imagine a relatively small, arid island with a large mainland-sized town built on the east coast, and you have some idea what Syros is like. An oddity among Greek islands, Syros was able to avoid the chaos and destruction encountered by most islands at the hands of pirates from the 17 c. on, thanks to the existence of a strong Roman Catholic community that sought and got the patronage and protection of the King of France. Thanks to the French connection, the island was able to retain its coastal settlements rather than retreat from them to inland centres, and even during the war of independence was able to maintain a precarious neutrality; making it a haven for refugees. The influx of refugees (notably from Chios) fleeing Turkish suppression also served to give the town economy a massive boost.

Building on this background, the main town of **Ermoupolis** ('The city of Hermes') developed rapidly in the 19 c. (thanks to its role as *the* mid-Aegean coaling port) to become the largest in the Cyclades and the capital of the group. The town is divided into three quarters. This might sound Greek but is perfectly logical given the geography; for the waterfront and its environs is backed by two building-clad hills — each topped with a church, one Roman Catholic the other Orthodox. Add to this a superb natural harbour and they combine to produce one of the most impressive approches when viewed from a ferry. Unfortunately, such favourable impressions are quickly dispelled by a closer look at the (rarely flattering) waterfront houses, for sad to say it, the refugees that flooded the rapidly growing town brought their architecture with them. Efforts are now being made to remove the air of dilapidation that once adorned the waterfront, but the cute Cycladic village look is never going to be a practical possibility. This might not sound very

encouraging, but for this very reason Ermoupolis does offer some interesting sightseeing as it sports a faded neo-classical charm of sorts that neighbouring islands cannot match: it is worth a visit just to capture the contrast.

The two town hills also contrast greatly with each other and the lower town. Catholic **Ano Syros** is easily the more interesting as the buildings on its upper slopes form the nucleus of the original island chora. On your left hand side as you enter the harbour, it has a meandering staircase running down to the lower town. Attempting this climb is the most popular sightseeing trip in town, and you can take in the British Cemetery half-way up the hill (where the victims of a World War One troopship sinking are interred). The Orthodox hill town on **Vrontado** only dates from the 19 c. and, bar the domed church that marks it out from the more Kastro-like church topping Ano Syros, it has little of interest.

The recent tourist influx has yet to make much impact on the rest of the island. North of Ermoupolis, tourists will find they have become the main local attraction; though ever increasing numbers of hill walkers head for the area. The main resort (courtesy of the best island beach) is at **Galissas** on the west coast. Between maintaining traditional agriculture and catering to the tourists, the patchwork village is a curiosity, with reedbeds and rural farming lying uneasily alongside a decidedly incongruous and little used concrete pitch and putt course.

South of Galissas is a second resort strip running from **Finikas** down to **Delagrazia** (alias **Poseidonia**). However, the beaches are much more scruffy, and one has to search pretty hard to justify stopping here with so many other good beach islands close to hand. The remaining southern half of Syros is, if truth be told, best seen from a bus: merely a collection of small villages scattered over low-lying countryside and lacking tourist appeal.

Ferry connections to and from Syros are 'adequate' but no more: long gone are the days when the Ermoupolis was the hub of the Cycladic ferry system. In fact Syros is somewhat out on a limb these days, seeing a greater variation in its island hopping possibilities each year than most other islands. The Port Police have a complete list of the day's sailings chalked up in the doorway of their barrack-like building. On buying a ticket establish where the boat will dock as some still tie up on the north side; though the majority now berth at the new bus stop and passenger stalls on the west. The island bus service is dominated by a large number of one-way services but frequency between the centres is good.

⊨

There are hotels and rooms aplenty in the port area of **Ermoupolis**; most of them are at the budget end of the market (the buildings aren't up to providing much more), and are advertised by a veritable forest of signs. Given the comparatively small numbers of tourists visiting Syros, finding a bed is rarely a problem. At the bottom end of the market are a couple of pensions offering rooms: notably *Tony's*, buried in the warren of streets behind the waterfront and the better located *Apollon* (☎ 22158) and *Athina* (☎ 23600). More up-market hotels are not so centrally placed. Nearest is the B-class *Hermes* (☎ 28011) with its own tiny section of private beach. On the west side of the port is the C-class *Europe* (☎ 28771), and to the north-east stands the A-class *Vourlis* (☎ 28440). Elsewhere on Syros beds are few except at **Galissas** which has a supply of rooms.

▲

Two sites exist on the west coast at the resort village of Galissas. Set in a pistachio nut-tree grove, cosy *Two Hearts Camping* (☎ 42052) is the better of them. Broken single hearts are also admitted. *Camping Yianna* (☎ 42418) is nearer the beach but bordering on run down. Mini-buses from both meet all boats.

👁

Ermoupolis offers the main sightseeing on Syros, and unusually for a Greek island town is well endowed with street names (the west European influence coming to the fore again). Several blocks up from the waterfront is the

impressive **Miaoulis Square**. Adorned with a statue of the Greek hero of the War of Independence after which it is named, and a bandstand, it acquires a cosmopolitan air once evening falls. To the west side of the town hall that dominates the square is a small **Museum** housing exhibits (courtesy of this being the capital of the Cyclades) from other Cycladic islands too small to possess one (the exhibits include a few Cycladic figures from Keros and Amorgos). Just north-east of the square you will also find a miniature version of the La Scala **Opera House** built in 1862, it has been closed for refurbishing ever since.

The hills north of **Kastri** offer possibly the most intriguing and (unless you like hard hill-walking) inaccessible sites on the island. Ringing one of the hilltops are the walls of one of the largest of the **Early Cycladic** culture villages yet discovered. Built towards the end of the period, it clearly was defensive in function (the odd horseshoe-shaped bastion aside, the surviving 'ramparts' look just like typical hill farm walls the world over), and was accompanied by a large cemetery that has yielded up a number of important Cycladic figurines.

☎

CODE 0281, TOURIST POLICE 22620, PORT POLICE 22690, POLICE 23555.

Tinos

ΤΗΝΟΣ; 193 km², pop. 7730.

The spiritual centre of modern Greece, mountainous Tinos even outshines Patmos for raw pilgrim-pulling power. Billed as the Lourdes of the Aegean, Sundays and the Virgin Mary-related festivals on the 25th March (Annunciation), and particularly the 15th of August (Feast of the Assumption), see the main centre of Tinos Town packed with the faithful. If you plan to stay, then you should try to avoid Tinos on Saturdays and in the week preceding these festivals. The focus of all this activity is an icon housed in the church that dominates the town: the Panagia Evangelistra (or Megalochari, meaning 'Great Joy'). However, the religious dimension is only one aspect to the spiritual importance of Tinos; for the island is also a focus of Greek nationalism, thanks to its history of being the last of the Greek islands to succumb to Turkish rule (when the Venetians finally abandoned it in 1715). The torpedoing of the visiting Greek warship *Elli* on Assumption Day 1940 by an Italian submarine (before Greece had formally joined the war on the side of the allies) was an outrage that also served to encourage Greek resistance during World War Two. As a result of this background, Tinos has thrived on Greek rather than foreign tourism (something all too evident in the all-Greek timetables outside ticket agencies), and it is only now starting to emerge as a foreign tourist destination.

Coated with a sprinkling of small villages and over 1200 picturesque dovecotes (the island speciality) Tinos is very attractive. However, it remains very much of a 'one town' island and is best explored via excursions from the port and centre of **Tinos Town**. A largely modern affair, it owes its existence solely to the church

and icon; and this shows, for as you approach by ferry, the seemingly thin scatter of buildings looks to have a rather tenuous hold on the foreshore. Its most conspicuous feature is the main street that runs up the hillside from the waterfront to the impressive walls and ornate plaster facade of the church at the back of the town. In fact, Tinos Town is dominated by three streets: the waterfront (replete with ticket agencies, restaurant, and a good supermarket south of the Port Police office), the pedestrianised Evagelistrais (lined with a number of particularly tacky souvenir shops that sell plastic bonsai trees among other things) and Leoforos Megalocharis, the main processional road to the church: on feast days devout pilgrims process up it on their knees, stopping off only to buy candles — some up to 2 m high — from shops along the way. This all sounds serious stuff, yet the town feels a very relaxed, laid-back sort of place, and is a nice base for exploration.

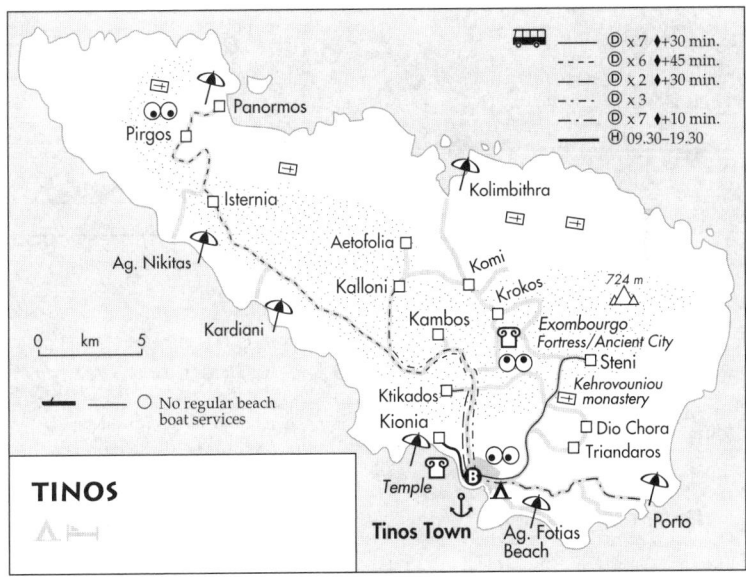

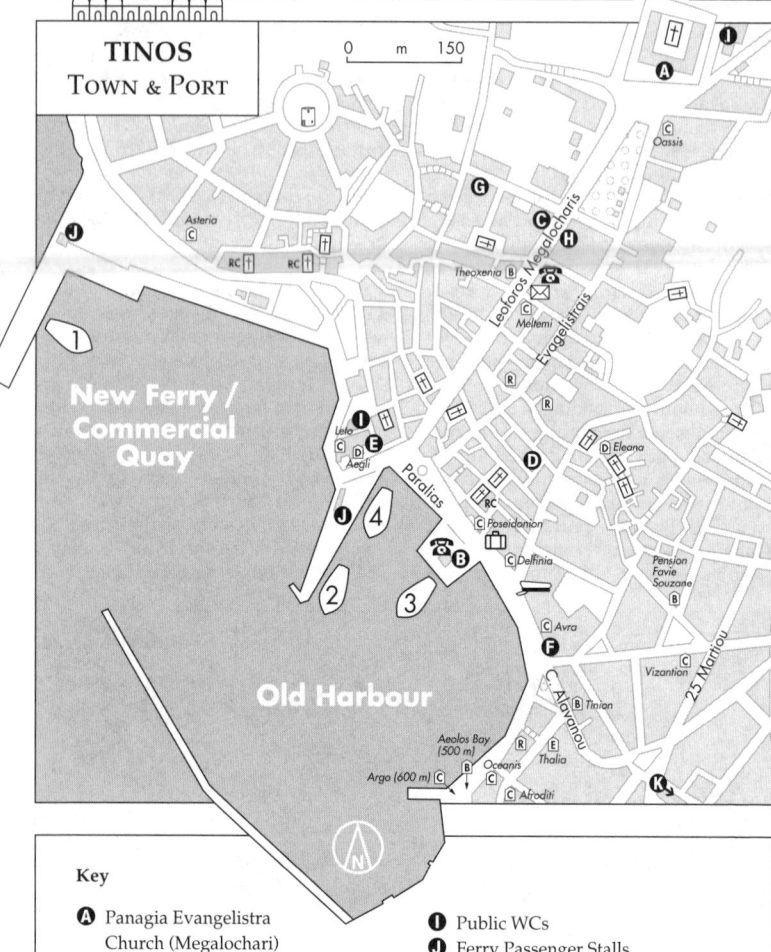

TINOS
Town & Port

0   m   150

New Ferry /
Commercial
Quay

Asteria
Oasis
Theoxenia
Meltemi
Lefa
Aegli
Paralias
Eleana
Poseidonion
Delfinia
Pension
Favie
Souzane
Avra
Vizantion
Tinion
Aeolos Bay
(500 m)
Argo (600 m)
Oceanis
Thalia
Afroditi

Old Harbour

1

4

2

3

Leoforos Megalocharis
Evangelistrais
25 Martiou
Alavanou

N

Key

A Panagia Evangelistra
Church (Megalochari)

B Bus Station (all destinations)

C Archaeological Museum

D Police Station

E National Bank of Greece

F Supermarket

G Cultural Centre

H Clinic / Medical Centre

I Public WCs

J Ferry Passenger Stalls

K Camping Tinos (150 m)

1 Quay for large ferries (unsheltered)

2 Inner Ferry Quay (sheltered)

3 Quay for smaller ferries /
   Catamaran / Hydrofoil Berth

4 Tourist boat departure point

Tinos Town also has a couple of beaches reasonably close to hand. The closest — Ag. Fotias beach — is a walk away; 500 m past the town's camp site. However, the best is at **Kionia** (now the island package tourist centre). Buses run frequently from Tinos Town, or if you are feeling energetic you can walk along the coast past the scanty remains of a temple to Poseidon and Amphitrite and a small stoa. Poseidon was the island's favourite deity after he relieved Tinos from a plague of snakes by sending along a flock of hungry storks ('Tinos' is derived from the Phoenician word for snake: *tenok*). These days finding a snake is very difficult and on a par with working out where your ferry is going to dock in Tinos Town. Depending on wind conditions, ferries can dock at one of three quays; you'll have to ask where your boat will berth.

Tinos Town aside, the island is very quiet (apart from the billing of tourists and the cooing of the doves that inhabit the island's distinctive 100-odd dovecots). The former capital lay on the upper slopes of **Mt. Exambourgo**. If you care to attempt the steep walk you will find the remains of the Venetian fortress behind a monastery and part of the Archaic city wall. The summit was an important landmark in ancient times when sailors navigated by always keeping in sight of land. Local tradition had it that when it was obscured by cloud it was a sure sign that unsettled weather was on the way.

The villages of Tinos are, in the main, pretty mountain-side affairs little visited by tourists, with the notable exception of attractive **Pirgos** (now home to a thriving painting community). Buses run daily (other villages have irregular bus calls); though Sunday services are not good. Buses also provide good links the 12 c. village-like monastery at **Kehrovouniou**; another popular excursion destination. If you are easily irritated by other people's personal habits then avoid sitting next to priests or little old ladies on the island

buses. These delightful souls indulge in the practice of crossing themselves every time they pass a chapel or shrine. There are said to be 643 chapels on Tinos.

🛏

Tinos Town has plenty of hotels. Prices are slightly higher than average, but on pilgrimless nights you can usually haggle advantageously. Budget beds are limited to a scatter of rooms and two D-class hotels: the quayside *Aigli* (☎ 22240) and the backstreet *Eleana* (☎ 22561). The majority of hotels are C-class establishments: the more appealing being those along the waterfront. These include the *Oceanis* (☎ 22452), the *Avra* (☎ 22242), the *Delfinia* (☎ 22289) and the B-class *Tinion* (☎ 22261).

A

Tinos Camping (☎ 22344): A reasonable site. Blown clean daily, it has plenty of tree cover, and a dovecote in lieu of a mini-market.

👓

The stucco plastered church of **Panagia Evangelistra** complete with the icon causing all the fuss is the main sightseeing destination to Tinos; though the latter is so encased in gold that it is difficult to get anything other than a brief impression. The **icon** is reputedly the work of St. Luke (the time involved in pursuing a second career as a painter no doubt explains why the author of the third gospel copied roughly 60% of Mark's gospel into his own), and if true shows a remarkable anticipation of later Byzantine art. Reputedly from a church destroyed by pirates in the 10 c., it is widely believed to be endowed with healing powers. It came to light in 1822 after a passing nun saw a hunky bronzed workman digging in a field and had a vision (of what, history hasn't recorded). Given instructions where to dig he unearthed the icon miraculously uninjured. The church was built on the discovery site. The icon's appearance during the birth throes of the Greek state has further enhanced its symbolical importance to the Greek people. Take care to observe the church dress code: it is strictly enforced here. Tinos Town also houses the island's **Archaeological Museum**; the exhibits include a late Hellenistic sundial and odd fragments recovered from the temple of Poseidon and the Mt. Exambourgo Kastro.

☎

CODE 0283, PORT POLICE 22348, POLICE 22100, FIRST AID 22210.

6

CYCLADES WEST

FOLEGANDROS · KEA · KIMOLOS · KYTHNOS
MILOS · SERIFOS · SIFNOS · SIKINOS

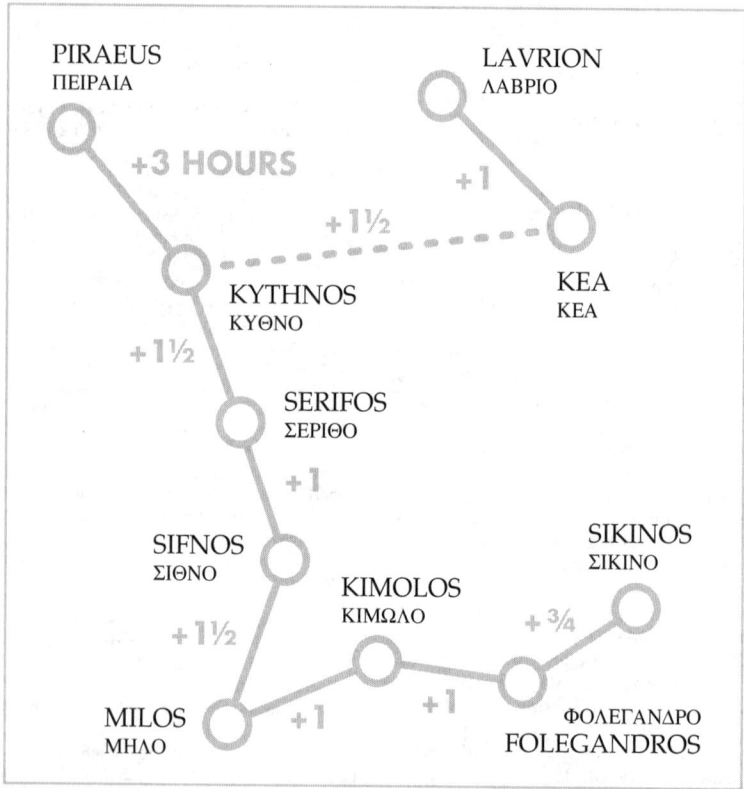

PIRAEUS
ΠΕΙΡΑΙΑ

LAVRION
ΛΑΒΡΙΟ

+3 HOURS

+1

+1½

KYTHNOS
ΚΥΘΝΟ

KEA
KEA

+1½

SERIFOS
ΣΕΡΙΘΟ

+1

SIFNOS
ΣΙΘΝΟ

SIKINOS
ΣΙΚΙΝΟ

KIMOLOS
ΚΙΜΩΛΟ

+¾

+1½

+1

+1

MILOS
ΜΗΛΟ

ΦΟΛΕΓΑΝΔΡΟ
FOLEGANDROS

General Features

The Western Cyclades Line runs in an irregular 'L'- shaped chain around the rim of the group. A paucity of camping sites and budget accommodation produces the odd combination of fewer backpackers and greater numbers of Greek holidaymakers than elsewhere; thus helping to keep the islands free from the worst trappings of mass tourism. In fact out of the High Season foreign tourists are thin on the ground. The chain is peculiar in that the nearer the island is to Athens, the fewer foreign tourists it tends to see. Northerly Kea — served by the mainland port of Lavrion — is very much of an Athenian's get-away-from-it-all weekend island, but very quiet in midweek. Kythnos and Serifos are quite off

the beaten track despite the frequency of Piraeus ferries. Sifnos, on the other hand, is the only island in the group that comes close to being labelled 'touristy' and even this is mild by Central Cyclades standards. While Milos — famous as the island where the Venus de Milo was discovered — attracts tourists by virtue of name recognition rather than the limited appeal that it has in its own right. Kimolos makes an interesting day excursion but is very much of a minor island as are the two at the tail end of the line; Sikinos and Folegandros. Bridging the Central and Western lines, they do not fit comfortably into either, being serviced by boats steaming down both; but as they are more characteristic of the Western Cyclades they are covered here.

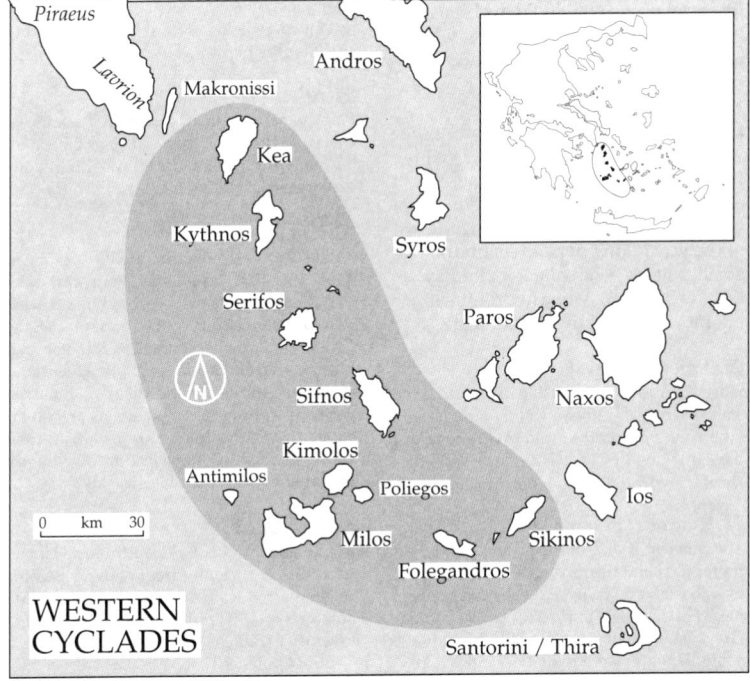

Suggested Itinerary
[2 Weeks]

Those looking for a fortnight's holiday that combines the sights of Athens with some relaxed island hopping without huge crowds of backpackers could do worse than the Western Cyclades. An atmosphere of quiet romanticism rules. The islands are close to the capital and fairly quiet, yet with enough going on so that you don't end up feeling as if you had been washed up at the back of beyond.

Arrival/Departure Point
None of the islands boast an international airport, and connections with other island groups are so poor that Athens is the only viable starting point. During the High Season Santorini becomes another possibility; though you could well have to hop to Paros for one of the daily boats running into the line from there.

Season
Daily services operate (somewhat irregularly) down the line from late June through to late September. The month either side of this sees ferries five days a week falling to three days during the rest of the year. Don't depend on finding the smaller Sifnos—Paros boats or the Piraeus (Zea) — Kythnos — Kea hydrofoil service operating out of July and August.

1 Athens [2 Days]
Since you can't spend all day in the sun at the start of a holiday anyway, you might as well take in the sights of the capital over a couple of days (picking up the NTOG ferry departure sheets/Hydrofoil timetable at the same time).

2 Kythnos [1 Day]
The quietest island in the group; you might prefer to spend the day elsewhere if you are new to island hopping. Experienced hoppers weary of the hurly burly of the more popular Greek islands will find more to savour in the somnolent atmosphere that pervades here.

3 Serifos [2 Days]
A day is all that is needed to take in the port and dramatic Chora hanging on the hill behind. After this you can retire to the beach and wait — if needs be for an extra day — for a *morning* ferry to Sifnos; enabling you to take your pick of the accommodation on arrival there.

4 Sifnos [4 Days]
As this is the best beach island in the group (and by this stage you should be better conditioned to enjoy more extended time in the sun), Sifnos offers the opportunity to enjoy a few days of complete relaxation.

5 **6** Milos/Kimolos [3 Days]
Milos provides the best sightseeing in the Western Cyclades. Three days can be happily spent between the catacombs, beach and if you are really feeling adventurous a day-trip to Kimolos via the Apollonia-based taxi-boats. (Don't leave a Kimolos trip until the last day just in case high seas result in you getting stuck for the night).

1 Athens [2 Days]
Finally, take a boat direct to Piraeus — spending the recommended clear day spare before your return flight finishing your exploration of the capital.

Alternative 1
Rather than returning direct to Piraeus, if you have the time available, you can take advantage of the new hydrofoil link to visit **Kea**. Once one of the most important of all the Greek islands it offers some good sightseeing. Ideally, you should aim to explore the island in mid-week as rooms disappear as the weekend approaches. You are also recommended to visit Kythnos in passing earlier in your itinerary to establish times if you are planning to catch the twice weekly ferry.

Alternative 2
In July and August **Folegandros** appears on schedules sufficiently frequently to become an alternative destination. However, boats do not run every day, and you should be prepared to return to Piraeus via ferries running up the Central Cyclades Line.

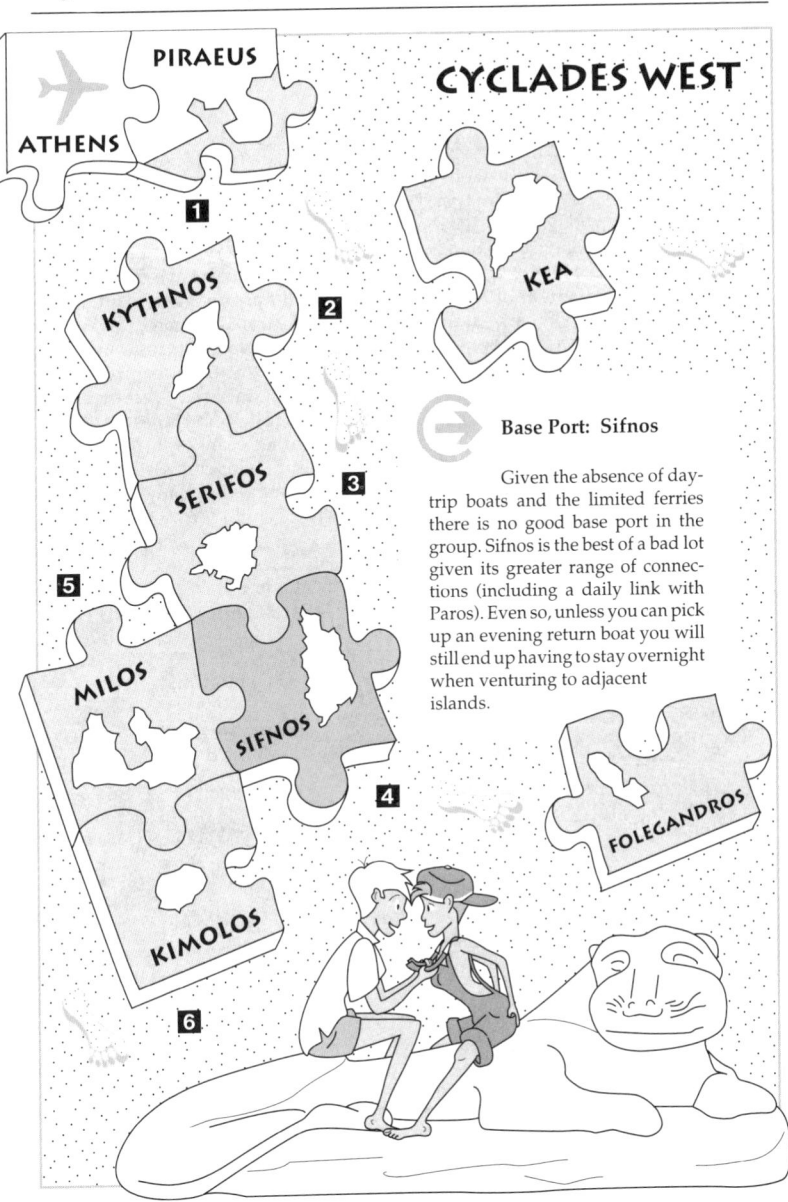

CYCLADES WEST

Base Port: Sifnos

Given the absence of day-trip boats and the limited ferries there is no good base port in the group. Sifnos is the best of a bad lot given its greater range of connections (including a daily link with Paros). Even so, unless you can pick up an evening return boat you will still end up having to stay overnight when venturing to adjacent islands.

PIRAEUS

ATHENS

1

KYTHNOS

2

KEA

SERIFOS

3

5

MILOS

SIFNOS

4

FOLEGANDROS

KIMOLOS

6

Cyclades West Ferry Services

Main Car Ferries

A combination of fewer tourists and a shorter sailing time to Piraeus results in an appreciably lower level of activity and competition than on other routes. For the last 5 years schedules have been dominated by the ferries (bar the *Georgios Express*) here with the pattern of services seeing only minor changes each summer (mostly one suspects to relieve the monotony). An odd characteristic of the line is that there is less of a regular 'run', almost every possible combination of ports attempted. Links with other routes remain poor, as does the amount of tourist boat activity. This is, however, set to change: pressures of tourism in the rest of the Cyclades are encouraging increasing numbers onto this line. Recent moves by hydrofoil operators into the region are further encouraging this trend.

C/F *Milos Express*

Lindos Lines; 1969; 4797 GRT.

The largest ferry now operating down the line, this elegant Lindos Lines boat (formerly the cross-Channel *Vortigern*) has been on this service for the last seven summers. Schedules have changed little during that time (though 1994 did see a major shake up). Fortunately, this didn't damage her invaluable cross-line links with the islands at the southern end of the Cyclades Central line. These remained intact; though days and times did change. Expect further changes in 1995. Out of High Season she operates less frequently on the line and occasionally deputises on others (e.g. running down the Peloponnese to Crete). Deck-class facilities are adequate, but showing her age (the other large boats on the line having a major competitive edge in this respect).

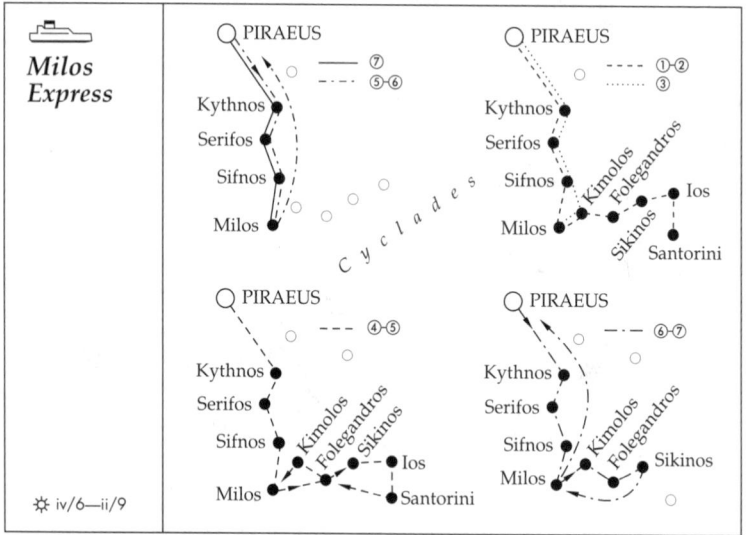

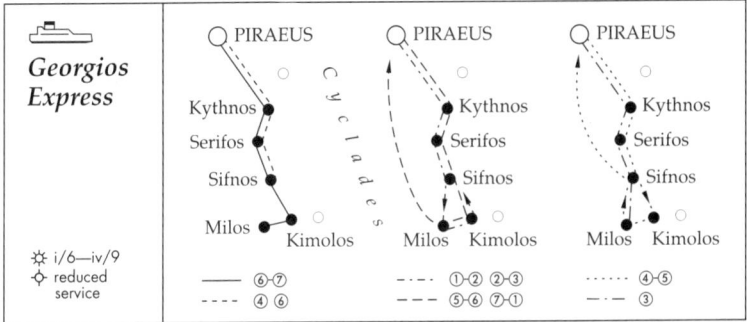

Georgios Express

☼ i/6—iv/9
✧ reduced service

PIRAEUS
Kythnos
Serifos
Sifnos
Milos
Kimolos
Cyclades

—— ⑥-⑦
- - - - ④ ⑥

PIRAEUS
Kythnos
Serifos
Sifnos
Milos Kimolos

- - - · ①-② ②-③
- - - ⑤-⑥ ⑦-①

PIRAEUS
Kythnos
Serifos
Sifnos
Milos Kimolos

· · · · · · ④-⑤
— · — ③

C/F *Georgios Express*

Ventouris Sea Lines; 1965; 3023 GRT.
One of the stately old ladies of the Greek ferry scene, the elderly *Georgioś Express* runs a 'try-every-island-combination' schedule down the Cyclades West line. Until 1993 she partnered the *Apollo Express 1* on the Cyclades Central line (a role still advertised on company hoardings and out-of-date posters), but like the other boats in the Ventouris Sea Lines fleet she was moved 'along one' in the fleet reshuffle that followed the arrival of the *Apollo Express 2*. Deck-class facilities are, if anything, better than either of the *Apollo*s. Clean and well maintained, the interior seating is not exactly in the luxury category, but is nonetheless adequate. Only the limited nature of buffet and restaurant facilities are a real source of complaint. On the plus side, she has a creditable record for reliability, and is arguably now the best ferry on this line.

Ventouris Sea Lines

C/F *Artemis*; 1960; 4952 GRT.
For the last five years Ventouris Sea Lines have run a regular service down this line — with several sorties down the Cyclades Central Line (see p. 135) and the Cyclades West—Rhodes service (see p. 228) via a now defunct ferry, the C/F *Sifnos Express*. Now sold, it remains to be seen which boat replaces her. The most likely candidate is

another VSL ferry: the *Artemis*. Formerly the *Panagia Tinou*, this boat was a mainstay of the Cyclades North Line. Designed at the end of the 50s, she is a slick-looking ferry with a conspicuous squashed funnel toward her stern. Reliable enough, she has a number of flaws. For a start she is an awkward boat to board and disembark from, partly because of a side car door, and also because her architect appears to have been a four foot midget with an obsession for stairwells and car decks adorned with quaint, but tripsy, little steps. She is also a poor night boat as her moulded plastic seating is not sleeping bag friendly.

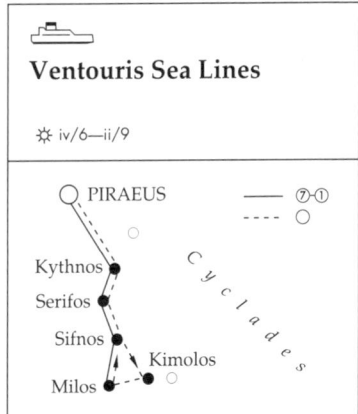

Ventouris Sea Lines

☼ iv/6—ii/9

PIRAEUS
Kythnos
Serifos
Sifnos
Kimolos
Milos
Cyclades

—— ⑦-①
- - - - ○

C/F *Anemoessa*
Local; 1975; 626 GRT.
For a brief period during 1994 the Western Cyclades saw one of Greece's less worthy ferries making occasional runs to the group. Operating out of Syros, she ran to Serifos, Sifnos, Kimolos and Milos on ② and ④, with an excursion to the Little Cyclades on ③. By the end of the summer she was employed in the Dodecanese, running a service from Rhodes to Karpathos, Kassos and Eastern Crete. A regular tub that looks far older than her age, she is a low, slow boat that used to be the mainstay of the Evia (Kimi)—Skyros service. Very unreliable, it is anyone's guess where she will try to make a living next. However, she is a boat to look out for — especially in the Low Season.

T/B *Margarita*
A very useful — if little known — service between the West and Central Lines, the *Margarita* links Sifnos and Paros 'daily' in July and August (June and September ① ③ ⑤ only). A large cabin-topped caïque, her size is her great problem; too small to be graced by the term 'ferry', she is no bigger than a tourist excursion boat and thus subject to the vagaries of the weather: the 3½ hour crossing is often cancelled several days running. Even in flat seas her wooden hull rolls so much that passengers are handed plastic bags after the tickets are collected: so many passengers are sea-sick on this boat that it is almost bad manners not to be so.

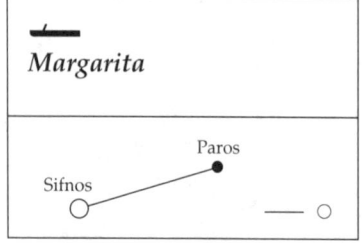

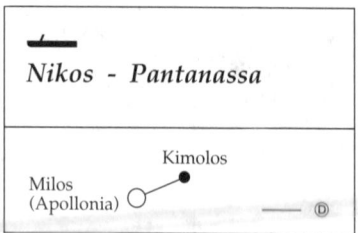

T/B *Nikos - Pantanassa*
These Apollonia-based taxi boats make the crossing to Kimolos three times daily in High Season. At £1 it's cheaper — if somewhat more choppy — than taking a ferry from Adamas.

Kea Channel Ferry Services
At the northern end of the Cyclades West Line lies the island of Kea. Ignored by virtually every Cycladic-bound ferry it floats adrift from the rest of the group and is served by ferries operating across the narrow Kea Channel from the mainland port of Lavrion. Until 1992, the ex-*Royal Daffodil* (one of the ferries across the Mersey) ran on the Kea—Lavrion crossing, initially as the *Iouis Keas II*, and latterly as the *Agia Kyriaki*. Sadly, this quaint ferry hasn't been seen of late, with the *Mirina Express* running solo in her place.

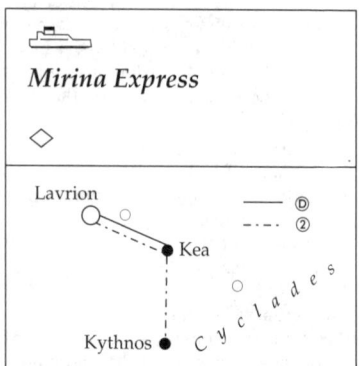

C/F *Mirina Express*
Goutos Lines; 1975; 1168 GRT.
The best ferry in the small Goutos Lines fleet, this vessel has become the mainstay of the Lavrion—Kea route; usually mooring overnight on Kea. Greek built, she has the traditional, but now rare, external staircases for passengers at her stern. Otherwise she is rather characterless, though the presence of a reasonable deck-class saloon means that there is no need to buy a higher class ticket to travel in reasonable comfort on this boat. Despite the arrival of hydrofoils in 1992, she has maintained her practice of previous years of providing a once weekly Kea—Kythnos service (though it has to be said that these trips see her running all but empty). Only black mark against her are the weekends when the Athenian commuter rush to cottage retreats in Kea means she is very full, even with extra sailings.

H/F *Flying Dolphin*
In 1992 Kea finally emerged from its isolation from the rest of the Greek ferry system courtesy of a daily hydrofoil link with Piraeus (Zea Marina) and Kythnos. This operates once daily either side of the summer and twice daily during the High Season. An additional call at the Apollo coast resort of Anavissos existed in 1992. Major changes are unlikely in 1995.

ILIO Hydrofoils
Running out of Rafina, ILIO introduced a hydrofoil service to Kea and the Western Cyclades in 1993. Schedules never bedded down (with considerable mid-season changes), and in 1994 were reduced from a daily to a once weekly run down the line. Further modifications (hopefully for the better) are probable in 1995. These are thus boats to look out for rather than rely on. Travellers to Kea should also note that some hydrofoils were putting in at the mock-windmill tourist resort of Koundouros as well as Korissia ferry port. These calls did not appear on timetables.

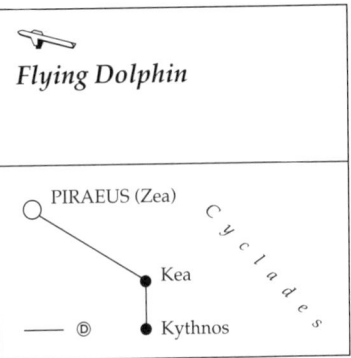

Flying Dolphin

PIRAEUS (Zea)

Kea

Kythnos

Cyclades

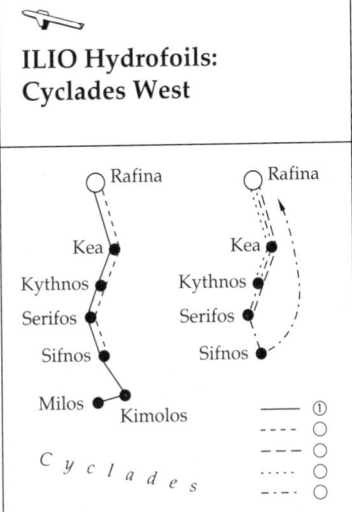

ILIO Hydrofoils: Cyclades West

Rafina   Rafina

Kea   Kea
Kythnos   Kythnos
Serifos   Serifos

Sifnos   Sifnos

Milos
Kimolos

Cyclades

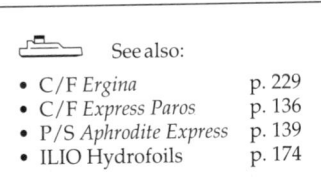

See also:

- C/F *Ergina*   p. 229
- C/F *Express Paros*   p. 136
- P/S *Aphrodite Express* p. 139
- ILIO Hydrofoils   p. 174

Cyclades West Islands & Ports

Folegandros

ΦΟΛΕΓΑΝΔΡΟΣ; 32 km²; pop. 650.

A 'romantic' island boasting one road and no large shops, Folegandros has long been known as a get-away-from-it-all sort of place. In the last few years it has attracted a select clientele of up-market island lovers drawn by the quiet laid-back atmosphere. The islanders, eager to get the economic benefits of tourism but not over-keen on the more tacky aspects of the trade, have happily promoted this image, with the result that Folegandros has managed to retain its traditional lifestyle yet also take advantage of a relatively small number of visitors with money to spend. If your object in island hopping is to find a port of respite from the modern world then you could do far worse than be washed up here — provided, of course, that your budget can stand it. This is not to say that those with limited funds should be put off visiting (those that do miss a lot); you just have to work on the assumption that this is one place where you might have to splash out a bit for a day or two. Much will depend on the time of year that you visit. Out of High Season Folegandros could never be described as crowded, but during July and August the island often seems to be so, simply because the port and town are very small and have difficulty coping with those that do call. In fact, compared to any of the 'popular' islands the numbers visiting are surprisingly low.

At first sight Folegandros appears to live up to its historical role as a place of exile, courtesy of its arid and rocky landscape, but as is so often the case with Greek islands, first impressions can be misleading. The dusty little port in Karavastasis bay doesn't do the island justice. Relatively new, it is little more than a motley collection of tourist-generated buildings trailed around a rather poor beach. Now used as the island caïque harbour, the fishermen weighing their catches and mending nets on the quay inadvertently add some colour, and with each season the port becomes a little more lively. The locals have tried to tart it up as best they can (latterly by adding an elaborate staircase down to a second poor beach over the quayside headland), but it remains more of a place to pass through rather than stay in. Two roads run out of the port. The first skirts the port beach and then round the bay and over a headland before running down to Livadi beach (an indifferent strand of sand) with the campsite on the hillside behind. The second is the main island road, running up to the Chora and the settlements behind. Buses run regularly between the two (times are posted up at the 'bus station' on the ferry quay).

Chora (also known as Folegandros Town) is the only large centre and lies 4 km from the port. One of the most attractive of the traditional whitewashed cubist Cycladic villages, it is a mini Mykonos Town without the crowds, and feels like the sort of place where everybody obviously knows everybody else and everybody else's grandmother besides. Part of the secret of its appeal is its location. Set atop a 200 m cliff on the northern coast it shares that 'living on the edge of the world' feeling common to the caldera towns on Santorini. However, unlike the latter, Chora doesn't look the dizzy views in the eye (though there are several good vantage points) but for the most part turns in on itself. The result is a cosy huddle of houses and churches centred on a couple of leafy squares (thanks to a number of large plane trees) decked with pots of red geraniums and check-cloth taverna tables that leave one feeling that

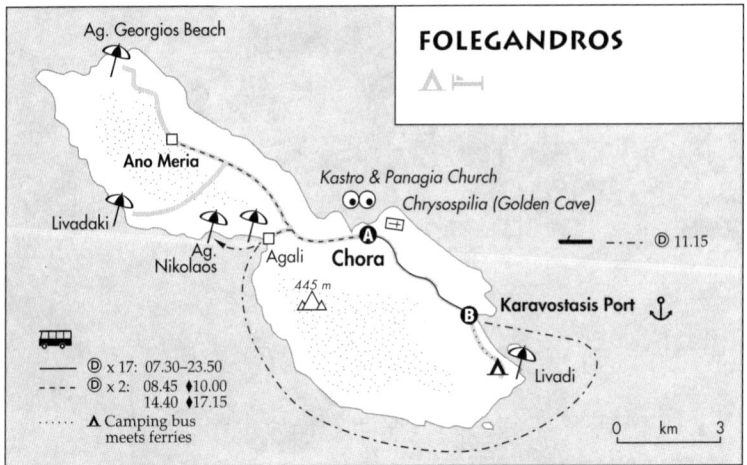

FOLEGANDROS

Ag. Georgios Beach

Ano Meria

Kastro & Panagia Church

Chrysospilia (Golden Cave)

Livadaki

Ag. Nikolaos

Agali Chora

445 m

Karavostasis Port

Livadi

Ⓓ x 17: 07.30–23.50
Ⓓ x 2: 08.45 ♦10.00
14.40 ♦17.15
Ⓓ 11.15
Λ Camping bus meets ferries

0   km   3

one is tucked away in the heart of a cosy provincial French hill village. Chora is a great place for romantic evening meals (to say nothing of futile cliff-edge gestures if all you end up with is a spot of unrequited love or the taverna bill). The best part of all is the old Kastro quarter of town. This neatly hides the cliff-edge from view, besides offering the best surviving example of the medieval house-stockade forts built to defeat Cycladic islands from pirate attacks. Its interior is a real delight; the flower-filled isles of whitewashed houses being adorned with brightly painted balconies and ranks of external staircases (each with its own cat). New development in the town is confined to strips along the access roads; the liveliest being along the dusty Ano Meria road which has several bars and a disco en route to the Fani Vevis pension.

After passing by Chora the main road runs west along the spine of the island. Although there is a bus service of sorts along it, it is also a ready made excursion if you are up to the walk. There are several possible destinations; the first being the excellent sand beach at **Agali** (also known

as Vathi, and just under an hour's walk from Chora) complete with a couple of tavernas offering rooms. From here a coastal path winds its way to a second good beach at **Ag. Nikolaos**. Both can also be reached by a daily beach caïque running from the port in High Season. If beaches aren't your thing you can continue to walk west along the windmill-clad island spine road (complete with superb views of Serifos and Crete) to **Ano Meria**: a very quiet little village that does little more than hug the island road it is hardly a major attraction in itself, but it at least provides a destination to aim for.

⊨

Rooms are available to rent in the port, but most tourists take the bus that meets all boats to **Chora**, which is both prettier and has more options. The most appealing of these is the small hotel in the old kastro, the E-class *Castro* (☎ 41230). Rooms are scattered around the town, but other hotels are confined to the outskirts. The best thing in town is the new C-class *Polik-ania* (☎ 41322) on the port road. The Chora—Panagia Church path also has some very plush furnished apartments along it. Somewhat more down-market rooms lie on the east side of town, along with the E-class

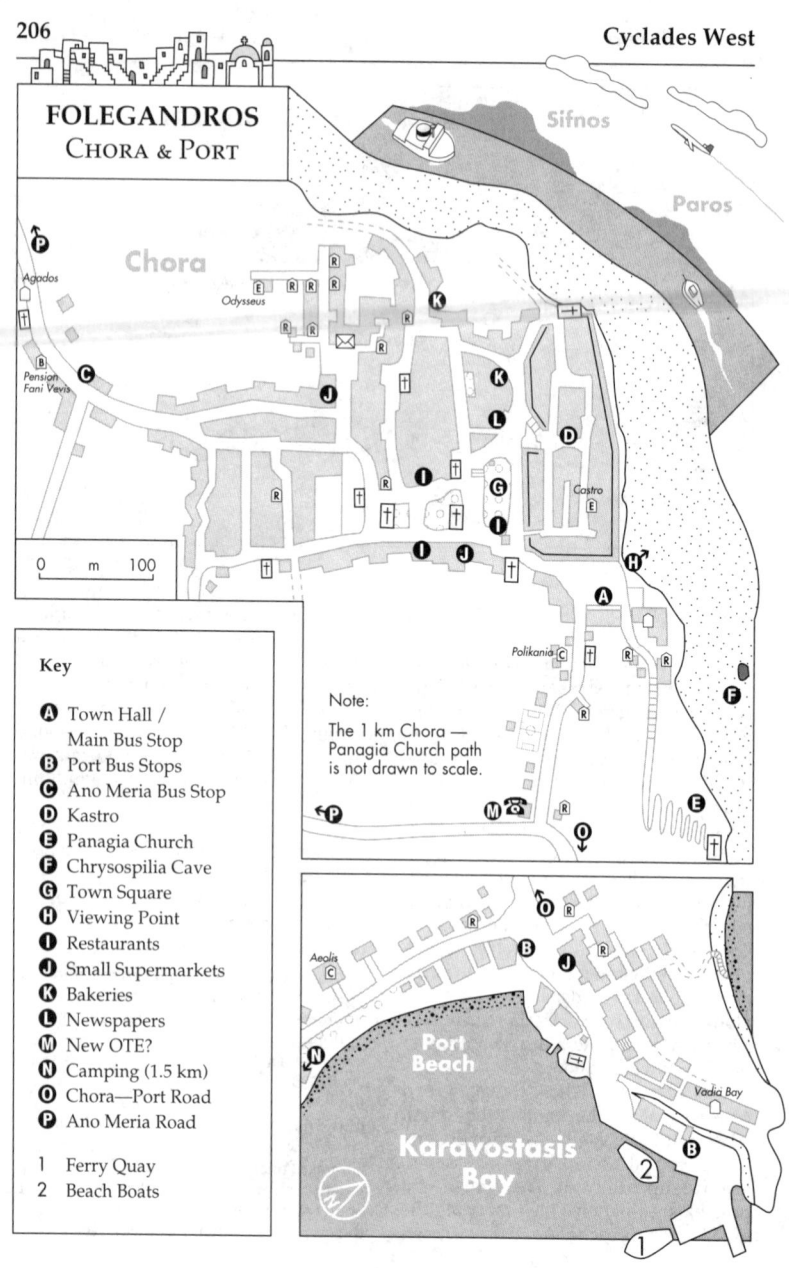

FOLEGANDROS
Chora & Port

Chora

Sifnos

Paros

Agados

Odysseus

Pension Fani Vevis

0   m   100

Castro

Polikania

Note:

The 1 km Chora — Panagia Church path is not drawn to scale.

Key

Ⓐ Town Hall / Main Bus Stop
Ⓑ Port Bus Stops
Ⓒ Ano Meria Bus Stop
Ⓓ Kastro
Ⓔ Panagia Church
Ⓕ Chrysospilia Cave
Ⓖ Town Square
Ⓗ Viewing Point
Ⓘ Restaurants
Ⓙ Small Supermarkets
Ⓚ Bakeries
Ⓛ Newspapers
Ⓜ New OTE?
Ⓝ Camping (1.5 km)
Ⓞ Chora—Port Road
Ⓟ Ano Meria Road

1   Ferry Quay
2   Beach Boats

Aeolis

Port Beach

Vadia Bay

Karavostasis Bay

Odysseas (☎ 4139). The Chora—Ano Meria road also has a couple of pensions including the deceptively dour-fronted B-class *Fani Vevis* (☎ 41237). **Karavastasis Port** also has several hotels including the C-class *Aeolis* (☎ 41205).

Δ

Camping Livadi (☎ 41204); 2 km west of the port along the coast path. Lack of competition (and water) all too evident with the very poor washing facilities — hence the freelance camping on the adjacent beach. Bring food-stuffs with you as the campsite restaurant takes full advantage of the longish walk to the port (a rusty mini-bus meets ferries). Tents are available for hire, but view before you pay: some of the 'two persons' jobs are *very* small.

👓

Only island sights are the **Chora** and its **Kastro** (built in 1212 AD). The attractive whitewashed **Panagia Church** lies on the cliff-hill on the north-east side of the Chora and stands on the foundations of the ancient city wall that stood on the site. Rare excursion boats also head for **Chrysospilia** (Golden Cave) set in the base of the cliff below the Chora just above sea level when conditions are calm enough.

☎

CODE 0286, POLICE 41249,
FIRST AID 41222.

Kea

KEA; 131 km²; pop. 1700.

Despite being only three hours from Athens, Kea (also transcribed as Tzia) is one of the hidden pearls of the Aegean, retaining much of its rural charm and now popular with those who like walking holidays. This is something of an unfamiliar role for an island that was home to an important Minoan outpost and was one of the cradles of Greek civilisation. Kea has always been, and remains, an island set apart from the rest. Not only did it manage to support four city states where most islands could barely manage one, but it was also a pioneer of social change by introducing a compulsory celebratory cup of hemlock when its citizens reached retirement age at 70. These days the locals buy holiday homes instead. Kea thus tends to fill up quickly on weekends with

Athenians escaping the city smog. Foreign tourists are comparatively thin on the ground, and nightlife is non-existent. If you intend to stay then plan for a mid-week arrival.

All ferries and hydrofoils dock at the small port of **Korissia**, a tapering hamlet sited on the west side of Agios Nikolaos bay. On the south side is a large beach and the port accommodation. Apart from these attractions there is little incentive to linger. Buses head regularly for the red-tile roofed main town of **Ioulis** or **Chora**. Visible from the port, it sits in a natural amphitheatre in the hills, overlooked by a handful of ruined windmills. The town itself clings to a couple of hillsides; the old Kastro dominating one, and the Chora the other. The streets are too narrow to admit vehicles, and this remains an attractive island working town. If you can find a room here you will find this is also the best base for exploring the island.

The rest of Kea is an odd mix of unspoilt countryside and holiday-villa filled villages. Best of these is the delightfully named **Pisses**. With a good beach backed by a fertile valley, it is now served by the barely adequate island bus service (time-tables seem to be geared to school times) along with the northern hamlets of **Vourkari** and **Otzias**. These are both holi-day villa centres of little interest. The south-west coast hamlet **Koundouros** is also a holiday home-lined bay, but rather more distinctive thanks to several large artificial windmill homes near the small quay that sees occasional hydrofoils call.

⊨

Rooms are on offer in Korissia and the Chora, Ioulis. Hotel and pension options are thin on the ground: though this shouldn't mean you have any difficulty finding a bed. **Ioulis** has one B-class pension, the *Ioulis* (☎ 22177), near the Kastro, and an E-class hotel, the *Filoxenia* (☎ 22057) in the northern quarter of the chora. **Korissa** has the C-class hotel *Karthea* (☎ 21204) and a B-class 'motel', the *Tzia Mas* (☎ 21305). **Koundouros** also has one hotel: the pricey B-class *Kea Beach* (☎ 31230).

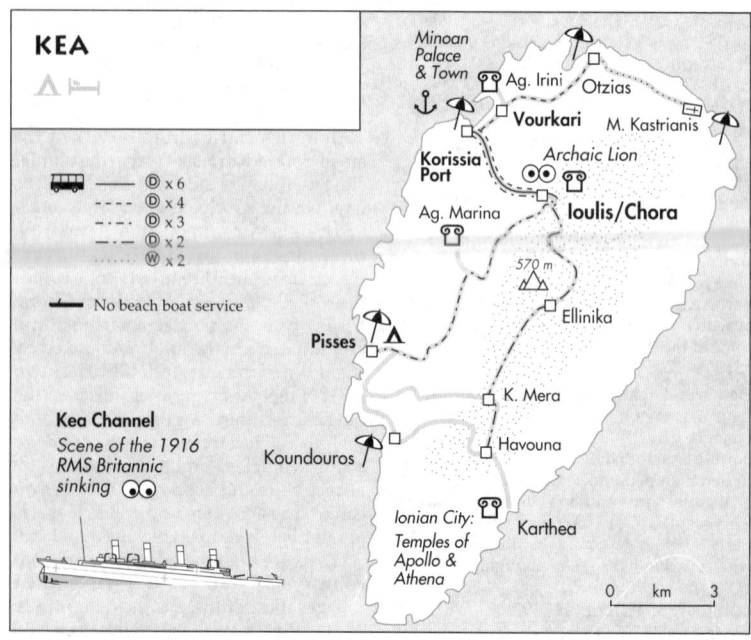

KEA

⊕ x 6
⊕ x 4
⊕ x 3
⊕ x 2
Ⓦ x 2

No beach boat service

Kea Channel
*Scene of the 1916
RMS Britannic
sinking* ◉◉

Minoan Palace & Town — Ag. Irini — Otzias — Vourkari — M. Kastrianis — Korissia Port — Archaic Lion — Ag. Marina — Ioulis/Chora — 570 m — Ellinika — Pisses — K. Mera — Havouna — Koundouros — Ionian City: Temples of Apollo & Athena — Karthea

0   km   3

A

Camping Kea (☎ 31335). A nice site on the best island beach at Pisses 16 km from the port, it suffers somewhat from its isolated location.

◉◉

Oldest and most accessible of the Kea sites is on the promontory north of the port: the foundations of a **Minoan Palace** at Ag. Irini. Of the four ancient cities surprisingly little remains except at remote **Karthea** for which you will need your own transport. **Ioulis** (home of the 5 c. BC poet Simonides) has the remains of a **Venetian Kastro** built out of the ruins of a temple to Apollo. There is also a **Museum** housing island finds in the town. The most impressive sight lies just to the north-east of the town, the 6 c. BC **Lion of Kea**: 6 m long, it is carved sphinx-like from an out-crop of rock and wears the enigmatic smile of one who has answered the sphinx's riddle ('What creature has four legs in the morning, two in the daytime and three in the evening?') The third city (Korissia) produced a famous

Kouros statue (now in Athens) but otherwise (like the fourth of Kea's cities Poiessa — near Pisses on the seaboard of Kea's market garden valley) there is little extant on the ground today. Elsewhere on the island you will find a **Hellenistic Watchtower** at **Ag. Marina** and a monastery at M. Kastrianis.

One final site of interest is the steamy, mirror-smooth **Kea Channel**. Although there is noth-ing to see except sea, sea, sea, the strait is the last resting place of the *Britannic* (sister-ship of the *Titanic*). Lying on her starboard side in 350 m of water she can now only be viewed via a Jacques Cousteau video. Originally laid down as the *Gigantic*, she was renamed for her launch in 1914, and sank off Kea after hitting a mine while serving as a hospital ship during the 1916 Dardanelles campaign. Like her fam-ous sister, she was the largest ship semi-afloat at the time of her sinking.

☎

CODE 0288, PORT POLICE 21344, POLICE 21100, FIRST AID 22200.

Kimolos
ΚΙΜΟΛΟΣ; 38 km²; pop. 800.

A good island to escape the crowds and the more commercial trappings of tourism, Kimolos is named after the 'kimolia' or chalk that was mined here before Fuller's Earth (used in the manufacture of porcelain) took over as the dusty mainstay of the local economy, leaving the northern hillsides badly scarred with open cast mines. This sounds singularly uninviting, yet it creates a very false impression, for the southern half of the island has a nice sleepy backwater atmosphere with a number of excellent sand beaches (notably at Aliki). Those looking for a tranquil holiday in traditional surroundings will find Kimolos a minor gem.

All ferries dock at the small port of **Psathi** on the south-east coast. Little more than a rather dour quay beside a beach lined with odd trees and fishermen's houses, it looks suitably like the back of beyond. The air of abandon is greatly enhanced by the crescent of hills behind the port, complete with 10 derelict windmills; relief coming only from the hill-top Chora dominating the sky-line. The chora and port are linked by a 1 km road — the main one on the island. Chora itself is a pretty, unspoilt, working island village; complete with a dominating cathedral and, hidden away in the ramshackle streets in its centre, another of those small house-stockade kastros built to protect the inhabitants from marauding pirates.

In the absence of any public transport the rest of Kimolos is very quiet, apart from Prassa which is busier thanks to the mining industry. The main means of travel to and from Kimolos is via caïques to Milos (Apollonia) departing from the ferry quay when numbers are sufficient (usually 4 x ⑩ in High Season).

🚤

The lack of anything approaching a hotel reflects the small number of overnight visitors to Kimolos. Fortunately, there is a reasonable supply of rooms. Most are in **Chora**, but the

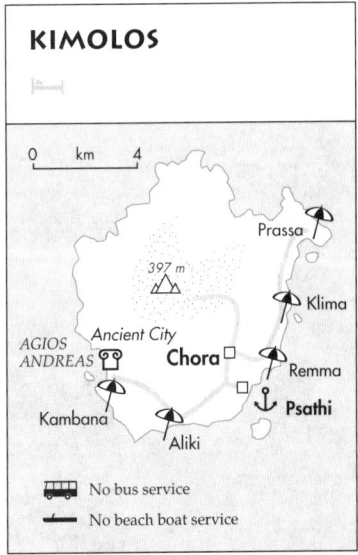

KIMOLOS

port at **Psathi** also has a block of holiday rooms on the road to Chora, and the tavernas backing on to **Aliki** beach also offer beds; notably *Taverna Aliki* (☎ 51340). Freelance camping is tolerated on the remoter beaches.

👓

Kimolos has, from its earliest history, been dominated by its large neighbour Milos. This limited development on the island, and with it possible sights. These do exist, but most are located in the remoter parts of the island and take some effort to visit. The **Chora** is the exception, and along with appealing views has the **Medieval Kastro**. The inner part dates from the 13 C., the outer walls from the 17 C. The chora aside, the main points of interest are a sulphur spring at the northern hamlet of **Prassa**, a surviving **Tower** of the ubiquitous ruined Venetian kastro (built on the slopes of the island's highest mountain, Paliokastro), and the site of the island's **Ancient Capital** on the west coast (now largely submerged between Kimolos and Ag. Andreas islet).

☎

CODE 0287, PORT POLICE 22100, POLICE 51205, FIRST AID 51222.

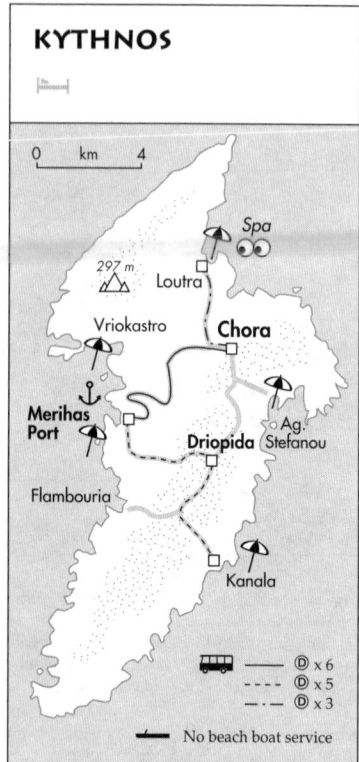

KYTHNOS

0   km   4

297 m

Spa

Loutra

Vriokastro

Chora

Merihas Port

Ag. Stefanou

Driopida

Flambouria

Kanala

🚌 —— Ⓓ x 6
---- Ⓓ x 5
—·— Ⓓ x 3

▬ No beach boat service

Kythnos

ΚΥΘΝΟΣ; 86 km²; pop. 1500.

A friendly, rocky little place three hours sailing south of Athens with few tourist facilities, Kythnos (also often transcribed as 'Kithnos') is not the sort of island where the casual island hopper will be tempted to linger. The main attraction of the place is its very lack of attractions: a feature more likely to appeal to the jaded palette of the experienced island hopper than a novice. None of the island centres has much on offer. The port of **Merihas** is strung around a small bay on the west coast and is slowly emerging as a resort village in lieu of better alternatives elsewhere. It has a beach of sorts, a couple of general stores and not a lot else. The coves to the north and south offer quieter and better beaches if you are prepared to walk (the former are considerably nearer than the southern Flambouria beach). The best island beach is on the east coast at **Ag. Stefanou**, but few venture this far.

The island bus service links the port (buses depart from just behind the beach: times are posted in the front windscreens) with the main towns on Kythnos. First among these (at least with the elderly Greeks who make up the bulk of the island's visitors) is the 19 c. spa resort and fishing port at **Loutra** on the north coast. Sadly, a thimbleful of the thermal waters has more fizz than all the holiday-makers here put together. Inland there are two more settlements of note; the new capital at **Chora**, and the former centre at **Driopida**. Chora has an ill assorted mix of architectural styles with everything from old style Cycladic houses (complete with the usual whitewashed-edged crazy paving paths—only tarted up with flowers painted on them) to ugly new electricity-generating windmills and red tile roofs reminiscent of Kea. More attractive Driopida has more going for it, and evolved around the only island 'sight' — the **Katafiki Cave** at the head of the valley in which the town lies.

🛏

Even in High Season you can't walk far from the ferry quay without islanders calling out 'Room?' Lack of tourists all but guarantees a cheap bed on demand. Hotel accommodation is rather thinner on the ground. The island has four C-class establishments; most are in the spa 'resort' of **Loutra**. At the bottom end of the range is the relatively inexpensive *Xenia Anagenissis* (☎ 31217). This is followed by the pricier *Kythnos Bay* (☎ 31218) and *Meltemi* (☎ 31271). **Merihas Port** has the popular *Possidonion* (☎ 31200) overlooking the bay.

☎

CODE 0281, TOURIST POLICE 31201, FIRST AID 31202.

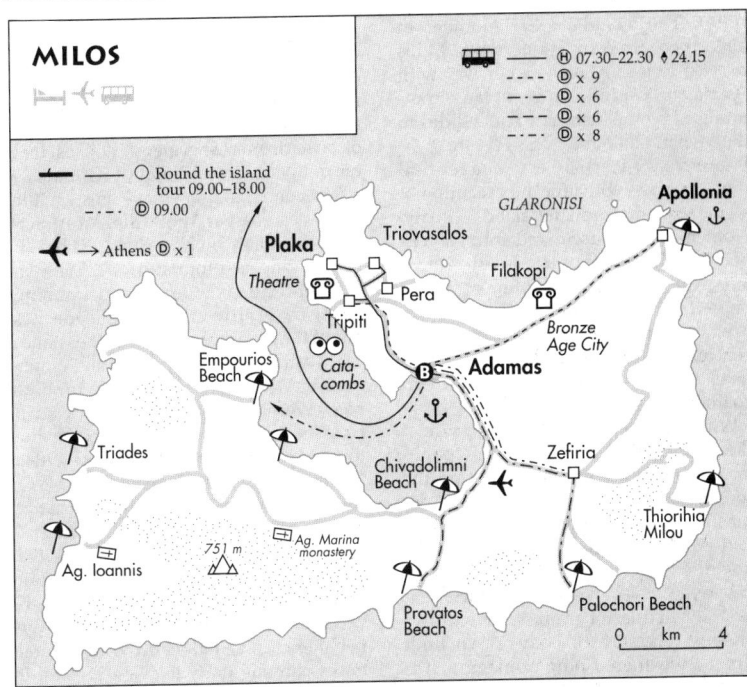

MILOS

🚌 —— Ⓗ 07.30–22.30 ♦ 24.15
---- Ⓓ x 9
—·— Ⓓ x 6
——— Ⓓ x 6
—··— Ⓓ x 8

—— Ⓞ Round the island
tour 09.00–18.00
—··— Ⓓ 09.00

✈ → Athens Ⓓ x 1

GLARONISI

Apollonia ⚓

Plaka   Triovasalos

Theatre 🏛   ◻ Pera   Filakopi 🏛

Tripiti

Bronze Age City

Empourios Beach ⚓

👁👁 *Cata-combs*

Ⓑ **Adamas** ⚓

Triades

Zefiria ◻

Chivadolimni Beach ⚓   ✈

Thiorihia Milou

751 m ⛰   🏠 Ag. Marina monastery

Ag. Ioannis

Provatos Beach

Palochori Beach

0   km   4

Milos

ΜΗΛΟΣ; 161 km²; pop. 4500.

Like its more scenic neighbour Santorini, Milos is volcanic in origin — with its primary port of Adamas located in the flooded interior of an old caldera. Comparisons however, are apt to end there for Milos has no dramatic scenery to draw the crowds and relies on mining as the mainstay of the local economy. This has not helped the development of the tourist trade, for although the island is famous thanks to the discovery of the beautiful Hellenistic statue of Aphrodite (the Venus de Milo), mining and the workings of archaeologists looking vainly for the statue's arms, have left the island looking sadly scarred. At first sight Milos is apt to disappoint those looking for typical Greek island charm, but this is misleading, for the island has its moments and if you are on a sightseeing driven holiday has enough of interest to make it worth stopping over for a couple of days.

Thanks to its large sheltered harbour Milos was an important centre in ancient times rivalling Naxos as a centre of Pre-Hellenic civilization with an important Minoan settlement developing on the northern coast at Filiakopi. Prior to this Milos appears to have been a major trading post thanks to the availability of obsidian, a volcanic glass that could be cut to make sharp tools. Mycenaean and Archaic settlement followed apace, and by the Classical era Milos was one of the more notable of the minor players in the internecine struggles of the Greek city states. The island's great moment in history occurred in 416 BC when Milos refused to join Athens in her war with Sparta and Corinth (an event later immortalised by the historian Thucydides in the Melian Dialogue in his *History of the Peloponnesian War*). By way of a reprisal the Athenians voted for the execution of all the adult males on the island. With the women and children sold into slavery and the island repopulated with Athenians, Milos kept a low profile from then on — apart from a short period in the 17 c. when it emerged as a notorious pirate centre, and World War One when it was used as a major allied naval base and coaling station.

With the exception of the north side of the island, Milos is very sparsely populated. Few tourists venture beyond the triangle of settlements made up of Adamas, Plaka (and its associated villages) and Apollonia. The port of **Adamas** is now the biggest of the three, and this is not saying a lot: like the island itself, at first sight it doesn't impress, but it grows on most who stay for a day or two. Built upon a weathered plug of magma, it is distinctive, even if the waterfront is not the prettiest in Greece — the views across the bay (which looks more like a lake as the entrance is hidden from view) are marred by the commercial ships serving the mining industry. Either side of the town are several small sandy beaches. There are also several discos in town that are the sum total of the island's nightlife.

North of Adamas lies the classical centre of Milos. This part of the island is dominated by a cluster of four villages the prettiest of which, **Plaka** , is the island capital. Easily the most photogenic part of Milos, it is an unspoilt whitewashed chora with the usual warren of streets to get hopelessly lost in, and with superb views and a couple of museums worth visiting. Dominating the town is another volcanic mound topped with a number of chapels: all that remain of the old Venetian Kastro-

cum-town. The other villages in the quartet are close enough to walk to: the best being **Tripiti** running down from a windmill topped hill to the remains of the ancient island capital and the lovely string of waterfront fishermens' houses that make up the tiny old port of **Klima**.

A second fishing village lies on the north-east coast at **Apollonia**. An attractive little village lining a sheltered bay, it is emerging as a tourist resort. Even in spite of the inevitable open-cast mining eating away an overlooking hillside, it is one of the more scenic parts of the island. The availability of caïques to neighbouring Kimolos also helps (along with some nice tavernas and rooms) to draw such tourists as come to Milos. Backing the town bay is a sand beach complete with a few trees, tents and a long neglected WC.

Around the rest of the island are a scatter of good and scantily occupied beaches — those in the monastery and goat inhabited west of the island inaccessible without your own transport. The best of these served by the reasonable bus system is the pebble beach at **Palochori** with several buses running daily in High Season. If you have your own transport you can do better, for Milos is blessed with a plentiful supply of attractive, but remote, beaches that are ideal for indiscrete nudism. A beach boat runs across the main bay to one at **Empourios**, and the island boat tour gives you a glimpse of the rest.

⊨

The Information Office (☎ 22445) at the end of the ferry quay hands out information sheets showing the location of all hotels on the island. Rooms on Milos tend to be 10–20% more expensive than elsewhere in the group. There are no campsites but unofficial summer beach camps spring up at Adamas (over the headland west of the port) and Apollonia.

Most of the hotels and pensions are in **Adamas**. These include the spiffy, pricey C-class *Venus Village* (☎ 22030) complex, complete with swimming pool and the port's best beach. Also ideally placed to take advantage of this are the C-class *Afrodite* (☎ 22020) and the D-

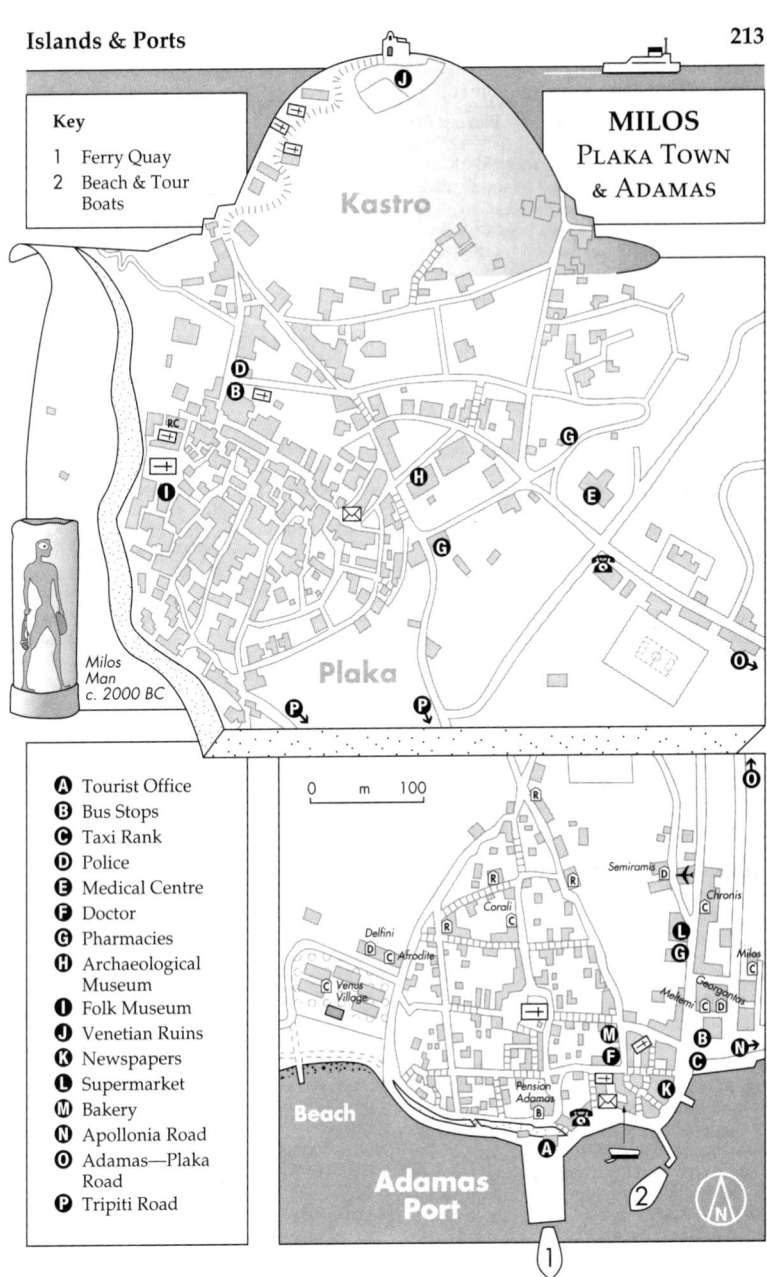

Key

1 Ferry Quay
2 Beach & Tour Boats

MILOS
PLAKA TOWN
& ADAMAS

Kastro

Milos Man c. 2000 BC

Plaka

A Tourist Office
B Bus Stops
C Taxi Rank
D Police
E Medical Centre
F Doctor
G Pharmacies
H Archaeological Museum
I Folk Museum
J Venetian Ruins
K Newspapers
L Supermarket
M Bakery
N Apollonia Road
O Adamas—Plaka Road
P Tripiti Road

0   m   100

Semiramis
Chronis
Corali
Delfini
Afrodite
Venus Village
Milos
Georgantas
Meltemi
Pension Adamas
Beach

Adamas Port

class *Delfini* (☎ 22001). More hotels are to be found on the east side of the port. Nearest the waterfront are the C-class *Meltemi* (☎22284) and *Milos* (☎ 22087) along with the D-class *Georgantas* (☎ 21955). On the Adamas—Plaka Town road behind are the C-class *Chronis* (☎ 22226) and the D-class *Semiramis* (☎ 22117). The Adamas 'hill' has less accommodation; with the C-class *Corali* (☎ 22204) augmented by the B-class pension *Adamas* (☎ 22322) and a number of rooms. Around the rest of the island the only hotel of note is the friendly D-class *Panorama* (☎ 21623) at **Klima**.

∞

Plaka and the surrounding villages have the main concentration of sights on Milos. The **Town Museum** is inevitably something of a disappointment as the main island attraction — the **Venus de Milo** (c. 320 BC) is now residing in the Louvre in Paris (it is represented here by a plaster replica). This famous statue was discovered by a farmer in a field in 1820. This was reported to the French ambassador to Constantinople who arranged for its purchase from the Turks and had it shipped to Paris. Rumours persist that when this plumpish lady was first unearthed she was not brachially disadvantaged (the first two Frenchmen who saw the statue reported their existence). Quite what happened to her arms is the subject of any number of tall tales; the best embracing ransom demands, with almost every islander having, if not an arm, then at least a hand in the business. Like the Elgin marbles, this piece of sculpture has been exploited by Greek government ministers seeking a popularist profile. The latest request to the French government for her return coming as recently as July 1994 from the Minister of the Aegean.

The **Ancient City**, down the road at nearby Tripiri, is worth wandering around; though to call the extant remains a city casts a very misleading impression given their scanty nature. Built on a relatively steep hillside, it was the island capital from around 1000 BC through to the Byzantine period. The best preserved remains are parts of the **city walls** along with a **Roman amphitheatre**. A plaque also stands on the site where *the* statue was discovered (there are plans to erect a copy of the Venus on the site): it is thought to have graced a niche in a gymnasium that stood near the stadium. The lower part of the city stood behind an ancient harbour and was dominated

by a small temple topped hill (a small church, built from the stones, now stands on the site).

Easily the most impressive remains of the ancient city are the **Catacombs**; the earliest known Christian site in Greece (they are thought to date from the 1 C. AD—St. Paul was shipwrecked on Milos). The site of Christian burials and worship for close on 400 years, they lie just outside the East Gate of the city wall. Dug into the easily worked volcanic rock they originally took the form of three unconnected tunnels (the longest being some 184 m) with secondary chambers leading off them. Since their discovery in 1840 connecting corridors have been dug between them and two of the three entrances closed off. Only the central catacomb is now occasionally opened up to the public (ask at the information office at Adamas about current opening times). If you are lucky enough to get the chance to visit you will find yourself in a long, floodlit chamber with burial niches in the walls and floor, along with cavities in the walls for oil lamps. Estimates as to the numbers interred in the catacombs range from 2000—8000, but as 'dem bones' appear to have risen up and legged it during the repeated pillaging of the catacombs in the island's piratical years (Milian skull and cross-bones flags were obviously very realistic exercises in black humour), it is all but impossible to arrive at an accurate figure.

The other major site on Milos is the **Bronze Age Town** at **Filakopi** on the Apollonia road. The site offers plenty of foundations for passing archaeologists to ponder on but little for the layman. The jumble of houses and city walls (extending under the sea) are not readily intelligible, but are nonetheless important as one of the largest Minoan towns outside Crete and Santorini. Later a major Mycenaean centre, it remained the island capital until decline set in c. 1100 BC. Some finds from the site are in the Plaka museum, but the best — including the flying fish fresco — is now in the National Archaeological Museum in Athens.

Boat trips around the island, although expensive, also make an interesting excursion; passing the strange volcanic pipe **Glaronisi** islets to the north of Milos, and the uninhabited (rare chamois goats excepted) and inaccessible island of **Antimilos** to the north-west.

☎

CODE 0287, PORT POLICE 22100, TOURIST OFFICE 22445.

Key

A Tripiri Village Bus Stop
B Main Path to Archaeological Site
C Entrance to the Catacombs
D Circular Bastion
E Internal Defensive Wall
F Stadium
G Discovery site of the Venus de Milo / Gymnasium
H Foundations of Baptistry & Early Christian Font
I Theatre
J Site of Main City Temple?
K Roman Baths
L Private Houses
M 'Hall of the Mystai' Mosaic
N Sections of City Wall
O Road to Triovasalos Village (1 km)
P Road to Plaka Village (1 km)
Q Road to Adamas Port (4 km)
R Current hiding-place of the Venus de Milo's arms

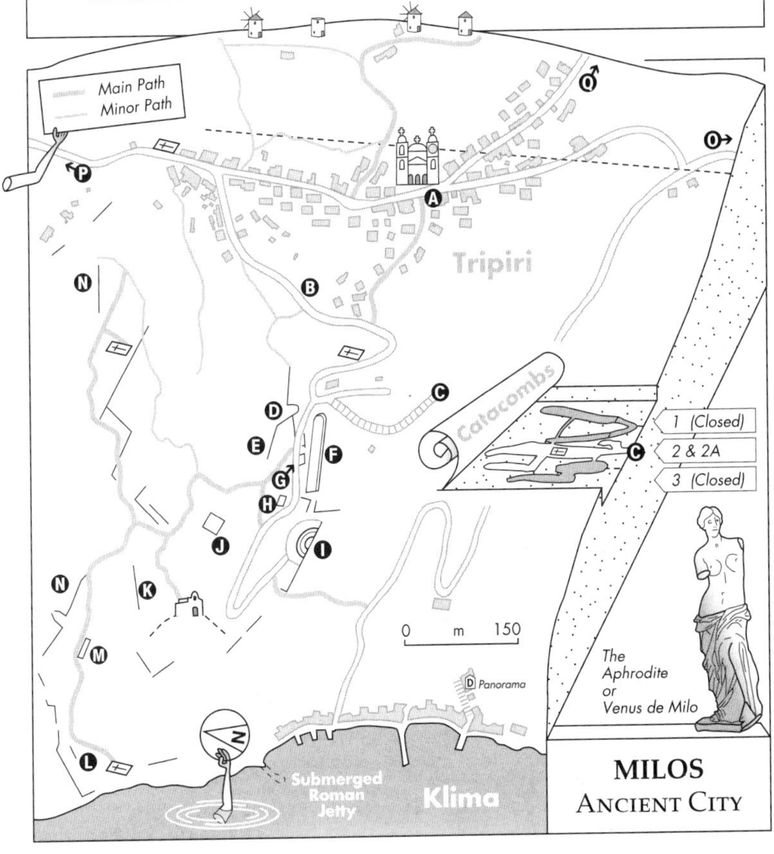

Main Path
Minor Path

P

O→

Q

A

Tripiri

N

B

Catacombs

C

1 (Closed)

2 & 2A

3 (Closed)

D

E

F

G

H

C

J

I

N

K

M

0   m   150

D Panorama

L

N

Submerged
Roman
Jetty

Klima

The
Aphrodite
or
Venus de Milo

MILOS
ANCIENT CITY

Serifos

ΣΕΡΙΦΟΣ; 70 km²; pop. 1100.

An undiscovered gem, sun-baked Serifos is blessed with a laid-back, relaxed ambiance. The island also offers a tantalizing glimpse of what Ios might have been like if it hadn't been discovered by the partying masses; for the setup is not dissimilar, with a small port overlooked by an appealing chora, coupled by a good beach a headland away. Serifos is as barren as Ios too, and as a result few venture beyond the port—chora—beach combination.

The only means of arrival and escape is the cosy pine-fringed harbour of **Livadi** (home to most of the island's facilities and a passable beach) set in a deep cut bay. Rising from the port, a dusty road winds up to the island's only town: **Chora**. Not to be missed, it deserves a visit for it is one of the most picturesque island choras around: a mini-Astipalea Town, complete with a ridge of windmills, and a hilltop Kastro. A path from Chora also winds down to the island's best beach — a long stretch of sand at **Psili Ammos**.

The dry interior of Serifos is a dull iron brown and littered with the rusting remains of the iron mining industry — now defunct. This landscape, relieved only by small green valleys and the **Taxiarchis** monastery on the north coast, tends to get a stony reception from tourists. An earlier island attraction got an even stonier reception; for Serifos was the home of Perseus, the Greek hero who (with the aid of winged boots and a mirror shield provided by his patron Athena) cut off the snake-haired head of the Gorgon Medusa (a personified shriek who, if seen, would turn the viewer into stone). Armed with this little trinket, Perseus went around the island flashing it at anyone who didn't take his fancy — much to the palaeofication of his king, Polydectes. These days, returning ex-islanders are coming home for nothing more than Sunday lunch, so weekend ferries to and from Athens are invariably very crowded.

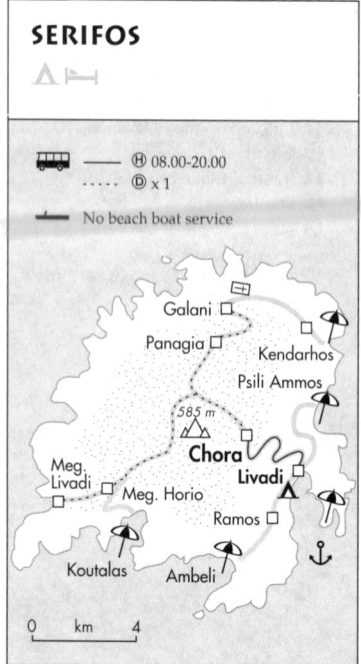

SERIFOS

⊞ 08.00-20.00
Ⓓ x 1

No beach boat service

Galani
Panagia
Kendarhos
Psili Ammos
585 m
Chora
Meg. Livadi
Meg. Horio
Livadi
Ramos
Koutalas
Ambeli

0   km   4

⊨

Almost all the accommodation on Serifos is to be found in and around the port of **Livadi**. This includes three B-class pensions: the *Areti* (☎ 51479), the *Naias* (☎ 51585) and the *Perseus* (☎ 51273). In addition there are two C-class hotels: the *Maistrali* (☎ 51381) and *Serifos Beach* (☎ 51209). At the budget end of the range is the D-class *Albatros* (☎ 51148) along with the E-class *Cyclades* (☎ 51315). A scatter of rooms — notably *Captain George Rooms* (☎ 51274) near the main square—complete the accommodation options.

Λ

Korali Camping (☎ 51500). 400 m west of the port. Very clean site but lacking shade; so it suffers from being both very hot and extremely windy. On site bungalows are also rented out.

☎

CODE 0281, PORT POLICE 51470, POLICE 51300, FIRST AID 51178.

Sifnos
ΣΙΦΝΟΣ; 89 km²; pop. 2200.

The most touristed island in the Cyclades West group, Sifnos is still fairly quiet by Central Cyclades Line standards. Much of the island's popularity can be attributed to a landscape sprinkled with typical white Cycladic villages and several good beaches. During the Archaic period Sifnos was very prosperous thanks to the discovery of gold on the island. By way of a thanks offering for this good luck the islanders were in the habit of making an annual gift of a golden egg to the god Apollo's shrine at Delphi (This wasn't as odd as it sounds for the oracle stone at Delphi, the *Omphalos* marking the centre of the world, was egg-shaped). The story has it that one year they sent a gilt egg

instead and surprise, surprise, their mines (which by now had extended out under the sea) were mysteriously flooded. This had a catastrophic effect on the island's fortunes and by the classical period Sifnos had ceased to be a major player among the islands and (until the advent of modern tourism) relied on pottery production for its livelihood — the islanders presumably working on the practical notion that if you can't dig up pots of gold you can at least make the pots).

These days Sifnos is one of those leading the pack in the second eleven of Greek Islands. All ferries and tour boats dock on the 'wrong' side of the island where a narrow gorge provides a natural harbour at **Kamares**. Here you will find tavernas by the score, travel agents and a sand

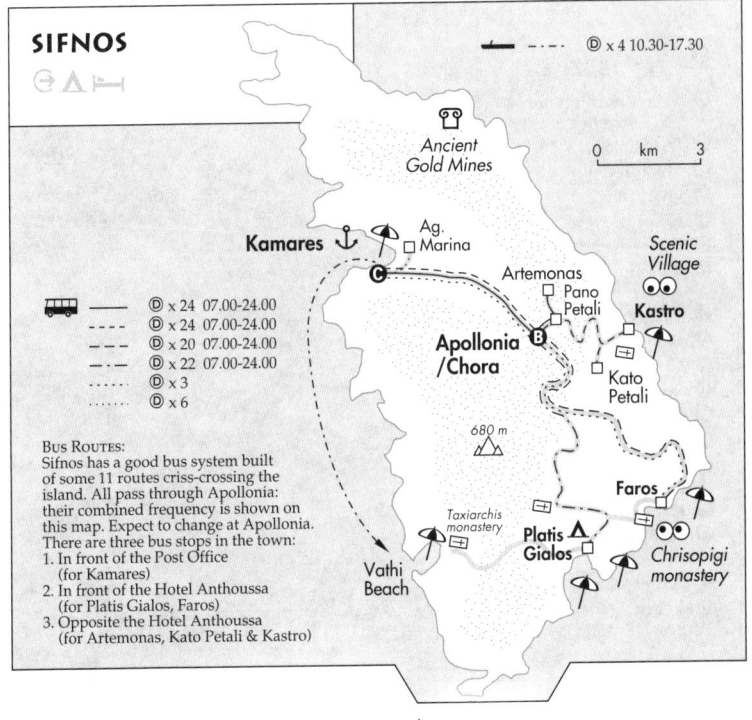

SIFNOS

ⓓ x 4 10.30-17.30

Ancient Gold Mines

0 km 3

Kamares ⚓

Ag. Marina

Artemonas
Pano Petali

Scenic Village

Kastro

Apollonia /Chora

Kato Petali

680 m

Faros

Taxiarchis monastery

Platis Gialos

Chrisopigi monastery

Vathi Beach

🚌 ——— ⓓ x 24 07.00-24.00
- - - - ⓓ x 24 07.00-24.00
— — — ⓓ x 20 07.00-24.00
—·—·— ⓓ x 22 07.00-24.00
· · · · · ⓓ x 3
· · · · · · ⓓ x 6

BUS ROUTES:
Sifnos has a good bus system built of some 11 routes criss-crossing the island. All pass through Apollonia: their combined frequency is shown on this map. Expect to change at Apollonia. There are three bus stops in the town:
1. In front of the Post Office (for Kamares)
2. In front of the Hotel Anthoussa (for Platis Gialos, Faros)
3. Opposite the Hotel Anthoussa (for Artemonas, Kato Petali & Kastro)

SIFNOS
CHORA & PORT

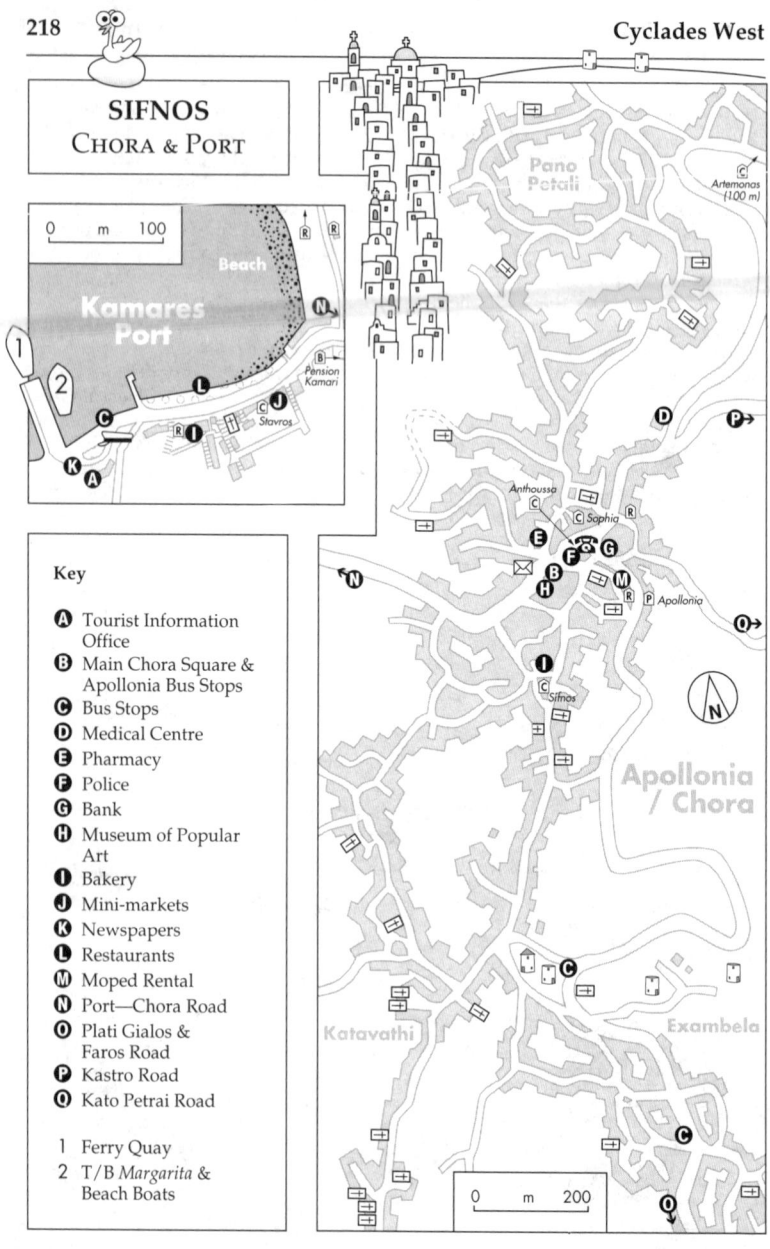

Beach

Kamares Port

Pension Kamari

Stavros

Pano Petali

Artemonas (100 m)

Anthoussa

Saphia

Apollonia

Sifnos

Apollonia / Chora

Katavathi

Exambela

Key

A Tourist Information Office
B Main Chora Square & Apollonia Bus Stops
C Bus Stops
D Medical Centre
E Pharmacy
F Police
G Bank
H Museum of Popular Art
I Bakery
J Mini-markets
K Newspapers
L Restaurants
M Moped Rental
N Port—Chora Road
O Plati Gialos & Faros Road
P Kastro Road
Q Kato Petrai Road

1 Ferry Quay
2 T/B *Margarita* & Beach Boats

0   m   100

0   m   200

beach of some length and dubious quality. Near the ferry quay there is also a helpful tourist information office. Considering how small the port is, it is a surprisingly lively place, defying the stark hills that crowd it against the water's edge. Buses run from the small turn-around point near the information office into the island's interior very frequently; making escape easy.

Given the High Season accommodation situation on Sifnos it is best to run from the ferry to the bus if you want to stay in the capital. Buses run frequently from the port, and the journey east and south (the northern third of Sifnos is unpopulated: the gold mines now being inaccessible) up a fertile valley filled with olive and fig trees that is a revelation in itself; for Sifnos is not the barren island that the port bay and coast suggest. The modern capital of **Apollonia** lies 5 km inland. As island capitals go it is a bit of an odd ball; being merely one of four closely placed hill villages that has grown (by virtue of its role as the island's cross roads) to become the de facto centre. Lacking a historical centre of note, the town has grown along the roads to the neighbouring villages rather than in a traditional manner. The other three villages of **Artemonas, Pano Petali** and **Kato Petali** effectively combine (along with the former fortified Chora and old harbour at **Kastro** on the east coast) as a Greek holiday home strip.

Foreign tourist activity is centred on the town square in Apollonia and the string of beaches along the south coast. Of these, the best (and most remote) is at taverna-backed **Vathi** — visited by regular caïques from Kamares port or by walking along a dirt track from the south-coast beach resort at **Platis Gialos**. Made up of tavernas, rooms and the odd hotel strung along the foreshore, Platis Gialos is the main beach on Sifnos. Further east lies the less popular small village of **Faros**; complete with three small beaches lined with a grubby brown sand.

⊨

Finding accommodation on Sifnos in High Season can be a problem as turn-over is slower than on other islands: it pays to arrive on a morning boat. Good tourist offices on the port waterfront and Apollonia main square are of some help. There are four of the latter in **Apollonia**, and all are C-class. Nearest the town square is the *Anthoussa* (☎ 31431), with the *Sophia* (☎ 31238) tucked away in a nearby street. Quieter than both is the *Sifnos* (☎ 31624) away to the south. The *Artemonas* (☎ 31303), 1 km to the north-east, is nice, but inconveniently placed. There is also a reasonable pension in town — the *Apollonia* (☎ 31490). **Kamares Port** also has some accommodation in the form of the C-class *Stavros* (☎ 31641) and the B-class pension *Kamari* (☎ 31641). Other towns also have hotels: **Faros** has the D-class *Sifneiko Archontiko* (☎ 31822) along with the expensive B-class *Blue Horizon* (☎ 31442), and **Platis Gialos** the B-class *Platys Gialos* (☎ 31324) and the D-class *Filoxenia* (☎ 322212).

A

Camping on Sifnos has been very poor to date. Kamares had a beach taverna which let tourists pitch a tent behind the building provided it couldn't be seen. Now forced to close, you now have to trek to *Camping Plati Gialos* (☎ 31786), an olive-tree hill site west of the bus stop. A new site is also supposed to be opening soon at Apollonia: *Camping Kinotiko*?

∞

The most popular sight is the small **Chrisopigi Monastery** sited on a small islet (linked to Sifnos by a causeway) lying west of Faros. Equally photogenic is the former island capital at **Kastro**. Largely built between the 14 — 19 C., it is now an impeccably kept little village that has retained most of its medieval character and shouldn't be missed. Not least among its sights are the old whitewashed houses complete with brightly painted wooden huts on their balconies: a Greek variation of the outside privy. Best of all is the unspoilt atmosphere; though tourists are now arriving in increasing numbers. Of the other small villages around Apollonia, Venetian-built **Artemonas** is the most attractive, with the Kohi church built on the foundations of a Temple of Artemis.

☎

CODE 0284, PORT POLICE 31617, TOURIST OFFICES 31977, 32190.

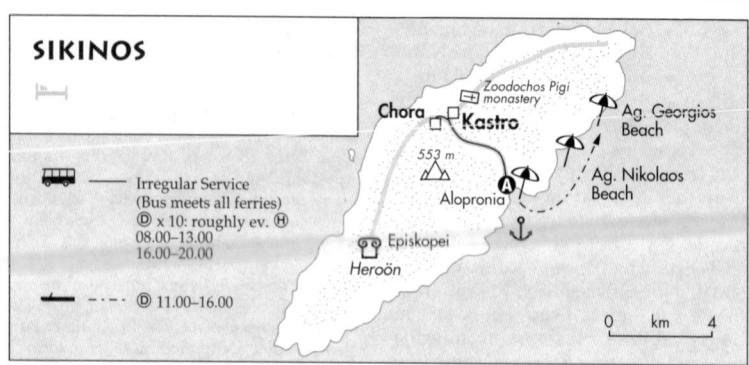

SIKINOS

Zoodochos Pigi monastery

Chora — Kastro

Ag. Georgios Beach

553 m

Aloproina

Ag. Nikolaos Beach

Episkopei
Heroön

Irregular Service
(Bus meets all ferries)
Ⓓ x 10: roughly ev. Ⓗ
08.00–13.00
16.00–20.00

Ⓓ 11.00–16.00

0   km   4

Sikinos

ΣΙΚΙΝΟΣ; 41 km²; pop. 330.

If you want to experience an 'unspoilt' Greek island you can't pick much better than Sikinos. A hilly gem close to Ios, it is only in recent years that a ferry quay, road and a hotel have appeared; changing the scruffy beach port bay but otherwise unspoiling the working island atmosphere. After Anafi, Sikinos is the least touristed large island in the Cyclades, and offers a unique insight as to what Ios and other popular islands were like in pre-tourist days. For apart from a restaurant in both village and port, there are few concessions to tourism (you are hard put to even find a postcard) and much of the island's attractiveness stems from the fact that the donkeys constantly processing through the only town are carrying water rather than tourists. Another plus is the hospitality of the islanders, who have the unusual distinction of being of Cretan stock (their ancestors re-populated the island in the 16 c.).

Sikinos is best visited via the day-trip excursion boat from Ios (see p. 137); running to the port at Aloproina. This has caïques to good beaches along the coast and buses to Kastro / Chora. As the duel name implies, the settlement consists of two closely sited villages. Climbing up the spines of opposing hillsides, they are delightful, picturesque examples of their kind. **Kastro** is the larger and its lower quarter is now the de facto 'town' centre. Shrunken **Chora** is now little more than a suburb, with a trail of ruined houses and mills running up the hillside behind.

🛏

A reasonable supply of rooms scattered around the port is augmented by a fewer number in Kastro / Chora. Few in the latter have signs: owners meet boats instead. The only hotel; *Porto Sikinos* (☎ 512 20), is new and expensive: rooms start at 13,000 GDR.

👓

Kastro / Chora aside, the only sights on Sikinos are two unusual defunct monasteries. Easily accessible is **Zoodochos Pigi**, overlooking the main town. Once fortified, it gives Kastro its name. The donkey path up to it is not in the best condition, but those without broken legs are rewarded with superb views. More ambitious sightseers have the option of making the scenic and windswept walk across the island to **Episkopei**, a delightfully adapted Roman templet now masquerading as a monastery. Originally thought to be a small Hellenistic temple to Hera (hence Heroön), it is now deemed more likely to have been a 3 c. AD mausoleum. It is the only surviving remnant of the ancient centre of the island which was here rather than at Kastro. Virtually intact, it was converted into a monastery in the 17 c.

☎

CODE 0286, POLICE 51222,
FIRST AID 51211.

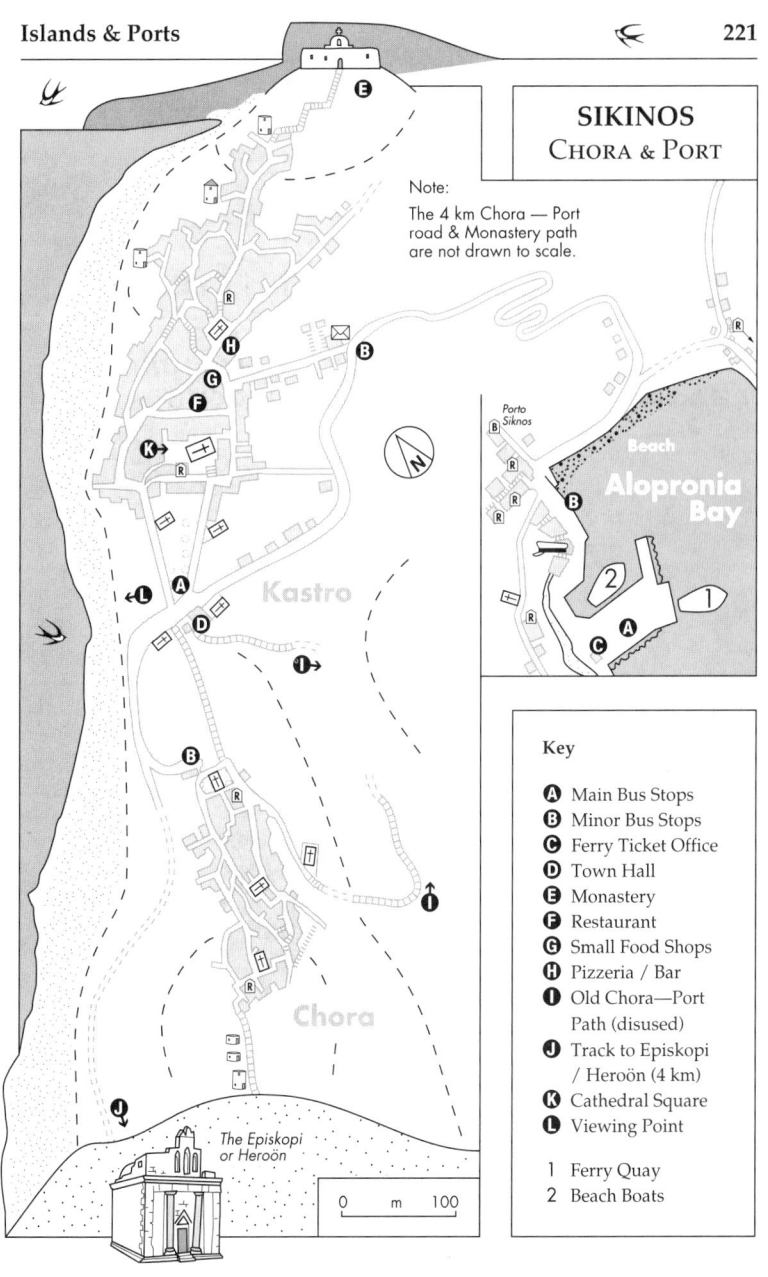

SIKINOS
CHORA & PORT

Note:

The 4 km Chora — Port
road & Monastery path
are not drawn to scale.

Porto Siknos

Beach

Alopronia Bay

Kastro

Chora

The Episkopi or Heroön

0   m   100

Key

- **A** Main Bus Stops
- **B** Minor Bus Stops
- **C** Ferry Ticket Office
- **D** Town Hall
- **E** Monastery
- **F** Restaurant
- **G** Small Food Shops
- **H** Pizzeria / Bar
- **I** Old Chora—Port Path (disused)
- **J** Track to Episkopi / Heroön (4 km)
- **K** Cathedral Square
- **L** Viewing Point

1 Ferry Quay
2 Beach Boats

7

CRETE & THE EASTERN CYCLADES

**AMORGOS · ASTIPALEA · CRETE: AGIOS NIKOLAOS
CHANIA · IRAKLION · KASTELI · PALEOCHORA · SITIA**

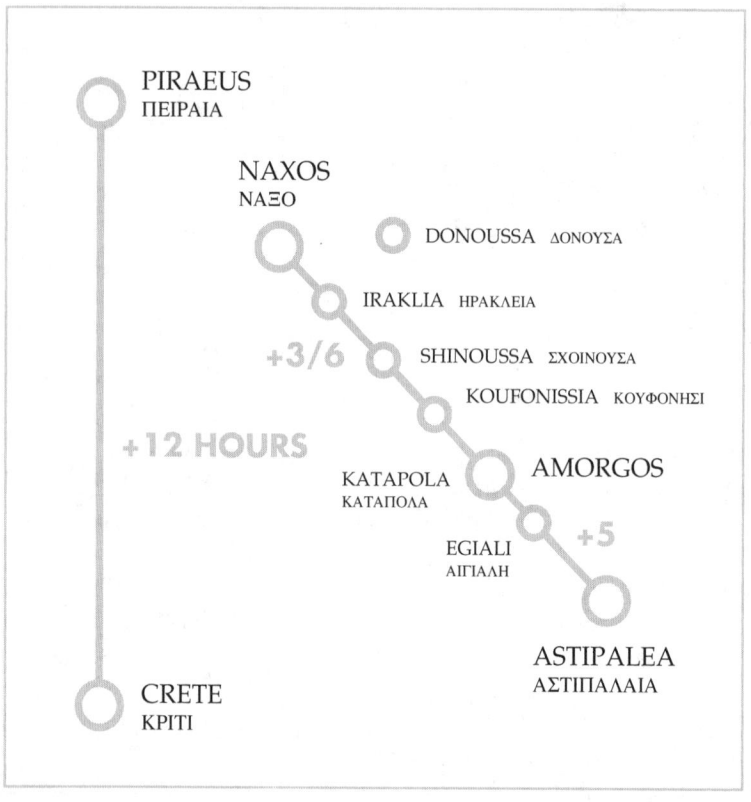

PIRAEUS
ΠΕΙΡΑΙΑ

NAXOS
ΝΑΞΟ

DONOUSSA ΔΟΝΟΥΣΑ

IRAKLIA ΗΡΑΚΛΕΙΑ

+3/6

SHINOUSSA ΣΧΟΙΝΟΥΣΑ

KOUFONISSIA ΚΟΥΦΟΝΗΣΙ

+12 HOURS

KATAPOLA
ΚΑΤΑΠΟΛΑ

AMORGOS

+5

EGIALI
ΑΙΓΙΑΛΗ

ASTIPALEA
ΑΣΤΙΠΑΛΑΙΑ

CRETE
ΚΡΙΤΙ

General Features

In the centre of the Aegean lie a number of islands that do not fall easily into chapters organised by ferry routes. Rather than distort the reader's perception of those routes by describing them elsewhere these islands are gathered together here. Not least of them is Crete (an island so large as to justify a separate volume in several popular guide series) which — with six major ports on its northern coast and an odd collection of associated islets — justifies separate treatment rather than being broken down over several chapters. Equally difficult to categorise is Astipalea; administratively one of the Dodecanese but more characteristic in appearance of the Cyclades and lying at the end of the line for several boats serving them. The relatively untouristed Eastern Cycladic islands (usually known as the 'little' or 'lesser' Cyclades) running east of Naxos to Amorgos make up the balance of this chapter.

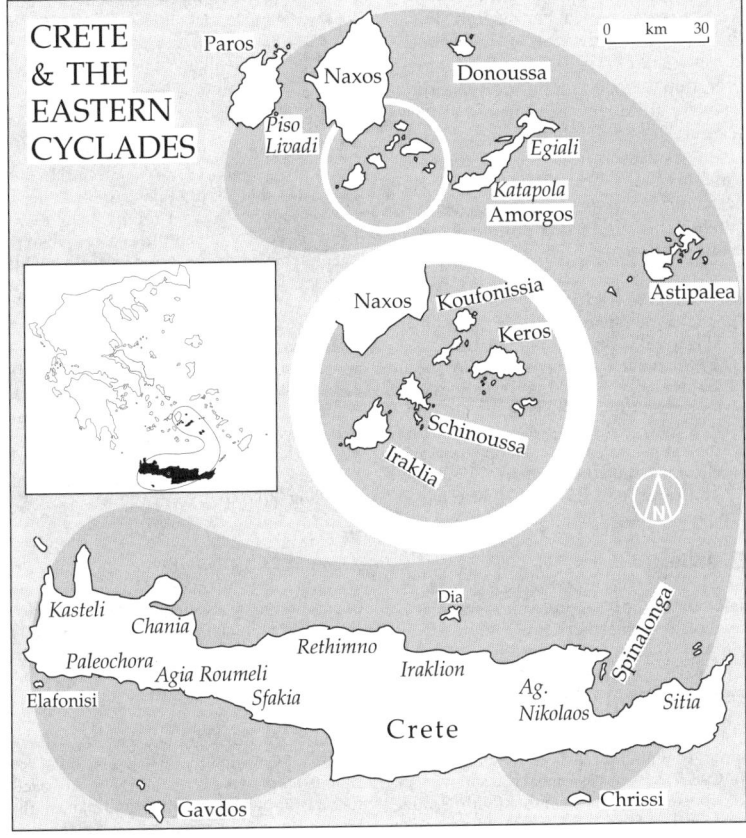

CRETE
& THE
EASTERN
CYCLADES

Paros

Naxos

Piso
Livadi

Donoussa

Egiali

Katapola
Amorgos

Naxos   Koufonissia

Keros

Astipalea

Schinoussa

Iraklia

Kasteli
         Chania
                        Rethimno
Paleochora
         Agia Roumeli   Iraklion
Elafonisi   Sfakia   Ag.
                                                Nikolaos
                                                           Spinalonga

                                                                      Sitia

                         Dia

                    Crete

         Gavdos   Chrissi

0   km   30

Suggested Itinerary [2/3 Weeks]

This chapter covers two islands — Amorgos and Astipalea — widely hailed as amongst the most attractive and unspoilt in the Aegean. Lying off the main ferry routes, they are passed over as impracticable by most island hoppers restricted to a fortnight's travelling. Yet, in fact they can easily be incorporated in to a tight timetable. The trick is to tackle them as primary objectives. By visiting them first you can easily build them into a wider ranging island-hopping holiday, and as Amorgos was a major centre of the Early Cycladic culture, the itinerary below takes in other islands similarly blessed. However, don't expect to find idols standing on every hilltop for the figures rarely exceeded 30–40 cm in height and are only visible as museum pieces and copies in souvenir shops. The itinerary can be undertaken in two weeks in the High Season, outside it, abandon Koufonissia or take a leisurely three.

1 Piraeus to Astipalea
Piraeus is the obvious starting point when seeking to get to Astipalea simply because of the comparative frequency of ferry connections. That said, you could still be faced with a two-day delay awaiting a boat. If your prospective ferry is heading elsewhere before arriving at Astipalea you can hop ahead and pick it up at the intermediate port. Alternatively, you can spend the time sightseeing in Athens or hopping south to nearby Aegina.

2 Astipalea
Your length of stay on Astipalea is going to be delimited by the paucity of a means of escape. Beyond saying that the overall pattern of ferry connections remains the same each summer it is difficult to generalise as ferry times at this end-of-the-line island tend to change each year. You should be able to plan on the assumption that a ferry will be running to Amorgos within three days. If Amorgos and the Cyclades have less appeal you should also find that ferries run to Kalimnos (with its links with the rest of the Dodecanese) twice a week.

3 Amorgos (Egiali)
The great majority of visitors to Amorgos head for Katapola, but if you didn't encounter a long delay at Athens, those who like quiet island ports should find themselves with plenty of time to stop off at Egiali first. When you are ready to move on you have the option of taking either a bus or ferry on to Katapola.

4 Amorgos (Katapola)
Once at Katapola you are effectively plugged back into the ferry mainstream. With daily boats to Naxos you are within easy striking distance of the Cyclades Central Line. Katapola is also the best jumping off point on Amorgos for the Little Cyclades and Koufonissia, but if the *Skopelitis* isn't running daily, you should allow for the possibility of being stranded on the beach a day longer than intended either here or on Koufonissia.

5 Koufonissia
Koufonissia offers a fair degree of small island escapism — but with the reassurance of having just enough by way of tourist facilities to hand. Even if you can't find a caïque-tour heading for Keros, the island is worth taking time out to visit. Allow a day in hand for a connecting service on to Naxos.

6 Naxos
An arrival at Naxos after the previous ports of call can be a bit of a shock for you will be back in tourist season. Even so, the northern coast of the town was host to a major Early Cycladic village, the museum has a clutch of idols, and a souvenir shop near the promenade is devoted to selling little else.

7 Paros
Although Parikia was also the site of an early Cycladic village the main reason to call now is to pick up a ferry or tour boat on to Antiparos. Besides, if you have found the other islands restful and idyllic you won't be tempted to linger for long here anyway.

8 Antiparos
The ideal place to wile away the last few days of a holiday, Antiparos is reasonably quiet yet close to Paros. It is easy to lounge on the beach for a day, nip across to Parikia and take a night boat to Piraeus for a final day in Athens.

EASTERN CYCLADES

Base Port: Naxos

Not the best collection of islands for springboard island hopping, **Naxos** offers the greatest number of possibilities with easy hops to Paros and Antiparos as well as tour boats to the Little Cyclades and Koufonissia. Links with Amorgos (a night stop destination) are daily in High Season and thrice weekly for most of the remainder of the year.

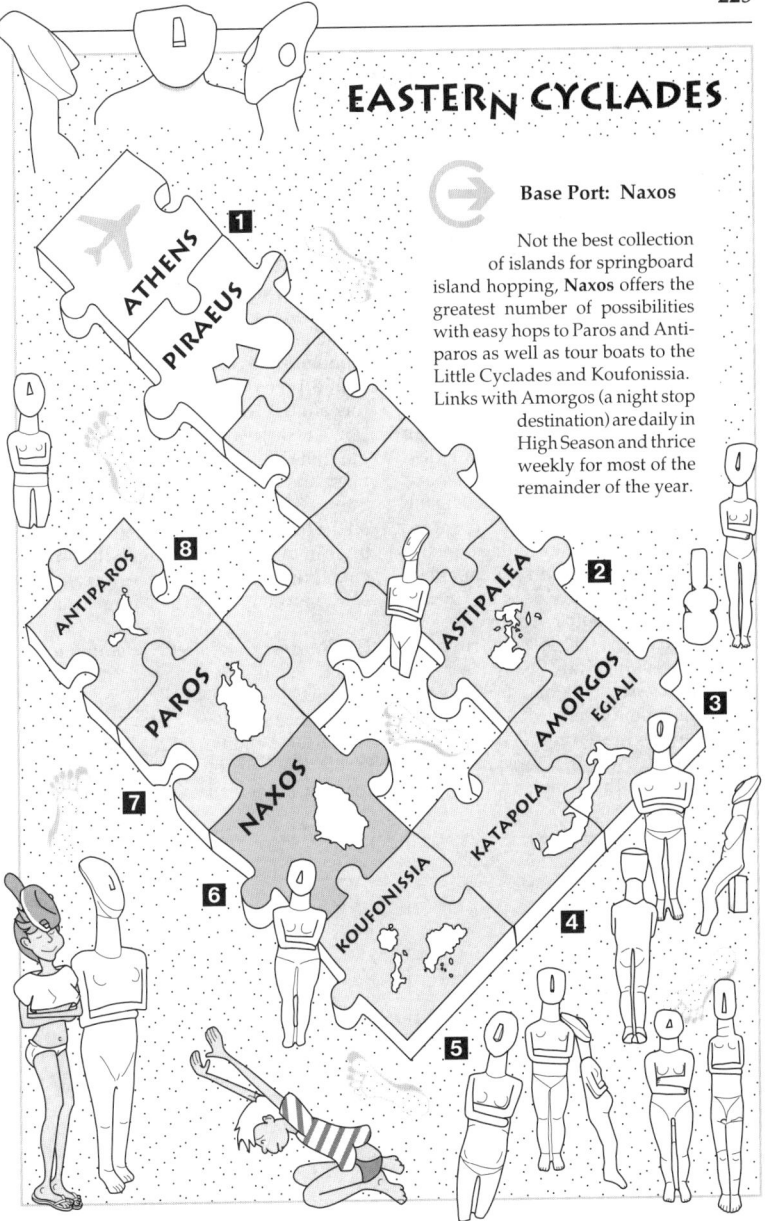

ATHENS
PIRAEUS
1

ANTIPAROS **8**

ASTIPALEA **2**

PAROS

AMORGOS
EGIALI **3**

NAXOS

KATAPOLA **4**

7

6

KOUFONISSIA

5

Crete & Cyclades East Ferries

Main Car Ferries

Crete is used as a springboard by several long-haul Greek ferries as well as being well served by direct boats. The latter are reliable and can be timed to the minute, however, it is not uncommon for indirect ferries to be four or more hours late; Crete is often at the end of scheduled routes and delays (thanks to the distance from Piraeus) tend to be longer than elsewhere in the Greek system. Such ferries either sail down from the Central Cyclades (adding Iraklion to their schedules) or ricochet off Crete, en route to Rhodes. Conditions on board direct ferries are significantly better as these ferries are for the most part deemed to be inter-changeable with the Trans-Adriatic boats operated by the same ferry companies. One invaluable High Season Cretan connection that should not be overlooked is provided by the C/F *Anemos;* running a thrice-weekly High Season service between Thessalonika and Iraklion via the Sporades and Cyclades island chains. Since she provides a unique service into the Northern Aegean she is described and mapped in that chapter (p. 326).

**C/F *King Minos* - C/F *N. Kazantzakis*
Minoan**

King Minos; 1972; 9652 GRT.
N. Kazantzakis; 1972; 10500 GRT.

These direct ferries are the primary link between Piraeus and the capital of Crete, Iraklion. They derive the bulk of their revenue from freight and vehicles. Tourist traffic, although important in the summer months, seems to count more as a bonus than a prerequisite for the existence of this annual service. Along with ANEK, Minoan share an effective monopoly of the route. Both companies possess large fleets and ferries are switched around at intervals so you could see other vessels on the route. Departure times could vary by an hour or so depending on the time of year. High Season also sees occasional extra morning departures from Piraeus.

**C/F *Kantia* / *Candia* - C/F *Rethimno*
ANEK**

Kantia; 1971; 7291 GRT.
Rethimno; 1971; 7291 GRT.

ANEK broke ranks with Minoan in the summer of 1994 by adding Milos to the majority of their boats' Piraeus—Iraklion

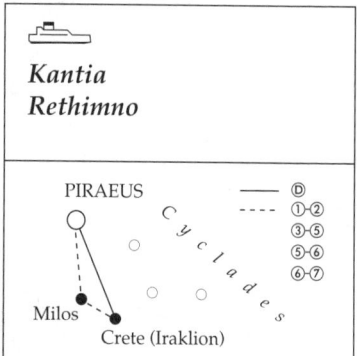

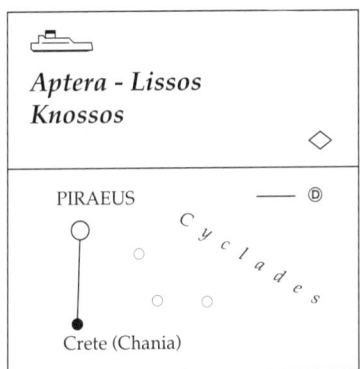

Aptera - Lissos
Knossos

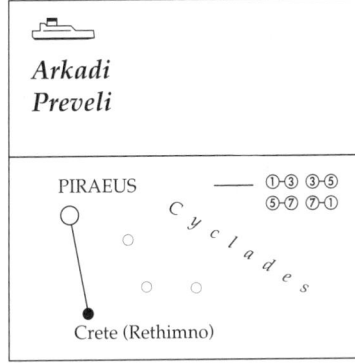

Arkadi
Preveli

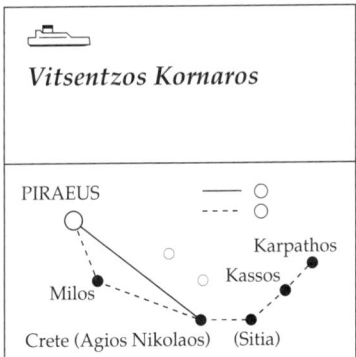

Vitsentzos Kornaros

sailings. Given that this must make these boats less attractive an option for those wishing to continue on to Crete it is to be doubted if this arrangement will continue: don't be surprised to find Milos off these boats' itineraries in 1995 (see below).

C/F *Aptera* - C/F *Lissos*
ANEK
Aptera; 1973; 7058 GRT.
Lissos; 1972; 9893 GRT.
C/F *Knossos*
Minoan Lines; 1966; 7262 GRT.
Given the size of Crete, ANEK have found a profitable niche offering a daily service to the north-western town of Chania (via its port at Souda). Minoan Lines devote a single ferry to this route and thus only run on alternate nights. In the High Season they manage to squeeze in an extra weekend sailing by turning the ferry around sharpish when she gets into port.

C/F *Arkadi* - C/F *Preveli*
Rethimno SA
Arkadi; 1983; 4097 GRT.
Preveli; 1980; 5683 GRT.
A newish ferry — the *Arkadi* put a new port on the ferry map in 1990, running from Piraeus to Rethimno 4 times weekly. Summer schedule has remained unaltered over the last four years, though this could well change to a daily service as the company is now advertising a new ferry (the C/F *Preveli*) alongside the *Arkadi*.

C/F *Vitsentzos Kornaros*
LANE Lines; 1976; 9735 GRT.
Crete sees several subsidised ferry runs, notably a thrice-weekly link from Piraeus to Agios Nikolaos and Sitia on the north-east coast (usually via Milos). Unfortunately, neither port offers lucrative pickings and several lines have tried and failed to make the link pay. In the absence of a boat in 1994 ANEK ran their Iraklion boats via Milos. A 'new' ferry, the *Vitsentzos Kornaros* (the ex-*Pride of Winchester*), is now being advertised on the route.

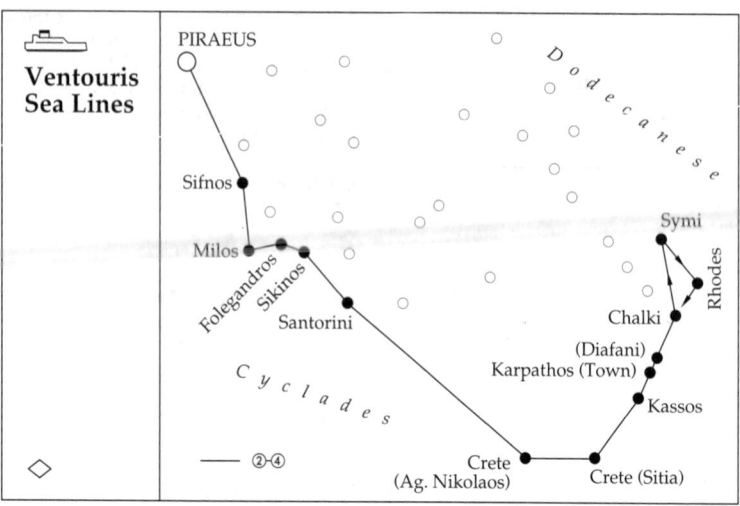

Ventouris Sea Lines

C/F *Artemis*; 1960; 4952 GRT.

Most of the more exotic subsidised 'life-line' ferry routes that a decade ago were a major feature of the Greek ferry scene have now vanished. The nearest to such a thing these days is a weekly itinerary most recently undertaken by Ventouris Sea Lines boats. The majority of their fleet have now had a turn on this annual service — including the *Georgios Express, Ergina* and now defunct *Sifnos Express*. Further change to the name of the boat or the day the service is run is guaranteed given that the latter boat was the latest to run this service, combining it with runs into the Cyclades. By rights the *Artemis* (see p. 201) is due to take a turn. It is also possible that the independently operated *Vitsentzos Kornaros* could take it on. A Ventouris Ferries boat — the *Pollux* has been advertised along with an itinerary running: Piraeus—Paros—Kastelorizo—Rhodes —Crete (Ag. Nikolaos, Iraklion, Chania) —Paros—Tinos—Piraeus, but don't expect too much as she has lately been deployed in the Adriatic.

C/F *Ionian Sea*

Strintzis Lines; 1961; 2455 GRT.

The Eastern Cyclades are the beneficiary of a regular one-off subsidised weekly run. In 1994 the *Ionian Sea* (see p. 258) took over from the *Penelope A* on the route.

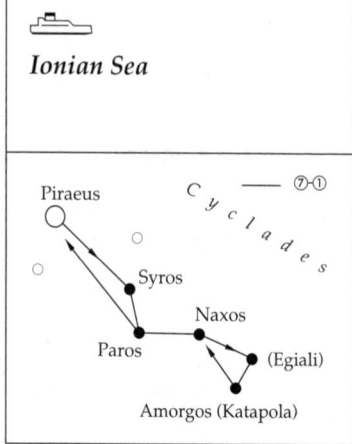

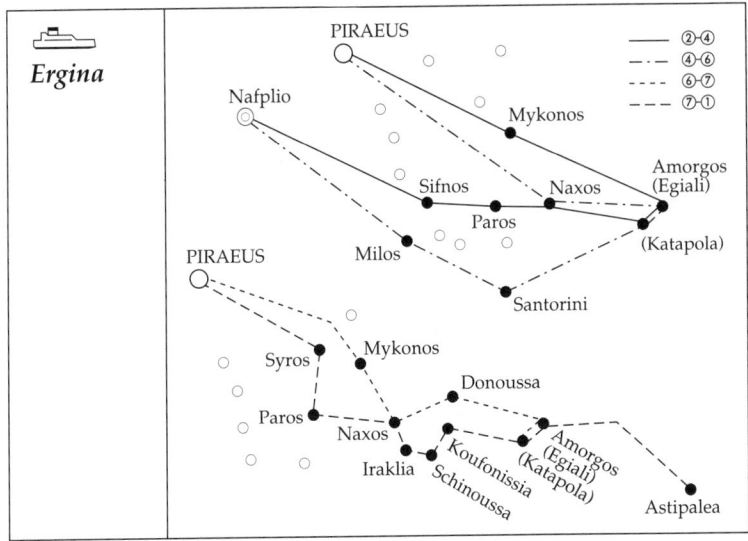

Ergina

C/F *Ergina*
Ventouris Sea Lines; 1962; 2607 GRT.
The number four boat in the Ventouris Sea Lines fleet, the *Ergina* has been steaming over the Aegean for over a decade as the *Kimolos*. Renamed in 1993 following her removal from her regular Cyclades West slot, she found herself on a mould-breaking twice-weekly Piraeus—Nafplio service (via the Eastern Cyclades, the Cyclades Central and West Lines). Given the 'experimental' cross-line nature of her 1993 itinerary, it was not surprising to see changes in 1994; this took the form of a change in days of sailing and the addition of an Astipalea run. Further change is not improbable in 1995 (the unemployed *Artemis* is a potential joker in the pack). Nonetheless, she will be a boat to watch out for. Not the prettiest ferry to look at, with poor sun-deck seating. Her saving grace is the recently refurbished deck saloon, complete with TV's, air conditioning, and original, if impracticable, 'VSL'- shaped bar tables.

P/S *Skopelitis*
(Map overleaf.) This invaluable, but tiny, rock-and-roll boat is the local bus for the small islands south-east of Naxos that make up the Little Cyclades. Like most Greek buses she is apt to get ludicrously over-crowded. A very small rusty passenger ferry with a curious side ramp adjacent to her stern (that enables her to carry 2—3 cars at a pinch), she traditionally runs from Amorgos (Katapola) to Naxos six days a week (on alternate days continuing on to the—otherwise unvisited — Parian port of Piso Livadi as well as Mykonos) in July and August. However, out of High Season, this is cut to a twice-weekly run. Naxos excepted, tickets are usually bought on board. Conditions there are poor: seating above decks is designed to let the wind blow as many passengers overboard as possible, while below the sea-sickies huddle in a cramped muddle. If Katapola is your destination you should also note that this boat is very slow; rarely arriving before 22.00.

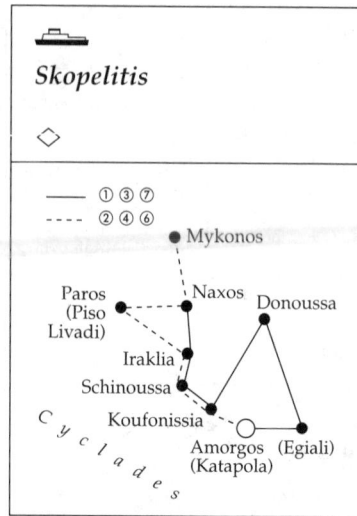

Skopelitis

◇

——— ① ③ ⑦
--- - ② ④ ⑥

● Mykonos

Paros ● Naxos Donoussa
(Piso ●   ●
Livadi)
Iraklia ●
Schinoussa ●
C y   Koufonissia ●
  c l   ○
    a d   Amorgos (Egiali)
      e s (Katapola)

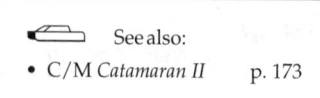

See also:
• C/M *Catamaran II*   p. 173

South Crete Line

Five small ferries operate along the south-west coast of Crete from the ports of Paleochora and Sfakia/Chora Sfakion. Their primary role is ferrying tourists disgorged from the mouth of the Samarian Gorge to adjacent coastline towns, but they also offer an irregular service to the remote island of Gavdos to the south (the most consistent from Sfakia). Timetables (albeit somewhat theoretical) are available from the NTOG branch in Iraklion and should be obtained before you reach this part of Crete. Although these boats are supposed to service the mountain-locked fishing hamlets along this coast they remain very tourist dependent, and only a limited service operates (April to October) out of the July—August peak. A weekly Sfakia—Gavdos service operates all year round (formerly this ran from Paleochora). Most of the boats are small passenger 'ferries' too small to survive commercially elsewhere; the one exception being a small car ferry charged with the vital task of bringing refrigerated ice-cream lorries to the roadless but tourist-full Agia Roumeli.

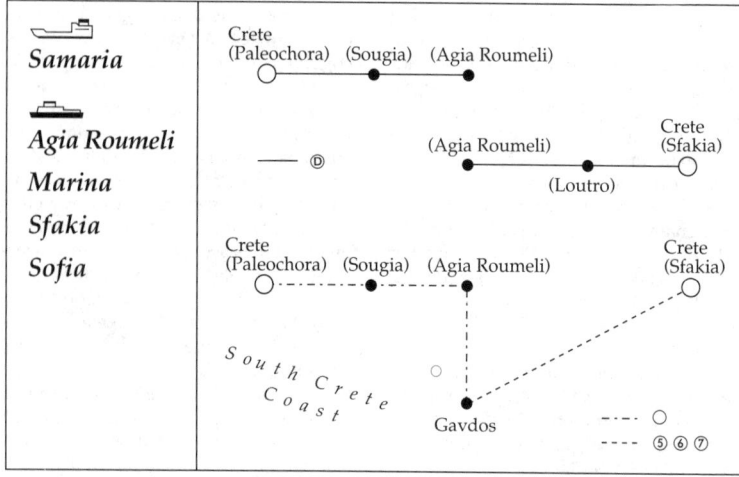

Samaria

Agia Roumeli

Marina

Sfakia

Sofia

Crete
(Paleochora)   (Sougia)   (Agia Roumeli)
○——————————●——————————●

——— ⑩   Crete
                (Agia Roumeli)   (Sfakia)
                ●——————————————○
                        (Loutro)

Crete   Crete
(Paleochora)   (Sougia)   (Agia Roumeli)   (Sfakia)
○- - - - - - - ●- - - - - ●   ○
                          ┊
S o u   ┊
   t h   C r e t e   ○
      C o a s t   ┊
                          ●   - - - ○
                        Gavdos   - - - ⑤ ⑥ ⑦

Cyclades East Islands & Ports

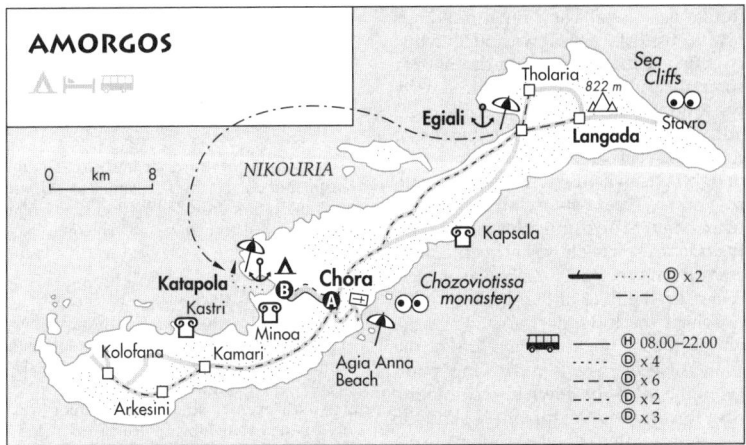

Amorgos

ΑΜΟΡΓΟΣ; 117 km², pop. 1720.

The most easterly of the Cyclades, Amorgos has been one of the least touristed of the large Aegean islands. This is rapidly changing as its reputation grows, for Amorgos *should* be on the itinerary of any Cycladic island hopper. It is rugged, mountainous, often battered by choppy seas, and at first sight more intimidating than many other islands. But once ashore, it turns out to be very friendly and charmingly unspoilt. The 'Amorgos' experience is dominated by the island's hilly terrain. One consequence of this is that the road system is very poor; the two main settlements at each end of the island are linked only by a dirt road more compatible with hikers than buses. As a result, even though a regular bus link between them has been established, ferries usually call at both centres (ticket agents also use port names in lieu of 'Amorgos' on timetables), and even the islanders tend to think of their end as separate from the other half.

Katapola, the principal port, lies on the more populous western half of Amorgos. Tucked into a suitably scenic bay on the north coast, it is rapidly acquiring all the trappings of a mini resort (a patisserie has just opened) besides offering the best facilities on offer on the island. This isn't saying a great deal as shopping — as elsewhere on Amorgos — is very limited. However, you will find tavernas and a road running the extent of the bay, along with various establishments offering rooms. The port beach is more for show than lying on, and a regular taxi boat chugs across the bay to the island's most popular beach (behind the eastern headland). Fanning out behind Katapola is a fertile plain bisected by a road that winds steeply up the hills behind to the island's capital at Chora (as ferries steam toward the bay it is just possible to make out the Chora windmills and satellite dish towers on the skyline). Frequent buses run between the Chora and port (Katapola, incidentally, means 'below the town').

Chora is a superb example of a Cycladic white-cubic town. Still geared to local island life, it has yet to acquire the bespoiling retinue of boutiques and tourist shops found elsewhere. The ruined buildings on the outskirts of the town and a skyline crowned with derelict windmills (for some unclear reason each extended family on Amorgos had to have its own mill) add greatly to the unspoilt character of the place. This is enhanced further by delightful small tree-filled squares and melting ice-cream-style churches that in turn generate a cosmopolitan touch via the odd artist sketching in dreamland.

The main street (inaccessible to vehicles) winds up the floor of the shallow valley in which the town lies, arriving at the windy top of the southern cliffs of the island. Here there is a viewing point (under one of the town's two satellite dish towers) and the top of the staircase that winds down to both the main tourist attraction on Amorgos: the monastery of Chozoviotissa and the road to the island's most popular beach at Agia Anna — a tiny pebble affair known for nudism (both can also be reached by island bus). To the north looms Mt. Protitis Ilias which, even in summer, is usually accompanied by a playful cloud chasing its tail around the upper slopes. This intimidating spectacle sets the tone for the island hinterland that is little frequented by tourists thanks to the paucity of bus services.

Egiali, the island's second port, is smaller but thanks to a better beach and a hill skyline topped with seven derelict windmills is more picturesque than Katapola. Set in a wide sandy bay with an absurdly long quay, it is overlooked by two hill villages. In past years backpackers have predominated, but it is cultivating a more up-market image. Much more accessible than even five years ago, it is very quiet and is a destination more likely to appeal to seasoned island hoppers: the most exciting thing in town is the dust cloud raised by the Katapola bus twice a day.

🛏

Hotels and rooms fill fast in High Season: try to arrive by noon. Rooms there are in Chora (usually not signed), Katapola and Egiali. Katapola has a number of pensions — including the *Amorgos* (☎ 71214) — in addition to the C-class hotels *Ag. Georgios Valsamitis* (☎ 71228) and *Minoa* (☎ 71480). Egali has more up-market establishments with the B-class *Egialis* (☎ 73393) and C-class *Mike* (☎ 73208).

Å

Camping Amorgos (☎ 71257): Inexpensive, and reasonable out of High Season; but can get intolerably over-crowded in August. Popular with French school groups it can sometimes feel like camping in a school playground during a fire drill.

👓

The island sight is the spectacularly impressive 11 c. **Chozoviotissa Monastery** complete with a miraculous icon of the Virgin (Ⓓ 08.00–14.00). Plastered into the side of a cliff 300 m above sea level, it justifies adding Amorgos to any itinerary; remember to wear 'formal' clothing if you want to gain admission.

Chora itself is more scenic than sight-filled. The best it has to offer is the finger of rock poking up from the whitewashed buildings: this is home to an unimpressive wall of a tiny 13 c. Venetian **Kastro**. Other sights are harder work. The most rewarding is to be found near Katapola at **Minoa** which has the remains of a classical town (fragments of a temple and the agora are visible). **Kastri** also has a poor site.

Hill Walking is possibly the best attraction that Amorgos has to offer. Shops on the island sell plain white island maps showing the main paths and suggesting itineraries and journey times. Topping the list is the 5–7 hour walk along the island spine from Katapola to Egiali; this offers sumptuous views — including the ex-leper colony islet of **Nikouria**, and the hillside at **Kapsala** where the largest **Cycladic Idol** yet discovered was unearthed. Almost life size at 148 cm long, it is also remarkably thin. It is now in the National Archaeological Museum in Athens. Not on the map list, the Egiali—Langada—Tholaria—Egiali round trip has also been recommended by one reader as 'one of the most delightful walks in Greece'.

☎

CODE 0285, PORT POLICE 71259, POLICE 71210, FIRST AID 71208.

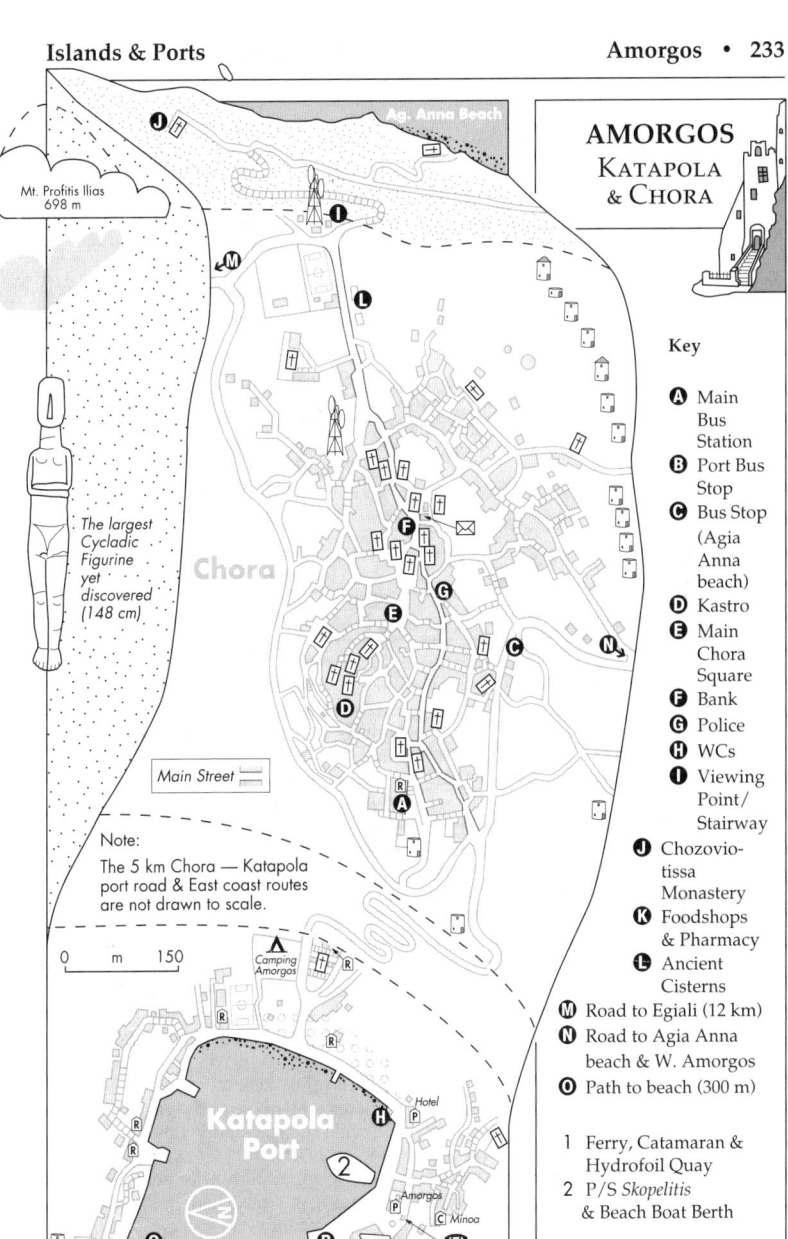

Ag. Anna Beach

Mt. Profitis Ilias
698 m

Chora

The largest
Cycladic
Figurine
yet
discovered
(148 cm)

Main Street

Note:

The 5 km Chora — Katapola
port road & East coast routes
are not drawn to scale.

0   m   150

Camping
Amorgos

Katapola
Port

Hotel

Amorgos

C Minoa

Valsamitis

AMORGOS
KATAPOLA
& CHORA

Key

A Main
Bus
Station

B Port Bus
Stop

C Bus Stop
(Agia
Anna
beach)

D Kastro

E Main
Chora
Square

F Bank

G Police

H WCs

I Viewing
Point/
Stairway

J Chozovio-
tissa
Monastery

K Foodshops
& Pharmacy

L Ancient
Cisterns

M Road to Egiali (12 km)

N Road to Agia Anna
beach & W. Amorgos

O Path to beach (300 m)

1 Ferry, Catamaran &
Hydrofoil Quay

2 P/S *Skopelitis*
& Beach Boat Berth

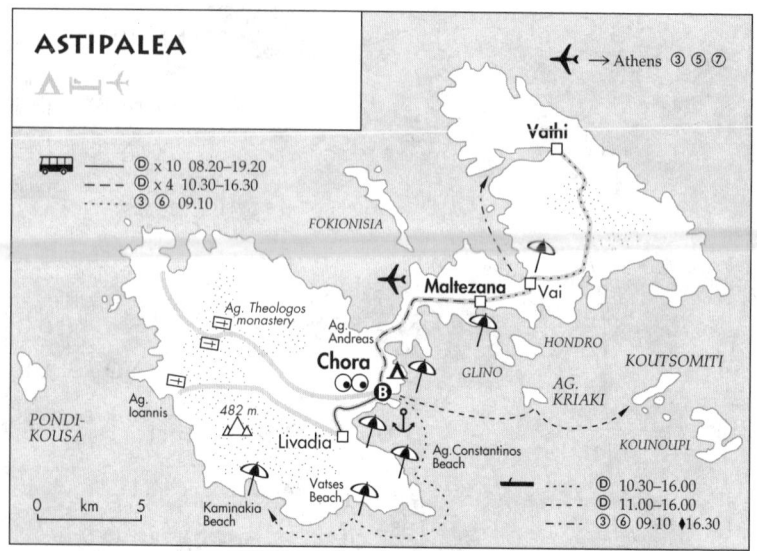

Astipalea

ΑΣΤΙΠΑΛΕΑ; 95 km², pop. 1150.

Administered from Kalimnos, butterfly-shaped Astipalea is technically a member of the Dodecanese group. Yet, in both appearance and frequency of ferry links, the island has far more in common with the neighbouring Eastern Cyclades, with a white-cubist house chora (complete with windmills and castle) and typical barren, arid hillsides. It's relative remoteness, lack of nightlife (there are only three discos!) and reasonable — but not spectacular — beaches have all conspired to keep the masses at bay. All this is now changing; for one only has to sail between the folds of Astipalea's wings and see the castle-topped chora for a certain fascination to take hold. The end-of-the-world sense of introspection that pervades is enhanced by the combination of the island's beachcomber scruffiness (there are insufficient tourists to fund municipal cleanups here) and the picturesque litter of islets around the coastline.

Astipalea is a perfect spot to quietly unwind and soak up the Greek island atmosphere, free from crowds, yet in tangibly exotic surroundings. Folks come here to clamber up the hillsides behind the town and drink in the views. Buffeted by the wind, this is an island which encourages you to feel exhilaratingly alive. Rich, blue sea-filled vistas drenched in a dreamy bright sunlight worthy of an Alpine ski-slope and all that sort of stuff.

Coming back down to earth, the only settlement of any significance is the main **Chora** and port complex; an odd mix of staircases and new buildings running up to one of Greece's nicer old towns. Finding your way around is not particularly difficult: just keep climbing and sooner or later you arrive at the castle entrance which offers a shady (and wind-free) retreat in the form of a passage that burrows quaintly under one of the two surviving whitewashed interior churches to the forecourt, and spectacular views of the coastline and beach islets to the south.

Most tourist facilities are to be found fringing the port, in the saddle-top windmill square above, and strung along the stairways and roads between the two. The popular port beach is lined with tavernas and mini-markets and is the nearest thing you will find to the centre of town: the chora square is usually too windy for those left standing to want to linger in it for long. Astipalea is too small to warrant having its own bank: the post office doubles up as a currency exchange for those with cash or Eurocheques. The National Bank of Greece also has a 'representative' (don't go expecting very much) via a shop next to the Aegeon hotel.

Reliable buses run from both the port and chora squares. The prime destinations are **Livadia** to the west of the port; site of the island's best beach and backed by a fertile valley that gave the island renown in classical times as a source of market garden produce, and east to **Maltezana** (also known as **Analipsis**), a former pirate lair noted as the spot where a French captain died in 1827 by firing his corvette to avoid capture; the closest Astipalea has to a resort beach, the nearest thing you'll see to skulls and cross-bones are paraded by elderly nudists.

The rest of the island lacks decent roads; buses crawling to Astipalea's second port at Vathi only twice a week. Blessed with a good beach and set in a deep fjord-like cove, this is a scenic village with a good cave, but it really only comes into its own during the winter months when heavy seas occasionally force ferries to berth here. Hill paths lead to several hilltop monasteries on the island and to a number of narrow tree-filled valleys.

⊨

Room supply is good, with owners meeting the boats and three inexpensive, but reasonable, hotels (all D-class) in the lower part of the town. The best of these — notably the clean but spartan *Paradissos* (☎ 61224) — and the *Astynea* (☎ 61209) are on the waterfront. The *Aegeon* (☎ 61236) lies on the chora road.

Rooms are also available in the houses on the north side of the port bay (these have great views of the floodlit Kastro at night) and also in the beach villages of Livadia and Maltezana.

A

Camping Astipalea (☎ 61238): a pleasant and well shaded — if isolated — pebble beach site 2.5 km east of the port. Mini bus meets ferries.

👓

Astipalea's great attraction is its imposing **Kastro**. Built on the site of the ancient acropolis, it is a 9 c. Byzantine fortification, later rebuilt after a fashion by the Venetian Quirini family that ruled Astipalea between 1207 and 1522. Never a traditional castle, it thereafter evolved into a medieval apartment block of sorts during the centuries of piracy that followed. In its prime it was home to some 4000 people: its walls containing a labyrinth of staircases and four-storey buildings (if contemporary accounts of it are anything to go by then the island has lost a quite amazing tourist attraction). This was extant until the 1920s, when the Italian building of the port shifted the axis of settlement away from the chora, prompting partial demolition. An earthquake in 1956 destroyed those buildings that hadn't been demolished along with the north-east wall, leaving the interior little more than a shell, with only the churches and the fragmentary remains of the houses that nestled against the window-choked walls (now a storey lower than in times past) surviving.

Little of pre-medieval Astipalea survives, thanks in part to the island's most famous son, an Olympic boxer by the name of Kleomedies. Disqualified for killing his opponent at the games he returned to Astipalea in disgrace and did a Samsun; pulling down the pillars of the island school and killing all the children along with himself (his late opponent obviously got in at least one good head blow). The fact that the school had pillars is about the only thing known of the island's classical architecture. Odd fragments of buildings are to be found in the Kastro walls and the island has yielded up a number of important inscriptions. The best remains are found at Maltezana, where a series of well-preserved zodiac mosaics from a **Roman Bathhouse** are on view.

☎

CODE 0243, PORT POLICE 71259, POLICE 61207, TOURIST OFFICE 61217.

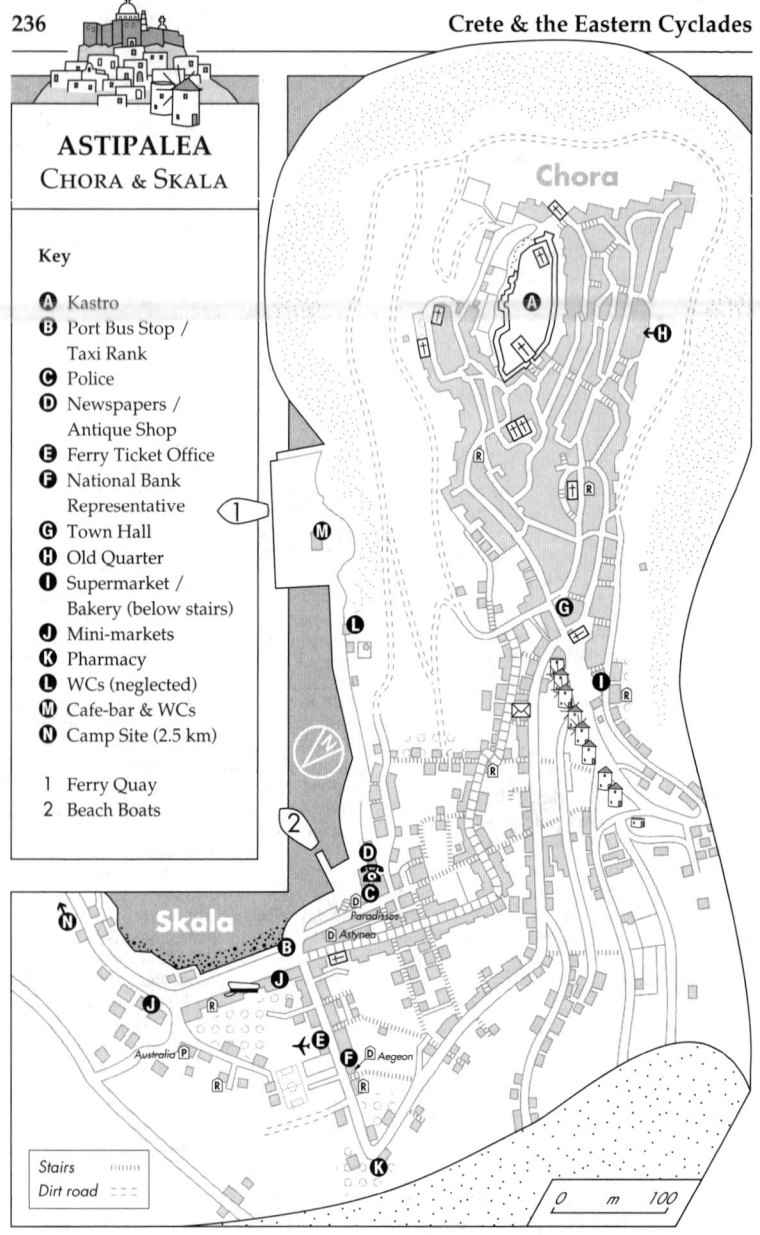

ASTIPALEA
Chora & Skala

Key

Ⓐ Kastro
Ⓑ Port Bus Stop /
   Taxi Rank
Ⓒ Police
Ⓓ Newspapers /
   Antique Shop
Ⓔ Ferry Ticket Office
Ⓕ National Bank
   Representative
Ⓖ Town Hall
Ⓗ Old Quarter
Ⓘ Supermarket /
   Bakery (below stairs)
Ⓙ Mini-markets
Ⓚ Pharmacy
Ⓛ WCs (neglected)
Ⓜ Cafe-bar & WCs
Ⓝ Camp Site (2.5 km)

1 Ferry Quay
2 Beach Boats

Stairs ∷∷∷∷∷
Dirt road ≡≡≡

0   m   100

The Little Cyclades

Between Naxos and Amorgos lie a cluster of small islands and islets (some 12 in all), little known and well off the beaten track. They are collectively known by various names (including the Little, Lesser, Minor, and Small Cyclades). Four of them are inhabited, and all are small enough to make you feel as if you really are on an island; since it is almost impossible not to loose sight of the sea no matter where you are, and you can explore them in a day. That, and the fact that they are untainted by tourism, is their great charm: these are *real* Greek islands!

If you are attracted by the prospect of a visit then you should take on board before you get off a ferry the fact that these islands lack banks, supermarkets, discos and almost everything else (water included). The fact that electricity has only recently made it to this part of the world says it all. This is, of course, the main reason for visiting, and the islands are a true delight — if you can live without your creature comforts. All have small, friendly populations that subsist mainly on fishing. During the winter months a goodly number of islanders now live in Athens and elsewhere in order to augment their income. However, as the increasing numbers visiting the Aegean reduce the number of 'unspoilt' Greek islands, tourism is beginning to make an impact. This is putting pressure on the limited number of rooms available on each island in High Season. Fortunately, freelance camping is widely tolerated. Each island can boast a shop and a couple of tavernas —though the cuisine is often limited to fish, salads and omelettes.

Donoussa aside, all are visited by ferry daily during the High Season (every other day during the remainder of the year). For those who just want to sneak a quick look you will find day-trips (at a price) are on offer to several of the Little Cyclades from both Paros and Naxos in High Season (see p. 175).

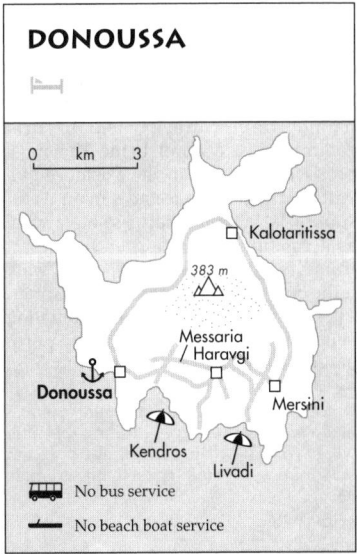

Donoussa

ΔΟΝΟΥΣΣΑ; 13 km², pop. 100.
Of the four inhabited Little Cyclades, Donoussa is the most isolated. Rising steeply out of the sea east of Naxos it looks a rather forbidding island from a ferry. It is also the most difficult to get to as, unlike the other islands, it lies too far north to be a convenient stop for Naxos—Amorgos ferries. It is also rare for tourist boats to call as the other islands are equally rewarding and much closer to Naxos Town. Connections are thus far fewer. For this reason it pays to work out how you are going to leave before you hop over. Once ashore, you will find that Donoussa is a tranquil, friendly place with several good sandy beaches on the south coast and three hamlets on the girdling coastal 'road'. Little English is spoken and there is only one shop. This is to be found in the port town of Donoussa (also known as Ag. Stavros) along with three tavernas and a bakery. Such rooms

as are available on the island are also mainly to be found here. The rest of Donoussa offers some rewarding walks and several excellent (and all but empty) beaches at Kendros and Livadi. The three hamlets are studies in small rural communities; Mirsini being the most prosperous thanks to the existence of a spring which is the island's main water supply. Isolated Kalotaritissa has appeal as a walking destination. In fact, apart from the beach, 'doing' the coastal walk is the only activity Donoussa has to offer. Those attempting a circumambulation should note that the 16 km trip requires good shoes and several bottles of water.

Rooms are not over-abundant; take up offers made when ferries arrive. Failing this, you will have to do what everyone else does and opt for freelance camping on Kendros beach.

☎

CODE 0285

Iraklia

IPAKΛIA; 17.5 km², pop. 110.

The largest island in the Little Cyclades constellation, **Iraklia** (also transcribed as Heraklia, and not to be confused with Heraklion / Iraklion, the capital of Crete) is the most accessible of the four thanks to regular day trips from Naxos Town. A hilltop sticking out of the sea that tapers away into 'dune hills' to the north, the island has the best sightseeing in the group. All boats call at the north coast port of Ag. Georgios. Set in a deep inlet it is a rather ramshackle affair which follows the main road out of town rather than the coastline. It is overlooked by the ubiquitous ruined windmill stump on the hill behind the town. From the upper village is a path winding on to Chora an hour or so's walk away. Ferries dock on the left-hand side of the bay (unlike Schinoussa where the dock is on the right as you enter the bay): this is a good means of establishing which island you have arrived at (the islands are apt to be difficult

for the initiated to distinguish when arriving by ferry: the ports of Iraklia and Schinoussa are a mere 10 minutes apart).

The port has now supplanted the inland island chora (reached via a mule track running up from the port) as the main settlement thanks to its being sited in the island's most fertile valley, and the economic pull of increasing day-tripper tourism. Even so, the old chora at Panagia is an attractive walking destination, and the east coast path takes you past the narrow fjord-cum-inlet of Livadi (where there is a good sand beach) and the remains of a tower dating from the days when these islands were notorious pirates' nests. A second mule path runs down the west coast and on to a cave (complete with the usual stalactites and stalagmites) overlooking Vourkaria Bay.

Room supply is reasonable with the bulk of the beds in the port.

☎

CODE 0285

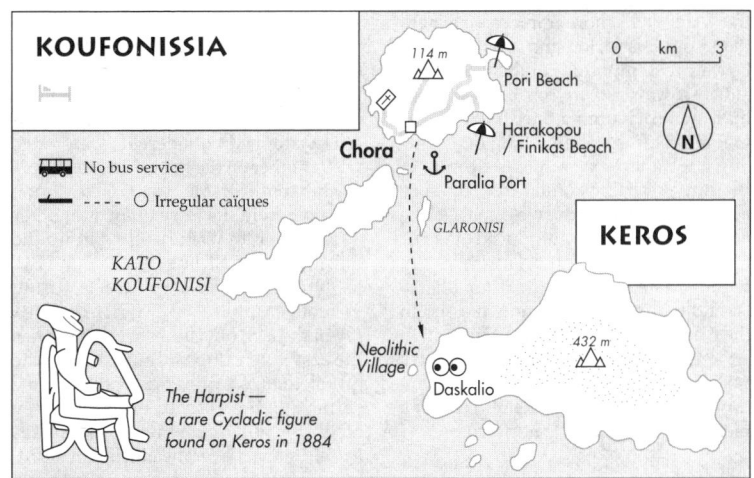

KOUFONISSIA

No bus service

---- O Irregular caïques

KATO KOUFONISI

*The Harpist —
a rare Cycladic figure
found on Keros in 1884*

114 m

Pori Beach

Chora

Harakopou
/ Finikas Beach

Paralia Port

GLARONISI

0   km   3

KEROS

*Neolithic
Village* o

Daskalio

432 m

Koufonissia

ΚΟΥΦΟΝΙΣΣΙ; 3.8 km², pop. 280.
This being Greece, it is not surprising that the smallest inhabited island in the Little Cyclades is the most heavily populated, and indeed, touristed. Koufonissia is becoming quite a trendy place to visit, for although it can offer only the usual mix of beaches and mule tracks, the former are of a high quality and the generally cosy beach island atmosphere gives it an edge over its companions. If you have time to visit only one of the Little Cyclades then Koufonissia is the island to go for. Truth to tell, part of its attraction is that it does have at least a modicum of facilities (i.e. a post office, tavernas and a hotel), and ferry connections are as good as any in the group.

Koufonissia is, in fact, the collective name for two islands: Ano (upper) Koufonisi and Kato (lower) Koufonisi — though these days the name is generally taken to mean the former. Ano Koufonisi is the main island (its low-lying companion being little more than a reef rising a few metres above sea level and used for grazing goats), and is home to the only settlement and the ferry quay. The island is easily identified thanks to the white-roofed windmill to the left of the quay as you view it from the ferry. In addition, it is low and flat, tapering gently down to the sea on the south side. Hemmed in by Kato Koufonisi and Glaronisi, with mighty Naxos dominating the northern horizon and the much taller island of Keros close by to the south, Koufonissia also has a wonderful little-kid-in-the-playground feel about it.

Needless to say there is not much to do except lie on a beach (the best are the long sandy strands at Pori and Finikas) and exploring the island mule paths. These all start from the port of Paralia which is a holiday home extension of the chora; with fishing caïques nestling in the lea of the ferry quay, a couple of windmills, and a beach of sorts. Caïques regularly make the crossing to Kato Koufonisi (there are several isolated farmsteads near the shore) and also make occasional trips to the Neolithic village site on neighbouring **Keros**. This large hilltop poking out of the water is far more impressive a sight than Koufonissia; looking as if it ought to be the most important of the Little Cyclades. However, apart from the obligatory mad monk, it is uninhabited and used for grazing. This is all something of a come down from its days as a major centre of the early Cycladic culture (c. 3000–2000 BC). Excavations on the west coast at the end of the last century produced over 100 Cycladic figures — the largest group found to date, including the famous harpist and flautist (both are now housed in the National Archaeological Museum in Athens — see p. 119). If you charter a caïque to take you across take care you don't end up instead at the remains of a medieval village on the north coast.

⊨

The port-cum-chora has a hotel in addition to a goodly number of rooms. Tavernas at both the port and Finikas beach offer rooms.

☎

CODE 0285

Schinoussa
ΣΧΙΝΟΥΣΣΑ; 8.5 km², pop. 100.
Tiny Schinoussa is the least visited of the four islands. Rooms are almost outnumbered by shops and there are only two of these. It is best to come prepared to camp on the beach. There are up to a dozen of these around the coast, but sadly, they are made of grey, course sand and are not on a par with those of the other islands; a fact that partly explains Schinoussa's relative unpopularity. Another feature which hardly encourages island hoppers to disembark is the harbour. It is little more than a couple of buildings (even the fact that one of these is a taverna does not make this the most reassuring of starts) and a ferry quay set in a small inlet. Note: some larger ferries prefer to dump travellers into caïques rather than enter the inlet. This can be a problem as they are apt to sound a horn in passing and then — if nothing appears in ten seconds

— steam gaily away. These discouragements are a pity, for Schinoussa has something to offer. Looking like a group of interconnected rock dunes, the island is made up of some nine hillocks (the northern two topped with derelict windmills, with another on the hill behind the beach to the south of the port). The Chora, invisible from the ferry quay, is another good reason to visit: lying 1 km up the hillside, it is small, but attractive and can justly claim to be one of the last truly unspoilt examples of its type. Ironically, given the lack of visitors Schinoussa has the best water supply of any island in the group thanks to the existence of three springs. In the absence of tourists they feed the wild chewing-gum bushes (mastica) that cover the hillsides instead.

⊨

Rooms in the quayside and chora tavernas.

☎

CODE 0285

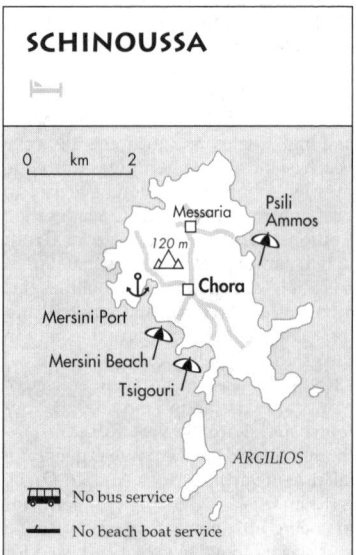

SCHINOUSSA

⊨

0   km   2

Messaria

Psili Ammos

120 m

Chora

Mersini Port

Mersini Beach

Tsigouri

ARGILIOS

No bus service

No beach boat service

Cretan Islands & Ports

Crete
KPITI; 8259 km², pop. 460,000.
The fifth largest island in the Mediterranean and the largest in Greece, Crete
justifies (and often gets) coverage in a
single volume separate from the rest of
Greece. There is certainly no shortage of
subject matter. Geography and history
have combined to mark the island out as
one of the most diverse in Greece. Long
and mountainous, it marks the southern
boundary of the Aegean Sea, blocking
any rain-clouds that might attempt to
venture further north as well as acting as
a giant breakwater for the southern Aegean as a whole. Crete is also an island of
great strategic importance, for without
control of it no power was able to fully
command the rest of the Aegean. As a
result, the island is littered with the
remains of all the great powers from the
region, and indeed, appears to have been
the power base of the earliest of them all
— the bronze age Minoan civilization.
Their palaces are among the top sightseeing destinations, though later Greek and
Roman temples, Byzantine churches,
Venetian fortresses, Ottoman mosques
and fountains, and WW2 German battlefields also lie thick on the ground.
    If this was not enough, Crete is also
very fertile and following in the tradition
of its role as an important grain producing
island in the ancient world, now is the
major supplier of market garden produce
to Greece. The self-sufficiency gained by
this has given the Cretans a reputation
for hot-headed independence and radical
politics. Tourism, although not vital to
the economy, is rampant thanks to good
beaches, impressive sightseeing and a
climate befitting an island lying further
south than the northern coast of Tunisia.
All major settlements lie on the north
coast which has developed into an
English-speaking tourist strip, leaving the
hinterland and south coasts; rugged and
mountainous, covered in pine forests and
wildly beautiful, untainted and inviting
exploration.
    The size of Crete has resulted in ferry
links with the mainland developing to
five ports on the northern coast. All large
towns in their own right, they provide
good bases for exploring the adjacent
coastlines and hinterland. They are linked
by the island's main road (which runs the
length of the northern coast, with feeder
roads running south from the main towns
to the mountain villages and the south
coast) and are served by frequent buses.
The island bus service is excellent; making
travel on Crete both easy and cheap.

Crete (Agios Nikolaos)
ΑΓΙΟΣ ΝΙΚΟΛΑΟΣ
The premier port of eastern Crete (though
given the paucity of ferry connections
this isn't saying a lot), Agios Nikolaos
(often called locally by its Venetian name
of San Nikolaos) is only a couple of hours
from Iraklion by bus. It is an attractive —
though all too obviously tourist — town,
perched on a tiny headland and noted for
having a lagoon-like sea lake harbour of
reputedly measureless depth. Apart from
a general 'prettiness', the town lacks sights
and beaches, but thrives on its reputation
as the 'Ios' of Crete (i.e. where the youth
element hangs out), thanks to its role as
the watering hole for a number of nearby
package tour resorts. As a result, the
harbour and downtown area is dominated by bars and discos filled with holiday
makers who haven't realized that if they
were on Ios or Paros they could enjoy a
similar nightlife filled to excess and plenty
of beaches as well. On the plus side,
Agios Nikolaos is the hub of the eastern
Crete bus system.

⊢

Accommodation fills up early in High Season. This is also one town where it pays to have a well-filled wallet. The easiest hotels to find lie on the waterfront on the opposite side of the harbour to the ferry quay. These include the C-class *Alcestis* (☎ 22454) — with a *Youth Hostel* (☎ 22823) tucked away in the street behind — and (250 m north-west) the B-class *Coral* (☎ 28363) and the B-class pension *Lida* (☎ 22130). Finally, the C-class *Mandraki* (☎ 28880) lies one block north of the bus station.

A

Nearest site to the town, *Gournia Moon Camping* (☎ 0842 93243) is well away from the town at Gournia, near a Minoan palace.

◑◑

The town itself has no buildings of particular merit. The one notable sight is the **Archaeological Museum** (located 500 m up Paleologou St., which starts at the inner harbour bridge), which is home to an impressive display of artifacts from nearby Minoan sites. Being a tourist town, a number of pleasure boats operate from the port, though most of them are ludicrously expensive, given the distances involved. The most popular excursion is to the Cretan version of Alcatraz — the island of **Spinalonga** (£5.50 Rtn.), billed as the 'island of the living dead' thanks to its history as a leper colony. Here you will find a well-preserved **Venetian Fortress** that was able to withstand Turkish attack for half a century after Crete had succumbed. Taxi boat services also operate to the resort of **Elounda** and the quiet village of **Plaka**. There are also excursions to the Roman city of **Olous** up the coast, as well as Bird and Kri-Kri (named after the local species of goat) islands. If you really feel like throwing money away you can go on a mystery boat tour (these visit the same islands but without an explanation as to where you are). In the High Season there is a ⑦ trip to **Chrissi** islet via the southern resort of **Ierapetra**.

☎

CODE 0841, TOURIST POLICE 223 21, POLICE 223 38, TOURIST INFO 223 57.

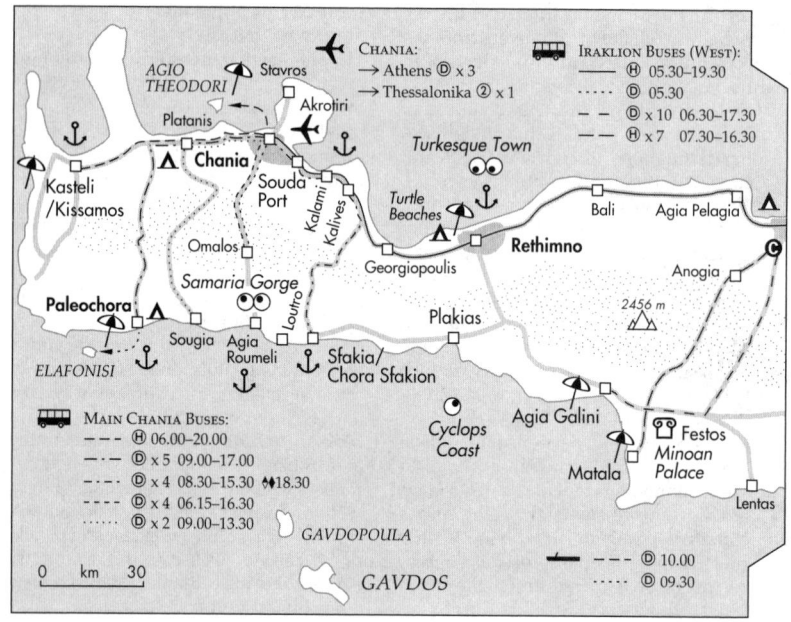

CHANIA:
→ Athens ⑩ x 3
→ Thessalonika ② x 1

IRAKLION BUSES (WEST):
—— ⊕ 05.30–19.30
····· ⑩ 05.30
— — ⑩ x 10 06.30–17.30
— — ⊕ x 7 07.30–16.30

AGIO THEODORI Stavros
Platanis Akrotiri
Kasteli /Kissamos **A** Chania Souda Port
Omalos *Turkesque Town*
Samaria Gorge Turtle Beaches
Paleochora Agia Roumeli Sfakia/ Chora Sfakion
ELAFONISI Sougia
Georgiopoulis **Rethimno**
Bali Agia Pelagia
Anogia
2456 m
Plakias

MAIN CHANIA BUSES:
— — ⊕ 06.00–20.00
—·— ⑩ x 5 09.00–17.00
—···— ⑩ x 4 08.30–15.30 ♦18.30
— — — ⑩ x 4 06.15–16.30
······ ⑩ x 2 09.00–13.30

Cyclops Coast
Agia Galini
Matala
Festos Minoan Palace
Lentas

0 km 30

GAVDOPOULA
GAVDOS

— — ⑩ 10.00
····· ⑩ 09.30

Crete (Chania)
XANIA

The capital of Crete until 1971, Chania (pronounced Han*y*a) is now the number two city on the island. As such, it is the beneficiary of the second daily direct service between Crete and Piraeus. Chania boasts one of the most attractive town centres on Crete, retaining much of its Venetian/Turkish heart and offering an attractive caïque-filled harbour lined with tavernas (complete with expensive package tourist orientated menus). Unfortunately, some of the outer suburbs are pretty ropy, and the town's modern port (thanks to the inability of the old harbour to handle large vessels) is located an inconvenient 6 kilometres to the east of the town centre — across the Akrotiri headland at Souda. In addition to the heavy package tourist trade, local prices are pushed by the military personnel from

the nearby Akrotiri NATO air and naval base. The military presence is strong in the area (i.e. 'photography banned' notices abound, and there are always plenty of unattached males in the local discos), but in the main it doesn't detract from the town. Inevitably, the harbour is the main centre of activity. Used as the set for the film *Zorba the Greek*, it is easily the most attractive on Crete — even with the crowds. Taxi boats run from here (ferry fans shouldn't miss the free raft across the harbour to the Fortella restaurant) to local beaches and the small islet of **Agio Theodori**. The winding streets behind the waterfront are inevitably very boutique laden, but also contain a fair number of easily found pensions. All the main services are to be found in the centre apart from the bus station which lies outside the old city walls, some five blocks in from the waterfront. Chania is the

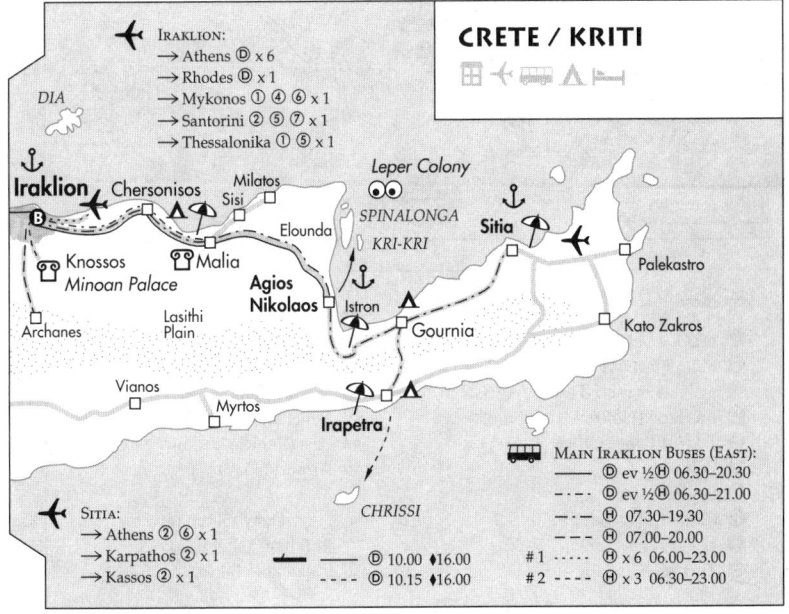

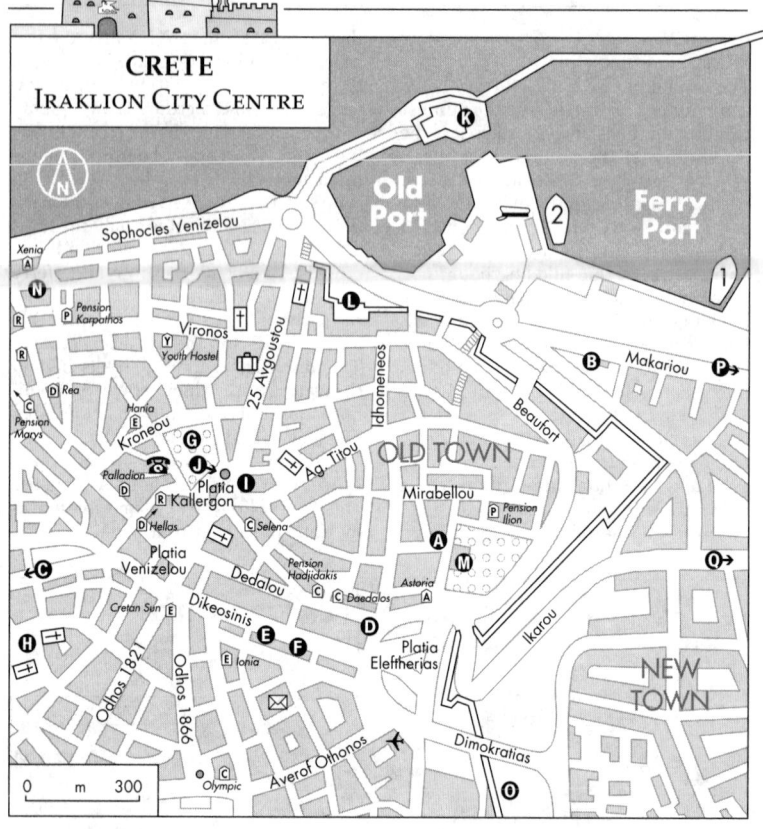

CRETE
IRAKLION CITY CENTRE

Key

A NTOG / EOT Office
B Main Bus Station / WCs
C SW Bus Station (Festos / Ag. Galini)
D Bus Stop (Hotels & Camping)
E Tourist Police Office
F Police
G El Greco Park
H Cathedral
I Loggia
J Turkish Fountain

K Venetian Fortress
L Venetian Arsenal
M Archaeological Museum
N Historical Museum
O Venetian City Wall
P Port (Vehicle Entrance 300 m)
Q Airport (4 km)

1 Ferry Quay (Ferry Terminal
   Building 200 m East)
2 Catamaran Berth

main junction for the Eastern Crete bus system with good links to Paleochora and the ports on the south Cretan coast as well as the villages in the White Mountains that rise behind the town.

⊨

Rooms are in limited supply, but pricier beds are less hard to come by. A NTOG / EOT office in a mosque on the waterfront can help you find a bed. The B-class *Samaria* (☎ 51551) is right next to the bus station and easily located, along with the nearby C-class *Canea* (☎ 913 60) and *Omalos* (☎ 95215). So too is the E-class *Piraeus* (☎ 54154) on the Old Port waterfront. Tucked behind the Nautical Museum are the much more expensive B-class *El Greco* (☎ 904 32) and A-class *Palazzo* (☎ 43255). The Old Harbour and the main street (Halidon St.) between the Old Harbour and the bus station have a number of pensions in the side-streets behind them. There is also a *Youth Hostel* (☎ 53565) at 33 Drakonianou St., south of the town centre.

A

Camping Chania (☎ 31138). A reasonable site 3 km on the road to Kasteli is backed up by *Camping Agia Marina* (☎ 68555) further west (take the Kasteli bus and ask for the camping).

👓

Known as the 'Venice of Greece' the town itself is the main sightseeing attraction. This being Greece it is without a single canal (unless you count the drains). Within the town, the main street is host to a 16 C. Venetian church that now houses an **Archaeological Museum**. The west side of the Old Harbour waterfront is also home to a **Nautical Museum**.

☎

CODE 0821, TOURIST POLICE 24477, NTOG 26426, EMERGENCY 22222.

Crete (Iraklion)
HPAKΛEIO

The main port and capital of Crete, Iraklion does its best to equal Athenian grime at its worst but doesn't quite make it. Instead, the city has to settle for looking as if it is suffering the effects of a catastrophic explosion at a local cement factory. However, it is not all dust and grime: the mollifying existence of the

well-preserved Venetian city walls, waterfront fortress and arsenal do something to redeem the ambiance and the Archaeological Museum (home to the greatest display of Minoan artifacts in the world) is enough to justify adding the city to any itinerary. Iraklion is a very popular starting point for Greek island hopping holidays, thanks to the international airport on the city limits (many prefer to start from here just to avoid the horrors of Athens). It is also the hub to the island bus system and an important ferry junction. Ferry links are adequate, if not brilliant. In addition to the daily service to Piraeus, in High Season you can also be fairly sure of at least one boat a day to Santorini and the Cyclades as well as increasingly frequent boats to Rhodes.

Ferry arrivals will find themselves on a long commercial quay; the east end being reserved for international boats. On the west side of the fence that separates this international section you will find a ferry passenger waiting-room/terminal with a G.A. Ferries ticket office. Boats arriving in the early hours tend to berth here regardless of line. Behind the commercial quay stands the New Town: an ugly expanse of concrete that is best ignored. A short walk west, however, will bring you to the main city bus station and the old town walls. These enclose the more appealing part of the town and run down and around to the old Venetian harbour (dominated by the wonderfully well-preserved kastro; its front entrance still adorned with a Venetian winged lion) and the old arsenal. From the west side of the latter, the city's main street (25 Augoustou) runs up to the main square (Platia Kallergon). Dominated by an ornate Turkish fountain (which backs onto an attractive and shady park) and the reconstructed Venetian Loggia, it is very lively of an evening and opens onto the side streets south of Dikeosinis St. which are home to the best of the tourist restaurants and shops.

⊨

There are few rooms on offer in Iraklion but plenty of hotel accommodation. Top of the range are the A-class *Xenia* (☎ 284000) on the waterfront and the *Astoria* (☎ 229002) overlooking leafy Eleftherias Square. C-class hotels lie pretty thick on the ground. These include the good *Selena* (☎226377), the *Olympic* (☎ 288861) and the *Daedalos* (☎ 224391). Being old and dusty, the old town also has plenty of D-class establishments close to the centre. There are three worth trying: the *Hellas* (☎ 225121), the *Palladion* (☎ 282563) and the *Rea* (☎ 223638). E-class hotels are a bit more dubious but will do for a night in a pinch. The *Cretan Sun* (☎ 243794) is too noisy for comfort, though the rooms are pleasant enough. Finally, in addition to a number of pensions there is a good *Youth Hostel* (☎ 286281) at 5 Vironos St.

A

Camping Iraklion (☎286380): Expensive trailer-park type site 5 km west of the city centre on the hotel strip. Hotel bus (#6) stops at the entrance. A better bet (provided you don't want to catch an early morning ferry from Iraklion) is *Camping Creta* (☎ 0897 41400); 30 minutes east of the capital via a #18 bus, then a 20-minute walk to the excellent beach site.

ᑫᗡ

Iraklion boasts two attractions that draw the crowds. The **Minoan Palace** at **Knossos** (see description opposite) is the big pull: 5 km from the town centre, it is an easy bus ride (#2 bus every 20 minutes from St Augustu St.) and is the most important Minoan site on the island. Other Minoan palace sites on Crete at Malia, Festos and Agia Triada have been left as excavated. The **Archaeological Museum** opposite the Iraklion NTOG / EOT is rich in associated finds, and offers a shady, fresco-filled retreat from the midday heat of the city street and a model reconstruction of the Knossos Palace complex. In addition to this popular museum there is also a less frequented **Historical Museum** with exhibits ranging from icons of saints and heroes of the independence struggle (Crete only joined Greece in 1913) to the German occupation of the island in the Second World War.

☎

CODE 081, PORT POLICE 282002, TOURIST POLICE 283190, NTOG 228203, EMERGENCY (FOR MOST OF CRETE) 100.

Knossos

The Palace of Knossos was the centre of Minoan civilisation between 3000—1400 BC. Its fame was such that faint memories of it, along with its name ('Knossos' is of pre-Greek origin) lingered on in Greek myth long after the site of the palace and the Minoan civilization were forgotten. By the Classical period, a thousand years after its destruction, beyond the myths and a belief that a Golden age had given way to an age of Silver, then Bronze, and that the world was now living in the age of Iron, no recollection of the pre-Greek Minoans had survived. As a result, when garbled tales came out of Egypt of a wonderful bull-worshipping maritime island-based civilization that lived 'in the far west' Plato looked around, saw no evidence of it, and, with a greater knowledge of geography than the Egyptian story tellers of a millennia earlier, placed this wondrous lost power in the 'far west' of his day — the Atlantic; giving us the tale of 'Atlantis'.

Incredible as it may seem, beyond the odd pot and some clay tablets baring a strange script, the Minoans remained completely unrecognised until Sir Arthur Evans began excavating the hill of Knossos in 1900. His discovery of a massive, elaborate, surprisingly modern looking palace adorned with modernistic frescoed walls, pillared light wells and drains (a feature not found on other sites for a thousand years), yet lacking defensive walls (suggesting an awesome military command of the region), was equal to any other archaeological discovery this century. Apart from an interruption due to the First World War, Evans continued to excavate at Knossos until the 1930s. As part of this exercise he undertook considerable rebuilding. This involved replacing the lost wooden pillars and beams with concrete substitutes, and had his sponsors not balked at providing additional funds for concrete he would probably have rebuilt the whole complex). Even so, the result today gives you plenty to see (even if this sort of 'reconstruction' is nowadays regarded as over-enthusiastic) and offers a nice compromise between the impression given of the former palace as it was and the warren of foundations that recall the palace of Greek legend: the famous Labyrinth where the Athenian hero Theseus fought the dreaded Minotaur before running off with the King's daughter, Ariadne. Worth recalling it ran something like this:

Far away and long ago there lived a King called Minos. He presided over a powerful maritime empire. Unfortunately for Minos, his wife, Queen Pasiphae, took a fancy for the idea of a night in bed with a large white bull that the king had refused to sacrifice to Poseidon (a strange desire which rather suggests that King Minos was King Minus when it came to the tackle department). Pasiphae sought out the chief craftsman — Daedalus — and ordered him to devise some kind of heifer-shaped sex aid that would allow her to… Well, anyway, one hell of a night and nine months later she gave birth to the Minotaur; the monstrous creature with the body of a man and the head of a bull. King Minos then ordered Daedalus to construct the labyrinth in which the Minotaur was hidden away. Here it lived on an annual diet of 14 Athenian youths and maidens who were pushed into the entrance and never seen again. Daedalus, meantime, was imprisoned to prevent him from divulging the secret of the labyrinth (to say nothing of indulging the queen's fancies) whereupon, with his son Icarus, he made some wings out of feathers and wax and flew to Sicily by way of Ikaria (where Icarus died after flying too near the sun). Meantime, back at the labyrinth, Theseus, the son of the king of Athens, disguised as one of the annual sacrificial youths, killed the Minotaur with the help of Ariadne, the daughter of King Minos, who gave him a ball of thread that enabled him to escape from the labyrinth. The couple then fled to Naxos where Theseus unceremoniously dumped his love, returning to Athens alone.

Visitors to the palace today no longer need a ball of string as plans are in hand to confine access to parts of the site due to heavy tourism wearing down the floors. You may therefore find that the traditional route around the site described below has changed. The site is multi-layered and complex, the palace being built around the sides of a flattened hill. The foundations of rooms, corridors and storage pits on four levels centre on this hilltop central court. Originally built c. 2000 BC, it was demolished in an earthquake and rebuilt c. 1700 BC. With the collapse of the Minoan civilization following the massive eruption of Santorini c. 1450 BC, Knossos appears to have been rebuilt by alien Mycenaean Greeks, before being finally abandoned c. 1400 BC.

On entering the site, you first pass a bust of Sir Arthur Evens. This stands on the palace forecourt that is dominated by **Ⓐ** the circular **Offering Pits**. Behind these is the reconstructed west façade. Known as **Ⓑ** the **Pillar Hall**, it is currently roped off. You can, however, look down into **Ⓒ** the **West Magazines** containing the pithoi jars used to store oil and wine. Passing these, the path brings you to **Ⓓ** the **Corridor of the Procession** (which takes its name from the fresco depicting gift-bearers and a goddess figure), before running on to the roped off **Ⓔ** the **South / High Priest's House**. This lay outside the palace and the tourist path now turns back, past the partially reconstructed **Ⓕ** the **Upper Propylon** (complete with a fake white tapered column), to **Ⓖ** the **Stairs** that led into the religious wing of the palace. A second path from the Propylon runs east to **Ⓗ** the **Central Court Corridor**, which contains a reproduction of the famous **Prince of the Lilies Fresco**. One of the most famous frescos found at Knossos, it shows a kilted youth wearing a crown of lilies and peacock feathers. It is probable he was leading a sacred animal of some kind, but these days he stands alone and has to make do with a new role as the symbol for the Minoan Lines ferry company. The corridor led to **Ⓘ** the **Central Court** — a feature common to all Minoan palaces, and the site where the famous bull-leaping contests or rites were performed. All the important palace buildings led off it.

Ⓙ the **Throne Room** is arguably the most interesting room on the site. Viewed via a basin filled anteroom, it was originally thought to be the throne of Minos, but is now believed to have served a High Priest. Made of gypsum, it has benches on either side, above which are frescos of griffins and lilies (dating from the Mycenaean occupation). This room is also a good example of the degree of reconstruction undertaken by Evens; photographs of the excavation show that the throne's back stood several feet above the height of the surrounding walls, with only the griffin's feet surviving from the frescoes. All of this room (and the storey above) from seat height is, therefore, 'fake'. The frescos, along with most of the others found, have been reconstructed from tiny fragments. Applauded at the time, they have come in for criticism following the discovery of the better preserved Akrotiri frescos. By comparison, the Knossos reconstructions

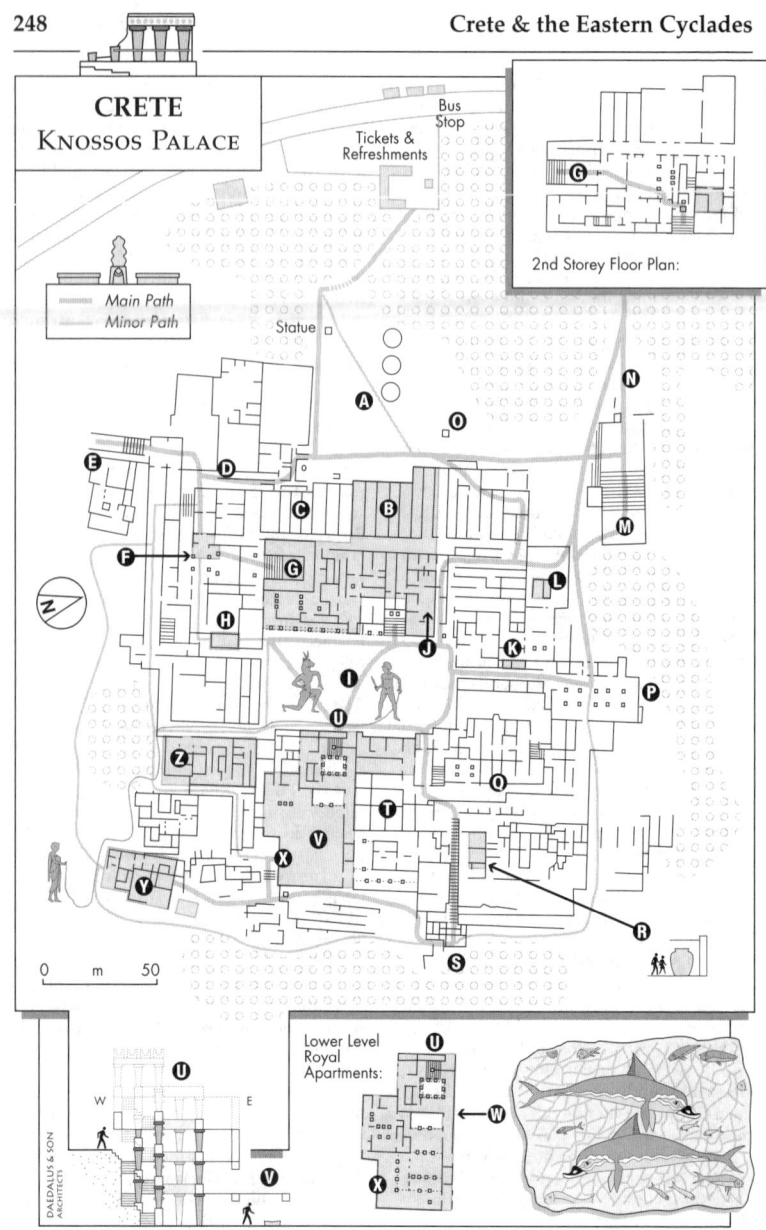

CRETE
KNOSSOS PALACE

Bus Stop

Tickets & Refreshments

2nd Storey Floor Plan:

Main Path
Minor Path

Statue

Lower Level Royal Apartments:

DAEDALUS & SON ARCHITECTS

0   m   50

look curiously lifeless, and in some instances the fragments were completely misinterpreted (notably the remains of a blue monkey which was reconstructed as the figure of a boy).

Turning north, the most prominent feature is the rebuilt tapered columns of ❻ the **North Entrance**. Complete with a **Racing Bull Relief**, it has been suggested that this wall was visible among the rubble during the Archaic period, giving rise to the legend of the Labyrinth and the Minotaur. Behind it rises another reconstructed feature, ❼ the **Lustral Basin**: a small sanctuary. The path runs past this to a feature of greater fame: ❿ the **West Court** or **Theatre** now thought to be Homer's 'dancing floor which Daedalus made for Ariadne in broad Knossos'. From it runs ❶ the **Royal Road**; described as the oldest paved road in Europe, it dates from the earliest palace period. Originally, it was lined with houses and led to the **Little Palace** and a nearby town (as yet unexcavated). Today the path turns back to the entrance court past ❶, one of two **Altars**.

Retracing your route past the court, the path runs on to ❷ the **North Hypostyle Entrance** of the palace, and the most impressive of the site's 'gateways'. To the east stood ❸ the **Servants' Quarters**, now little more than a jumble of foundations, with the singular exception of the re-roofed room containing ❹ the **Giant Pithoi Jars**, that stand over 2 m high. The best means of seeing these is to take the staircase running from the central court to ❺ the **East Bastion**. These divide the servant's quarters from ❻ the **Workshops**, where the palace craftsmen did their stuff.

The south-east sector of the palace was the most luxurious part of the complex. Today it is reached via ❼ the reconstructed **Grand Staircase**, that in its prime stood five storeys high. Built around a light well, it takes you down to ❽ the **Royal Quarters.** The most impressive of these is the **Queen's Bathroom** (complete with hip-bath). The staircase has also been used to display reconstructions of a number of frescoes, notably the Mycenaean-period figure of eight shields and ❾ the lovely **Dolphin Fresco** (the originals are on display in the Iraklion Archaeological Museum). Emerging from ❿ the **Royal Apartment Lower Entrance**, the path takes you to ❶ the **South-East House**, and ❷ the **Shrine of the Double Axes** (another popular Minoan motif), before returning to the Central Court.

Crete (Kasteli)
ΚΑΣΤΕΛΛΙ
A small, rather drab town on the western edge of Crete offering all the essential facilities but no more, Kasteli is often called, by ticket agents and maps alike, by its older name of **Kissamos**. The only ferry connections are the subsidised services to Kithera, Piraeus and the southern Peloponnese: a fact reflected in the location of the ferry quay, over 2 km west of the town centre on a particularly quiet stretch of coastline. The solitude of the surrounding countryside — particularly to the Gramvoussa Peninsula to the west — is the only real attraction, given that the town (complete with a uninspiring centre and a comparatively poor beach) itself lacks zip at all times of the day. Despite being the local transportation hub, the absence of frequent buses means you will need to hire a moped or car to explore the wilds.

᛫᛫

Plentiful supply of rooms are on offer in the town square and waterfront even at the height of the season. There are also a number of reasonable hotels including the C-class *Kissamos* (☎ 22086), *Castle* (☎ 22140) and the *Peli* (☎ 22343). There is also one B-class hotel/pension, the *Astrikas*, and one D-class outlet with expensive apartments, the quaintly named *Mandy* (☎ 22825).

A

Camping Mythimna (☎ 31444): very quiet, 5 km east of the town centre on an excellent beach (take a Chania-bound bus and ask to be dropped at the campsite). There is also a semi-official site closer to hand — *Camping Kissamos* (☎ 23444). Complete with pool, it lies 200 m west of the town centre.

ᴑᴑ

Sightseeing is a bit thin on the ground if you don't have your own wheels. The best thing on offer is the 7 km trek (buses are rare) inland to the village of **Polirinia** which has the substantial remains of an **ancient city** (complete with an aqueduct commissioned by Hadrian) on the hillside above the current centre.

☎

CODE 0822.

Crete (Rethimno)
ΡΕΘΥΜΝΟ

Unlike most of the other large towns along the northern coast of Crete, Rethimno has preserved much of its old waterfront and city centre and, along with it, its atmosphere. This is more flavoured than with other Cretan towns as the Venetian core has a particularly strong Turkish overlay that adds a touch of the exotic to the town. Complemented by a very attractive harbour (complete with a very helpful NTOG / EOT office on the waterfront), and the largest Venetian castle in Greece, it is not surprising that Rethimno is now very much of a package tourist resort town. Hotels are mushrooming up all over the place (particularly along the coastal strip east of the town) and doing little to enhance the ugly suburbs around the old town. Ferry connections, however, are scanty and consist of boats running direct to Piraeus augmented with occasional tourist boats to Santorini.

⊢

The popularity of Rethimno leads to higher prices than in other towns, so you could have to ask around; though there are rooms and pensions aplenty — most within a block of the town beach or waterfront. There is also a *Youth Hostel* (☎ 22848) at 41 Tombasi St. With some forty hotels in the town or its environs finding a bed isn't difficult. Finding a cheap bed is a bit more tricky. The best bets are the D-class *Minoa* (☎ 22508), *Kastro* (☎ 24973), *Acropole* (☎ 27470) and the E-class *Achillion* (☎ 22581). Higher up the range is the C-class *Valari* (☎ 22236) near the National Bank and the B-class *Olympic* (☎ 24761) by the bus station.

A

Camping Elisabeth (☎ 28694) and *Camping Arkadia* (☎ 28825): reasonable sites 4 km east of the town. There is also a third site further out: *Camping Agia Galini* (☎ 91386).

◠◡

The **Venetian Kastro** is the main attraction in the town. In its prime its walls almost held a town in themselves, but most of the interior buildings have gone now and you have to make do with the lovely views over the town.

The alleyways of the old town (complete with **Venetian Fountains**, a **Loggia**, and overhanging balconies) make for interesting walking. You can also climb the minaret of the **Nerandzes Mosque** (the nearest to the castle) for a view over the castle and town. Rethimno also has poorish **Archaeological** and **Historical Museums** to the south of the castle.

☎

CODE 0831, TOURIST POLICE 28156, POLICE 25247, NTOG OFFICE 29148.

Crete (Sitia)
ΣΗΤΕΙΑ

The most easterly port on Crete, scenic Sitia is very much the poor relation compared to the other towns along the northern coast when it comes to ferry connections. However, it beats the pants off Agios Nikolaos as an attractive destination. Set in a wide bay with a reasonable beach, the Venetian-built town attracts its share of tourists in High Season, thanks in part to its lovely fishing port atmosphere. The town is also blessed with a reasonable sand beach and a couple of days of sightseeing for those who want it. The municipal tourist office in the main square offers information on these and accommodation in the town.

⊢

Rooms are plentiful (except for the end of August Sultana Festival), with over a dozen hotels in the centre. For a reasonable bed try the B-class pension *Denis* (☎ 28356) on the waterfront. At the budget end of the range is the D-class *Archontiko* (☎ 22993), and the *Pension Artemis* (☎ 22564). There is also a *Youth Hostel* (☎ 22693) 500 m from the town centre (towards Iraklion) at 4 Therissou St.

◠◡

Thanks to a good **Archaeological Museum**, a passable **Folklore Museum** in the town and a **Venetian Kastro** on the hill behind, there is enough to keep one occupied if you have to wait for a boat. Crowded tourist buses also head east to **Vai**: home to the only natural **Palm Forest** in Europe (now a national park).

☎

CODE 72300, TOURIST POLICE 24200, POLICE 22266, FIRST AID 24311.

Crete: South Coast Ports

The southern coast of Crete is very quiet with poor roads. It escapes the attentions of *meltemi* wind that slams into Crete's northern coast and thus the more exposed southern shore-line — which by rights ought to be rougher — boasts calmer seas during the summer months. The only large town is at Irapetra. This rather ugly tourist resort has a good beach, the odd campsite and not a lot else. Occasional boats filled with crowds seeking to escape the crowds run to the small nature reserve islet of **Chrissi**. A second 'resort' has developed at Matala. This part of the Cretan coast is famed as Cyclops country. Unfortunately, during the 1960s these hapless giants failed to keep a spare eye out for squatters and the hippy brigade moved in, changing all the boulders on the caves, and generally making a nuisance of themselves. Most have now become company executives so things have calmed down a bit. Even so, this part of Crete is still an odd mixture of local conservatism and discrete foreign liberalism.

The only ferries on this coast run between the small fishing communities on the western side. Biggest and best is **Paleochora**; an attractive peninsular town with a daily beach boat to the brush-covered islet of **Elafonisi** to the south-west. **Sfakia** (also known as **Chora Sfakion**) is the next in size and lies at the other end of the line (main attraction is the bus service with Chania). **Agia Roumeli**, at the mouth of the Samarian Gorge, is a tourist trap of little merit, while **Lutro** and **Sougia** are tiny fishing hamlets.

⊨

Rooms available in all ferry ports, but supplies are necessarily limited.

Λ

Camping Paleochora (☎ 0823 41120); 2 km east of the town in olive grove behind pebble beach.

◯◯

18 km long and ranging from 3.5 km down to 3 m wide, the **Samarian Gorge** (Crete's Lilliputian Grand Canyon) runs to the south coast village of Agia Roumeli. Buses run daily from Iraklion (05.30) and (more socially) from Chania to the village of Omalos at the northern entrance to the Gorge. The trek takes about 6 hours with good shoes and is very pretty — particularly in the spring. High Season travellers will find the walk less attractive; the numbers of trekkers turning a communion with nature into a noisy hobbit's walking party. It is best to do the walk early in the day to be sure of picking up a Sfakia-bound ferry in time for the last bus (usually 18.30).

Gavdos

ΓΑΥΔΟΣ; 34 km², pop. 50.

The most southerly part of Europe, Gavdos is worth a visit if only for curiosity value. Sun-baked and isolated (bring food and essentials), it is home to about forty people living on in otherwise abandoned villages. The island is best reached via Paleochora (Brown's travel agency runs tour boats to the island). If you want a quiet beach in August then you could do worse than make for Korfos at the mouth of a small fertile valley. Occasional caïques also venture to uninhabited **Gavdopoula**.

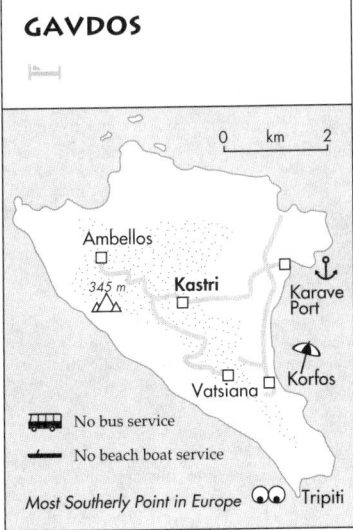

GAVDOS

⊨

0   km   2

Ambellos

345 m   Kastri   Karave Port

Vatsiana   Korfos

🚌 No bus service

▬ No beach boat service

Most Southerly Point in Europe ◯◯ Tripiti

8
DODECANESE LINES

KALIMNOS · KARPATHOS · KASSOS · KOS · LEROS
LIPSI · NISSIROS · RHODES · SYMI · TILOS

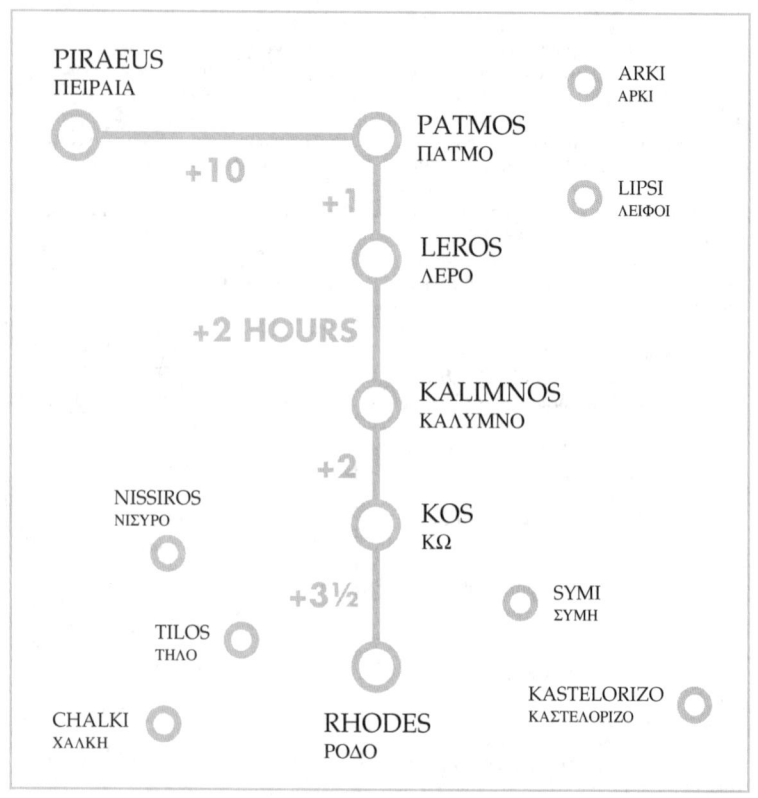

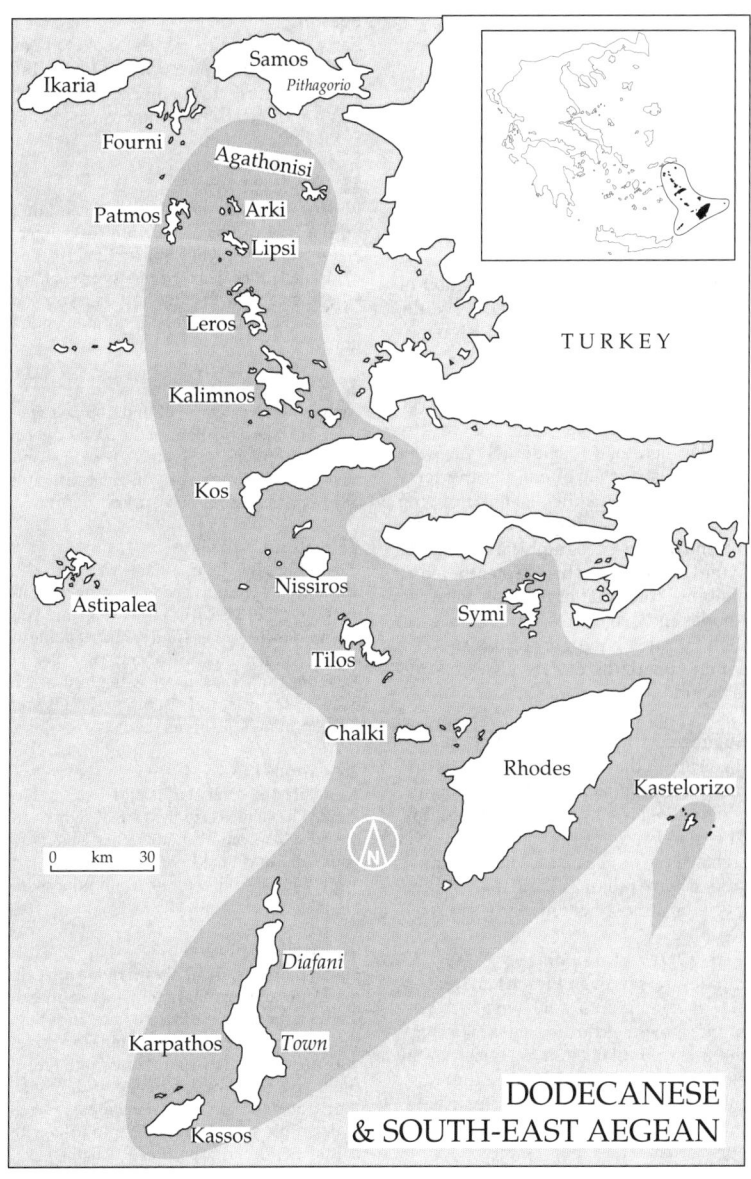

Ikaria

Samos
Pithagorio

Fourni

Agathonisi

Patmos

Arki

Lipsi

Leros

TURKEY

Kalimnos

Kos

Astipalea

Nissiros

Symi

Tilos

Chalki

Rhodes

Kastelorizo

0   km   30

Diafani

Karpathos   *Town*

Kassos

DODECANESE
& SOUTH-EAST AEGEAN

General Features
Running down the Aegean coastline of Turkey, the Dodecanese Islands derive their name from the Greek 'dodeka' or 'twelve', after the number of major islands (or more accurately administrative centres) that make up the chain. The islands possess a unique character thanks to a combination of the strong architectural heritage inherited from the Knights of St. John (who left at least one castle on every island), the Italian occupation of the islands between 1913 and 1943, the allure of day trips to the Turkish mainland — visible from most islands — and the duty-free status that has accompanied their late entry into the Greek state. The tourist influx has resulted in the development of a considerable pleasure boat industry that augments the ferry infrastructure, making island hopping easy. Ferry connections tend to overflow beyond the strict geographical boundaries of the Dodecanese. This chapter therefore includes the smaller islands between Rhodes and Crete to the south. Astipalea, though part of the group, has more in common with the Eastern Cyclades and is included in Chapter 7.

Suggested Itinerary [2 Weeks]
If you aren't the most adventurous island hopper the Dodecanese chain offers the prospect of an easy and relaxed holiday. The islands offer a popular mix of good sightseeing and beaches. The only down side is an Italian rather than typical Cycladic atmosphere in many towns.

Arrival/Departure Point
Rhodes, Kos or even Piraeus are reasonable starting points. All have good entry points into the group. Rhodes is perhaps the most popular (so it is chosen in the example here); though lying at the end of the chain with poorly connected islands immediately north of it, it is an indifferent springboard/base port island.

Season
Early June through to the end of October sees a high level of services. Out of this period ferries only run 3—4 days per week and the all-important tourist boats are far less evident.

▌1▐ Rhodes [2 Days]
Rhodes is a good starting point if venturing up the Dodecanese chain; with easy flights and plenty to see while you acclimatise. The city tourist office also distributes current ferry schedules and with these in hand you can start to fill in the details of your intended itinerary.

▌2▐ Kos [4 Days]
Arriving on Kos you will find yourself well placed to take advantage of the island's good base port options by staying a few days and alternating between days on the beach and day hops to Nissiros and Turkey (Bodrum).

▌3▐ Kalimnos [2 Days]
Can be happily 'done' as a day trip from Kos if you don't want to change your accommodation. Otherwise, it is an easy hop and you can head on to Mirities and spend a couple of days between the beach and the islet of Telendos. Kalimnos also has the best beach boats to the island of Pserimos should you want to try out the beach there.

▌4▐ Patmos [3 Days]
A suitably spectacular island to aim for, Patmos has a nice lazy mixture of sights and beaches. You can also add other islands to your tally and take boat trips to Lipsi and Marathonisi/Arki before catching the overnight ferry back to Rhodes.

▌1▐ Rhodes [3 Days]
One of the great advantages of flying direct to the Dodecanese is that your final couple of days are spent in far nicer surroundings than those offered by Athens. Returning to Rhodes with plenty of time to spare before your return flight you can take advantage of the many tourist boats down the coast to Lindos, as well as day trips to the islands of Symi and — with a little more circumspection — Chalki.

Base Port: Kos

Lying in the centre of the Dodecanese chain, Kos is one of the best springboard islands in Greece, provided that you are prepared to dig a little deeper into your pocket and take advantage of the numerous tour boats operating out of Kos Town (regular ferries do not run at times conducive to day-trip hopping). On a 2 week holiday you can take advantage of day trips to Pserimos, Kalimnos, Nissiros, Rhodes, Tilos, Patmos, and Leros, as well as the attractive town of Bodrum on the Turkish coast.

Dodecanese Ferry Services

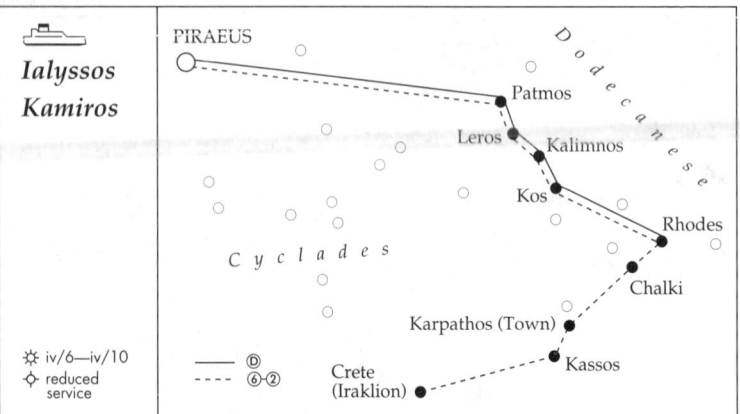

Ialyssos
Kamiros

PIRAEUS

Dodecanese

Patmos

Leros Kalimnos

Kos

Rhodes

Chalki

Cyclades

Karpathos (Town)

Kassos

Crete
(Iraklion)

☼ iv/6—iv/10
◇ reduced
   service

——— Ⓓ
- - - Ⓖ-②

Main Car Ferries

Because the Dodecanese are beyond the range of Piraeus day-return ferries the chain relies on day out, next day return, ferry runs. Unfortunately, this line is currently undergoing one of those periodic phases of major adjustment that beset most groups once in a while; so you should expect more changes than on other lines in 1995. Even so, moving around is easy enough, though ferries on this line tend to have awkward evening and night time arrivals/departures, leaving anyone wishing to travel during the mornings having to rely on inter-island tourist boats.

C/F *Ialyssos* - C/F *Kamiros*
D.A.N.E Sea Lines
Ialyssos; 1966; 8586 GRT.
Kamiros; 1966; 7466 GRT.
These reliable *Canberra* look-a-like ferries have long been the mainstay of the line (their traditional run being Piraeus to Rhodes via Patmos, Leros, Kalimnos and Kos), providing a daily service each way in High Season. Their schedules change

little from summer to summer; with the *Ialyssos* making an extended weekend run down to Crete, and the *Kamiros* running thrice weekly to Rhodes. Out of High Season services are maintained at the *4 days per week* level with the boats also covering other lines. Both old and rather grubby boats and now decidedly inferior to almost all the competition, there is little to choose between them. The *Ialyssos* has the better sun-deck, while the *Kamiros* has the better interior, with reasonable leather seats only made uncomfortable by the dangerously restricting gates and locked doors between classes. She also has a self-service cafeteria. Fate decides which of the pair you end up on, but either way at Piraeus it pays to board and grab a space early as possible in High Season as both can get ludicrously overcrowded. You should also note that D.A.N.E Sea Lines are one of the few companies who sell deck tickets on board with a 20% mark-up using the tourist class fare loophole (see p. 31), so it always pays to buy ashore.

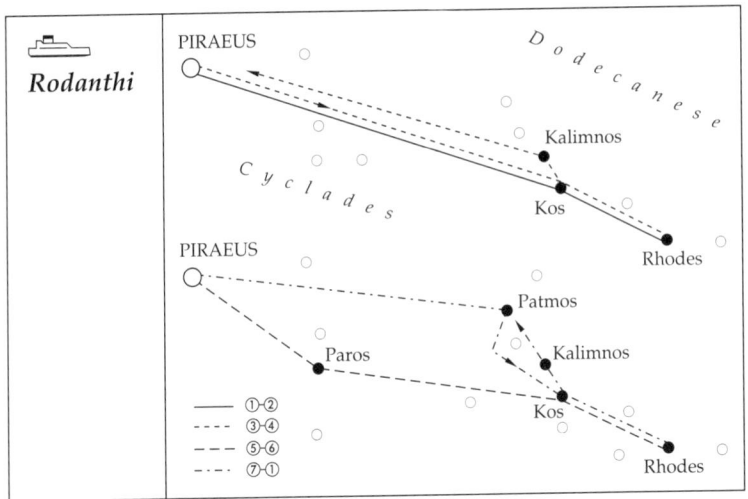

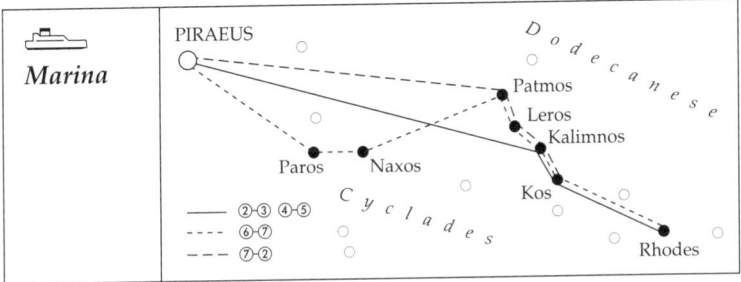

C/F Rodanthi
G.A. Ferries; 1974; 8273 GRT.

As her name implies, the *Rodanthi*, was christened with a regular Rhodes link in mind. After three years providing a very consistent service (running via Crete in tandem with the *Daliana*) she was transferred to the Adriatic in 1993 causing chaos to schedules. In 1994 she returned to the Dodecanese concentrating on the south half of the chain. Some further changes are likely in 1995 as schedules are 'tweaked' further. A comfortable boat, bar her limited exterior deck-class seating.

C/F Marina
G.A. Ferries; 1971; 5941 GRT.

Advertised on company literature as long ago as 1991, the Marina finally deigned to make her debut in 1994. Not the largest of ferries, she is nonetheless a nice boat, and usually running several hours behind the D.A.N.E ferry mid-day Piraeus departures, offers the possibility of a day in Athens along with a night trip to the Dodecanese. As with her companion ferry —the *Rodanthi* — schedules have yet to survive more than a season so times could see changes in 1995.

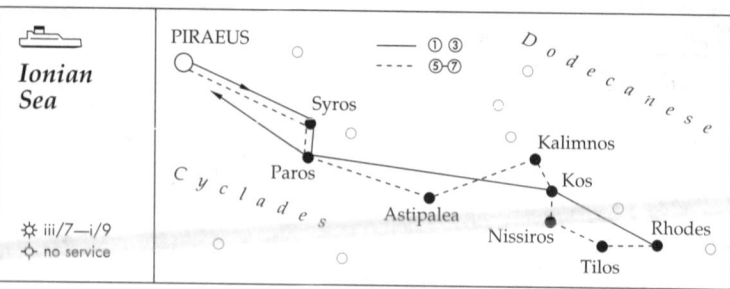

C/F *Ionian Sea*

Strintzis Lines; 1968; 5257 GRT.

For several summers past Strintzis Lines have provided a regular mainland—Rhodes service (usually running out of Rafina). Unfortunately, neither boats nor schedules have been very consistent (the *Ionian Sea* was the third boat in as many years to take on this role). Now operating out of Piraeus, there is at least some hope that things will stabilize a little. Ticket agents have been issued with expensive advertising hoardings; which suggests that this boat will be running again in the summer of 1995. Times could see some adjustment however, as this elderly, but reasonably comfortable ferry was often running several hours late in 1994. Given the heavy competition on the route a return to Rafina cannot be ruled out either.

C/F *Patmos*

D.A.N.E Sea Lines; 1972; 7480 GRT.

The new boat down the Dodecanese in 1992, the *Patmos* is a large, if rather boring, boat. She is nonetheless a cut above the rest of the D.A.N.E fleet in the deck-class facilities on offer. Her Rhodes—Kos—Thessalonika route was also a new addition to Aegean schedules, though its value to island hoppers is sadly diminished by the paucity of ports of call along the way. Expect changes to schedules in 1995 as she now has to cover the Piraeus departures of the *Rodos* when she goes on her extended Cyprus runs.

C/F *Rodos*

D.A.N.E Sea Lines; 1973; 6475 GRT.

The fourth of the D.A.N.E ships running between Piraeus and Rhodes. Unlike her overworked cousins, she is able to maintain facilities at a higher standard because the numbers aboard are smaller, thanks to her direct Piraeus—Rhodes routing (completing the passage in 12 hours; to the 18 taken by ferries calling at the islands of the Dodecanese). This did not stop her engines catching fire in June 1991, forcing

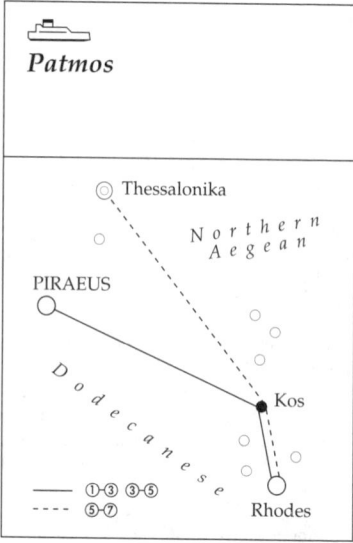

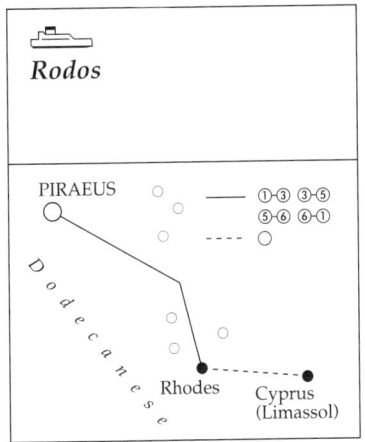

Rodos

PIRAEUS

①-③ ③-⑤
⑤-⑥ ⑥-①
○

Dodecanese

Rhodes

Cyprus
(Limassol)

passengers to be transferred mid-Aegean to a rescue boat. Since then she has run without a problem — though of late she has been running an extended itinerary from Rhodes to Limassol. A fifth D.A.N.E vessel — the C/F *Lindos* — also appears on some timetables, but is an ugly non-passenger-carrying ro-ro.

See also:

- C/F *Romilda*   p. 135
- C/F *Artemis*   p. 228
- C/F *Ergina*   p. 229

C/F *Nissos Kalimnos*
Local; 1988; 754 GRT.

The only small car ferry sailing solely within the Dodecanese, this Greek-built, homely vessel operates out of Kalimnos and provides an invaluable service to adjacent islands. Run by a one-boat company, timetables have tended to be made on the hoof — though they have not changed much over the last three years. For the most part reliable — if occasionally very late — this ferry broke down in July 1992, leaving her passengers with nought to do but admire the view while listening to the soporific 'lip-lip' of the sea kissing the ship's sides. This is called tradition in this part of the world, for, if not exactly the place where old ferries come to die, the Dodecanese has seen a succession of small elderly boats attempting to eke out a living via the government subsidy for providing the small island of Kastelorizo with its only link with the civilized world. The *Nissos Kalimnos* was initially forced to deputise for these boats only to end up taking on the role for good (an Epirotiki cruise ship deputised for her in turn while she was out of action). Given this backdrop, the probability is that the *Nissos Kalimnos* will be running with minor changes in 1995, and if not, a substitute will be found to run the Kastelorizo service. One feature common to all ferries providing the Kastelorizo link is the use of a separate quay at Rhodes harbour (see p. 291) — even on runs to other islands.

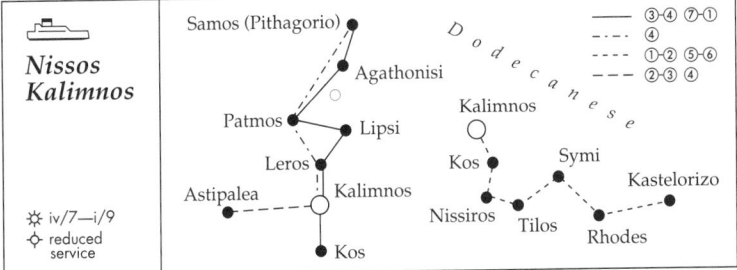

Nissos
Kalimnos

Samos (Pithagorio)

Agathonisi

Dodecanese

——— ③-④ ⑦-①
-·-·- ④
----- ①-② ⑤-⑥
——— ②-③ ④

Patmos

Lipsi

Kalimnos

Leros

Kos

Symi

Astipalea

Kalimnos

Kastelorizo

Nissiros

Tilos

Rhodes

Kos

☼ iv/7—i/9
◇ reduced
  service

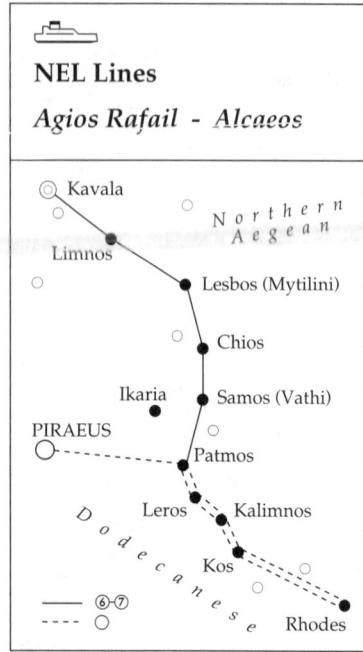

NEL Lines

Agios Rafail - Alcaeos

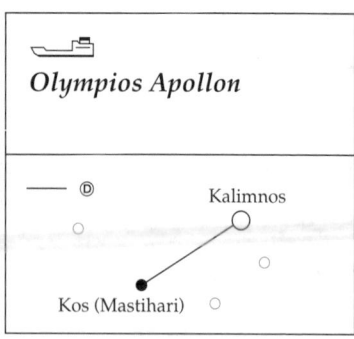

Olympios Apollon

fully restored in 1995. A second connecting service is made via the tour-boat *Cassandra*: a small 1956-built vessel that rolls further than many stomachs care for. If you think yours is to be numbered among them then the daily hydrofoils (see p. 262) might be a safer bet.

C/F *Olympios Apollon*
A large, insipid landing-craft ferry, this vessel has operated out of Kalimnos to the resort town of Mastihari on Kos for the last 5 years. Running the service three times daily, she provides a useful evening service for those day trippers who have missed their tour boat and have found themselves marooned on Kalimnos.

T/B *Chalki*
A small, white and orange wooden-hulled boat that provides the island of the same

Samos—Dodecanese Links
For nigh on a decade now, each summer has seen a once weekly ferry link from the Dodecanese to the Northern Aegean provided by NEL Lines (see p. 300). In 1994 a reduced service operated (stopping at Patmos). It is unclear if this link will be

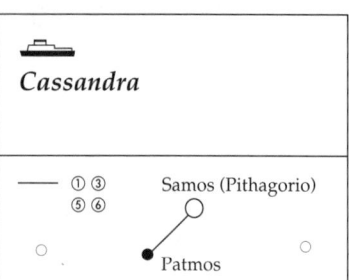

Cassandra

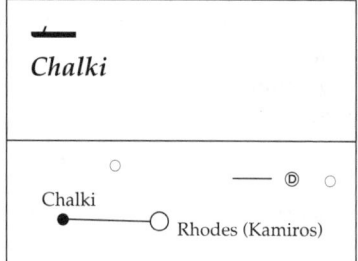

Chalki

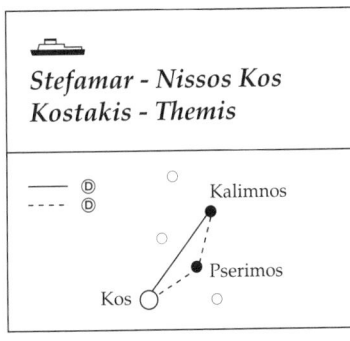

Stefamar - Nissos Kos
Kostakis - Themis

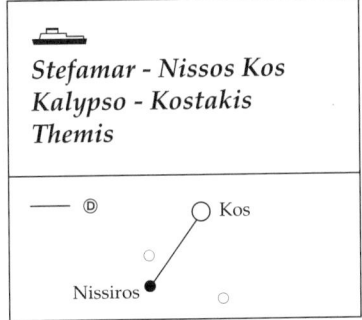

Stefamar - Nissos Kos
Kalypso - Kostakis
Themis

name with its main link with the wider world. If past experience is anything to go by, times (listed on the boat's side) should be treated with caution.

Dodecanese Tour Boats

The inconvenient departure times of many ferries in the Dodecanese means that most island hoppers resort to at least one of the tourist craft shown on this page. Although they cost a bit more, the convenience value makes them worth it. Kos is the main base for tour boats with two large and comfortable vessels — the Stefamar and the Nissos Kos — augmented by several smaller boats. They swap destinations several times a week, but in practice combine to run a daily service to Nissiros, Kalimnos and Pserimos: a quick wander along the waterfront the night before will enable you to find out which

one you want. Tickets can be bought on board. You can also pick them up just on their return runs. The same is true of the smaller boats operating out of Patmos to Lipsi, and the larger Rhodes—Symi tour boats. The most useful of these is the Symi I: a small passenger ferry that carries several cars in a pinch. Worth looking out for as — charging ferry rates — she is cheaper than other tourist boats, usually running an early morning Symi—Rhodes service. The catamaran Symi II runs in tandem with her, starting from Rhodes. Both boats are now suffering, following the arrival of hydrofoils (see overleaf) which cream off much of the route's tourist traffic. A second Rhodes' catamaran was also operating in 1994; named the Aegean Princess, she operated to various islands but is prohibitively expensive (e.g. Rhodes to Kuşadası 19,000 GDR!).

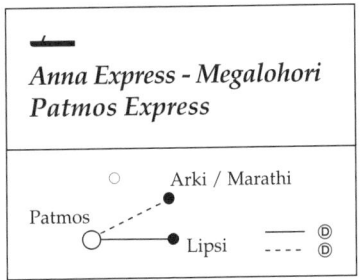

Anna Express - Megalohori
Patmos Express

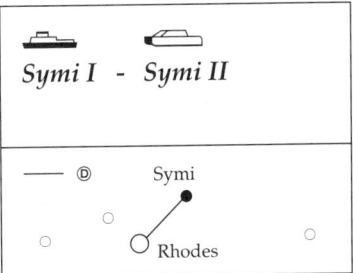

Symi I - Symi II

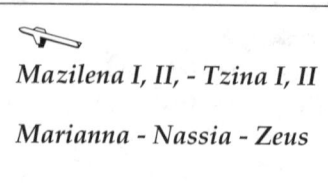

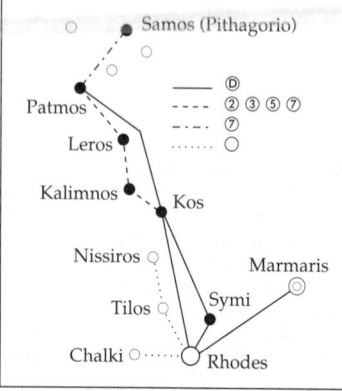

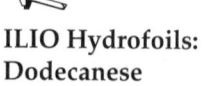

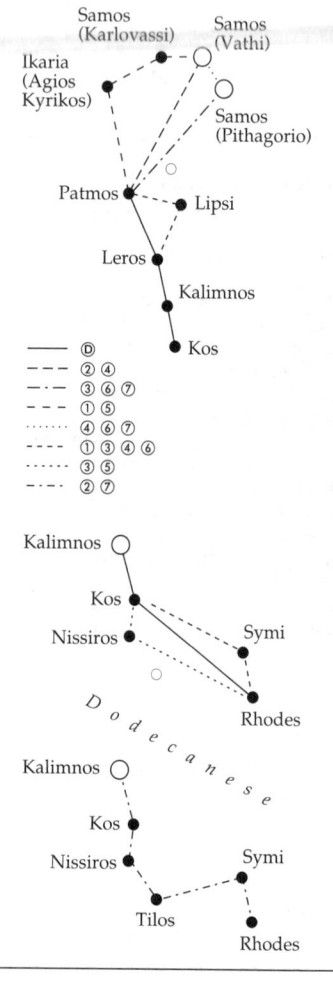

Dodecanese Hydrofoils

Recent years have seen a rapid expansion in Dodecanese hydrofoils. The down side is that there are considerable fluctuations in levels of activity and itineraries, so it is very much a case of looking to see what is running when you arrive. The only links that you can confidently expect to find are daily Kos—Rhodes and Samos—Kos runs. ILIO Hydrofoils arrived in a big way in 1993, with boats operating out of Kalimnos and Samos (from Vathi or Pithagorio, or both). Schedules have yet to settle down, with boats running from Samos direct to Kos and then doubling back to less attractive ports. Dodecanese Hydrofoils run the *Mazilena I, II,* and *Tzina I, II* between Kos and Rhodes with extended runs up to Samos. Zeus Lines' *Marianna, Nassia* and *Zeus* are more excursion orientated, running daily out of Rhodes to Symi and Marmaris in Turkey.

Dodecanese Islands & Ports

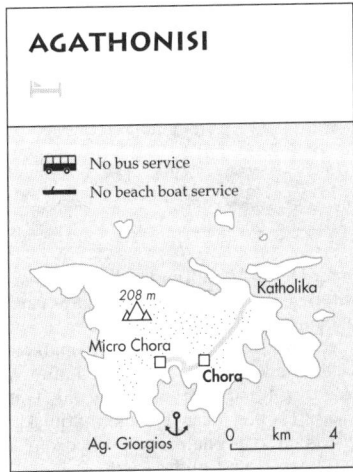

AGATHONISI

No bus service
No beach boat service

208 m

Katholika

Micro Chora

Chora

Ag. Giorgios

0 km 4

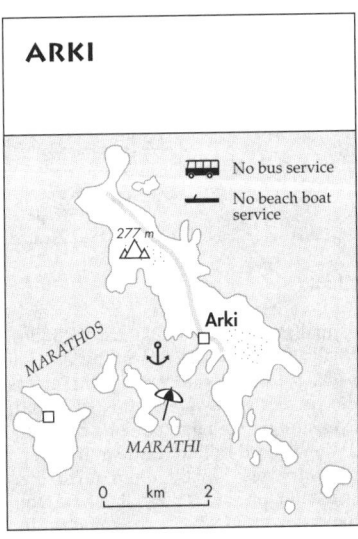

ARKI

No bus service
No beach boat service

277 m

MARATHOS

Arki

MARATHI

0 km 2

Agathonisi

ΑΓΑΘΟΝΗΣΙ; 13 km², pop. 110.

Poorly connected Agathonisi is home to a small fishing community, six islets (all uninhabited), and a large ferry quay. An uninspiring hilly island covered with thorn bushes, it remains the preserve of the odd northern European grimly determined to get away from it *all*. The best reason to visit is the sense of elation that comes on leaving it; you can guarantee that you will return from your holiday feeling you have really achieved something. Unfortunately, the sum of the parts is considerably less than the whole. The two tiny hamlets aren't worth spending three days on the island for and the only activity on offer is walking the donkey path to an abandoned village at Katholika.

Two pensions in the port offer 12 beds and the only island accommodation.

☎
CODE 0247, PORT / REGULAR POLICE 23770.

Arki

ΑΡΚΟΙ; 7 km², pop. 50.

Consisting of scrub-covered dune-hills unrelieved by anything of interest, one dour fishing village and a dozen odd islets, Arki is not on the tourist map. The island also has no ferry quay, so boats steam aimlessly around on the off-chance of meeting a passenger-filled caïque. More important, there is no regular caïque to nearby uninhabited islet of **Marathi** (complete with a delightful beach backed by a couple of seasonal tavernas) — the destination for most 'Arki' advertised Patmos boats (check your exact destination if taking one of these). Marathi excepted, visitors should bring their own food, shelter, spade and nut-bucket.

Accommodation is limited to two tavernas offering rooms in Arki village. One of the tavernas on Marathi also offers summer rooms.

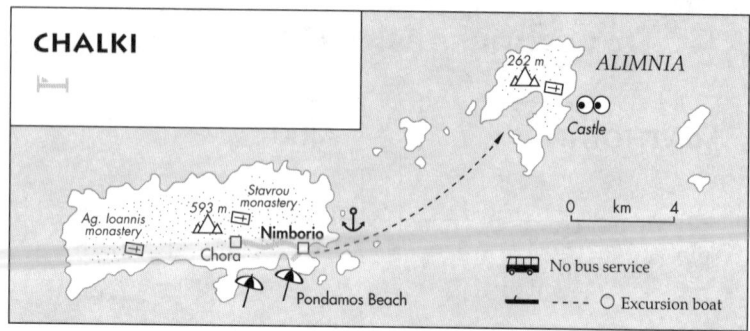

CHALKI

ALIMNIA

262 m

Castle

Stavrou monastery

Ag. Ioannis monastery

593 m

Nimborio

Chora

Pondamos Beach

0   km   4

No bus service

---- ○ Excursion boat

Chalki

ΧΑΛΚΗ; 28 km², pop. 300.

A small island to the south-east of Rhodes, Chalki has been discovered by enough package tour operators (who market it as the perfect get-away-from-it-all island) to ensure that in High Season accommodation is hard to find. Little more than a bone-dry rock, Chalki (often transcribed as Khalki, or Halki) takes its name from the bronze that was once mined on the island (it thus shares the name with other bronze mine islands — see p. 423).

The port town of **Nimborio** houses most of the small population. A mass of richly painted Venetian (or if you prefer Symi) style houses set against a skyline topped by three ruined windmills, it is very attractive — though there is little to do here except admire the view. The best of these is from a ferry: looking at the town cupped within the comforting folds of a deep U-shaped bay. The ferry quay juts out of the centre of the bay, and rising close behind it, the tallest campanile in the Dodecanese. Given the small size of the port (strung along the shoreline, it is only a few streets deep) the bare minimum of facilities are close to hand and easily found; with the nearest beach a 15-minute walk away. On the down side, the island has no fresh water supply, and water tankered in from Rhodes is heavily augmented with sea water. Drink from a tap

on Chalki and you'll end up thirstier than before you started. Ferry links are very poor and have actually declined in recent years: the island now largely depends on a daily link with the village of Kamiros Skala on Rhodes provided by the T/B *Chalki*. The best means of making a quickie visit is via occasional excursion hydrofoils and boats from Rhodes town.

Accommodation is scarce and pricey, however, the island tourist office (☎ 57330) —located near the ferry quay — can usually help you find a bed. Phone ahead in July and August when demand exceeds supply. There are two options in Nimborio: the B-class pension *Kleanthi* (☎ 57334), and the C-class *Markos*.

The only other settlement on Chalki (and only 'sight' is the former **Chora** (topped with a chapel-filled castle built by the Knights of St. John). Set safely inland, it is now all but abandoned, and sees almost as few tourists as it did pirates: faced with the choice between a very steep walk from the port (the road rises 300 m in 2 km) and a very easy walk to the good sand beach at Pondamos most opt for the latter.

The main sightseeing excursion is a caïque ride away on the adjacent island of **Alimnia**. Blessed with some excellent beaches and an impressively well preserved castle straddling a ridge on the south-eastern side.

☎

CODE 0241, PORT POLICE 57255, POLICE 71273, FIRST AID 57206.

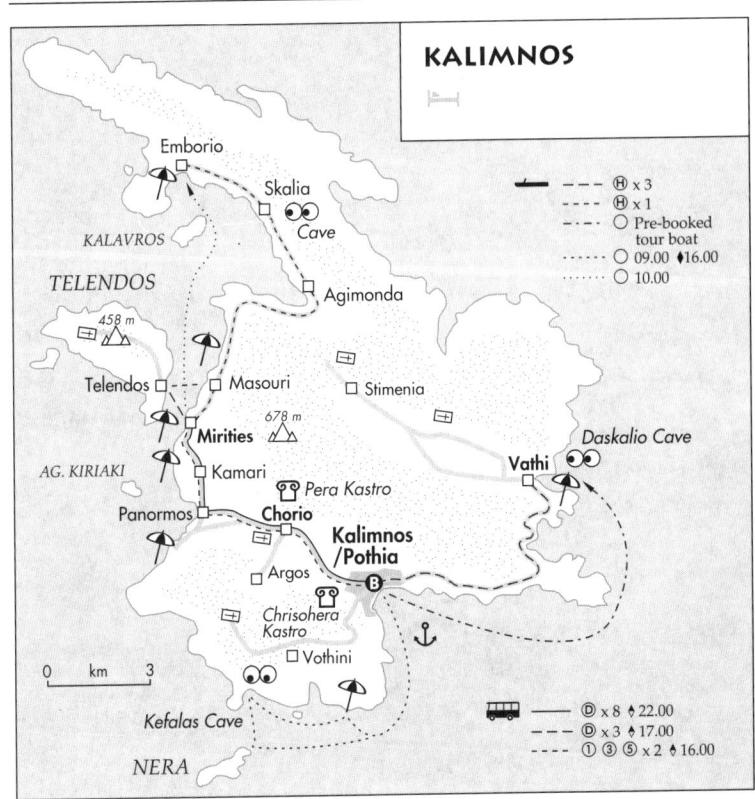

KALIMNOS

Emborio

Skalia

Cave

KALAVROS

TELENDOS

458 m

Telendos Masouri Stimenia

678 m

Mirities

AG. KIRIAKI Kamari

Pera Kastro

Panormos Chorio

Kalimnos /Pothia

Argos

Chrisohera Kastro

Vothini

0 km 3

Kefalas Cave

NERA

Agimonda

Daskalio Cave

Vathi

Ⓗ x 3
Ⓗ x 1
○ Pre-booked tour boat
○ 09.00 ♦16.00
○ 10.00

Ⓓ x 8 ♦ 22.00
Ⓓ x 3 ♦ 17.00
① ③ ⑤ x 2 ♦ 16.00

Kalimnos

ΚΑΛΥΜΝΟΣ; 111 km²; pop. 14,500.

Yet to embrace mass tourism, Kalimnos is a medium-sized island north of Kos that hides its attractions behind superficially forbidding mountains and one of the most dour and largest of island towns (population 11,000) in the Aegean. First impressions are, however, misleading for between the mountains lie dark pockets of verdant vegetation, and there is certainly enough on the island to see if you don't mind poking around in dark holes to find it. In fact, dark holes are something of an island speciality, with three caves visited by irregular excursions and a hole lot more scattered around the island for you to risk getting irrecoverably lost in (*Cave* all of them). Ferries call at the capital, Pothia (also known as Kalimnos Town), set in a wide, sheltered bay on the south coast. The object of daily excursion boats from Kos Town, the Italianesque waterfront is arguably the best of its type in the Dodecanese. Lined with trees and tavernas, it manages to offset the unappealing size of the town surprisingly well; offering an attractive spot in which to watch the world go by. Sadly, this is the problem with the rest of the town; for

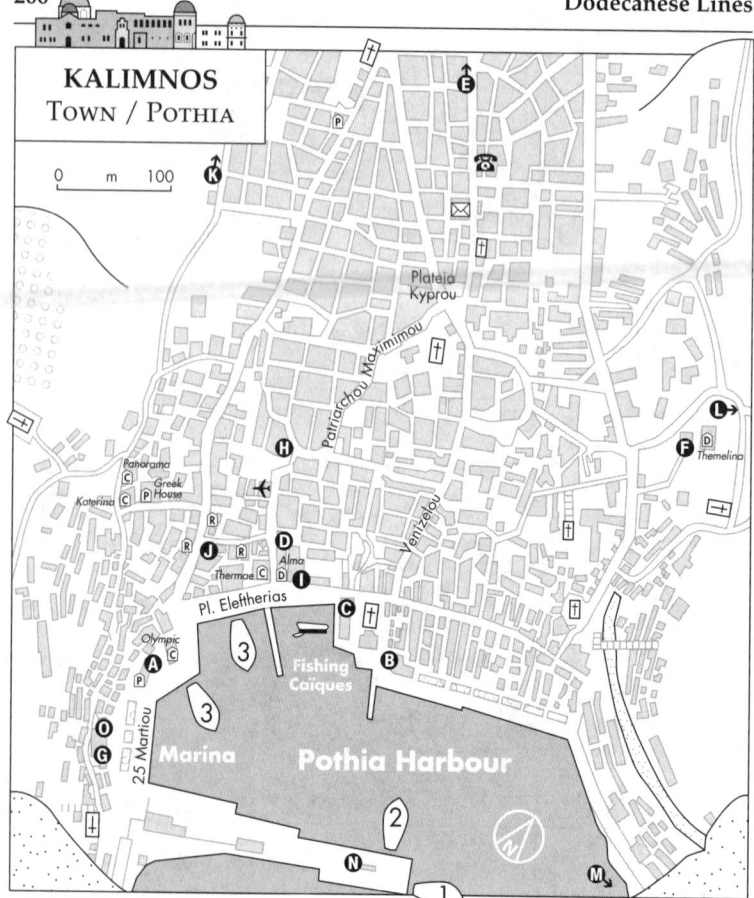

KALIMNOS
TOWN / POTHIA

0   m   100

Key

A Tourist Information
Office

B Bus Station

C Tourist Police

D National Bank of Greece

E Hospital (400 m)
& Ag. Varvara Cave

F Museum

G Sponge 'Factory'

H Supermarket

I Newspapers

J Moped Rental

K Kastro Chrisso
Cherias (300 m)

L Acropolis (300 m)

M Vathi Road

N Passenger Stalls

O *Nissos Kalimnos* Office

1   Large Ferry Berth

2   Hydrofoils &
Kos (Mastihari) Ferry

3   Excursion Boats

the locals treat the narrow streets as if it were a motorbike rally course and walking the town is positively dangerous.

The island has long been one of the sponge fishing centres of the Aegean — though there is little now to show for it, bar a shop just off the ferry quay where you can see the bleaching process under way. The rest of the waterfront is almost okay but otherwise the town offers little temptation to linger. Most tourists head on to the rapidly expanding resort/beach strip running between the villages of **Mirities** (complete with caïque service to Leros and Telendos) and **Masouri**.

The rest of the island tends to be little explored even by those tourists staying more than a day or two. Best alternative destination is the small port of **Vathi** on the east coast. Set in a market garden valley, it offers a hotel, a few rooms and a sea cave. The north of the island is very quiet, with a limited bus service. There is an interesting cave just outside the village of **Skalia** and the isolation of the beach village **Emborio** is now attracting a growing number of those in the know.

ᗷ

Surprisingly for such a large island there is no camping. There are, however, plenty of beds available, most in Pothia and Mirities. The island has a helpful tourist office housed in an old beach hut 200 m from the ferry quay behind an ugly modern bronze of Poseidon. **Pothia** has a pretty mixed collection, starting with the waterfront C-class *Olympic* (☎ 28801) and *Thermae* (☎ 29425), along with the D-class *Alma* (☎ 28969). A quieter D-class hotel — the *Themelina* (☎ 22682) stands near the town museum. A clutch of establishments lie up in the backstreets rising behind the harbour. These include the C-class *Panorama* (☎ 23138) and *Katerina* (☎ 22532), along with the pension *Greek House* (☎ 22559). **Mirities** also has over a dozen hotels including the D-class *Myrties* (☎ 47512) and E-class *Paradise*.

ᐧᐧ

From Pothia tour boats run to the main sea cave: Kefalas's Cave. Famous for its stalagmites and stalactites, this cavern is said to be that in which the god Zeus hid from his

immortal father before killing him (gods can do *anything*). These boats also often stop off at the islet of **Nera** to the south-west, where there is a small monastery. Other tour boats irregularly visit the Daskalio Cave at Vathi. Elsewhere on Kalimnos you will find two reasonable castles: the one outside Pothia is better preserved, but a better excursion is to be had visiting the other (Pera Kastro), just outside the old capital of Chorio, thanks to its impressive views. When you get down to earth again Mirities below has little to offer except an indifferent beach. You will do better to take one of the taxi boats across the narrow straits to the small volcanic island of **Telendos** sitting like a giant boulder off-shore and offering a nice beach, a few rooms and a castle besides. Originally joined to Kalimnos, Telendos was born in 554 AD when an earthquake struck: the ancient capital of the island doing a 'Port Royal' in the process. If you take a caïque across at the turn of the tide, 'tis said you can hear them bells' tolling from the city on the sea-bed.

☎

CODE 0243, PORT POLICE 29404, POLICE 22100, HOSPITAL 28851.

Karpathos

ΚΑΡΠΑΘΟΣ; 301 km²; pop. 5400.

Along with Kassos to the south and Saria to the north, the island of Karpathos forms a small archipelago midway between Rhodes and Eastern Crete. A lovely destination if you are looking for a quiet, unspoilt Greek island, it remains a relatively difficult spot to get to and from. Given the irregularity of ferry links you should allow a couple of days in hand if you visit to effect your escape.

Like Amorgos, Karpathos enjoys a history of division with the two sides of the island effectively separated by inhospitable terrain; with the result that ferries call at two island ports. The similarities end there, however, because Karpathos is graced with some excellent beaches and — thanks to the large expatriate community (many now in the US) who send back funds — is now among the most affluent islands in the Aegean.

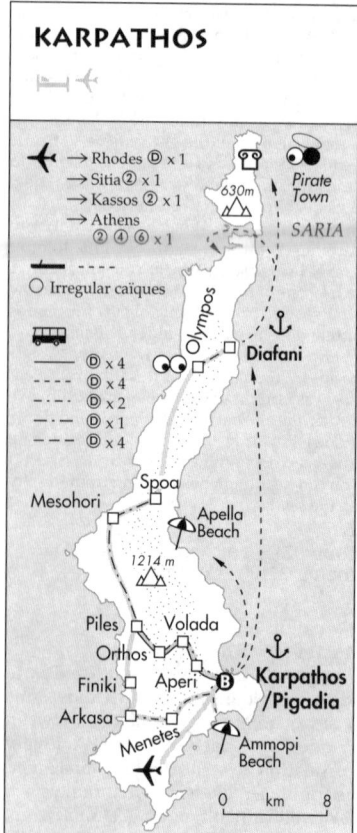

KARPATHOS

→ Rhodes ⓓ x 1
→ Sitia ② x 1
→ Kassos ② x 1
→ Athens
  ② ④ ⑥ x 1

○ Irregular caïques

───── ⓓ x 4
─ ─ ─ ⓓ x 4
─··─ ⓓ x 2
─·─ ⓓ x 1
── ── ⓓ x 4

630m
Pirate Town
SARIA
Olympos
Diafani
Spoa
Mesohori
Apella Beach
1214 m
Piles Volada
Orthos
Finiki Aperi
Arkasa
Menetes
Karpathos /Pigadia
Ammopi Beach

0   km   8

In spite of the appearance of the first charter flights, tourism has yet to take off on the island, with the somewhat paradoxical effect of creating a surplus of demand for what limited facilities do exist. Buses run to the most popular island beach at Ammopi, but the bus service is otherwise generally poor. Sundays see tour buses running between the pretty island villages. The capital, **Pigathia**, is called 'Karpathos' by locals and timetable writers alike and lies at the more popular

southern end of the island. Relatively new, it is attractive in an unspectacular way with a long sandy beach running for several kilometres north of the town. In spite of this, the main tourist resort lies to the south at **Ammopi** where three small bays backed by tavernas offering rooms play host to the growing number of tourists. Other beaches around the island remain the preserve of the taxi boat.

The rest of the island is divided between a dozen villages (most of which lie in the southern half). First among these is **Aperi**, the former chora and still home to the island cathedral. It competes with **Piles** and **Orthos** in the island's accessible scenic village contest — though thanks to a poor bus service many other worthy contenders don't get a look in. The villages in the northern part of Karpathos fall into this category, with the small port of **Diafani** deriving much of its tourist traffic from those wanting to explore **Olympos** — easily the best village on the island. True to its name it straddles a steep hill ridge, and complete with windmills galore, is famous for retaining a traditional village lifestyle (complete with original dress), that is, sadly, increasingly for the tourists' benefit.

There is no camping on Karpathos bar an unofficial site at Diafani. Fortunately, beds are plentiful, even in High Season. Most budget accommodation is in **Karpathos Town**. At the bottom end of the range are a couple of pensions offering rooms: *Harry's Rooms* (☎ 22188) north of the bus station, and *Carlos Rooms* (☎ 22477) along with two E-class hotels: the *Zephyros*, and the *Avra* (☎ 22388), a block inland. Moving up the price range, the D-class *Coral* and *Anessis* (☎ 22100) are topped by the C-class *Karpathos* (☎ 22347) and *Atlantis* (☎ 22777). In **Diafani** you will also find several pensions and several hotels including the quayside E-class *Chryssi Akti* (☎ 51215).

Sightseeing is very limited, the best thing on offer being the High Season taxi boats (the *Adelais* and *Chrisovalandou*) that run up the

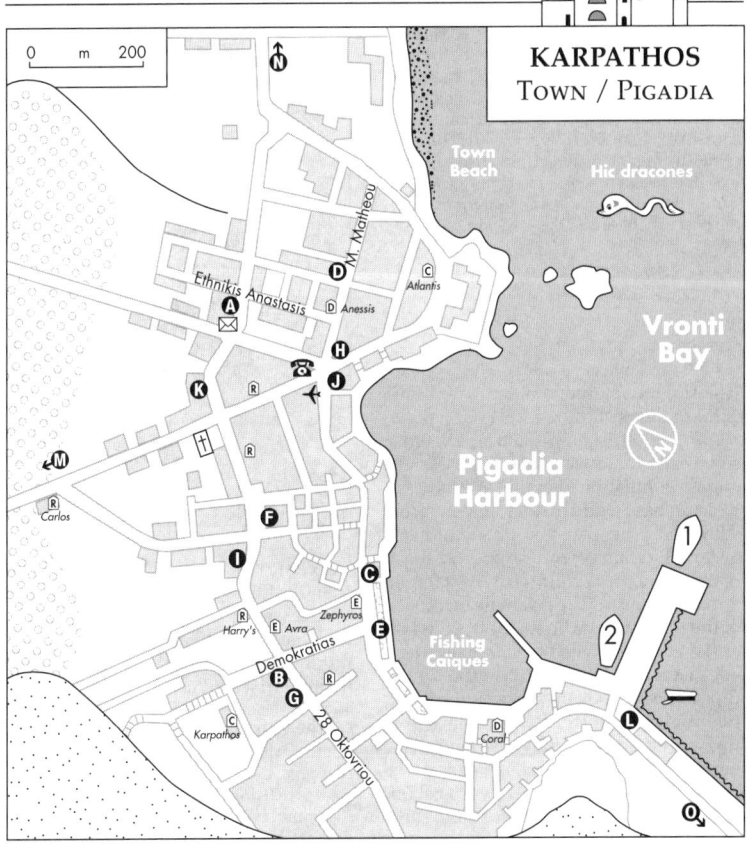

KARPATHOS
TOWN / PIGADIA

0   m   200

Town Beach

Hic dracones

Vronti Bay

M. Matheou

Ethnikis Anastasis

Ⓐ

Ⓓ   Ⓓ Anessis   Ⓒ Atlantis

Ⓗ

Ⓚ   Ⓡ   **Ⓙ**

Ⓡ

Ⓜ

Ⓡ Carlos

Pigadia Harbour

Ⓕ

Ⓘ

Ⓒ

Ⓔ Zephyros   **Ⓔ**

Ⓡ Harry's   Ⓔ Avra   **Ⓔ**

Demokratias

Ⓑ
Ⓖ   Ⓡ

Fishing Caiques

Ⓒ Karpathos   28 Oktovriou   Ⓓ Coral

Ⓛ

1

2

Ⓞ

Key

Ⓐ Tourist & Regular Police
Ⓑ Bus Station
Ⓒ National Bank of Greece
Ⓓ Hospital
Ⓔ Waterfront Clock Tower
Ⓕ Town Hall
Ⓖ Supermarket
Ⓗ Pharmacy

Ⓘ Bakery
Ⓙ Newspapers
Ⓚ Moped & Car Hire
Ⓛ WCs
Ⓜ Airport & Menetes Road
Ⓝ Aperi, Spoa & Diafani 'Road'
Ⓞ Ammopi Beach Road

1 Ferry Quay
2 Beach & Excursion Boats

coast to **Diafani** daily with stops at various beaches. The latter boat also visits the uninhabited island of **Saria** beyond, complete with a deserted 'pirate' town noted for having the remains of some oddly shaped houses (i.e. cone-like roofs). This can also be reached via caïque from Diafani, which has an expanding bus link to Olympos. Tour buses in all but name, their Karpathos town counterparts offer the best way of seeing the southern villages.

☎

CODE 0245, TOURIST POLICE 22218, POLICE 22222, HOSPITAL 22228.

Kassos

ΚΑΣΟΣ; 66 km²; pop. 1184.
An arid, mountainous island with more cliffs than beaches, Kassos is definitely not on the tourist map and has seen ferry services dwindle over the last four seasons and its population over the last two centuries. It has an odd history, having been subjected to an attack by a band of marauding Egyptians who carried off most of the women and children in 1834 for no apparent reason. The few male members of the population who were not killed or enslaved were invited to Suez a few decades later on a goodwill visit (no doubt they hoped to look up a long lost wife or two) and only allowed home when they'd dug the odd canal. Sadly, the Egyptians have not offered ferry links since and it is best to allow at least three days to get off the island or take advantage of the lifeline flights to Rhodes and Crete.

All ferries berth at the small taverna-backed harbour of **Emborio** 1 km round the bay from the capital **Fri** (which also has a lovely small caïque harbour too small for ferries to enter). Also transcribed as **Phry**, the town is a ramshackle affair, but it has a certain scruffy charm and the inhabitants are all smiles. Behind the 'town' lie four closely located villages, all exhibiting signs of gentle decay — particularly **Ag. Marina**, the old capital, and **Panagia**, which has yet more of those derelict early 19 c. mansions so typical of the islands of the southern Dodecanese.

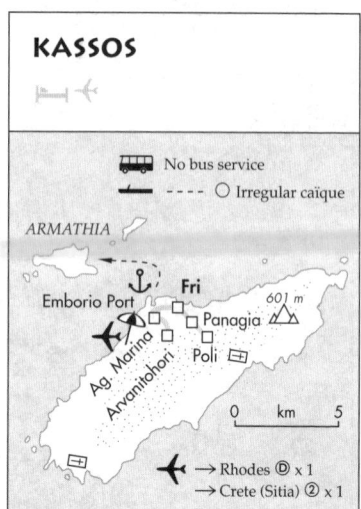

Lacking roads or beaches the rest of the island is little visited. **Armathia**, an islet just west of Kassos, sees caïques heading for a good sand beach when sufficient numbers can be generated, otherwise the main tourist activity is hill walking.

⊨

So few tourists call that facilities are very poor. Harbour tavernas offering rooms and two poor C-class hotels combine to cater for the few that do call (they can more than handle the number of visitors, even in High Season). Best is the *Anagenissis* (☎ 41323), with the *Anessis* (☎ 41201) limping in behind.

👓

Kassos is not noted for its sightseeing. That said, there are sights of a sort. Most notable is the **Sellai Cave** near the airfield, complete with all the usual subterranean accoutrements. The village of **Poli** is also of some interest; being located (as its name suggests) on the site of the **Ancient City** (complete with Acropolis). A Byzantine church now adorns the site. A second church of note is that at **Arvanitohori**, which is partly carved out of the bedrock of the hillside.

☎

CODE 0245, POLICE 41222.

Kastelorizo
ΚΑΣΤΕΛΛΟΡΙΖΟ; 9 km²; pop. 240.

Lying 90 km east of Rhodes and under 3 km from the coast of Turkey, Kastelorizo is the most easterly part of Greece and feels like it. Sometimes known as Megisti ('large'), the island is the largest in a small archipelago of 14. Once very wealthy, thanks to its position on the east—west trade routes (the island is the only safe shelter on the Asiatic coast between Beirut and Makri), extensive depopulation in the last century and a half has left Kastelorizo feeling like a ghost town (the islanders totalled 17,000 in 1850) with the attractive pastel-mansioned waterfront hiding rows of derelict houses. You almost expect to see tumble sea-weed skitting across the magnificent, wide, U-shaped harbour bay. Needless to say, Kastellorizo is another of those islands plagued by the politics of the region. Like Symi, decline set in with the arrival of the Italians in 1918. Cut off from Turkey she lost much of her commercial strategic significance. This was followed by most of her town buildings when the allies bombed the Italians out in 1943 and then forced the entire population to evacuate the island until the end of the war: they returned to find their town a derelict ruin.

The number of tourists calling is very small; for although the island offers a superb castle, a cathedral and good sea-food, it lacks even the smallest of beaches. Kastelorizo's isolation is eased by flights to Rhodes and a twice-weekly ferry.

╘╛

There are plenty of rooms: owners meet boats. The only hotel is the expensive B-class *Xenon Dimou Meghistis* (☎ 49272); rooms from 8,000 GDR. This is augmented by several signless pensions on or near the waterfront.

∞

Thanks to a roadless, and hilly interior, sightseeing is limited to boat excursions to Fokiali Cavern — the best sea-cave in Greece if not the Med. Occasional caïques run to the outlying islands of **Strongili** and **Ro** (whose famous last inhabitant — a little old lady — herically ran up the Greek flag each day until her death in 1986), and offer day trips to Turkey (though you can't formally cross the frontier here).
Within the town the 1380-built **Kastro** (known as Red Castle; it gave the island its name) is home to a small **Museum** — both of which are worth a look. Some way beyond the latter, cut out of the rock, is the only **Lycian Tomb** to be found in Greece; though there are plenty on the coast opposite. The **Cathedral** is also of interest as the columns in the nave were taken from the temple of Apollo at Patara in Lycia.

☎

CODE 0241, POLICE 29068.

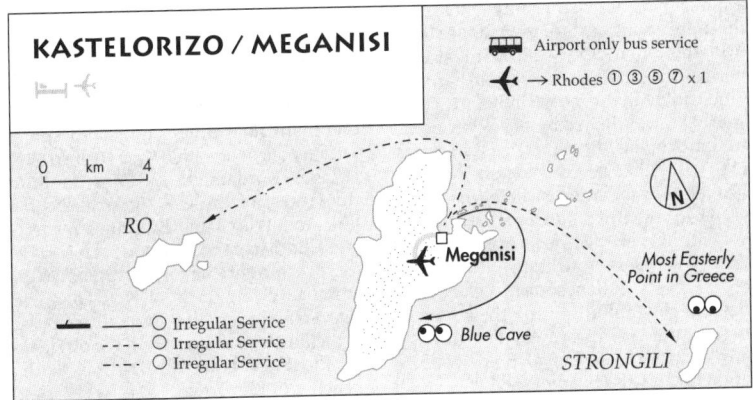

KASTELORIZO / MEGANISI

╘╛ ✈

🚌 Airport only bus service

✈ → Rhodes ① ③ ⑤ ⑦ x 1

0 km 4

RO

□ ✈ Meganisi

Ⓝ

Most Easterly
Point in Greece

∞

━━━ ○ Irregular Service
- - - ○ Irregular Service
-·-· ○ Irregular Service

∞ *Blue Cave*

STRONGILI

Kos

ΚΟΣ; 290 km²; pop. 21,500.

Thanks to an attractive mixture of sand and sights Kos (often transcribed as Cos) is a justifiably popular package tourist destination. Lying mid-way down the Dodecanese, it is also the de facto hub of ferry activity on the chain, with virtually every ferry putting in an appearance and an unsurpassed number of tourist craft operating to neighbouring islands and the Turkish coast. Large for a Greek island (45 km long), Kos was an important centre in the ancient world until it was devastated by an earthquake in the 6 c. AD. Much of its fame was derived from an odd mix of figures and famous associations. In the former category were Hippocrates (460–357 BC) — the so-called 'Father of Medicine' — who was born and had his school here, and a famous painter contemporary of Alexander the Great by the name of Apelles. The island was also a noted producer of fine wine, and scandalously, in the Roman era, see-through silk garments beloved by Senators' wives and the Emperor Caligula.

Kos Town, the main port and capital of the island, lies on the sandy east coast with views across to Turkey. It is a gentle, wide-avenued centre of flowers and trees that would be very restful if it wasn't for a spot of mass tourism. For the most part the more scenic parts of town have stood up to this remarkably well, but the streets north of the castle-dominated old harbour (and indeed, the coastline north and south) are dominated by a heavy concentration of hotels, discos and tee shirt shops that will either be your idea of holiday heaven or a variation of hell: this is the secret for the town's success for there is something here likely to appeal to all tastes — unless you like solitude. The centre is very Italianesque in feel, having been largely rebuilt during the interwar occupation years (courtesy of a devastating earthquake in 1933). Some consolation for the loss of any tangible 'Greek' atmosphere is to be found in the Italian disinclination to rebuild over any archaeological remains that came to light, leaving Kos Town with wide, open, ruin-topped vistas along with the boulevards. Hotels are strung out along the east coast from Lambi to Ag. Fokas. Lined with equally common sand beaches, a cycleway now runs alongside the coast road (bicycle hire being uniquely popular on Kos). This hotel-strip road is also served by city buses (timetables from the office at ⓐ), which also run to the main sightseeing attraction on Kos — the Asklepieion — a sanctuary that became a major focus for healing pilgrimage thanks to the fame of Hippocrates. Local guides will give you a detailed life-story of this figure, though in fact his story is rather illusive. The earliest advocate of a 'scientific' practice of medicine he seems to have gained fame by travelling the Aegean stopping plagues and other little mass infections by advocating the novel idea of boiling drinking water and the isolation of the sick from the healthy. Thereafter, almost every medical practice and book around was ascribed to him; glorying in the association. The most recent manifestation of this is the ancient tree he is supposed to have taught under standing near the castle.

The rest of Kos is fertile but rather scruffy and littered with military encampments thanks to the close proximity of Turkey. It is served by very overcrowded buses (timetables from ⓑ) running along the one main road down the island spine, with feeder roads linking it with coastal villages. **Kardamena** and **Mastihari** are the largest of these with regular ferry links to Nissiros and Kalimnos respectively. Both have become tourist resorts in their own right, the former almost managing to outdo parts of Kos Town for discos and beach shops. Equally popular is the north coast beach village of Tigaki — the alternative destination to the beaches of Kos Town.

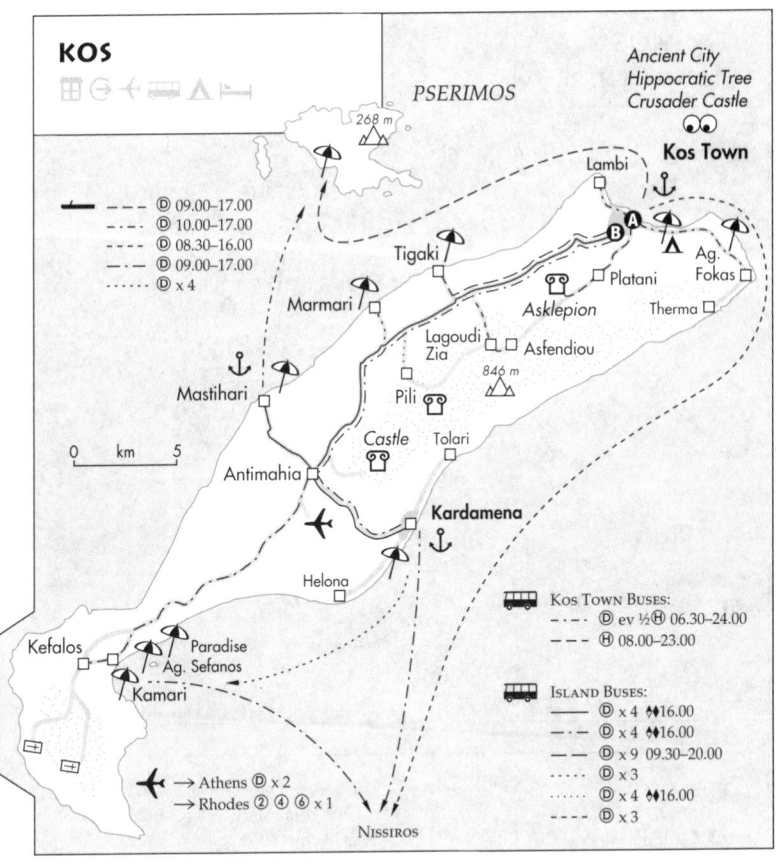

KOS

PSERIMOS

268 m

Ancient City
Hippocratic Tree
Crusader Castle

Kos Town

Lambi

ⓓ 09.00–17.00
ⓓ 10.00–17.00
ⓓ 08.30–16.00
ⓓ 09.00–17.00
ⓓ x 4

Tigaki

B A

Ag.
Fokas

Marmari

Platani

Asklepion

Therma

Lagoudi
Zia

Asfendiou

Mastihari

846 m

Pili

0   km   5

Castle

Tolari

Antimahia

Kardamena

Helona

Kos Town Buses:
ⓓ ev ½Ⓗ 06.30–24.00
Ⓗ 08.00–23.00

Kefalos

Paradise
Ag. Sefanos

Kamari

Island Buses:
ⓓ x 4 ♦♦16.00
ⓓ x 4 ♦♦16.00
ⓓ x 9 09.30–20.00
ⓓ x 3
ⓓ x 4 ♦♦16.00
ⓓ x 3

→ Athens ⓓ x 2
→ Rhodes ② ④ ⑥ x 1

Nissiros

Inevitably, the more attractive destinations are harder to get to. The best beaches are tucked away under the western 'fin' of the island beneath the hilltop windmilled village of **Kefalos**, 45 km from Kos Town. This is easily the best part of Kos, quieter and more fertile than the rest of the island (particularly the pine woods south-west of Antimahia known as Plaka: now an attractive picnic spot for island coach tours and those with their own transport); it is largely unspoilt, with a lovely sandy beach at **Kamari**, and an equally good, but more crowded affair at **Paradise**. Both are backed by tavernas.

Those looking for sightseeing will find Kos replete with options. In addition to those outlined overleaf, the hills above Kardamena are crowned with the Knights of St. John-built Antimahia castle, to the north-east is the village of **Pili** alongside its beautiful ruined medieval counterpart, while at **Therma**, a 4 km walk from **Ag. Fokas**, hot springs run down to the sea.

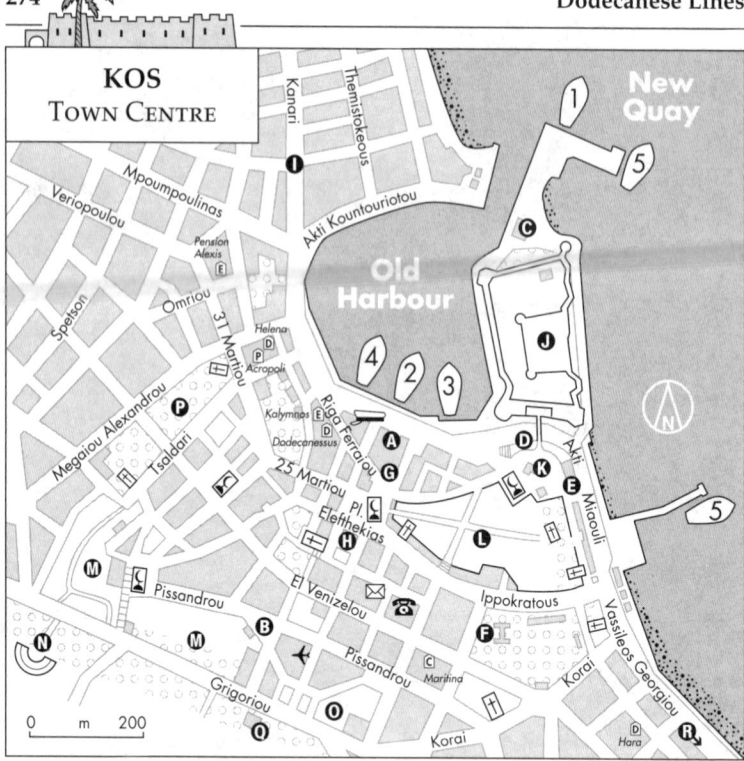

KOS
TOWN CENTRE

Key

- **A** Customs Office / City Bus Stop
- **B** Bus Station
- **C** Ferry Terminal Building
- **D** Taxi Rank & WCs (beneath bridge)
- **E** Tourist Police Office
- **F** Hospital
- **G** Museum
- **H** Fruit Market Building
- **I** 'Disco' Alley
- **J** Crusader Castle
- **K** Plane Tree of Hippocrates / Castle Entrance & Turkish Fountain

- **L** Agora (Marketplace) Ruins
- **M** Acropolis & Roman Forum Ruins
- **N** Ancient Odeon (restored)
- **O** Altar of Dionysos
- **P** Site of the Stadium
- **Q** Casa Romana
- **R** Camping Kos (3 km)

1 Ferry Quay
2 Tourist Boats
3 Turkish Boats Departure Point
4 Bodrum Day Excursion Boats
5 Hydrofoil Berths

⊨

High Season sees a rush for the available hotel space and rooms, and understandably so for Kos, an island overloaded with upper and mid range package tour hotels, is poorly supplied with budget accommodation given the number of visitors it sees. It thus pays to arrive on a morning boat (i.e. Rhodes hydrofoil rather than afternoon ferry). The limited budget rooms available in **Kos Town** are divided between seven establishments. To the south of the ferry quay the D-class *Hara* (☎ 22500) lies one block behind the beach road that is home to package tour hotels for a kilometre each side of the town (if funds aren't too much of a problem then finding a bed in one of them is never very difficult). Alternatively, you can try the C-class *Maritina* (☎ 23241) near the OTE. Although it is on a busy street, it is not as noisy as the clutch of hotels overlooking the Old Harbour. These consist of the E-class *Kalymnos* (☎ 22336), the D-class *Helena* (☎ 22986) and *Dodecanessus* (☎ 28460) and one good pension — the *Acropoli* (☎ 22244). To the north lies a second, the *Alexis* (☎ 28798). There are also a limited number of rooms around the town: owners are in the habit of only meeting the major boats.

Each of the main tourist villages on Kos has more hotels than most islands can muster. At the budget end of the range: **Mastihari** has the D-class *Faenareti* (☎ 51395) and the E-class *Zevas* (☎ 22577), **Kardamena** the D-class *Paralia* (☎ 51205) and the E-class *Olympia*, and **Kefalos**, the D-class *Sidney* and E-class *Eleni* and *Maria* (☎ 71308). Rooms are also available at all the above as well as at **Tigaki** and **Kamari**.

Α

Camping Kos (☎ 23275): 3 km south of Kos Town on the main beach road. Well maintained and friendly site. Mini-bus meets ferries.

👓

Kos is one of the best islands going when it comes to sightseeing. First and foremost there is the **Asklepieion**, one of the greatest shrines in Greece, it is described overleaf). Kos town itself is the other big crowd-puller.

Kos Town

By mixing sightseeing, shady trees, and the occasional drink at a passing taverna, the town offers a relaxed and interesting day's sightseeing. The most obvious attraction is the inappropriately named **Crusader Castle**

(all sites on Kos open ②–⑦ 08.30–15.00). Started in 1450 it was built by the Venetians out of masonry and columns from the ancient city and Asklepieion. A road now runs through its land-side moat under the castle's entry bridge. Standing opposite the bridge is the impressive 14 m girthed (and now hollow) **Plane Tree of Hippocrates** — its not so plain limbs artistically supported with scaffolding and cut-up tractor tyres. Supposedly the one he taught under, it is only in fact about 500 years old. It shades a Turkish fountain (dry) constructed from fragments of ancient buildings and the best of Kos Town's several mosques: **Gazi Hassan Pasha Mosque** (1786).

Immediately to the south of the mosque lies the largest excavated area of the ancient city: the unenclosed market-place or **Agora**. Now consisting of little more than foundation stones and the inner cores of temples (only the long gone exteriors were faced with marble) it is the preserve of lizards during the day and couples serenading the moon at night. Unfortunately, a lack of the usual carved stones telling you what you are looking at renders most of the site unintelligible. More interesting is the town **Museum**, housing the finds not shipped by the Italians to Rhodes.

The **Roman Forum** area to the east of the town centre is (thanks to Italian restorers) the best of the ancient sites. A number of pillars that formed the forum's peristyle court have been 'reconstructed', and the street still bears the ruts worn into the stones by ancient carts. The excavations near the bus station also have walls complete with original painted plasterwork, though the ancient Acropolis isn't visible. The mosqueless minaret on the hill bisecting this area stands on the site. To the south of these excavations lie two other popular attractions: the restored **Odeon** and also a rebuilt example of a Roman Villa: the **Casa Romana**, a mixture of pools and mosaics. Well worth a look: don't be put off by the singularly ugly cement exterior of the building.

Finally, Kos has boat excursions aplenty, with craft running daily across the 5 km straits to **Bodrum** in Turkey and to all the adjacent Greek islands, including **Persimos**, a crowded beach island reserved for day-trippers seeking (in vain) to escape the crowds.

☎

CODE 0242, PORT POLICE 28507,
TOURIST POLICE 28227, HOSPITAL 22300.

The Asklepieion

The remains of one of the most imaginative and effective creations of Greek architecture lies on a hillside 4 km west of Kos Town. Overlooking both the town and the Turkish strait, the Asklepieion was the leading medical sanctuary in the Greek world. Dedicated to the God of Healing, Asklepios (a son of Apollo whose symbol was a snake curling up a staff), it was (thanks to the revenue that accompanied the pilgrims that flocked there) an architectural and cultural centre. The sanctuary was initiated a century after the death of Hippocrates (357 BC) and because of his associations rapidly developed thereafter. Built on four terraces (the upper one being a grove in the sacred wood responsible for the siting of the sanctuary) it was considered a masterpiece of Hellenistic architecture in its day and boasted a series of famous paintings by Apelles to heal the spirit when they couldn't manage the body. Offices to the latter were undertaken by a priestly order supposedly descended from the god. The sanctuary also offered the right of asylum.

Despite losing some of its most notable art works to Rome, the Asklepieion thrived until the 6 c. AD when it was reduced to rubble either by the Anatolian attack on Kos in 554 AD or an earthquake. The ruins lay undisturbed until 1450 when the Castle of the Knights was constructed in Kos Town: the need for building blocks being sated by the readily available ancient masonry in the town and at the Asklepieion. As a result the site was all but stripped bare of architectural members and passed out of memory. One of the lost great shrines only known through literary sources, the long search for the Asklepieion began in 1896; its location eventually being pinpointed by a local antiquarian, G. E. Zaraphtis, in 1902; though his German archaeologist sponsor Herzog took the credit for the discovery, undertaking a 'grub and grab' dig until 1904. Under Zaraphtis systematic excavation continued until his death in the 1933 earthquake. Thereafter Italian archaeologists did as much building as excavating. The site is therefore as much of a 'fake' as Knossos on Crete, but as in that case, this is of great value to those seeking an appreciation of its former grandeur.

Today the Asklepieion is approached via a 400 m road lined with cypress trees. This ends with the ticket kiosk at the entrance to the site.

At this point you have to choose between taking the path up the south side of the site and then walking down the terraces from the upper terrace or taking the ancient route (i.e. walking up the staircases). The description below assumes the latter; if only because it is easier to climb, rather than descend, stairways without hand rails.

Passing the foundations of several unidentified buildings that lie to the south, the first structure of note is **ⓐ** the **Entrance Stairs**. Consisting of 24 steps they climb to the **Lower Terrace** and the site of the formal gateway to the sanctuary: **ⓑ** the **Entry Propylon**. Long since reduced to foundations, the vision, on passing through it, of the wedding-cake terrace layers leading up to the main temple, is now to be only dimly gleaned. The enclosed 'courtyard feel' of the Lower Terrace that **ⓒ** the **Galleries** — pillared, stoa-like buildings which once ran from either side of the gate to the middle terrace wall — created is also considerably diminished. Even so, the Lower Terrace retains the wide, open aspect that graced it in antiquity and it was probably on this terrace that athletic contests associated with festivals honouring the god were held. Unfortunately, the votive statues that were such a feature of the terrace have long gone. All that remains are **ⓓ** the **Statue Bases** (usually running parallel to the gallery foundations), and the **Statue Niches** in **ⓔ** the **Middle Terrace Wall**. In one of these niches stood a famous statue of antiquity now lost — the Aphrodite by Praxiteles. Walking along to the north side of the terrace wall you arrive at **ⓕ** the **Fountains**. Fed by both sulphurous and iron-rich springs they were revered for the supposed healing properties of the water. The later Romans somewhat debased the atmosphere by building **ⓖ** the **Latrines** nearby (no doubt the steady tinkle of water dribbling into the sacred pool helped bring on the idea).

Returning back along the terrace you come to **ⓗ** the **Second Staircase**. Running up to the Middle Terrace via 30 steps it brings you on to the real heart of the sanctuary; for directly in front of you is **ⓘ** the **Great Altar of Asklepios** (4 c. BC), the oldest building of the Asklepieion. Now reduced to its foundations, it was similar to the Great Altar at Pergamon, with a central stairway running up to the winged-base. The base was also roofed, and one of the ornate roof coffers lies on the edge of the foundations.

THE HIPPOCRATIC OATH

I SWEAR BY APOLLO PHYSICIAN, BY ASCLEPIUS, BY HYGEIA AND PANACEA AND BY ALL THE GODS AND GODDESSES, MAKING THEM MY WITNESSES, THAT I WILL CARRY OUT, ACCORDING TO MY ABILITY AND JUDGEMENT, HIS OATH AND THIS INDENTURE.

TO HOLD MY TEACHER IN THIS ART EQUAL TO MY PARENTS: TO MAKE HIM PARTNER IN MY LIVELIHOOD: WHEN HE IS IN NEED OF MONEY TO SHARE MINE WITH HIM, TO CONSIDER HIS FAMILY AS MY OWN BROTHERS, AND TO TEACH THEM THIS ART, IF THEY WANT TO LEARN IT, WITHOUT FEE OR INDENTURE.

TO IMPART INSTRUCTION WRITTEN, ORAL AND PRACTICAL, TO MY OWN SONS, THE SONS OF MY TEACHER AND TO INDENTURED PUPILS WHO HAVE TAKEN THE PHYSICIAN'S OATH, BUT TO NOBODY ELSE. I WILL USE TREATMENT TO HELP THE SICK ACCORDING TO MY ABILITY AND JUDGEMENT, BUT NEVER WITH A VIEW TO INJURY AND WRONG DOING. NEITHER WILL I ADMINISTER A POISON TO ANYBODY WHEN ASKED TO DO SO ... ETC. ETC.

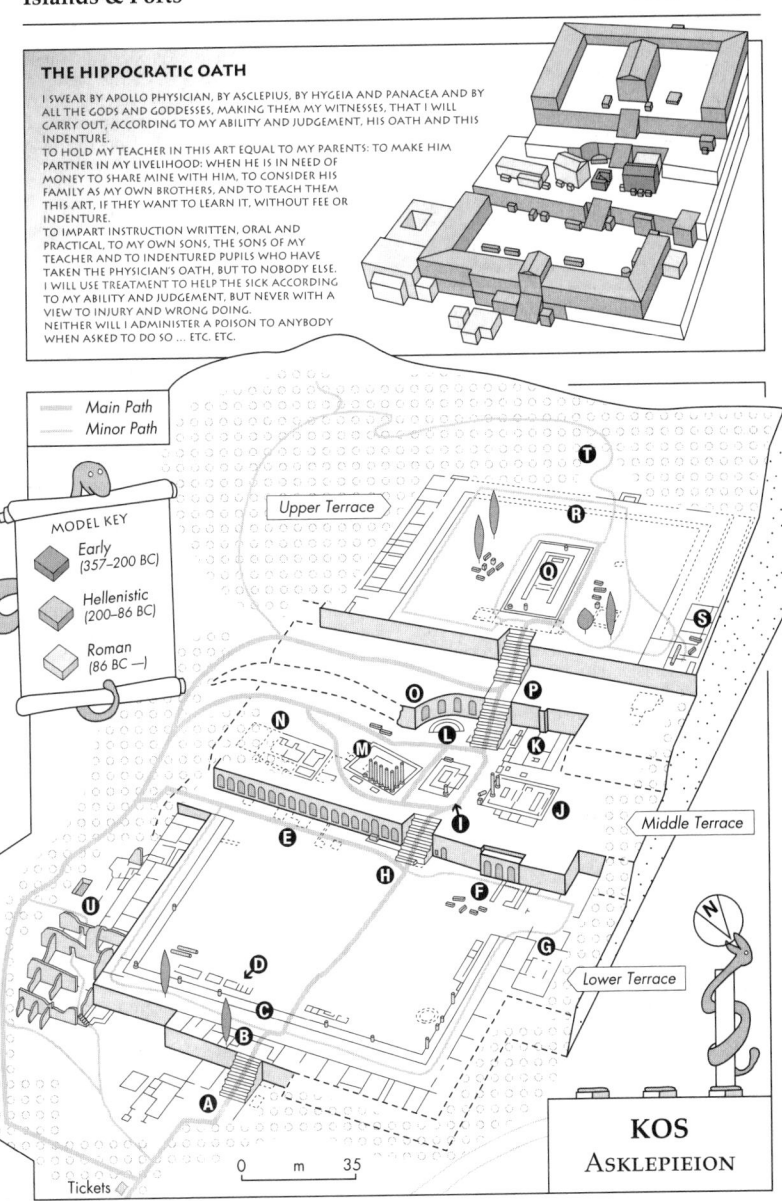

Main Path
Minor Path

MODEL KEY

Early (357–200 BC)

Hellenistic (200–86 BC)

Roman (86 BC —)

Upper Terrace

Middle Terrace

Lower Terrace

KOS
ASKLEPIEION

0   m   35

Tickets

To the north lies the oldest temple in the sanctuary: ❹ the **Asklepios Small Temple**. Dating from the 4 C. BC, it was built in the Ionic style (two of the columns have been restored) and functioned as the sanctuary treasury after it was replaced as the main shrine on the site. In this capacity it housed a series of wooden panel paintings by Apelles. One in particular — the Aphrodite Anadyomene — was widely regarded as a masterpiece of ancient art. It was carried off to Rome by the Emperor Augustus. On the Lower Terrace side are the bases for lost votive statues, while tucked away on the Upper Terrace side is a Roman building standing on Greek foundations (❾), believed to have been the **Priest's Quarters**.

Opposite the Priest House are the semicircular foundations of ❺ the **Exedra / Public Platform**. An odd building, with no clear function, suggestions as to its purpose have ranged from a public bench to an assembly point for priests or doctors. The terrace wall behind it has several more statue niches. To the east, the Romans in-filled the terrace by building ❿ an irregularly orientated **Temple of Apollo**; now the most visable of all the buildings on the site thanks to the seven fake columns erected by the Italians to give you something to look at. Two of them contain fluted fragments of the original pillars.

To the south, now little visible and largely overgrown with trees, are the foundations of ⓫ usually known as the **Lesche** or **Conference Hall** — though the precise function of the building remains unclear. Given the snake cult associated with the god Asklepios, it is somewhat surprising that the Asklepieion does not appear to have possessed a snake house (its counterpart at Epidavros had a magnificent Tholos built for this purpose); so perhaps this was it. Snake pits were quite common at medical shrines, for these lovely little critters were deemed to have healing powers given the numbers of lame men who suddenly acquired the ability to run very fast when faced with one. Add to that the numerous compulsive stammerers suddenly able to say Asklepieion three times in as many seconds at the first time of asking, and the evidence was irrefutable.

Behind the buildings on the Middle Terrace is ❻ the first stage of the double **Upper Terrace Wall**. In fact, the Middle Terrace can be divided into two (hence the four terraces), but as the upper part of the Middle Terrace is too small to contain buildings, it is viewed as merely a half-way point up ❼ the **Monumental Staircase**. This consists of two closely positioned flights that rise in 60 steps to the **Upper Terrace** and its superb views over both the site and Kos Town.

Dominating the centre of the Upper Terrace is ❽ the **Large Temple of Asklepios**. Built in the 2 C. BC, this was the main temple on the site to the God. Doric in style, it was an irregularly shaped 6 x 11 columned building, notable for having the lowest of its three steps made of black marble. Today only the foundations and part of the interior floor survive. Around the side and back perimeter of the terrace ran ❾ the **Galleries**, forming an peristyle backdrop to the temple. At some later date the side galleries were extended to provide, what are thought to have been, ❿ **Patients' Rooms**.

From the back of the terrace the path winds into ❶ the **Sacred Wood** that surrounds the site, eventually emerging at the back of ⓪ the **Roman Baths**. Dating from the 1 C. AD, this is a late, but major structure, and is so described because of the well-preserved plunge bath inside the remains; but some maintain that this building was more likely to have been the official house of a general or someone of similar status. Either way, it is easily the best preserved building on the site (the remains here are the genuine article for once!).

Leros

ΛΕΡΟΣ; 53 km²; pop. 8200.

Leros is a real oddity among the Greek islands. Conveniently placed between the popular islands of Patmos and Kos, it is sufficiently attractive to deserve its fair share of the crowds — even despite its comparative lack of sights — and yet, although it is very well served by ferries, the island remains stubbornly off the tourist trail. There is, of course, a reason and that is its rather unsavoury reputation. This is so bad that information leaflets issued to tourists by the Municipality of Leros are, unusually, forced to acknowledge the problem thus: 'In 1958 the Community of Psychopaths was established at Leros, which is still here today, under the name of 'State Therapeutical

Hospital of Leros'. Stemming from that, by mistake or sometimes in purpose, an infamous picture of Leros has been promoted, which in no way can identify with the island and its people. Since 1989 various press reports in Greek and foreign press presented in excess the negative sides of such an establishment'. In short, a past Greek government came up with the idea of conveniently placing all lunatics and severely mentally handicapped adults in one location — Leros. The media reports in question were humiliating accounts, widely publicised across Europe, that patients in the hospital were being kept in concentration camp-like conditions. Further damage was done when it was revealed a year or so later that the improvement in those conditions promised by the authorities had not materialised. Happily, thanks to international pressure, things have now improved; though the legacy of this episode lives on in the lack of visitors.

Greek tourists tend to avoid the island anyway (its name has become a byword in Greece carrying much the same resonances that 'Bedlam' has acquired in English). In many ways this is unfortunate, because Leros has a fair bit going for it in a down-beat sort of way, and you are likely to find that the islanders are both welcoming and almost pathetically grateful that you have paid a visit.

Its reputation not withstanding, Leros is not by any means a typical Greek island. Superficially, it is not dissimilar to Patmos; being small and hilly, with a deeply indented coastline offering a number of sheltered bays complete with beaches. However, the years of Italian rule between the world wars have left a greater mark on this island than on any other in the chain, and it is fair to say that Leros still retains the atmosphere of an Italian island. This is largely because the crumbling plastered 1930s vintage buildings, the harbour works and military roads (lined

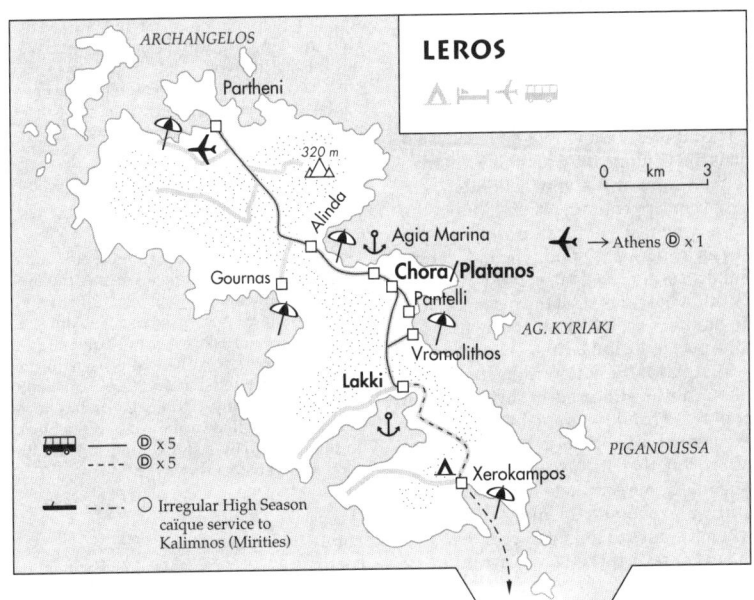

with plane trees) are Italian built, with the tiny nucleus of the Greek Chora failing to make an impact.

Most visitors to the island arrive at the port of **Lakki**, set in a deep inlet on the south-west coast. Thanks to the shelter offered by this bay, Leros was a major Italian naval base during the last war, and saw action when it was captured by the allies in 1943 with 25,000 casualties (war cemeteries are scattered around the island). The memory of this does little to relieve the atmosphere that is set by the airfield-like lights of a mental hospital complex (used to detain political prisoners by the Colonels) on the southern shore. The port town is a very artificial affair; revealing its planned Italian origins. The roads were laid out, impressive waterfront buildings were erected and then, well, not a lot really; as the local economy has never grown enough to allow a town to fully develop in the space provided. The result is a mix of odd buildings and clumps of trees that is a bit ghost-townish. On the plus side, accommodation is easily found here, along with all the essential services, and in summer the promenade has been known to play host to a travelling circus, complete with little top.

The bus service on Leros is so poor that taxis thrive along the walkable 3 km road to the Chora at **Platanos**. Slightly more Greek in appearance, it lies under the protecting walls of the imposing Kastro, but is somewhat spoilt by indifferent buildings and the busy road running through the centre. All the main services lie on the road which runs down to the little port of **Agia Marina.** The 19 C. main port, Agia Marina is now rather neglected (though it is still used by hydrofoils in poor wind conditions and by the island's excursion boats). It has a more attractive waterfront than its successor, and boasts a pebble beach complete with a windmill gracing a submerged mole. However, when it comes to tourist appeal, it looses out to **Pantelli**, tucked away in a little bay

to the south-east of the Chora, for this hamlet has a much better beach that is an attractive mix of pebbly sand (like the beach at the resort hamlet of **Alinda**) and the odd fishing boat besides.

The rest of Leros is fertile, quiet and little visited thanks to the poor bus service. None of the island villages are of any great merit, though **Xerokampos**, on the south coast, has a pebble beach of sorts and, more importantly, a regular summer caïque service that runs daily to Mirities on Kalimnos.

⊨

Offers of rooms meet the large ferries: arrive any other way and you will find an empty quay. **Lakki** has a number of hotels including the D-class *Miramare* (☎ 22043) and the E-class *Katerina* (☎ 22460), both one block in from the waterfront. More up-market establishments lie further inland, with the attractive C-class *Artemis* (☎ 22416) supported by the B-class *Agelou Xenon* (☎ 22514). **Chora** also has a couple of pensions: most conspicuously the *Platanos* (☎ 22608) housed in an incongruously tall modern building overlooking the main square, and the nicer *Elefteria* (☎ 23550) on the Lakki road. **Agia Marina** has a few apartments on the beach road but no other advertised accommodation. **Pantelli** (off the map) also has a scatter of Pensions and taverna rooms, as does the package resort village at **Alinda**.

A

Camping Leros (☎ 23372): at Xerocampos. Olive grove site with more trees than tents.

👓

The 12 c. **Castle** built by the Knights of St. John on the site of a Byzantine fortress is the one and only attraction. It contains a church and offers panoramic views of the island and the large number of islets nearby. Tourists can visit (the stairway to the castle starts to the right of a small florist just off the Chora main square). The nearest thing Leros has to a museum is contained in the tourist office block on the ferry quay: a single room filled with odds and ends (mostly WW2 memorabilia, including unexploded shells).

☎

CODE 0247, PORT POLICE 22224, POLICE 22222, HOSPITAL 23251.

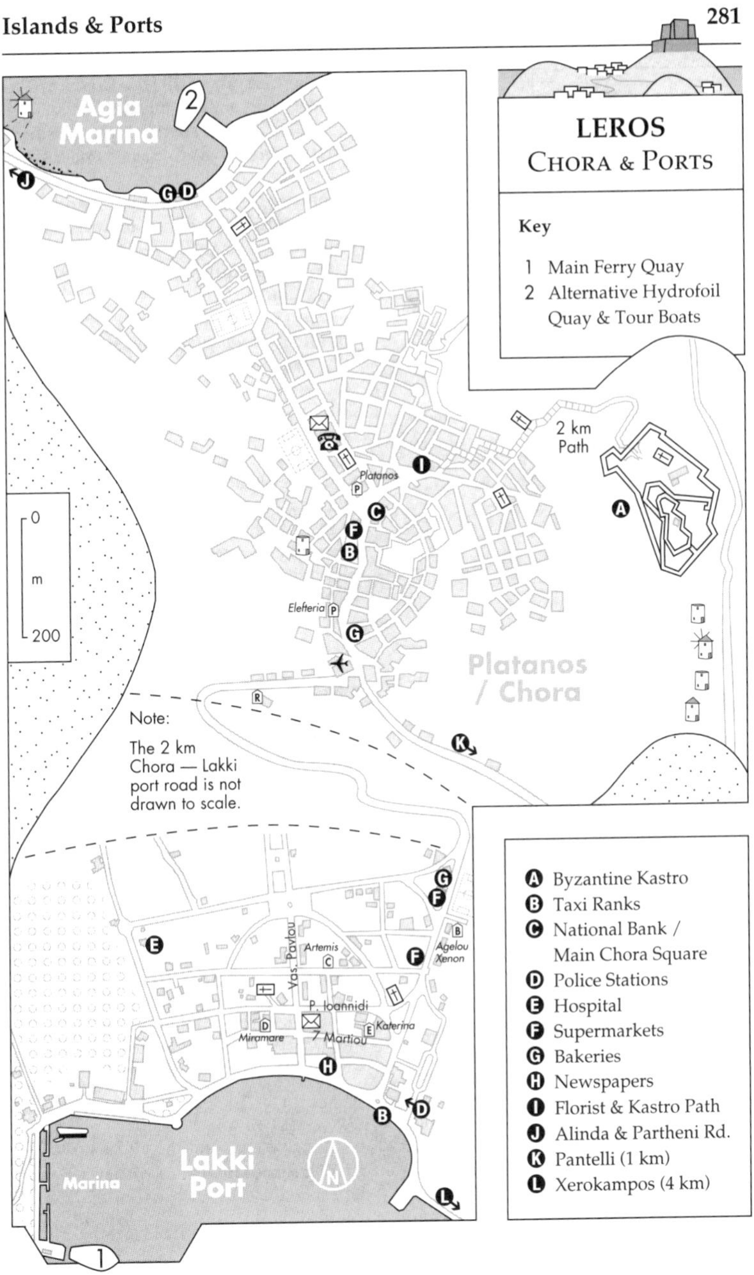

LEROS
CHORA & PORTS

Key

1 Main Ferry Quay
2 Alternative Hydrofoil
   Quay & Tour Boats

Agia Marina

2 km Path

Platanos

Elefteria

Platanos / Chora

Note:

The 2 km Chora — Lakki port road is not drawn to scale.

Yas. Tavlou

Artemis

Agelou Xenon

P. Ioannidi

Miramare

7 Martiou

Katerina

Marina

Lakki Port

A Byzantine Kastro
B Taxi Ranks
C National Bank /
   Main Chora Square
D Police Stations
E Hospital
F Supermarkets
G Bakeries
H Newspapers
I Florist & Kastro Path
J Alinda & Partheni Rd.
K Pantelli (1 km)
L Xerokampos (4 km)

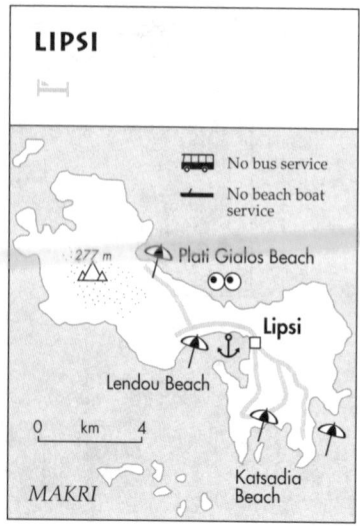

LIPSI

No bus service

No beach boat service

277 m

Plati Gialos Beach

Lipsi

Lendou Beach

0   km   4

MAKRI

Katsadia Beach

Lipsi

ΛΕΙΨΟΙ; 16 km²; pop. 650.

The most developed of the small islands north of Patmos, charming Lipsi offers good beaches and a get-away-from-it-all atmosphere. Perpetually hovering somewhere between being a mere beach-boat island and a ferry destination in its own right, Lipsi sees most of its visitors in the form of day-trippers from Patmos and Leros (there are daily beach boats from both). The island takes its name from the goddess Calypso: local tradition has it that it was here that Odysseus was imprisoned as a sex slave for seven long, hard, years. Almost as many other Mediterranean islands have laid claim to this piece of notoriety, but only this one has sought to make the claim by virtue of its name. Further circumstantial support for this claim is derived from the fact that this is the sort of spot where loving couples might feel tempted, when confronted with an empty beach and a full moon (Note: if you are caught doing 'it' in public in Greece you can get up to three years).

Be they ferry or tourist boat, most arrive at Lipsi's only settlement: the small village of Lipsi set into a deep bay on the south coast. From a boat it looks to be a singularly uninspiring place; with a prominent blue-domed church surrounded by a rather grim collection of whitewashed houses backed by low, arid hills (one with the ubiquitous ruined windmill turret); but this is misleading, for once ashore you will find shady streets and squares and very friendly islanders.

If it wasn't for the lack of a bus service (the locals make do with offering visitors 'lifts' in pick-up trucks) Lipsi would be the perfect beach island. As it is, most visitors 'do' the town and then head for the nearest beach within walking distance (at Lendou close by the port). It pays to be more adventurous and head for the coves that make up Katsadia beach (complete with a taverna offering rooms), or Plati Gialos (wide and sandy; easily the best beach on the island) on the north coast. It is close on an hour's walk — unless you avail yourself of one of the truck 'taxis' that run between it and the town.

🚍

Day-tripper tourism has left a dearth of budget accommodation, with the result that beyond several outfits offering pricy rooms and the waterfront D-class hotel *Kalypso* (☎ 41242), there is nought but the beach to head for. At the height of the High Season it is as well to consider the option of picking up a returning beach boat to bedded parts if your attempts to find accommodation come to nought.

👀

Only sight on Lipsi is a girls' **Carpet Weaving School** (complete with occasional quayside performances designed to stitch up passing day-trippers) beloved by postcard photographers. Not to be outdone, the town information office-cum-**Museum** is even more of a rip off (and considering that entrance is free, this is really saying something). Prize exhibits are an assortment of plastic bottles full of 'Holy' water (allegedly) and the remains of a passing American's pet rock collection.

☎

CODE 0247

Nissiros
ΝΙΣΥΡΟΣ; 41 km²; pop. 1100.

A small island just to the south of Kos, Nissiros is to be numbered among the more picturesque Dodecanese islands; attracting considerable day-tripper traffic and worthily so. It is easily the best day-trip destination from Kos (Rhodes excepted); thanks to a lovely small island atmosphere and a real Jekyll and Hyde personality. For Nissiros is the cone of a volcano jutting out of the Aegean. In shape not unlike the Aeolian islands north of Sicily, it looks oddly out of character in this part of the world. Another feature that contrasts markedly with other southern Aegean islands is that it is (thanks to the volcanic soil) remarkably fertile, with outer slopes thickly planted with vineyards, fig and almond trees and wild flowers. These combine to make this a gorgeous island to visit in the spring and an excellent shady walking destination any time of the year. Climb the hillside however, and you will see the other face of Nissiros, for the verdant outer slopes conceal a very different interior: this takes the form of a deep and barren crater caked with a yellow sulphurous mud that smells as bad as it looks. Tradition has it that when the Olympian gods arrived in Greece they had to fight a race of giants for control of the earth. Nissiros was formed as the result of a battle between Poseidon and the giant Porphyris; the god speared a lump of Kos and dumped it on the giant, burying him alive — hence the volcano's rumblings.

The island has one town (**Mandraki**), and two hamlets (Emborio and Nikia) on the crater rim. Mandraki is an attractive centre that manages to cater to the tourist hordes without losing its whitewashed narrow street charm. Not very large, it is really just a main street ribboning along the northern shore. Starting from the ferry quay on the east side of the town, it gradually rises to the first of the island's castles to the west. With only small side

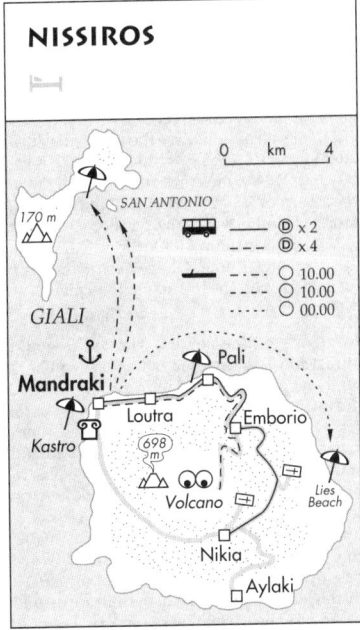

streets branching off to either side it is difficult to get lost and a hour's exploration is sufficient for you to establish where all the salient landmarks are. Buses run from near the ferry quay to the volcano crater floor and the crater rim villages. Both **Nikia** and **Emborio** have view and sniff points over the crater along with steps/paths down into it.

Like Santorini, Nissiros has black or red sand beaches, but in the main these are poor affairs, the best being at Pali (people generally come to Nissiros to have a day off from shading a beach). There are hot water springs to be found just outside Nikia and also at **Loutra**; now the home of a rather run down spa.

Ferry connections are surprisingly poor, but daily tour boats from Kos (Town and Kefalos) and Rhodes hydrofoils, make Nissiros easily accessible.

🛏️

There are plenty of rooms in Mandraki, with some in Pali and Nikia. Hotel accommodation is adequate, even if there isn't much at the top of the range. The nearest Nissiros comes to luxury is the C-class *Porfyris* (☎ 31376). Hotels just to the left as you leave the ferry quay include the *Three Brothers* (☎ 31344) and the *Romantzo* (☎ 31340), these are on a par with the B-class pension *Haritos* (☎ 31322) in the town. More down market is the pension *Drosia* (☎ 31328); again in the town. Outside of Mandraki the only hotel of note is the C-class *White Beach* (☎ 31497/8) on the hill above the Pali road.

👓

Even without the volcano **Mandraki** would attract tourists: a scenic whitewashed chora built on a black lava and with 2 castles. Above the town stands the Knights of St. John **Castle** (1315) which contains a multi-iconed monastery within its walls, while 1 km inland stands an older and more impressive **Kastro** built out of suitably imposing black lava on the site of the ancient acropolis. Occasional Mandraki boat excursions are also available to **Giali** (a small double-hilled island which has a pleasant beach surprisingly unmarred by the pumice quarrying in the hillside behind it), and to a beach on the islet of **San Antonio**.

The **Volcano** is the great attraction, and better done first thing if you are on a day trip. Tour buses meet the daily boat flotilla, running direct to and from the crater floor. The island buses only run as far as the rim, visiting both semi-abandoned **Emborio** and thriving **Nikia** (easily the better viewing point and with a stepped trail down into the crater). As with other Greek volcanos, Nissiros is not all fountains of ruby magma and pillars of steam, but more a lunar landscapey hole — in this case some 4 km across with five shallow craters set in the main crater floor. These chronicle the history of the volcano very neatly. The last few eruptions have produced these small craters; all being very minor affairs. The last was in 1933 and followed in sequence to similar outbursts in 1888 and 1871–73. The main crater is the product of the last major eruption which occurred in 1552 when the island literally blew its top off.

☎

CODE 0242, PORT POLICE 31222, POLICE 31201, FIRST AID 31217.

Patmos

ΠΑΤΜΟΣ; 34 km²; pop. 2600.

Volcanic in origin, cosy Patmos (famous as the island where St. John the Evangelist wrote the Book of Revelation) is an attractive mix of small hills and beach-lined bays. In spite of being one of the most heavily touristed Greek islands it manages to retain a very relaxed atmosphere, and most who visit place it near the top of their list of better islands. Religious tourism is the mainstay of the local economy and a procession of cruise liners release a flood of tourists overwhelming attempts to maintain a reverential image. In a recent effort to stem the tide, the Patriarch of Constantinople declared Patmos a holy island, and extra backing has come via a government decree outlawing 'promiscuity and looseness'. Nudity and discos are theoretically banned. In practice however, this delightful monastery-topped island is far less forbidding than all this sounds and on all but the town beach you will still encounter a happy ratio of a hundred boobs to every brother.

The island's success in mixing things spiritual and tourists temporal has come about by a tacit separation of the two. This happy compromise confines religion to the heights, while the island's playgrounds grace the shoreline. The centre of activity is the port of **Skala**. Now the largest resort village on the island, it is an attractive little place made up of tavernas, Cycladic-style whitewashed houses, and fringed with a marina replete with beach boats. Despite the fact that the locals are doing their best to ruin it (latterly by cutting down the trees lining the port beach in order to widen the road used by maniac mopeds), it is still a long way from the worst excesses of mass tourism found on other islands. No large hotels or Tinos-tacky souvenir shops here. The only obvious concession to the numbers visiting is the inordinately large quay built to accommodate the cruise liners whose tear-and-bunting departures enliven evening promenades along the waterfront. Most only stay long enough for passengers to be whisked by bus up to impressive looking Chora for a quickie tour of the monastery.

Chora is a very insipid sort of place — lacking shops, rooms for rent and any 'lived-in' sense at all. A maze of white-washed buildings skirting the high dark walls of the monastery, it is too quiet for its own good, and filled with churches has become little more than a glorified outer precinct to the monastery itself. Only the windmills crowning the ridge at the edge of the town remind one that the chora once had a less sanitised role. The monastery aside, the best reason to visit Chora is the excuse it gives to walk the old 3 km mule path that runs up from the port. An easy walk (most people prefer to bus up and then return on foot), it is an excellent way of taking in the island.

The rest of the island has much more going for it; being a lovely mix of bays and beaches tucked away within the folds of an intricate coastline. Beach caïques run from Skala to the best of these — **Psiliamos** to the south and the multi-coloured pebble **Lampi** on the north coast, as well as to the adjacent beach islands of Lipsi and Arki (most 'Arki' taxi boats in fact go to a beach and taverna on the adjacent islet of Marathi). The only other settlements of any size at all are at **Kambos** — which is a pleasantly unspoilt hill village complete with a pebble beach — and **Grikos**; billed as a 'resort' village (though it has fewer hotels than Skala).

In addition to the beach boats, Patmos has a good bus service running between the main centres. Photocopied timetables for these and all regular ferries are available from the island information office located behind the post office.

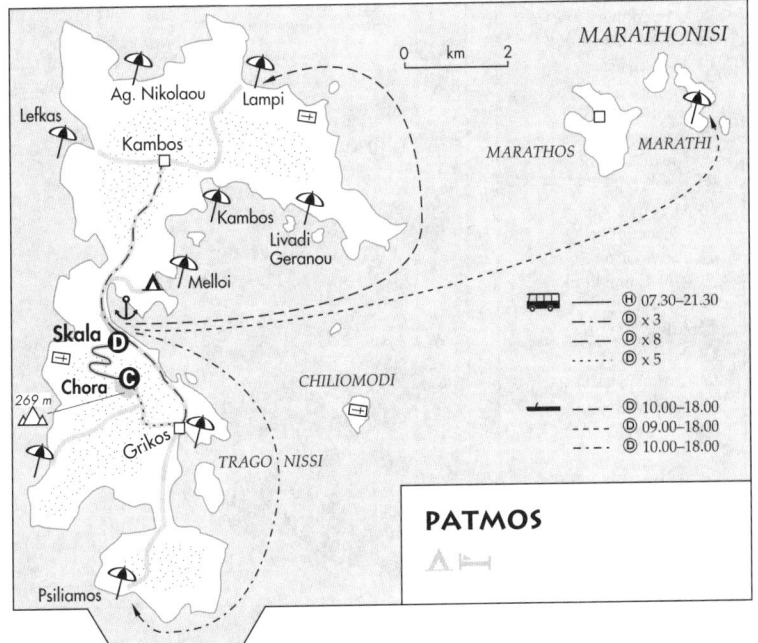

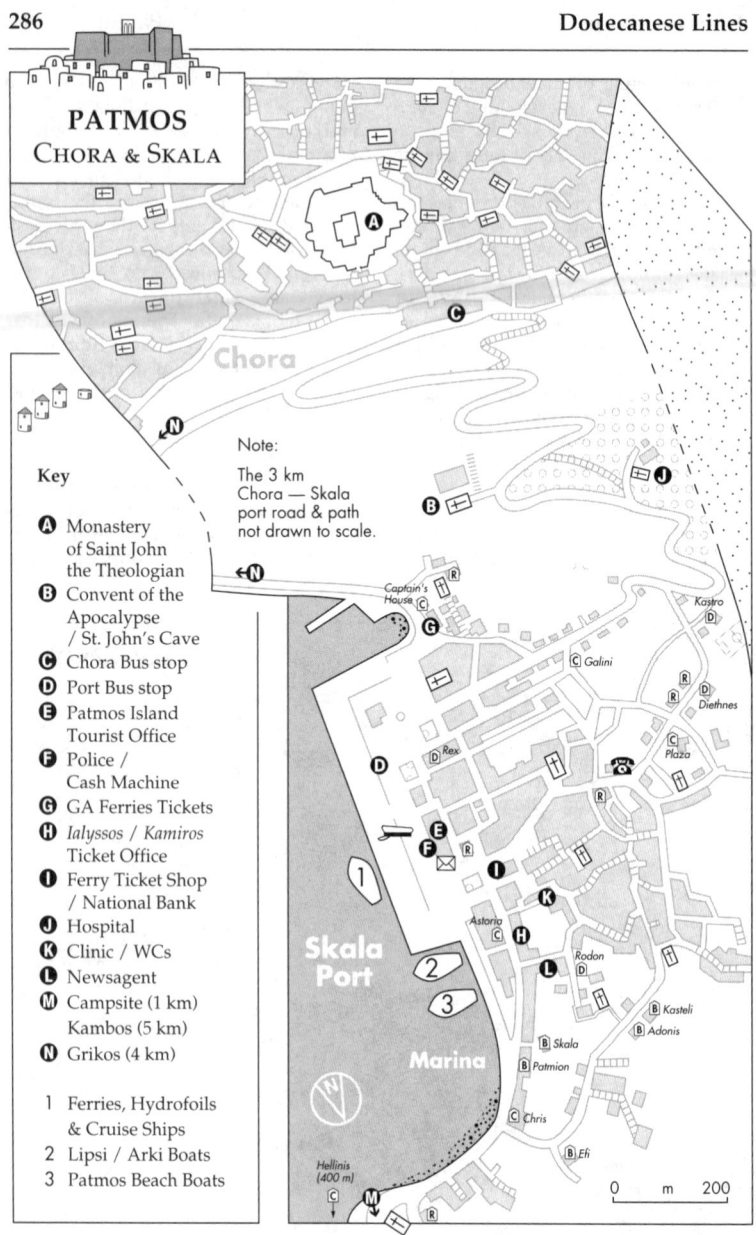

PATMOS
CHORA & SKALA

Key

A Monastery
of Saint John
the Theologian
B Convent of the
Apocalypse
/ St. John's Cave
C Chora Bus stop
D Port Bus stop
E Patmos Island
Tourist Office
F Police /
Cash Machine
G GA Ferries Tickets
H *Ialyssos / Kamiros*
Ticket Office
I Ferry Ticket Shop
/ National Bank
J Hospital
K Clinic / WCs
L Newsagent
M Campsite (1 km)
Kambos (5 km)
N Grikos (4 km)

1 Ferries, Hydrofoils
& Cruise Ships
2 Lipsi / Arki Boats
3 Patmos Beach Boats

Note:
The 3 km
Chora — Skala
port road & path
not drawn to scale.

Chora

Skala
Port

Marina

Captain's
House

Kastro

Galini

Rex

Diethnes

Plaza

Astoria

Rodon

Kasteli

Skala

Adonis

Patmion

Chris

Efi

Hellinis
(400 m)

0   m   200

ᖶᖯ
Plenty of rooms available, thanks to the island's
pilgrim status. Offering hordes meet all boats.
The island tourist office also has lists of hotels.
The majority are to be found in Skala, which is
also the name of the premier hostelry — the B-
class hotel *Skala* (☎ 31343). At the north end of
the port, it is close by other up-market estab-
lishmets including the waterfront *Patmion* (☎
31313). Best of the mid-range hotels are the C-
class *Chris* (☎ 31001) and *Hellinis* (☎ 31275).
Cheaper hotels are also plentiful. Just off the
quay is the D-class *Rex* (☎ 31242), and behind
the town are the *Kasto* (☎ 31554), the *Plaza* (☎
31217), and cheaper *Rodon* (☎ 31371).

Λ
Patmos Flowers Camping (☎ 31821): 2 km
around the harbour and over the hill at Melloi.
A bambooed site — one of the best in Greece,
but suffers from the island's water shortages.

👁👁
Main attraction is impossible to miss: the castle-
like **Monastery of St. John the Theologian**.
Surly monks do wonders for the atmosphere
— successfully repelling all boarders since the
monastery's foundation in 1088. As a result it
is something of a treasure house containing
over 890 early Christian manuscripts (notably
an early 6 c. version of St. Mark's Gospel), a
large collection of icons and the most important
collection of monastic artifacts on display in
Greece. Built on the site of the ancient acropolis,
fragments of an earlier temple of Artemis are
scattered around the building.

Half-way up the Skala—Chora road and
mule-track you will come to the second major
monastery on Patmos: the **Convent of the
Apocalypse**, built over the cave where St.
John saw and dictated (to his disciple Proch-
oros) all. Quite why he was disposed to conjure
up such happy notions as 'And I looked, and
behold a pale horse: and his name that sat on
him was Death, and Hell followed with him'
remains a mystery; modern Patmos encourages far happier thoughts, and the island in St.
John's day (complete with a picturesque temple in place of the rather forbidding monastery)
had even more going for it. Perhaps the excellent souvlaki-pita outlet on the main street
leading to the OTE had yet to set up in business.

☎
CODE 0247, PORT POLICE 31231,
POLICE 31100, TOURIST OFFICE 31666.

Rhodes
ΡΟΔΟΣ; 1398 km²; pop. 60,000.

The largest island in the Dodecanese,
Rhodes also lays claim to being the
sunniest island in the Aegean. A substantial package tourist industry has thus
emerged, making it one of the premier
destinations in Greece, with visitors all
year round. Inevitably there is a down
side to this, for Rhodes comes expensive,
and the island clearly doesn't feel the
need to cater for independent travellers
in any great numbers. On the plus side,
the heavy tourist presence has encouraged
a proliferation of pleasure boat services
augmenting the ferries that call — thanks
to the island's role as a terminus on the
domestic ferry network and point of call
for most international services to Cyprus,
Israel and Egypt. The combination makes
Rhodes an attractive point from which to
start an island-hopping holiday.

The principal town and port is **Rhodes
City** on the north-eastern tip of the island.
Founded in 408 BC, it rapidly emerged as
a trading and cultural crossroads and
was one of the great Hellenistic centres of
Greek power; the mighty bronze Colossus
acting as a lighthouse to guide shipping
into port. Ferries today are greeted by
less artistic, but in their own way equally
impressive, massive red stone walls of
the medieval city that mark Rhodes out
as the former home of the Knights Hospit-
allers of St. John (an order of crusading
knights founded in 11 c. Jerusalem, who
were driven west by the Saracens and
Turks to Rhodes in 1309, and after Rhodes
fell in 1522, on to Malta). After 1919
Rhodes became the capital of the Italian
Dodecanese and an Italianesque new
town emerged adjacent to Mandraki harbour (the departure point for beach boats
and hydrofoils). The result of all this has
been to leave Rhodes City looking remarkably cosmopolitan in the grandest way,
though over-expensive old town souvenir
shops and new town bars and discos try
their best to turn it into a tourist trap. All

facilities are located near the centre of town: the southern part of Mandraki harbour. This is just as well because the city can get unbearably hot and humid. Protected from the meltemi wind, street temperatures often exceed 100° F, and simply walking from the port to the tourist office can be hard work. However, the profusion of sights, excursions (including Turkey day trips) and cheapish old town rooms justify being based in the capital.

The rest of the island has much to offer. The **East Coast** from Rhodes City to Lindos is heavily touristed with many boats running down each morning, stopping at resorts and sand beaches en route. Preferable to taking a bus (and cooler), they call en route at the faded 1920s Italian spa town of **Kalithea**, the youth disco city resort of **Faliraki, Ladiko** (also known as the 'Antony Quinn' beach), and the resort beach of **Kolimbia, Tsambika** (with a monastery-topped hill behind the beach offering good views of the coastline), and the **Archangelos Town** beach of **Stenga**.

Lindos itself is an attractive white cubist town (now preserved from further development by government order) huddled around the most impressive acropolis in Greece after the better known example at Athens. The dramatic ruins and their majestic setting (see description below) justify the effort and cost of the trip, but Lindos is not really up to coping with the numbers visiting. The town has a less pleasant side to it as well. In the summer of 1994 Lindos received considerable publicity for flying a EU Blue Flag on its beaches while independent scientific tests made in 1992 revealed that 'the waters of Lindos Bay and its surrounds are heavily contaminated with bacteria specifically associated with human sewage'. Bacterial levels have been recorded up to 100 times more than is allowed by EU regulations. The problem is the result of an obsolete town sewage system. Lindos has received a £1 million EU grant to replace it; but this

has yet to be built. As a result you would be wise to avoid swimming on this stretch of the coast for the foreseeable future.

South of Lindos the coast is quiet, with buses reduced to a trickle: the town of **Kattavia** sees a service only three times weekly, while the beach islet of Prassonissi (linked by a beach causeway to Rhodes) is only accessible via your own transport. Car hire is worth considering when exploring Rhodes.

The **West Coast** is greener and quieter than the east, thanks to the winds that hit this side of the island. Beaches tend to be pebble rather than sand. Tourist development on this side is largely confined to the coast between Rhodes City and the airport at **Paradisi**. Thereafter you are into excursion country, with buses running to **Trianda** (the stop for the ancient city of Ialyssos), **Petaloudes** (the inland butterfly valley where millions of moths are scared into flying by almost as many tourists) from June to September, and **Kamiros** (a second abandoned ancient city), before terminating at **Monolithos** — a poor beach resort with a castle perched on an overlooking hill. En route, buses call in at the village of **Kamiros Skala** (not to be confused with the ruins), which has a daily summer link to Chalki (times on the ferry timetable sheet issued free in Rhodes City). Lastly, the hilly interior of Rhodes remains surprisingly untouristed — the territory of 'scenic' bus tours and the car rental brigade.

ᴴ

City tourist office offers a room-finding service as well as free maps. Reasonable supply of rooms — mostly in the old walled city; but you will find rates higher than on other islands. At the bottom end of the range you will find pensions aplenty: one of the best being the *Nikos* (☎ 23423). The shabby but atmospheric *Pension Steve* (☎ 85293) is also worthy of consideration. Thanks to the competition, E-class hotels are all pretty reasonable. These include the *Spot* (☎ 34737), *Sydney* (☎ 25965) and *Teheran* (☎ 27594). However, the *Kastro* (☎ 20446) near the Turkish baths is noisy. D-class hotels

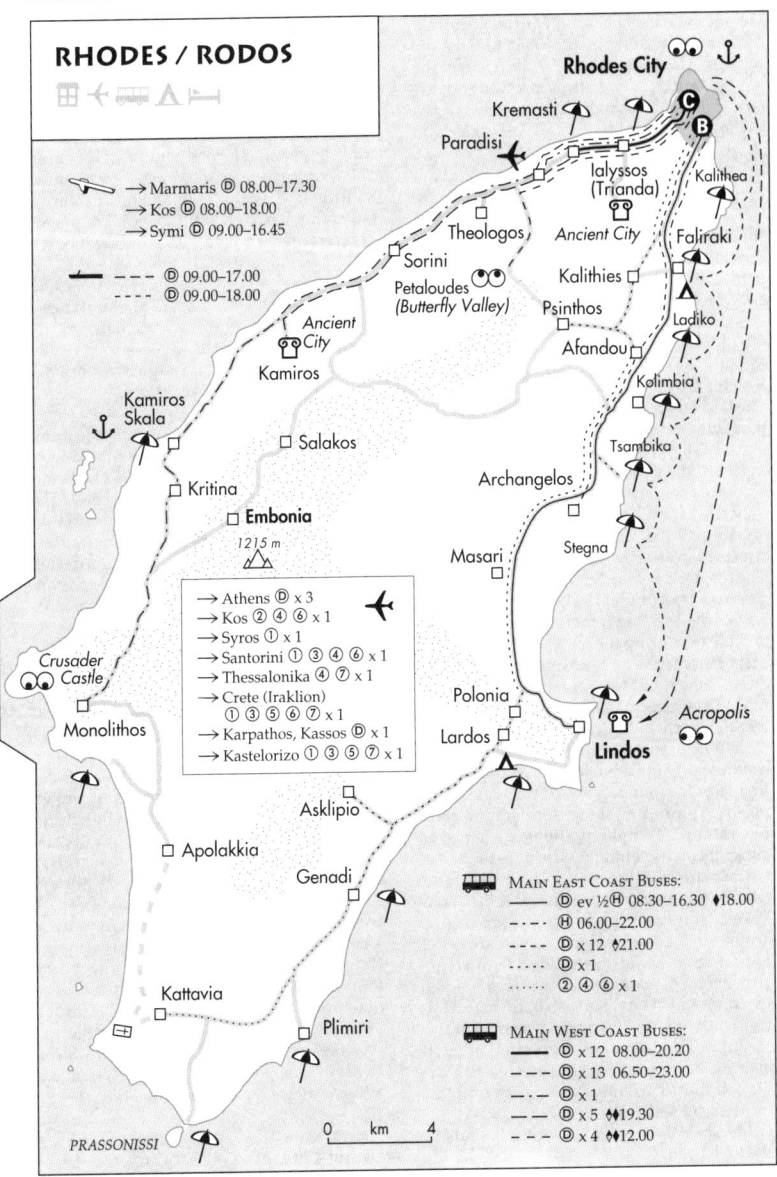

RHODES / RODOS

✈ → Marmaris Ⓓ 08.00–17.30
→ Kos Ⓓ 08.00–18.00
→ Symi Ⓓ 09.00–16.45

━━━ ‑‑‑ Ⓓ 09.00–17.00
‑‑‑‑‑ Ⓓ 09.00–18.00

Rhodes City ⚓

Kremasti

Paradisi

Ialyssos
(Trianda)
Ancient City

Kalithea

Theologos

Faliraki

Sorini

Kalithies

Petaloudes
(Butterfly Valley)

Psinthos

Ladiko

Ancient
City

Afandou

Kamiros

Kolimbia

Kamiros
Skala

Salakos

Tsambika

Kritina

Archangelos

Embonia

1215 m
△△△

Masari

Stegna

→ Athens Ⓓ x 3
→ Kos ② ④ ⑥ x 1
→ Syros ① x 1
→ Santorini ① ③ ④ ⑥ x 1
→ Thessalonika ④ ⑦ x 1
→ Crete (Iraklion)
   ① ③ ⑤ ⑥ ⑦ x 1
→ Karpathos, Kassos Ⓓ x 1
→ Kastelorizo ① ③ ⑤ ⑦ x 1

Crusader
Castle

Polonia

Acropolis

Monolithos

Lardos

Lindos

Asklipio

Apolakkia

Genadi

MAIN EAST COAST BUSES:
━━━ Ⓓ ev ½Ⓗ 08.30–16.30 ♦18.00
‑·‑· Ⓗ 06.00–22.00
‑‑‑ Ⓓ x 12 ♦21.00
····· Ⓓ x 1
······ ② ④ ⑥ x 1

Kattavia

Plimiri

MAIN WEST COAST BUSES:
━━━ Ⓓ x 12 08.00–20.20
‑‑‑ Ⓓ x 13 06.50–23.00
‑·‑ Ⓓ x 1
━ ━ Ⓓ x 5 ♦♦19.30
‑‑ ‑ Ⓓ x 4 ♦♦12.00

PRASSONISSI

0   km   4

include the excellent *Kava d'Oro* (☎ 36980) and the better placed *Paris* (☎ 26356). Most of the top range hotels are on the waterfront on the west side of the city off the top left edge of the city opposite, with more D and E-class hotels in the streets around Orthonas Amalias St.

Δ

Rhodes has two beach camp sites, both well away from Rhodes City. *Camping Faliraki* (☎ 85358) is the most accessible. A nice site 16 km south, it can easily be reached by bus or beach boat. It is popular with Brits and boasts its own swimming pool, as does less busy *Agios Georgios Camping* (☎ 0244 44203) south of Lindos at Lardos.

👀

Rhodes has sights to fill a 2–week holiday:

Rhodes City:

The **Old Town** offers plenty of sightseeing for those who care to walk the streets in the heat. Bounded by a complete city wall breached by 11 gates, the Old Town is divided into two sections: the northern section containing the Master's Palace/Castle of the Knights and the 'inhabited' quarters made up of a maze of streets to the south. Main attractions are:

The Master's Palace: rebuilt in 1856 after a fire destroyed the original building, it houses the best of the Kos Town mosaics discovered by the Italians during the inter-war years. South of the Palace runs cobbled **Ipaton Street** — the Street of the Knights; one of the best preserved medieval streets in Europe. At the eastern end lies the **Archaeological Museum** (⊘ ex ① 08.30–15.00), home to finds on Rhodes, notably a statute of Aphrodite known as the Marine Venus. Some foundations from a 3 c. BC **Temple of Aphrodite** (along with fragmentary remains of a **Temple of Dionysos** famed in antiquity for its paintings) also lie to the east of the museum near the city walls. The rest of the Old Town is a very picturesque maze of narrow streets (you can happily get lost wandering around in the knowledge that you are never too far from a wall gate) filled with reconstructed medieval inns, derelict or converted mosques and even a **Turkish Bath**. In fact this residential quarter has retained a very Turkish feel to it. The **City Walls** also offer an interesting excursion, but can be accessed only via guided tour (currently ②, ⑥ 14.15 from the north-east Palace Gate).

Other sites also worth exploring lie outside the Old Town:

The **Mandraki Harbour**, guarded by 2 bronze deer was the port of ancient Rhodes. Somewhere in this area the Colossus (see p. 62) stood and fell. One survival from those days is the ancient harbour mole — now home to 3 medieval windmills and the turret fort of St. Nicholas (now adorned with a lighthouse). The ferry quay was once similarly adorned with no less than 13 windmills and a defensive tower (known as the Mill tower). Fragments of several of the mills hide behind the modern buildings. The ancient acropolis is also hidden away; lying to the west of the current Old Town. Now laid out as a park, the site offers a shady view of a well-preserved **Stadium** and small **Theatre**, as well as several standing columns of a **Temple of Apollo** (over-heavily restored by its Italian excavators).

Lindos:

Until 408 BC Rhodes was host to three medium-sized classical cities: at Kamiros on the west coast, at Ialyssos 5 km south-west of Rhodes City and at Lindos on the eastern coast. The three communities agreed to join up and build a new centre commissioning the famous town planner Hippodamos of Miletus to design Rhodes City. Only Lindos survived this development, and this was in large part due to its having the major shrine on Rhodes as its centrepiece on a well-fortified acropolis. One of the most spectacular archaeological sites in Greece, the **Acropolis of Lindos** has been drawing tourists since antiquity. Perched between two small bays with a whitewashed chora village beneath on the landward side, the 116 m rock still contains substantial remains of the **Temple of Athena**. Built in 348 BC it replaced an earlier temple on the site. In addition to the temple, remains of a formal gateway or **Propylaia** (407 BC) and a large 42 column double-winged **Stoa** (208 BC) are extant. During the Byzantine period the rock was fortified with protective walls and these were developed further into a castle by the Knights of St. John. In the town below are the foundations of a temple and a theatre. The other two pre-408 BC cities can also be visited via the island buses. **Kamiros** is easily the best — with much of the city plan visible, but it lacks any notable major buildings. The remains at **Ialyssos** are far more fragmentary.

☎

TOWN CODE 0241, PORT POLICE 28666, TOURIST POLICE 27423, OFFICE 35945.

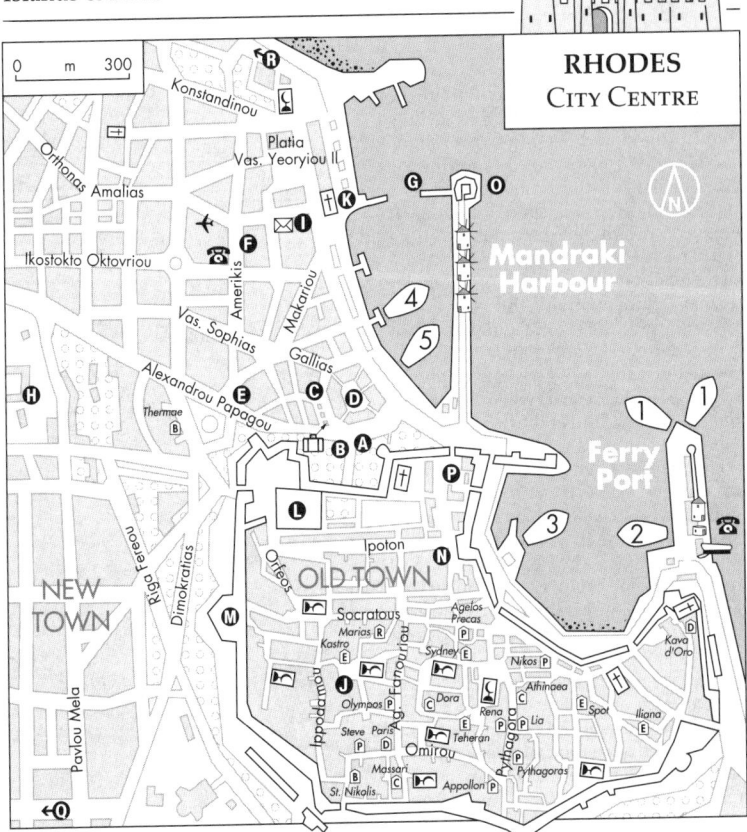

RHODES
CITY CENTRE

Mandraki
Harbour

Ferry
Port

NEW
TOWN

OLD TOWN

Key

- **A** Tourist Office (Bus & Ferry Times)
- **B** Bus Station (Lindos & E. Rhodes)
- **C** Bus Station (Airport & W. Rhodes)
- **D** New Market / Newspapers
- **E** NTOG Office
- **F** Tourist Police Office
- **G** Bronze Deer
- **H** Hospital
- **I** Police
- **J** Turkish Baths
- **K** Cathedral
- **L** Master's Palace
- **M** City Walls
- **N** Archaeological Museum
- **O** Fort of St. Nicholas
- **P** Temple of Aphrodite
- **Q** Temple of Apollo / Stadium (500 m)
- **R** City Aquarium (200 m)

1 Ferry Quay
2 Turkey (Marmaris) Ferry Berth
3 Kastelorizo Ferry Berth
4 Symi & Kos Tourist boats / Hydrofoils
5 East Coast & Lindos beach boats

Symi

ΣΥΜΗ; 58 km²; pop. 2500.

A small island half tucked within the folds of the indented Turkish coast, hilly Symi (pronounced 'See-me') was once one of the most prosperous islands in the Aegean thanks to the combined industries of shipbuilding and sponge fishing. It enjoyed considerable autonomy during the period of Ottoman rule and by the end of the 19 c. had a population of just under 23,000. Unfortunately, the rise of the steamship and the loss of the all-important wood supplies from mainland Turkey (needed to maintain the island output of over 500 caïques a year) when the Italians took over the island at the end of the first world war reduced the island to comparative poverty. Gialos, the capital, graced by opulent mansions was reduced to a ghost town and has only come to life in the last 20 years after Symi emerged as a popular Rhodes' day excursion following the invasion of Cyprus (when Turkish Marmaris was out of bounds). Since then it has become ever more popular; overly so in the eyes of many island hoppers.

Once heavily wooded, Symi is now barren with a small population (living mainly off tourism and sponge fishing), a few cars and a coastline of steep cliffs and sandy bays. The port of **Gialos** is pure magic — with serried tiers of neo-classical mansions (many abandoned) set in an amphitheatre bay. The scene is particularly attractive at night when the banked, orange street and house lights seem to roll into the sea like the glowing embered lip of a lava flow. The waterfront (complete with a campanile near the ferry quay) is crowded during the daytime, but quickly reverts to its normal sleepy self once the tour boats have gone. The upper town retains an air of tranquillity, thanks to the need to climb a 500-step path running from the port to the castle on the site of the ancient acropolis. This is more than enough to dissuade the day-trippers who push up quayside prices.

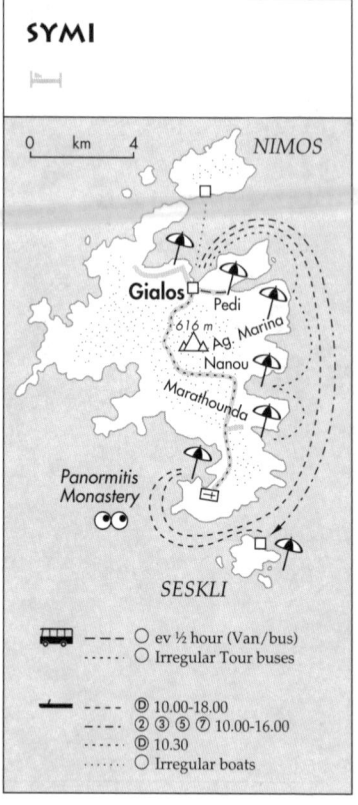

The rest of Symi has nought but odd farmsteads, hamlets and goat-tracks galore; this makes it a good hill-walking island. The only bus runs between Gialos and the beach hamlet at Pedi. Gialos is also host to a stream of beach caïques running to bays down the east coast.

⊨

There are a few rooms in Gialos and several expensive hotels — including the A-class *Akiki* (☎ 71665) and the cheaper *Horio* (☎ 71800) and *Grace* (☎ 71415). There are also three pensions in town: the *Dorian* (☎ 71181), *Albatros* (☎ 71707) and *Metapontis* (☎ 71491). The lack of a campsite or much budget accommodation puts great pressure on accommodation in High Season when it pays to book ahead by phone.

Along with Galos Town, **St. Panormitis Monastery** on the south coast is the prime target of the tourist boats. This institution (named after the patron saint of sailors, the Archangel Michael) owns the largest of Symi's satellites — the islet of **Seskli**, which provides fruit and produce for the monks. Some tours have visits in their itineraries, including a twice-weekly excursion from Gialos. Occasional taxi boats also make the short trip to **Nimos**, a hilly islet lying to the north of Gialos.

CODE 0241, TOURIST OFFICE 71215, FERRY INFORMATION 71307.

Tilos

ΤΗΛΟΣ; 63 km²; pop. 320.

A very sleepy island even in High Season, Tilos abounds in hills topped with castles (seven in all), quiet lush orchard valleys and empty beaches. Quite why it is not on the tourist map is not clear. Rumours of internecine feuds between the islanders (resulting in few tourist facilities emerging) whisper up and down the Dodecanese, but there is nothing on Tilos to support them: the islanders are generally very friendly and welcoming.

Having abandoned several villages, the population is now divided between the port of **Livadia** (behind an attractive 1 km tree and beach-lined bay) and the small castle-topped pretty capital of **Megalo Chorio**. The two are connected by the only good road on Tilos and a mini-bus that meets all ferries (space is usually pre-booked with arriving hydrofoils or Rhodes' tourist boats). When you can get a ride you will find the mini-bus runs past the derelict village of Micro Chorio (home to a grotto where the fossilised remains of a species of small mammoth have been found). In High Season the mini-bus also visits Eristos beach. Note: all mini-bus times vary greatly depending on the time of year.

There are rooms in both settlements (and the good beach at Eristos) as well as 2 hotels: the C-class *Irini* (☎ 53293) and E-class *Livadia* (☎ 53202) — both in Livadia port. The bulk of the island rooms are here, behind the beach. Freelance camping is also widely tolerated.

Main attraction is the 1470-built fortified hill **Monastery of Agios Panteleimon** on the north-west side of Tilos, past the island's best red-sand, volcanic (courtesy of neighbouring Nissiros) beaches. A series of little castles run down the spine of the island, including one at Megalo Chorio. East of Livadia lies an abandoned castle village of **Mikro Chorio** which is worth the walk, while sun-lovers at **Agios Andonios Beach** have a sobering reminder of the dangers of over-exposure thanks to the petrified remains of three 7 c. BC (Pompeiian?) sailors who were caught napping by an eruption of Nissiros c. 600 BC.

CODE 0241, POLICE 532 22, FERRY INFO 53259, FIRST AID 53294.

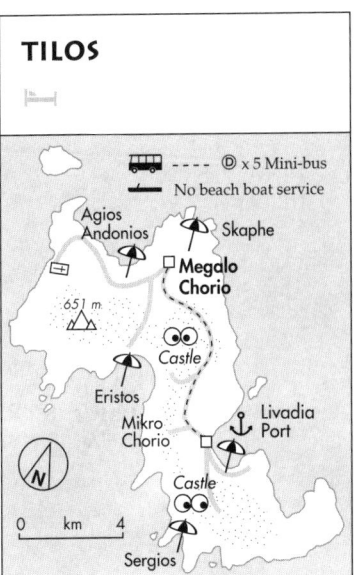

TILOS

━━━ ---- Ⓓ x 5 Mini-bus
━━ No beach boat service

Agios Andonios
Skaphe
Megalo Chorio
651 m
Castle
Eristos
Mikro Chorio
Livadia Port
Castle
0   km   4
N
Sergios

9

EASTERN LINES

CHIOS · FOURNI · IKARIA · LESBOS · PSARA · SAMOS

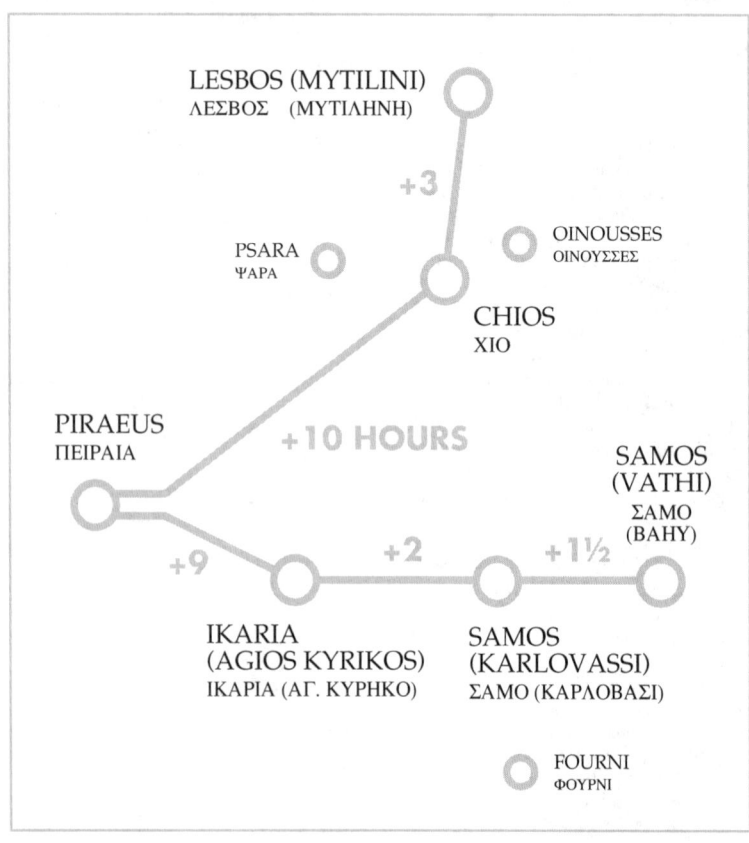

LESBOS (MYTILINI)
ΛΕΣΒΟΣ   (ΜΥΤΙΛΗΝΗ)

+3

PSARA
ΨΑΡΑ

OINOUSSES
ΟΙΝΟΥΣΣΕΣ

CHIOS
XIO

PIRAEUS
ΠΕΙΡΑΙΑ

+10 HOURS

SAMOS
(VATHI)
ΣΑΜΟ
(ΒΑΗΥ)

+9

+2

+1½

IKARIA
(AGIOS KYRIKOS)
ΙΚΑΡΙΑ (ΑΓ. ΚΥΡΗΚΟ)

SAMOS
(KARLOVASSI)
ΣΑΜΟ (ΚΑΡΛΟΒΑΣΙ)

FOURNI
ΦΟΥΡΝΙ

General Features

The Eastern Aegean Line is made up of two separate routes running from Piraeus east across the Aegean to those Greek islands adjacent to the Turkish coast north of the Dodecanese. All the ferries operating Eastern Line services follow the natural geographical division of the islands into the two sub-groups, either running Piraeus—Ikaria—Samos, or Piraeus—Chios—Lesbos (Mytilini).

The more southerly route takes in the large and increasingly popular island of Samos as well as the less well known Ikaria. Each boast two regular ports at which ferries can call, giving scope for alternations in schedules. The more northerly route runs across to Chios and then running along the Turkish seaboard to Lesbos (Mytilini); both are large islands

which have remained economically independent of the tourist hordes but which are increasingly attracting Grecophiles jaded by the over-tourism encountered elsewhere. Northern route sailings are almost exclusively confined to the major ports of Chios Town and Lesbos (Mytilini), but a number of ferries then continue on into the northern Aegean to varying ports of call. Both groups also include minor islands little visited by tourists: Fourni and Samiopoula off Samos, Oinousses and Psara accessible from Chios. Links between the two lines remain poor, but are slowly improving with a connecting Chios—Samos service three days a week. Equally indifferent are connections with the Dodecanese which are so thin on the water that locals utilize Patmos-bound tourist boats.

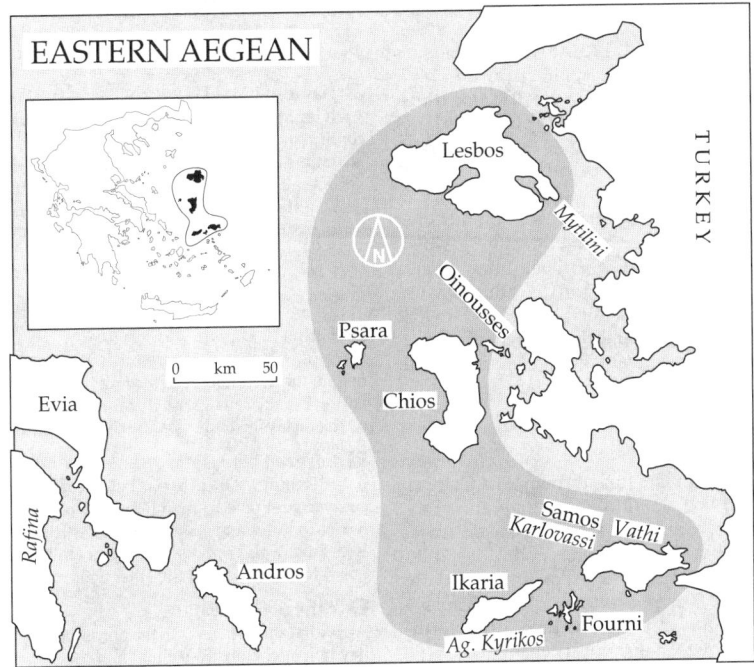

Suggested Itinerary [2 Weeks]

An itinerary based on the Eastern Lines is for those who prefer a scattering of trees rather than High Season crowds with their Greek islands and are happy to settle for quiet taverna eating and making their own entertainment. It is unlikely to appeal to those who like to boogie between boats. The islands en route are comparatively quiet thanks to a mix of fewer ferry connections and the need to get a bus to the nearest reasonable beach (on the popular Cycladic islands you only have to fall overboard near to port to find yourself on one). The crowds are missing more than they realise.

Arrival/Departure Point

On a fortnight's holiday there are two easy flight options: Athens and Samos (more poorly served Lesbos (Mytilini) is a third possible option). Athens is the easiest to get back to in a rush. Samos is an equally accessible point provided you travel in an anticlockwise direction (thus ensuring you can pick up one of the daily Piraeus—Samos links in the latter part of the trip if needs be). If you have three weeks at your disposal then a start from Mykonos, Santorini or Kos can also be considered as viable starting points. However, unlike Athens and Samos, neither will give you advance information on the 2—3 *days per week* link in the itinerary: the Samos—Chios crossing, and this is a disadvantage given that you will have to structure your plans around the days it runs.

Season

Travel in late June through late October and you shouldn't encounter any problems. Low Season sees difficulties in crossing between the Samos and Chios lines; ferries along both decline from the daily High Season services to the usual 3—4 days a week level, with links to the Northern Aegean disappearing altogether.

1 Athens [2 Days]

Quite apart from the city sights, Athens offers agents in Piraeus who do anything if there is the prospect of getting you to buy a ticket, including showing you the latest Miniotis Brothers Co. timetable when you ask about ferry links between Chios and Samos. With this information you can then work out how many days you have either side of this weak link and allocate nights and stops accordingly.

2 Paros [2 Days]

As there are not usually morning and evening boats out of Piraeus along the Samos line it is often more convenient to make for better connected Paros and then jump from there onto a Samos boat. It also breaks up an otherwise 12-hour voyage and offers a quick dash down to Naxos and the Cyclades Central Line if you have a third week to hand.

3 Ikaria [1 Day]

An optional island (it is a good idea to build in extra flexibility by having one in any itinerary) you can fit (time willing) into a tight schedule.

4 Samos [3 Days]

Arriving at Vathi the number one priority is to confirm the Monday and Friday boat to Chios is running (in the unlikely event of this service not operating — and it has for the last six years — you always have the option of heading south by picking up a tourist boat from Pithagorio down to Patmos and the Dodecanese). This established, you can fill the available time on excursions to Pithagorio and Turkey.

5 Chios [2 Days]

Once on Chios you have optional hops to neighbouring Oinousses, to Turkey for a day and even adjacent Psara if the notion of a couple of days of untouristed isolation appeals.

6 Lesbos [2 Days]

A nice island on which to relax before catching an overnight boat back to Piraeus. Irregular ferries to Volos and Rafina (via the Northern Aegean) are also options if you don't mind a bus ride into Athens at the other end.

1 Athens [2 Days]

Arrive back in Athens with the precautionary day in hand before your flight home.

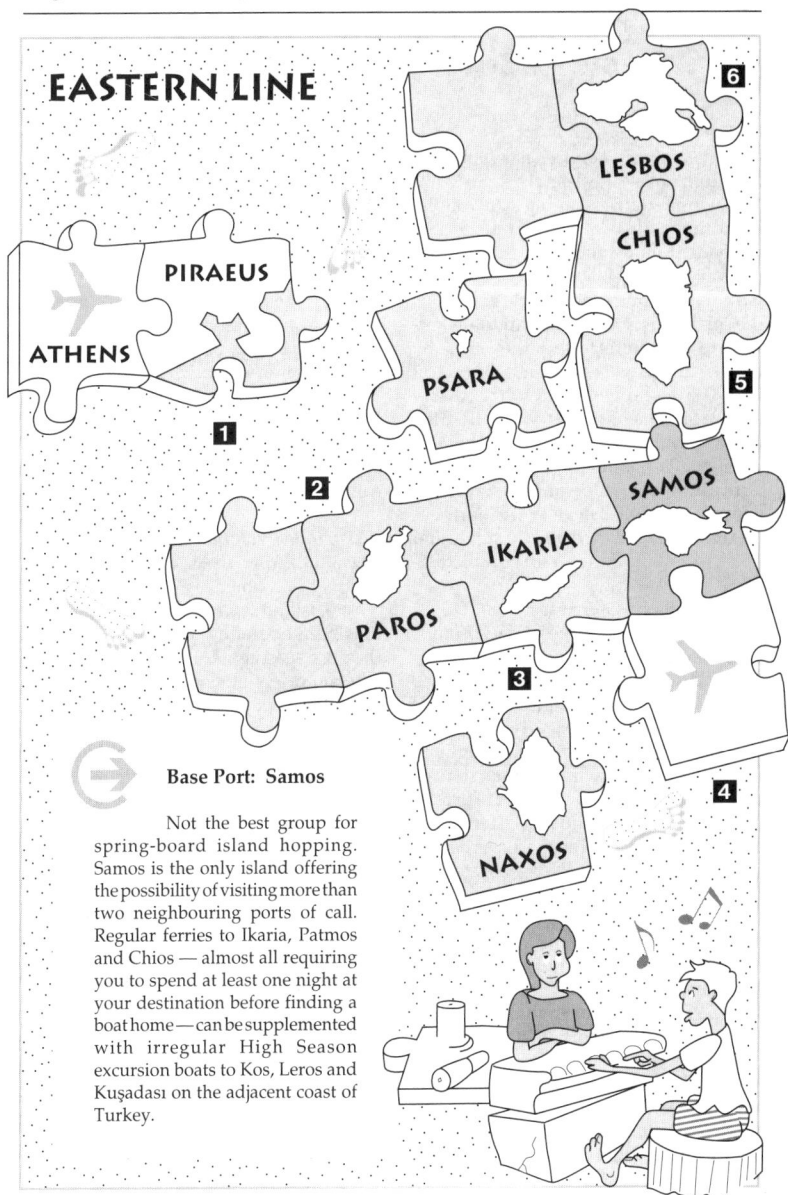

EASTERN LINE

PIRAEUS

ATHENS

1

LESBOS

CHIOS

6

PSARA

2

5

PAROS

IKARIA

SAMOS

3

NAXOS

4

⊖ **Base Port: Samos**

Not the best group for spring-board island hopping. Samos is the only island offering the possibility of visiting more than two neighbouring ports of call. Regular ferries to Ikaria, Patmos and Chios — almost all requiring you to spend at least one night at your destination before finding a boat home — can be supplemented with irregular High Season excursion boats to Kos, Leros and Kuşadası on the adjacent coast of Turkey.

Eastern Line Ferry Services

Main Car Ferries

The level of ferry services has remained consistent over the last six years with only two new ferries coming in to complement the older boats. Traffic is far less dependent on tourism than some other parts of the Greek system, with regular daily connections in both directions as the ferries are providing important services to what are all fairly large islands by Greek standards. The islands of Fourni and Psara, however, are irregularly served by Piraeus ferries with calls often only added to schedules at the last moment. These links should be treated with caution. Low Season sees services at a four-days-a-week level, with Northern Aegean links all but non-existent, and services to Turkey severely curtailed.

Piraeus—Samos Ferries:

Samos — one of the largest Greek islands — is an important destination for Piraeus ferries. The traditional route of Piraeus—Ikaria—Samos has seen a reduction of services of late, as larger and faster ferries have come along and have sought to increase revenue by calling elsewhere en route. Many boats now come via Paros or Naxos; thus opening up the Eastern Lines to more tourism than they had seen before.

C/F Milena

G.A. Ferries; 1970; 5491 GRT.

This large, well-equipped vessel moved onto the Eastern Line in 1990 and has run back and fourth along the route ever since. Although she offers an 'annual' service, her timetable has seen a fair amount of minor juggling of times and ports of call in recent summers. Of late this has been to the benefit of Paros and Naxos, where, in 1994, she was scheduled to call at both; thus abandoning her direct Piraeus—Ikaria—Samos service. Time-

table juggling aside, the *Milena* is a reliable ferry, and arguably the best on the line.

C/F Samaina

Arkadia Lines; 1962; 3783 GRT.

A small, squat, elderly car ferry with a reputation for reliability, she has run this direct Piraeus—Ikaria—Samos route for many years. Both route and times have remained largely unchanged during that time despite several changes of owner. Only High Season variation is usually in the form of some chopping and changing to her Ikaria ports of call. Facilities on board are adequate, but she lacks the plush interior of the *Milena*.

C/F Golden Vergina

Agapitos Ferries; 1966; 4555 GRT.

Widely acclaimed as one of the worst Greek island ferries, the *Golden Vergina* has been operating on this route for the last six seasons. A large grime-bucket, she shudders along; not due to engine vibration, but with the collective disgust of the passengers thanks to the conditions on board. Even the locals avoid her if at all possible. Even in High Season she can offer a quiet night Paros—Piraeus run. Unfortunately, the plastic moulding seating is not sleeping-bag compatible. If all this isn't discouragement enough, this boat has a poor record in keeping to her scheduled times. It is not uncommon for her to be anything up to four hours late. Better than no boat at all; but only just.

    See also:

- C/F *Alcaeos*   p. 327
- C/F *Dimitra*   p. 170
- C/F *Nissos Kalimnos* p. 259

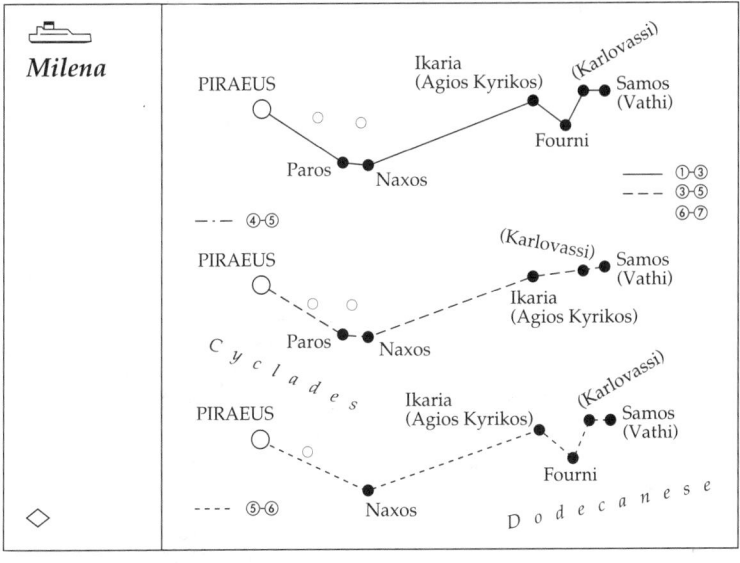

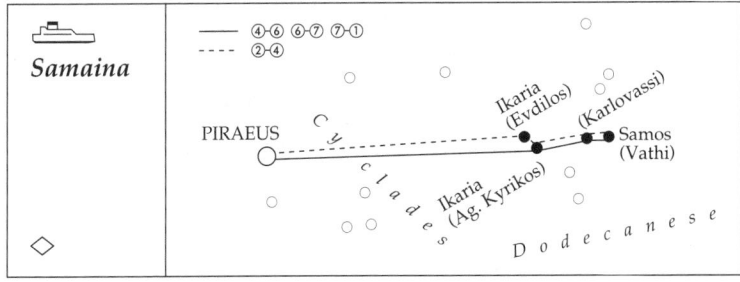

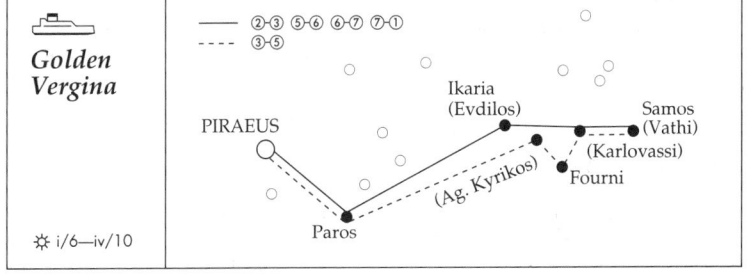

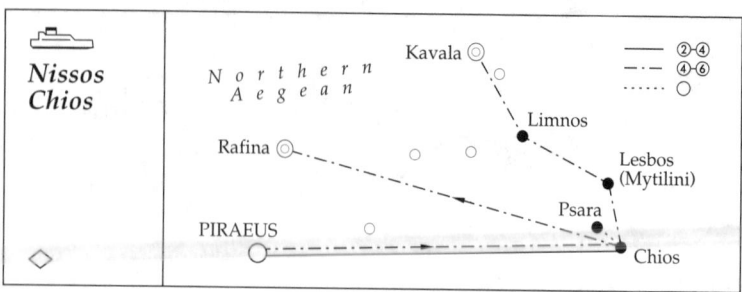

Piraeus—Chios Ferries:

Piraeus to Lesbos and Chios links suffer from a chronic lack of competition and are dominated by one company: the Maritime Co. of Lesbos (NEL Lines). The company is something of a timetable compiler's bane: not only does it tend to pool its boats with changes to the advertised vessel on any given service, but has also been in the habit of adjusting timetables during the summer (though the pattern of services is little altered). For these reasons all the services opposite are mapped together rather than by individual boat.

C/F Nissos Chios

Local; 1967; 3118 GRT.
The only competition to NEL Lines comes in the form of an elderly ferry run by a single boat company. True to her name she has long served the island of Chios with a thrice weekly run to Piraeus and irregular calls at Psara. In 1994, however, she took on a much more wide ranging itinerary thanks to the absence of the *Hellas Express*, with runs to Kavala and Rafina (see p. 327). Conditions on board are on a par with most of the competition — that is to say: 'elderly but adequate'.

C/F Agios Rafail

NEL Lines; 1968; 2262 GRT.
This small ferry (complete with lopsided funnel, scaffold sun decks) is arguably the least comfortable major ferry in the Aegean. Very much the number four boat,

she is shoved around from year to year (in 1994 running a regular direct ser-vice to Lesbos). Previous summers have seen her deployed on a six weekly ferry link between the Dodecanese and the Northern Aegean (see p. 260). Changes are more than possible in 1995.

C/F Alcaeos

NEL Lines; 1970; 3930 GRT.
Somewhat long in the tooth, the medium-sized *Alcaeos* is reliable, once you establish which of the NEL schedules she is running. She tends to move around a lot, getting the odd ball runs (e.g. Lesbos to Volos), and in 1995 had a timetable that consisted of little else with runs to Kavala, Rafina and Patmos thrown in (see p. 260, and 327). On-board facilities are okay, but distinctly utilitarian.

C/F Mytilene

NEL Lines; 1973; 6702 GRT.
One of the biggest Greek domestic ferries, the *Mytilene* is the new boat in the NEL fleet and even has the locals a-talking. Once aboard, it is difficult to imagine one is on a Greek boat at all, such is the plush interior. Her size is something of a problem; the search for the sun deck or the WCs is apt to be hard on the feet, and her turnaround times are not good due to the limited entry/exit facilities given the numbers she can carry. The company had problems getting her up and running in 1992, but she settled down in 1993, taking

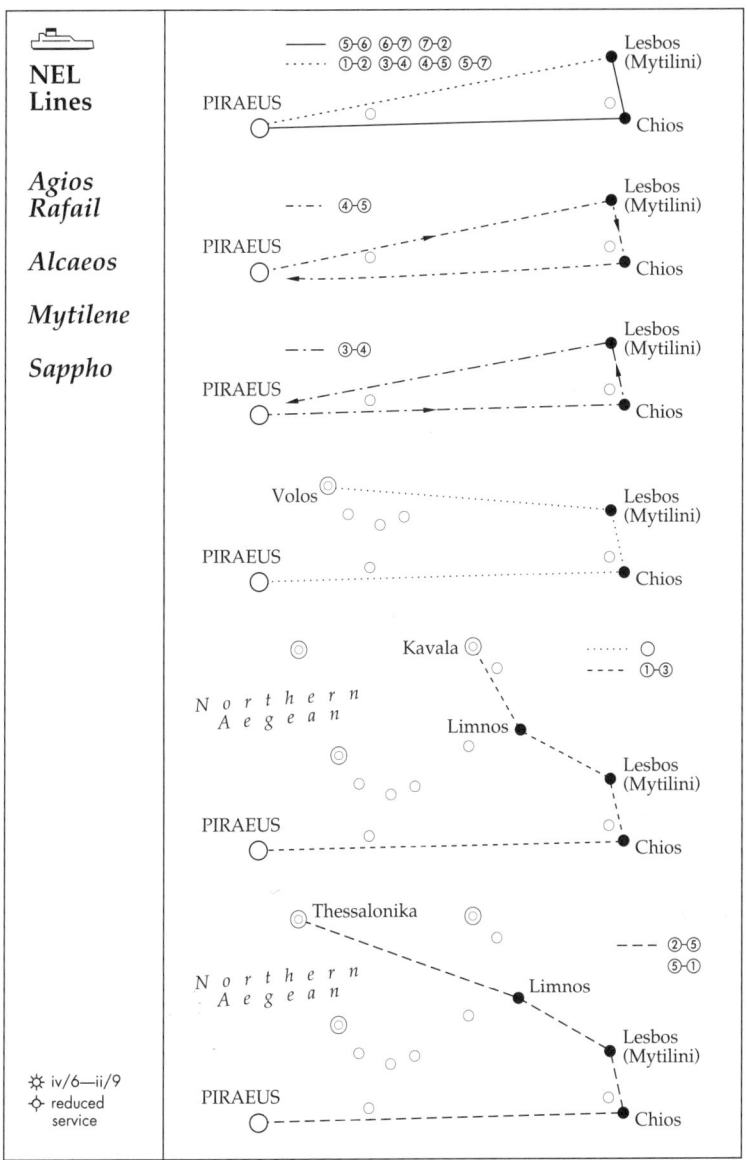

on the 'glamour' routes to Thessalonika and Kavala. Easily the best overnight boat on the Piraeus—Lesbos line, long standing island hoppers rushing aboard may well find a certain nostalgia creeping on; the escalators waiting to whisk them to the upper decks are a long way removed from the antiquated external hull staircases of Greek ferries of old.

C/F Sappho
NEL Lines; 1966; 6500 GRT.
Named after the famous Lesbian poet of antiquity, this old maid (built 1966) was displaced as the largest NEL boat in 1992. As a consequence she lost all bar one of her sorties to the North Aegean in favour of the workhorse role of providing the bulk of the overnight Piraeus—Chios—Lesbos return services. Now running for the last three years, this pattern is unlikely to change much in 1995.

Local Chios-based Boats:
Chios is the home of a small, and delightfully amateurish, ferry company: Miniotis Brothers. Advertising its services as far as Piraeus, they provide the bulk of Chios links to Psara, Samos, Ikaria and Turkey. Unfortunately, they shuffle their four tiny boats around a fair bit. The only services that you can rely on are the Chios—Samos (Vathi) and Chios—Psara runs. Thereafter island hoppers have to check out island timetables.

C/F Capetan Stamatis
Miniotis Bros.; 1967; 436 GRT.
Named after a local war hero (her interior is a veritable shrine to his exploits), this small Miniotis Brothers ferry (20 vehicles) splits her time between runs on the Chios—Turkey (Çeşme) link and operating an invaluable Chios—Samos (Vathi) linking service. A regular tub, she is thrown around a fair bit, besides being very slow. Coupled with the stuffy saloon you have a perfect recipe for seasick passengers galore.

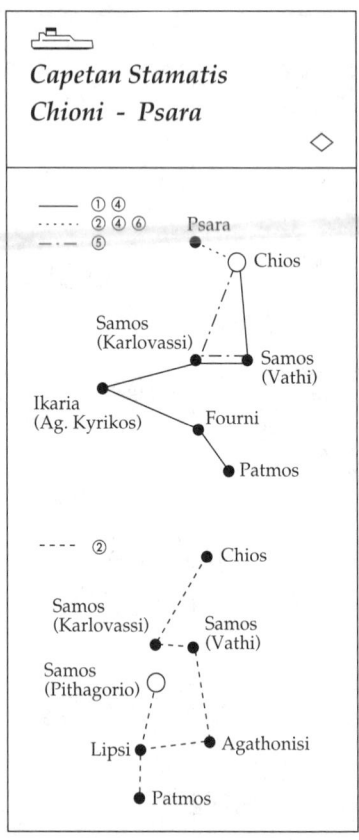

Capetan Stamatis
Chioni - Psara

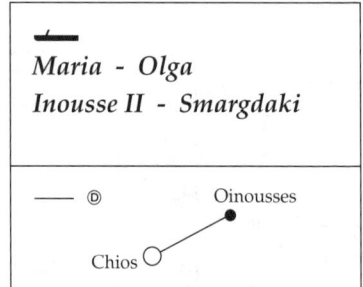

Maria - Olga
Inousse II - Smargdaki

C/F *Chioni*
Miniotis Bros.; 1968; 572 GRT.
This small ferry was bought by Miniotis in 1991 and has freely interchanged with the *Capetan Stamatis* above. Timetables will name one; but either could turn up. The *Chioni* has the better interior facilities though this is not saying a lot. Providing a useful connecting link between Samos and the Dodecanese, the value of their runs south of Samos is sadly diminished by a lack of consistency.

C/F *Psara*
Miniotis Bros.; 1963; 250 GRT.
Almost too small to be considered a car ferry at all, this rusty boat provides Psara with her primary link with the outside world. Seas permitting, she makes the run from Chios thrice-weekly throughout the year, in the summer also running to nearby Oinousses and Turkey.

T/B's *Maria - Olga - Inousse II - Smargdaki*
Chios is home to a number of tourist caïques that run to the small island of Oinousses. These range from the *Maria* (run by Miniotis Lines) to more tourist orientated day boats. They combine to provide a daily service—though be careful to check that your boat will be returning the same day; some remain at Oinousses overnight.

Hydrofoil Links
Since 1993, hydrofoils have provided a summer service in the Northern Aegean. However, services are very erratic; so these remain boats to look out for rather than rely on. ILIO are the largest operator and run out of Lesbos south to Samos and to the mainland ports on the Northern Aegean coast. Connections tend to be expensive due to the distances involved. In 1994 a new company, Giaimar Lines, ran an invaluable boat out of Chios down to Patmos (thus making lovely Fourni a day trip destination for the first time). With luck it will be running again in 1995.

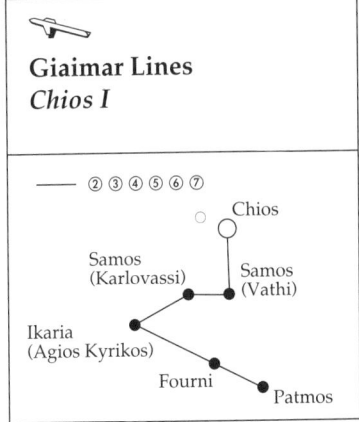

Giaimar Lines
Chios I

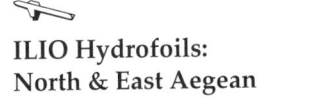

ILIO Hydrofoils:
North & East Aegean

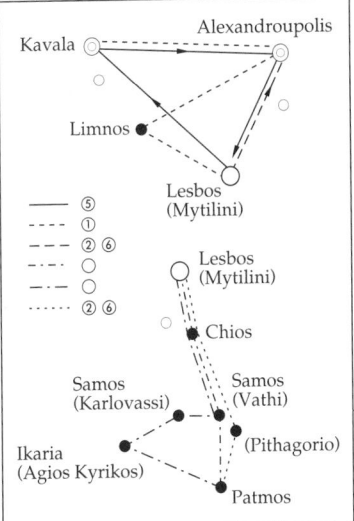

⚓ Eastern Line Islands & Ports

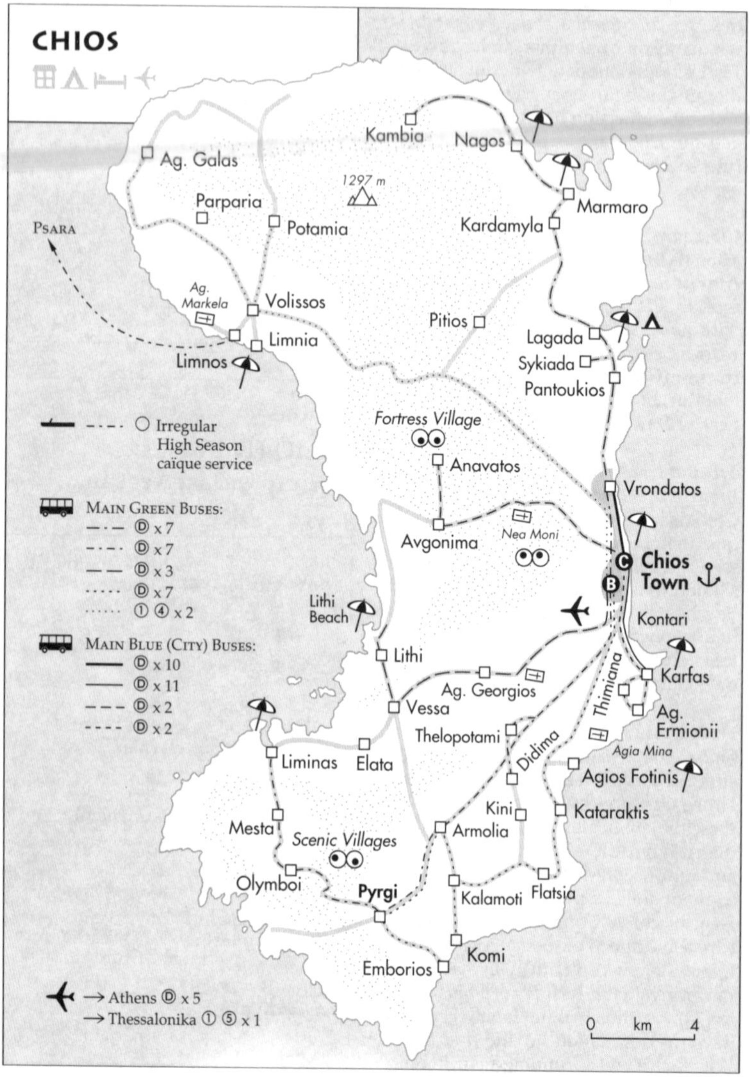

CHIOS

PSARA

Ag. Galas

Parparia

Potamia

Kambia

Nagos

1297 m

Kardamyla

Marmaro

Ag. Markela

Volissos

Pitios

Lagada

Limnia

Sykiada

Limnos

Pantoukios

Fortress Village

Anavatos

Nea Moni

Avgonima

Vrondatos

C Chios Town ⚓

B

Kontari

Lithi Beach

Lithi

Ag. Georgios

Karfas

Vessa

Thelopotami

Thimiana

Ag. Ermionii

Didima

Agia Mina

Liminas

Elata

Agios Fotinis

Kini

Kataraktis

Mesta

Scenic Villages

Armolia

Olymboi

Pyrgi

Kalamoti

Flatsia

Komi

Emborios

⊙ Irregular High Season caique service

🚌 MAIN GREEN BUSES:
— ·— Ⓓ x 7
— ·· — Ⓓ x 7
— — Ⓓ x 3
···· Ⓓ x 7
······ ① ④ x 2

🚌 MAIN BLUE (CITY) BUSES:
——— Ⓓ x 10
——— Ⓓ x 11
— — Ⓓ x 2
- - - Ⓓ x 2

✈ → Athens Ⓓ x 5
→ Thessalonika ① ⑤ x 1

0   km   4

Chios

ΧΙΟΣ; 852 km²; pop. 54,000.

Relatively untouristed (thanks to an ugly main port with no good beaches close by) nor offering much in the way of photogenic sightseeing, the large island of Chios remains quiet with its low-key attractions hidden away. To do the island justice you need to take time to explore away from the capital: Chios has a merited reputation for having some of the most fertile and attractive terrain found in the Aegean. Indeed, in many ways the landscape is the best thing about Chios, as well as being the source of its quiet affluence: thanks to the growing of mastica (the sticky stuff used to make paint adhere to walls and chewing-gum to everything else). The island is mountainous with the mastica bush crop covering much of the south, while the north is forested — though major fires in 1981 and 1987 inflicted considerable damage to this region. A more recent and lucrative contribution to the local economy has come via shipping; for almost every Greek shipping tycoon in sight seems to hail from here or the neighbouring satellite of Oinousses.

The capital — Chios Town — has an industrial port waterfront with little to recommend it. Demolished by a major earthquake in 1881, subsequent rebuilding has left the town an inadequate harbinger to the attractiveness of the rest of the island. Host each summer to a large expatriate North American community, the back streets behind the waterfront offer an incongruous mix of crumbling 19c. mansions, pool bars and New Yorker run pizza bars. The quayside is more reminiscent of a vast and empty version of Piraeus than any other harbour in Greece. The centre of activity lies near the north-western corner: this is where all the large ferries dock, with the most scenic part of the town behind (complete with a closed mosque and a large tree-filled square/park). In an attempt to humanize the waterfront, the western side is now pedestrianised during the evening; the local mosquitos taking full advantage of the humans taking in the night air (this is one harbour where it can be quite potent).

Most of the major villages on Chios are linked by the island bus service. Blue city buses run well beyond the town environs to cover the central portion of the island, less consistent Green island buses (both start from their own terminals near the town park) serve the rest. Timetables for both services (and ferries) are provided by an official NTOG/EOT office on Kanari St. (a side-street off the north-eastern corner of the harbour).

Southern Chios has most to offer the tourist thanks to a series of scenic medieval fortress villages in the mastica growing region. **Pyrgi** is the biggest and prettiest of these so-called 'mastic' villages; the whitewashed houses adorned with a wide variety of geometric blue patterns that extend even to the underside of the balconies. **Mesta** is also worth exploration, for although smaller it retains more of its medieval buildings and with it its old world atmosphere (as does **Olymboi** on the road between the two). It also has a port at **Liminas** that until four years ago saw the occasional ferry. Nowadays only the occasional tourist hydrofoil disturbs the waves. Just to the south of Chios Town are a couple of other popular destinations: **Karfas** — offering the nearest reasonable beach, and the monastery of Agia Mina — site of another massacre by the Turks.

North of the town, buses run frequently to **Vrondatos** and the Daskalopetra or 'teaching rock', which tradition associates with Homer. North of this resort Chios is quiet. The largest village is at Kardamyla; though it isn't much bigger than its equally rustic and undisturbed neighbours. Whitewashed Volissos on the west coast has more to offer, with remnants of a fortress and a pretty little harbour at **Limnos** with caïques to Psara.

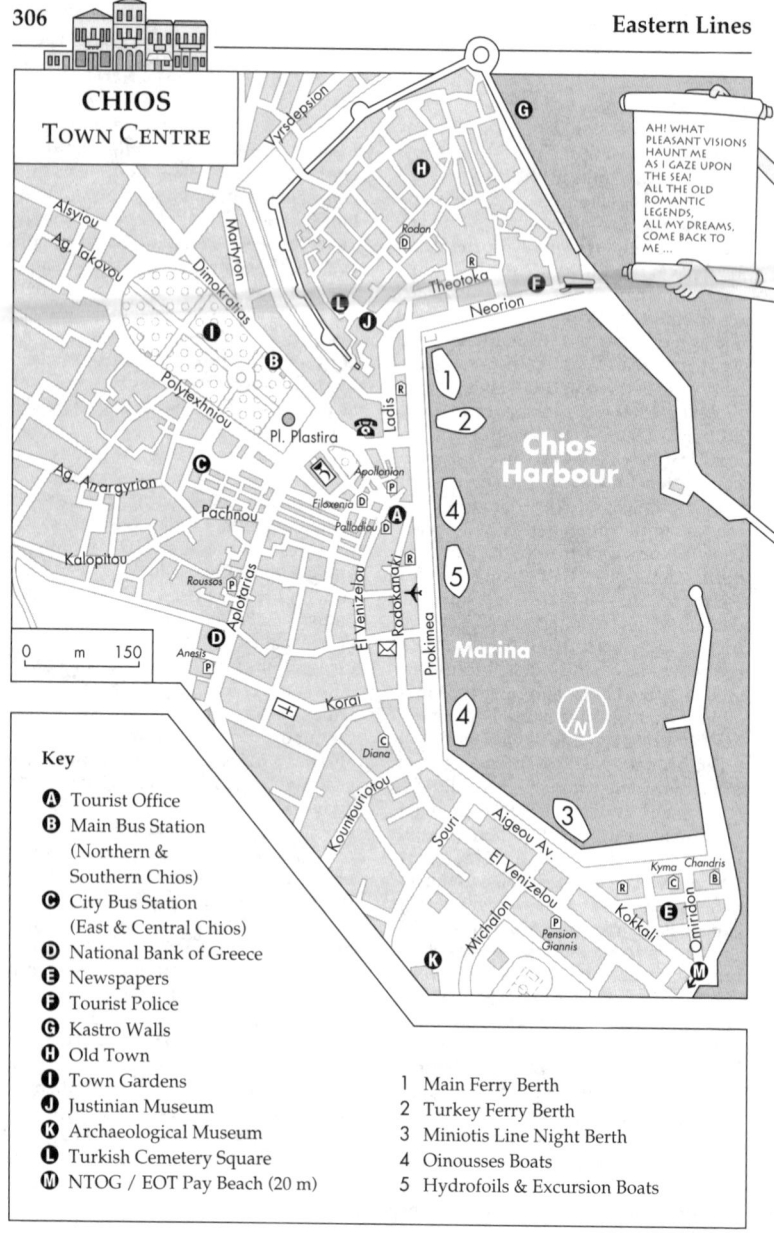

CHIOS
TOWN CENTRE

AH! WHAT PLEASANT VISIONS HAUNT ME AS I GAZE UPON THE SEA! ALL THE OLD ROMANTIC LEGENDS, ALL MY DREAMS, COME BACK TO ME ...

Chios Harbour

Marina

0   m   150

Key

Ⓐ Tourist Office
Ⓑ Main Bus Station (Northern & Southern Chios)
Ⓒ City Bus Station (East & Central Chios)
Ⓓ National Bank of Greece
Ⓔ Newspapers
Ⓕ Tourist Police
Ⓖ Kastro Walls
Ⓗ Old Town
Ⓘ Town Gardens
Ⓙ Justinian Museum
Ⓚ Archaeological Museum
Ⓛ Turkish Cemetery Square
Ⓜ NTOG / EOT Pay Beach (20 m)

1 Main Ferry Berth
2 Turkey Ferry Berth
3 Miniotis Line Night Berth
4 Oinousses Boats
5 Hydrofoils & Excursion Boats

⊢⊣

The lack of tourists means that accommodation options are adequate but not vast. Chios Town has the most beds, but in High Season finding an empty one come the evening can be a problem; ticket agencies will phone around for you. Best (and most expensive) hotel in town is the *Chandris* (☎ 25761), hiding in the street below the harbour. Nearby is the popular mansion *Kyma* (☎ 44500). The *Radon* (☎ 24335) in the old town also offers a quiet atmosphere and reasonable prices. Noisier, but clean are the *Diana* (☎ 24656) and cheaper *Filoxenia* (☎ 22813). Rooms along the waterfront are also popular and generally good value for money though the best lie in the old town. Most of the main island towns also have several hotels (Karfas being the best served with five) along with a scatter of rooms in Pyrgi and Mesta.

▲

Chios Camping (☎ 74111): exposed, isolated beach site 14 km north of Chios town.

෴

Lacking any notable sites from the Classical, Hellenistic or Roman periods, the main attraction on Chios is an 11 C. **Byzantine Monastery** at **Nea Mona**, 15 km west of Chios Town. Set in the foothills, it is home to some of the finest Byzantine frescos and mosaics known (dating from the monastery's foundation in 1042). The charnel house is also home to a ghoulish display of skulls. Victims of the 1822 massacre of the island's population by the Turks, they stare at visitors in serried rows like a hungry crowd of evangelicals looking for converts. East of the monastery lies another popular sight: the abandoned cliff village of **Anavatos** whose inhabitants did a collective jump as the Turks approached (sightseeing on Chios is not for the squeamish). Chios Town has few sights worth hunting out bar the remains of the Genoese **Kastro** (1433) housing the **Turkish Quarter** to the north of the harbour. The only part of the town to survive the 1881 earthquake, it was badly damaged, but patched up and boasts an impressive moat. Less inspiring are the town's poor **Archaeological Museum** and Cathedral: two good reasons to splash out on a day-trip to the Turkish town of **Çeşme** on the coast opposite.

☎

CODE 0271, TOURIST OFFICE 24217, TOURIST POLICE 26555.

Fourni

ΦΟΥΡΝΟΙ; 37 km²; pop. 970.

A small rocky archipelago lying between Ikaria and Samos to the north and Patmos to the south. The bulk of the population lives in the villages of Fourni and Chrisomilia on the main island of **Fourni**. Formerly the home of Byzantine pirates, the island is quiet even in High Season, only recently emerging as a regular ferry destination and still lacking proper roads. Fourni village is a pretty little place, overlooked by derelict windmills and with a caïque-laden sandy port beach. Emptier beaches lie to the north and south of the village. All this adds up to a lovely, unspoilt island: one of the few genuine articles left in Greece. The second islet of **Thimena** (complete with one untouristed hillside hamlet) can be visited by hiring a caïque or via the caïques that stop here when running between Fourni and Ikaria.

⊢⊣

No hotels, but Rooms in Fourni village.

☎

CODE 0275, PORT POLICE 51207.

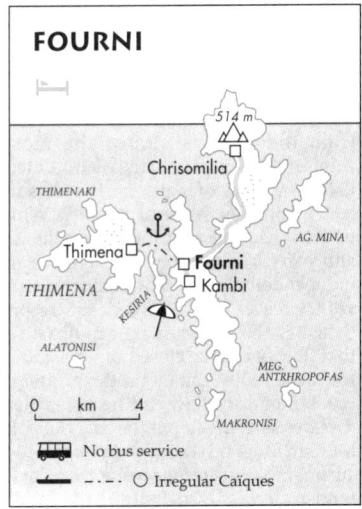

FOURNI

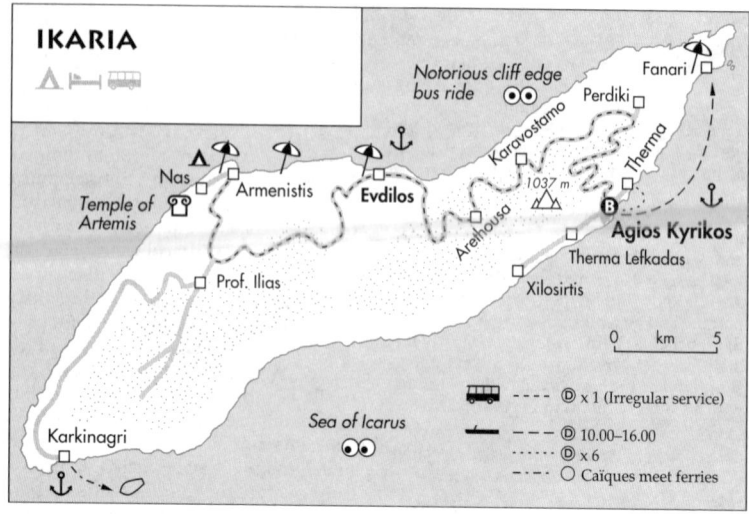

IKARIA

Notorious cliff edge bus ride

Fanari

Perdiki

Karavostamo

Therma

Nas

Armenistis

Evdilos

1037 m

Temple of Artemis

Agios Kyrikos

Therma Lefkadas

Prof. Ilias

Arethousa

Xilosirtis

0   km   5

Sea of Icarus

Karkinagri

⊕ x 1 (Irregular service)

⊕ 10.00–16.00

⊕ x 6

○ Caïques meet ferries

Ikaria

IKAPIA; 260 km²; pop. 9500.

Named after the unfortunate Icarus who fell and drowned (in the sea of the same name), after the wax holding the feathers to his man-made wings melted on flying too near the sun, wing-shaped Ikaria is a mountainous island with a thin covering of trees standing on the slopes like so many pins in a cushion. In fact, the view from the ferry is almost the most comfortable thing about the island. Often used as a place of exile, Ikaria seems to lack a coherent sense of identity. With five changes of name in the last two thousand years, a three-month existence as an independent state in 1912 before union with Greece, a failed 19 c. spa resort (boasting thermal springs so radioactive that they had to be closed down), and a freelance hippy colony on the northern coast monopolising the best beaches (besides seeming to put the islanders off tourism for good) this is perhaps not too surprising. But it does leave the island with a decidedly faded air: the locals haven't got much and don't seem to expect much either. The few tourists who call are often left feeling much the same; though if you are prepared to grub around, with a bit of effort Ikaria can at least offer an 'interesting' variation of the Greek island theme.

The main town of **Agios Kyrikos** lies on the south-east coast. Having evolved as the port serving the 19 c. resort spa of Therma, it hasn't developed much beyond a street or two behind the waterfront and is filled with the cheaper and uglier type of Aegean mansion house. The only quarter with any atmosphere lies north of the Hotel Adam; a warren of streets filled with shoeshops. On the plus side, the backstreets clambering up the hillside behind the boulder-strewn waterfront exude an air of quiet small town domesticity (Agios Kyrikos is another of those Greek towns filled with cats), and the whole town is well endowed with trees. The waterfront is the focus of all life; with all the usual facilities and several tavernas doing their best to inject a (very) little

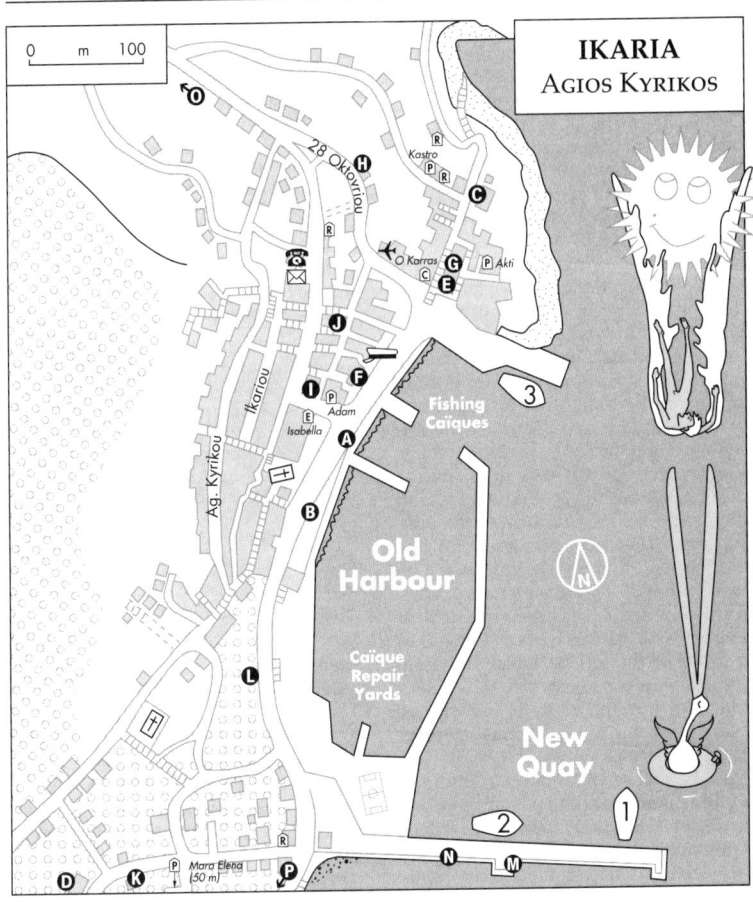

0   m   100

IKARIA
AGIOS KYRIKOS

28 Oktovriou

Kastro

O Karras

Akti

Ikariou

Ag. Kyrikou

Adam

Isabella

Fishing Caïques

Old Harbour

Caïque Repair Yards

New Quay

Mara Elena (50 m)

Key

Ⓐ Main Square
Ⓑ Bus Stop
Ⓒ Police Station
Ⓓ Hospital
Ⓔ Bank
Ⓕ Newspapers

Ⓖ Pharmacy
Ⓗ Supermarket
Ⓘ Bakery
Ⓙ Pizzeria
Ⓚ Rex Cinema
Ⓛ Moped Rental
Ⓜ Sculpture of Icarus

Ⓝ Passenger Stalls
Ⓞ Evdilos Road
Ⓟ Xilosirtis Road

1 Ferry Berth
2 Hydrofoil Berth
3 Therma/Fourni Caïques

bonhomie into things. There isn't much to see or do in town except stroll along the ferry quay and admire the modernist sculpture of Icarus that greets all arrivals. Quite why the failed aviator is depicted caught in what appears to be the beak of an enormous bird isn't immediately clear. (Truth to tell, it isn't any clearer if you come back five years later.) Perhaps the sculptor decided to spice the story up a bit by adding a mythical Halcyon bird quietly nesting on the waves when Icarus decided to drop by. Most tourists who visit Agios Kyrikos are doing little more, for the main attraction of the town is its role as the local transportation hub. In addition to the caïques (and in the summer of 1994 daily hydrofoils) to Fourni, it is the starting point for the only island bus link; a service that is very unreliable — often terminating at Evdilos — and departing when full rather than on schedule. The only thing going for it is the journey: a cliff-edge ride that will leave you with a vivid insight as to what Icarus saw and felt as he fell to sea. Most tourists who use this bus are doing so as a result of the ferries, which although they provide a daily service throughout the year, are apt to chop and change island ports both from summer to summer and between seasons.

At the end of the mountain road lies **Evdilos**, Ikaria's second port and a village in decline. Huddled around a small bay, it offers few temptations to linger. Ferry links remain good thanks to the hippy hoppers that collar this side of the island during the High Season. Most disembarking here are those in the know — heading for the beaches at Armenistis 8 km along the coast: now witness to the first signs of Ios-like disco/taverna development. Some 2 km further on lies the pretty hamlet of Nas, after which roads degenerate into dirt tracks. This end of the island is little visited, with rare ferries stopping off the hill village **Karkinagri** in lieu of a terrestrial means of access.

🛏

Gloomy Therma has a monopoly on faded up-market waterfront hotels, while Agios Kyrikos has a motley collection of cheaper establishments including the B-class pension *Adam* (☎ 22418), the C-class *O Karras* (☎ 22494) and E-class hotel *Isabella* (☎ 22839) — all on the waterfront. More attractive is the pension *Kastro* (☎ 22474), which offers rooms overlooking the town. Rooms are scarce on the island — though some exist at Evdilos. There are unofficial campsites at Evdilos (at Livadi), Armenistis and Nas (the best of the three).

👓

Only site of interest on Ikaria is a **Temple of Artemis** at Nas: foundations of which survive. **Agios Kyrikos** sees frequent water taxies running to the ugly spa and hotel hamlet of Therma 4 km from the town, a reasonable beach at Fanari, and more interesting daily High Season caïques to the Fourni archipelago. Waterfront signs pointing out the town museum (150 m south of the hospital) take you on a town walk to a long abandoned building.

☎

CODE 0275, TOURIST POLICE 22222, PORT POLICE 22207, HOSPITAL 22330.

Lesbos

ΛΕΣΒΟΣ; 1630 km²; pop. 104,600.

The third largest Greek island, Lesbos (pronounced Lesvos) is more popular with locals rather than with foreign holiday-makers (this latter category largely confined to those individuals who go everywhere and sundry loving couples (usually female) searching out their feminist roots). Thanks to good olive oil and ouzo (the aniseedy Greek national drink) brewing industries, the island is economically self-sufficient with little need to develop tourism. This is somewhat intimidated anyway by the size of Lesbos and the nature of bus services, which are inconveniently centred on the east coast capital of Mytilini and infrequent: making quick movement difficult without your own transport. Given that sights are spread inconveniently around the island and that much of the stark landscape

LESBOS

Main Green Buses:
— Ⓓ x 4 ⬆18.00
— — Ⓓ x 6 ⬆18.00
—··· Ⓓ x 2/3
—·— Ⓓ x 2/3 ⬆13.15
— — — Ⓓ x 1 13.15

Main Blue (City) Buses:
---- Ⓗ 07.00–20.00
········ Ⓗ 07.00–18.00
·········· Ⓗ 06.30–20.00

Skala Sikamias

Castle
Molivos/
Mithimna
Petra
Mantamados

Anaxos

0   km   10

Moni Perivolis

Agios
Paraskevi

Kalloni
Temple of
Aphrodite

Spa
Pirgi Thermis

Castle &
Theatre

Moni Limona

Aqueduct

Sigri   Andissa
Petrified Trees

Lambou Mili

Mytilini

Eressos

Gulf of
Kalloni

Varia

Skala
Eressou

Agiassos

968 m
Paleokipos

Gulf of
Gera

Loutra

Feminist
Beach

Polihnitos
Vrissa
Temple of
Dionysos   Vatera

Skopelos

Ag. Isidoros

Agios
Ermoyenis
Beach

Plomari

Tarti Beach

✈ → Athens Ⓓ x 2
→ Thessalonika Ⓓ x 1
→ Limnos ① ⑤ ⑦ x 1

— --- Ⓓ x 2
—·— Ⓓ x 2
○ Irregular Service

🚢 — Ⓓ x 8

reflects the island's volcanic origins, it is perhaps not surprising that most island hoppers confine themselves to Mytilini and the lovely northern resort town of Mithimna/Molivos.

Mytilini, the island capital, is the destination for all ferries and is one of those ports which operators prefer to refer to direct in preference to the island name. At first sight very appealing, straddling a promontory adorned with a impressive castle and a busy harbour crowned with a prominent pineapple-domed church, this large town is something of a disappointment on closer inspection: being little more than a conglomeration of drab, dusty streets that are filled to bursting in the week, but dead to the world on Sundays. One of these, Ermou — running from the harbour to the northern town bay — doubles as the town bazaar with a suitably bizarre collection of junk shops. All the facilities are within a drachma's throw of the inner harbour waterfront. Along the quay to the west lie the city bus station (with a frequent service to Pirgi Termis — a popular spa and beach resort to the north), a Folk Art

Museum, a Byzantine Museum and the main bus station. This latter landmark is the best way out of town with daily links to all parts of the island. You may wish to take advantage of this sooner rather than later for although the Mytilini towns-people are friendly enough they are more superstitious than most, and leapt into the world's press in 1994 when, during an excavation of a 19 c. Muslim cemetery, a stone-lined crypt hollowed out of the city wall was found to contain a vampire's coffin. The inhabitant, a middle-aged man, had been nailed through his neck, pelvis, and ankles to the casket base in order to prevent him from rising again. This was a common enough practice in Greece at the time (as was the habit of nailing horseshoes to a deceased's hands and feet so that if they were to go walkies the locals would hear them coming). Quite what this particular unfortunate had done to deserve his fate is not known. Rumour, probably malicious, has it that he was a misogynist who rashly spoke out of turn in a lesbian bar; but this is unlikely given that he appears to have been dead before he was nailed down.

Thanks to the olive-grove lined Gulfs of Gera and Kallonis, Lesbos is effectively divided into three parts with Mytilini and the peninsula below hanging on like the island's tail. Links between the three are all but non-existent: hence the difficulty in moving around. To date, the northern part of the island has been the focus of the tourist industry, thanks to the attractive castle-topped northern coast town of **Molivos** (usually known by its older name of **Mithimna**) 55 km from Mytilini. **Petra** 5 km to the south is also emerging as a resort thanks to its better beach. The best island beaches however, lie elsewhere. **Vetera** has an amazing 7 km stretch of sand and can be reached direct by bus or beach boat from the indifferent south coast resort of **Plomari**. The bus route is better as it takes in the lovely old (and government protected)

hill village of **Agiassos** carved out of a pine forest with cobbled streets and old timber houses. The west side of Lesbos is comparatively quiet with the singular exception of Eressos and its impressive beach at Skala Eressou. Home to the feminist poet Sappho and the island's lesbian movement, the long sandy beach is comparable with that at Vetera — apart from the scattered bodies of local youths driven to suicide by their failure to successfully chat up foreign fluff. Lone males will do better to head for the pretty fishing village of **Sigri** — an ideal spot for quiet romance away from the crowds.

⊨

A semi-friendly Tourist Police office lies just off the ferry quay offering (if you ask nicely) accommodation details. Unfortunately most of it is well away from **Mytilini Town**. In town (which is where you often need to be thanks to ferry departure times that prohibit sleeping elsewhere) options are more limited. Out of High Season the scatter of rooms around the town offer the best value for money; for this reason they fill quickly in the summer. Most are on or near Ermou St.; though the best lie on the south side of the harbour. The hotels are a pretty diverse collection. The B-class *Blue Sea* (☎ 23994) just off the ferry quay offers the prospect of an easy, if pricey, bed but this is deceptive thanks to a 'strictly no riff-raff' admissions policy (note: if you are under 40 or wearing a backpack then *you* are 'riff-raff'). The C-class *Sappho* (☎ 28888) on the other side of the harbour is much more accommodating, but too popular by half (phone ahead in High Season). If you can afford the odd 10,000 GDR a night, the nearby B-class *Lesvion* (☎ 22038) offers an attractive option.

Usually the last hotel in town to fill is the C-class *Rex* (☎ 28523): a leading candidate for the weirdest hotel in Greece, it looks like a down-beat Addams Family mansion, and boasts hollowed mattresses so old that getting into bed is not unlike getting into a coffin. Add to this the cloves of garlic embellishing the wrought iron trellis of the front door and the photograph of a naked two-headed Siamese infant boy adorning the hotel reception and the result is the cheapest hotel in Mytilini. Usually half empty, even in High Season, it is

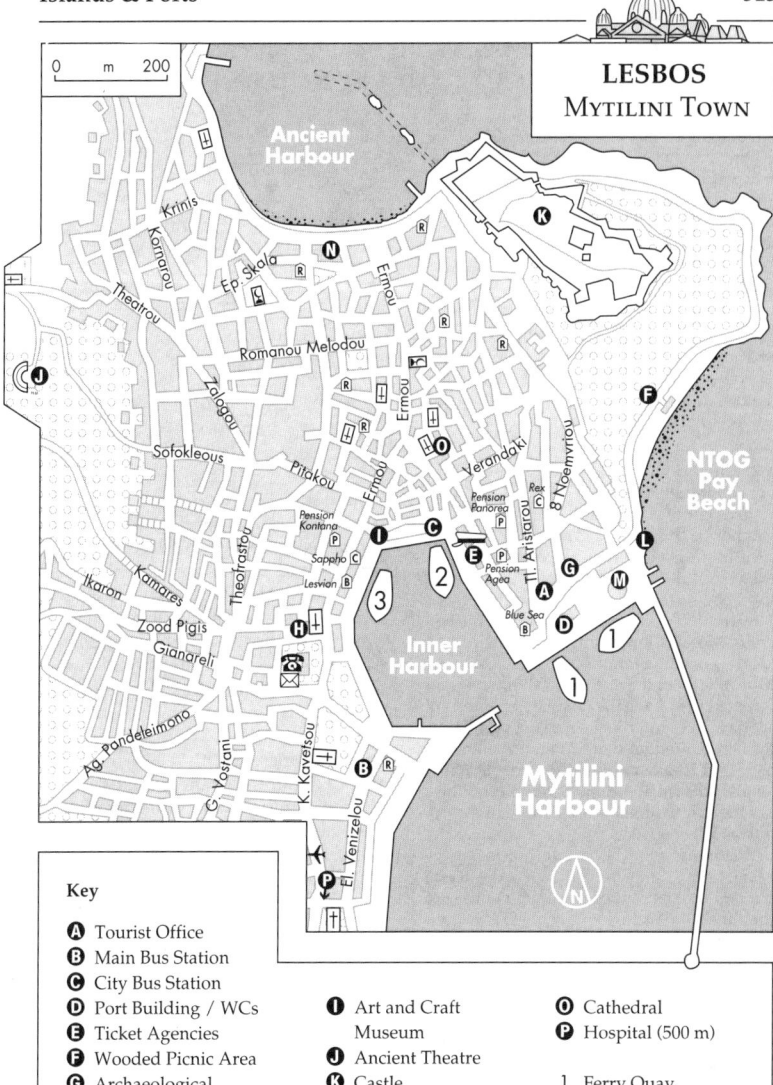

0   m   200

LESBOS
Mytilini Town

Ancient Harbour

Krinis
Kamarou
Theatrou
Ep. Skala
Ermou
Romanou Melodou
Zalagou
Sofokleous
Pitakou
Ermou
Ermou
Verandaki
Noemvriou
T. Aristarou
Ikaron
Kamares
Theofrastou
Zood Pigis
Gianareli
Ag. Pandeleimono
G. Vostani
K. Kavetsou
El. Venizelou

Pension Kontana
Sappho
Lesvian
Pension Pariorea
Pension Agea
Rex
Blue Sea

NTOG Pay Beach

Inner Harbour

Mytilini Harbour

N

Key
A Tourist Office
B Main Bus Station
C City Bus Station
D Port Building / WCs
E Ticket Agencies
F Wooded Picnic Area
G Archaeological Museum
H Byzantine Museum / St. Theodore's Church
I Art and Craft Museum
J Ancient Theatre
K Castle
L Statue of Liberty
M Swimming Pool
N Flea Market
O Cathedral
P Hospital (500 m)

1 Ferry Quay
2 Turkey Ferry Overnight Berth
3 Tourist Boat Berth

a family-run concern with a 'Wednesday Addams' look-alike daughter on reception.

In **Mithimna / Molivos** there is so much hotel and room accommodation on offer that one is spoilt for choice . The tourist office near the bus stop can help find a bed, but given the hilly nature of the town it pays to check how far from the waterfront any bed is before you accept it. The town has B-class hotels in abundance and precious little else; including the *Poseidon* (☎ 0253 71570) close by the bus stop, and the waterfront *Sea Horse* (☎ 0253 71320).

A

Camping Mithimna (☎ 0261 71169): reasonable, and popular beach site: 2 km east of Mithimna. *Camping Dionysos* (☎ 0252 61340), on the other hand, is a new site just inland from Vatera and has yet to really get going.

☙

Mytilini is dominated by the **Castle**, built in 1373 on the site of the old acropolis: it can be visited, but overlooking the Turkish coast is another of those photographically sensitive sites. Impressive views of the castle can, however, be gleaned from the hillside that is home to the bowl (sans seats) of the 3 c. BC **Hellenistic Theatre** that marked the edge of the ancient town. Mosaics found in excavations nearby are now residing in the good **Archaeological Museum** 50 m north-east of Mytilini's ferry quay. 4 km outside the town at the hamlet of Moria are the impressive remains of a 3 c. AD **Roman Aqueduct** that watered the ancient city. Odd fragments survive along its 20 km length notably at Lambou Mili. Lesbos also has the scanty remains of Temples of Aphrodite and Dionysos.

Mithimna offers the best sightseeing on the island courtesy of the 14 c. Genoese **Kasto** built on the site of the ancient acropolis, and the almost too picturesque cobbled and stone house town that lies below. Finds from the ancient town (including sarcophagi) are in the Mithimna **Museum** in the town hall. The west side of Lesbos has what are claimed to be the remains of **Sappho's Home** and, on off the road to Antissa, the grossly over-rated remains of a petrified forest in the shape of three desultory tree stumps. Finally, Sigri, on the west coast has a good 18 c. Turkish Fortress.

☎

MYTILINI CODE 0251, PORT POLICE 28888, NTOG OFFICE 22776, HOSPITAL 28457.

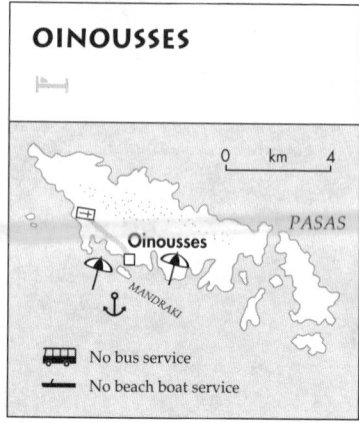

OINOUSSES

No bus service

No beach boat service

Oinousses

ΟΙΝΟΥΣΣΕΣ; 16 km²; pop. 420.

A small island blessed with several good beaches and one large town that feels more like a city suburb on the slide than an island capital. The home of several of Greece's richest shipping owners, Oinousses has strong seafaring tradition that sees many of the menfolk working away: the result is a curious mix of affluence combined with boarded-up summer holiday homes. For this reason tourism is all but ignored as the islanders have enough coming in to be able to resist the temptations to turn their home into a resort island. The most obvious consequence of all this is that tourist facilities are scarce to the point of being non-existent, and the usual welcoming attitude typical of most Greek islanders is thin on the ground if you try to sleep on it. Those that recourse to the only hotel fare better.

The lack of tourists has in its turn made the island difficult to visit, as the local boats linking it with Chios Town are mostly based on Oinousses; forcing you to stay overnight. Given this, the island is best visited by the Chios Town day-tripper boats (frequency varies greatly according to the time of year). In addition to visiting Oinousses proper, tripper boats also stop at the church islet of **Mandraki** 300 m from the town quay.

👓

Oinousses is relatively bereft of things to see or do other than lie on the beach (the best lie in quiet coves to the west of the town). The town is no great shakes and can only boast a **Maritime Museum** (that is invariably closed). This means that most visitors are reduced to doing the coastal walk to the **Evangelismou** convent on the western tip of the island. Home to the mummified corpse of a shipping billionaire's daughter who snuffed it after becoming a nun, the monastery was rebuilt as a shrine to her memory by her parents. The fact that her body hadn't decomposed after its traditional three-year stint underground (in Greece graves are re-used, so once the flesh has rotted the bones of the deceased are removed and interred elsewhere) was taken as a (fortuitous) sign of sainthood.

🛏

No rooms, but one nice, if pricey, D-class hotel in the town; the *Thalassoporos* (☎ 51475).

☎

CODE 0272, POLICE 51222.

Psara

ΨΑΡΑ; 45 km²; pop. 460.

Barren and dusty Psara rarely figures on tourist itineraries and, ignored by most ferry operators, wallows quietly in the shadows of its own grim history. An obscure island in ancient times, it came to prominence (along with the Saronic islands of Hydra and Spetses) in the early 19 c., thanks to an indigenous fleet of merchant adventurers. Psara was thus well placed to play a prominent part in the early liberation struggle of the independent Greek state, but — lying just off the Turkish mainland — very badly placed when it came to avoiding the wrath of the Turks that came after. By way of setting an example to would-be rebellious islands the Turks laid waste to the island in 1824; killing the bulk of the population (inflated by refugees from other islands) of 20,000 (3,000 escaping by boat to found a town on Evia: Nea Psara). Psara has

never really recovered from the event the Greeks call the 'holocaust'. Some survivors drifted back, but the descendants only number around 600. Almost all live in the one island town of **Psara** and not surprisingly they remain somewhat luke-warm toward visitors. The government takes a different view and in past years has offered free ferry tickets in the Low Season as well as providing (through the NTOG/ EOT) accommodation in the converted town jail. Bar this dubious establishment, and a few pre-war mansions the town (dominated by one over-tall church like Naoussa on Paros) has little to offer apart from walks to empty beaches (most of sadly poor quality) and a monastery on the north side of the island.

🛏

The thin supply of Rooms (rarely full) in High Season, are augmented by an A-class hotel/ pension, the *Miramare*, the cheaper *Xenonas Pension* (☎ 61293) and the NTOG/EOT *Guest House* (☎ 61293).

☎

CODE 0274

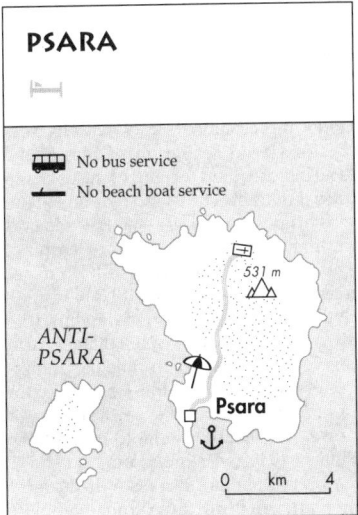

PSARA

🛏

🚌 No bus service

⚓ No beach boat service

531 m

*ANTI-
PSARA*

Psara

0   km   4

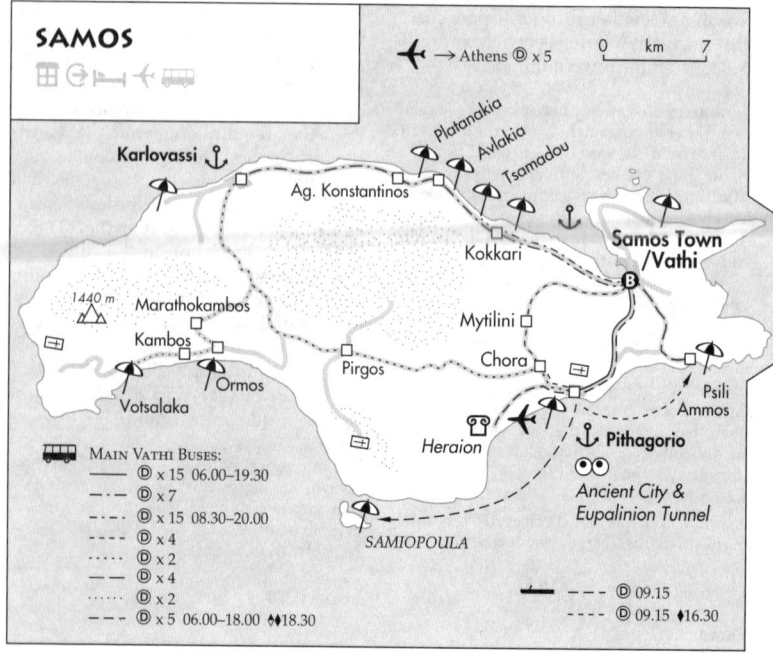

SAMOS

→ Athens ⓓ x 5   0   km   7

Platanakia
Avlakia
Tsamadou

Karlovassi ⚓

Ag. Konstantinos

Kokkari

Samos Town /Vathi
Ⓑ

1440 m
Marathokambos

Mytilini

Kambos

Chora

Pirgos

Ormos

Votsalaka

Psili Ammos

Heraion

Pithagorio

Ancient City & Eupalinion Tunnel

SAMIOPOULA

MAIN VATHI BUSES:
—— ⓓ x 15 06.00–19.30
—·— ⓓ x 7
—·–·– ⓓ x 15 08.30–20.00
––––– ⓓ x 4
·········· ⓓ x 2
—— ⓓ x 4
·········· ⓓ x 2
—––– ⓓ x 5 06.00–18.00 ◆◆18.30

––– ⓓ 09.15
–––– ⓓ 09.15 ◆16.30

Samos
ΣΑΜΟΣ; 472 km²; pop. 41,500.
A large island just to the north of the
Dodecanese, Samos is known for its tree-
clad slopes, a scattering of reasonable
sand beaches, and top end of the package
tourist market. The island was one of the
most important in the ancient world and
particularly noted as a centre of learning.
This reputation was derived from her
most famous sons: Aesop (of fable fame),
Pythagoras, Epicurus, Aristarchus (the
astronomer who worked out that the earth
revolved around the sun), and the Colum-
bus of the ancient world — the navigator
Kolaios — who dared to sail a ship (later
preserved near the Heraion) through the
Pillars of Hercules in 650 BC.
  Most of Kolaios's successors in the ferry
line attract little fame and even less

fortune sailing to the island's largest port
of **Samos Town** (or **Vathi** as it is want to
appear on all timetables). Like all of the
large island ports along this section of the
Turkish coast it is commercial in appearance (i.e. a drab and dingy collection of 19
c. buildings) without the obvious charm
of the harbours of the smaller islands that
make up the Dodecanese: the sort of place
you can happily spend a few hours in —
though you wouldn't travel across Europe
just to visit it. This is something of a surprise if you venture here by way of Pithagorio to the south, as from the hills
overlooking the town, Vathi looks to be a
very attractive place. As it is, most tourists
confine their wanderings to the waterfront, the streets running in parallel to it,
and the small, but pleasant, town park
abutting the post office and the towns'

archaeological museum. Despite this, Samos town figures on the itineraries of a lot of island hoppers as Vathi is the terminus for all Piraeus—Ikaria—Samos ferries, with small (but invaluable) linking services on to Chios. Turkey and the well preserved ancient Greek city of Ephesus is also a popular hop away from here, as you will find if you venture into the multi-stepped ticket agency near the ferry quay: they aren't over interested in selling anyone trips to anywhere else. As usual in this part of the world political tensions are evident: the Port Police are very sensitive when Turkish boats are in, and are quick to shepherd interested spectators away from these boats. Sleeping on the ferry quay is also a non-starter thanks to the attentions of mice and men (or in Vathi's case rats and policemen). Tourist activity in the town is low key; with most of the package tour hotels being located along the coast at the pretty beach resort of **Kokkari**, an easy bus ride away.

The second of the island's ports is commercial **Karlovassi**. Also on the north coast, but an hour's steaming closer to Piraeus, it had its heyday when boats were slower and it formed the nearest convenient link with the mainland. Even today most Vathi-bound ferries call en route, though few tourists disembark. The run-down 19 c. neo-classical warehouse back-drop to the port (inconveniently placed on the outskirts of the town proper) is neither prepossessing nor relived by an equally drab town beyond. It does, however, have some residual value as a place to pick up boats after touring the length of the island.

The third Samian port of **Pithagorio** on the south coast offers a complete contrast to the northern ports. Now the centre of the island's tourist industry, it has a very attractive atmosphere and the bulk of the island sights, but bar a few tourist boats and a daily summer hydrofoil (most heading for Patmos) it is poorly connected with the ferry network with only a couple of regular departures each week. Despite

the large numbers of package tourists in town, Pithagorio manages to retain a surprisingly dreamy air (at least until evening falls), with a snug taverna and tree-lined small harbour backed by red-roofed town behind. Unfortunately, all this means that Pithagorio is very expensive by Greek standards — a reflection of the top-island-resort status it enjoys (hotels line the coast on either side) and the number of day-trippers calling: the modern town lies over the ancient capital of the island. Known at the time as Samos, it is not to be confused with the modern town of that name on the north coast. In fact, Pithagorio has changed names several times, and the current name only dates back to 1953 when the town was re-christened in honour of the island's most famous son: the mathematician Pythagoras. Between the middle ages and 1953 the town was called Tigani. Local prices are high — reflecting the top island resort status it enjoys (hotels line the coast on either side). Tourism has at least ensured the existence of taxi boats to Psli Ammos beach as well as to **Samiopoula** islet (visiting a north-side beach and taverna).

Buses run from Samos Town calling at almost all the main island towns and villages twice daily. The busy routes however, are along the north coast to Karlovassi and south to Pithagorio. The north coast buses thus pass through Kokkari, the beaches at Tsamodou and Avlakia before arriving at Ag. Konstantinos: an ugly tourist town better seen from the bus and Karlovassi. The southwest coast can be reached from here: an appealing mix of taverna-lined beaches and fishing villages this is the most relaxed and unexploited part of Samos.

⊢

Samos is unusual for a popular Greek island in having no camping facilities. Budget accommodation is also thin on the ground in the popular towns. As a result Samos can be a very tricky island on which to find a reasonably priced bed in August — particularly if you

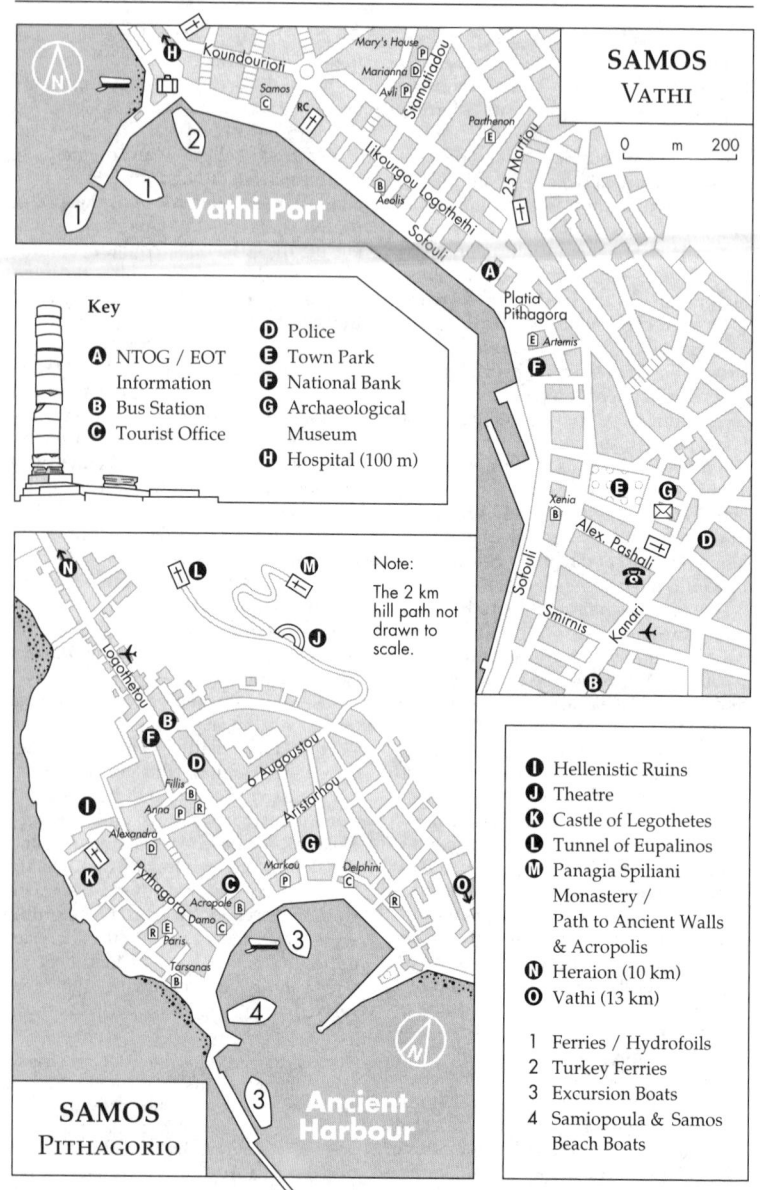

SAMOS
VATHI

Mary's House
Marianna
Avli
Parthenon
Koundourioti
Samos
RC
Shamiadou
Likourgou Logothethi
Aeolis
Sofouli
25 Martiou

0   m   200

Vathi Port

1
2
1

Key

Ⓐ NTOG / EOT
   Information
Ⓑ Bus Station
Ⓒ Tourist Office

Ⓓ Police
Ⓔ Town Park
Ⓕ National Bank
Ⓖ Archaeological
   Museum
Ⓗ Hospital (100 m)

Platia
Pithagora
Ⓔ Artemis
Ⓕ
Xenia
Ⓑ
Ⓔ   Ⓖ
Alex. Pashali
Ⓓ
Sofouli
Smirnis
Kanari
Ⓑ
Ⓐ

Ⓝ
Ⓛ
Ⓜ
Ⓙ

Note:
The 2 km
hill path not
drawn to
scale.

Logothetou
Ⓑ
Ⓕ
Ⓓ
6 Augoustou
Aristarhou
Fillis
Ⓑ
Anna
Ⓟ Ⓡ
Ⓘ
Alexandra
Ⓓ
Ⓗ
Ⓚ
Pithagora
Acropole
Damo
Ⓒ
Markou
Ⓟ
Ⓖ
Delphini
Ⓒ
Ⓔ
Ⓒ
Ⓡ
Paris
Ⓡ
Tarsanas
Ⓑ
Ⓞ
Ⓡ

3
4
3

SAMOS
PITHAGORIO

Ancient
Harbour

Ⓘ Hellenistic Ruins
Ⓙ Theatre
Ⓚ Castle of Legothetes
Ⓛ Tunnel of Eupalinos
Ⓜ Panagia Spiliani
   Monastery /
   Path to Ancient Walls
   & Acropolis
Ⓝ Heraion (10 km)
Ⓞ Vathi (13 km)

1 Ferries / Hydrofoils
2 Turkey Ferries
3 Excursion Boats
4 Samiopoula & Samos
   Beach Boats

arrive in the latter part of the day: at this time of the year it pays to phone ahead. Ticket agencies have lists of accommodations as do the Tourist Police.

Vathi, the capital, is not really a primary tourist destination and this is reflected in the accommodation; with most of the beds in hotels strung along the coast well away from the town centre. In the town are a number of better placed establishments. The waterfront has a number of hotels including the B-class *Xenia* (☎ 27463) at the south-east end of the harbour and the better placed *Aeolis* (☎ 28904), and the C-class *Samos* (☎ 28377) which occasionally has reasonably priced rooms and always boasts a main staircase with overhangs designed for midgets. Nearer the budget end of the range is the waterfront E-class *Artemis* (☎ 27792). The hilly backstreets behind the harbour are also a rich source for beds with the E-class *Parthenon* (☎ 27234) and several pensions (principally along Stamatiadou St.).

Pithagorio has a tourist office/booth just off the main street with accommodation information. The quayside has a number of pricey but justifiably popular hotels hidden behind the tavernas, including the B-class hotel / pensions *Tarsanas* (☎ 61162) just off the ferry quay, and the *Acropole* (☎ 61261), along with the almost as pricey C-class *Damo* (☎ 61303) and *Delphini* (☎ 61205). The streets behind offer the prospect of better hunting. On the main street is the B-class *Fillis* (☎ 612 96) and behind, the budget D-class *Alexandra* (☎ 61429) and E-class *Paris* (☎ 61513). These are augmented by several minor pensions and a limited number or Rooms.

Karlovassi is an ugly place and finding a bed is rarely a problem. Cheapest option is the Youth Hostel behind the large Panagia Church, but there are some 14 hotels in town. At the bottom end of the range are the D-class *Morpheus* (☎ 32672), the *Astir* (☎ 33150) and the *Aktaeon* (☎ 32356) near the port. At the top end of the range is the A-class *Arion* (☎ 92020).

👓

Given that Samos was one of the better endowed islands with monuments in ancient times, the extant remains are something of a disappointment: much has gone and the remainder can comfortably be taken in during the course of a day trip to the island. **Pithagorio** is *the* sightseeing town on Samos. During the 6 c. BC it was the island capital and ruled by the tyrant Polykrates, who seemed intent on leaving a series of monumental works behind him. No doubt it was a considerable source of satisfaction to him when, crucified (by the Persians in 522 BC) on the Turkish coast opposite the town, he hung around and surveyed the wondrous constructions he had commissioned. All survive (in various states of repair) today. First among these is the **Temple of Hera** — more usually known as the **Herion**. It is the main archaeological attraction on Samos, though it is more likely to appeal to archaeological devotees rather than casual sightseers, consisting of no more than foundations and a single lone (hastily reassembled) column that is now the island's totem. Quite a famous building, it was also accredited the status of the eighth of the seven wonders of the world (getting into later lists that excluded inaccessible Babylon). The foundations of its associated buildings include one of its predecessors (the earliest known temple built in the classic 'Greek' style) as well as the earliest known 'true' Stoa. In ancient days the temple was connected by a 10 km Sacred Way running direct to Pithagorio, known to have been lined with over 2000 statues; the road has been irreparably damaged by the island airport runway which now bisects it.

The best preserved of the Polykratic monuments is the **harbour mole**; now the ferry quay most tourists walk its length without knowing it to be any different from quays the islands over. The quay reflects the fact that Pithagorio hides all but scant remains of the ancient city of Samos. Beyond odd collections of stones and some Hellenistic houses behind the **Castle of Legothetes** (built in 1824 by a hero of the independence movement) only the ruinous **Theatre** and **City Walls** on the hill behind give a hint as to what was here before. Tourists can sometimes enter the first 70 m of the 1 km **Tunnel of Eupalinos** (named after its architect and completed in 524 BC) hewn through the mountain; it was designed to guarantee water supplies to the city as well as offering a means of escape (though Polykrates failed to take advantage of it. The town also has an **Archaeological Museum** — though the best of the Heraion exhibits are to be found in the **Vathi Archaeological Museum**.

☎

CODE 0273, TOURIST OFFICE 28530, PORT POLICE 27318, HOSPITAL 27407.

10
NORTHERN AEGEAN

**ALONISSOS · LIMNOS · SAMOTHRACE · SKIATHOS
SKOPELOS · SKYROS · THASSOS · THESSALONIKA**

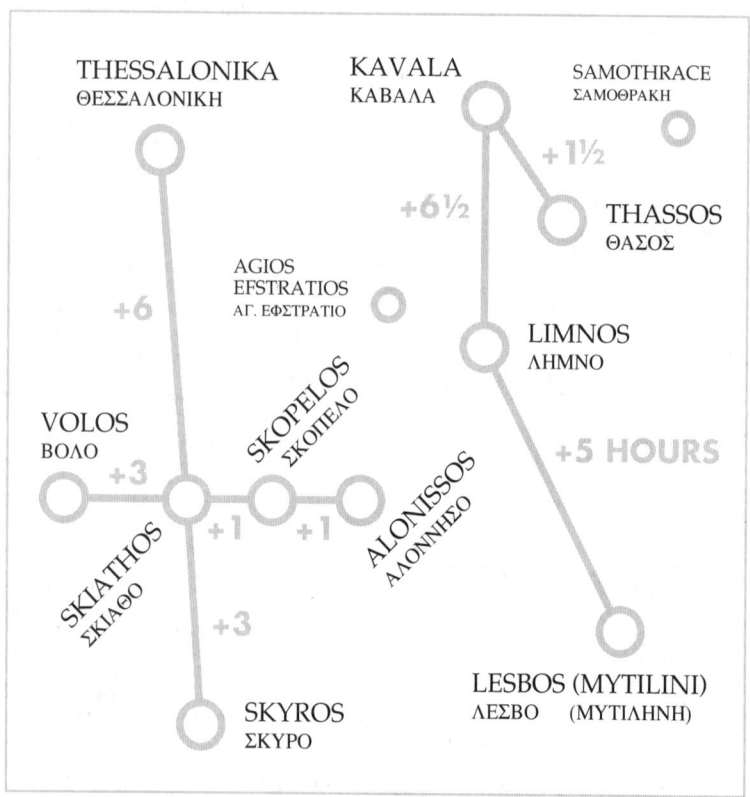

THESSALONIKA
ΘΕΣΣΑΛΟΝΙΚΗ

KAVALA
ΚΑΒΑΛΑ

SAMOTHRACE
ΣΑΜΟΘΡΑΚΗ

+1½

+6½

THASSOS
ΘΑΣΟΣ

AGIOS
EFSTRATIOS
ΑΓ. ΕΦΣΤΡΑΤΙΟ

+6

LIMNOS
ΛΗΜΝΟ

SKOPELOS
ΣΚΟΠΕΛΟ

VOLOS
ΒΟΛΟ

+5 HOURS

+3

ALONISSOS
ΑΛΟΝΝΗΣΟ

+1   +1

SKIATHOS
ΣΚΙΑΘΟ

+3

SKYROS
ΣΚΥΡΟ

LESBOS (MYTILINI)
ΛΕΣΒΟ   (ΜΥΤΙΛΗΝΗ)

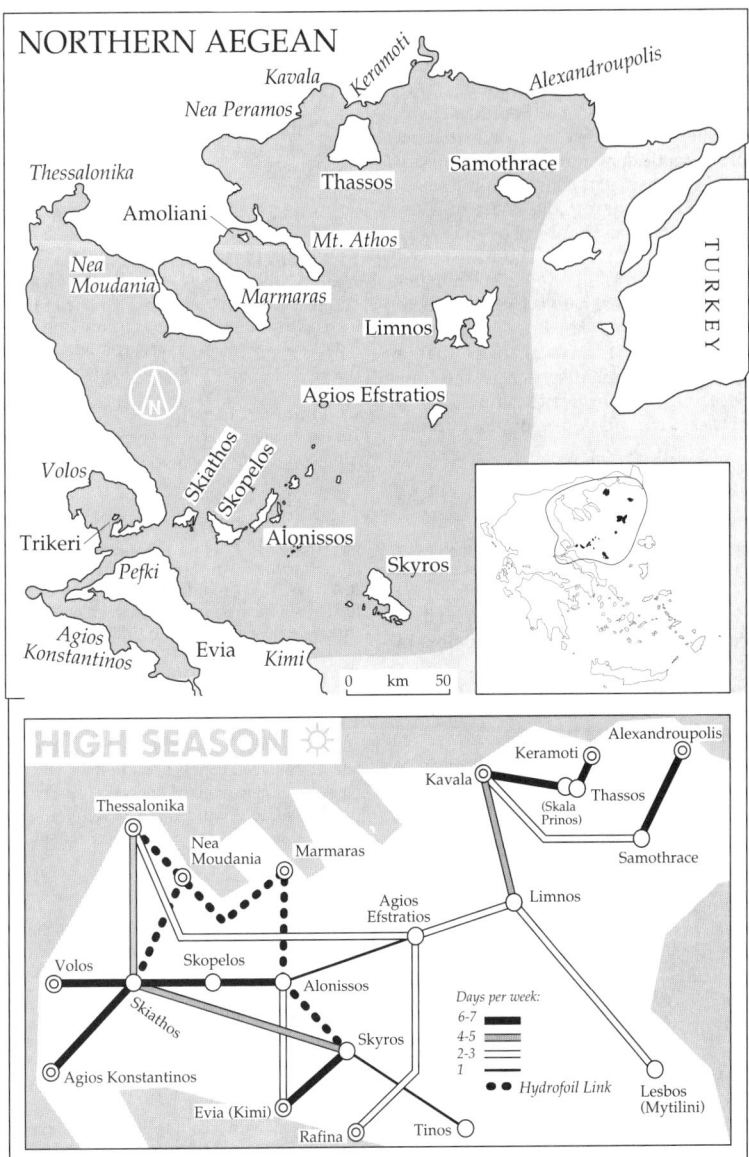

General Features

The Northern Aegean is characterised by a combination of poorly connected large islands and mainland ports, coupled with an easily accessible small Sporades chain. Travel is either very easy or extremely problematic depending upon where you are. The 'easy' part consists of the small, wooded islands off the coast of Evia: Skiathos, Skopelos, Alonissos and — to a lesser extent — Skyros. These are linked by a good hydrofoil service. The remainder of the northern network requires more time and really can only be happily negotiated by those with more than a fortnight at their disposal. In the Low Season the lack of ferries running north of Lesbos curtails non-Sporades options.

Suggested Itinerary [3 Weeks]

The Northern Aegean offers some of the nicest Greek island hopping, but at the price of a loss of flexibility as you are constrained by the few boats available. This itinerary has been achieved in 8 days with a lot of luck. It is more usual to encounter delays, and allowing time to explore, you should allow three rather than two weeks to complete the circuit.

Arrival/Departure Point

There are charter flight airports at three points on the circuit: Athens, Kavala and Thessalonika and you can happily operate from any of them. Athens is the best should you need to get back in a rush. Similarly, as you are visiting poorly connected ports it is better to travel anti-clockwise as the latter destinations all have easy ferry links to the mainland and bus links to the capital: reducing any danger of finding yourself caught out and missing a flight home.

Season

July and August only : the months either side see reduced services sinking away to all but nothing in the Low Season.

1 Athens [3 Days]

An easy starting point with access to NTOG ferry departure sheets from which you can deduce departure times further up the line.

2 Chios [2 Days]

Well worth a stop-over, Chios has a lot to offer. You can establish in Athens when subsequent boats are running down the line and thus deduce the times of Chios—Lesbos ferries.

3 Lesbos [2 Days]

A nice island, which is just as well given that you will probably have to wait a day or two for a boat north. Depending on how long you have to wait you can either stay in Mytilini or head up to much prettier Mithyma.

4 Limnos [2 Days]

Unless you have to change here you can treat Limnos as an optional port of call that can be missed if your Lesbos boat north leaves you running late.

5 Kavala [4 Days]

An attractive town in which to rest up for a few days. You should take advantage of the ferries to **Thassos** and the less regular **Samothrace** boat — stamina and time permitting.

6 Thessalonika [1 Day]

Athens buses run every hour from Kavala so you can run across at your leisure and pick up either hydrofoil or ferry to Skiathos. This is one of the weak connections in the chain as weekend services out of Thessalonika can be booked solid. Should this happen you can take a train to Volos and then a Skiathos-bound hydrofoil or ferry from there (p. 237).

7 Skiathos [3 Days]

Another nice resting point with good Athens links if the need arises via Volos. Even so, try to find time to continue on to Skyros.

8 Skyros [2 Days]

The final island in the loop with daily ferry links with Kimi and the waiting bus to Athens.

1 Athens [2 Days]

Arrive back with a couple of days to spare if you have a flight pre-booked.

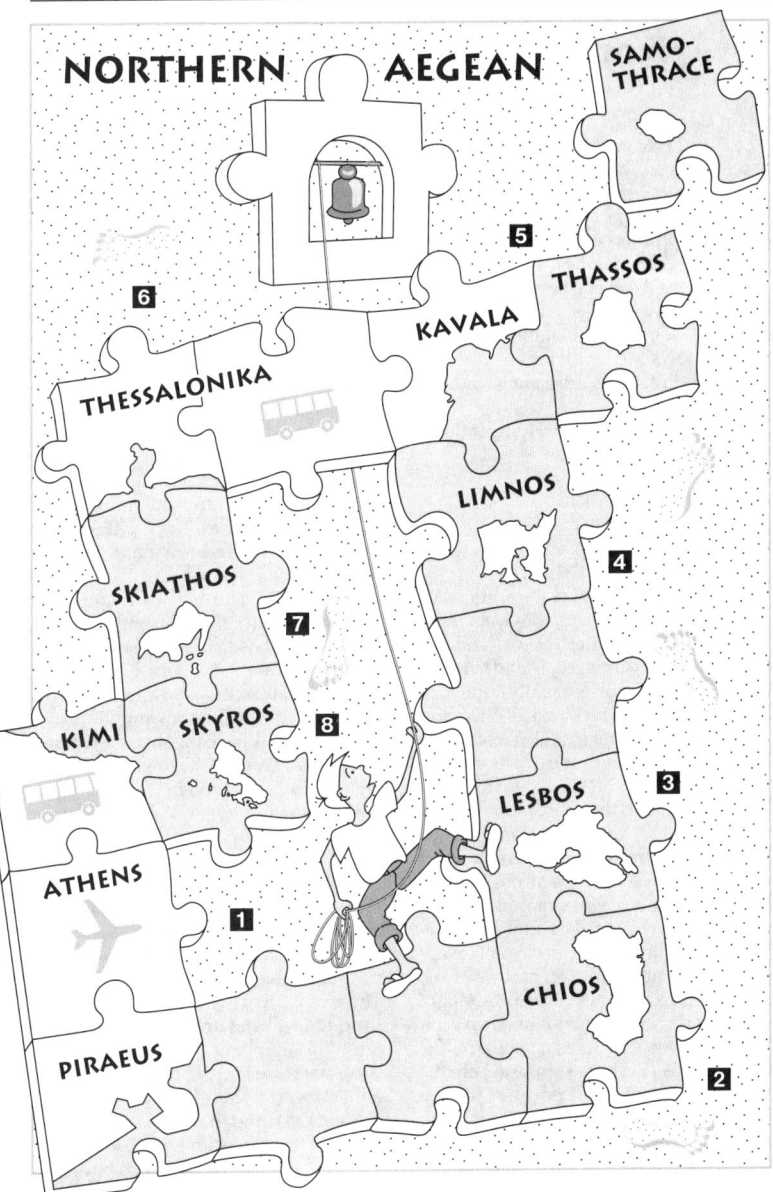

Northern Aegean Ferry Services

Main Car Ferries

The Northern Aegean ferries fall into three groups. The first is a collection of small car ferries bustling back and forth along the small Sporades line, the second is made up of large ferries that operate irregular, wide-ranging itineraries across the northern Aegean (the majority being summer-only services operating via Lesbos — see p. 300). Finally, there are a number of short-haul ferries offering mainland links with adjacent islands.

Sporades Line Ferries & Hydrofoils
Nomikos Lines;
Lemnos; 1976; 1787 GRT.
Macedon; 1972; 1974 GRT.
Skopelos; 1965; 1414 GRT.
Goutos Lines;
Papadiamantis II; 1973; 1060 GRT.

The Greek islands were traditionally divided into two groups: the Cyclades or those islands 'circling' Delos, and the Sporades or 'scattered' islands. Nowadays the latter term is usually applied to just the small archipelago of Skiathos, Skopelos and Alonissos (also referred to as the Northern Sporades). These small wooded islands attract considerable tourist traffic and therefore ferry activity.

Four small car ferries run along the line, most starting from the mainland town of Volos, but some from Agios Konstantinos. Three (the *Lemnos*, *Macedon*, and *Skopelos*) are owned by Nomikos Lines and together they combine to run virtually every possible combination of ports in their schedules. Exact times vary by the month but a good service is maintained all year, with summer schedules changing little. Itineraries A and B (see opposite) are the most widely run. Most ports see at least one ferry berthed overnight in order to provide a very early morning service to the mainland — a feature that largely accounts for schedules of C and D. E is run twice a week in High Season but days are apt to change each year. One independent boat — *Papadiamantis II* — provides the only competition. As usual with this company, timetable information is hard to come by (though her current schedule is well advertised at all ports).

Strong competition to the ferries down the Sporades line is provided by the growing hydrofoil system. Although they only operate a restricted service outside of the High Season, with the usual hydrofoil constraints of being confined to daylight hours and calm sea conditions, they do cream off considerable passenger traffic. In addition to running the same routes as the ferries, the CERES *Flying Dolphins* also operate to a number of destinations otherwise inaccessible by ferry, with a daily High Season morning departure from the islands south to Skyros (H) — usually filled with day-trippers, and to ports along the northern coastline of the Aegean. A daily hydrofoil (I), leaves Thessalonika for Skiathos and the rest of the Sporades during the summer, calling four days a week at the town of Moundania en route — though this often gets booked solid in advance. Moundania is also the starting point for a hydrofoil (J), four days a week, heading (after a call at Marmaras) for Alonissos and ending at either Volos or Agios Konstantinos. Finally, a number of small ports around Evia and Volos (G) are served by hydrofoils running otherwise regular schedules. These calls seem to be aimed at attracting the odd local and are of little interest to the island hopper. The most notable of these ports are Pefki (a beach resort cum hamlet with a campsite, on the north coast of Evia) and the fishing hamlet clad islet of Trekeri nestling like a lone tooth just inside the mouth of Volos bay.

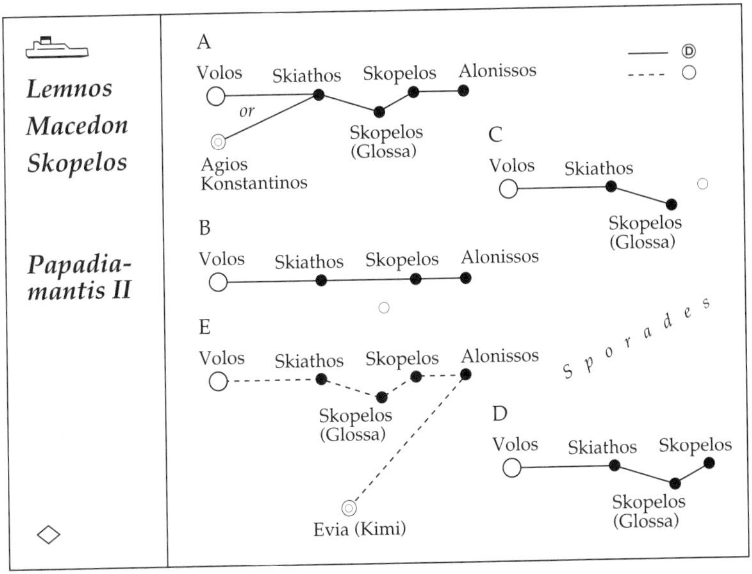

**Lemnos
Macedon
Skopelos**

**Papadia-
mantis II**

◇

A
Volos — Skiathos — Skopelos — Alonissos
or
Agios Konstantinos — Skopelos (Glossa)

C
Volos — Skiathos — Skopelos (Glossa)

B
Volos — Skiathos — Skopelos — Alonissos

E
Volos — Skiathos — Skopelos — Alonissos
Skopelos (Glossa)
Evia (Kimi)

D
Volos — Skiathos — Skopelos — Skopelos (Glossa)

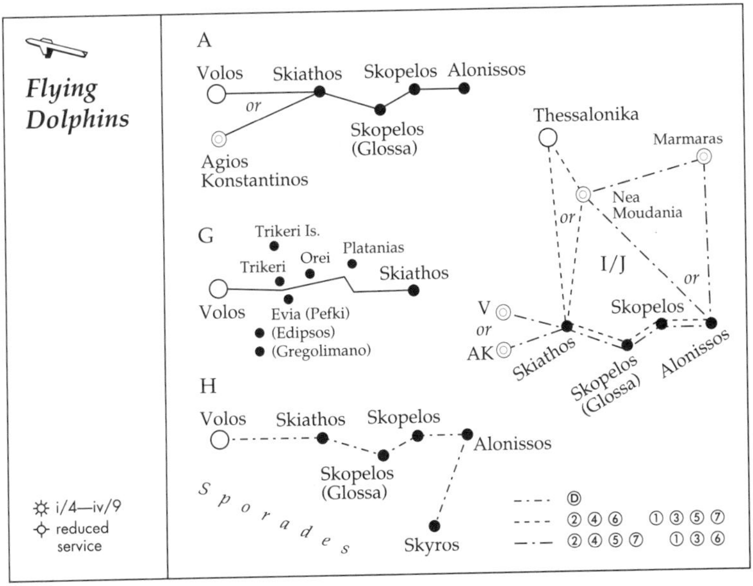

Sporades

**Flying
Dolphins**

☼ i/4—iv/9
◇ reduced service

A
Volos — Skiathos — Skopelos — Alonissos
or
Agios Konstantinos — Skopelos (Glossa)

G
Trikeri Is. — Trikeri — Orei — Platanias — Skiathos
Volos — Evia (Pefki) — (Edipsos) — (Gregolimano)

H
Volos — Skiathos — Skopelos — Alonissos — Skopelos (Glossa) — Skyros

Thessalonika — Marmaras — Nea Moudania
or
I/J
V or AK — Skiathos — Skopelos — Alonissos — Skopelos (Glossa)
or

Sporades

—··— Ⓓ
----- ② ④ ⑥   ① ③ ⑤ ⑦
—·— ② ④ ⑤ ⑦   ① ③ ⑥

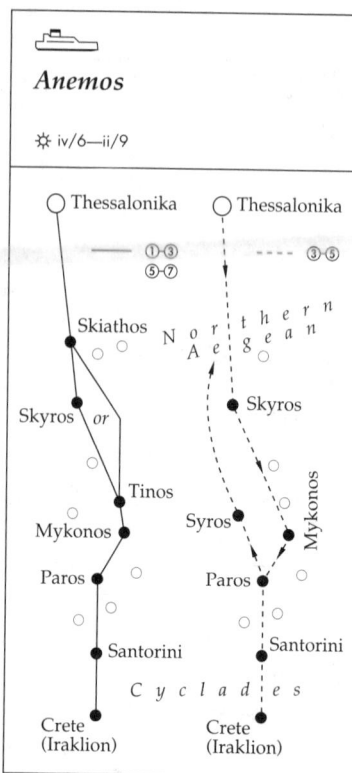

Anemos

☼ iv/6—ii/9

Thessalonika   Thessalonika

——— ①-③   ---- ③-⑤
      ⑤-⑦

Skiathos   N o r ț h e r n
            A e ï g e a n

Skyros *or*   Skyros

Tinos

Mykonos   Syros

Paros   Paros

Santorini   Santorini

            C y c l a d ¦ e s

Crete   Crete
(Iraklion)   (Iraklion)

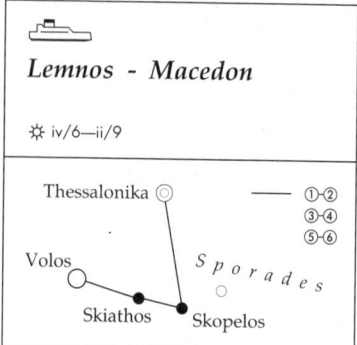

Lemnos - Macedon

☼ iv/6—ii/9

Thessalonika ◎   ——— ①-②
                              ③-④
                              ⑤-⑥
Volos   S p o r a d e s

      Skiathos   Skopelos

C/F *Anemos*

Nomikos Lines; 1976; 1787 GRT.

This large, chunky, but comfortable ferry has been running this fantastic trans-Aegean route since 1989. Although each year has seen some slight variation to her itinerary the overall pattern has not changed much with two call-at-all sailings each end of the week sandwiching an express run to the popular southern Cycladic ports. Skyros and Syros are the ports that see some changes each summer — usually being missed on either the outward or return runs. Either end of the High Season the mid-week express run is dropped and the slower runs move days: departing from Thessalonika on Tuesdays and Thursdays (same times). The popularity of this boat should limit changes in 1995. Unusually for a large Greek domestic ferry you will probably have to buy tickets in advance for Thessalonika High Season departures as the entire city often seems to be aboard. During the Low Season the Thessalonika—Crete run is discontinued, with the *Anemos* running a skeleton Northern Aegean itinerary.

C/F *Lemnos* - C/F *Macedon*

Demand by local holiday-makers fleeing the delights of Thessalonika prompts several of the small Sporades chain boats to run up to the city in High Season. Both boats are on the small side; so at the height of the season they are likely to be booked solid when running south. The *Macedon*, recently refitted on coming into service, is by far the better of the pair.

Rafina—Kavala Ferries

The mainland ports of Rafina and Kavala have been connected for a number of years by a regular 'lifeline' ferry service that takes in the poorly connected islands of Agios Efstratios and Limnos (with occasional calls at Skyros as well). Of late, one ferry — the *Hellas Express* — took on the route, but she was sold in 1994 and two other ferries amended their itineraries

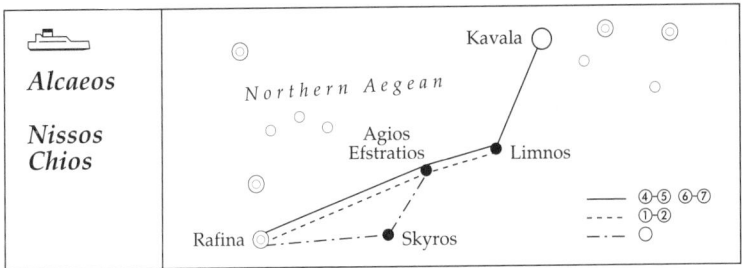

to fill the gap: the *Alcaeos* (see p. 300) and the *Nissos Chios* (see p. 300). Both adopted routes so bizarre that they are unlikely to go unaltered in 1995. Expect changes to both days and boats — though the thrice-weekly link is sure to continue. Athens newspapers (see p. 33) carry current times of Rafina and Kavala departures.

C/F *Lykomides*
Skyros Line; 1973; 1169 GRT.
A small car ferry operated by a one boat company, the *Lykomides* runs solely between the ports of Evia (Kimi) and Linaria on Skyros. A little-changing daily 'lifeline' service runs throughout the year, with a second and an occasional third trip in High Season. Reliability is good

and facilities are reasonable given the lack of competition. Athens buses link up with Kimi sailings (see p. 100).

H/F *Santa*
A solo hydrofoil, the *Santa* has operated a six times daily High Season service between mainland Kavala and Thassos Town since 1992. Popular with tourists and locals alike (she is much faster than taking a ferry to Skala Prinos and then a bus on to Thassos Town with only a 50p difference in the price), she makes additional Kavala day tripper runs to ports down the island's west coast. Operated as a bus service (unusually for a hydrofoil, tickets are bought on board). Other hydrofoils are expected on the route soon.

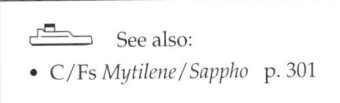

See also:
- C/Fs *Mytilene/Sappho*   p. 301

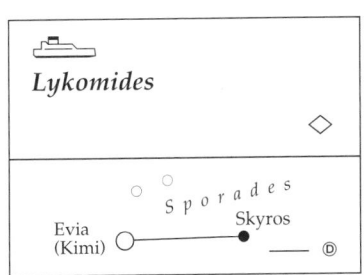

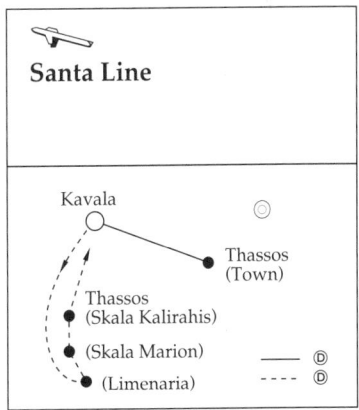

Thassos — Mainland Ferries

A service provided by nine landing-craft
car ferries. Most are run by the local
A.N.E.T. Line and are named along the
lines of *Thassos I*, *Thassos II* etc. Tickets are
bought from kiosks on the quayside. The
primary service is the 70-minute crossing
between Kavala and the Thassos port of
Skala Prinos. A 30-minute crossing between Thassos Town and Keramoti
attracts more vehicles. Reliability and
frequency (every 2 hours) of these boats
is good. Skala Prinos ferries also provide
a four times daily (mainly commercial
vehicle) service to the roadside hamlet of
Nea Peramos 20 km west of Kavala.

C/F *Arsinoe*

Local; 1980; 800 GRT.

Named after a temple on Samothrace,
this is the only ferry linking Samothrace
and Alexandroupolis with the rest of the
Greek ferry system. She has seen a steady
increase in the number of High Season
excursions to Kavala over the last few
years. A bit of an odd boat all around: for
a start tickets can't usually be bought on
board. Secondly, she retains one of those
— now so rare — traditional Greek
chapels on her sun deck. Thirdly, it is not
locked, but open to the passengers and
their prayers. Finally, the sinks in the
WCs are regularly polished with a Greek

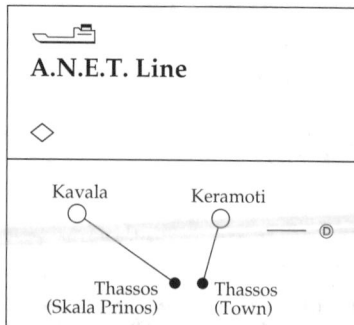

version of 'Flash': proving that even the
most wistful of prayers can occasionally
be answered in one.

C/F *Saos*

Local; 1964; 707 GRT.

One of those little car ferries now reduced
to eking out an existence in remoter
corners of the Aegean, this is one of the
tubbiest, smallest and oldest still running.
Operating a daily service from Alexandroupolis to Samothrace, she is worth
seeking out just for a peek at her antiquated appearance: distinguished by a
lack of portholes and the retention of
external staircases along her sides. She
has run an odd-ball, once-weekly, run to
Limnos in each of the last two summers.

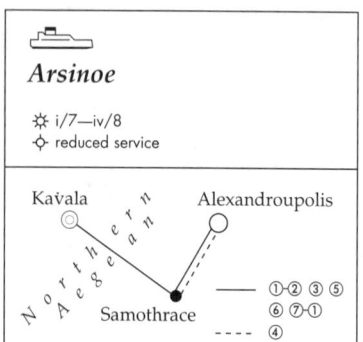

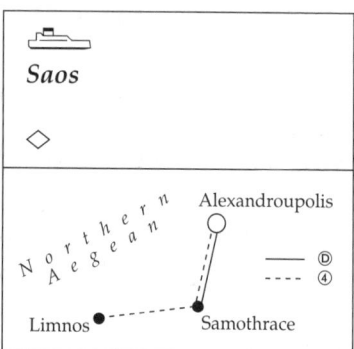

Northern Aegean Islands & Ports

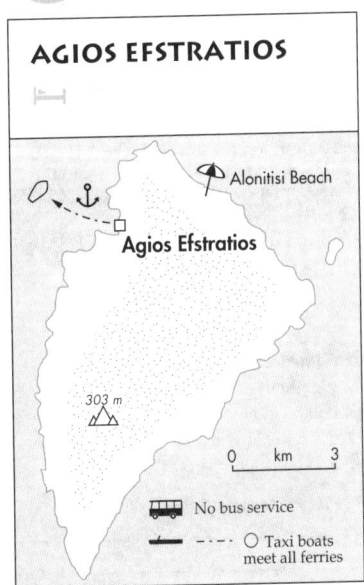

AGIOS EFSTRATIOS

Alonitisi Beach

Agios Efstratios

303 m

0   km   3

No bus service

---··· ○ Taxi boats
              meet all ferries

Agios Efstratios
ΑΓΙΟΣ ΕΥΣΤΡΑΤΙΟΣ; 43 km²; pop. 300.

A remote, sunbaked island with vegetation (mostly scrub and scattered oak trees) hidden away in the folds of the hills, Agios Efstratios sits like a drowned camel's hump to the south-west of Limnos (from where it is administered). Rarely visited by tourists, it offers close on the ultimate in 'get-away-from-it-all' experiences, and is one of the last islands without a deep water quay (blue and white taxi boats meet ferries off the port — when sea conditions are calm enough!). Used as a camp for some 5000 political prisoners during the 1930s, the island has never been popular. Any chance of its emerging as a tourist destination was effectively demolished in 1968 when an earthquake put paid to the picturesque houses of the

only settlement on the west coast. This in itself was unlucky enough, but unfortunately the military junta ruling Greece at the time decided to help out and sent the army to the rescue. Helpfully demolishing the damaged town, they rebuilt it with ugly concrete prefabricated buildings laid out in military formation. They also bulldozed the town beach beyond repair in the process. The islanders have been in mourning ever since.

Given the attractions of the town, most visitors take to hill walking. This does offer some consolation, for the island is criss-crossed with goat tracks that wander into hidden folds in the hills and down to deserted beaches. The best is a long strand of volcanic sand on the north coast.

Tourists are so few that despite there being only a couple of pensions/tavernas offering rooms there is rarely a shortage of facilities.

Agios Konstantinos
ΑΓΙΟΣ ΚΩΝΣΤΑΝΤΙΝΟΣ

Figuring larger on ferry schedules than in real life, this port is a distinct non-entity as a destination in its own right. Little more than a stopping point on the main road to Athens, four blocks deep and backing onto the mountains of Attica, there is scant reason to stay. Most visitors therefore take advantage of the Athens buses laid on to meet the *Flying Dolphins* hydrofoils (buy your bus ticket along with the hydrofoil ticket: 2000 GDR) or repair to the bus station (buses hourly to Athens) several blocks in from the quay.

Alexandroupolis
ΑΛΕΞΑΝΔΡΟΥΠΟΛΗ

A rather drab modern town on the northern Aegean coast redeemed only by a lively promenade decked with a lighthouse, Alexandroupolis is named after an obsure 19 c. king of Greece rather than

Alexander the Great (who renamed half the cities of Asia after himself during his campaigns). This fact eloquently sums the place up, and not even the annual July through August wine festival can dispel the 'okay, but not a great place' impression. On the plus side, this port is quite difficult to get to (thanks to its location near the Turkish border), and from a ferry point of view this is definitely the end of the line. No reason to come here apart from the daily boat to Samothrace. Most non-Greek tourists are just passing through via the seven Kavala buses a day and the Athens railway link.

🛏️

The wine festival produces considerable pressure on the limited accommodation available in High Season. The Tourist Office has lists of rooms in the town, but if you arrive after midday the only option likely to be open to you is an expensive (£25) US-style motel just off the waterfront 2 km west of the ferry quay. There are, however, a number of hotels in town worth a try first; the best bets being away from the waterfront. These include the D-class *Ledo* (☎ 28808) and *Majestic* (☎ 26444) and the C-class *Alex* (☎ 26302) and *Alkyon* (☎ 23593/5).

☎

CODE 0551, TOURIST OFFICE 24998, POLICE/TOURIST POLICE 26418.

Key

🅐 NTOG / EOT Information Office
🅑 Bus Station
🅒 Railway Station
🅓 Police Station
🅔 National Bank of Greece
🅕 Main Square (Platia Politechnou)

🅖 Cathedral / Ecclesiastic Art Museum
🅗 Lighthouse (built 1880)
🅘 Ferry Tickets
🅙 Road to Motel & Komotini
🅚 Road to Kipi & Turkey

1 Ferry / Hydrofoil Quay

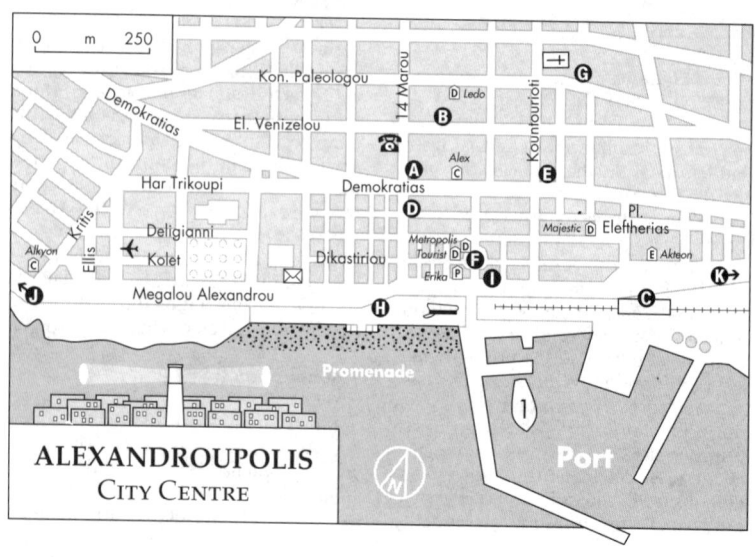

ALEXANDROUPOLIS
CITY CENTRE

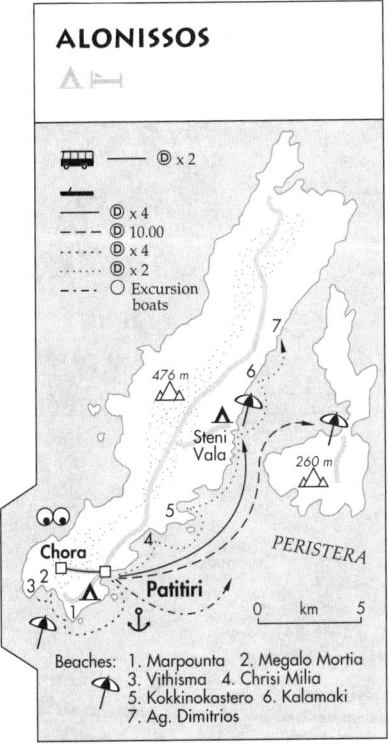

ALONISSOS

⊕ x 2

⊕ x 4
⊕ 10.00
⊕ x 4
⊕ x 2
○ Excursion boats

7

476 m

6

Steni
Vala

260 m

5

Chora

PERISTERA

3 2

Patitiri

0   km   5

Beaches: 1. Marpounta 2. Megalo Mortia
3. Vithisma 4. Chrisi Milia
5. Kokkinokastero 6. Kalamaki
7. Ag. Dimitrios

Alonissos

ΑΛΟΝΝΗΣΟΣ; 62 km²; pop. 1500.
The least populated of the regular Sporades, Alonissos is less green than its companions and has also suffered two major economic blows since the war with its vineyards wiped out in 1950 (prompting considerable depopulation as the islanders were forced to look elsewhere for a living) and a disastrous earthquake in 1965. Thanks to tourism, recovery is well under-way, and the island can get quite busy (for a 'quiet' island) at the height of the season. The fact that it is less touristed than its neighbours makes it appealing to increasing numbers of

visitors attracted by the quiet beaches (accessible only via a flotilla of caïques thanks to the impassable dirt track roads), the friendly islanders and the overwhelmingly cosy ambiance of the place. Given this, it is best to allow for extended stays here when planning your holiday.

The largest settlement is now the port of **Patitiri** as the former Chora is only now being reclaimed following the 1965 earthquake. After it struck, the military junta ruling Greece decided to 'abandon' the Chora and all but forced the islanders to resettle in the rebuilt port. Nestling in a delightfully piratesque cliff and taverna-decked cove the port has managed to retain plenty of atmosphere despite being rebuilt in concrete.

Other settlements on Alonissos remain tiny; the most substantial being at **Steni Vala** half way up the east coast, which boasts several tavernas, a shop of sorts and the official HQ of the Hellenic Society for the Protection of the Monk Seal (the islands to the north of Alonissos are home to some 20 pairs of a world population of under 900). Some island maps also show an airport in anticipation of the year 2020.

A good supply of well-signed rooms in the port augment 14 hotels (most in the port, but several in Votsi bay some 20 minutes walk to the north). Most are B and C category establishments and all are pricey. The most expensive is the B-class *Alkyon* (☎ 65450) above the port. At the bottom end of the range are the E-class *Ioulieta* (☎ 65463) and *Liadromia* (☎ 65521).

Two semi-official summer sites exist on the island — the most accessible lies just south of the port. The second, *Camping Ikaros* (☎ 65258) is at Steni Vala and is reached via taxi boats.

In addition to being a prime day-tripper destination in its own right (with its pirate cove port and deserted hill chora behind), Alonissos is also the springboard to a number of attractive satellite islets. The largest of these is **Peristera**; lying across a narrow strait off the east coast it is a popular beach destination.

Other islets can be visited but the onus is on you to arrange a boat. The two worth a look are **Gioura** (with yet another of those 1000 stalagmite caves with Cyclops legends attached), and **Piperi** — an official wildlife sanctuary due to monk seal breeding grounds. A visitor's permit is needed from the EOT in Athens should you want to land.

☎

CODE 0424.

Amoliani & Mt. Athos

Accessible via bus from Thessalonika, the island of Amoliani and the neighbouring Mt. Athos peninsula are well off the ferry lanes and thus tend to be the preserve of the mainland tourist rather than the island hopper. Amoliani island is about as far removed as you can get from the rest of the Greek ferry system, and really only on the hit lists of island hoppers determined to do every Greek island. The one hamlet offers a few rooms as well as dirt roads over the island to good beaches at Ftelis and Tsarki (also known as Alikes) bays. Passenger boats run from Tripiti, a quay on the Ouranopolis road. **Ouranopolis** is the last settlement before the 'border' that delimits Mt. Athos (the closed collection of medieval monasteries) from the rest of the world. The town is now a bit of a tourist trap, but does offer boat trips to the Dhenia islets offshore as well as along the coast of Mt. Athos. Most simply cruise along the coast, but each morning you will find one doing the 'provision' run, stopping at various monasteries en route to Dafni where the few males (females, both human and animal, are banned from Mt. Athos) with the almost impossibly hard to obtain permits to visit disembark. Tourist and provision boats also run down the east coast from Ierissos. Buses call at both, passing the scanty remains of the canal dug in 480 BC for the invading Persian fleet (en route to the Battle of Salamis) of King Xerxes (his abortive invasion of 491 BC having come to grief when his fleet was wrecked off the tip of Mt. Athos).

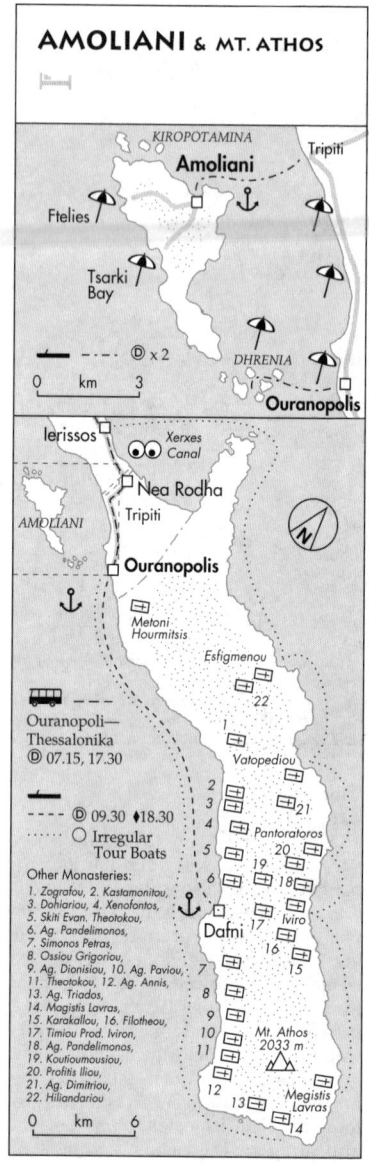

AMOLIANI & MT. ATHOS

KIROPOTAMINA
Amoliani
Tripiti
Ftelies
Tsarki Bay
⊕ x 2
0   km   3
DHRENIA
Ouranopolis

Ierissos
Xerxes Canal
Nea Rodha
AMOLIANI
Tripiti
Ouranopolis
Metoni Hourmitsis
Esfigmenou
22
Ouranopoli—Thessalonika
⊕ 07.15, 17.30
Vatopediou
2
3   21
---- ⊕ 09.30 ♦18.30
4   Pantoratoros
······ ○ Irregular Tour Boats
5   20
19
6   18
Other Monasteries:
1. Zografou, 2. Kastamonitou,
3. Dohiariou, 4. Xenofontos,
5. Skiti Evan. Theotokou,
6. Ag. Pandelimonos,
7. Simonos Petras,
8. Ossiou Grigoriou,
9. Ag. Dionisiou, 10. Ag. Paviou,
11. Theotoku, 12. Ag. Annis,
13. Ag. Triados,
14. Magistis Lavras,
15. Karakallou, 16. Filotheou,
17. Timiou Prod. Iviron,
18. Ag. Pandelimonos,
19. Koutioumousiou,
20. Profitis Iliou,
21. Ag. Dimitriou,
22. Hiliandariou
Iviro
Dafni   17
16   15
7
8
9
10   Mt. Athos
11   2033 m
12   Megistis
13   Lavras
14
0   km   6

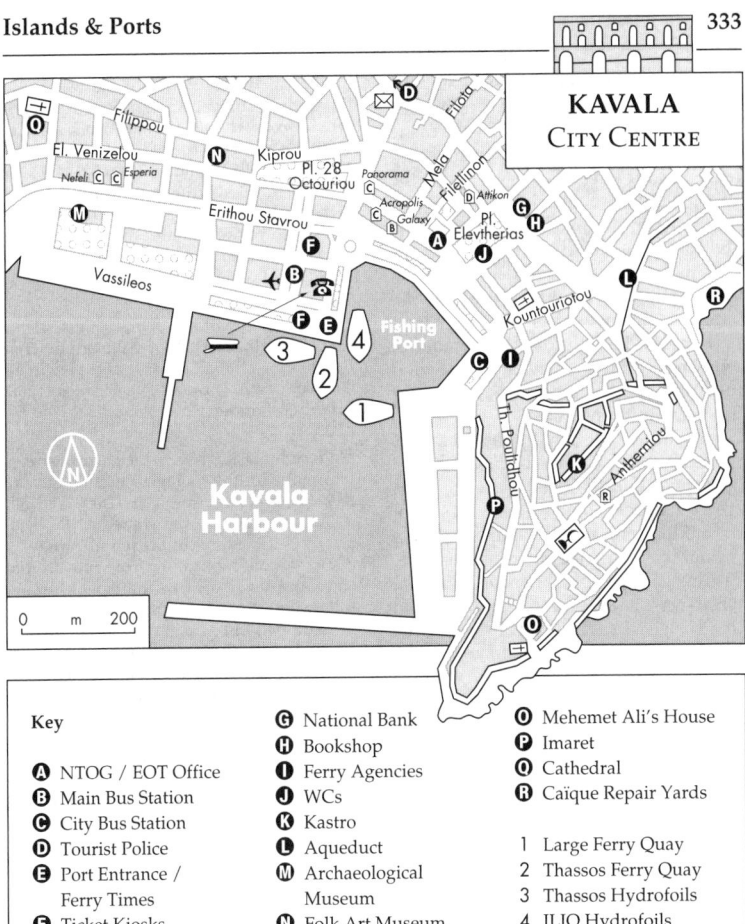

KAVALA
CITY CENTRE

Kavala Harbour

Fishing Port

0 m 200

Key

A NTOG / EOT Office
B Main Bus Station
C City Bus Station
D Tourist Police
E Port Entrance /
   Ferry Times
F Ticket Kiosks

G National Bank
H Bookshop
I Ferry Agencies
J WCs
K Kastro
L Aqueduct
M Archaeological
   Museum
N Folk Art Museum

O Mehemet Ali's House
P Imaret
Q Cathedral
R Caïque Repair Yards

1 Large Ferry Quay
2 Thassos Ferry Quay
3 Thassos Hydrofoils
4 ILIO Hydrofoils

Kavala
ΚΑΒΑΛΑ

If you exclude hydrofoils from the equation, Kavala (ancient Neapolis) is easily the premier port of the Northern Aegean, with good links to the otherwise unconnected islands of Thassos and Samothrace, and also — in High Season — the Athenian port of Rafina, the Dodecanese and Rhodes. If this wasn't reason enough to venture in this direction, the city itself is one of the nicest in Greece; set against a backdrop of rolling hills, it nestles snugly between their lower folds and the shoreline, with a picturesque old Turkish quarter topped with an imposing castle, an aqueduct and traditional caïque-building thrown in for good measure. Sadly, however, the strong tourist presence is very evident in local prices.

The city centre is surprisingly compact, dividing into two quarters. To the east lies the old town dominated by the castle set upon the building-clad promontory ringed by the old city wall (known as the Panagia Quarter). Outside the walls, the old town continues to the north under the arches of the delightful aqueduct that once took water to the castle. The inlet to the east is littered with boat-builder's yards. To the west lies the old fishing harbour. Still home to a fair number of working caïques, they sit somewhat incongruously against a backdrop of 'modern' buildings (and the ugly main city square — Pl. Elevtherios) that now make up the new town behind the very busy road that divides the two. Things are a bit more relaxed on the west side of the old harbour, with several reasonable restaurants with views over the castle backing onto a long promenade, complete with sun-bleached lawns and the odd tree for good measure. The rest of the new town isn't up to much, but has the merit of a reasonable scatter of shops (though supermarkets are thin on the ground) and a very busy bus station.

The absence of many competing ferry companies means that ticket agents are confined to three outlets on the quayside serving the large boats and ticket kiosks for the Thassos boats on the quay. Buy in advance if you can as it is much more common in this part of Greece to buy tickets before boarding. The main quay has ferry times up at the entrance gate kiosk (in Greek) and a procession of large landing-craft type car ferries and a hydrofoil heading for Thassos. The Samothrace ferry berths on the east side of the harbour under the castle walls.

⊨

A good NTOG/EOT office on the edge of Eleftheria Sq. has free city maps and will help you find where the one empty bed is to be located. Hotel accommodation is rather limited, and at the bottom end of the scale very poor; this is one city where it pays to look up-market a

bit. Within an easy walk of the waterfront there are a number of C-class establishments: the *Acropolis* (☎ 22 3643) and *Panorama* (☎ 22 4205) — both near the old harbour, and the *Esperia* (☎ 22 9621) and *Nefeli* (☎ 227441) near the museum. Best of the down-market options is the D-class *Attikon* (☎ 22 2257) a couple of blocks behind the EOT office. If you can afford to splash out then the waterfront B-class *Galaxy* (☎ 22 4521) is the best hotel in the centre.

▲

Nearest to the port is a poor, treeless NTOG site 3 km to the west. 5 km to the east lies *Irini Camping* (☎ 22 9776): a good trailer park grass site. Better still is the site on Thassos (Skala Prinos) a short ferry hop away.

∞

Main sights in Kavala are the maze of streets that make up the **Panagia Quarter** and the **Byzantine Kastro** (⊙ 10.00–17.00), the old quarter spanned by the **Aqueduct** (c. 1550) and an **Archaeological Museum** (home to a disparate collection culled from sites around Kavala). There is also a **Municipal Museum** full of the usual round of bric-a-brac dating from the early 19 c. on. If you have more than a day in Kavala then you should consider venturing 15 km north-east of the city to the remains of the ancient city of **Philippi**: the site of the battle in which Octavian (later the Emperor Augustus) defeated the murderers of Julius Caesar, Cassius and Brutus in 42 BC. Straddling the main road, the remains are substantial and include a well-preserved latrine (this is more than modern Kavala can boast). Buses run every ½ hour from Kavala.

☎

CITY CODE 051, POLICE 222905, NTOG/EOT OFFICE 222425.

Keramoti
ΚΕΡΑΜΩΤΗ

An isolated 'port' that owes its existence solely to the fact that it is the nearest point on the mainland to Thassos. Definitely not a foot passenger's destination, there is little more here than a quay, a quiet beach and a motor-park-style campsite. Package tourists often pass through via the landing craft ferries serving Thassos Town en route for Keramoti airport some 20 km to the north-west.

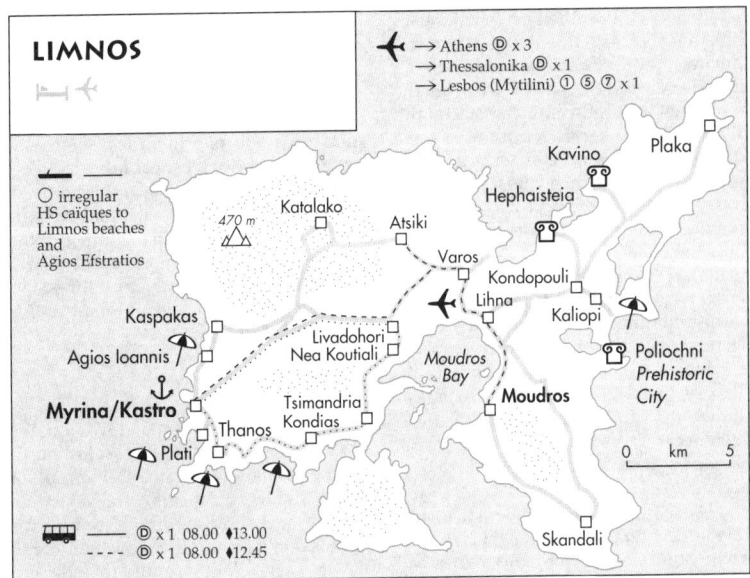

LIMNOS

→ Athens ⑩ x 3
→ Thessalonika ⑩ x 1
→ Lesbos (Mytilini) ① ⑤ ⑦ x 1

○ irregular
HS caïques to
Limnos beaches
and
Agios Efstratios

470 m

Katalako

Atsiki

Varos

Kavino

Plaka

Hephaisteia

Kondopouli

Lihna

Kaliopi

Kaspakas

Agios Ioannis

Livadohori
Nea Koutiali

Moudros
Bay

Poliochni
Prehistoric
City

Myrina/Kastro

Tsimandria
Kondias

Moudros

Thanos

Plati

0   km   5

⟬⟬⟬ ── ⑩ x 1 08.00 ♦13.00
    ---- ⑩ x 1 08.00 ♦12.45

Skandali

Limnos

ΛHMNOΣ; 477 km²; pop. 16,000.

The home of Hephaistos, the divine smith, Limnos (also commonly transcribed as 'Lemnos') is a fertile, volcanic island opposite the entrance to the Dardanelles — a strategic location that inevitably attracts a strong military presence. An accompanying lack of tourists (who are missing a lovely island) has ensured a continuation of the traditional island culture now sadly absent elsewhere. This, coupled with good beaches, very friendly islanders and an attractive (in a weird volcanic molehill, lumpy, sort of way) main port of Myrina, are all the more reason to visit. **Myrina** (also known as Kastro thanks to the floodlit castle built on the ancient acropolis) is very much the centre of island life and is a prosperous little working town with an interesting warren of backstreets leading off from the main street that snakes its way from the cute little square backing on to a small

caïque harbour near the constantly enlarging ferry quay, under the castle walls and then east into the suburbs. Lined with an odd mix of hardware shops, discos and men's clothing outlets (it is difficult to forget that Limnos has a large army garrison) it is very much the focus of town life. Either side of the castle are the town's sandy beaches; the one to the north being decidedly more up-market.

Limnos is a lovely island to visit if you have your own transport and very frustrating — given the almost non-existent bus service — if you haven't. The two halves of the island contrast greatly. The east side is flat and fertile, with two lakes adding to the oddly un-Greek landscape of cornfields and grazing cattle, while the west has a starker rocky volcanic terrain and the bulk of the best beaches. Apart from Myrina the only large settlement is at **Moudros** (the forward allied military base during the ill-fated Gallipoli campaign; thanks to the sheltered bay, it also safely housed the allied generals). Buses link the town with the capital, but unfortunately, the service is geared to moving islanders into Myrina for work in the mornings and returning them at night. With only two services offering a same day return to Myrina, buses are all but useless for tourism purposes. Short of hiring a moped, the best way to see the remote sites of interest on Limnos is to take the once-a-week bus excursion (on ⑦ in 1994). Ferry services are adequate in High Season and the island's role as a mini-junction for Rafina and Lesbos ferries results in the *Greek Travel Pages* carrying ferry departure information. Tourist maps of the Northern Aegean show a ferry link with Samothrace to the north-east. This hasn't operated in years, so expect to be disappointed.

�︎

No camping on the island as you are definitely off the tourist trail. In High Season a Tourist Police office is open in Myrina's town hall which will help you find a bed. This usually means directing you to one of the **Myrina** hotels (of which there is a reasonable selection). On the waterfront the D-class *Aktaion* (☎ 22258) and the C-class *Lemnos* (☎ 22153) are easily found and reasonable. Harder to find is the C-class *Sevdalis* (☎ 22691), which lies in a side street one block beyond the OTE square on the town's main street. More up-market establishments tend to lie near the beaches. These include the B-class *Paris* (☎ 23266) and the expensive *Kastro Beach* (☎ 22148) which lies at the east end of the town's north beach.

👓

Limnos was an important island during the Archaic period: the primary archaeological site at **Poliochni** predating Troy on the adjacent Turkish coast. Tours visit this rather confused site along with the site of the classical city at **Hephaisteia**, built on the spot where the god Hephaistos landed and lamed himself after Hera threw him from the summit of Mt. Olympus in a fit of 'peak'. The tangible remains include a temple to the god and an odeon.

☎

CODE 0254, TOURIST OFFICE 24110, PORT AUTHORITY 22225.

Marmaras
ΜΑΡΜΑΡΑΣ

A resort on the middle fork (known as Sithonia) of the Halkidiki peninsula, Marmaras (also called Nea Marmaras) is now on hydrofoil itineraries. An expensive resort with a reasonable beach, good bus links to Thessalonika and a campsite, the main incentive to visit is the boat tour along the coast offering a glimpse of the monasteries of Mt. Athos. For Marmaras is the easiest departure point for island hopper's wanting a look; the daily excursion costs £15.

Nea Moudania
ΝΕΑ ΜΟΥΔΙΑΝΑ

An over touristed small town on the Northern Aegean's west coast just north of the left hand fork (alias Cassandra) of the Halkidiki peninsula, Nea Moudania is the weekend getaway resort for Thessalonika, and now sees a number of hydrofoils calling en route to and from the Sporades. Beyond the crowded beach, some over-expensive hotels and a crowded campsite, it has very little to recommend it — unless you are in a hurry to continue onto Cassandra. Hourly buses to Thessalonika offer frequent means of escape.

Nea Peramos
ΝΕΑ ΠΕΡΑΜΟΣ

Unless you have a vehicle, this mainland port 15 km east of Kavala is not really a practical proposition given the 'inter-city' nature of local buses. However, host to several daily landing-craft ferries running to Thassos, it offers a short-cut to motorists arriving from or departing west. Set in a cosy, open-mouthed bay, this hamlet (complete with its own beach, kastro and campsite) is an infinitely more relaxing jumping off point to Thassos than Kavala. If you are prepared to stop overnight, Nea Peramos is worth considering as a quiet 'night-trip' destination for those staying on Thassos.

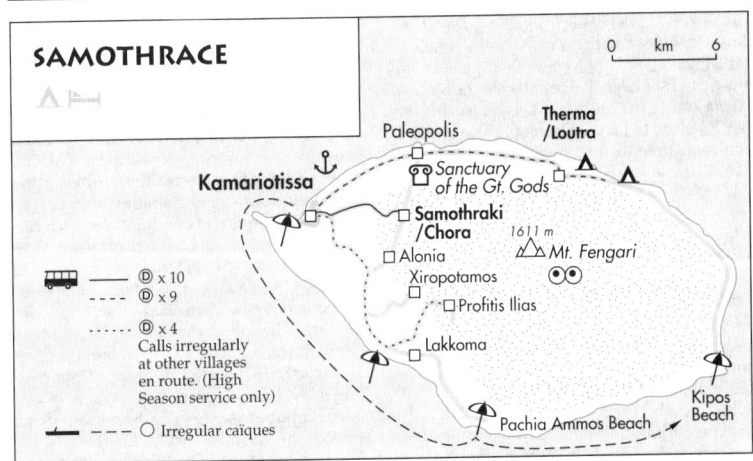

SAMOTHRACE

0   km   6

Paleopolis
Therma /Loutra
Kamariotissa
Sanctuary of the Gt. Gods
Samothraki /Chora
1611 m
Mt. Fengari
Alonia
Xiropotamos
Profitis Ilias
Lakkoma
Kipos Beach
Pachia Ammos Beach

Ⓓ x 10
Ⓓ x 9
Ⓓ x 4 Calls irregularly at other villages en route. (High Season service only)
Ⓞ Irregular caïques

Samothrace

ΣΑΜΟΘΡΑΚΗ; 178 km²; pop. 2800.

A dramatic heavily wooded mountain peak rising from the sea, Samothrace was an island of spiritual pilgrimage in the ancient world; partly one suspects because it was as difficult to get to then as it is now. First impressions of a comparatively bleak and mountainous island are enhanced by the almost apologetic way the main island town and port of **Kamariotissa** clings to the foreshore against a backdrop of undulating hills devoid of vegetation bar the odd wind-broken tree and stubbly cornfields. A couple of horribly modern electricity-generating windmills on the long western spur do nothing to relive the almost forbidding sense of isolation. This tends to do Samothrace something of a disservice for once ashore it is quite a friendly place. All the nightlife and essentials are to be found in the port along with most of the accommodation. For once on a Greek island, English is little spoken as most visitors are German or Scandinavians.

Almost all tourist activity is confined to the northern coast thanks to the impressive archaeological remains of the Sanctuary of the Great Gods at Paleopoli and the spa-village at Therma. Other island villages see few tourists. Buses run regularly to the whitewashed island capital at **Chora**; a jumble of whitewashed houses tucked comfortably out of sight in a fold in the foothills, it is devoid of hotels and all the other trappings of modern tourism and topped with the remains of a lovely castle. Equally attractive is the pretty hill village of **Profitis Ilias** (buses also head for here calling irregularly at other villages en route). Buses also run direct to the campsite via **Therma** (also known as Loutra). As the name implies, this is a spa resort of sorts and now the main tourist centre on the island, though trees out-number tourists for the greater part of the year. Not really a beach island, Samothrace does have two excellent examples that are sadly only accessible by dirt track or irregular caïque on the south coast at Pachia Ammos and delightfully remote Kipos.

Rooms, pensions and hotels are scattered thinly between the port, Paleopolis, Therma and Chora. Low numbers of visitors means low prices. At the **Port** you will find, at the eastern end of the waterfront, the C-class *Niki Beach* (☎ 41561), with the pricey B-class Aeolis (☎ 41595) close by, along with a pension — the *Kyma* (☎ 41268). **Paleopolis** has the B-class *Xenia* (☎ 41230) and the C-class *Kastro* (☎ 41850) close to hand. **Therma** is also blessed with a couple of reasonable establishments: the B-class *Kaviros* (☎ 41577) and the C-class *Mariva* (☎ 41759).

▲

There are two High Season only sites on the north coast: *Camping Loutra* (☎ 41784), a poor site 3 km east of Therma. *Multilary Camping* (☎ 41759) is a much better site 2 km further on.

◌◌

Samothrace offers two great attractions: the most obvious being **Mt. Fengari** (the 'Mountain of the Moon'). Used by Poseidon as a seat while he observed the Trojan war, mortals seeking serious hill walking (via Therma) find that when they get to the summit after a day's climb that the ground is still warm.

The **Sanctuary of the Great Gods** at Paleopolis sees far more visitors. The remains of one of Greece's premier places of pilgrimage (the first historian, Heroditos was initiated into the rites, and Alexander the Great's parents met and fell in love here), it is sadly diminished, but is located in a marvellous woody ravine setting that more than makes up for the limited remains. The sanctuary was pre-Greek in origin, being originally dedicated to the Great Mother Earth goddess Axieros and a fertility god, Kadmilos. The Greeks quickly conflated these figures with their own Demeter and Hermes and so kept local traditions going for the best part of a millennium. What those traditions were is still something of a mystery. Ancient writers were loath to mention them thanks to the belief in shadowy demon figures (known as the Kabeiroi) who were thought to harbour implacable wrath towards any that divulged the sanctuary's secrets. However, it is known that anyone could be initiated into the sanctuary's mysteries and that the torch-lit night-time ceremony had two stages (the first involving purification, the second, initiation into the rites). Despite earthquakes and the odd pirate attack the sanctuary (politically independent throughout its life) was only abandoned with the formal adoption of Christianity by the Roman Empire, and most of the important buildings were rebuilt several times during the course of their working life.

Access to the site today is via a footpath running inland from the main coast road. Walking past the hotel and the museum along the path running parallel with the central ravine stream, on your right you will see the remains of ❶ the **Milesian Building** (so called because of an inscription associated with it), and behind it ❷ the remains of a **Byzantine Fort** built from stones from the sanctuary.

The most important buildings were all located on the 'island' of land bounded by the (usually dry) streams running down the ravines. Crossing the stream brings you to ❸; the rotund **Arsinoeion** was also an important structure though of much later date. Built c. 285 BC, it was the largest circular building ever constructed by the ancient Greeks. Commissioned by Queen Arsinoe of Thrace, it was used for public sacrifice. To the north is ❹ the **Anaktoron** (also known as the 'Hall of the Lords'); it was one of the oldest buildings on the site, being in continuous use from the 6 C. BC to the 4 C. AD. It was used for the first stage of the initiation rites. In the Roman period a robing room, (❺ the **Sacristy**) was added to the building when it was substantially rebuilt.

Turn south of the Arsinoeion and you come to ❻ the **Temenos** (an open air precinct with a ceremonial entrance on the north-east side), and ❼ the **Hieron**. Now the most prominent building on the site thanks to the columns re-erected in 1956, the temple was the location for the second stage of the initiation. The remains of spectator seating line the interior walls. On its west side lie the scanty foundations of ❽ the **Hall of Votive Gifts** (c. 540 BC), little evident now, but important in that it survived for close on a thousand years without rebuilding. Next door is the much better preserved **Altar Court** at ❾, dedicated by a half-brother of Alexander the Great. The path now crosses a culvert that ran under the theatre stage. ❿, the site of the **Theatre** is now just a tree-covered depression and barely recognisable as almost all the seats were removed for the construction of later fortifications.

Once you have passed the theatre, the paths divide. The eastern path wanders over the stream and a hill (that was home to ⓫ the **South Necropolis**) before coming to the substantial foundations of ⓬ the **Propylon of Ptolemy II**, a formal gateway constructed for the use of the local townspeople (the ancient capital — Paleopolis proper — stood to the

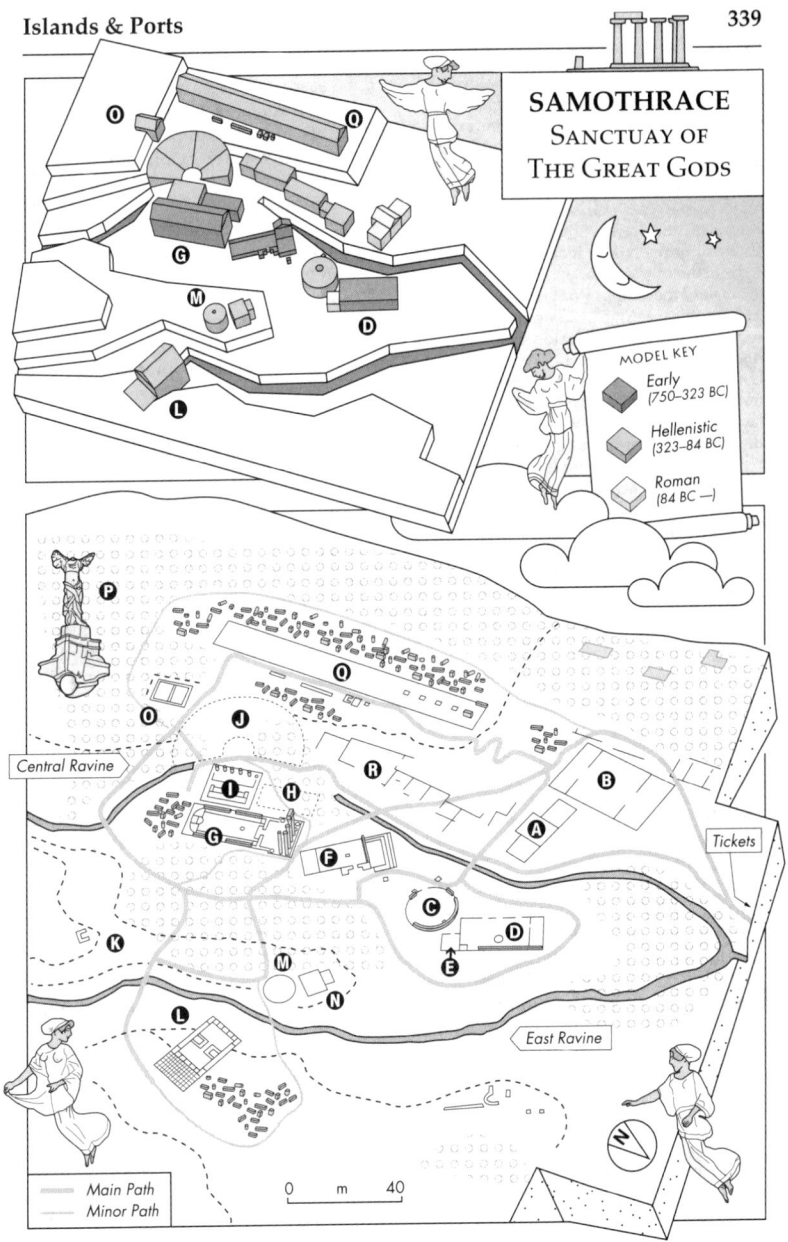

SAMOTHRACE
SANCTUAY OF
THE GREAT GODS

MODEL KEY

Early
(750–323 BC)

Hellenistic
(323–84 BC)

Roman
(84 BC —)

Central Ravine

Tickets

East Ravine

Main Path
Minor Path

0   m   40

east of the sanctuary). When originally built it had the stream channelled to emerge through it. On the west side of that stream are two rather obscure buildings: **Ⓜ** a **Circular Building** and **Ⓝ** a **Doric Structure** dedicated by Phillip III and Alexander IV.

The western path turns west up the hillside behind the theatre, bringing you to the foundations of **Ⓞ** the **Nike niche**: a small building cut into the hillside that was built specifically to house **Ⓟ** the famous **Winged Nike (Victory) of Samothrace**. Made of Parian marble, this sculpture is the site's greatest archaeological find, and (bar the missing head) is now in the Louvre. It takes the form of an 'angel' standing on the prow of a ship. The Nike niche was in fact a fountain house, and the prow stood in a double-level floor basin filled with water.

From the Nike building the path continues up the hill to the higher level behind the theatre and **Ⓞ** a **Stoa**. Plenty of fragments of this large structure lie scattered around but nobody has yet found the time to reassemble them. Between the stoa and the central ravine stream at **Ⓡ** lie scanty remains of **Hellenistic Buildings** (purpose unknown). Finally, returning to the main path you come back to the **museum**; well laid out and worth a visit; though the most important sculpture found on the site is now in French and Austrian museums.

☎

CODE 0551, POLICE 41203, FERRY INFORMATION 26721.

Skiathos

ΣΚΙΑΘΟΣ; 61 km²; pop. 4900.

The mini-Corfu of the Aegean, Skiathos is the most attractive and touristed island in the Sporades — thanks to a combination of a delightful pine-clad landscape, excellent sand beaches, good ferry links and a heavily used charter flight airport. Unfortunately, the cosy 'ideal family holiday' atmosphere is now under siege in High Season thanks to the sheer number of visitors (it is particularly popular with up-market British package tourists and Italians of all descriptions), with the result that those in the know mark Skiathos down as one of the best Greek islands going for spring/early summer visits and a spot to be avoided during the height of

the season. That said, even with the crowds it remains a friendly place, and there are plenty of quieter spots you can escape to if you are so minded.

As with many of the smaller Greek islands Skiathos has one substantial settlement and no other major centres. Considering how many tourists pass through, Skiathos Town weathers the storm remarkably well. Set in a islet littered bay, it is a picturesque mixture of red tile roofs, white buildings and bell towers. The crowds that throng the narrow streets have had a major impact, but fortunately, this has taken the form of boutiques, patisseries and bars rather than neon lights and discos. The restaurant-lined waterfront also adds greatly to the cosmopolitan ambiance of the town; complete with beach boats tied up in the old harbour, wooded Bourtzi islet, and assorted portrait painters, sponge sellers and street entertainers (to say nothing of campaigners protecting the endangered monk seals that breed in this part of the world) it is ideal for interesting evening promenades. The downside to all this are restaurant and bar prices — which are very expensive compared to most islands. Most of the facilities are to be found within easy distance of the waterfront or along the main town artery (Papadiamantis St.) along with pharmacies, a reasonable supermarket and the main sight in town: the house of the island's most famous son; a 19 C. poet by the name of — yes, you guessed it — Papadiamantis.

Almost all the large package tour hotels lie outside the town, strung irregularly, like so many octopi out to dry, along the sheltered southern coast. This isn't as depressing as it sounds as the coast is a mix of headlands thickly wooded with umbrella pines and small bays hosting a number of golden sand beaches; the hotels are almost lost amidst this attractive jumble. The south coast road (the only one made up on the island) is naturally very busy, but at least it is almost impossible

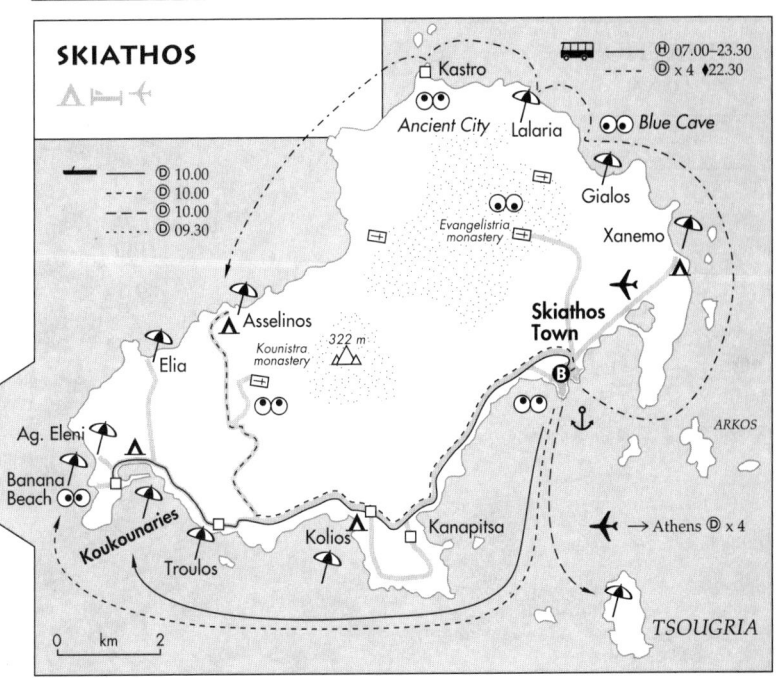

SKIATHOS

Kastro

⌖ 07.00–23.30
⌖ x 4 ♦22.30

Ancient City   Lalaria

Blue Cave

⌖ 10.00
⌖ 10.00
⌖ 10.00
⌖ 09.30

Gialos

Evangelistria
monastery

Xanemo

**Skiathos
Town**

Asselinos

Kounistra
monastery   322 m

Elia

ARKOS

Ag. Eleni

Banana
Beach

Koukounaries

Kolios   Kanapitsa

→ Athens ⌖ x 4

Troulos

TSOUGRIA

0   km   2

to get lost, and there are frequent bus stops and taxis along its length. The primary destinations lie at each end; in the evenings everyone is heading for Skiathos Town, while in the mornings the big draw is **Koukounaries** beach; a long crescent-shaped stretch of sand filled with bodies of various hues and sporting a lagoon of sorts with yet more umbrella pines behind it. A short walk away is quieter **Banana** Beach — reputedly the best naturist beach in the Mediterranean, most of the bananas on display tend to be middle-aged and Italian.

The north coast is very quiet, without hotels or settlements of note, thanks to a lack of roads and the strong winds that turn the beaches into a beachcomber's paradise. In fact, the only easily accessible point is at **Asselinos** (via the camping

buses that brave the dusty woodland track past the odd stud farm to a blissfully quiet and verdant little valley only let down by a rather tatty beach. Equally underdeveloped is the wooded interior of the island which is popular with hikers and those who have found the frequent, but horribly overcrowd, bus service too much to cope with. The east coast is similarly the preserve of those looking for a quiet life; the one blot on their happiness being the island airport which is so close to the main road that the road is closed every time a flight leaves. There is a poor beach and campsite at **Xanemo**, but you will have to recourse to beach boats if you want to do better. **Lalaria** on the northeast corner is the best bet; a very picturesque tapering pebble beach at the base of a cliff, it is more Beachy foot than head.

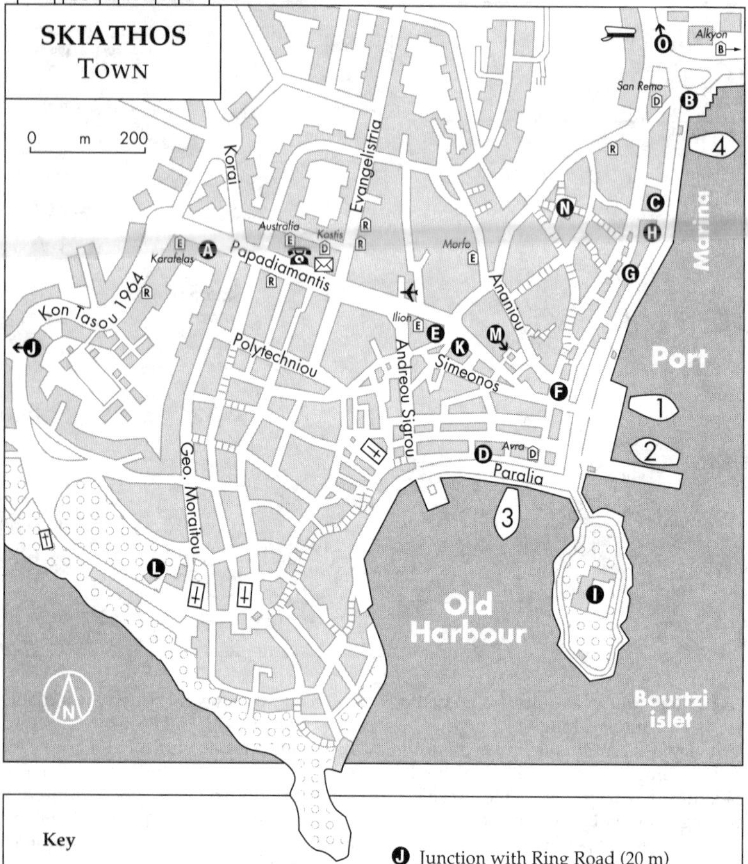

SKIATHOS TOWN

0   m   200

San Remo **ⒹⒷ**

Alkyon **Ⓑ**

Ⓞ

④

Marina

Ⓝ **Ⓒ**
Ⓗ

Australia
Karafelas **Ⓔ** **Ⓐ** Marfo **Ⓔ**
Papadiamantis Kostis **Ⓓ**
Ⓡ **Ⓡ**
Ⓡ Anamiou **Ⓖ**

Kon Tasou 1964 **Ⓡ**

←Ⓙ

Polytechniou

Ilioti
Ⓔ **Ⓚ**
Ⓜ
Simeonos
Ⓕ

Port

①

②

Andreou Sigrou

Geo. Moraitou

Ayra **Ⓓ**
Ⓓ
Paralia

③

Ⓛ

Old Harbour

Ⓞ

Ⓝ

Bourtzi islet

Key

- **Ⓐ** Police Station
- **Ⓑ** Bus Station
- **Ⓒ** Asselinos Bus / Moped Car Rental
- **Ⓓ** Newspapers & Books
- **Ⓔ** National Bank of Greece
- **Ⓕ** Nomikos Lines Ticket Office
- **Ⓖ** C/F *Papadiamantis* Ticket Office
- **Ⓗ** *Flying Dolphin* Ticket Office
- **Ⓘ** Site of Old Kastro (replaced with school: now abandoned)

- **Ⓙ** Junction with Ring Road (20 m)
- **Ⓚ** Pharmacy
- **Ⓛ** Hospital
- **Ⓜ** Papadiamantis House Museum
- **Ⓝ** Spyglass Church with Campanile
- **Ⓞ** Town Ring Road to all destinations

1 Ferry Quay
2 Hydrofoil Berth
3 Tourist & Beach Boat Quay
4 East Coast Beach Boat Quay

⊨

Rooms can be very hard to come by in High Season; you might have to rough it a bit on your first night. A quayside kiosk just north of the ferry quay has been built to offer accommodation advice. Offers of rooms made when getting off the boat are not to be ignored. Hotels there are aplenty on Skiathos. Most are block-booked by package tour operators. Seeking out untaken up rooms is an option, though you will find almost all the A to C class hotels are well out of town bar the B-class *Alkyon* (☎ 22981) on the airport road. Within Skiathos Town there are a number of budget establishments. D-class hotels are the poor *Avra* just off the waterfront, the *San Remo* (☎ 22078) at the other end of the harbour and the *Kostis* (☎ 22909) behind the post office. E-class hotels are mostly to be found on or near Papadiamantis St. These include the *Ilion* (☎ 21193), the *Morfo* (☎ 21737), the *Australia* (☎ 22488) and the *Karafelas* (☎ 21236).

Λ

There are four sites on Skiathos: nearest to the port is a municipal campsite at Xanemo. Under the airport flight path, it does a roaring trade but attracts few campers. The newest site is at *Koukounaries Camping* (☎ 49290) and is easily the best for the beach of the same name and buses to Skiathos Town. If camping in green pastures (with nought but fellow camper's nocturnal impressions of the birds and the bees to distract you) is more to your taste, then laid-back *Asselinos Camping* (☎ 49312) is to be recommended (served by orange buses; tickets from the travel agent near the bus pick-up point). Unfortunately, this cannot be said of *Camping Kolios* (☎ 49249), a very poor site that takes full advantage of its roadside position between the beaches and Skiathos town to prey on the unwary.

👓

Skiathos Town is the island's main attraction. The only 'sight' as such is the well-preserved turn-of-the-century home of the poet **Alexandros Papadiamantis**. A sort of Greek Lord Tennyson without the title, you will find a simple islander's homestead likely to appeal to minimalists and creaky floorboard fans. Unfortunately, this poet had as few possessions as his fellow islanders and the house reflects this wonderfully. Most tourists visit at least once a day if only to pick up the daily tour boats heading on to Skopelos and Alo-

nissos, the beach boats (most heading for Koukounaries, Banana and a beach on the adjacent islet of **Tsougria**), or the anticlockwise island boat tour.

The island boat tour also stops briefly at the **Blue Cave**, a sea cave on the east coast, and at **Kastro**, site of the medieval centre of the island until it was abandoned in the last century after piracy was no longer a threat to the islanders' security. Set on an all but impregnable headland, it is now a picturesque ruin of houses, streets and churches (a couple of which are still kept in good order).

Tourist excursions also run to two monasteries: **Kounistra** to the west (for the view) and to **Evangelistria** (a popular donkey ride destination north of Skiathos Town, famed throughout Greece as the place where the Greek flag was first raised in 1807 by a group of conspiring independents).

☎

CODE 0427, TOURIST POLICE 21111, FIRST AID / HOSPITAL 22040.

Skopelos

ΣΚΟΠΕΛΟΣ; 96 km²; pop. 4700.

The largest island in the Sporades group, Skopelos has less sparkle than neighbouring Skiathos. The beaches are not as good (most are pebble), there is less sightseeing, and the main town has far less going on. Even so, it is a very nice island — covered in pine forests and (thanks to flatter terrain) more agriculture as well. With the easy links to the airport on Skiathos, Skopelos has seen a dramatic rise in tourism as package tour operators have moved in; promoting the island as an ideal quiet family-holiday destination. Independent travellers are far less visible, but their numbers are growing as the appeal of Skiathos wanes, and many are apt to rank it ahead of Skiathos thanks to its more relaxed, laid-back atmosphere.

The main settlement is **Skopelos Town**, set in a deep bay on the northern coast. This is something of a disadvantage as, lying on the exposed side of the island, ferry and hydrofoil services can be subject to disruption. On windy days these, and other tourist boats, are often diverted to a small inlet quay at **Agnontas** on the sheltered south side (free buses into town are laid on in this event). Skopelos Town has retained much of its whitewashed traditional appearance despite being badly damaged in the 1965 earthquake that put paid to the Chora on neighbouring Alonissos. The town rises from a tree-lined waterfront steeply up the hillside to the west of the bay. It also has a crowded sand beach running the width of the bay offering ringside views of the procession of docking hydrofoils and ferries. Once you start wandering around the steeply stepped backstreets (reputably home to some 120 churches) you soon leave the trappings of tourism aside. At the top you will find meagre remains of a Venetian kastro and a view across the bay to the monastery clad hillside opposite.

Given that there is only one metalled road and a good bus service (the Skopelos Town bus stop is located at the end of the tree-lined harbour promenade by the town beach), visiting the rest of the island is very straightforward. Most of the bus stops are at beach hamlets. **Stafilos** offers the overcrowded main island beach, **Panormos** (windsurfing and unofficial camping) and **Milia** (a quiet beach). Buses run on to **Elios** (the nearest thing Skopelos possesses to a resort village) then **Klima** (an abandoned one — after the 1965 earthquake) before arriving at the island's second major settlement of **Glossa**. Quite a large village, it is perched idyllically on a hillside 3 km above the small port of **Loutraki**. Relatively untouristed, Glossa attracts a few devotees and more ferries. Note: be careful when reading timetables in Skopelos Town — they sometimes also list Glossa departures (indicated by the Greek ΓΛΟ after the time) amidst those of Skopelos Town as not all ferries call at both. Elsewhere on the island, caïques run to otherwise inaccessible, but attractive, beaches at Glisteri from Skopelos Town and to Limnonari from Agnontas.

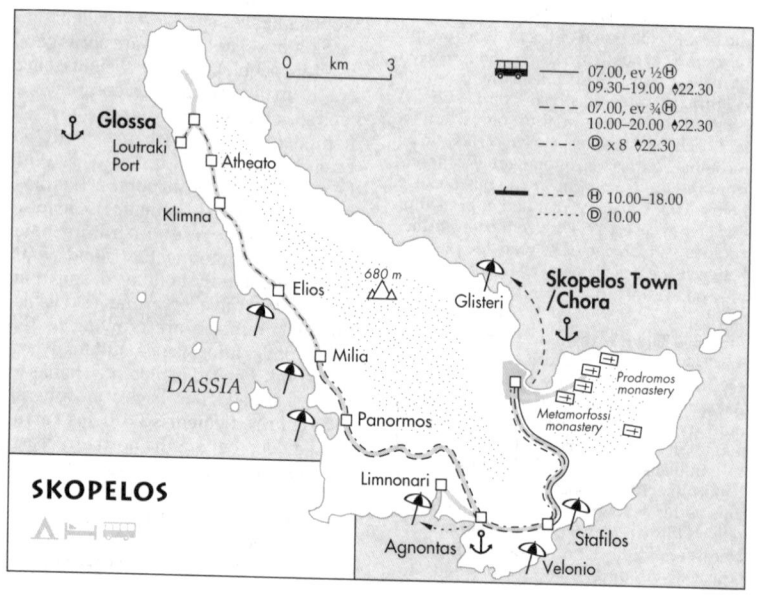

⊨

Plenty of rooms in **Skopelos Town** (a kiosk on the ferry quay offers information). Hotel beds are also reasonably plentiful. Most of the most conveniently placed establishments are within striking distance of the ferry quay. The most prominent of these is the pricy C-class *Delfini* (☎ 23015), but nearby you will find the D-class *Eleni* (☎ 22393), the *Amalias* (☎ 000 00) and the E-class *Stella* (☎ 22081) and *Rania* (☎ 22486). **Glossa** also has some rooms on offer, as well as a hotel: the C-class *Avra* (☎ 33550).

Λ

There are no official campsites, but freelance camping is tolerated at Velonio (the unofficial nudist beach), and at Panormos beach; now the recognised 'camping strip' on Skopelos.

👓

The town and beaches are the main attractions; sightseeing comes in a poor third. **Skopelos Town** has a tiny **Folk Art Museum** hidden away in the backstreets, and that is just about it. Coach trips around the island are quite popular, and usually take in at least one of the island monasteries. Three of these open their doors to visitors, **Prodromos** and **Evangelismou** (both dating from the 18 c. and now occupied by nuns) and 16 c. **Metamorfossi** (now uninhabited; so you can be a bit more uninhibited when it comes to observing the dress code). In addition, tour boats operate daily out of Skopelos Town to Alonissos and Skiathos. Ticket Agencies also offer day coach trips to Athens for a day of quickie sightseeing (albeit at a price).

☎

CODE 0424, POLICE 22235,
FIRST AID/HOSPITAL 22220.

Skyros

ΣΚΥΡΟΣ; 208 km²; pop. 2900.
A gem of an island to the east of Evia, Skyros offers an appealing mix of one of the best Cycladic-style choras and a history laced with everything from transvestism and a Greek Excalibur to pirates and poets. The weak spots that have prevented it emerging as a major tourist destination are the limited number of good beaches and the fact that it is too far from regular ferry routes (out of High Season links with other islands are non-existent).

The main settlement of **Skyros Town** lies hidden from view from the sea in the folds of a hill on the east side of the island — a 20-minute bus ride from the west coast port hamlet of **Linaria**. This desire for seclusion was prompted by the piracy of the 16 and 17 c., but did not prevent 'Three Entrance Bay' at the southern end of the island becoming a notorious Pirate Lair. During the Heroic Age the warrior Achilles had much the same hideaway idea with equally little success; for foreseeing his death at Troy, he hid on Skyros disguised as a girl only to let his frock slip when Odysseus (offering a particularly heroic sword for sale) discovered him and dragged him by the heel to its date with destiny (see p. 409). Surprisingly, there is nothing commemorating this event in the town. Instead, you will find a bronze of another poetic warrior who died with a sore point — Rupert Brooke, the First World War poet who came off worse in a fight with a mosquito, dying unheroically here of his wound in 1915, en route to Gallipoli. If he sauntered around the island wearing as little as his statue it is not surprising that he was smitten and, all things considered, was lucky not to share the fate of the third notable to come a cropper here — the hero Theseus who was thrown over a cliff onto a nudist beach by the then king of Skyros, Lykomides. These days the townsfolk are much more friendly, in part because the chora has managed to retain much of its unspoilt charm thanks to the bulk of the island accommodation being located a bus ride away on the beach. The chora — a car free zone — is dominated by the castle and the main street which winds up the hill towards it, and is particularly appealing in the evenings when the streets are thronged with gossiping locals. It is, however, often quite windy.

Rupert Brooke's grave aside, the rest of the island is little visited by tourists: most visitors to Skyros confine themselves to

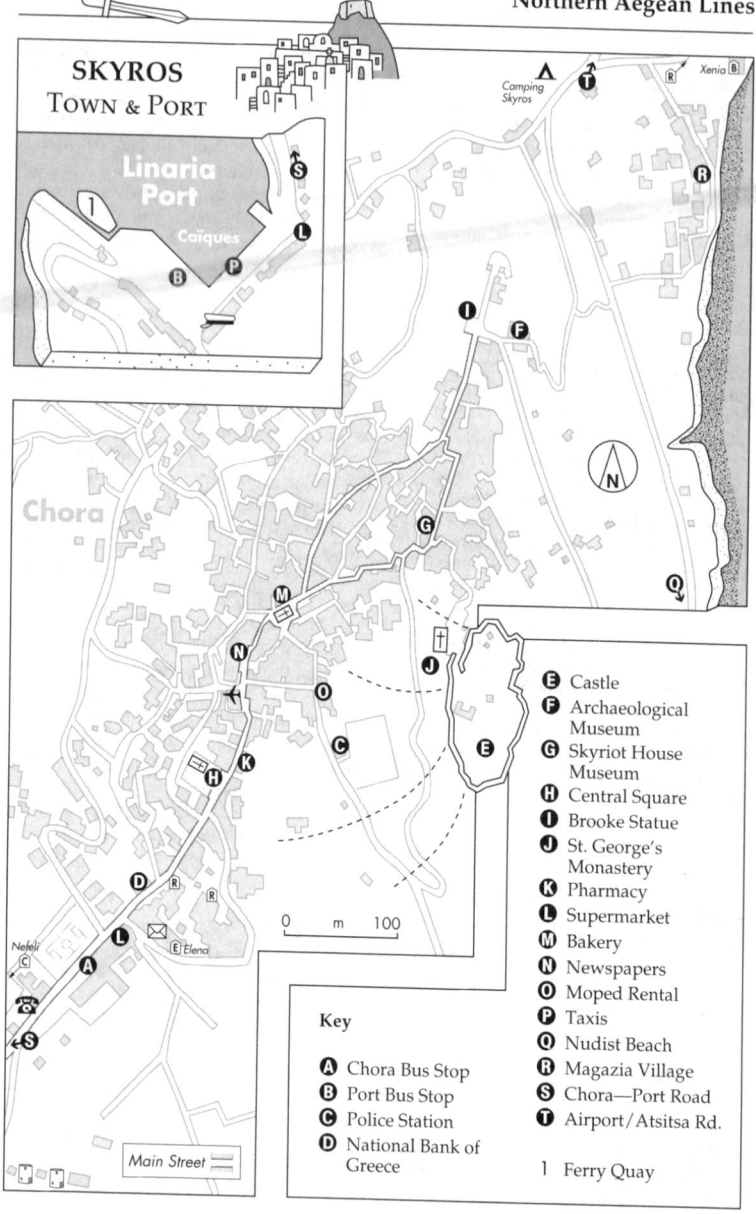

SKYROS
TOWN & PORT

Linaria Port

Caïques

Chora

Camping Skyros

Xenia **B**

N

E Castle
F Archaeological Museum
G Skyriot House Museum
H Central Square
I Brooke Statue
J St. George's Monastery
K Pharmacy
L Supermarket
M Bakery
N Newspapers
O Moped Rental
P Taxis
Q Nudist Beach
R Magazia Village
S Chora—Port Road
T Airport/Atsitsa Rd.

Nefeli

Elena

0   m   100

Key

A Chora Bus Stop
B Port Bus Stop
C Police Station
D National Bank of Greece

1 Ferry Quay

Main Street

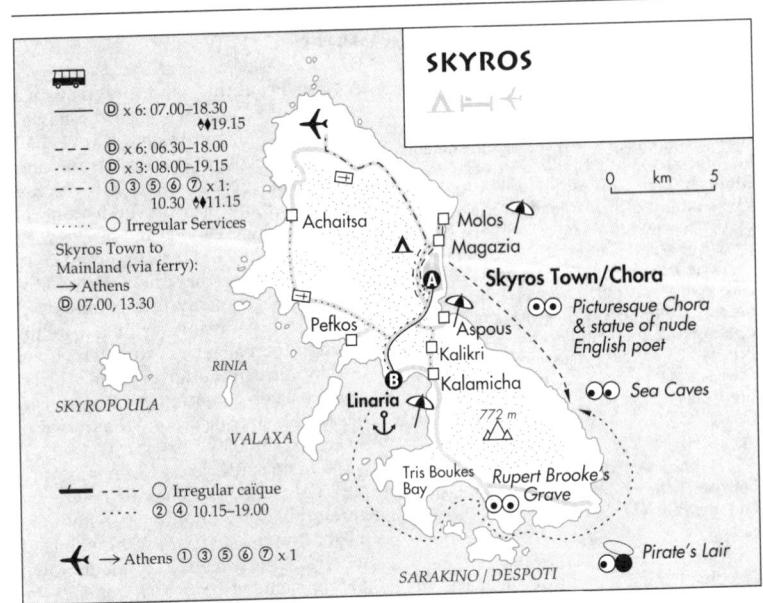

the chora and the relatively new beach villages of **Magazia** and **Molos** (the island bus service isn't geared to getting tourists anywhere else). Those hiring their own transport to explore further will find the expense well worth it. The southern half of Skyros is mountainous, the north flatter and more fertile, and the whole delightfully unspoiled and well wooded with pine trees (making this excellent hill walking country).

The island has attracted considerable media attention thanks to a 'holistic holiday community' that has established itself at Achaitsa (or Atsitsa) on the north-west coast. Offering mind/body/spirit courses for those asking questions like 'Where am I going?', 'What do I need in my life?' or 'What is stopping me from being who I really am?' (the London NTOG can supply a brochure full of this stuff — and to do this 'community' justice most people who go on these courses return swearing by them) they have taken over Achaitsa

bay, and have a centre in the chora, but otherwise have had no impact on the island — beyond leaving the locals asking 'Why us?' First someone comes along and erects a bronze nude of a poet they have never heard of right in the middle of town (at a time when most chaste village maidens wouldn't have known what a poet's lyric metre was, still less seen one), and now they have ranks of middle management types in mid-life crises skinny dipping in between 'painting the soulscape' and asking 'Where am I going?' On Skyros, this question at least, is easy to answer as ferry connections are such that there is rarely much choice. The island has its own ferry — the *Lykomides* — that runs to and from the Evian port of Kimi (some 5 hours by bus from Athens). High Season sees daily hydrofoils running down from the Sporades (though they are often full of day-trippers on the outward leg and you could have difficulty getting a seat north if you haven't booked).

⊨

There is a reasonable supply of rooms on Skyros spread between the town and the beach villages of Magazia and Molos. Hotels are thin on the ground and rather pricey; though the island is worth it. The best establishments are also in the beach villages to the north. **Molos** has the new A-class *Skyros Palace* (☎ 91994) on the beach (a large apartment complex on the beach with its own pool), the B-class *Angela* (☎ 91764), and the new C-class *Paradissos* (☎ 91220). Closer to the town lies the B-class *Xenia* (☎ 91209), a lovely hotel on the beach under the kastro at **Magazia**. Hotel options in Chora are much more limited; your best bets being the C-class *Nefeli* (☎ 91964) on the road just before you enter the town and the E-class *Elena* (☎ 91738) behind the Post Office.

Δ

Skyros Camping (☎ 92458): quiet field site between the beach and the chora hill. Adequate and inexpensive.

◑◑

The **Chora**, with its traditional Skyriot houses and blue and white 'Delftware' pottery is the main attraction on the island. The streets are so narrow vehicles are confined to the outskirts. The town climbs to an impressive **Venetian Kastro** of Byzantine origin with fantastic views over the town and island as well as housing a small **Archaeological Museum**. Below the castle walls is the **Monastery of St. George**. The chora also has a folk museum in the form of a traditional house (known as the **Faltaits Museum**) decked out with examples of the island wares (though most of the town houses retain the fittings and platters that give the museum its atmosphere).

The grave of **Rupert** ('If I should die, think only this of me: That there's some corner of a foreign field that is forever England') **Brooke** is set under a small grove of olive trees in the **Pirate Bay** on the south of Skyros, and is the premier destination of tourist caïques (which occasionally also visit the pirate base — once one of the largest in the Aegean — of **Despot's Island**) and island bus tours (easily the most accessible way of seeing Skyros. The east coast cave was also a **Pirate Grotto** in its heyday.

☎

CODE 0222, POLICE 91274,
FIRST AID 92222.

Thassos

ΘΑΣΟΣ; 398 km²; pop. 16,000.

A large, beautiful island tucked against the northern Aegean seaboard, Thassos is mountainous and green, with over half of its surface covered with cedar, oak and pine forests (now criss-crossed with fire gaps to keep any forest fires under control) and fringed with good sand beaches. As a result the island has emerged as a popular (if somewhat pricy) north European package-holiday destination as well as attracting caravaners willing to motor through the Balkans. Fortunately, hotel development, although evident, is by no means over-conspicuous thanks to reasonable spacing around the attractive 95 km coastline.

The main settlement at **Limenas** (also popularly known as **Thassos Town**) lies in a large bay on the north coast — offering the shortest crossing point to the mainland (12 km). A pleasant mix of modern town and ancient city ruins, it reflects the island's history as a quietly prosperous state during the ancient period (its wealth generated by gold and silver mines and marble quarrying). With a scatter of later Turkish houses, infilled with modern (invariably tourist related) buildings, the town is probably akin to what Kos Town would have looked like today if both Crusaders and Italians had not come a-building. Even the presence of tourist outlets and discos accompanying the holidaymakers fails to diminish the appealing relaxed atmosphere.

Activity naturally centres on the waterfront, which is surprisingly diverse with three distinct zones: the ferry quay (home to most of the services and shops), the ancient harbour (base for tour and beach boats, starting point for town tours, and offering leafy night-time waterfront promenades), and the popular town beach (backed by restaurants and tavernas). The leafy streets behind are thinly lined with buildings that are rarely more than one deep.

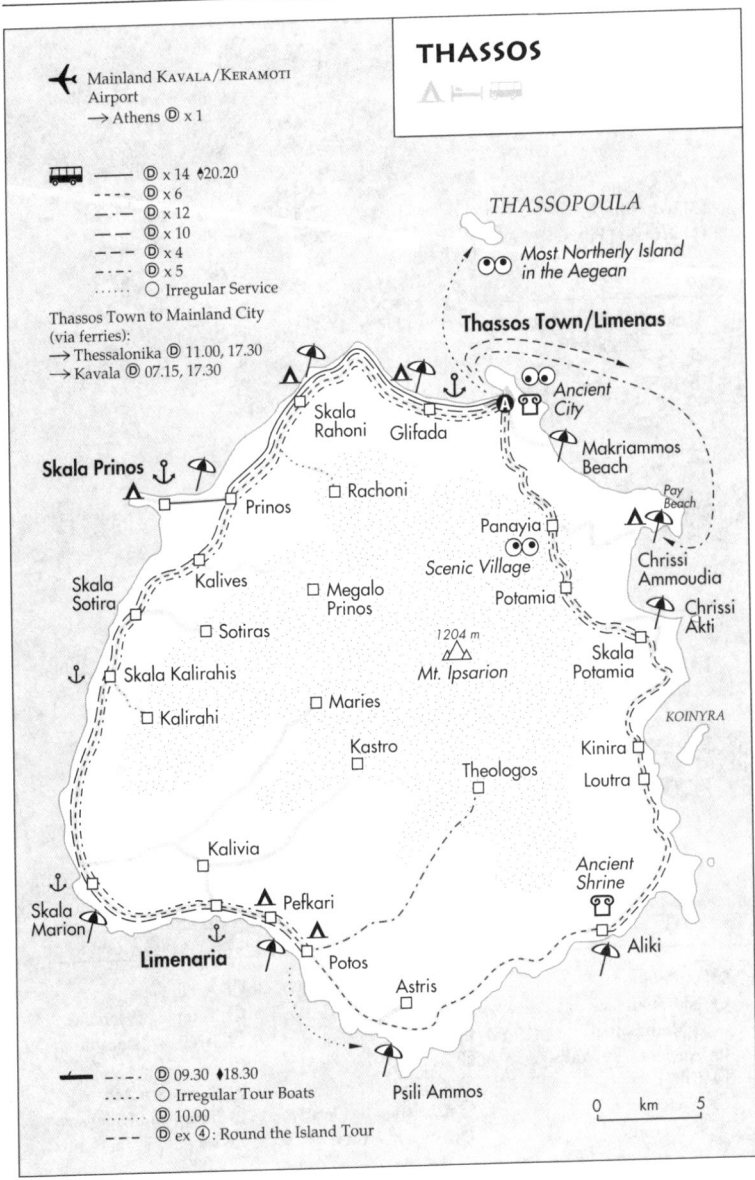

THASSOS

Mainland KAVALA/KERAMOTI
Airport
→ Athens Ⓓ x 1

——— Ⓓ x 14 ⬧20.20
- - - Ⓓ x 6
-·-·- Ⓓ x 12
— — Ⓓ x 10
- - - Ⓓ x 4
-··-··- Ⓓ x 5
········· ○ Irregular Service

Thassos Town to Mainland City
(via ferries):
→ Thessalonika Ⓓ 11.00, 17.30
→ Kavala Ⓓ 07.15, 17.30

THASSOPOULA

Most Northerly Island
in the Aegean

Thassos Town/Limenas

Ancient
City

Makriammos
Beach

Skala
Rahoni   Glifada

Skala Prinos ⚓

Pay
Beach

Prinos   Rachoni

Panayia

Chrissi
Ammoudia

Scenic Village

Skala
Sotira

Kalives

Megalo
Prinos   Potamia

Chrissi
Akti

Sotiras

1204 m

Skala
Potamia

Skala Kalirahis   Mt. Ipsarion

KOINYRA

Kalirahi   Maries

Kastro   Kinira

Theologos   Loutra

Kalivia

Ancient
Shrine

Skala
Marion   Pefkari

Limenaria   Potos   Aliki

Astris

—·-·- Ⓓ 09.30 ⬧18.30
········· ○ Irregular Tour Boats
········· Ⓓ 10.00
— — Ⓓ ex ④ : Round the Island Tour

Psili Ammos

0   km   5

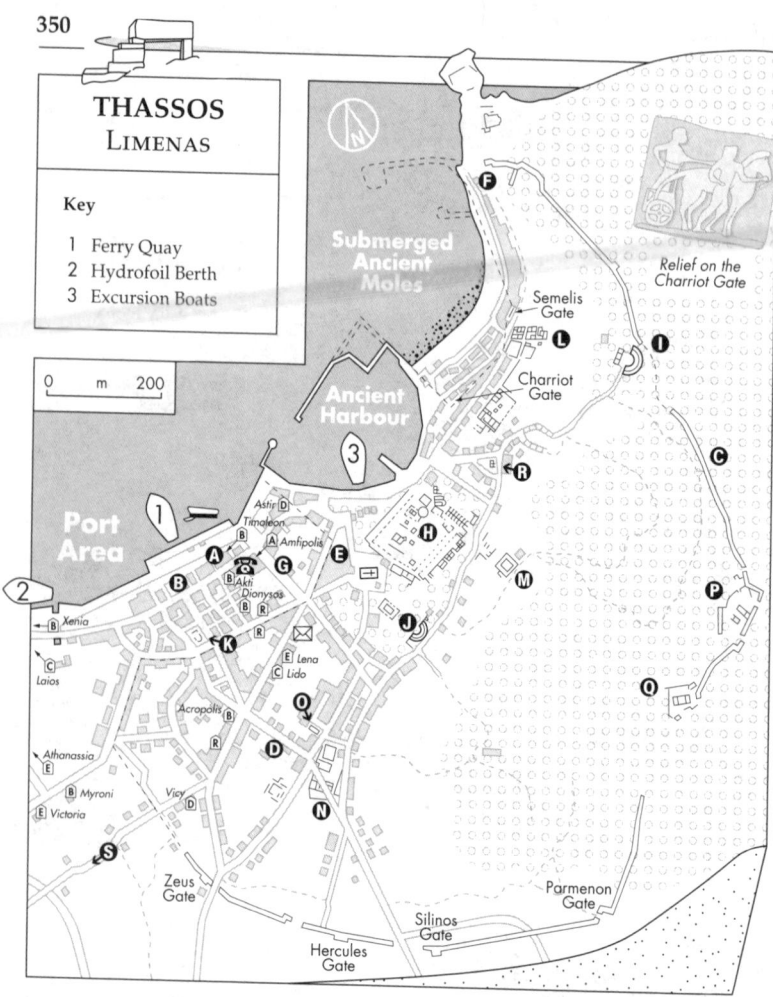

THASSOS
LIMENAS

Key

1 Ferry Quay
2 Hydrofoil Berth
3 Excursion Boats

0   m   200

Port Area

Submerged Ancient Moles

Ancient Harbour

Relief on the Charriot Gate

Semelis Gate

Charriot Gate

Astir
Timaleon
Amfipolis
Akti Dionysos
Xenia
Laios
Athanassia
Myroni
Vicy
Victoria
Acropolis
Lena
Lido

Zeus Gate

Silinos Gate

Hercules Gate

Parmenon Gate

- **A** Bus Station / Police
- **B** National Bank of Greece / Main Square
- **C** Ancient City Walls
- **D** Clinic
- **E** Archaeological Museum
- **F** WCs
- **G** Newspapers
- **H** Agora
- **I** Theatre
- **J** Odeon
- **K** Christian Basilica
- **L** Ancient Houses
- **M** Artemision
- **N** Temple of Hercules
- **O** Arch of Caracalla
- **P** Acropolis
- **Q** Temple of Athena
- **R** Temple of Dionysos
- **S** Road to Skala Prinos

Movement around Thassos is dominated by the coast road that runs in a rough circuit around the island. Most buses travel in an anticlockwise direction to connect with the main port of **Skala Prinos** perched on an east coast spit: a tourist dominated hamlet, but with more going for it than many Greek ports. South of Skala Prinos the west coast is fairly quiet with the bulk of the island's low-key agriculture and scattered beach villages until it reaches **Limenaria** on the south coast. The island's main resort and the only other large town, it is largely a product of the mining industry in the early years of this century; though this fact is somewhat misleading as the only dark holes these days are provided by the local discos. These exist in numbers, as if trying to compensate for the damaged landscape around the town: this southern part of the coast is the most spoilt part of Thassos thanks to extensive forest fire damage in recent years. Those in search of scenery will do better to head on to neighbouring resort villages of **Pefkari** and **Potos**.

The beach at **Makriammos** aside, the east coast of Thassos is the best on offer. More scenic (the road deviates from the coast to take in the lovely mountain villages of **Panayia** and **Potamia**; the latter a popular tour destination in consequence) it runs down to the picture-postcard village of **Aliki** and, arguably the most attractive part of the island; the long golden sand pine-backed beach running from **Kinira** to **Psili Ammos**.

🛏

Thassos Town is the best place to stay on the island. Rooms are around but are never plentiful in High Season. You shouldn't ignore offers on disembarking. There are also a wide range of hotels in Thassos Town, most behind the ferry quay. Prices are generally higher than average, and the balance of accommodation is towards the upper end of the range. At the top is the A-class *Amfipolis* (☎ 23101). B-class hotels include *Xenia* (☎ 71270) and the pensions *Acropolis* (☎ 22488), *Myroni* (☎ 23256),

Akti (☎ 22326) and *Dionysos* (☎ 22198). C-class hotels are confined to the *Lido* (☎ 22929) and *Laios* (☎ 22309). At the bottom end of the range are the D-class *Astir* (☎ 22160), and E-class *Victoria* (☎ 22556), *Lena* (☎ 22793) and *Athanassia* (☎ 22545).

Δ

There are several sites at Skala Prinos including a good NTOG / EOT site: *Camping Prinos* (☎ 71171) 700 m west of the ferry quay. Of the other sites around the island, *Camping Ioannidis* (☎ 71477) at Skala Rahoni is also worth considering. Even better is south coast *Pefkari Camping* (☎ 51190) and east coast *Chryssi Ammoudia Camping* (☎ 61207).

👓

Thassos Town offers an easy day's sightseeing, along with a readily accessible beach. Ancient remains are scattered liberally around the town, though in almost every case nothing but foundations survive. Most obvious of these is the **Agora**, which backs onto the ancient harbour and houses the remains of a couple of Roman stoas, a tholos and several monumental altars. Nearby is a well-stocked **Archaeological Museum**. To the south lies a small **Odeon** fronted by a tiny remnant (50 m) of a paved **Hellenistic street**. This would have led to the triumphal **Arch of Caracalla** when both were in their prime. The latter is now reduced to some impressively large foundations. Other survivals consist mainly of temples to assorted gods along with a well-preserved **Theatre** (used for performances each summer) hidden in the woodland north of the Agora.

Perhaps the most impressive feature of the ancient town are the well preserved 4 C. BC **City Walls**, these are largely complete along with city gates that each take their name from the Archaic reliefs carved on them. Walking the (now wooded) circuit, finding and identifying each gate in turn is a great way of escaping for a day. Another alternative is one of the irregular boats running to **Thassopoula** — a desolate rock bedecked with scrub vegetation and a solitary lighthouse. Buses around the scenic coast road are also popular. Tourists make for the east coast villages of **Panayia** and **Aliki** (the latter offering the remains of a small Doric shrine and ancient marble quarries).

☎

CODE 0593, TOURIST POLICE 22500, FIRST AID 22190.

Thessalonika
ΘΕΣΣΑΛΟΝΙΚΗ

The second city of Greece, Thessalonika (often abbreviated to plain 'Salonika') commands attention as an important bus and rail junction, but the city has to work hard to keep the many tourists passing through. With a population approaching half a million, along with all the smog, crowds and concrete of the capital Athens — but without the mitigating grace of an Acropolis complex — Thessalonika has limited appeal unless you are prepared to venture well away from the waterfront.

Founded in 316 BC by the Macedonian commander Cassander (husband of Alexander the Great's half-sister), the city, unlike most other important centres in Greece, was never a major city state in its own right (hence the lack of classical antiquities), instead, ideally placed on the trade route between the Levant and the Balkans, it has thrived as a major staging post from the Roman era (when it became the capital of the province of Macedonia) to the present day. Its history, therefore, is one of repeated changes in ruler as the warring powers in the region through the centuries have fought to secure its strategic position; leaving a legacy of impressive Byzantine churches and an even more spectacular city wall. Poets and philosophers are conspicuous by their absence: Thessalonika just wasn't their sort of town. Trade has always been the order of the day and with it came waves of immigrants (notably 1492 when 20,000 Spanish Jews settled in the city, and 1923; when Greeks emigrating from Turkey arrived in numbers).

The last hundred years have not been particularly kind to the city. Victim of a devastating fire in 1917 (which resulted in the waterfront and commercial centre being totally destroyed and then reconstructed on a grid system, with only the odd rebuilt church or ancient monument poking incongruously amid the new buildings giving a reminder of the city of old), Thessalonika saw its commercial stuffing all but knocked out during World War Two when the occupying German forces deported the large Jewish population to the death camps. This was followed by a major earthquake in 1978 that inflicted considerable damage to the rich legacy of Byzantine churches (many only recently rebuilt after the fire). These three events have combined to take much of the zip out of the city's step, and the pervading down-town atmosphere is one of utilitarian commercialism; this is all rather a pity given that this city is often the first port of call for visitors to Greece — courtesy of its position on the main railway line to Europe. Even so, while this isn't Greece at its best, there is certainly enough sightseeing to fill a couple of leisurely days. If you are looking for something more, then you would be better advised to move on, for although the city has a fairly active nightlife, beaches and bathing are two non-starters: tucked up in the Thermaic Gulf, the seas hereabouts are not as clean as they might be.

No matter how you arrive in the city, the easiest way of getting your bearings is to head for the waterfront. The helpful NTOG/EOT office located mid-way along the promenade have free city maps. Though finding your way around the centre is easy enough provided you stick to the main streets. Most of the sights are to be found in the north and eastern sections of the city. The former (just to the north of the area shown on the map opposite) includes the well-preserved city walls and the only part of the pre-1917 town to survive the flames. Now known as the Kastra district, it is an atmospheric maze of tiny streets more reminiscent of a Turkish town and offers a considerable contrast with the bland wide boulevards (albeit fairly leafy ones) running between the large city squares of the rebuilt centre.

As befits a major city, bus links are good all year round, though the bus stations are poorly marked, hard to find and are

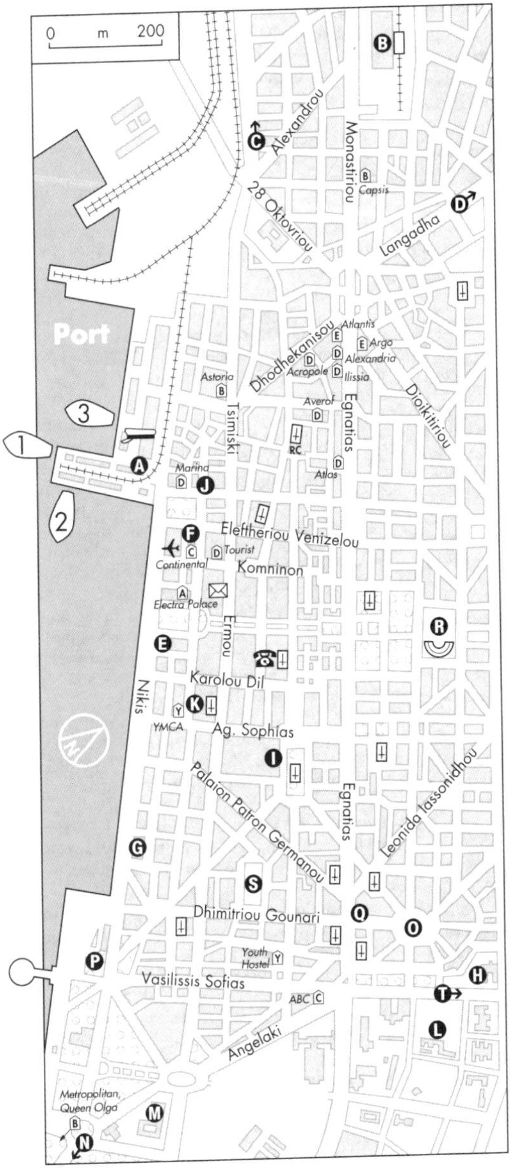

0 m 200

Port

3

1

2

Key

Ⓐ Port Entrance /
   Customs Building

Ⓑ Railway Station
   (all destinations)

Ⓒ Main Bus Station:
   Athens & West
   (700 m)

Ⓓ Bus Station:
   Kavala & East
   (1 km)

Ⓔ NTOG / EOT Office

Ⓕ British Consulate

Ⓖ US Consulate

Ⓗ Hospital

Ⓘ Tourist Police

Ⓙ Banks

Ⓚ Cathedral

Ⓛ University

Ⓜ Archaeological
   Museum

Ⓝ Folk Museum
   (800 m)

Ⓞ Rotunda
   (Ag. Georgios)

Ⓟ White Tower

Ⓠ Arch of Galerius

Ⓡ Roman Agora

Ⓢ Palace of Galerius

Ⓣ Acropolis & City
   Walls (500 m)

1 Domestic Ferries

2 International Ferries

3 Hydrofoil Berth

Alexandrou

Monastiriou

28 Oktovriou

Langadha

Ⓑ Capsis

Atlantis

Dhodhekanisou

Ⓔ Argo

Ⓔ Alexandria

Acropole

Ⓓ Ilissia

Astoria

Dioikitiriou

Averof

Tsimiski

Egnatias

RC

Atlas

Marina

Ⓓ Ⓙ

Ⓐ

Eleftheriou Venizelou

Ⓕ Ⓒ

Continental

Ⓓ Tourist

Komninon

Electra Palace

Ⓔ

Ermou

Nikis

Karolou Dil

Ⓚ Ⓨ

YMCA

Ag. Sophias

Ⓘ

Palaion Patron Germanou

Ⓡ

Egnatias

Leonida Iassonidhou

Ⓖ

Ⓢ

Dhimitriou Gounari

Ⓠ

Ⓞ

Youth
Hostel Ⓨ

Vasilissis Sofias

ABC Ⓒ

Ⓟ

Ⓣ

Ⓗ

Angelaki

Ⓛ

Metropolitan,
Queen Olga

Ⓜ

Ⓑ

Ⓝ

best reached via taxi. However, Thessalonika is not well served by ferries; though island hoppers can justify a visit by virtue of those boats (admittedly often booked solid) that do run. Thessalonika is a little-known jumping off point for the islands, and a preferable alternative to an uncomfortable night train-bound to Athens. Those prepared to pay and in the know can happily get into the Sporades: ferries and hydrofoils run down to Skiathos most days of the week. These services, however, only exist in High Season.

⊨

As the nearest camping is 25 km away at Agia Triada (via a #72 or #73 bus) most budget travellers head for the hotels near the railway station; these include the D-class, *Alexandria* (☎ 536185) and the *Ilisia* (☎ 528492). All tend to get filled to bursting and at the height of the season you will do better nearer the port. Both the D-class *Marina* (☎ 538917), and the C-class *Continental* (☎ 277563) offer reasonable rooms. To the east lies the expensive A-class *Electra Palace* (☎ 232221). There is also a *Youth Hostel* (☎ 225946) at 44 Alex. Svolou St.

👓

If you only have a short time in Thessalonika then you should abandon all other sightseeing for the **Archaeological Museum**. Housing the contents of Phillip II of Macedon's (Alexander the Great's father) tomb at Vergina (closed to tourists) it contains a collection of art and goldware not to be missed, including the gold casket decorated with the star of Macedon in which Phillip's partially cremated bones were interred. They are now laid out near the casket. The museum has gained, in both prominence and the number of visitors, from the dispute over the use of the name Macedon by the former Yugoslav republic to the north. Phillip II's remains are seen as irrefutable proof that 'Macedonia is Greek'; in this respect the Greeks do have a point as the population of ancient Macedon were Greek speakers (albeit regarded by the sophisticates of Athens and main stream Greece as quaintly accented provincial cousins) and not Slavs.

The city's main sights all lie to the south-east of the port/railway station area and can be divided into ancient and Byzantine / medieval categories. Most impressive in the former cate-

gory is the excellently preserved **Rotunda**: an intact Roman building dating back to 306 AD. Having served as everything from a museum to a mosque (the surviving abandoned minaret is very conspicuous), it is now the university church of Agios Georgios, but is usually closed to tourists. Other ancient remains are more fragmentary but more accessible. The **Arch of Galerius** (303 AD) is the best preserved of them, and was erected to celebrate the Roman Emperor's victory over the Persians at Armenia and Mesopotamia. It is decorated with reliefs depicting the battles. Galerius also built a **Palace** in the city but only foundations of this, the Roman **Agora** and **Hippodrome**, are extant and there is little on public display.

The great architectural jewels in Thessalonika's crown are the Byzantine churches dotted around the city and the Medieval fortifications. Most famous of the churches is the rather plain looking **St. Demetrius** standing near the Agora (it lies over the remains of the Roman city baths). Noted for its fine mosaics, it was badly damaged in the 1917 fire, and the current building is a copy in all but name. More substantive (and venerable) are the largely intact **City Walls** to the north of the down-town area. Originally they extended east as far as the **White Tower**. Otherwise known as 'Lefkos Pirgos', this is a medieval construction built on older foundations, and now the nearest the city has to an identifiable emblem. Used for executions during Turkish rule it was christened the 'Bloody tower' by the locals after the sultan imprisoned and massacred his rebelling personal bodyguards here in 1826. The sultan took umbrage at the burgers' new name for his little home from home and painted the tower white by way of a response. It is now open to tourists, and contains a **Byzantine Museum** that is put to shame by the city views available from the top of the tower.

Provided you have your passport to hand you can also get into the least publicised of the city's attractions. This is the home of the founder of modern Turkey, **Kemal Attaturk**, who was born in Thessalonika in 1881. Now maintained by the Turkish government, and guaranteed to be closed whenever Greco-Turkish tensions run high, the house lies east of the Kastra district, on Apostolou St.

☎

CODE 031, TOURIST POLICE 544162, NTOG OFFICE 263112, POLICE 100.

Volos
ΒΟΛΟΣ

The number four city of Greece, Volos (or Bolos) is set deep in a bay north of Evia, and is the mainland jumping-off point for the Northern Sporades island chain. Long an important port, the modern town lies atop the ancient city of Iolkos, home of Jason the Argonaut, from whence he set out in search of, and returned with, the mythical Golden Fleece. Sadly, there is little to show of this pastoral ancestry these days — except the ugly appearance of a city that looks as if it ought to be the sort of place which manufactures sheep dip. As a result, most visitors just pass through, being either day-trippers from the islands or Athens-based groups 'doing a Greek island' or using the town as a jumping off point for the very attractive oak-wooded Mount Pelion peninsula rising up behind. This popular tourist attraction (hence the helpful NTOG tourist office in Volos town centre) was home to the half-men, half-horse Centaurs that have long since hoofed it from the city-clad foothills to quieter parts, despite the existence of a good Archaeological Museum on Volos's bustling waterfront. The means of getting away are very good; with a dozen buses a day to Athens as well as a rail link to Larissa. Ferry connections with the Sporades are good all year, though other sea connections (including the uninspiring fishing hamlet-clad islet of **Trikeri** to the south) are less consistent.

⊢⊣

Both the D-class *Iassson* (☎ 26075) and E-class *Europa* (☎ 23624), just off the ferry quay, provide indifferent rooms that serve in a pinch. Private room availability is very poor.

☎

CODE 0421, PORT POLICE 38888, NTOG OFFICE 23500.

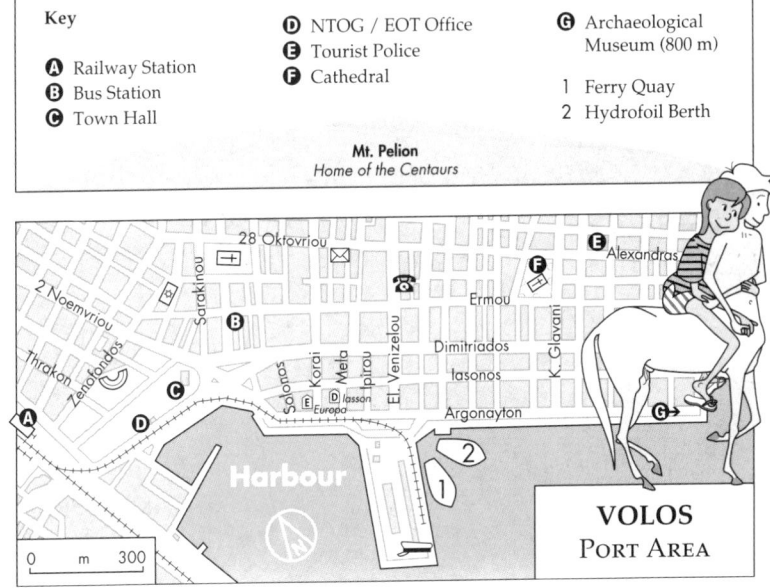

Key

A Railway Station
B Bus Station
C Town Hall

D NTOG / EOT Office
E Tourist Police
F Cathedral

G Archaeological Museum (800 m)

1 Ferry Quay
2 Hydrofoil Berth

Mt. Pelion
Home of the Centaurs

28 Oktovriou

2 Noemvriou

Thrakon

Zenofondos

Sarokinou

Solonos

Korai

Mela

Ipirou

El. Venizelou

Ermou

Dimitriados

Iasonos

Glavani

K. Glavani

Alexandras

Argonayton

D Iasson
E Europa

Harbour

VOLOS
PORT AREA

0   m   300

11
ARGO-SARONIC LINES

AEGINA · ANTIKITHERA · GYTHIO · HYDRA · KITHERA MONEMVASSIA · NEAPOLI · POROS · SALAMIS · SPETSES

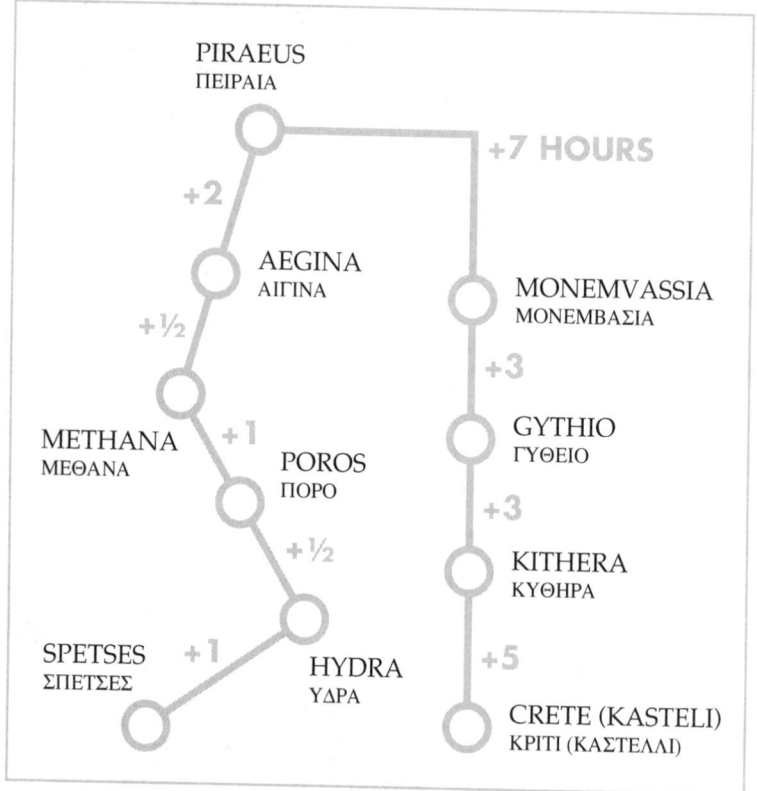

PIRAEUS
ΠΕΙΡΑΙΑ

+7 HOURS

+2

AEGINA
ΑΙΓΙΝΑ

MONEMVASSIA
ΜΟΝΕΜΒΑΣΙΑ

+½

+3

METHANA
ΜΕΘΑΝΑ

+1

GYTHIO
ΓΥΘΕΙΟ

POROS
ΠΟΡΟ

+3

+½

KITHERA
ΚΥΘΗΡΑ

SPETSES
ΣΠΕΤΣΕΣ

+1

HYDRA
ΥΔΡΑ

+5

CRETE (KASTELI)
ΚΡΙΤΙ (ΚΑΣΤΕΛΛΙ)

General Features

This 'Argo-Saronic' chapter encompasses ferry services to islands within the Saronic Gulf proper, as well as those running down the so-called 'Argoid' or East Peloponnesian coast to Kithera and Crete. Ferries confine their runs within one of the two branches; the all important linking services being provided by hydrofoils. The islands and ports also reflect this divide and range from among the most heavily touristed in Greece (within the Saronic Gulf, where the short distance to the capital provides a ready tourist and commuter market), to coastal hamlets further south that hardly deserve to be on the ferry network at all, and only are so thanks to subsidies. Connections reach their nadir on Antikithera, the small island most poorly served by regular ferry in the Aegean. There is thus little middle ground between the two groups. Ports are either over-touristed with a veritable procession of landing-craft type ferries and hydrofoils running around (Aegina, Poros, Hydra, and Spetses all qualify for this category thanks to their popularity as day-tripper and European package tour islands), or they can be almost too quiet for comfort (the Peloponnese and island of Kithera) relying on a couple of infrequent ferries and an occasional long-range High Season hydrofoil. Aristotle and his golden mean clearly never found much favour in these parts.

If you like the idea of island hopping against a background of such extremes, then this route offers a happy mix of days when you can visit up to eight ports in 24 hours (if you feel mad enough to try it), with others when you have to wait as long for a ferry. One set of boats definitely to be avoided are the widely advertised 'three-island' day cruise trips starting from Piraeus and taking in Aegina, Poros and Hydra. You can do this yourself using the hydrofoils for half the price, and save even more using the local ferries.

1 Angistri
2 Methana
3 Souvala

4 Ag. Marina
5 Kosta
6 Porto Helio
7 Galatas

PIRAEUS
Corinth Canal
Salamis
Aegina
Nafplio Epidavros
Tolo
Ermioni
Poros
Hydra
Spetses
Leonidio
Kiparissi
Gerakas
N
Gythio
Neapoli
Monemvassia
Agia Pelagia
Elafonissos
Kithera
Kapsali
Antikithera
0   km   30

SARONIC GULF & EAST PELOPONNESE

Suggested Itinerary [2 Weeks]
The mix of over-touristed and relatively inaccessible ports of call offers an interesting holiday for those who like a variety. Even so you will have to be prepared to compromise and adjust your schedule (particularly the latter part). Arrive on a favourable day and it is quite possible to get down the group (returning either via Crete and a direct boat back to Piraeus or by bus back up the Peloponnese). Otherwise you will have to skip a port.

Arrival/Departure Point
Athens is easily the best airport on offer. If you are offered a cheap flight to either airports on the Peloponnese or Crete ignore the temptation; they are just too difficult to get back to in an emergency.

Season
If you are prepared to give it an extra week then this itinerary could be followed all year round or you could return via the Central Cyclades Line. Otherwise the usual High Season advantages in terms of frequency of service apply.

◼ Athens [2 Days]
An easy starting point and an easy first hop: all the boats start from the same quay at Piraeus and offer frequent starts for Aegina so you won't have to hang around for long.

◻ Aegina [1 Day]
An interesting first port of call with enough to fill a day with sightseeing. But the inescapable evidence of mass tourism does little to nurture a get-away from it all Greek island atmosphere. Accommodation can also be a problem so if you are having real difficulty you could take an evening boat on down the line or alternatively, pick up an evening ferry to the neighbouring small beach island of Angistri.

◻ Poros [1 Day]
The town itself can be done in a couple of hours but this does make a good base of operations if you prefer to 'do' the adjacent islands as outings from one base. Mainland excursions to Mycenae and the famous theatre at Epidavros are possible from here too.

◻ Spetses [2 Days]
The best beach island in the group and thus the best place to rest up for a couple of days while you wait for a hydrofoil or ferry south. The mainland village of Kosta is also easily accessible, with buses to nearby tourist sites.

◻ Monemvassia [2 Days]
After being pampered by the profusion of services thus far the jump to Monemvassia can come as something of a shock. It seems like the end of the world but in fact it is quite a civilized little place. If a hydrofoil or the ferry is not offering your required hop on south you can always take a bus to Napoli and pick up the ferry from there.

◻ Kithera [2 Days]
This quiet island offers a complete contrast with its northern Saronic sisters and is a worthy destination to aim for in its own right. That said, the first priority on arrival must be establishing when you can get off. If the wait for a boat on to Crete is too long you always have a boat to Gythio or Napoli on the Peloponnese (both offering bus links with Athens) as a safety option to fall back on. Alternatively, if you have tarried too long in the Saronic Gulf you can give the island a miss and head directly on to Crete.

◻ Crete [2 Days]
Dumped on the eastern end of Crete you will have to get a bus from Kasteli to Chania and then another on to Iraklion. Here you can take time out to visit Knossos and the Archaeological Museum before taking the overnight boat back to Piraeus.

◼ Athens [2 Days]
If you are planning to venture as far down this line as Crete you could do worse than skip a day in the capital at the beginning of your hoilday to give you an extra day's safety at the end of your trip. Either way, as usual give yourself at least one clear day back in Athens before your return flight.

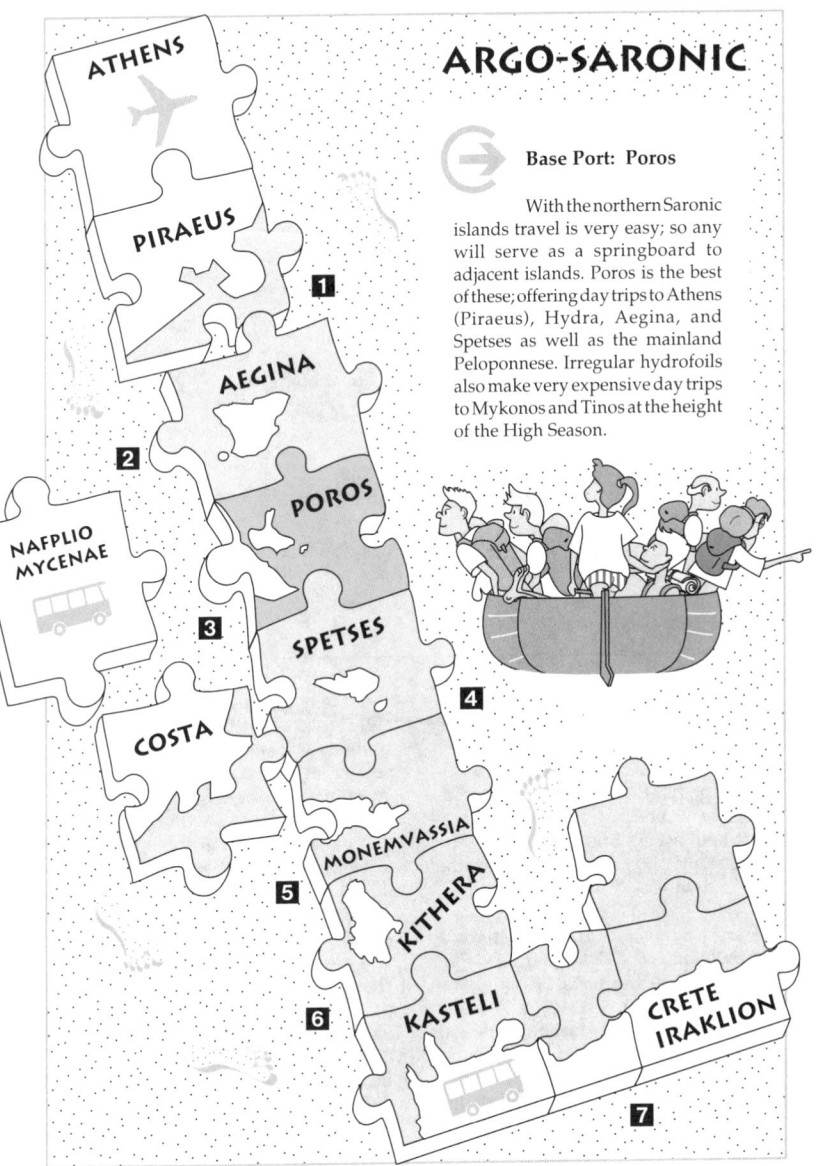

ARGO-SARONIC

Base Port: Poros

With the northern Saronic islands travel is very easy; so any will serve as a springboard to adjacent islands. Poros is the best of these; offering day trips to Athens (Piraeus), Hydra, Aegina, and Spetses as well as the mainland Peloponnese. Irregular hydrofoils also make very expensive day trips to Mykonos and Tinos at the height of the High Season.

ATHENS

PIRAEUS

1

AEGINA

2

NAFPLIO
MYCENAE

POROS

3

SPETSES

4

COSTA

MONEMVASSIA

5

KITHERA

CRETE
IRAKLION

6

KASTELI

7

Argo-Saronic Ferry Services

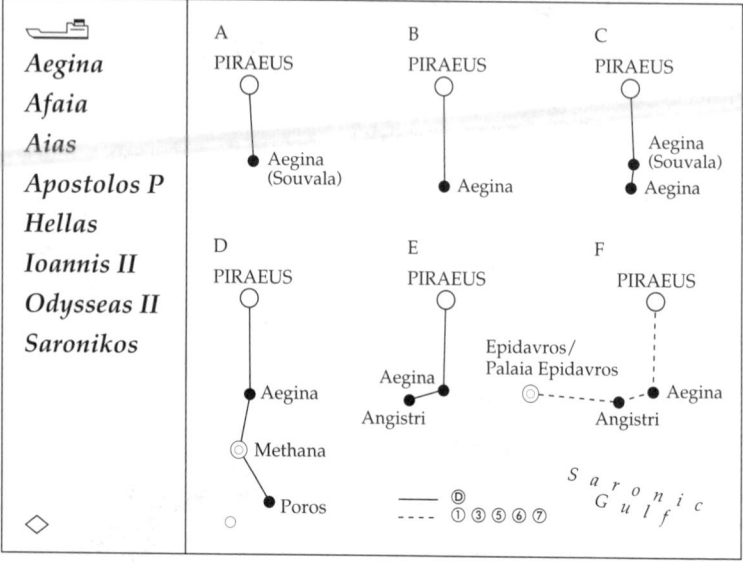

Aegina
Afaia
Aias
Apostolos P
Hellas
Ioannis II
Odysseas II
Saronikos

Main Car Ferries
The mix of small islands tucked closely against the mainland along with either massive popularity or none at all has conspired against the existence of large car ferries on the line. Ferry operations are all short-haul affairs and competing more against tourist boats and hydrofoils rather than each other.

C/Fs *Aegina, Afaia, Aias, Apostolos P, Hellas, Ioannis II, Odysseas II, Saronikos*
The 8 landing-craft ferries running into the Saronic Gulf operated by Poseidon Co. berth in the Great Harbour at Piraeus just south of the bus station/ferry terminal building. Departure times do not appear on NTOG ferry sheets but are posted up in Greek (for a 48-hour period) on a small Port Police kiosk (who are usually very

ready to help non-Greek readers) on the quay. Tickets for these boats are bought from stalls beside the ferry. Each runs one or several of the above routes with additional weekend sailings. The boats are interchangeable, with little between them in terms of facilities or their bland all-white colour scheme. Most display destination boards and nursery clocks showing their departure time. Most boats — if not offering a direct service to Aegina Town — include it on extended schedules. Departures for Aegina (Souvala) are primarily for commercial vehicles. None of these boats heads further south than Poros but offer the cheapest (and slowest) travel down the line. All services are duplicated by smaller passenger craft, but these landing-craft car ferries offer the cheaper tickets.

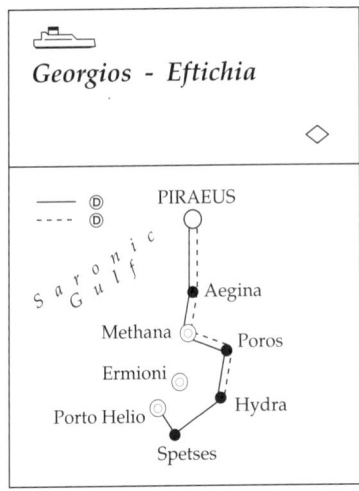

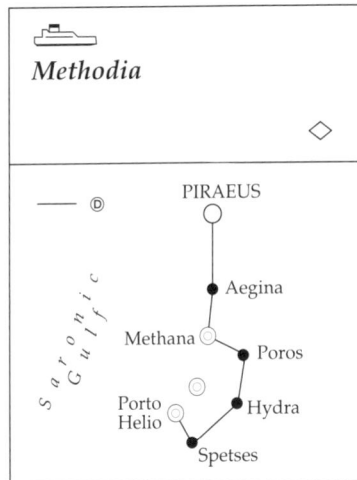

C/F *Georgios*
Local; 1990; 1820 GRT.
The large number of hydrofoils in the Saronic Gulf means that the smaller car ferries that run this route have to work pretty hard to compete: they do so by being very well kitted out. The largest of these small ferries is the *Georgios*. Well maintained, she is worth looking out for, but bring a pullover as the air conditioning works too well for comfort. From her arrival in 1991, she has run a daily service to Spetses (in previous years with irregular calls at Ermioni). However, since 1994 she appears to have come to a tacit arrangement with a rival — the *Eftichia*; the two alternating runs, with one boat going all the way to Porto Helio while the other starts later and turns back at Hydra.

C/F *Eftichia*
Local; 1974 (rebuilt 1993); 869 GRT.
The sharp-nosed, but reliable, *Eftichia* — a converted passenger boat — is the smallest ferry on the line. Usually overcrowded to busting as a result, she offers a less relaxed journey than her larger rivals.

C/F *Methodia*
Ventouris Lines; 1972; 1903 GRT.
The good 'ol *Kyklades* is back! Long standing island hoppers will know that once upon a time, far away and long ago, there was a little ferry that every three weeks left Piraeus on a wondrous voyage to almost every island you could name — running via Milos and Kastelorizo to Kavala on the North Aegean coast. It didn't matter if nobody knew when she was going to turn up as, thanks to (now defunct) subsidies, she could make a profit without anyone ever travelling on her at all. She also got a mention in every guidebook going. After a number of years laid-up she has now reappeared as the *Methodia*. Taking on the itinerary of her new partner, the *Agios Nektarios* (see overleaf), she operates daily down the line to Porto Helio. Times could change in 1995 as this new service is adjusted. Those looking to renew acquaintance with this boat will be pleased to hear that conditions on board are improved; though she has managed to retain both her external staircases and her reputation for running late.

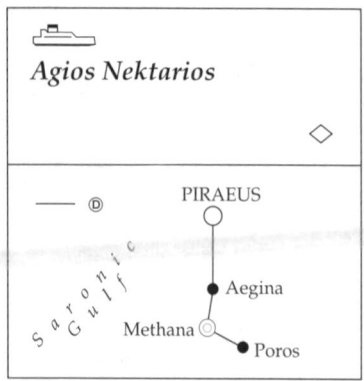

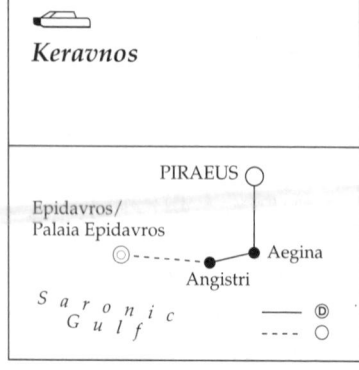

C/F Agios Nektarios

Ventouris Lines; 1964 (rebuilt 1993); 2355 GRT.
This Ventouris Ferries' boat has run down this line under several company flags and names since her arrival in Greece (latterly as the elderly *Hydra*). In 1992 she disappeared while she underwent an extensive rebuild, re-emerging in 1993 as an all but new boat (including name). Now a worthy rival to any ferry, her facilities include a good restaurant, carpeted sun decks and a plastic adobe deck bar. Running twice daily to Poros she has surrendered her former longer runs to Porto Helio to her new companion ferry the *Methodia*.

P/S Poros Express
Ventouris Lines

Posing as a 'jet boat' this tiny, large windowed tourist boat has rattled (ear-plugs are mandatory) her way to Aegina and Poros (Routes C and D) for a number of years as the *Delfini Express*. Recently bought and renamed by Ventouris, she spent the summer of 1994 sitting idle in Piraeus Harbour. Quite what her itinerary will be in 1995 remains a mystery. Too small to venture out of the Saronic Gulf she is almost as fast as the hydrofoils and equally reliable. However, hydrofoils have the edge in all the creature comforts.

C/M Keravnos

For the last few years a rather tatty catamaran has run around the upper reaches of the Saronic Gulf. Formerly known as the *Super Cats*, this small catamaran is similar to the Cycladic *Nearchos* and equally the worse for wear. Schedules are inconsistent, with an invaluable daily 1993 Epidavros link being abandoned in favour of a much more prosaic Piraeus—Aegina—Angistri service in 1994. Expect the changes to be rung again in 1995.

Small Passenger Boats

In addition to the regular ferries, a number of smaller passenger craft operate along the Saronic Gulf line. For the most part

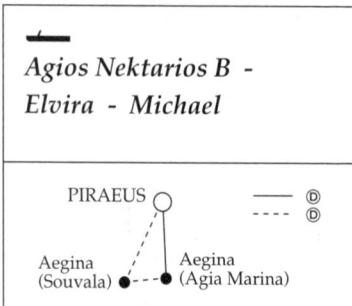

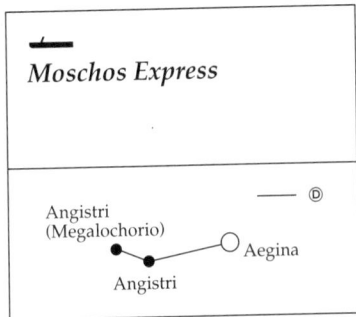

means of access is via a large caïque — the **T/B *Moschos Express*** — that runs (well, okay, rolls) from Aegina Town, calling at both the main ferry quay at Skala as well as Megalochorio along the coast. Finally, there is the **P/S *Manaras Express***; she also ventures to Angistri (via Aegina) but is less prepossessing; being a tiny tub of a boat that looks to have been cobbled together out of old banana boxes. She runs for the benefit of those who like to live dangerously.

small vessels incapable of journeying far, they rely on commuters and day-tripping tourists for their custom; each boat running several times daily to its own set destination. Departures are posted up on the Port Police 48-hour kiosk (they are listed separately at the end of the regular ferry departure times). Tickets for any of these boats are either bought on board or from ticket 'desks' on the quayside.

Most likely to be of use are flashy *Elvira*, the **P/S *Agios Nektarios B*** (not to be confused with her larger namesake, this is a tiny boat boasting an upturned tin bath masquerading as a dummy smokestack) and **P/S *Michael***: all three providing a link with the resort of Agia Marina on Aegina. Also of interest is the **P/S *Kitsolakis Express*** which heads direct to the 'beach' island of Angistri. A more popular

H/F *Flying Dolphins*
CERES
For reasons that aren't clear, hydrofoils heading direct to Aegina depart from Piraeus (Great Harbour) rather than from Zea Marina. Tickets are bought from a kiosk on the quay (see p. 123).

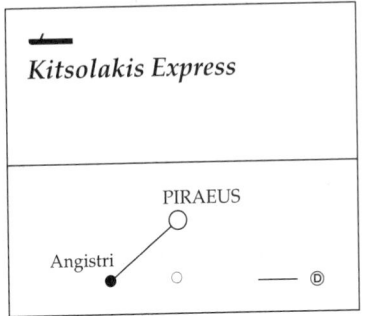

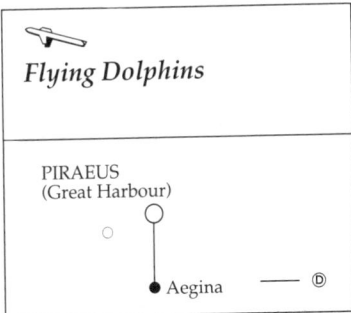

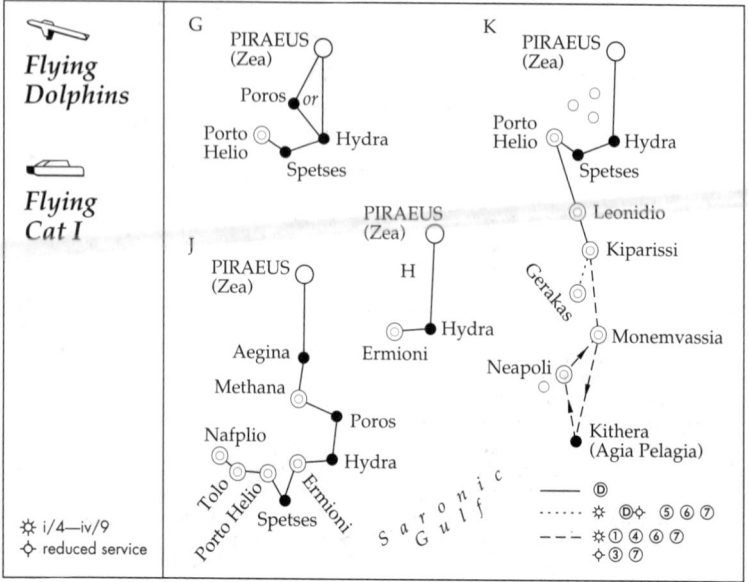

☀ i/4—iv/9
✧ reduced service

H/F *Flying Dolphins*
CERES

Provided your budget will stretch to a £5 hydrofoil ticket, the yellow and blue CERES *Flying Dolphins* are both the most versatile and quickest way of hopping around the Saronic Gulf. So much so, that some islands (e.g. Hydra) largely depend on them. Easy to use, if only because comprehensive timetable booklets (in English and Greek) are available from the ticket agencies covering every port of call and give times for the whole of the hydrofoil year (April to October). For the most part reliable (the protected Saronic Gulf waters ensure that most of these services run reasonably to schedule), your only real problem is likely to be their popularity; in some instances it pays to buy a return ticket: this is particularly true for (1) last hydrofoils from any given port, and (2) hydrofoils between Poros and Aegina, and Spetses and Poros, which

are relatively few in number. Apart from the services to Aegina (see previous page) which use the Great Harbour, all services arrive and depart from Piraeus (Zea Marina). Itinerary G is the most consistent of the routes run, but the timetables are dominated by one-off irregular itineraries — particularly at the weekend. Most of these take in ports along J, which is run every afternoon (returning the next day). During the High Season there is a service (K) down to Kithera four days a week: but days are apt to change each summer.

C/M *Flying Cat I*
CERES

Operating alongside the hydrofoils is one very swish catamaran; usually running itinerary G twice daily. Times are included in the hydrofoil timetable and ticket prices are the same. This being so, take this boat if you can: the ride is a lot faster, smoother, and quieter into the bargain.

C/F *Theseus*

Miras Ferries; 1975; 2353 GRT.

One of the few subsidised ferry routes left in Greece runs down the Peloponnese coast and on to Crete. The itinerary has changed little in years; though the days of operation and boats have. In 1993 the *Milos Express* provided a mid-week stop-gap service after the previous ferry sort of sank. The possibility of a new boat (the *Laburnum*?) appearing cannot be ruled out. Meantime, the *Theseus* (a rather ugly, chunky-looking boat) combines the Peloponnese service with her primary role; offering a regular ferry link between the hitherto unconnected Peloponnese city of Kalamata and Crete (Kastelli). In order to do this, she makes sojourns to the Peloponnese from Crete before making the return leg of her Piraeus runs.

C/F *Martha*

Miras Ferries; 1968; 825 GRT.

A small ferry, too past her prime to make a go of it elsewhere, the slow *Martha* provides the main link between Kithera and the mainland. A martyr to inconsistent timetabling, she does nought but a daily service out of Elafonissos to Gythio via Kithera. Schedules could see more than the usual amount of change in 1995 as they are juggled with those of the *Theseus*.

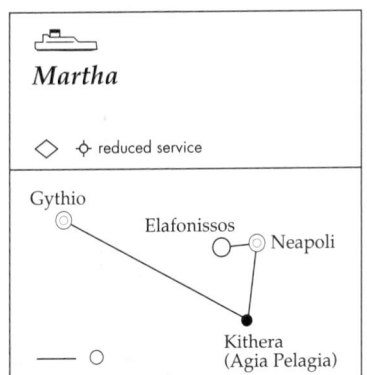

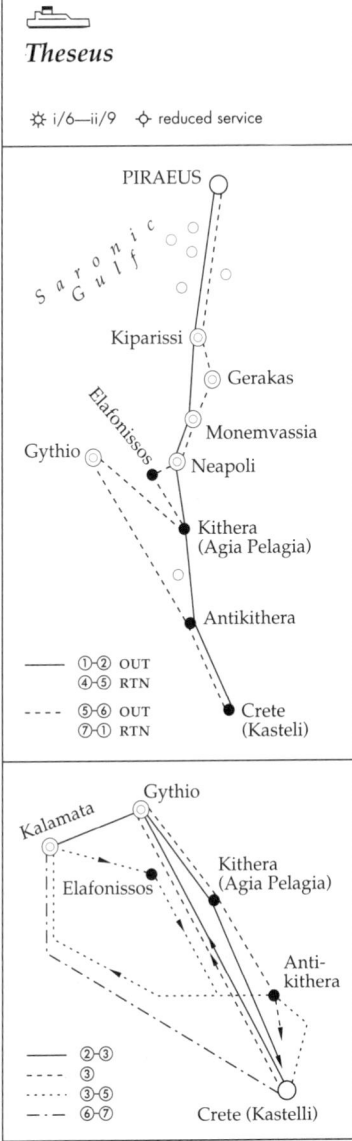

⚓ Argo-Saronic Islands & Ports

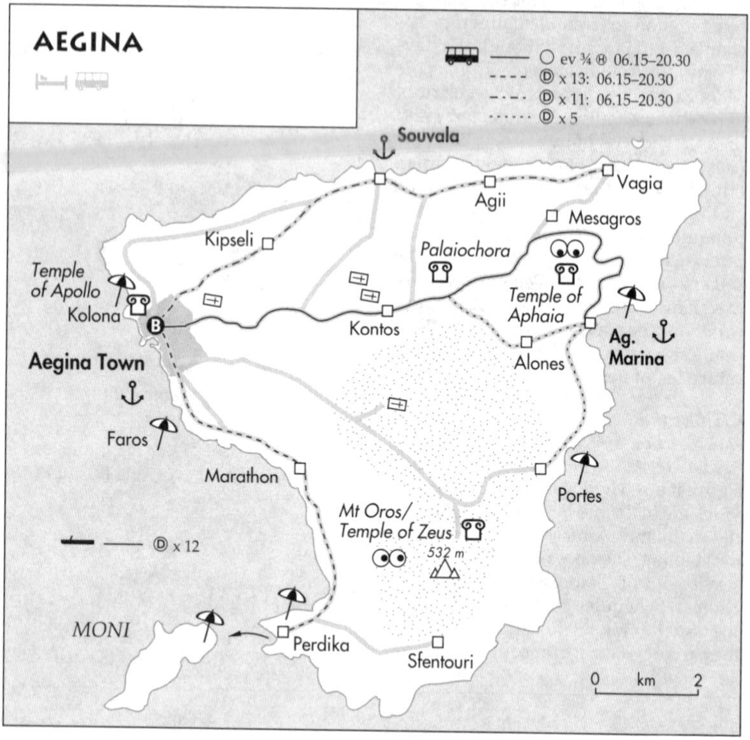

AEGINA

○ ev ¾ ⊕ 06.15–20.30
Ⓓ x 13: 06.15–20.30
Ⓓ x 11: 06.15–20.30
Ⓓ x 5

Souvala

Vagia

Agii

Mesagros

Kipseli

Palaiochora

Temple of Apollo
Kolona

Ⓑ

Temple of Aphaia

Aegina Town

Kontos

Ag. Marina

Alones

Faros

Marathon

Portes

Ⓓ x 12

Mt Oros/
Temple of Zeus

532 m

MONI

Perdika

Sfentouri

0   km   2

Aegina

ΑΙΓΙΝΑ; 84 km²; pop. 10,000.

Lying a mere 20 km south of Piraeus, Aegina (pronounced 'Ye–nah') is among the most touristed of the Greek islands. Its close proximity to Athens makes it a popular package tourist destination (and incidentally, an ideal spot in which to fill a day in hand before a flight home), but despite this, out of August it is not noticeably overcrowded. If you don't mind commuting each day, the island is actually quite a nice base for 'doing' the capital,

besides offering pleasant wooded, low-lying mountain scenery and plenty of sand beach coves for (given the cleanliness of the water) somewhat dubious bathing.

Aegina has had a very up and down history: emerging during the 5 c. BC as a serious rival to Athens, it lost the inevitable regional power struggle that followed. Forcibly re-populated by the Athenians, the new inhabitants deemed it safer to grow pistachio nuts rather than dream of power: Aegina is now the nut capital of Greece. In 1829 Aegina Town briefly again came to the fore when it became the first capital of the Greek state (before losing out to Athens for a second time).

Aegina Town, complete with its neoclassical frontage from its days as the capital, is the main centre and by far the best of the possible ferry destinations. The waterfront is lined with tavernas and tourist shops (pistachio nuts figuring prominently in the displays of wares) near the ferry quay, but once you move along the waterfront or inland a street or two, Aegina Town reveals itself to be a surprisingly unspoilt small island town surrounded by nut orchards and offering a day of gentle tourism. The town is very much centred around the ferry quay, the tourist presence all too evident by the existence of horses and carriages standing along the promenade awaiting a fare. But either side of this the waterfront is attractive. To the south, in the ancient commercial harbour, you will find full-to-overflowing caïques selling fruit and veg. (note: *no* pistachio nuts) with a fresh fish market housed in a quayside ally opposite. To the north lies the remains of the ancient naval trireme harbour backed by the lightly wooded former acropolis at Kolona (with good views over the Saronic Gulf and the town and the good beach to the north). Along the beach road lie the bus ticket kiosk and several budget hotels and restaurants. Ticket agencies are surprisingly thin on the ground; the quayside Port Police kiosk has ferry departure times posted up daily (in Greek), with ticket kiosks (often only staffed half an hour before the ferry is due to depart) either side. Note: if you are planning to return to Athens via late afternoon/evening hydrofoil you should buy your ticket on arrival as they tend to get booked up.

Aegina's bus service is limited but good running frequently along the northern coast to the island's second town of **Agia Marina**. Linked by small passenger ferry to Piraeus, it is about as resortified a place as you can get in Greece. Disco-city on the sand. If night-life is a priority then it will appeal, otherwise the walk up the hill to the Temple of Aphaia is likely to be of greater interest. Other coastal villages are gradually falling to the tourist hordes, or failing this, have become villa-filled suburbs for the more affluent Athenians. The small fishing port of **Perdika** on the south-west coast is the most attractive, and surprisingly unspoilt, with some rooms on offer besides boats to the delightfully quiet pine-clad islet of **Moni**. The third of Aegina's ports, **Souvala**, is a resort village with a reasonable beach and a large quay used by lorries unwilling to negotiate the streets of Aegina town.

🛏

Most of Aegina's hotels are pre-booked by tour operators or inconveniently placed. In town there are plenty of options in the middle price range. The best of these are: the *Brown* (☎ 22 271) at the south end of the town, along with the hotels north of the port; the *Marmarinos* (☎ 23 510) just has the edge, though there is little between the *Plaza* (☎ 25600), *Avra* (☎ 22 303), *Artemis* (☎ 25195) and the budget *Togias* (☎ 24242). Those looking for something a little different should try the *Pension Pavlou* (☎ 22 795); which offers pricey, but atmospheric, rooms in an old town house. Regular rooms fill up quickly; so arrive early.

👁

The island's major draw is the 5 c. BC **Temple of Aphaia** (a minor daughter goddess of Zeus ignored elsewhere); set atop a pine tree-clad hill 10 km from Aegina Town, it is one of the best preserved in Greece with a unique 2-storey inner colonnade. The pedimental sculptures, however, now reside in Munich. Similarities with the Acropolis in Athens extend beyond 'lost' sculptures: it is advisable to visit as soon as the site opens (◑ 08.00–15.00/17.00) to avoid the crowds.

Aegina also has other temples of interest. Largest of these is the **Temple of Zeus** on the peak of Mt. Oros. Only the foundations survive, with few tourists venturing up the mountain path. The crumbling lone column of the **Temple of Apollo** stands as a marker indicating the site of Aegina's ancient acropolis on the northern edge of the town. The walls were demolished by the Athenians so little but jumbled foundations remain. The temple

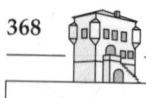

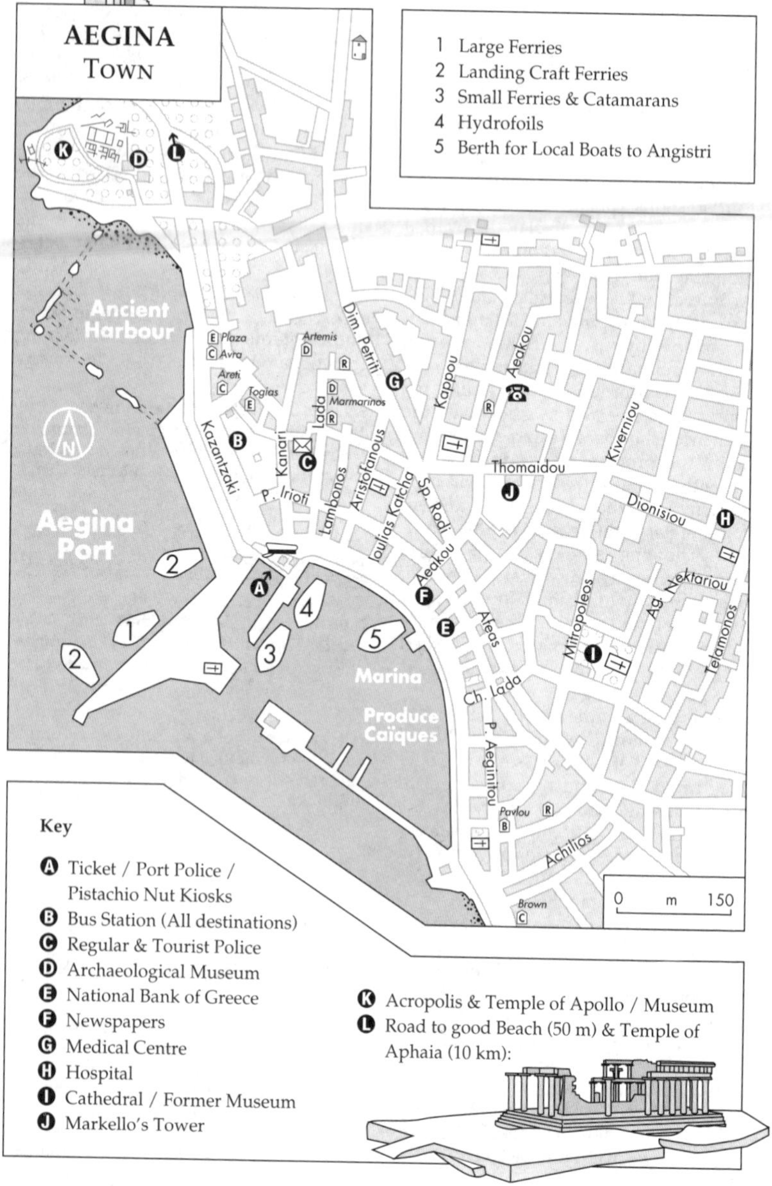

AEGINA
Town

1 Large Ferries
2 Landing Craft Ferries
3 Small Ferries & Catamarans
4 Hydrofoils
5 Berth for Local Boats to Angistri

Ancient Harbour

Aegina Port

Aegina Town (map labels):

Plaza, Avra, Areti, Togias, Artemis, Dim. Petriti, Marmarinos, Lada, Kanari, Kazanizaki, P. Irioti, Lambonos, Aristofanous, Laulas Katcha, Sp. Rodi, Aeolou, Kappou, Aeolou, Thomaidou, Kiveniou, Dionisiou, Mitropoleos, Ag. Nektariou, Telamonos, Ateas, Ch. Lada, P. Aeginiou, Achilios, Pavlou, Brown

Marina

Produce Caïques

Key

Ⓐ Ticket / Port Police / Pistachio Nut Kiosks
Ⓑ Bus Station (All destinations)
Ⓒ Regular & Tourist Police
Ⓓ Archaeological Museum
Ⓔ National Bank of Greece
Ⓕ Newspapers
Ⓖ Medical Centre
Ⓗ Hospital
Ⓘ Cathedral / Former Museum
Ⓙ Markello's Tower
Ⓚ Acropolis & Temple of Apollo / Museum
Ⓛ Road to good Beach (50 m) & Temple of Aphaia (10 km):

0   m   150

once resembled the temple of Aphaia but you would be hard pressed to know it now. This site (known as Kolona or 'column') is also home to Aegina's reasonable **Archaeological Museum** (08.30–15.00 ex ①), which houses finds from around the island, notably coins (Aegina was the first island to mint its own currency) and the 6 c. BC 'Aegina Sphinx'. The rest of Aegina Town is stronger in atmosphere than sightseeing detail; the one exception being the oddly turreted **Markello's Tower**. Built in 1802, it was the office/home of Greece's first Governor and the tiny ground floor is now a home for local art exhibitions.

The final site of note on Aegina is the monastery of **St. Catherine** on the road east of Aegina Town. It lies west of the abandoned former hill capital of **Palaiochora** on the site of a Temple of Aphrodite.

☎

CODE 0297, TOURIST POLICE 22100, HOSPITAL 22 20990.

Angistri
ΑΝΓΙΣΤΡΙ; 17 km²; pop. 530.

A small satellite of Aegina increasingly absorbing the overflow of her larger neighbour, but lacking sights or centres. Local caïques take tourists to the island primarily for the lone sand beach at Skala (a wind-blown and dusty all-hotels-and-nothing-else resort on the north-east coast) — some also calling at Megalochorio (alias Miloi); the port below the main island village of Angistri. Very quiet, like the rest of this pine-wooded island, (buses run from the port to the untouristed village of Limenaria) the only attraction is the escape from the crowds.

⊨

Reasonable supply of rooms and some 22 D and E-class hotels, but these are apt to fill with Athenian 'weekenders' from Friday on.

☎

ISLAND CODE 0297.

Antikithera
ΑΝΤΙΚΥΘΗΙΡΑ; 29 km²; pop. 115.

Occupying the straits between the Peloponnese and Western Crete, this island is a dry rock that would only appeal to extreme get-away-from-it-all fanatics. The tiny population live in two dusty hamlets and see few strangers. In fact Antikithera is best known for its shipwrecks; one of which yielded up the bronze Ephebe of Antikithera now in the National Archaeological Museum in Athens. The Elgin marbles were also temporarily sunk here en route to Britain. Most ferries steer well clear and out of High Season links are reduced to one a

week: so the island is inaccessible for all practicable purposes. If you want a quick look you can stop off when the ferry is en route to Crete and then rejoin her on her return north some 6 hours later.

🛏

Take a room and double an islander's income!

Elafonissos
ΕΛΑΦΟΝΗΣΙ; 19 km²; pop. 270.

An attractive, isolated, small beach island lying off the southern Peloponnese coast town of Neapoli, Elafonissos ('deer's island') was linked to the mainland by a causeway until 1677. The only settlement lies at the site of this divide: a church now standing in glorious isolation (along with Elafonissos's only tree) from the other buildings on a spit of land tapering towards the mainland. Elafonissos town is a pretty fishing village that offers an ideal base if your notion of getting away from it all includes an absence of banks and other tourists. In addition, the island is blessed with clean seas and a superb sand beach 4 km south of the village. It is accessible via a dirt road or an irregular boat. Daily caïques augment ferry links, running to Neapoli (30 minutes east).

ELAFONISSOS

🛏

🚢 ---- Ⓓ x 2

0 km 4

⛵ Elafonissos
⚓

276 m
⚠

Sarakiniko

Levki Bay

🚌 No bus service

--- Ⓓ 10.00–16.00

There is also a rusty landing craft mainland service operating to a track running off the Neapoli—Peloponnese road.

🛏

Some rooms and 2 B-class pensions in the village: the *Asteri Tis Elafonissou* (☎ 61271) and the cheaper *Elafonissos* (☎ 61268).

☎

ISLAND CODE 0734.

Epidavros
ΕΠΙΔΑΥΡΟΣ

So named on timetables, this resort village is actually the small Peloponnese port of **Palea Epidavros.** Host to three campsites, and a dozen hotels, the main reason to stop off here (the beach aside) is the archaeological site of ancient Epidavros 15 km away (taxis and buses run direct; the latter also to nearby Ligourio en route for **Nafplio** — which also has a direct bus service to the site). An important sanctuary to the healing god Asclepius (of staff and serpent fame), the site is home to a theatre (4 c. BC) that was recognised by the ancients themselves as the most perfect ever constructed. Fortunately, it is also the best preserved, and with seating for 14,000 it is a sightseeing must. Tours run weekly from all the nearby islands.

Ermioni
EPMIONI

A suburb commuter town on the Peloponnese coast. Tourists with any sense avoid disembarking here as there is nothing to see or do: the town lacking even a serviceable beach. Majority of vessels calling are hydrofoils.

Gerakas
ΓΕΡΑΚΑΣ

Located in a mini-loch half-way down the eastern Peloponnese, this small and singularly uninspiring hamlet does have the benefit of a road into the interior. No buses or beach, and if it wasn't given a subsidy to call, one can't imagine there would be a ferry either.

Gythio
ΓΥΘΕΙΟ

The most important town on the south coast of the Peloponnese, Gythio offers an attractive Venetian house-fronted promenade, decked out with fish restaurants and set against the green foothills of Mt. Laryssion. A good base for exploring the region, it is a pretty — if somewhat over-touristed — port with quite a history. Sparta's naval base during the Peloponnesian war, it was sacked by Athens in 455 BC, (relations are now on a friendlier footing, with 4 buses daily via Sparta). During the Roman era the town became an important production centre for murex — the imperial purple dye — extracted from sea molluscs by a method now lost. Most of ancient Gythio is now equally invisible: the only survival of note being a small theatre 400 m north of the current town. Ferry links are also rather poor as Gythio lies tucked 2/3 hours steaming up the Gulf of Lakonia. Along with the occasional tourist boat, they combine to provide an almost daily service to Kithera and its links with the outside world.

⊨

A dozen hotels, but they tend to be expensive: this is package tour country. The cheapest are the waterfront D-class *Akaion* (☎ 22294) and *Kranae* (☎ 22249). Fortunately rooms are on offer and well sign-posted around the harbour area of the town.

▲

Several quiet olive grove sites lie just off a good beach 5 km south of the town. Buses run hourly past the camping strip.

👓

The main sight lies just to the south of the promenade: the small causeway-linked islet of **Marathonisi** (ancient Kranai). Famed in antiquity as the spot where Paris spent his first night with Helen (whose face launched the first thousand Greek ferries) while carrying her off to Troy, the islet attracted the curious from the first, prompting the erection of a Hellenistic temple of Aphrodite and a number of other shrines. As late as 1770, garbled tales of the Jolly Roger prompted the islet's Turkish masters in far away Istanbul to sanction the

building of a fortress tower (newly restored) to keep nonexistent local brigands in hand. Apart from this construction, a couple of chapels, and a suitably phallic lighthouse, Marathonisi has no other buildings but is disappointingly covered in shrubby trees and hosts an annual summer pan-Hellenic mosquito convention so large that one wonders if any mortal has ever managed an untroubled night's sleep here.

☎

CODE 0733, PORT POLICE 22262, POLICE 22271.

Hydra
ΥΔΡΑ; 52 km²; pop. 3000.

A hilltop sticking out of the Aegean lacking roads or beaches, Hydra (pronounced 'EE-dra') has overcome the disadvantages of a generally dour appearance to become one of the most touristed spots in Greece. This is due to a combination of a very attractive fortified harbour town and the close proximity of Athens (making it a perfect day-tripper island). Sadly, the numbers calling have turned the place into a tourist trap and the island is now arguably the least idyllic in the whole

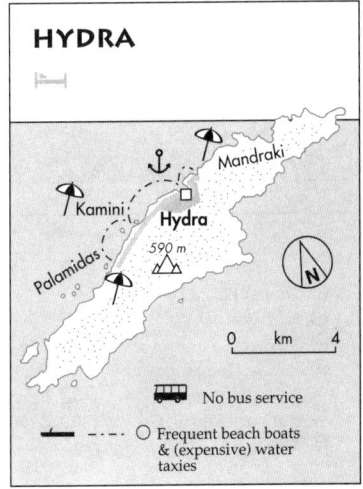

HYDRA

No bus service

Frequent beach boats
& (expensive) water
taxies

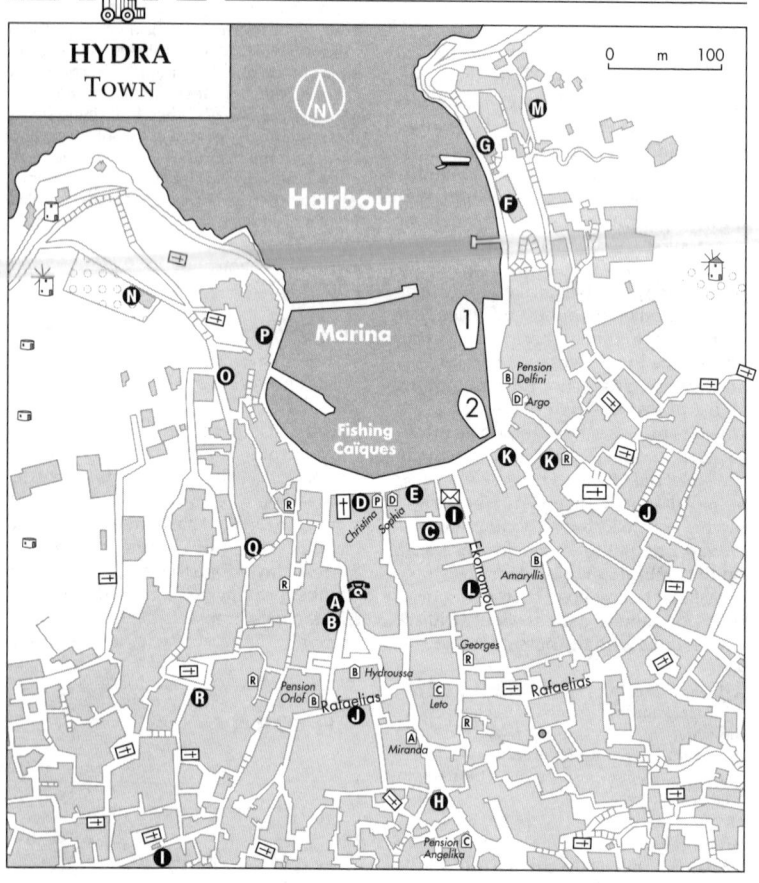

HYDRA TOWN

Harbour

Marina

Fishing Caïques

0　m　100

Pension Delfini B

Argo D

Pension Orlof B Rafaelias

Hydroussa B

Leto C

Miranda A

Pension Angelika C

Georges R

Amaryllis

Sophia

Christina

Ekonomou

Rafaelias

Key

A Tourist Police
B Hospital
C Market
D Panagia Monastery / Clock Tower
E National Bank of Greece
F Museum
G Old Arsenal / Port Police
H Doctor
I Supermarket
J Pharmacy
K Bakery
L Cinema
M Kriezis Mansion
N Koundouriotis Mansion
O Tombasis Mansion
P Voulgaris Mansion
Q G. Voulgaris Mansion
R L. Koundouriotis Mansion

1　Ferry / Hydrofoil Berth
2　Taxi Boats

Aegean, with a constant procession of hydrofoils and tour-boats bringing in the crowds and encouraging the most expensive island prices in Greece. Poor and insignificant in ancient times, Hydra's transformation into a gold and jewellery boutique has its origins in the 17th and 18th centuries, when, lying on the periphery of both Turkish and Venetian spheres of influence, the island bred a succession of autonomous buccaneer flash Harry's who successfully exploited the growth of Euro-Levantine trade. The town thrived and grew to support a population of 28,000 before post-independence decline reduced the numbers to around 3,000, eking out an existence by sponge fishing until tourism took off.

Apart from the town, with its harbour walls adorned with cannon, Hydra has little to offer. Decked with steep hill paths and a scattering of monasteries and with a car and motorbike ban, it is often touted as a hill walking destination given the absence of anything else to do. Bathing areas are confined to three northerly beaches that are small, poor, crowded and served by expensive taxi boats.

⊢⊣

Pricey hotels and rooms. Book ahead if at all possible. The A-class *Miranda* (☎ 52230) and B-class *Hydroussa* (☎ 52217) are the premier hotels in town and with prices to match. Those on a tighter budget will fare better trying the C-class *Leto* (☎ 53385), the pension *Angelika* (☎ 53202) or the D-class *Argo* (☎ 52452). Also on the waterfront is the rather run down D-class *Sophia* (☎ 52313). Right under the monastery belfry, certain disadvantages become apparent on the hour, every hour.

👀

For most tourists **Hydra Town** is Hydra. Very photogenic, it is snugly tucked into a fold in the barren hills and consists of neo-classical mansions built during the years of prosperity fanning up the hillsides behind the port. The packed-to-bursting waterfront is distinguished by the 18 c. **Panagia Monastery**; built from the stones of the famous Temple of Poseidon on Poros. On the hillsides either side of the harbour are the early 19 c. mansions built by the leading pirate families of the day. The **harbour fortifications** are also impressive and do wonders for the feel of the town. Carefully restored (boutiques aside), it is worth stopping off for a look before catching a hydrofoil to the next port of call when you feel a comparatively inexpensive drink coming on.

☎

CODE 0298, PORT POLICE 52279, TOURIST POLICE 52205.

Kalamata
ΚΑΛΑΜΑΤΑ

The second city of the Peloponnese (after Patras), Kalamata is a sprawling conurbation as ugly as any other large Greek urban centre and well off the regular ferry trail. Tucked away in the deepest recess of the Messiniakos Gulf, it has a rail link with the rest of Greece and regular buses to both Athens (8 daily) and Patras (2 daily). The bad news is that the bus station is 3 km from the port which saw its first ferry service at the end of the 1993 summer season. From the island hopper's perspective Kalamata is thus an unattractive destination.

⊢⊣

Limited number of budget hotels on or near the waterfront including the *Plaza* (☎ 82590) *Nevada* (☎ 82429) and the *Pension Avra* (☎ 82759). Offers of rooms are very rare.

A

Camping Patista (☎ 29525): 2 km east of the ferry quay; an okayish beach site.

☎

CODE 0721, TOURIST POLICE 23187, PORT POLICE 22218.

Kiparissi
ΚΥΠΑΡΙΣΣΙ

An idyllic hamlet on the Peloponnesian coast offering a pleasant mixture of red-tiled houses, trees and a good shingle beach that attracts the occasional day-tripper hydrofoil. The ferry only seems to call in order to pick up the occasional stranded motorist who — having braved the mountain track to get here — finds himself without the nerve to drive back.

Kithera

KYΘHPA; 278 km²; pop. 2,600.

Arguably deserving of the title of the last unspoilt large Greek island, Kithera lies in glorious isolation from other island chains like a lump of rare meat falling off the Peloponnese fork. Historically it has always been deemed to be part of the Ionian chain, and although sharing a similar history (of Venetian rather than Turkish rule), its appearance is more in common with the Cycladic islands.

These days Kithera is administered from Athens. Lack of ferry connections and an ambivalent attitude towards tourists have contrived to keep most at bay. A majority of the population have become economic migrants (notably to Australia), but keeping either holiday homes or retiring back to the island. While welcoming, they are not keen to see their dream island degenerate into yet another tourist resort. The lack of tourists is reflected in the level of services. Public transport is poor (the school bus runs down the road bisecting the island twice daily in the summer; with frequent, but expensive, taxis making the most of this).

Most visitors arrive via the northern port of **Agia Pelagia**, which sees the bulk of the ferry traffic as well as all the hydrofoils. There is little here apart from a long ferry quay with a taverna and a small ticket office. Unless they have or hire their own transport, most tourists head straight for the scenic hill-top capital of **Chora** (home to a lovely whitewashed village that meanders up the spine of a hill to an impressive, but sadly ruinous castle) and the resort port of **Kapsali** — the focus of Kithera's day and nightlife thanks to two excellent sand beaches in a bay divided by a small headland. The rest of the island is home to empty villages on rolling low hills with little vegetation; the best lying along the main island road.

Hotels are scattered thinly around the island. At **Agia Pelagia** the D-class *Kytheria* (☎ 33321)

and the B-class *Filoxenia* (☎ 33610) mop up evening arrivals to the island. **Chora** has the pricey, but lovely, B-class *Margarita* (☎ 31694) and a couple of cheaper pensions — notably *Pension Keti* (☎ 31318) and some rooms. **Kapsali** has the luxury B-class pension *Raikos* (☎ 31629), both rather pricy. Budget accommodation is limited to the D-class *Aphrodite* (☎ 31328) and rare rooms along the beach.

▲

Camping Kapsali (☎ 31580): a nice (pine-wood) site on the out-skirts of Kapsali, but only open mid-June through to mid-September.

∞

The **Chora**, straddling a narrow 500 m ridge, and the Venetian **Kastro** (built in 1503) are the most accessible attractions that Kithera has to offer. The latter looks impressive from a distance but the remains are rather 'bitty'. The best reason to visit are the panoramic views of Kapsali and the coast. In Chora there is also a small town **Museum**. The most popular excursion is to the pretty village of **Milopotamos** with its impressive **Cave of Agia Sophia**, and nearby, a Venetian castle and town. Between Chora and Milopotamos lies the village of **Livadi**, complete with a bridge dating from the period of English rule (1814–1864). Looking incongruously out of place on a Greek island, it would happily pass as a railway viaduct anywhere in southern England.

Kithera was noted in antiquity as the place where the goddess Aphrodite was born (or drawn) out of the sea (a claim also made by Cyprus). Kithera's claim was not disputed in antiquity and the ancient centre (at **Paleopolis**) was home to a **Temple of Aphrodite** that the travel writer Pausanias deemed to be the oldest, most beautiful, and most venerated in the world. A church constructed from the temple stones now stands on the site. The final site of note is the medieval town of **Paleochora** — abandoned after the population was sold into slavery by the pirate Kemal Reis in 1537.

☎
CODE 0735, POLICE 31206, PORT POLICE (AG. P) 33280, (KAP) 31222.

Leonidio
ΛΕΩΝΙΔΙΟ
A small coastal town served by hydrofoils in the summer months. Commuters and the odd tourist escaping the crowds are the only beneficiaries of the service: there isn't any reason to stop off here.

Methana
ΜΕΘΑΝΑ
Another small port — this time on a peninsular jutting north from the Peloponnese into the Saronic Gulf. Ferries as well as hydrofoils call but most of the traffic is local rather than tourist. Like Leonidio most visitors ship out on the same boat they arrive on.

Monemvassia
ΜΟΝΕΜΒΑΣΙΑ
A distinctive small town at the southern end of the Peloponnese that lives off the tourism generated by the mini Gibraltar-cum-boulder offshore. From the ferry both look a bit austere but this is deceptive: there are souvenir shops and tavernas aplenty on the mainland, while the boulder town lies on the southern flank out of view. They are linked by a causeway that also provides a convenient quay for both ferries and the near-daily hydrofoils.

⊨
Plenty of rooms available as well as a number of hotels. These include the E-class *Akroyali* (☎ 61306) and D-class *Aktaeon* (☎ 61234); both are near the causeway along with the C-class *Minoa* (☎ 61209). The A-class pension *Kastro* (☎ 61413) provides a more pricey alternative.

A
Camping Paradise (☎ 61680): a lovely and relatively quiet site 3½ km south of the town.

∞
The 350 m 'Rock' looks barren at first sight but, in fact, is complete with a fortress dating back to Homeric times and a medieval village. The main Byzantine centre on the Peloponnese, its (largely abandoned) upper and lower towns offer an interesting day's exploration, besides being the site of an important event in the struggle for Greek independence: the massacre of the Turkish garrison in 1821.

☎
CODE 0732.

Nafplio
ΝΑΥΠΛΙΟ
Tucked into the Peloponnese coastline, stately and popular Nafplio — briefly capital of the embryonic Greek state (1827–34) between Aegina and Athens — is visited by occasional hydrofoils. The tourist presence is high thanks to the combination of a building programme which stalled when 'capital' status was lost, leaving the best preserved Venetian town in Greece, along with the daily influx from the nearby beach resort of **Tolo** (also linked by bus and Nafplio hydrofoil).

Rooms aren't thick on the ground but there are plenty of budget hotels and a *Youth Hostel* (☎ 27754) in the new. The side streets near the ferry quay hide small hotels including the musty D-class *Acropole* (☎ 27796). Best of the mid-range hotels is the *Agamemnon* (☎28021). Finally, at the top of the range, there is an A-class *Xenia* (☎ 28981) in the town.

Λ

Nearest is *Tolo Camping* (☎ 59133); a crowded site 8 km to the east.

ω

The old town is worth a day's exploration; the highlights being three impressive castles (the most impressive is the islet of **Bourtzi** — a mini Alcatraz; daily taxi boats make the 20 minute crossing 09.00–13.00, 16.00–19.00), and a small **Archaeological Museum** with an interesting display of Mycenaean artifacts.

☎

CODE 0752

Neapoli
ΝΕΑΠΟΛΗ

The most southerly port on the Peloponnese, Neapoli is tucked in the lip of the Gulf of Lakonia. Not that there is much to be laconic about, for there is nought here but a poorly connected and dusty town. The austere, 'end of the known world' feeling that pervades (that led to the ancients believing that the entrance to Hades — the underworld — lay at the southern tip of the Peloponnese) will do little for the tourist who likes his nightlife, though this is a resort town of sorts thanks to the long narrow beach bisected by the ferry quay. Most holiday-makers seem to be Greeks escaping the crowds elsewhere. If you are looking to get away from it all then Neapoli might have appeal — and nearby Elafonissos offers some attractive consolation.

⊨

Limited rooms, and three B-class pensions: the *Alivali* (☎ 22287), the *Arsenakos* (☎ 22991), and the *Limira Mare* (☎ 22208).

☎

CODE 0732

Poros
ΠΟΡΟΣ; 28 km²; pop. 4500.

The island that marks the limit for the landing-craft ferries running out of Piraeus, Poros is actually made up of two islands (**Sphalria** and **Kalaureia**) separated by a narrow canal and connected by a bridge. This double island combination takes its modern name from the narrow strait (360 m) that separates it from the mainland: 'Poros' meaning 'passage'. In fact Poros is an extremely odd island; for the straits — rather than the island itself — are the focus of activity, with settlement running along the shores on either side and the bulk of the island relegated to hinterland. The 'island' sensation is strangely thin, with an atmosphere more reminiscent of a large coastal town ribboned around a narrow bay. Perhaps because of this and a lack of good beaches, Poros attracts less tourism than her neighbours. However, it is a nice base for doing the mainland sights and adjacent islands.

Poros Town is the only settlement of any significance; occupying most of Sphalria Island. It consists of whitewashed and red-tile houses banked between the long quay and a stubby hill topped with a campanile. On first arriving, the waterfront can come as a bit of a shock; for not only is it the third smelliest in the Aegean (after Piraeus and Chios) but is adorned with several of the tackiest tourist shops to be found in Greece. Fortunately, the further you walk south from the ferry quay the better it gets; developing into an attractive mix of tavernas and yachts, with a myriad of taxi-boats and small car ferries scuttling across the straits to the mainland village of Galatas (the path ends at some rocks where the town children bathe). The backstreets are also reasonably attractive in a downbeat sort of way: but it is difficult to imagine anyone coming to Poros for the architecture. One suspects the main reason some tourists come back year after year is the low-key 'niceness' of the island: though if truth be told you don't have to go far to find better. Perhaps this is why cycle hire is so popular on the island — as they offer easy access to better mainland beaches.

Settlement on the wooded main island of Kalaureia is largely confined to tourist developments along the straits (served by frequent buses). The coast south of the town is the busiest, with the bulk of the island's poor beaches (all pebble) and the now unused but pretty monastery of **Kalavrias** (alias Zoodochos Pigi). At the other end of the strait lies Russian bay; home to a 1828 nautical conference in which the great powers (Britain, France and Russia) discussed the future of the independent Greek state. En route you will pass the beach at Neorio: arguably the best of the island's poor collection. Walk inland, and you will find yourself on the best part of the island: the abundance of trees being some compensation for the demolition of the public WCs on the waterfront of Poros Town.

Galatas is much more dowdy than Poros Town; though some efforts have been made to tart up the waterfront of late. Unless you are heading for the campsite there is now great reason to venture in this direction.

🛏

Poros Town offers the best chance of finding a Room south of Aegina. There are also a number of easily located hotels along the waterfront. Closest to the ferry quay is the B-class *Latsi* (☎ 22392), the *Saron* (☎ 22279) and the C-class *Aktaion* (☎ 22281). More expensive hotels tend to be out of town on Kalavrias; the largest being the B-class *Poros* (☎ 22216). There are also several waterfront hotels in **Galatas** if you draw a blank in Poros Town. These include the D-class *Saronis* (☎ 22356) and the C-class *Galatia* (☎ 22227) and *Papasotiriou* (☎ 22841).

▲

Camping Kirangelo (☎ 24520): friendly small mainland site 1 km inland on the road north of Galatas. Avoid the tent village on the coast north of Galatas: this is a hospital resort run by the Greek health service for the elderly insane.

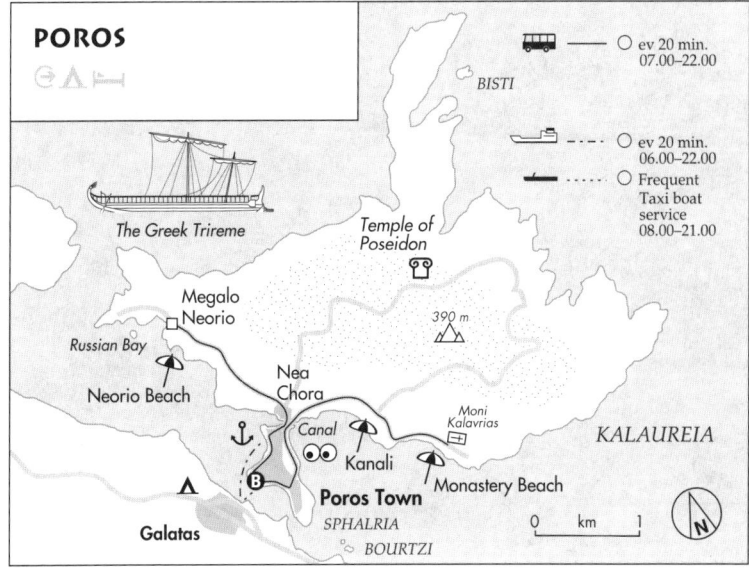

POROS

BISTI

🚌 ——— ○ ev 20 min.
07.00–22.00

⛴ – – – ○ ev 20 min.
06.00–22.00

■ · · · · · ○ Frequent
Taxi boat
service
08.00–21.00

The Greek Trireme

Temple of
Poseidon

Megalo
Neorio

390 m

Russian Bay

Neorio Beach

Nea
Chora

Moni
Kalavrias

KALAUREIA

Canal

Kanali

Monastery Beach

Poros Town

SPHALRIA

0   km   1

Galatas

BOURTZI

N

POROS
POROS TOWN

Key

Ⓐ Campanile
Ⓑ Bus Stop
Ⓒ Police / Supermarket
Ⓓ National Bank
Ⓔ Doctor
Ⓕ Pharmacies
Ⓖ Taxi Rank

Ⓗ Grocery Stores
Ⓘ Bakery
Ⓙ Newspapers
Ⓚ Restaurants
Ⓛ Camping (700 m)
Ⓜ Museum
Ⓝ Nautical School

1   Large Ferries
2   Hydrofoils
3   Landing Craft Berths
4   Taxi Boat Berths

Trireme Berth

Poros
Island

Marina

Papadopoulou

Latsi

Georgiou Michail

Demosthenos

25 Martiou

Manessi

Saron

Aktaion

7 Brothers

Mitropoleos

Galatas
(Mainland)

Fishing Caïques

25 Martiou

Galatia

Papasotiriou

Saronis

Vasiliadou

Note:
the 360 m wide
strait is not
drawn to scale

0   m   100

∽
Poros Town has little of sightseeing interest beyond the waterfront itself and a small **Archaeological Museum** south-east of the ferry quay (the Venetians preferring to fortify one of the Bourtzi islets rather than build in the town). On the north side of Sphalria lies Greece's **Naval Cadet School** in the former home of the 19 c. Arsenal. As a result, when she isn't on good will voyages up the Thames, it is occasionally possible to see the replica **Greek Trireme** (so named because such vessels were powered by three banks of oars) tied up at the end of the ferry dock (a nightwatchman is kept permanently aboard to stop tourists doing untold damage). Now officially part of the Hellenic Navy, the cadets have the dubious pleasure of rowing her each summer along with parties of invited foreign oarsmen.

Once out of the town you will find Poros is all pine trees and hills with an inland road around Kaleureia. This circuit offers a day's gentle strolling, taking in the views from the hills as well as the remains of the ancient city of Kaleureia. This settlement was home to one of ancient Greece's premier religious centres in the form of the 6 c. BC **Temple of Poseidon** (later demolished to furnish the masonry for Hydra Town's quayside monastery); here the great orator Demosthenes committed suicide in 322 BC (by nibbling on his poisoned pen while writing a farewell epistle — the original poison pen letter — to his family when his creditors seized him from the temple where he had sought sanctuary).

☎
CODE 0298, PORT POLICE 22274, TOURIST POLICE 22462.

Porto Helio
ΠΟΡΤΟ ΧΕΛΙ
An extremely large tourist town that is better avoided. This resort has become the natural terminus for ferries and hydrofoils running down the islands in the gulf — so most depart northwards (up to ten daily). Irregular smaller craft do put in occasionally, but the local market is insufficient to generate much traffic.

⊨
Pre-booked hotels predominate; but some pricey rooms available.

Spetses
ΣΠΕΤΣΕΣ; 22.5 km²; pop. 3500.
Sufficiently far from the capital to escape the worst of the day-trippers, yet still close enough to be served by daily Piraeus ferries (just), Spetses is a gentle, small, pine-forested island particularly popular with English tourists (suburbia rather than the fish-and-chips brigade). This is in part due to the island being the setting for John Fowles' novel *The Magus*; a popular tome that has ensured that many holiday-makers come to Spetses disposed to admire the place. The horses and traps that run along the waterfront of Spetses Town don't hurt either, though the paucity of good beaches results in a daily mass migration around the island that is not conducive to relaxed holiday-making.

Mansioned **Spetses Town** is apt to disappoint on first acquaintance: considering that it is the only settlement of any size on the island, the centre area is poorly laid out without the natural charm of most of the Cycladic island choras. It is also comparatively expensive. The tourist area is firmly focused around the streets near the new port. This is rather sad, as the too shallow old port is now reduced to a little visited yacht marina. In fact, it is much the more attractive of the two; with the headland to the south graced with three windmills for good measure.

An island-wide ban on cars has served to increase the suburbs of Spetses Town while restricting the growth of other tourist centres. Movement around the island is thus greatly restricted. As a result, crowded buses run along the northern coast hotel strip as well as to the most popular beach on Spetses — at Ag. Anargiri. Better reached by beach boat (you don't have to fight for a place like you do on the afternoon buses heading back to Spetses Town), it offers the best sand beach on the island. Beach boats also run across the straits from Spetses Town to the adjacent beach near the quiet village of **Kosta**; supplementing the

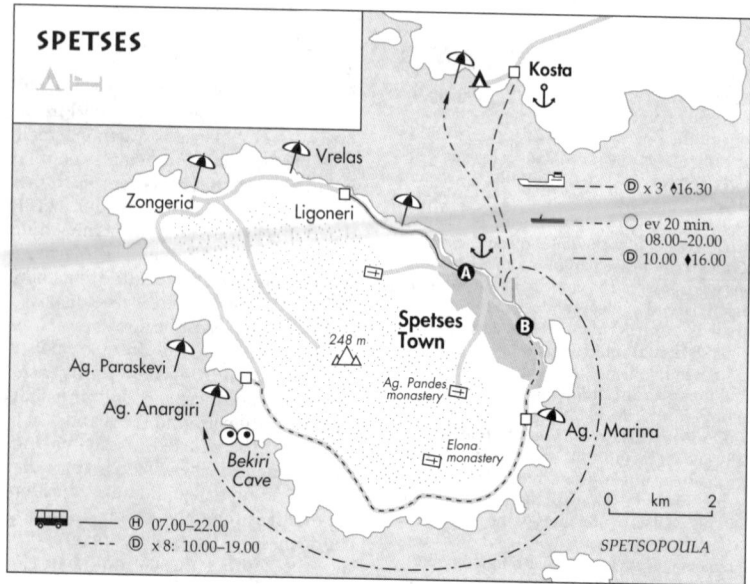

landing craft ferry running to the village itself several times a day. Tourist boats also make the crossing to here and Porto Helio. Be very wary of some of these boats: they divide up into 'normal' multi-passenger beach boats and so-called sea 'taxis' individually hired and charging ludicrous 'tourist' fares (2500 GDR as opposed to a mere 300 GDR).

⊨

Arrive early: block bookings by package tour operators means that beds are scarce. Tourist agencies east of the ferry dock have lists, and one *Takis Travel* (☎ 72888) — sited near the ferry quay — acts as agent for most of the island hoteliers; the residue being covered by *Pine Island Tours* (☎ 72464). Close by the ferry quay are a number of hotels worth a try. These include the budget E-class *Alexandri* (☎ 73073), the D-class *Saronikon* (☎ 73741), and the C-class *Faros* (☎ 72613). Near the town beach are the D-class *Klimis* (☎ 73777) and *Stelios* (☎ 72364); the latter complete with restaurant. Those with money to spend should try the A-class Edwardian *Posidonion* (☎ 72308).

A

Camping Kosta (☎ 51571). Reasonable site on the mainland 1 km west of Kosta village.

∞

Spetses, like Aegina and Hydra, played an important part in the struggle for Greek independence, furnishing the rebels with a cross between a Greek Boudicca and Lord Nelson in the form of a female admiral, Laskarina Bouboulina. Spetses Town has a **Museum** in one of the 18 c. mansions housing her bones and other independence material. The 8th of September also sees the islanders commemorate an 1822 naval victory when a Greek fireship forced an attacking Turkish fleet to withdraw from the island. This is re-enacted with the burning of a cast adrift taxi-boat each year. Apart from the Bekiri sea cave at Ag. Anargiri beach Spetses lacks sights: ticket agencies making a killing selling tours to attractions on the Peloponnese such as Epidavros and Corinth.

☎

CODE 0298, PORT POLICE 72245, TOURIST POLICE 73100.

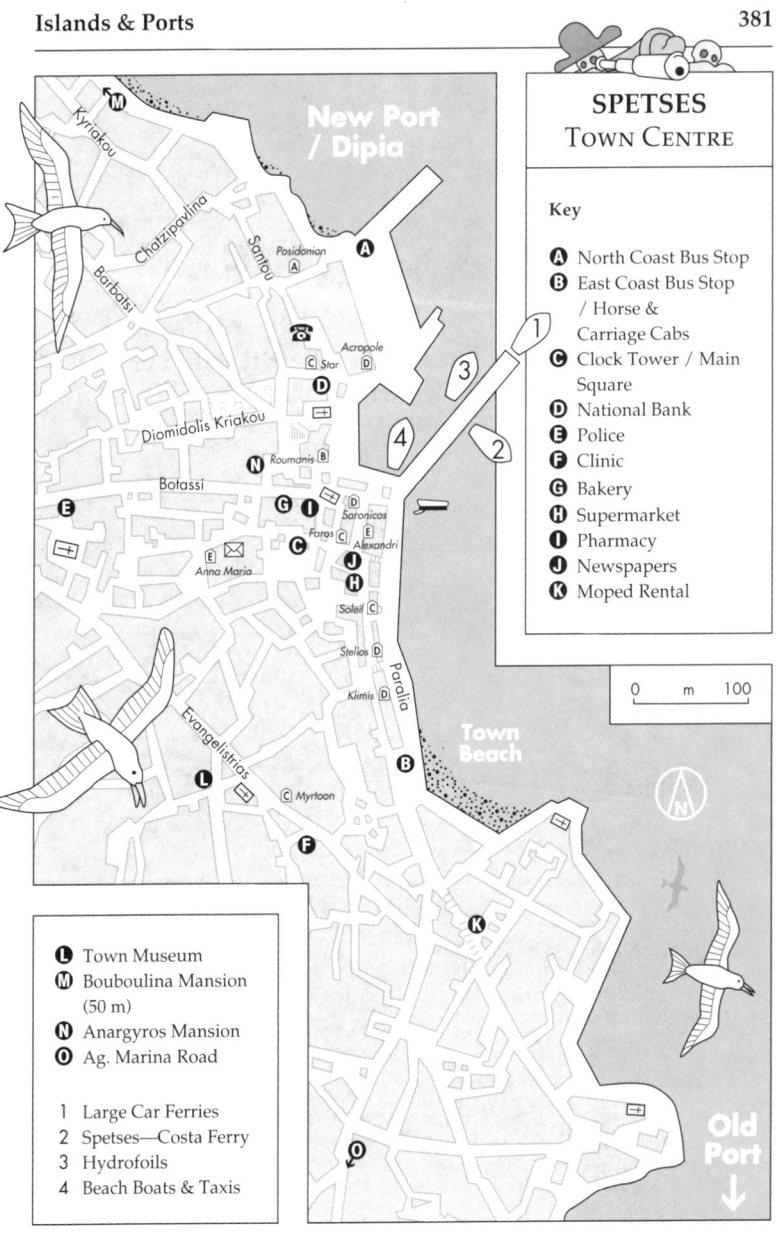

SPETSES
Town Centre

Key

- **A** North Coast Bus Stop
- **B** East Coast Bus Stop / Horse & Carriage Cabs
- **C** Clock Tower / Main Square
- **D** National Bank
- **E** Police
- **F** Clinic
- **G** Bakery
- **H** Supermarket
- **I** Pharmacy
- **J** Newspapers
- **K** Moped Rental

0   m   100

- **L** Town Museum
- **M** Bouboulina Mansion (50 m)
- **N** Anargyros Mansion
- **O** Ag. Marina Road

1 Large Car Ferries
2 Spetses—Costa Ferry
3 Hydrofoils
4 Beach Boats & Taxis

12
IONIAN LINES

ANTIPAXI · ITHACA · KEFALONIA · KILINI · LEFKADA
PAXI · ZAKINTHOS / ZANTE

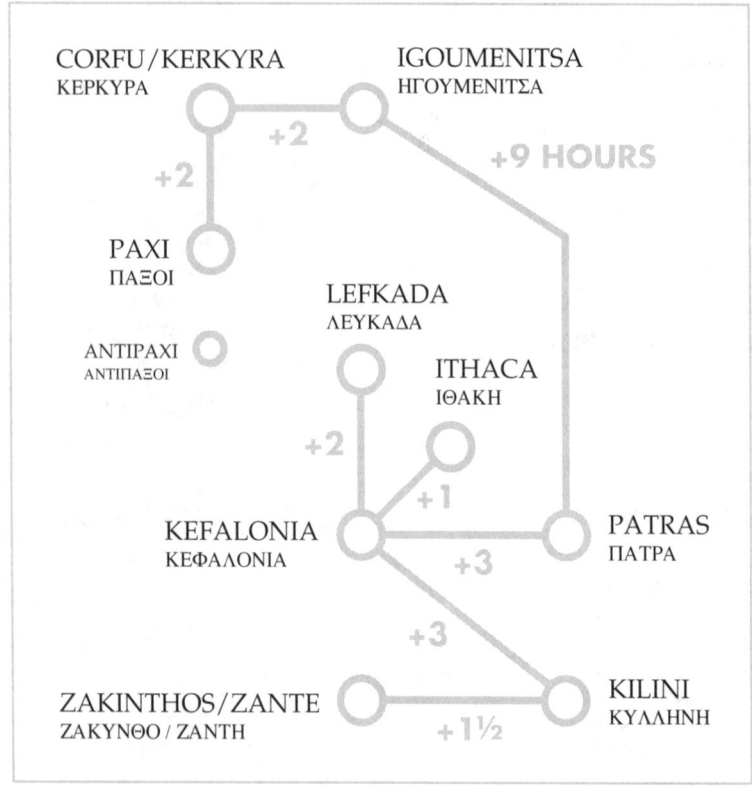

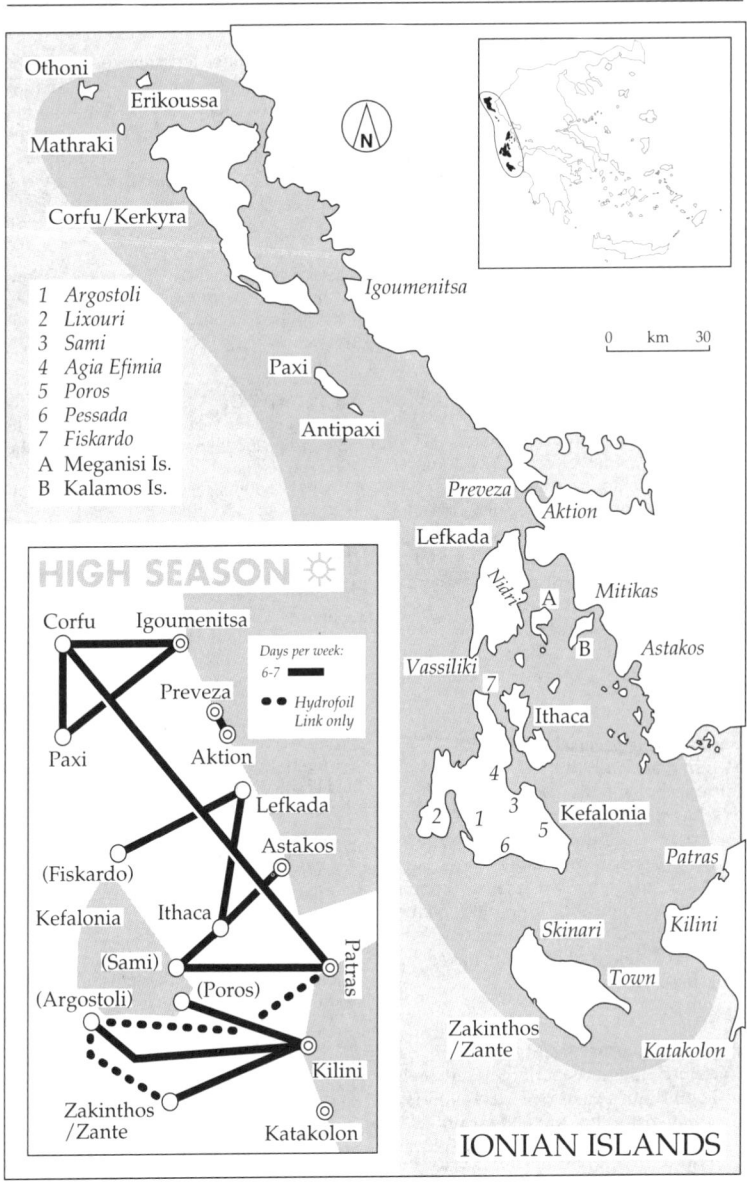

Othoni
Erikoussa
Mathraki
Corfu/Kerkyra

1 Argostoli
2 Lixouri
3 Sami
4 Agia Efimia
5 Poros
6 Pessada
7 Fiskardo
A Meganisi Is.
B Kalamos Is.

Igoumenitsa

0   km   30

Paxi
Antipaxi

Preveza
Aktion
Lefkada
Nidri
Mitikas
A
B   Astakos
Vassiliki
7
Ithaca
4
3   Kefalonia
2   1
5
6
Patras
Skinari   Kilini
Town
Zakinthos
/Zante   Katakolon

HIGH SEASON ☼

Corfu   Igoumenitsa
Preveza
Aktion
Paxi
Lefkada
Astakos
(Fiskardo)
Kefalonia   Ithaca
(Sami)
(Argostoli)   (Poros)   Patras
Zakinthos
/Zante   Kilini
Katakolon

Days per week:
6-7
●● Hydrofoil
Link only

IONIAN ISLANDS

General Features

The Ionian islands lie uncomfortably adrift from the rest of the Greek ferry system, guarding the entrance to the Adriatic Sea. By Greek standards most are on the large side, but as they have comparatively small population ratios and lie close to the mainland, a fully integrated ferry structure has never emerged. Poor ferry links are not helped by the profusion of airports; with Corfu, Zakinthos, Kefalonia and mainland Preveza/Aktion near Lefkada all offering viable arrival points. With the exception of Corfu, the islands see fewer independent travellers than their Aegean counterparts. Zante is a popular package tourist destination but at the southern extremity of the group attracts few ferries. Kefalonia is quiet and lacking a conveniently placed population centre. Ithaca (of Odysseus fame), along with Paxi and Antipaxi, are all too small to figure strongly on ferry schedules. Finally, as the great majority of travellers to and from Corfu/Kerkyra (p. 82) and the mainland ports of Igoumenitsa and Patras (p. 87) are using international services, these ports are described in Chapter 2.

Suggested Itinerary [2 Weeks]

Moving around the Ionian group is difficult but practicable on a one-hop a day basis; given that there is often only one boat between poorly connected ports and bus services are equally poor. The plus side to going Ionian lies in some lovely beaches and pine-clad island scenery coupled with shimmeringly clean water that looks as if Poseidon has set his waternymphs to giving each wavelet a lick and a rub daily.

Arrival/Departure Point

Corfu is the obvious starting point: given its good flight and ferry links, but Kefalonia and Zakinthos are better options if you are prepared to do a smaller circuit and drop Corfu from your itinerary.

Season

Most of the limited ferry network operates on an annual basis; consisting of essential mainland to island services. So travel is equally easy/difficult in April as it is in August. During the winter months less popular links either see reduced services or are suspended.

1 Corfu [2 Days]

This is one group where it is better to explore in the earlier part of a holiday; leaving the beach until later. So, after a couple of days on Corfu, take one of the international overnight ferries to Patras.

2 Patras [1 Day]

Having booked a seat on the afternoon bus to Kilini you will have a few hours to explore the city. You also have the option of heading on to Athens (3½ hours) for a couple of nights if you want to visit the capital.

3 Zakinthos [3 Days]

The Patras bus arrives at Kilini in time for the late afternoon ferry on to Zakinthos. Worth a couple of days exploration, when you are ready to move on you can take the morning ferry back to Kilini and pick up the connecting afternoon service on to Kefalonia (Argostoli).

4 Kefalonia [2 Days]

From Argostoli move on to the port of Sami for the best beds and daily boats to Lefkada and Ithaca. You could also stay longer and do the islands as day trips from here.

5 Lefkada [2 Days]

Arriving on the first boat you can use Vassiliki as a base for exploring Lefkada before taking the ferry on to Ithaca.

6 Ithaca [1 Day]

After exploring Ithaca, finish in the capital of Vathi — and its daily ferry link with Patras.

2 1 Patras/Corfu [3 Days]

Returning to Patras you can pick up one of the limited number of international ferries (e.g. Minoan Lines) offering travel within Greece to get back to Corfu, where you will have a couple of days to take in Paxi and Antipaxi, or lie on the beach before your flight home.

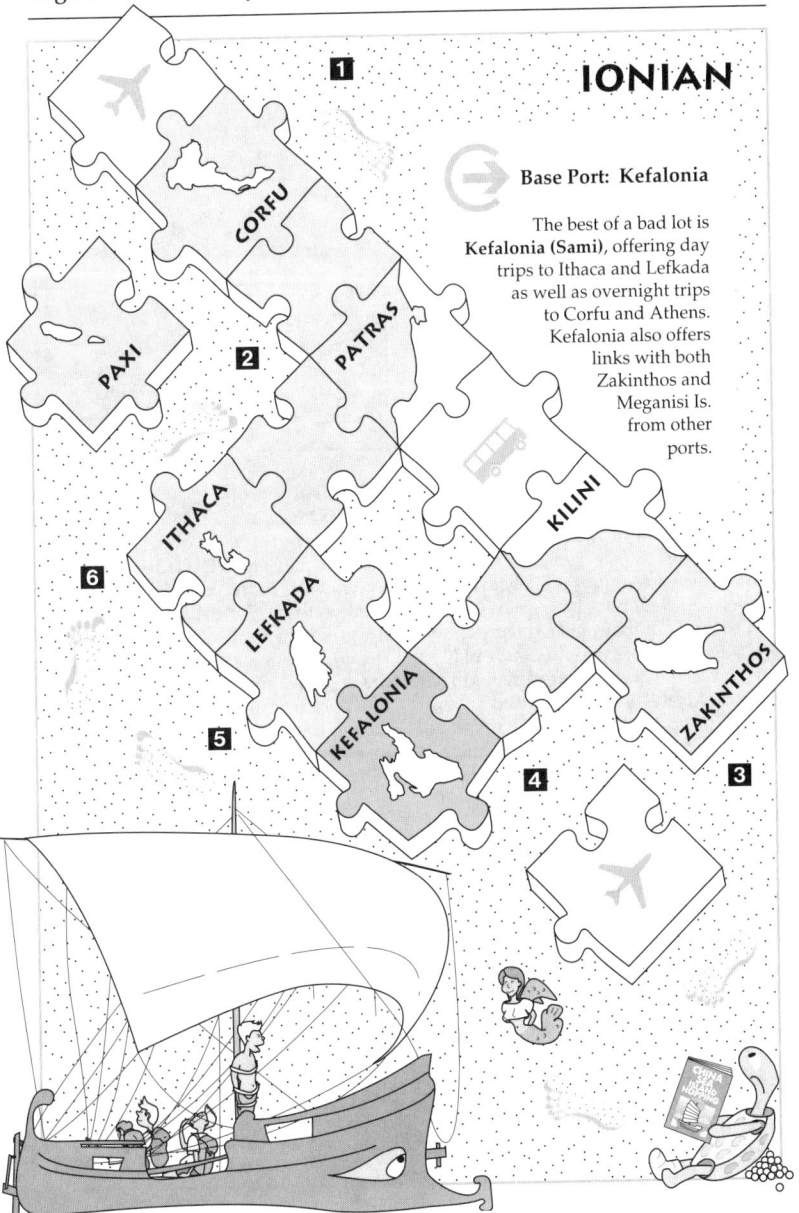

IONIAN

Base Port: Kefalonia

The best of a bad lot is **Kefalonia (Sami)**, offering day trips to Ithaca and Lefkada as well as overnight trips to Corfu and Athens. Kefalonia also offers links with both Zakinthos and Meganisi Is. from other ports.

1

CORFU

PAXI

2

PATRAS

ITHACA

6

LEFKADA

KILINI

5

KEFALONIA

4

ZAKINTHOS

3

Ionian Ferry Services

Main Car Ferries

Given the lack of any obvious pattern of progression between islands it is not surprising that most services are either small landing-craft ferries or elderly larger boats operating out of a mainland port to an adjacent island, rather than running up or down the chain. Moving between islands therefore often involves bouncing off the mainland by changing ferries at a mainland port. Moreover, useful interconnecting ferries often run solo on routes and you are pretty vulnerable should they not be operating. In 1991 none of the four most useful boats was operating during High Season; making travel around the group difficult to say the least. Things have improved since, but the potential for change remains. The big joker in the pack in 1995 is likely to be the ex-*Hellas Express*; bought by a new Corfu-based ferry company and renamed the *Agios Spiridon*, she will no doubt play a major role, but quite where remains to be seen. Hydrofoils are advertised in the Ionian group, but it is only since 1993 that they achieved any degree of reliability.

C/F *Myrtos*
Local; 1977; 2052 GRT.

An old friend in new clothes, the *Myrtos* has run this daily link between Argostoli (the capital of Kefalonia), and the mainland port of Kilini for years as the *Argostoli*. Now refurbished with a large deck-class passenger lounge (with air conditioning that works for good measure) she returned to her old route and schedule in 1992. Her new owners operate their boats in tandem with Strintzis Lines whose agents issue common tickets. If heading for Argostoli be careful to state your destination: this ferry deposits most of its passengers at the large town of Lixouri some ten minutes before arriving at Argostoli.

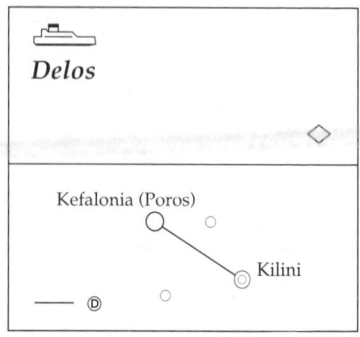

C/F *Delos*
Strintzis Lines; 1965; 2286 GRT.

A reliable ferry, the *Delos* operated out of Rafina to the Central Cyclades until larger ferries with more panache eroded her position there. For the last six years she has provided an all year service between Kefalonia (Poros) and Kilini. Choice of the vehicle port of Poros makes her unattractive to foot passengers. During the High Season she does the round trip thrice daily. Schedules unlikely to change in 1995. Formerly the SNCM *Villandry*, period facilities on board are adequate, and reflect her cross-Channel pedigree.

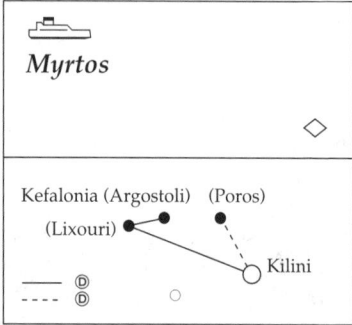

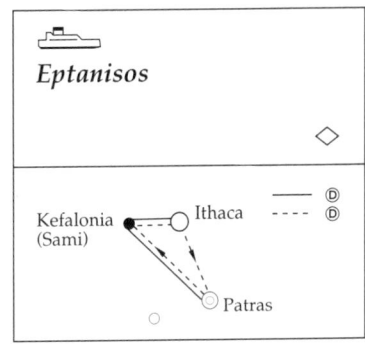

C/F *Dimitrius Miras* - C/F *Proteos* - C/F *Zakinthos I*
Local
Dimitrius Miras; 1972; 2160 GRT.
Proteos; 1973; 998 GRT.
Zakinthos I; 1973; 500 GRT.
Three ferries provide the link between the mainland and Zakinthos/Zante. The service runs eight times daily to the capital in the summer months, but only three times a day during the Low Season. All independently operated, the boats do the route by rota and you thus buy a ticket for a particular time of crossing rather than a specific boat. Although not the largest of the three, the *Zakinthos I* is easily the best, with more deck space and working air conditioning. The *Proteos* follows grubbily on. The final member of the trio, the *Dimitrius Miras*, is a converted cargo vessel used for heavy goods vehicle runs.

C/F *Eptanisos*
Strintzis Lines; 1965; 2963 GRT.
The Strintzis Line *Eptanisos* (ex SNCM *Valencay*) followed her sister ship — the *Delos* — into the Ionian Sea in 1992. With a tried and tested timetable, this boat operates the main morning service from the islands to Patras. As such it is unlikely to change much in 1995 (her predecessor ran the same schedule). Not surprisingly, the *Ephanisos* is almost identical to the

Delos, with distinctly utilitarian facilities by today's standards. Even so, she is well maintained, and commendably clean.

C/F *Aphrodite L*
This is an unusual landing-craft ferry (courtesy of the passenger seating on extended gangways either side of the car deck), and has operated a useful and largely unchanged twice-daily schedule for the last six years between Kefalonia, Ithaca and Lefkada (Vassiliki). In 1990 an early morning run between Sami and Ithaca was added to her summer timetable. Usually reliable, 1991 saw this vessel out of action after a little collision with an uninhabited islet: quite an achievement given their scarcity along her route.

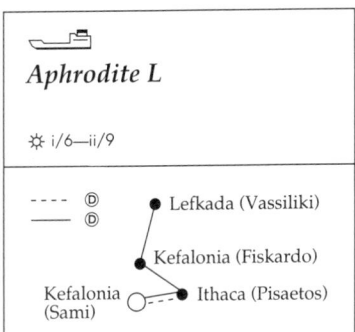

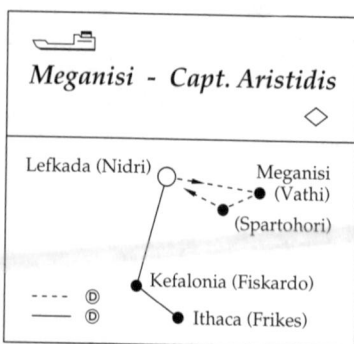

Meganisi - Capt. Aristidis ◇

Lefkada (Nidri) — Meganisi (Vathi) — (Spartohori) — Kefalonia (Fiskardo) — Ithaca (Frikes)

- - - - Ⓓ
───── Ⓓ

C/F *Meganisi - Capt. Aristidis*

After providing Meganisi with its main link with the outside world, small landing-craft ferries supplement their income with a (horribly over-loaded) twice-daily High Season service from Lefkada to the nearest (and remotest) ports on Kefalonia and Ithaca. A popular Italian motorist's link; car owners should arrive on the quayside early for a place.

C/F *Ionion Pelagos*

Each summer sees this stumpy small landing-craft ferry operate the shortest crossing between Kefalonia and Zakinthos. However, unless you have your own transport, this is a next to useless link given the absence of bus services to and from either of her ports of call.

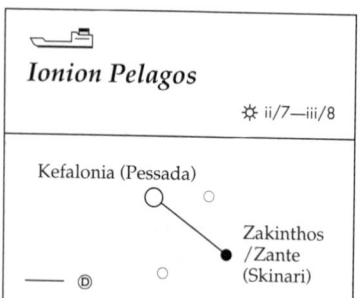

Ionion Pelagos

☼ ii/7—iii/8

Kefalonia (Pessada) ○ — Zakinthos /Zante (Skinari) ●

───── Ⓓ

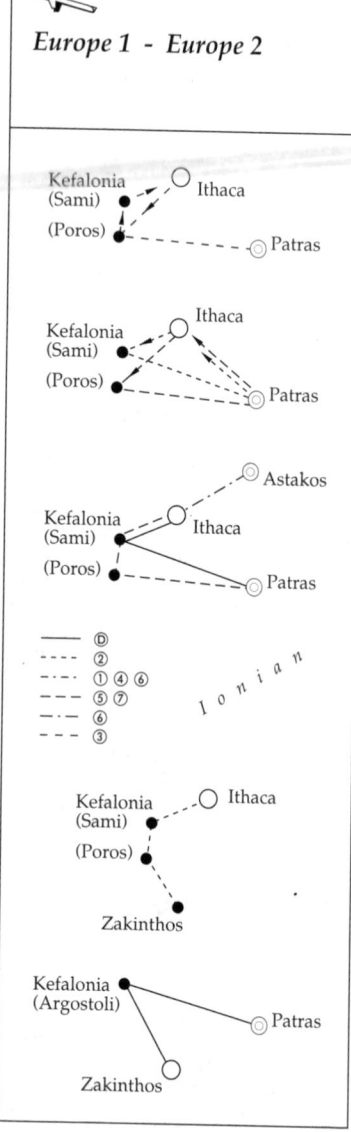

Europe 1 - Europe 2

Kefalonia (Sami) ● — Ithaca ○
(Poros) ● - - - - - - - Patras

Kefalonia (Sami) ● — Ithaca ○
(Poros) ● - - - - - - - Patras

Kefalonia (Sami) ● — Ithaca ○ —·— Astakos
(Poros) ● - - - - - - - Patras

───── Ⓓ
- - - - ②
—·—·— ① ④ ⑥
- - - - ⑤ ⑦
—·— ⑥
- - - ③

Ionian

Kefalonia (Sami) ● - - - Ithaca ○
(Poros) ●
Zakinthos ●

Kefalonia (Argostoli) ● — Patras
Zakinthos ○

H/F *Europe I* - H/F *Europe II*

For a number of summers hydrofoil services have been advertised in the Ionian islands only to be woefully absent at the height of the season. The appearance of two hydrofoils running their advertised schedules, and on time, was thus one of the great surprises of 1993. The only fly in the ointment was the failure of the company to notify local agents of the full timetable; a problem still evident in 1994. Changes to times and itineraries last year were considerable, and it would be unwise to rely on finding anything beyond the daily Patras—Kefalonia—Ithaca and Patras—Kefalonia—Zakinthos links. On both routes passengers needed to book a day in advance in 1993.

C/F *Thiaki*

Local; 1961; 499 GRT.

An elderly, tiny, car ferry. Operated by the owners of the *Myrtos* and in tandem with Strintzis Lines her route is something of an oddity: preferring to steam out of the remote port of Agia Efimia and travelling to the equally obscure mainland hamlet of Astakos (usually via Ithaca). Not a foot passenger's boat, the bulk of her custom is made up of commercial vehicles.

C/F *Zephyros*

Local; 1970; 1070 GRT.

Formerly the Nomikos Lines' *Aegeus* this cute little ferry now operates as an independent boat out of Paxi, providing the main daily link between that island and

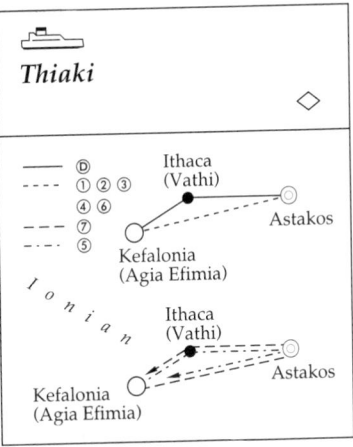

both Corfu and Igoumenitsa. Her summer 1992 schedule was modified in 1993, but remained unchanged in 1994. Further variations are likely to be confined to times as she has no other obvious places to go. At Corfu Town she tends to berth on the more exposed easterly quay of the Old Port. Often crowded with backpackers, the *Zephyros*'s daily Corfu Town to Paxi service is also augmented by a small tourist boat — the P/S *Pegassus* — which carries around 70 passengers. Significantly more expensive than the ferry, this small boat's one saving grace is that (unlike the *Zephyros*) it berths at the Old Port on Paxi, rather than the New Port 1 km north-west of Paxi Town.

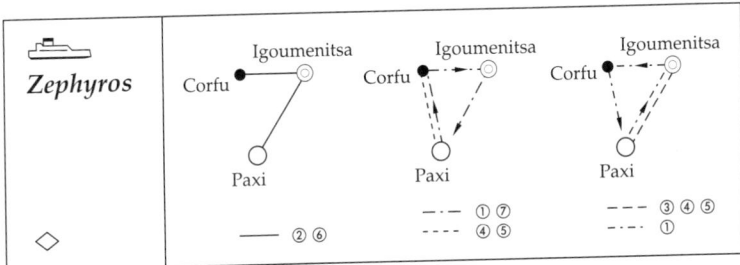

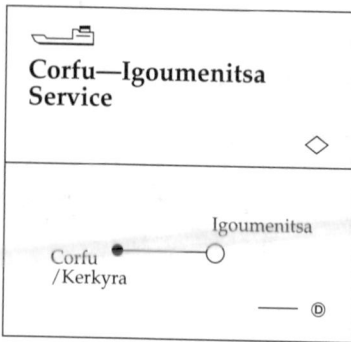

Corfu—Igoumenitsa Services

The 90-minute Corfu—Igoumenitsa crossing has some dozen landing craft operating an hourly service on a rota basis from a quay 400 m north of Corfu Town's International ferry terminal building. Unchanging schedules are posted up on the Port Police kiosk on the quay.

Corfu Local Ferries

Corfu also has a number of minor services with limited tourist appeal. The most useful of the mainland links is the 5 x ⓓ service between the island's second port of Lefkimi and Igoumenitsa. Prior to the arrival of the *Zephyros* Lefkimi also had an inconsistent link with Paxi (times for all the boats opposite are listed in the Corfu Town tourist office). Tourist boats (the P/S's *Rena S/II*, *Petrakis*, *Sotirakis*, and *Sotirakis II*) also offer extra Paxi, Antipaxi and Plataria connections (albeit at a price) as well as an Albania service (see p. 81).

P/S *Alexandros K II*

Corfu Town also has a limited service to the three minor islands to the north of Corfu. One small passenger boat departs soon after dawn several days a week. Times don't change much, but (Orthoni aside) these islets are more frequently visited via tourist boats from the north Corfu resort town of Sidari.

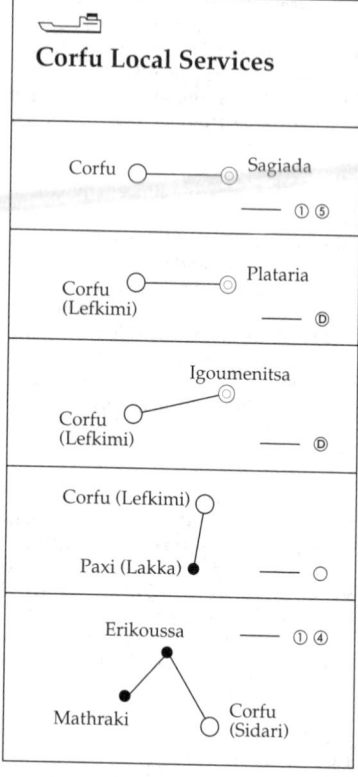

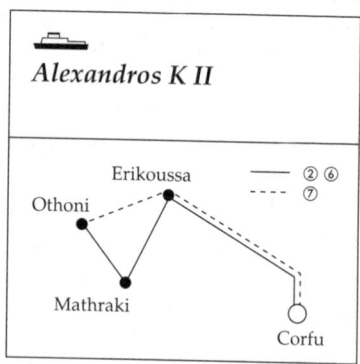

Ionian Islands & Ports

Astakos
ΑΣΤΑΚΟΣ

A small village on the mainland west coast, Astakos is the home port of a single ferry (the C/F *Thiaki*) running daily to Ithaca and Kefalonia. It is also the departure point for the produce caïques that keep the small fishing community that struggles along on the isolated island of Kalamos (which lies to the north-west) supplied with essentials. However, its connections aside, Astakos has little going for it. In truth, the beach aside, the most interesting thing in town is the bus stop.

⊨

Astakos has three hotels that cater for the few that get caught here. Top of the range is the B-class *Stratos* (☎ 41096). There are also two budget hotels in town: the D-class *Beach* (☎ 41135) and the *Byron* (☎ 41516).

☎

CODE 0646

Gulf of Corinth & Mainland Ports

Running north of the Peloponnese from the Corinth Canal to the entrance to the Ionian Sea lies the Gulf of Corinth. Two landing-craft ferry links make the crossing; foot passengers are something of a rarity. Easterly link runs from **Agios Nikolaos** on the north coast to **Egion** on the Peloponnese. Westerly link is from **Andirio** to **Rio** 10 km north-east of Patras. Both run frequently day and night.

There is also a regular ferry service between the mainland ports of **Aktion**, just north of Lefkada, and **Preveza** (home to the remains of a notable Roman city), a town on the headland to the north (see p. 397). This service is far less frequent and if you are bussing up or down the coast between Corfu and Astakos or the Peloponnese you might well have to stay the night at Preveza (there are a goodly number of hotels on the waterfront).

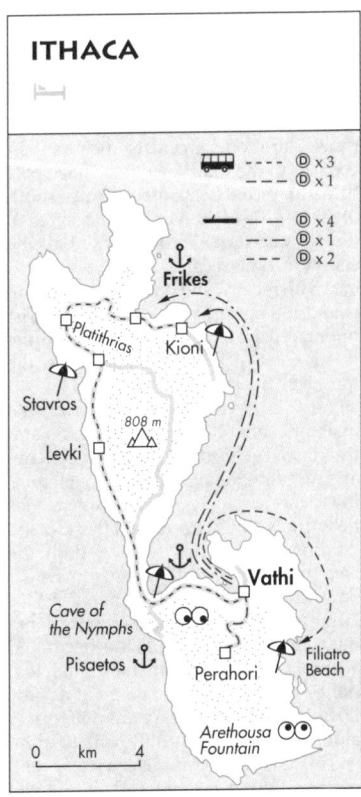

ITHACA

Ithaca
ΙΘΑΚΗ; 96 km², pop. 4000.

A small and very hilly island, Ithaca lies steeped in the romance of myth rather than offering much in reality beyond a quiet tranquillity. The legendary home of Odysseus (alias Ulysses), hero of the Odyssey — and the siege of Troy too in a way (he was the bright spark who came up with the idea of the wooden horse), there is little to do here except walk the hills, indulge in a little quiet romance and wonder why the hero spent ten years trying to get back. His palace (home to his wife Penelope, her suitors and attendant orgy girls) was supposedly in the north of the island, but unlike other attributed sites in Greece, Ithaca has yielded little significant archaeological evidence to suggest it was a centre of power at the time. The modern centre, such as it is, consists of the red-tile house village port of **Vathi** tucked deep into a bay just south of the middle of the island. Devastated in the 1953 earthquake that rocked all the southern Ionian islands, it has been rebuilt sympathetically, and offers a taste of rural island life spiced with the more tourist orientated waterfront looking onto the prison islet of **Lanroito** that graces the mouth of the bay.

Ferry links are good considering the insignificance of Ithaca as a tourist island (thanks largely to poor pebble beaches and few obvious sights) with boats running to three island ports. All large ferries head for Vathi, with daily High Season landing-craft ferries serving both the small northern port of **Frikes** (from Lefkada) and at **Pisaetos** (from Kefalonia). This latter 'port' is no more than an isolated quay below a steep hillside decorated with a switchback dirt track road that defies the island bus and sees as few taxis. Ithaca has a solitary bus that teeters along the precipitous hill roads to uninspiring **Stavros** (complete with several places offering rooms) and the hamlet villages on the northern half of the island, as well as to **Perahori**, the former centre in pirate-troubled days. High Season also sees taxi boats running from Vathi to the attractive pebble beach villages of **Kioni** and Frikes. Formerly quiet fishing villages, they now offer a gentle spot in which to spend a day or two.

⊨

Accommodation on Ithaca is pretty limited, and what there is tends to be expensive. **Vathi** has some rooms and two B-class hotels: the

Mendor (☎ 32433), on the waterfront near the caïque harbour, and the western edge of town the hotel/pension *Odysseus* (☎ 32381) — also on the waterfront. There is also a C-class hotel in **Frikes**: the *Nostos* (☎ 31644), and a B-class hotel in Kioni: the *Kioni* (☎ 31362). A few rooms are also on offer at both.

∞

Vathi is host to a small **Archaeological Museum** which in truth has limited appeal. More interesting by far is the **Cave of the Nymphs** — a large cavern 1 km west of Vathi, said to have been used by Odysseus and the goddess Athena to hide the treasure the Phaeacians gave him immediately prior to his return from Troy. A second site with Homeric associations lies on the south-east corner of the island: the **Arethousian Fountain** offers a splendid excuse for some pleasant hill walking, but bring liquid with you as your objective is often drunk dry.

☎

CODE 0674, POLICE 32205, FERRY INFORMATION 32145.

Katakolon
ΚΑΤΑΚΟΛΟ

A sleepy little port on the west coast of the Peloponnese, Katakolon hovers on the fringe of the ferry system, appearing every other year or so on a new boat's itinerary before commercial realities set in and it returns to somnolent isolation. The reason for these calls by irregular ferries and cruise ships is the port's ready access to the site of ancient Olympia (27 km), home to the most important Temple of Zeus and the Olympic games. Actually, the port is quite attractive itself, with an impressively long beach, several tavernas and hotels. Buses connect with the town of Pirgos (12 km away) and its links with Olympia (where you will find three campsites and a youth hostel).

⊨

Accommodation options in town are confined to three establishment: the A-class pension *Zefyros* (☎ 41170), the C-class hotel *Ionio* (☎ 41494), and the D-class *Delfini* (☎ 41214).

☎

CODE 0621

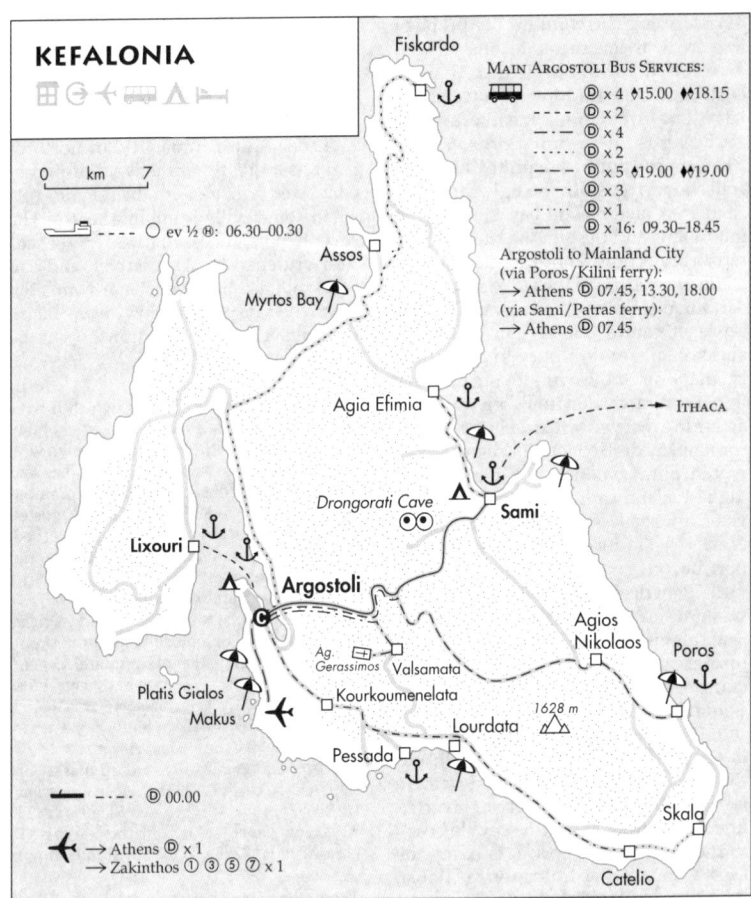

KEFALONIA

Fiskardo

MAIN ARGOSTOLI BUS SERVICES:
—— Ⓓ×4 ♦15.00 ♦♦18.15
---- Ⓓ×2
—·— Ⓓ×4
······ Ⓓ×2
—— Ⓓ×5 ♦19.00 ♦♦19.00
—··— Ⓓ×3
······ Ⓓ×1
—— Ⓓ×16: 09.30–18.45

Argostoli to Mainland City
(via Poros/Kilini ferry):
→ Athens Ⓓ 07.45, 13.30, 18.00
(via Sami/Patras ferry):
→ Athens Ⓓ 07.45

0   km   7

Ⓞ ev ½ ⓑ: 06.30–00.30

Assos

Myrtos Bay

Agia Efimia   ITHACA

Drongorati Cave   Sami

Lixouri   Argostoli

Agios
Nikolaos   Poros

Ag.
Gerassimos   Valsamata
Platis Gialos   Kourkoumenelata
Makus   1628 m
                    Lourdata
            Pessada   Skala

Ⓓ 00.00   Catelio

→ Athens Ⓓ × 1
→ Zakinthos ① ③ ⑤ ⑦ × 1

Kefalonia

ΚΕΦΑΛΛΩΝΙΑ; 781 km², pop. 31,800.

The second largest island in the Ionian group, Kefalonia is a quiet beach-holiday island offering spectacular mountain scenery and considerable vexation in moving around if you are without your own transport. If all you want to do is divide time between a small hotel and a quiet beach then the island has a lot going for it, otherwise it is apt to disappoint. Size is Kefalonia's problem: the island is too big while the population centres are too small. As a result of both this, and the misfortune of the island capital growing up in a superb sheltered bay on the far west side when all ferry links are either with the mainland or islands on the other three sides of the compass, an amazing seven island ports have emerged offering ferry services. This wouldn't be a problem if there was an adequate bus service between them but unfortunately there is not, and from midday on you usually have to resort to the expensive taxi service (Argostoli—Sami approx. £10).

Kefalonia's ports are a pretty disparate collection. **Argostoli**, the ugly capital, is sited in a picturesque bay beneath the mountains and despite the lack of good ferry connections and the prefab architecture that arose in the wake of the 1953 earthquake, has managed to retain some sense of centre but very little else: it abjectly fails to do justice to its setting. From the air or the overlooking hillsides it looks attractive enough, but once you arrive in town you will find yourself surrounded by drab concrete structures that would put Kefalonia very high in any 'ugliest island capital' contest. Even the waterfront lacks sparkle. There is a good NTOG/EOT office just south of the ferry port, but otherwise there is little reason to visit. Even the locals prefer to live on the western side of the bay at **Lixouri**, a port town almost as large as the capital, made up of nought but suburbs. A small landing-craft ferry (the C/F *Agios Gerasimus*) runs frequently between the two.

Of the other ports: the village of **Sami** has become the 'international' berth and the nearest thing Kefalonia has to a main ferry port. With an attractive, taverna-lined waterfront and a fine pebble beach to the north of the port, it is easily the most attractive place to stay on Kefalonia. Nightlife, such as it is, is centred here, but no-one comes to Kefalonia to party. The remaining ports have even less going for them; the hamlet of **Poros** is the favoured starting point for the Kilini ferry (with connections on to Zakinthos) but is difficult to get to from Sami. It is connected to Argostoli by the same road that branches south to the undeveloped village of **Skala**, with beaches to the east a second home to the Loggerhead turtles (see p. 402), this time minus tourists.

Fiskardo, perched on the northern finger, is the only village to retain a majority of pre-earthquake buildings around its petite tree-lined bay, but is host to day-trippers from the rest of the island and Lefkada. **Agia Efimia**, 10 km north of Sami, is a quietly attractive, but poorly connected, village with the remains of a small Roman villa crumbling nearby. The seventh port, at **Pessada**, has ferry schedules written by local taxi drivers and is to be avoided unless you have your own means of transport (its ferry link to Zakinthos is met by no public transport at the other end either).

🛏

Hotels plentiful on Kefalonia, which thrives on its reputation as a sedate package-holiday island. This end of the market, combined with a large number of Italian motorists, has had the unfortunate consequence that accommodation is pricey. NTOG/EOT office in Argostoli offers help in tracking down a spare hotel bed, along with free maps, bus timetables and some ferry information.

Sami has several convenient hotels. Two, the C-class *Ionion* (☎ 22035) and D-class *Kyma* (☎ 22064), both one block behind the promenade (the latter off the town square). Several blocks further back with good bay views across to Ithaca is the D-class *Melissani* (☎ 22464).

Argostoli has hotels aplenty; for a good, budget hotel try the D-class *Allegro* (☎ 22268) or *Parthenon* (☎ 22246). More up-market are the C-class *Tourist* (☎ 22510), *Agios Gerassimos* (☎ 28697) or more expensive *Mouikis* (☎ 230 32). If you want to splash out, then there is a B-class *Xenia* (☎ 22233) at the north end of town.

▲

There are several reasonable sites on the island: most convenient is *Caravomilos Beach* (☎ 0674 22480) at **Sami**. A nice, mature tree-filled site behind a pebble beach, but (thanks to the large number of Italian motorists) very expensive. Management dictate where you pitch your tent. *Argostoli Beach* (☎ 0671 23487) is 2 km north of **Agostoli** and offers marginally better value, but similar on-site conditions apply.
👓

Apart from a poor **Archaeological Museum**, the only 'sight' Argostoli has on offer is a small monument on the road causeway across

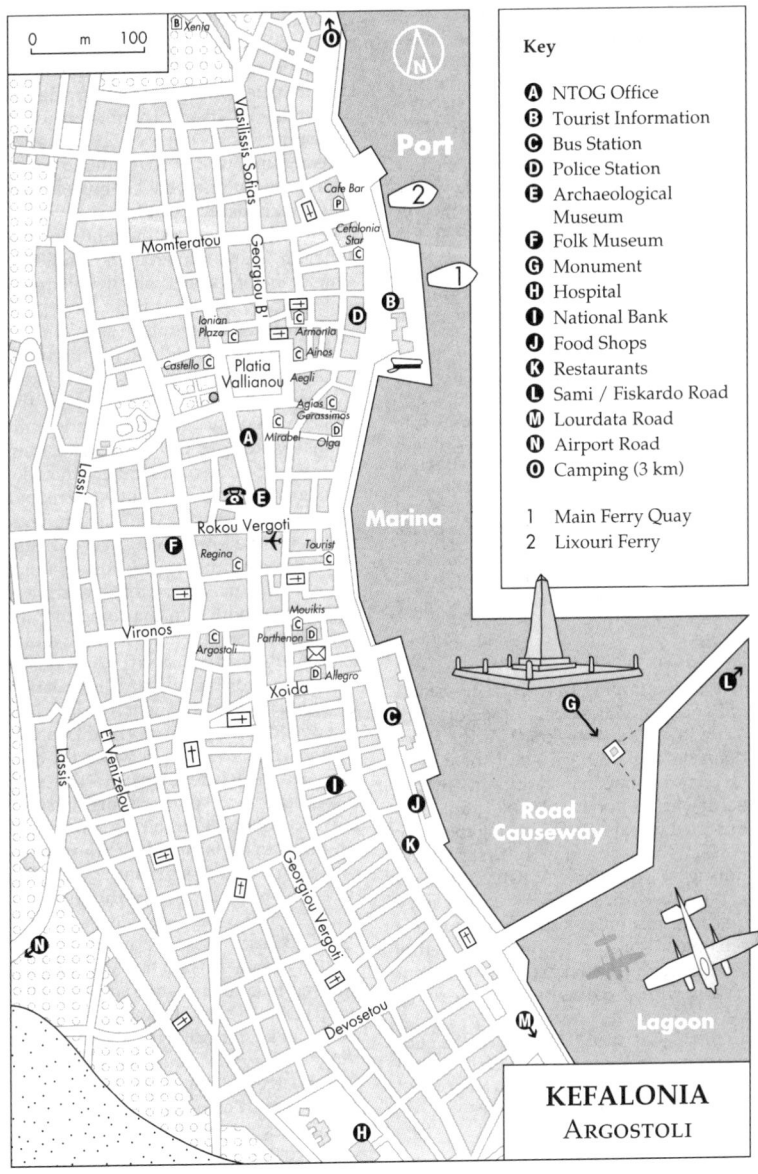

0   m   100

Xenia

Port

Café Bar

P

Cefalonia
Star

C

Vasilissis Sofias

Momferatou

Georgiou B.

D

B

Ionian
Plaza

C

Armonia

C Ainos

Castello **C**

Platia
Vallianou

Aegli

Agias **C**
Gerassimos

A

Mirabel

C

Olga

D

E

2

1

Lassi

Rokou Vergoti

F

Regina

C

Tourist

C

Marina

Mouikis

Vironos

C

Parthenon

D

Argostoli

C

Xoida

Allegro **D**

C

I

El Venizelou

Lassis

Georgiou Vergoti

J

K

**Road
Causeway**

G

L

N

Devosetou

M

Lagoon

H

KEFALONIA
ARGOSTOLI

Key

A NTOG Office
B Tourist Information
C Bus Station
D Police Station
E Archaeological
       Museum
F Folk Museum
G Monument
H Hospital
I National Bank
J Food Shops
K Restaurants
L Sami / Fiskardo Road
M Lourdata Road
N Airport Road
O Camping (3 km)

1 Main Ferry Quay
2 Lixouri Ferry

the neck of the bay south of the town — built to commemorate the glory of the British Empire (the British built most of the island roads during 50 years of rule in the 19th century); it is now inscription-less but otherwise intact. During 1992, the mayor of Sami (a part time archaeologist) discovered a major 14 c. BC Mycenaean beehive-shaped tomb on the outskirts of the town, reopening speculation as to whether Kefalonia was the true 'Ithaca' of Odysseus — given the absence of finds there and the better topographical 'fit' of Kefalonia to the island described by Homer. This discovery will presumably be open to the public at some point. Meantime, excursions out of Argostoli are very popular. These include **bus tours** around the island (visiting the impressive red-walled **Drongarati Caves** south-west of Sami — complete with a subterranean lake), and, combining buses with local ferries and hydrofoils to (1) **Zakinthos** (via Pessada), (2) the ruins of ancient **Olympia** — home to the original Olympic Games and the famous Temple of Zeus (via Poros and Kilini), and (3) day trips to **Ithaca** and **Lefkada**.

☎

SAMI CODE 0674, ARGOSTOLI 0671,
ARGOSTOLI NTOG OFFICE 22248.

Kilini
ΚΥΛΛΗΝΗ

The major jumping-off point to the island of Zante, Kilini is a dusty little port with a beach on the west coast of the Peloponnese some 30 km south of Patras. Overland connections are poor; simply getting to this port is apt to be a pain. Two buses a day leave Patras during the week (08.00, 14.55), with only the first running during the weekends. At Kilini they stop at the ticket office block behind the ferry quay, usually only skidding into town at breakneck speed a few minutes before ferries are due to depart. An indifferent train service also runs between the ports.

⊢

Tourist Police (☎ 92211) office on the quay will point you in the direction of the limited (but rarely full) rooms in the port. The nearest hotels are 5 km to the south at **Kastro**.

☎

CODE 0623.

Lefkada / Lefkas
ΛΕΥΚΑΔΑ; 303 km², pop. 23,000.

An island sufficiently close to the mainland to have a road link (via a bridge to the capital of Lefkada Town), Lefkada is barren and austere but spectacular thanks to its mountains and islet-littered coast. Tourist development has largely confined itself to the east and southern coasts, but is comparatively restrained; offering an appealing mix of taverna and tradition. Unusually for a Greek island, the capital — Lefkada Town — is not a ferry port. With the lagoon to the north now home to a yachting marina, and salt flats between it and the mainland, it doesn't feel like a coastal town. Tradition has it that the Lefkada was joined to the mainland until a canal was dug in the 5 c. BC separating the town from the mainland. Earthquake damage is also all too evident here, but fortunately most of the Venetian churches that make the town have survived, and the ad hoc rebuilding of houses (now limited to a maximum of two storeys high) has produced a charming tin roof and plaster touch. This is one town that has actually been enhanced by earthquake 'repairs'. Unfortunately, accommodation is limited in the town and it is best visited as a day trip from one of Lefkada's ports.

Buses run frequently between the capital and main island towns; most passing through the resort port of **Nidri**, the starting point for boat tours circumnavigating a number of islets including **Skorpios** — owned by the Onassis family. A number of boats (including an embarrassing caïque done up as a mock Odysseus boat (the T/B *Boat Odysseia*) advertise swims *on* the island. In practice you are not allowed to land and you swim from the boat just offshore. Despite this, these excursions offer value for money thanks to the visit to the sea cave on Meganisi. One boat even goes to Lefkada's best sand beach at **Porto Katsiki** — also visited by caïques from the port of **Vassiliki**. Home to the best windsurfing in Europe

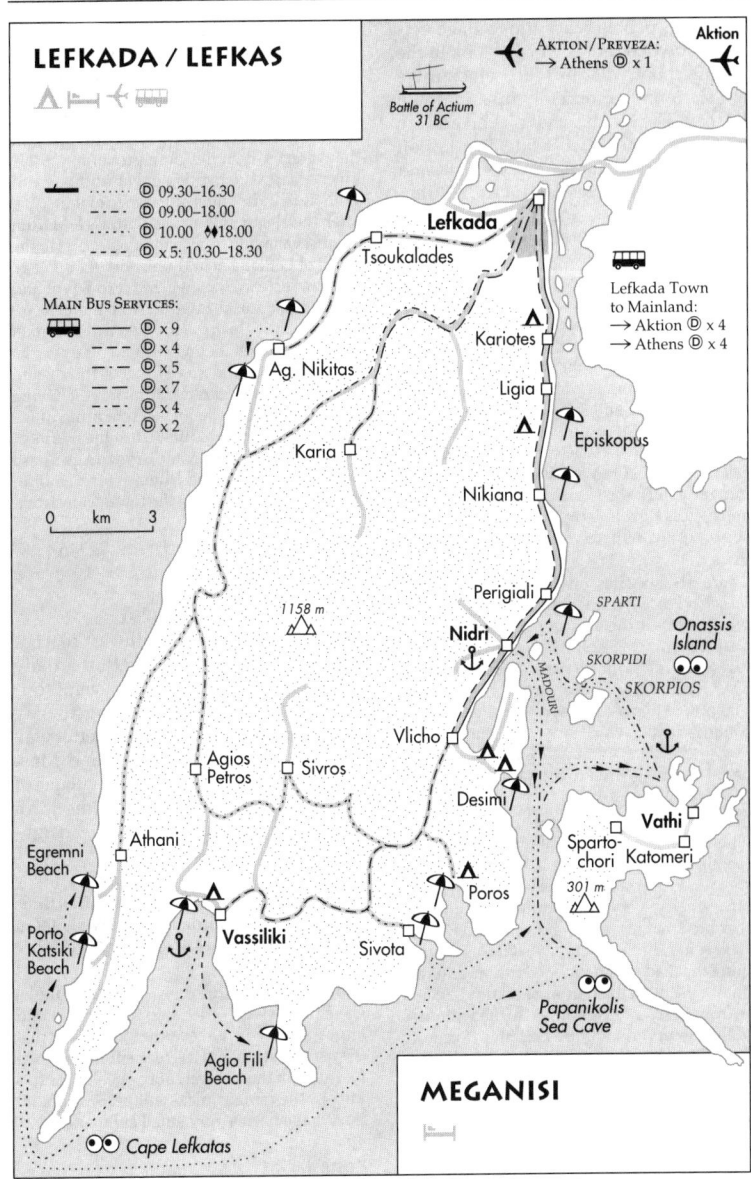

LEFKADA / LEFKAS

AKTION/PREVEZA:
→ Athens Ⓓ x 1

Aktion

Battle of Actium
31 BC

Ⓓ 09.30–16.30
Ⓓ 09.00–18.00
Ⓓ 10.00 ♦18.00
Ⓓ x 5: 10.30–18.30

MAIN BUS SERVICES:

Ⓓ x 9
Ⓓ x 4
Ⓓ x 5
Ⓓ x 7
Ⓓ x 4
Ⓓ x 2

Lefkada Town
to Mainland:
→ Aktion Ⓓ x 4
→ Athens Ⓓ x 4

0   km   3

Lefkada

Tsoukalades

Kariotes

Ligia

Episkopus

Ag. Nikitas

Karia

Nikiana

Perigiali

SPARTI

Onassis
Island

1158 m

Nidri

SKORPIDI

SKORPIOS

MADOURI

Vlicho

Agios
Petros

Sivros

Desimi

Vathi

Sparto-
chori

Katomeri

Egremni
Beach

Athani

301 m

Porto
Katsiki
Beach

Vassiliki

Poros

Sivota

Papanikolis
Sea Cave

Agio Fili
Beach

Cape Lefkatas

MEGANISI

off a poor pebble beach, this village gets very crowded, but is worth a look in the late afternoon when up to 100 windsurfers are skimming effortlessly up and down the bay. The best beaches on Lefkada are all on the remoter west side. In addition to Porto Katsiki there is an excellent sand beach behind the headland at **Ag. Nikitas**.

⊢⊣

High package tourist presence (courtesy of the airport at Aktion: sometimes advertised as Lefkada airport) has driven up prices and reduced the available accommodation. **Lefkada** is the most likely town to have beds on offer. The E-class *Patrae* (☎ 22359) near the Agricultural bank in the central square has a good reputation, as does the C-class *Santa Mavra* (☎ 22342) and the nearby E-class *Vyzantion* (☎ 22629). More up-market are the expensive promenade B-class *Niricos* (☎ 24132) and *Lefkas* (☎ 23916). **Vassiliki** also has some budget hotels: the C-class *Lefkatas* (☎ 31229) and E-class *Paradissos* (☎ 31256), and a plentiful supply of B-class hotels full of package tourists.

A

There are six sites on the island: *Camping Vassiliki Beach* (☎ 31308) full to bursting with windsurfers is the most convenient, *Camping Desimi Beach* (☎ 95225), 3 km south of Nidri, is less so but offers more space. *Camping Kariotes Beach* (☎ 23594) is the nearest to Lefkada Town. The other sites — *Episkopos Beach* (☎ 92410), *Santa Mavra Camping* (☎ 95493) and *Poros Beach* (☎ 95452) running down the east coast, are primarily geared to motorists.

👓

Lefkada's sights are more made up of places where things happened rather than things to see; the island being a veritable shrine to the sticky side of romance. Story has it that Aristotle, when a very old man, was asked if he regretted that his manly 'powers' had waned. He is said to have observed that it was the best thing that had ever happened to him, as it was 'like being unchained from a lunatic'. Lefkada is, from top to tail, a testament to the acuteness of this observation. **Cape Lefkatas** (formerly Cape Doukato) became the Beachy Head of the ancient world after Sappho (the famous lesbian poet of antiquity) jumped off after experiencing a touch of unrequited love — for a middle-aged man. The tip of this peninsula housed a **Temple of Apollo** (fragmentary

remains are extant) whose priests thought this action a terribly good idea and took to chucking sacrificial victims — with lover's dove wings tied to their limbs — over the edge in years thereafter (there is some evidence that they were collected by boat after they hit the water). Given the close proximity of this lover's leap, it is surprising that Anthony and Cleopatra didn't take advantage of it in 31 BC after the disastrous naval **Battle of Actium** against Octavian, which took place just to the north of Lefkada near the airport of Preveza / Aktion. Instead, they winged it to Egypt and jumped into the next world from there. Romance struck again in the 19 c. when the German archaeologist Wilhelm Dörpfeld hit upon the idea that Lefkada was Homer's Ithaca and then spent futile years trying to prove it. Dying of old age before the total discrediting of his theory could prompt him to test the merits of Sappho's leap, he left some **Bronze Age Tomb** excavations south of Nidri and a commemorative statue of himself on the town waterfront.

☎

CODE 0645, TOURIST POLICE 22346

Meganisi

ΜΕΓΑΝΗΣΙ; 23 km², pop. 250.

A small island off the south-east coast of Lefkada, Meganisi is linked by a daily ferry from Nidri as well as several tour boats. If you are not planning to stay overnight then the latter are a better way of quickly seeing this gentle island. Most boats also call at the fishing village of **Vathi**, the largest settlement on the north coast, and occasionally at its tidier neighbour — **Spartochori** — as well.

⊢⊣

A reasonable supply of rooms exist in all three villages. There is also an expensive hotel in Katomeri: the A-class *Meganissi* (☎ 51639).

👓

Nidri tourist boats run daily to the **Papanikolis Cave** on the west coast; said to be the second largest sea cave in Greece, the locals claim that they successfully hid a Greek submarine in it for much of the last war, but appealing as this idea is, the more cynical will perceive that it must have been a very small submarine.

☎

CODE 0645

Paxi / Paxos

ΠΑΞΟΙ; 25 km², pop. 3000.

Lying just south of Corfu, tiny Paxi (also commonly known as 'Paxos') is subject to daily invasions by day-trippers from both Corfu town and the mainland resort of **Parga**. When added to the vast crowds of Italians who come to stay (seemingly outnumbering the 200,000 olive trees that now cover almost the entire upland area of the island) this makes Paxi a comparatively expensive destination in season. The rest of the year (and once High Season day-trippers have gone) it is a much more tranquil spot reverting to a Patmos-like cosiness. This is easily the best time to visit as the island assumes an air of enchanted tranquillity — just waiting for a Peter Mayle to write a book and ruin it.

The main port and island centre is at **Gaios Town**. Protected by a Venetian fortress on Agios Nikolaos islet nestling within 100 m of the quay (accessible by taxi boat), it has more charm than many island capitals, despite the inevitable 1953 earthquake damage. Most of the lovely red-tiled houses that line the horse-shoe waterfront survived unscathed, and the two tree-clad islets that all but fill the bay (giving the impression that the town lies on the banks of a sea canal) provide a leafy and appealing backdrop. Because of the narrowness of the channel — which makes up the 'Old Port' and is more suited to caïques and tour boats — ferries dock at the so-called 'New Port'; a quay 500 m along the coast road.

The rest of the island (along with Antipaxi to the south) can be characterised by simply saying that it consists of low hills on the east side and dramatic cliffs and views on the west. Add to this the carpet of ancient olive groves and the island's homely size and the result is a near perfect walking island. Beaches, however, are harder to find — hence the taxi boats to Antipaxi. Taxi boats also run to the two islets to the south-east of Paxi: most heading first to the small beach at **Mogonisi**.

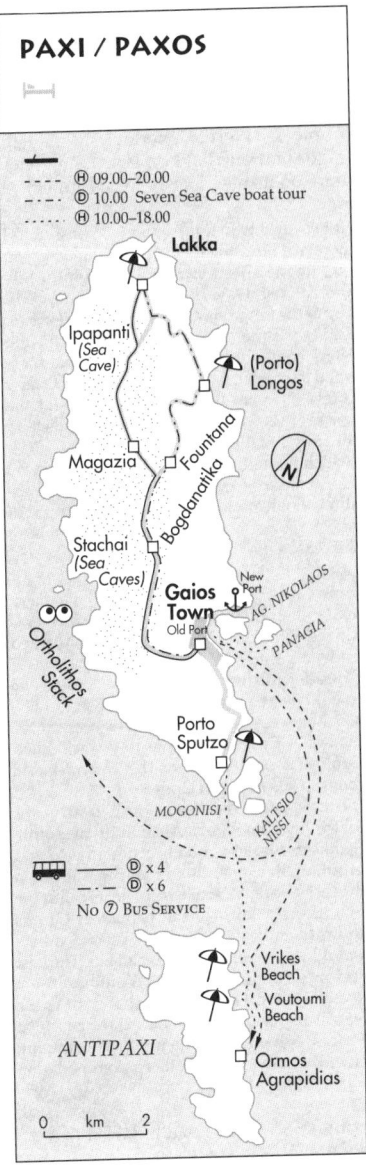

PAXI / PAXOS

---- Ⓗ 09.00–20.00
--·- Ⓓ 10.00 Seven Sea Cave boat tour
····· Ⓗ 10.00–18.00

Lakka

Ipapanti
(Sea Cave)

(Porto) Longos

Magazia   Fountana

Bogdanatika

Stachai
(Sea Caves)

Gaios Town

New Port

Old Port

AG. NIKOLAOS

PANAGIA

Ortholithos Stack

Porto Sputzo

MOGONISI

KALTSIO-NISSI

🚌 —— Ⓓ × 4
   —·— Ⓓ × 6
No ⑦ Bus Service

Vrikes Beach

Voutoumi Beach

ANTIPAXI

Ormos Agrapidias

0   km   2

Buses run across the island from Gaios to the small hamlet ports of Lakka and Longos (both of which have seen local boat links with Corfu in the past). **Longos** is the more attractive of the two, with a couple of tavernas overlooking a small caïque harbour. Lakka is larger, but relies more on its narrow bay for its appeal.

🛏

Hotels are few in number and expensive and there are no campsites on the island. If you can, phone ahead to reserve a room in July and August. **Gaios** has the bulk of the beds. Top of the range are the B-class *Paxos Beach* (☎ 32211) and the *Adamantia* (☎ 31121). The first offers bungalows, the latter traditional furnished apartments. There are also two E-class hotels in town: the *Ilios* (☎ 31808) and the *Lefkothea* (☎ 31807). Elsewhere on the island the only hotel is at **Lakka**: the D-class *Erida* (which offers furnished apartments), as well as a couple of pensions. In addition to the above hotels there is a reasonable supply of pricey rooms in Gaios except at the height of the season. Lakka also has a few rooms.

👓

From Gaios there are excursions to the mainland village of **Parga** and Corfu (the former is a lovely whitewashed chora-style town tucked under a hillside decked with trees and with a Crusader fortress on a headland beside the town). Nearer to home, excursion boats also visit the west coast of Paxi, which has three major **Sea Caves** and a limestone stack called **Orolithos** poking out of the waters like a monsterous finger of stone.

Tourist boats also leave hourly from Gaios for the large satellite of **Antipaxi** to the south, thanks to a lack of good beaches on Paxi and a proliferation of sandy strands running down the east side of Antipaxi. Most boats call at the two largest, north of the hamlet of **Ormos Agrapidias**, leaving you to walk to others should you want greater seclusion. The best and most popular beach is **Voutoumi** — a lovely stretch of golden sand that justifies the walk from the first (and most visited beach) at **Vrikes** — home to some unofficial camping given the absence of any other accommodation on the island.

☎

CODE 0662, PORT POLICE 31259, POLICE 31222, FIRST AID 31466.

Zakinthos / Zante

ΖΑΚΥΝΘΟΣ; 402 km², pop. 30,200.

One of the most popular Greek islands, Zakinthos (known to the Venetians as 'Zante') was once described as 'the flower of the Orient'. Regrettably, what was once an undeniably attractive island has been badly scarred by the unhappy combination of a major earthquake (in 1953) and insensitive package tourist development that leads some visitors wishing for another one. The island does not see vast numbers of island hoppers as it is inconveniently placed at the foot of the Ionian chain with poor ferry connections: the only link of note running from mainland Kilini to Zakinthos Town.

Rebuilt after the earthquake, **Zakinthos Town** is a considerable improvement on similar reconstruction on Kefalonia, with all the churches and important buildings being restored to something approaching their pre-earthquake state. That said, all look somewhat artificial and the town could never be described as cosy. This is in part due to the exceptionally large harbour that runs the length of the town. Ferries normally dock on the northern quay, but if the berths are full it is not unknown for new arrivals to disgorge their passengers on the southern quay (at the end of which stands Ag. Dionissiou church and its distinctive campanile — like its more famous model adorning St. Mark's Square in Venice, it is a reconstruction of a collapsed original).

All the main facilities are to be found along the waterfront; with the exception of the bus station which lies a block behind. The main focus of town life, however, lies to the north of the port, which is bordered by a reasonable NTOG / EOT pay beach. Hills rise quite steeply behind the town, limited development to the coastal strip. On a crest above the town are the remains of a Venetian kastro. Severely damaged by the earthquake, it is no longer a major attraction, though the views over the town are impressive.

ZAKINTHOS / ZANTE

Blue Caves

Smuggler's Cove

Skinari

Volimes

Alikanas

Drosia

Tsilivi

Anafonitrias   Katastari

Apo Gerakari

Planos

Tragaki

756 m

Zakinthos Town

Galarou

Argassi

Macherado

Kalamaki

Ag. Leontos

Vassilikos

Laganas

Lithakia

Agalas

PELUZO

MARATHONISI

Caves   Keri

Laganas/Turtle (soup) Bay

⛴ ---- Ⓓ 08.00–18.00
— --·-- Ⓓ 10.00
······ O Speed Boats (now banned)
✈ → Athens Ⓓ x 1
  → Kefalonia ② x 1

MAIN BUS SERVICES:
—— Ⓓ x 15
---- Ⓓ x 8
-·-· Ⓓ x 9
— — Ⓓ x 3
— — Ⓓ x 2
-··- Ⓓ x 9
······ Ⓓ x 4

Zakinthos Town to Mainland City (via ferries):
→ Athens Ⓓ 07.30, 12.30, 14.15, 17.30

0   km   3

Zakinthos offers an enjoyable combination of a fertile plain running the length of the island's east side, and a mountainous western half, made more accessible via regular coach excursions. Tourist activity is spread along the southern bay and the east coast (popular with cyclists) either side of Zakinthos Town itself. To the north it is centred on the resortified villages of **Planos/Tsilivi** and more attractive **Alikanas**, to the south at **Argassi**. Argassi aside, the southern peninsula is arguably the prettiest part of the island

— offering a succession of cove beaches backed by a wooded interior that climbs to the summit of Mt. Skopos that rises up between **Kalamaki** and Argassi. The low peak is adorned with the scant remains of a temple of Artemis. Marring all this, on the south coast lies the truly awful disco and beach resort of **Laganas**. Now the second largest settlement after Zakinthos Town, its main arteries resemble a giant 'T'; the upper stroke running along the beach, with an over-long hotel and restaurant alley running inland.

The island bus service is good; serving all the major tourist areas as well as running twice daily to all the other villages on the map opposite — with the notable exception of the northern hamlet of **Skinari** from whence the ferry to Kefalonia departs. Zakinthos Town is also the starting point for irregular tour boats and a catamaran (book in advance) service to sights on the scenic north of the island. Pricey at around £15 (tourist boats on Zakinthos are, on average, more expensive than any other Greek island), this is one instance when they are worth it.

⋈

The absence of large numbers of backpackers has limited the number of rooms on offer in the town. Hotels there are in profusion on the island. Most, however, are pre-booked solid by package tour operators. **Zakinthos Town** has the bulk of hotels likely to have empty beds. At the top end of the range is the waterfront B-class *Xenia* (☎ 22232), with the pricey new C-class *Palatino* (☎ 27780) 100 m behind. Nearby lies the *Diana* (☎ 28547). Cheaper options are the *Apollon* (☎ 22838) and *Aegli* (☎ 28317). Budget options are the D-class *Ionian* (☎ 22511) north of the Post Office and the *Omonia* (☎ 22113) in the southern suburbs.

A

Several sites on Zakinthos though, unusually, camping buses do not meet ferries. The nearest to the town is the reasonable *Camping Zante* (☎ 24754) at Tsilivi Beach (reached via regular bus from the bus station). Further up the coast is *Camping Paradise* (☎ 61888), near the village of Meso-Gerakari and Drosia Beach. Laganas Bay is also home to a couple of sites: *Camping Laganas* (☎ 51585) in an olive grove 1 km west of the end of the town beach is one of the worst sites in Greece. Further west lies the better *Tartarouga Camping* (☎ 51417): a quiet site down the road from the village of Lithakia.

👓

All over Greece you will find postcards of a rusty wreck of a cargo-ship set in a crescent beach of golden sand backed by towering cliffs: a catamaran (the C/M *Love Boat* — Sic) runs daily to **Smuggler's Cove** (for such is its name) as well as the **Blue Caves** on the northern tip of the island — generally reckoned to be among the best sea caves in Greece.

Island coach tours are popular as they enable tourists to take in the island sights without recourse to the main bus routes that tend to head direct to the destination rather than take in the island. Most tours include a mountain monastery, cliff-edge sunset views and esoteric sights such as the salt-pans on the beach north of Alikanas (known as Alikes beach).

Laganas Bay (also known as **Turtle Bay**) offers you a sight of the unacceptable face of package tourism. Blessed with a number of gently shelving beaches of a particularly fine sand, it has been the nesting area for some 80% of the Mediterranean's population of the shy **Loggerhead Turtle** for thousands of years, only to find a disco-city tourist resort of the tackiest kind (**Laganas**) develop on the main beach. Unfortunately the tourist and turtle nesting seasons are the same with dire consequences for the turtles. Coming ashore at night they lay eggs in the sand a mere 50 cm below the surface (when they can find a spot where the sand hasn't been packed hard by tourists). These hatch (assuming they haven't had a sun-umbrella pole rammed through the nest) at night, some eight weeks later, and the baby turtles then crawl towards the nearest bright light (in years past this was the moonlit sea: these days it is more likely to be the nearest disco). Meantime the female turtles, in between laying batches of eggs (or jettisoning them at sea rather than approach a neon-lit shore), bask in the bay; until recently only to be regularly run down and killed, or lose limbs to the speed boats (banned since last summer) that ignored government imposed zones limiting their speed to 6 knots or — near the east bay beaches of Sehania, Dafni and Gerakas (near Vassilikios) — forbidding them altogether. The situation is so bad that the World Wildlife Fund and Greenpeace have called for the entire bay to be declared a marine national park to protect the beaches. Some locals disagree: the owner of Marathonisi islet (also used by turtles and sun-lovers) is seeking to build a hotel, while boat operators engage in sporadic beach punch-ups with outraged conservationists. All in all you will do better to avoid Laganas; there are plenty of good beaches on the east coast and less environmentally destructive nightlife elsewhere.

☎

CODE 0695, PORT POLICE 22417, POLICE 22200, HOSPITAL 22515.

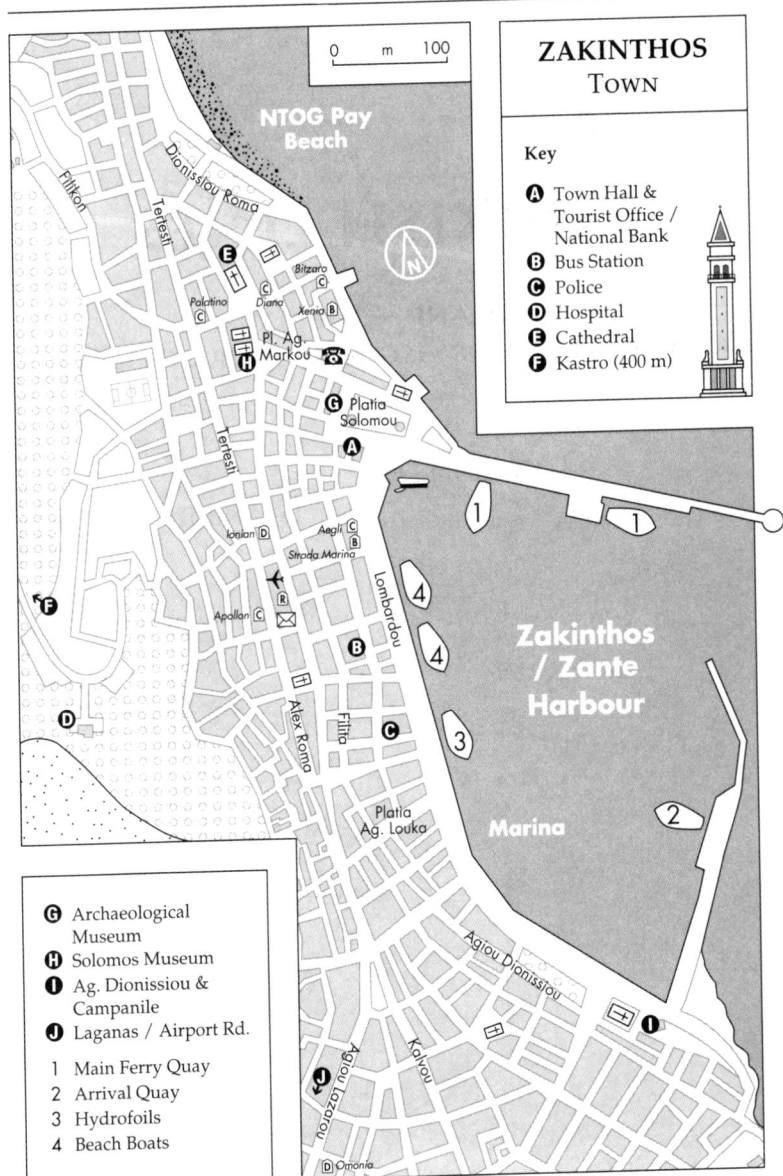

0   m   100

ZAKINTHOS
TOWN

Key

Ⓐ Town Hall &
Tourist Office /
National Bank
Ⓑ Bus Station
Ⓒ Police
Ⓓ Hospital
Ⓔ Cathedral
Ⓕ Kastro (400 m)

NTOG Pay
Beach

Flitkon

Dionissiou Roma

Tertesti

Ⓔ

Bitzaro

Palatino

Diana

Xenio

Ⓒ

Ⓒ

Ⓑ

Pl. Ag.
Markou

Ⓗ

Ⓖ Platia
Solomou

Ⓐ

Ionian **Ⓓ**

Aegli **Ⓒ**

Ⓑ

Strada Marina

Apollon **Ⓒ**

Ⓕ

Ⓓ

Tertesti

Lombardou

Filita

Alex. Roma

Ⓑ

Ⓒ

Platia
Ag. Louka

**Zakinthos
/ Zante
Harbour**

Marina

① ①

④

④

③

②

Agiou Dionissiou

Kalvou

Agiou Lazarou

Ⓘ

Ⓙ

Ⓓ Omonia

Ⓖ Archaeological
Museum
Ⓗ Solomos Museum
Ⓘ Ag. Dionissiou &
Campanile
Ⓙ Laganas / Airport Rd.

1 Main Ferry Quay
2 Arrival Quay
3 Hydrofoils
4 Beach Boats

13

TURKISH LINES

GREEK ISLAND — TURKEY LINKS
DARDANELLES · İSMİR · İSTANBUL · TURKISH ISLANDS

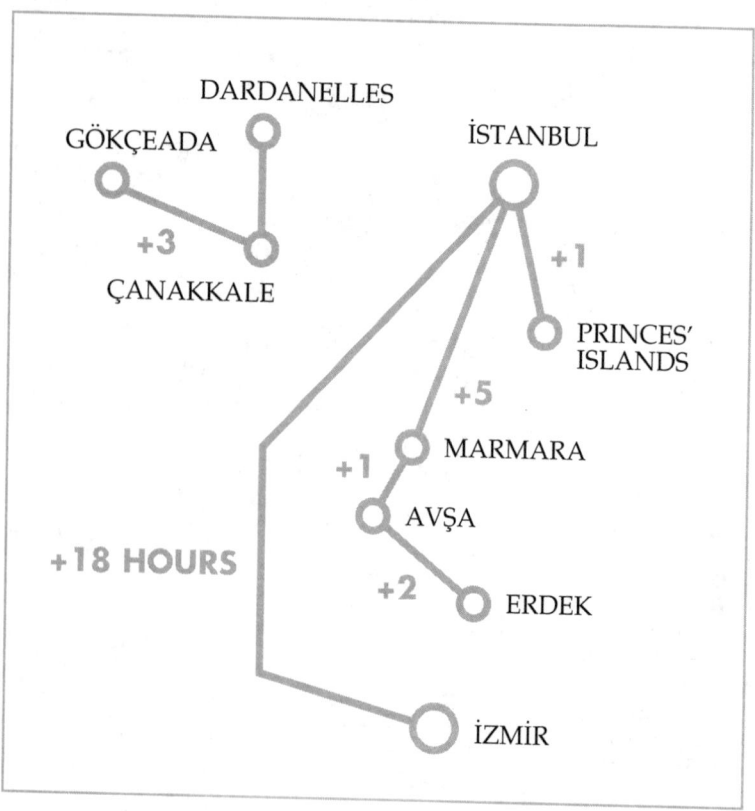

General Features

Given its size, Turkey is endowed with a remarkably poor ferry system. This is a historical accident born out of modern Turkey's failure to retain any of the large Aegean islands (apart from those guarding the entrance to the Dardanelles) once controlled by the Ottoman empire. As a result, ferries on the Turkish Aegean seaboard are — with the odd exception — confined to small international boats providing day trip excursions to adjacent Greek islands: the on-going political tension between Greece and Turkey preventing the emergence of more substantial links. Such islands where Turkey has sovereignty are tiny affairs that serve only to encourage local taxi boats bringing day-trippers from nearby resorts, rather than acting as the necessary catalyst for the emergence of a ferry system. South of the Dardanelles, Turkey is the land of the local bus rather than the ferry. This absence of anything that could remotely be called an Aegean ferry system means that hopping in Turkish waters is, for most tourists, usually a day trip option while following a Greek domestic route.

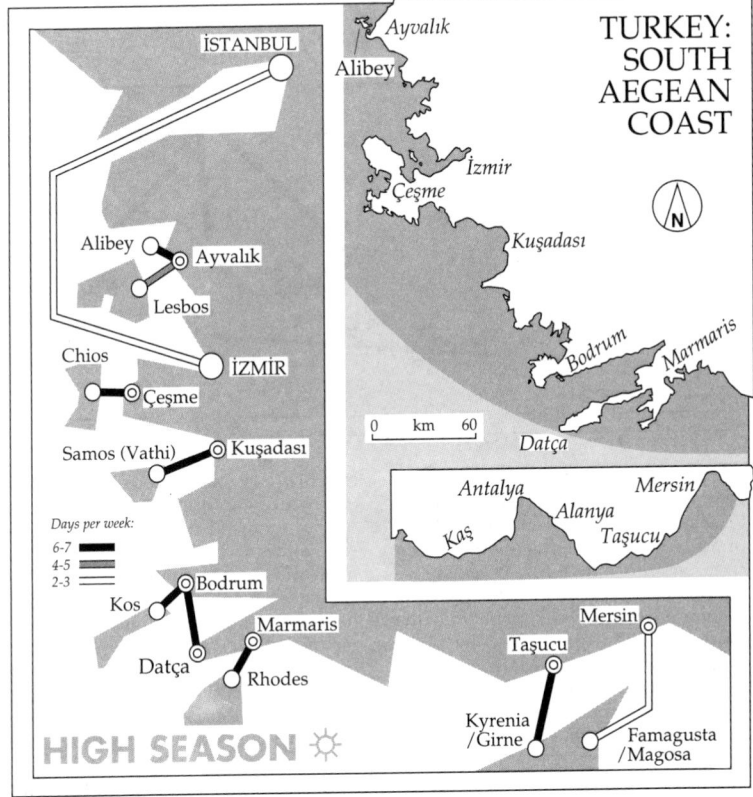

TURKEY: SOUTH AEGEAN COAST

Days per week:
6-7
4-5
2-3

HIGH SEASON ☼

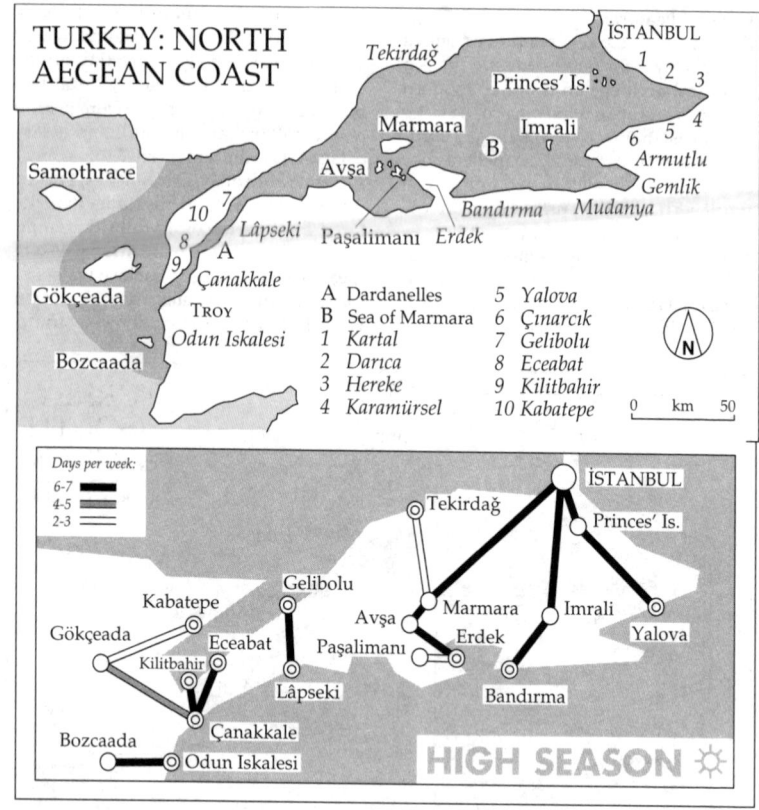

TURKEY: NORTH AEGEAN COAST

A Dardanelles
B Sea of Marmara
1 Kartal
2 Darıca
3 Hereke
4 Karamürsel
5 Yalova
6 Çınarcık
7 Gelibolu
8 Eceabat
9 Kilitbahir
10 Kabatepe

0   km   50

Days per week:
6-7
4-5
2-3

HIGH SEASON ☼

From the Aegean entrance of the Dardanelles through the Sea of Marmara to İstanbul, a very different state of affairs prevails, with something approaching a coherent ferry network in existence (backed up by short bus hops), courtesy of some dozen ex-'Greek' islands. For the most part these are served by boats provided by Turkish Maritime Lines (Turkey's national flag line). This excellent company is responsible for the bulk of the Dardanelles and Sea of Marmara services as well as the commuter boats operating along the Bosphorus. However,

effective ferry competition does not really exist since the only other companies operating out of Turkish ports are confined to routes and ships too insignificant to interest Turkish Maritime. Moreover, this company often has a controlling interest in Turkish ports and charges a steep levy for use which discourages competition on all but the most popular routes.

The islands are little touristed (except by holidaying Turks), and are very much a product of the messy aftermath of the border drawn up following the Greco-Turkish war of 1920–23. Home to almost exclusively ethnic Greek populations, the inhabitants found themselves on the 'wrong' side of the border, and though largely exempted from the forced population exchanges that occurred between the World Wars, most have subsequently left for Greece (thanks in part to cultural intimidation — something ethnic Turks 'stranded' in Greece also encountered). Home to new Turkish populations, they all have something of a 'someone's-sleeping-in-my-bed' air; with churches either abandoned or converted into mosques and the old Greek place names replaced with suitably Turkish successors.

From the Greek perspective these are very much the 'unlucky Greek islands' — all 13 of them — and reflect the fact that the modern border between Greece and Turkey is historically and archaeologically a very artificial one; something akin to a cultural Berlin Wall enhanced by enforced population exchanges. For most of history the power that reigned supreme on one side of the Aegean also held sway on the other. The Turkish Aegean seaboard is thus littered with cities that to the ancients were as 'Greek' as Athens or Corinth are today. Ironically, the archaeological remains tend to be better preserved than their Western Aegean counterparts, for deforestation of the mountains of Asia Minor caused extensive silting up of harbours on the Eastern Aegean seaboard leading to these cities being abandoned by the end of Roman rule, while prominent Greek cities elsewhere remained inhabited and grew into the built-over population centres of today. Hopping across to Turkey for a day for a spot of ancient 'Greek' city sightseeing combined with a Turkish coffee, and — it has to be said — a good whiff of the Orient besides, has thus become a popular feature of Greek island-hopping holidays.

In the past the omnipresent threat of hostilities between Turkey and Greece — that reached its peak with the 1974 Turkish invasion of Cyprus after a military

Cypriot regime sought union with Greece — has severely limited, and for a time curtailed ferry links. This uncomfortable situation has eased considerably in recent years but a number of reciprocal measures enforced after the Cyprus invasion have had a major impact on Greek island—Turkey services. Decrees that passengers could only travel to the other country on the ship of the country they were departing from (producing two fleets at every crossing point) are no longer enforced (though the competing fleets remain). A second charter-flight ticket issuing requirement that tourists who have entered Greece cannot spend a night in Turkey without losing their right to use the return half of their ticket is more serious and *remains in force*.

Fares

Turkey offers very good value for money, with the general cost of living — ferry tickets included — about 25% cheaper than Greece. However, even small boats running between the islands and Turkey attract international port taxes. The Greek government threatened (later backing down) to put up this tax from 1,500 GDR (£3) to 10,000 GDR (£25) in 1992.

Language

A relative of Finnish, modern Turkish is not the easiest of tongues to grapple with. Along the coast tourists can happily get by with a mix of English and German, but place names are often a bit of a mouthful. If you are planning to do more than a day trip or hop to İstanbul you should bring a language guide with you. Otherwise you can just about get by pronouncing:

Turkish	English
C	J
Ç	Ch
I	U
İ	E
J	S
Ö	Eu
Ş	Sh

Suggested Itineraries

Turkey has justly become a popular Greek-island-hopping day-excursion destination. If you find yourself on one of these islands offering excursions you should hop across; the contrast in culture and atmosphere is an experience well worth the cost of tickets. If you are on something longer than a two-week charter flight return ticket, then Turkey offers some interesting island hopping possibilities too.

Arrival/Departure Point

The lack of anything other than local boats making the crossing to Turkey means that the islands of the Dodecanese and Eastern Aegean are the best starting points. Rhodes, Kos and Samos all have frequent charter flights.

A: Day Trips to Turkey

Day trips operate from Rhodes to Marmaris, Kos to Bodrum, Samos to Kuşadası, Chios to Çeşme and Lesbos to Ayvalık. Prices tend to be broadly similar regardless of which crossing you use and average around £30 for a day trip (including the high port taxes). You are usually left to your own devices in Turkey, but you can travel from Samos as part of a tour if so minded. Greek craft from Kos and Rhodes tend to be excursion boats while their Turkish counterparts are closer to ferries. This distinction can become quite important, for if you travel by ferry you will be deemed an independent traveller and your passport will be stamped on entering and leaving the country. Travellers on excursion boats, because they have a return ticket, are issued with a landing pass while passports (unstamped) are held by passport control. Ferries also have well-advertised return times. Excursion boats don't — so be careful to establish when excursion boats depart for home; they do NOT wait for late passengers. Miss the boat and you'll have to stay overnight; thereby jeopardising your right to your charter flight home. Finally,

it is all but impossible to change Greek currency in Turkish banks or visa versa. Have another currency on you if you want to change cash. Traveller's cheques are no problem. If you do return from a day trip armed with wads of Turkish banknotes the best way of changing them is to offer them to day-trippers boarding the next day's boat.

B: Turkish Excursion [10 Days]

Those with time to hand will find that a trip to Troy and Constantinople (both dear to Greek hearts) is easily achieved:

1 Lesbos

The closest crossing point to Troy, Lesbos offers regular ferries to Ayvalık. Crossing points further south are also practicable options if you don't mind changing buses up the Turkish coast.

2 Ayvalık [1 Day]

Worth a day's exploration; with nearby Alibey to visit. Thereafter you can get a bus on to Çanakkale.

3 Çanakkale [3 Days]

Easily the best base for exploring the region, with plenty of accommodation and easy access to Troy and the battlefields of Gallipoli. Each offers a day of leisurely tourism, before heading on to Bandırma by bus.

4 5 Bandırma / Princes' Is. [1 Day]

From Bandırma you have several options. You can either take a regular ferry to İstanbul or break the journey with a visit to the Princes' Islands or travel via Erdek and Avşa.

6 İstanbul [3 Days]

Three days gives you time to do the sights and hop up the Bosphorus. Thereafter you can consider the options for returning to Greece.

Return [2 Days]

Most direct route out of High Season is the weekly ferry from İstanbul to Piraeus. Otherwise the fastest route is via ferry to İzmir (though you can always return via ferry to Bandırma and then an İzmir train) and then bus to Çeşme and ferry to Chios.

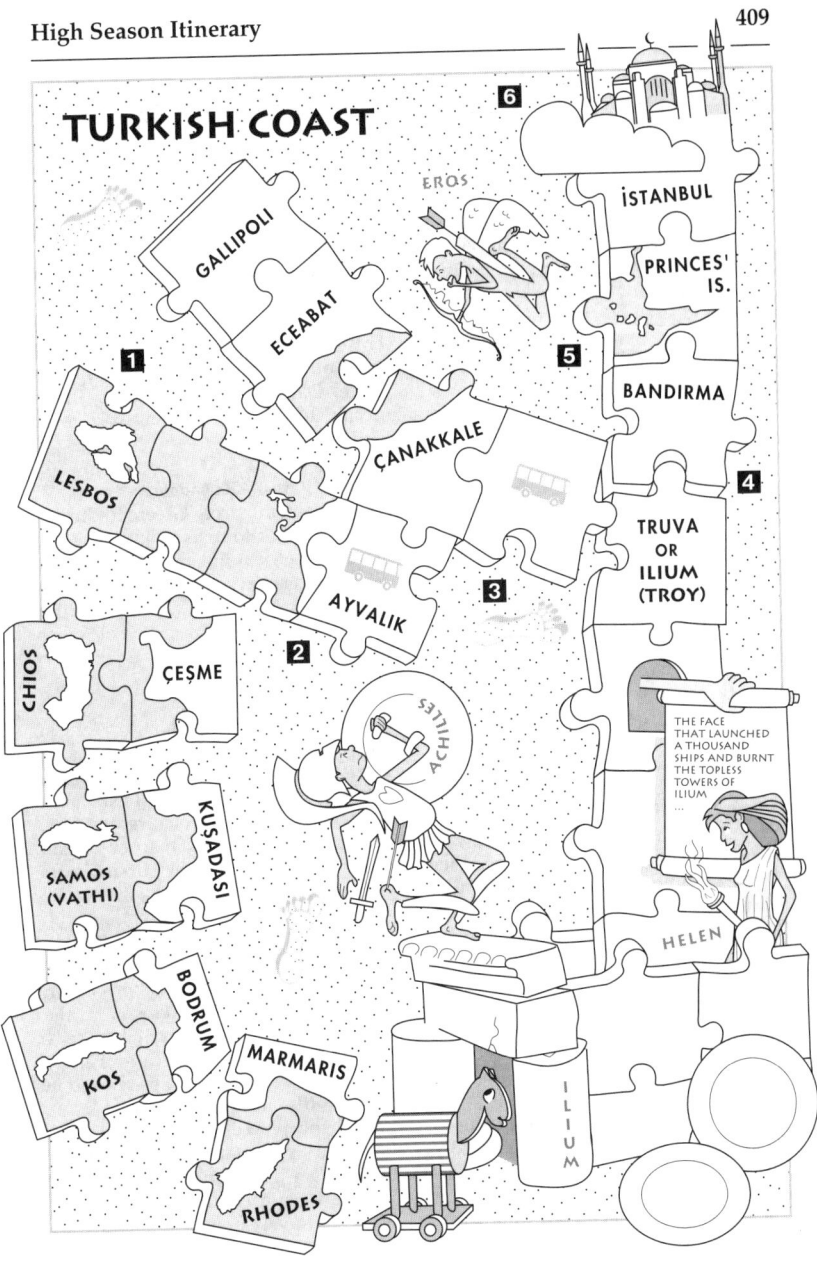

Greek Island — Turkey Links

Crossing between Greece and Turkey you must use a designated crossing point. Five Greek islands adjacent to the Turkish Aegean coast have ferry connections. However, the level of service varies greatly. Most are only advertised on a local basis, and exist courtesy of tourist day trippers and a small contingent of holidaying Greeks, off to visit towns and villages that were once home to parents or grandparents before the population exchanges. Services are thus drastically curtailed out of High Season. This tourist driven system is also reflected in the type of ferry, with the southern Rhodes, Kos and Samos crossings largely the prerogative of pricey passenger craft (these can often take one or two cars driven aboard with the aid of a couple of planks of wood as a makeshift ramp) operated on a day trip basis; thus enabling them to spend six to eight hours 'waving the flag' in the opposing nation's port (in the case of some of the Turkish boats: flags, large and lots of). The northern Chios and Lesbos crossings are more car orientated. It is standard practice at all ports to buy your ticket a day in advance, leaving your passport with the ticket agent. In practice, foot passengers can usually get on a boat, provided they arrive a couple of hours before departure on the Greek side (to clear immigration and customs control); and by midday for a late afternoon boat on the Turkish.

Crossing points:
Lesbos (Mytilini)—Ayvalık
The most northerly and utilitarian crossing point. Fewer tourists than elsewhere and atmosphere is rather low key. Very small car ferries (primarily the quaint — all bow and no stern — *Aeolis*) supposedly run daily during July and August, otherwise on alternate days. It is best to plan on the assumption of a 24-hour wait here.

Chios—Çeşme
Best crossing point for vehicles. Miniotis Brothers' car ferry service is well advertised (though you can't be sure which of their boats will be doing the run) and tickets can be bought as far afield as Piraeus. Like Lesbos, a do-it-yourself crossing point. Though occasional tourist boats offer more 'sheltered' day trips at a price. Daily High Season ferry links decline to ① ③ ⑤ sailings in April/May and October.

Samos (Vathi)—Kuşadası
Traffic is mainly from Greece to Turkey in the form of tourists heading for the remains of nearby Ephesus. Also popular with longer stay backpackers heading into Turkey. Occasional tourist boats also make the crossing often calling at Samos (Pithagorio) and even Leros en route.

Kos—Bodrum
Tourist boats make the 1-hour crossing in equal numbers from both directions, as both centres are popular tourist resorts. Greek boats tend to be small expensive cruisers, Turkish, more picturesque large caïque affairs. Cars and motorcycles can be taken across here on the Turkish boats — if you don't mind 'driving the plank'.

Rhodes—Marmaris
The most southerly crossing point. As Greek boats find day excursions down the Rhodian coast to Lindos or to the island of Symi, more profitable daily hydrofoils dominate Greece to Turkey traffic, and all travel must be booked in advance (the turning up several hours beforehand ploy doesn't seem to work here). Turkish boats coming to Greece for the day are mostly rust-bucket affairs. Weekday services are consistent, but weekend travel cannot be guaranteed.

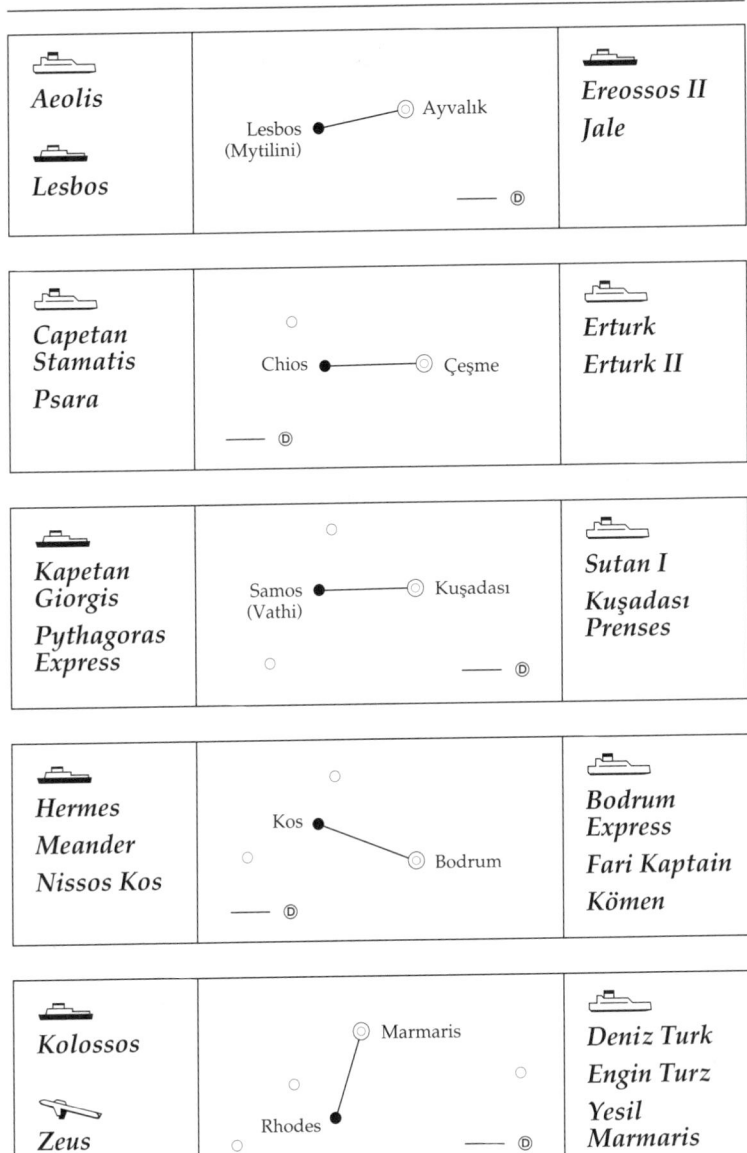

Aeolis

Lesbos

Lesbos (Mytilini) ● — ◎ Ayvalık

— Ⓓ

Ereossos II
Jale

Capetan Stamatis Psara

○

Chios ● — ◎ Çeşme

— Ⓓ

Erturk
Erturk II

Kapetan Giorgis Pythagoras Express

○

Samos (Vathi) ● — ◎ Kuşadası

○

— Ⓓ

Sutan I
Kuşadası
Prenses

Hermes Meander Nissos Kos

○

Kos ●

○ — ◎ Bodrum

— Ⓓ

Bodrum Express
Fari Kaptain
Kömen

Kolossos

Zeus

◎ Marmaris

○

○

Rhodes ●

○

— Ⓓ

Deniz Turk
Engin Turz
Yesil Marmaris

Turkey: Ferry Services

C/F *Ankara* - C/F *Truva*
Turkish Maritime Lines
Ankara; 1983; 10,552 GRT
Truva; 1966; 3,422 GRT

This is the only regular Turkish Aegean internal service of major significance. Frequency varies according to the time of year. The ⑤ departure from İstanbul service (returning from İzmir the following ⑦) is annual; the others run summers only. The ferries are large and run on the same basis as the company's international vessels (i.e. food and beverages are bought using coupons purchased from the purser's office). Bunks and seats usually have to be reserved well in advance during the summer season, but a limited number of deck tickets are sold on board (some two hours prior to departure). Unfortunately, these boats pass through the Dardanelles at night on both legs so that from a scenic point of view this 18-hour service is not all it could be; though the arrival at İstanbul is impressive enough.

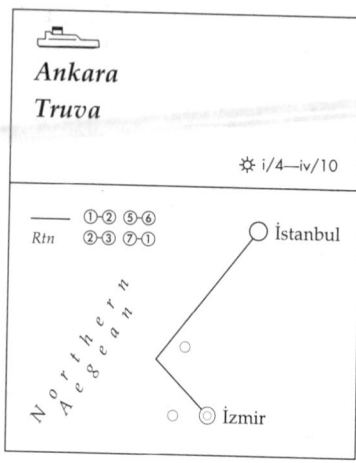

Sea of Marmara Services (East)

İstanbul is the starting point for a large number of passenger ferries heading up the Bosphorus, to the Princes' Islands and the towns on the south coast of the Sea of Marmara (including Bandırma and its rail link with İzmir). Most are crowded commuter services running several times daily. Monthly timetables are posted up on ferry quays. Most of these are passenger services operated by Turkish Maritime Lines with a large fleet of superbly maintained ferries. Excursions to the Princes' Islands and up the Bosphorus should be seriously considered if only for the waterside views of the İstanbul skyline. TML is not the only ferry operator in İstanbul. A catamaran/hydrofoil service is provided by Deniz Otobüsleri to the suburbs and the Princes'

Islands. Services start from a floating quay (you get sea sick before you even board) on the other side of the Golden Horn at Karaköy. This is the berth for the express ferries to the Princes' Islands. Slower ferries start with the rest at Eminönü.

Sea of Marmara Services (West)

The western Sea of Marmara is dominated by TML boats running out of the Kapıdağ peninsula town of Erdek and İstanbul. Both the islands of Avşa and Marmara are served daily by passenger ferries. These are augmented by a number of irregular private craft: Deniz Otobüsleri run a High Season daily service to the islands from İstanbul, while private daily local boats ship the odd car to the islands from Erdek and the Kapıdağ peninsula villages of Ilhan and Narli to the north.

Dardanelles Services

Turkish Maritime Line operates a number of impressive ro-ro ferries. These are odd looking affairs with a large open car deck,

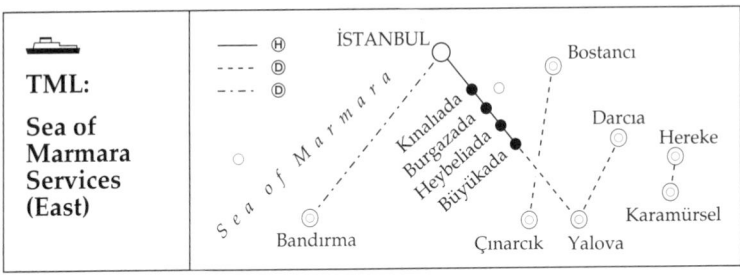

TML:

Sea of Marmara Services (East)

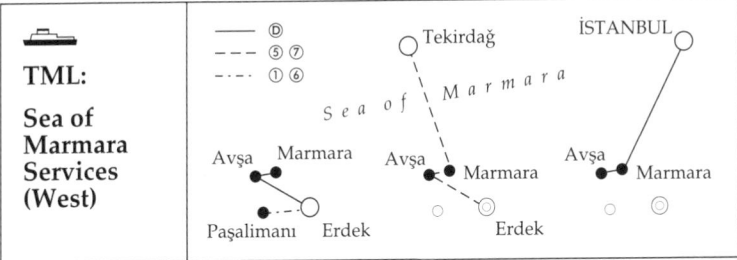

TML:

Sea of Marmara Services (West)

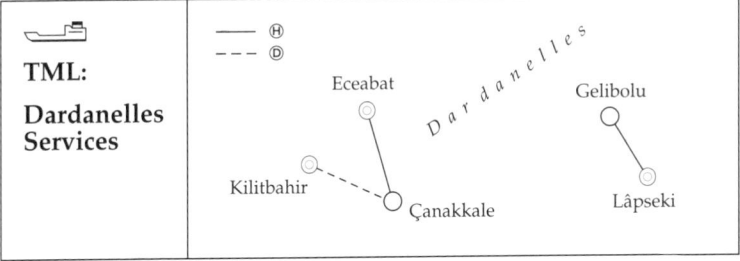

TML:

Dardanelles Services

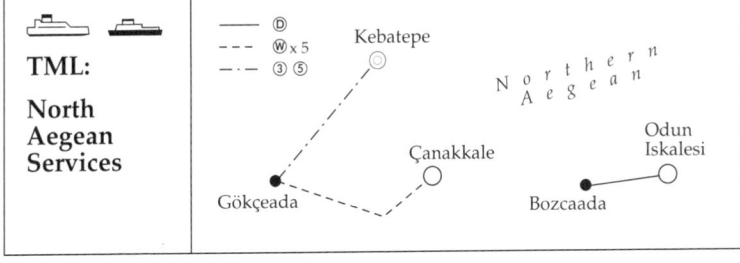

TML:

North Aegean Services

over the centre of which are the ship's bridge and cabin-space sitting atop an overhead gantry. Very much sheltered water craft, they run between Çanakkale and Eceabat and Gelibolu and Lâpseki. The Kilitbahir—Çanakkale boat is not nearly as large and runs on demand rather than hourly.

Turkish North Aegean Services

Both the islands of Gökçeada and Boz-caada are served exclusively by Turkish Maritime Line boats. Bozcaada has a twice daily service (falling to once daily out of High Season), while Gökçeada is served five days a week from Çanakkale, the remaining two days from the small Geli-bolu port of Kabatepe. Out of High Season the bulk of sailings are from this latter port. Current timetables for both islands are available at Çanakkale.

T/B *Bodrum Queen*

The old quay in Bodrum harbour is cluttered with elaborate wooden hulled tourist boats offering excursions to the adjacent islets. The *Bodrum Queen* is typical of these craft, running to assorted offshore islets. Most common are sailings to **Otok Is.** or a combination of **Korada Is.** (beach and hot springs) and **Ada Is.** (aquarium). Most set sail around 10.00, and all are on the pricey side.

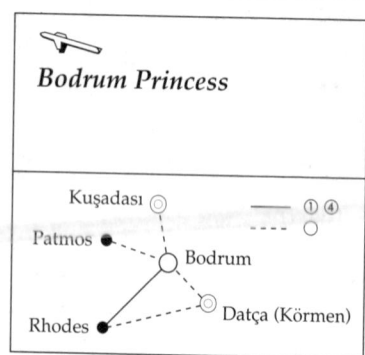

Bodrum Princess

H/F *Bodrum Princess*

An under-utilised Turkish operated hydrofoil operates out of Bodrum during the High Season. Painted a natty red and adorned with the inevitable Turkish crescent, this vessel has operated a direct service to Rhodes two days a week (① ④) since 1991. Other excursions along the north and south Turkish coast and day trips to Patmos long advertised in Bodrum but nowhere else have yet to materialise.

C/F *Bodrum Express* - C/F *Ege Express* - C/F *Fari Kaptain I*

The coast south of Bodrum is so indented that several small car ferries profit from this geography by offering a twice-daily

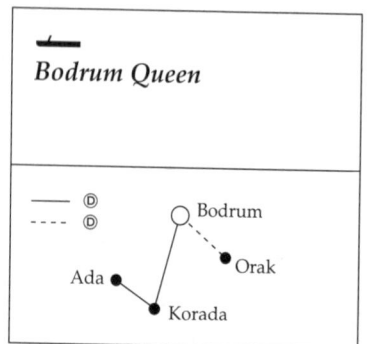

Bodrum Queen

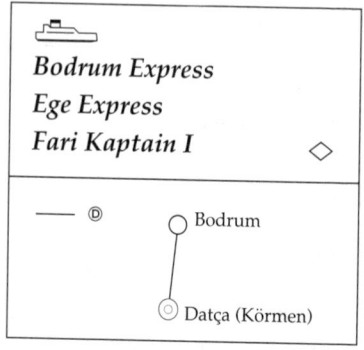

Bodrum Express
Ege Express
Fari Kaptain I

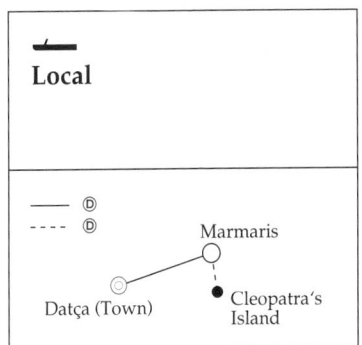

crossing from Bodrum (09.30, 17.00) to the quay at **Körmen** (09.00, 17.00) some 7 km north of Datça (bus service into town included in the price of the ferry ticket). When not running this route these ferries operate as the part of the Turkish fleet on the Bodrum—Kos run.

Marmaris Taxi Boats
Daily taxi boats run from Marmaris along the coast of the Datça peninsula to the town of Datça (some even continuing on to the ancient city of Kindos). In doing so they open up the possibility of doing a loop running Rhodes—Marmaris—Datça—Bodrum—Kos—Rhodes.

Turkey—North Cyprus Services:
Mersin—Famagusta
Occupied northern Cyprus is served by boats out of two Turkish south coast ports. From the Turkish perspective these are full blown international services. However, as Turkey is the only country which recognises the legitimacy of the so-called Turkish Republic of Northern Cyprus, these ferry links are de facto internal Turkish services. Mersin (ancient Tarsus) — a large noisy seaport with nothing to recommend it beyond the ferry link — is the best of the Turkish ports with the thrice-weekly Turkish Maritime Lines' elderly C/F *Yeşilada* operating to the war-ruined derelict resort of Famagusta (now Turkish **Magosa**). Weekend sailing continues on to Syria (Lattakia).

Taşucu—Kyrenia
Slightly closer to the Aegean is the resort town of Silifke and its port Taşucu. Again there is nothing of any interest in the place except the means of leaving it. Small ferries (*Liberty* and *Ertürk*) and hydrofoils make the 7-and 3½-hour crossings respectively to the once attractive port of Kyrenia (now **Girne**) daily in High Season, three times weekly during the rest of the year (though days and times are never very consistent).

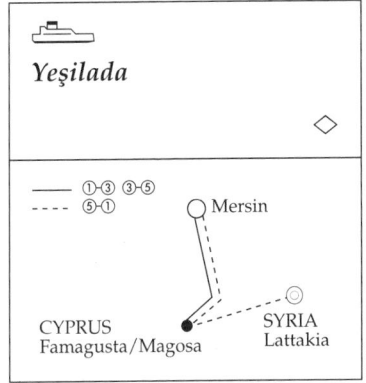

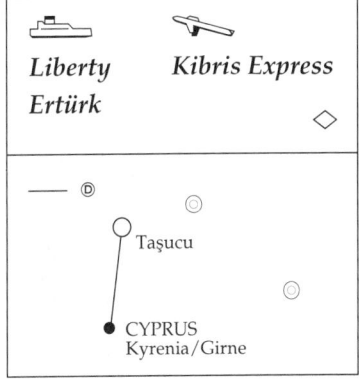

⚓ Turkish Islands & Ports

ALIBEY / CUNDA / MOSCHONISSI

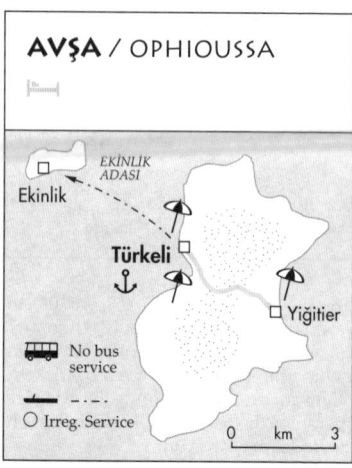

AVŞA / OPHIOUSSA

Alibey / Cunda

A small island north of Ayvalık, Alibey (alias Cunda) is linked by causeway to the mainland. This had a major impact on the former Greek population, which unusually, were forced out and replaced by displaced Cretans of Turkish stock between the wars. The background of the new population has at least ensured that the island retains a 'Greek' atmosphere, with a typical resortified town (linked by both ferry and hourly bus to Ayvalık), and several reasonable beaches. The best of these are on the west coast. The north of the island is very quiet and contains the nearest thing to the island 'sight' in Poroselene bay: famous in antiquity as the home of a dolphin who saved a drowning boy and did other party tricks for passing writers — notably Pausanias.

Avşa

The most popular central Sea of Marmara island, Avşa has emerged in recent years as the getaway destination for the better off in İstanbul and its environs. The only town is a mass of hotels and not much else (the nearby beaches and vineyard landscape being the great attraction). In addition to frequent ferry links occasional taxi boats head out to nearby Ekinlik.

Ayvalık

A new (thanks to earthquake damage) and low-key town, more ramshackle than scenic, Ayvalık owes its present importance to the nearby attractions of Troy and the Çanakkale—İzmir road running through the town. Alibey aside, the only ferry link is the 'daily' Lesbos service. A good base for exploring the region with regular buses to Bergama (and the ruins of Pergamum) and nearby Alibey island.

Budget rooms thick on the shore. Tourist office is 1 km south of the centre.

Bandırma

The main city on the Sea of Marmara south coast, Bandırma is a major transportation hub, with regular buses to all the major Aegean and Marmarian towns, an important rail link to İzmir, and regular ferries to İstanbul. Home to both cement and sulphuric acid factories, the city is not likely to be in many visitor's lists of Turkish trip highlights, but is tolerable enough if you are just passing through.

Bodrum

A resort town built on the ancient city of Halicarnassus opposite the island of Kos. These days it is the large, intact crusader castle of St. Peter along with the ruins of the original Mausoleum that are the main attractions, but the mosque and bazaar-filled town is one of the prettiest in the Aegean (the quayside girl selling drinks from inside a large plastic orange aside) and worth a day's visit in its own right. In addition to the daily half-dozen boats that head for Kos or the Datça peninsula, boats also head for beaches and islands nearby (see p. 414). These should be avoided by day trippers because they don't return before Kos boats return.

⊨

Rooms can be hard to find in High Season: best arrive on a morning boat. Tourist information office is in the castle.

⋀

Town boasts a couple of quite horrible sites. Best is *Uçar Camping* at Dere Sok.

Bozcaada

A small Aegean island a few kilometres south-west of Troy, Bozcaada was known for over two millennia by the name recorded by Homer — Tenedos. Closed to tourists until the late 80s for military reasons (check with the tourist office in Çanakkale for the latest information regarding the need for possible visitor's permits), the island is one of the least spoilt and most attractive around. The only town lies on the north-east corner

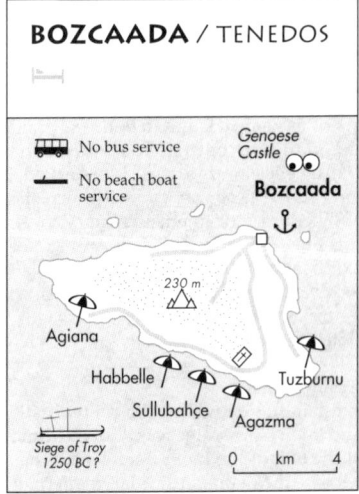

and is dominated by a well-preserved Genoese castle the equal of any in the Aegean. It lies on the site of Justinian's warehouses; for the island was used as a granary storage base in the Byzantine era. South of the town the shoreline is fringed by a succession of sand beaches; the best on the south coast proper, and it was to here that the Greek fleet retreated out of sight when they left the wooden horse outside the gates of Troy. The island economy depends on viticulture; mass tourism has yet to discover the delights of the — still very Greek — cobbled town, with its restaurant-fronted waterfront and dusty hotels in the streets behind.

Çanakkale

The largest port and best stopping point on the Dardanelles (known to the Greeks as the Hellespont), Çanakkale is a pretty town offering plenty to do thanks to the combination of a well-preserved castle (home to a naval museum), a well-stocked archaeological museum, the ferry link across the Dardanelles, and the half-hourly buses from the town centre to

Truva and nearby ancient Troy. The centre of town boasts a conspicuous clock tower, and in close proximity to this landmark you will find all the essentials — including the city tourist office. Nearby tour operators offer day packages to both Troy and the Gallipoli battlefields across the Dardanelles (tours to this latter destination are the best way to visit given the absence of a good peninsula bus service). Bus links from Çanakkale however, are excellent, with hourly connections to all local centres as well as İstanbul and İzmir.

Hotels and rooms are plentiful in the town.

Çeşme

A quaint little town with a pretty castle and interesting waterfront. Out on a limb at the end of the İzmir peninsula, it has become the main port for large international ferries along with the regular Chios boats — the pull of İzmir (a 90-minute bus ride away) being great. An appealing place to spend one's time with plenty of accommo-dation and camping to hand.

Datça

Deftly placed on one of the most attractive stretches of the Turkish coast, this quiet town and surrounding green pine forest and turquoise bay-lined Datça peninsula, is the real reason to hop from Rhodes to Marmaris. Taxi boats (and around 14 buses) run daily to Datça from there. The town has plenty of rooms, a campsite and is the jumping-off point (via occasional boat or expensive taxi) for Kindos 34 km away on the tip of the peninsula. An important city in classical times it was home to the masterpiece of the sculptor Praxiteles — a (lost) statue of Aphrodite.

Eceabat

Main destination for Çanakkale ferries crossing to the Gelibolu peninsula. Not much here beyond the ferry terminal itself: Kilitbahir being the traditional landing point adjacent to Çanakkale.

Erdek

An attractive (courtesy of a lack of modern building) town on the Kapidağ peninsula, Erdek is the main jumping-off point for the Sea of Marmara islands. The town has all the necessary tourist facilities (behind the tree and restaurant-lined waterfront). Dolmuş taxis run frequently to nearby Bandirma, with its bus links to Çanakkale and other major centres.

Gelibolu

Known to most by its former name of Gallipoli, Gelibolu is the major port on the European side of the Dardanelles, giving its name to the whole peninsula (and of course, the disastrous ww1 Gallipoli campaign in which the allies fought the Turks). Ferries dock on the outer quay, behind which lie two inner harbours bisected by a bridge. Pretty enough in a quiet sort of way, the town is home to a castle and also boasts a quayside statue of its most famous son, Riri Reis, a 16 c. cartographer and navigator. Hourly buses to İstanbul make Gelibolu more accessible than ferry links would suggest.

Gökçeada

The only large Aegean island in Turkish hands, Gökçeada is still widely known by its former Greek name of Imbros (or Imroz). Heavily fortified thanks to its strategic position at the entrance of the Dardanelles, tourist access was prohibited until the late 80s when visitors with permits were admitted (information regarding any current requirements can be obtained from the tourist office in Çanakkale). Red tape has relaxed further since, but the number of tourists remains very small. Visits to Gökçeada remain the preserve of the dedicated island hopper intent on 'doing' every Greek or Aegean island rather than the casual tourist. Green and very hilly, the island certainly offers a get-away-from-it-all atmosphere, but there is little disguising that of all the Turkish islands, this one more than any

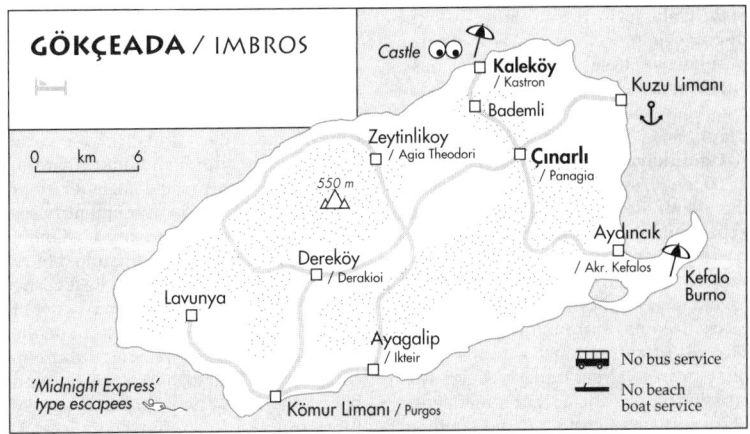

GÖKÇEADA / IMBROS

Castle

Kaleköy / Kastron

Kuzu Limanı

Bademli

Zeytinlikoy / Agia Theodori

Çınarlı / Panagia

0   km   6

550 m

Aydıncık / Akr. Kefalos

Kefalo Burno

Dereköy / Derakioi

Lavunya

Ayagalip / Ikteir

No bus service

'Midnight Express' type escapees

No beach boat service

Kömur Limanı / Purgos

other feels — thanks to the heavy military presence — like an occupied island. Although exempted from the 1920s population exchanges, the exclusively Greek inhabitants have been driven out over the last 30 years — unsung casualties of the Cyprus conflict. Faced with living in a military camp, the forced closure of Greek schools and the building of an open prison (from where the 'hero' of the film *Midnight Express* swam to freedom) most have gone, leaving Turkish settlers to move in. The island is very quiet. In the absence of a bus service, tourism is confined to the former chora (now Çinarli), and the town of Kaleköy — home to the island's best beach and an impressive castle. Both are linked by dolmuş taxi to the ferry port at Kazu Limanı.

Imrali

The former Greek island of Kalolimno, Imrali is very much the unlucky 13th of the inhabited Turkish islands. Home to a high security prison, the island is a latter-day Alcatraz. Ferries running from İstanbul to Gemlik do call; but unless you are dressed as a warder or have done a murder you won't be allowed to disembark.

İstanbul

Still one of the great cities of the world, İstanbul is well worth almost any amount of effort involved in getting there. The combination of the Topkarı Palace (home to the Sultans and their hareems and one of the greatest displays of crown jewels), the Agia Sophia (the great cathedral church of the Byzantine Empire), the beautiful Blue Mosque, the ancient Hippodrome and City Walls, and the bustle of the Grand Bazaar is hard to beat. The city owes so much to the sea and boasts a skyline so atmospheric that arrival by boat easily remains the most attractive way to approach. This can be done either by taking the ferry from İzmir or one of the boats operating between İstanbul and the islands and ports on the southern shore of the Sea of Marmara. İstanbul's principal port is located at Eminönü adjacent to the Galata bridge over the Golden Horn. All large ferries depart from here (a convenient quay as it backs on to the old part of the city that is home to all the major sights and the bulk of the budget accommodation). However, the İzmir ferry often lands its passengers at a quay 2 km to the north, on the far side of the Golden Horn. Eminönü is also the departure point for cruises up the Bosphorus. These are just regular passenger ferries calling at all the European and Asian ports up to the entrance of the Black Sea. Boats normally stop at **Anadolukavağı** for a couple of hours (♦♦ 15.00, 17.00) so passengers can get off on the Asian shore and buy over-priced kebabs and seafood dishes. Other ferries cross the Bosphorus — either to the port directly on the other side or visiting several ports on both. Normally you buy brass tokens emblazoned with the Turkish Maritime Lines insignia at the quay or from street traders. A one-way crossing will set you back about 10 pence. Ferries are numerous on the southern crossings. Timetables can be found on quaysides (European ports shown in black; Asian in red).

⊨

Most budget accommodations are in the Old City in the small streets backing on to Agia Sophia and the Blue Mosque. The total of five youth hostels includes one IYHF hostel at 6 Caferige Cad. The helpful City Tourist Office is at 31. Divan Yolo on the old Hippodrome and can advise on accommodation as well as offer plenty of blurb on the major sights.

A

Noisy short-stay site at *Londra Mocamp* near the city airport.

İzmir

The largest city on the Turkish Aegean coast İzmir (formerly the Greek Smyrna) is now a major metropolis. Sadly, little architecture of character remains in what is now one of the ugliest cities (not many Aegean towns are lumbered with a 'Park of Culture') in one of the Mediterranean's most attractive bays: the Gulf of İzmir. The bulk of the old town was burnt down with the collapse of the abortive Greek attempt to take the coast of Asia minor in the war of 1919–22. The sheer size of the rather uninteresting (an ancient Agora and Fortress aside) wide-boule-varded modern city does at least ensure a regular ferry link with İstanbul and a far less frequent international service with Piraeus. Most foreign visitors are taking advantage of either these or the railway (this is the only Turkish city on the Adriatic coast with such a link), or are en route to the ruins of the ancient city of Pergamum (reached via frequent buses to the new town of Bergama). İstanbul ferries leave from the international ferry berth (complete with a dusty locked-up duty-free centre) at the eastern corner of the gulf. The centre of the city lies on the south side. The accompanying suburban sprawl spreads far to the west and around the northern side hence the existence of three trans-bay commuter services: 1. From **Konak** quay (west of city centre) to **Urla** (south side of the gulf midway between İzmir and Çeşme). 2. From Konak quay to **Karşıyaka** (on the north of the gulf). 3. From **Pasaport** quay (centre of the city seafront) to **Alsancak** (200 m west of the International Ferry dock).

⊨

Finding a bed for the night in İzmir is rarely a problem. Cheap pensions and hotels are densest around the railway station. The city bus station also houses a helpful tourist office.

A

Nearest sites are at Çeşme. The village has several sites: notably *Fener Mocamp* on the promontory north of the harbour.

Kabatepe

A small town on the west side of the Gelibolu peninsula, Kabatape has an infrequent ferry link with Gökçeada, an excellent beach backed by a museum dedicated to the 1915–16 Gallipoli campaign. Local taxis run to nearby ANZAC cove and the many cemeteries that house the 200,000 dead. Local public transport is relatively poor over the whole peninsula: buses or dolmuş taxis from Eceabat are the best means of getting to the town. Accommodation is thin on the ground as most visitors are on official tours.

Kilitbahir
The narrowest crossing point on the Dardanelles runs between Kilitbahir and Çanakkale (1300 m) — hence the minor ferry link between the two. Worth a visit thanks to the castle, built by Mehmet the Conqueror in 1452, that gives substance to the town's name which means 'Key to the sea'. It was once linked by a massive chain rope to its Çanakkale counterpart, to control shipping in the Dardanelles.

Kuşadası
A relatively small, but pleasant, tourist town midway down Turkey's Aegean coast. Named 'Pigeon Island' — after a fortified islet linked to the town via a causeway — it draws the hordes thanks to its role as the jumping-off point to the nearby ruins of Ephesus: the best preserved of ancient Greek cities. Its appeal is such, that a stream of cruise ships call, upping prices to Greek levels. The port used to figure more prominently on ferry schedules until the last couple of years.

Ⱶ

Plentiful supply of rooms via ticket agencies.

Λ

Camping Önder: 2 km north of the town. Reasonable facilities.

Lâpseki
A small port that owes its existence to adjacent Gelibolu on the opposite side of the Dardanelles, Lâpseki is very much of an overspill town, relying on the ferry link between the two.

Marmara
The largest island in the Sea of Marmara, and from which the sea takes its medieval name, Marmara is a mountainous, and rather inhospitable-looking place. The island was famous in the ancient world as one of the best sources of white marble. In fact, the whole northern half is composed of little else, leaving a wind-swept landscape with little vegetation and well scarred with three thousand years of quarrying. The southern half of Marmara has more going for it, with a fringe of pine trees and the best of the small population centres. Ferries stop at assorted points around the coast — so check ports of call when boarding. Boats to the main centre of Marmara town (home to two budget hotels and the island bank) often stop at Gundoğdu en route, and the former island capital at Saraylar (replete with locals offering en promptu quarry tours) sees boats running north.

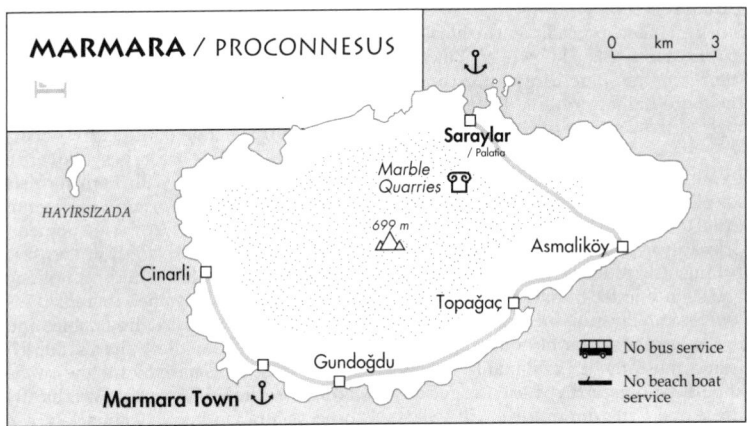

Marmaris

The most southerly Turkey—Greece crossing point, Marmaris has grown from a small fishing village to one of Turkey's leading tourist resorts. The town ribbons along the coast at the head of an islet-littered bay against an attractive backdrop of mountains and pine trees, but lacking anything approaching a major 'sight', seeing is reduced to souking up tourism with a Turkish flavour. There is enough going on to keep you happily occupied for a day but this is arguably the least interesting of Turkey's day-tripper ports. The ferries and hydrofoils to Rhodes are now the only regular services; though previous years have seen long-haul international ferries calling. Taxi boats run along the coast to Datça and to nearby **Cleopatra's Island** (sand imported from Egypt courtesy of one Marcus Antonius). Now sadly overrated and overcrowded.

◨

The few rooms and pensions fill early in High Season. Tourist Office opposite the ferry quay offers maps and a room-finding service. There is also an IYHF Youth Hostel at Iyiliktaş Merki.

⋀

Several sites on the town outskirts. Nearest is *Camping Berch* west of the port.

Odum Iskalesi

Small mainland port adjacent to the island of Bozcaada. Also known as Yukyeri, there is nothing here of interest, excepting the twice-daily ferry link. Dolmuş taxis meet ferries and run to Çanakkale.

Paşalimanı

An oddly-shaped, low-lying island with little tourism. The island economy is primarily driven by viticulture and shell fishing. All settlements are very small and even 'hamlet' implies more than you will find on the ground. Most ferries run to the largest cluster of houses (and the island mosque) at Paşalimanı, but you should be aware that boats (especially those operating out of the small village

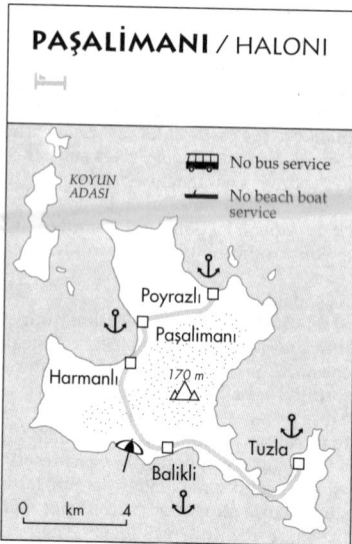

PAŞALİMANI / HALONI

No bus service

No beach boat service

KOYUN ADASI

Poyrazlı

Paşalimanı

Harmanlı

170 m

Tuzla

Balikli

0   km   4

ports north of Erdek on the Kapıdağ Peninsula often prefer to dock at other points — notably the wooded settlement of Balikli. Facilities ashore are all but nonexistent, so bring provisions with you. Best way to visit is via a day trip; crossing by private boat on one of the days that a scheduled ferry offers a means of return.

Princes' Islands

A group 20 km to the south of the Bosphorus, these nine car-free islets (four accessible by ferry — though the express boats usually only call at the largest two) are a popular destination with both tourists and locals alike; performing the role of city parks. The largely Armenian populations are now being displaced by increasing numbers of jetsetters building holiday homes. The islands gained their name as places of exile for Byzantine nobles and then members of the Sultan's family. Sadly, these days harems are few on the ground — though one island was briefly used as a rabbit farm. Nomenclature is something of a problem with the island names acquiring or losing the suffix 'ada' ('island') at random: e.g. Büyükada = Büyük. **Büyük** is the largest of the islands, and its Greek title (Prinkipo) gave the name to the group. Today it has become a resort in its own right, with a plethora of restaurants, full hotels, horses and carriages (offering pricey island tours), and gardens. **Heybeli**, is a quieter version of the same, with a naval collage and a Greek Orthodox school of Theology. The interiors of both islands are wooded, as is smaller **Burgaz**, the only other of the islands in the group to boast a reasonably sized settlement. Northerly **Kınalı** is home to one tiny hamlet, and along with **Sedef**, exists as a beach-island destination. The remainder of the group are little more than rocks with only **Kaşik** readily accessible (via beach boats from Heybeli). **Yassi** is now a prison and thus closed to tourists, while **Sivri** has an odd history as dumping ground for lighthouses and stray dogs rounded up from the streets of İstanbul, and **Tavsan** is uninhabited.

Tekirdağ
The only port of note on the northern Sea of Marmara coast, Tekirdağ is poorly connected with the rest of the Turkish ferry system, but offers good bus links with İstanbul. A growing resort town, outlying beaches are the main attraction.

Yalova
The destination of a number of İstanbul—Princes' Island ferries, Yalova is a commuter town on the southern Sea of Marmara coast. Yalova also has several daily links with **Darıca** and **Kartal** on the adjacent coast, as does **Çınarcık**, which also sees occasional Princes' Island boats. These are best of a number of uninspiring local services (the service between the towns of **Hereke** and **Karamürsel** being the other notable link) between equally uninspiring towns off the tourist map.

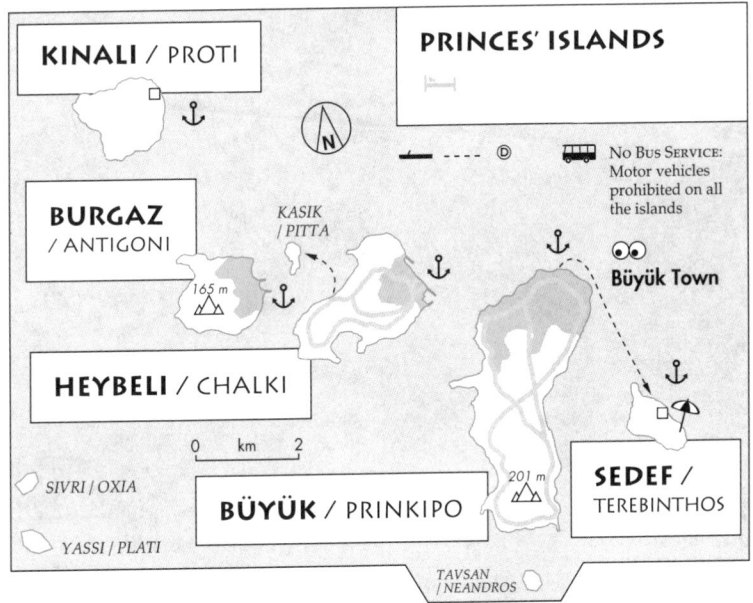

PORT TABLES

Note:

The following Port Tables show *typical* High Season ferry times. Islands and ports are listed alphabetically. Those islands that are known by two common names (eg. Santorini / Thira) are listed under the first (eg. Santorini). Island ports are not listed separately by name but appear under their respective island's name. Minor ferry services already shown on island maps are not listed again here.

Aegina

Argo-Saronic
p. 366

Ⓓ
06.10	Poseidon Co.	Piraeus.
07.15	Poseidon Co.	Piraeus.
07.40	*Keravnos*	Piraeus.
08.40	*Agios Nektarios*	Methana. Poros.
08.45	Poseidon Co.	Piraeus.
08.55	*Methodia*	Methana. Poros. Hydra. Spetses. Porto Helio.
09.00	Poseidon Co.	Methana. Poros.
09.10	*Eftichia*	Methana. Poros. Hydra. Ermioni. Spetses.
09.30	*Georgios*	Methana. Poros. Spetses.
009.30	*Moschos Express*	Angistri.
10.00	*Keravnos*	Angistri.
10.00	Poseidon Co.	Piraeus.
11.30	Poseidon Co.	Piraeus.
11.45	*Keravnos*	Piraeus.
12.00	*Moschos Express*	Angistri.
12.00	Poseidon Co.	[⑦ 11.30] Methana. Poros.
12.20	*Agios Nektarios*	Piraeus.
12.30	Poseidon Co.	Piraeus.
14.00	*Moschos Express*	Angistri.
15.15	*Keravnos*	Angistri.
15.45	Poseidon Co.	Piraeus.
15.50	*Moschos Express*	Angistri.
16.30	Poseidon Co.	[⑦ 14.15] Methana. Poros.
17.00	Poseidon Co.	Piraeus.
17.20	*Agios Nektarios*	Methana. Poros.
17.30	*Methodia*	Piraeus.
17.55	*Eftichia*	Piraeus.
18.30	*Georgios*	Piraeus.
19.00	*Moschos Express*	Angistri.
20.30	*Agios Nektarios*	Piraeus.

① ③ ⑤
| 13.30 | Poseidon Co. | Angistri. Epidavros. |

⑤ ⑥ ⑦
14.15	Poseidon Co.	Piraeus.
16.30	Poseidon Co.	Piraeus.
18.00	Poseidon Co.	Piraeus.
19.15	Poseidon Co.	Piraeus.
20.00	Poseidon Co.	Piraeus.

🐬 *Flying Dolphins* include:
Ⓗ 08.00–19.00   Piraeus (Great Harbour).
Ⓓ 09.45 17.15   Poros. Hydra. Spetses.

Aegina (Agia Marina)

Ⓓ
06.30	*Elvira*	Piraeus.
09.30	*Michael*	Piraeus.
13.00	*Agios Nektarios B*	Piraeus.
17.00	*Michael*	Piraeus.
18.45	*Agios Nektarios B*	Piraeus.

Aegina (Souvala)

Ⓓ
| 08.15 | Poseidon Co. | Piraeus. |
| 12.00 | Poseidon Co. | Piraeus. |

Ⓓ ex ⑥
| 17.30 | Poseidon Co. | Piraeus. |
| 19.30 | Poseidon Co. | Piraeus. |

⑥
| 16.30 | Poseidon Co. | Piraeus. |

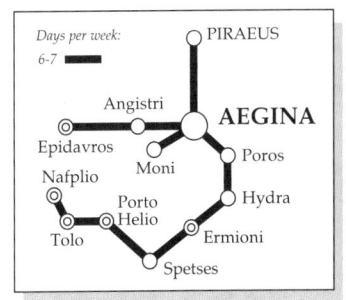

Days per week:
6-7 ▬

Agathonisi

Dodecanese p. 263

③
07.35	ILIO H/F	Kos. Kalimnos. Leros (Agia Marina). Patmos.
13.05	*Nissos Kalimnos*	Samos (Pithagorio).
18.10	*Nissos Kalimnos*	Patmos. Lipsi. Leros. Kalimnos. Kos.
19.30	ILIO H/F	Samos (Pithagorio).

④
| 09.00 | *Chioni* | Arki. Lipsi. Patmos. |
| 14.00 | *Chioni* | Samos (Pithagorio). Chios. |

⑦
| 13.05 | *Nissos Kalimnos* | Samos (Pithagorio). |
| 16.45 | *Nissos Kalimnos* | Patmos. Lipsi. Leros. Kalimnos. Kos. |

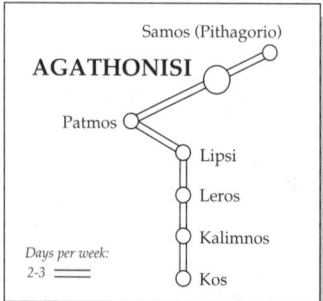

Agios Efstratios

Northern Aegean p. 329

①
| 00.30 | *Nissos Chios* | Rafina. |

②
| 05.40 | *Nissos Chios* | Limnos. |
| 08.30 | *Nissos Chios* | Piraeus. |

④
| 07.30 | *Alcaeos* | Limnos. Kavala. |
| 21.30 | *Alcaeos* | Skyros. Rafina. |

⑥
| 04.00 | *Alcaeos* | Limnos. Kavala. |
| 18.30 | *Alcaeos* | Lesbos (Mytilini). Chios. Samos (Vathi). Patmos. |

⑦
| 03.40 | *Nissos Chios* | Limnos. Kavala. |

Days per week:
4-5 ▭ Kavala — Limnos — **AGIOS EFSTRATIOS** — Rafina

Agios Konstantinos

Northern Aegean p. 329

①
| 09.00 | *Macedon* | Skiathos. Skopelos. Alonissos. |
| 21.00 | *Macedon* | Evia (Orei). Skiathos. Skopelos. Thessalonika. |

②
| 14.30 | *Lemnos* | Skiathos. Skopelos (Glossa). Skopelos. Alonissos. |

③ ⑤
| 09.00 | *Macedon* | Skiathos. Skopelos. Alonissos. |
| 21.00 | *Macedon* | Skiathos. Skopelos (Glossa). Skopelos. |

④ ⑦
| 12.00 | *Macedon* | Skiathos. Skopelos. Alonissos. |

⑥
| 11.00 | *Macedon* | Skiathos. Skopelos. |
| 21.30 | *Macedon* | Skiathos. Skopelos. Alonissos. |

〰 *Flying Dolphins*:
Ⓓ x 3 Skiathos. Skopelos. Alonissos.

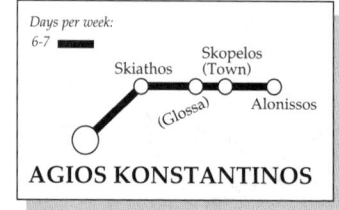

Days per week:
6-7 ▬ Skiathos — Skopelos (Town) — Alonissos (Glossa)
AGIOS KONSTANTINOS

Agios Nikolaos

Ionian p. 391

Ⓓ
08.30 12.00 15.30 18.00 20.30
    Panagia T. II   Egion.

Alexandria

Egypt p. 68

○
00.00   *Romantica*   Cyprus (Limassol).
                        Haifa.

Alexandroupolis

Northern Aegean p. 329

①
08.00   *Saos*   Samothrace.
15.00   *Saos*   Samothrace.
16.15   ILIO H/F   Lesbos (Mytilini).

②
08.00   *Saos*   Samothrace. Limnos.
09.00   *Arsinoe*   Samothrace.

③
09.00   *Saos*   Samothrace.
14.15   ILIO H/F   Limnos. Lesbos (Mytilini).
17.00   *Saos*   Samothrace.

④ ⑥
08.00   *Arsinoe/Saos* Samothrace.
15.00   *Saos*   Samothrace.

⑤
08.00   *Arsinoe*   Samothrace.
10.00   *Saos*   Samothrace.
10.45   ILIO H/F   Kavala. Lesbos (Mytilini).
17.00   *Saos*   Samothrace.

⑦
08.30   *Saos*   Samothrace.
12.00   *Arsinoe*   Samothrace.
17.00   *Saos*   Samothrace.

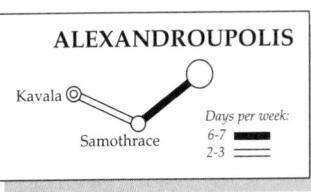

ALEXANDROUPOLIS

Kavala

Samothrace

Days per week:
6-7 ▬▬▬
2-3 ═══

Alonissos

Northern Aegean
p. 331

①
06.30   *Lemnos*   Skopelos. Skiathos. Volos.
14.30   *Macedon*   Skopelos. Skiathos.
                        Ag. Konstantinos.

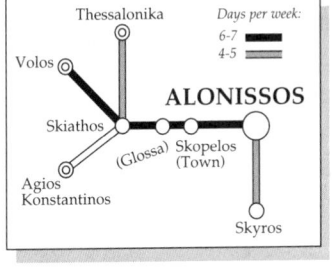

Thessalonika   Days per week:
                     6-7 ▬▬▬
Volos   4-5 ═══

ALONISSOS

Skiathos

(Glossa) Skopelos
          (Town)

Agios
Konstantinos

Skyros

15.00   *Skopelos*   Skopelos. Skopelos (Glossa).
                        Skiathos. Nesi. Volos.

②
06.10   *Lemnos*   Skopelos. Skopelos (Glossa).
                        Skiathos. Agios Konstantinos.
23.15   *Skopelos*   Skopelos (Glossa). Skiathos.
                        Volos.

③
05.15   *Papadia. II* Skopelos. Skopelos (Glossa).
                        Skiathos. Volos.
13.45   *Skopelos*   Evia (Kimi).
14.30   *Macedon*   Skopelos. Skiathos.
                        Ag. Konstantinos.
19.45   *Skopelos*   Skopelos. Skopelos (Glossa).
                        Skiathos. Volos.

④
18.00   *Macedon*   Skopelos. Skiathos.
                        Ag. Konstantinos.
23.10   *Skopelos*   Skiathos. Volos.

⑤
05.15   *Papadia. II* Skopelos. Skopelos (Glossa).
                        Skiathos. Volos.
06.30   *Lemnos*   Skopelos. Skiathos. Volos.
14.30   *Macedon*   Skopelos. Skiathos.
                        Ag. Konstantinos.
23.35   *Skopelos*   Skopelos. Skopelos (Glossa).
                        Skiathos. Volos.

⑥
19.00   *Skopelos*   Evia (Kimi). Limnos.
24.00   *Lemnos*   Skopelos.

⑦
05.00   *Macedon*   Skopelos. Skopelos (Glossa).
                        Skiathos. Ag. Konstantinos.
13.15   *Papadia. II* Skopelos. Skopelos (Glossa).
                        Skiathos. Volos.
16.15   *Skopelos*   Skopelos. Skiathos. Volos.
18.00   *Macedon*   Skopelos. Skiathos.
                        Ag. Konstantinos.

🚢 *Flying Dolphins* include:
Ⓓ 07.15 13.45 16.00
         Skopelos. Skopelos (Glossa). Skiathos.
         Ag. Konstantinos.
11.00   Skopelos. Skiathos. Volos.

Amorgos (Egiali)

Eastern Cyclades
p. 232

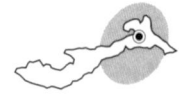

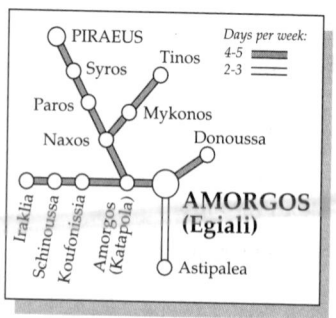

①
02.00	Ergina	Astipalea.
07.10	Ergina	Amorgos (Katapola). Koufonissia. Schinoussa. Iraklia. Naxos. Paros. Syros. Piraeus.
07.15	Skopelitis	Donoussa. Koufonissia. Schinoussa. Iraklia. Naxos.
19.45	Skopelitis	Amorgos (Katapola).
24.00	Dimitra	Astipalea.

②
| 05.00 | Dimitra | Amorgos (Katapola). Mykonos. Syros. Piraeus. |
| 23.00 | Ergina | Amorgos (Katapola). Naxos. Paros. Sifnos. Nafplio. |

③
07.15	Skopelitis	Donoussa. Koufonissia. Schinoussa. Iraklia. Naxos.
13.45	ILIO H/F	Amorgos (Katapola). Koufonissia. Schinoussa. Iraklia. Santorini. Ios. Naxos. Paros. Mykonos. Tinos. Syros.
19.45	Skopelitis	Amorgos (Katapola).
23.40	Ergina	Mykonos. Piraeus.

④
02.40	Express Olympia	Amorgos (Katapola). Naxos. Paros. Syros. Piraeus.
06.45	Dimitra	Astipalea.
12.30	Dimitra	Amorgos (Katapola). Koufonissia. Donoussa. Mykonos. Syros. Piraeus.
14.20	ILIO H/F	Koufonissia. Naxos. Paros. Mykonos. Tinos. Andros (Batsi). Rafina.
23.10	Ergina	Amorgos (Katapola). Santorini. Milos. Nafplio.

⑤
| 02.00 | Express Santorini | Astipalea. |
| 07.00 | Express Santorini | Amorgos (Katapola). Naxos. Paros. Piraeus. |

⑥
| 00.40 | Ergina | Naxos. Piraeus. |
| 23.30 | Ergina | Amorgos (Katapola). |

⑦
01.15	Ergina	Donoussa. Naxos. Mykonos. Piraeus.
07.15	Skopelitis	Donoussa. Koufonissia. Schinoussa. Iraklia. Naxos.
19.45	Skopelitis	Amorgos (Katapola).
20.15	Ionian Sea	Amorgos (Katapola). Naxos. Paros. Piraeus.

Amorgos (Katapola)

Eastern
Cyclades   p. 231

①
01.10	Ergina	Amorgos (Egiali). Astipalea.
06.00	Skopelitis	Amorgos (Egiali). Donoussa. Koufonissia. Schinoussa. Iraklia. Naxos.
08.00	Ergina	Koufonissia. Schinoussa. Iraklia. Naxos. Paros. Syros. Piraeus.
23.00	Dimitra	Amorgos (Egiali). Astipalea.

②
06.00	Dimitra	Mykonos. Syros. Piraeus.
06.00	Skopelitis	Koufonissia. Schinoussa. Iraklia. Paros (Piso Livadi). Naxos. Mykonos.
23.40	Ergina	Naxos. Paros. Sifnos. Nafplio.

③
06.00	Skopelitis	Amorgos (Egiali). Donoussa. Koufonissia. Schinoussa. Iraklia. Naxos.
14.15	ILIO H/F	Koufonissia. Schinoussa. Iraklia. Santorini. Ios. Naxos. Paros. Mykonos. Tinos. Syros.
15.30	Catamaran II	Koufonissia. Schinoussa. Iraklia. Naxos. Paros. Syros. Mykonos. Tinos. Andros. Rafina.
23.00	Ergina	Amorgos (Egiali). Mykonos. Piraeus.

④
| 06.00 | Dimitra | Amorgos (Egiali). Astipalea. |
| 06.00 | Skopelitis | Koufonissia. Schinoussa. Iraklia. Paros (Piso Livadi). Naxos. Mykonos. |

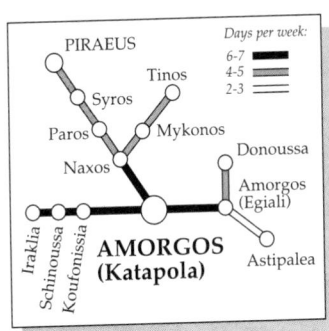

07.00	*Express Olympia*	Naxos. Paros. Syros. Piraeus.
13.30	*Dimitra*	Koufonissia. Donoussa. Mykonos. Syros. Piraeus.
24.00	*Ergina*	Santorini. Milos. Nafplio.

⑤
01.15	*Express Santorini*	Amorgos (Egiali). Astipalea.
07.45	*Express Santorini*	Naxos. Paros. Piraeus.

⑥
00.05	*Ergina*	Amorgos (Egiali). Naxos. Piraeus.
06.00	*Skopelitis*	Koufonissia. Schinoussa. Iraklia. Paros (Piso Livadi). Naxos. Mykonos.

⑦
00.20	*Ergina*	Amorgos (Egiali). Donoussa. Naxos. Mykonos. Piraeus.
06.00	*Skopelitis*	Amorgos (Egiali). Donoussa. Koufonissia. Schinoussa. Iraklia. Naxos.
21.30	*Ionian Sea*	Naxos. Paros. Piraeus.

Anafi

Cyclades Central   p. 140

②
09.00	*Express Santorini*	Santorini. Ios. Naxos. Paros. Syros. Piraeus.
15.00	ILIO H/F	Santorini. Ios. Naxos. Paros. Mykonos. Tinos. Syros.

③
18.00	*Express Santorini*	Santorini. Ios. Naxos. Paros. Piraeus.

⑥
04.45	*Apollo Express 1*	Santorini. Ios. Naxos. Paros. Piraeus.

Ancona

Italy   p. 82

Ⓓ
21.00	Minoan Lines	Igoumenitsa. Corfu. Patras.

①
13.00	Strintzis Lines	Corfu. Igoumenitsa. Patras.
17.00	*Kydon*	Igoumenitsa. Patras.
19.00	Adriatica	Dürres.

②
13.00	Strintzis Lines	Igoumenitsa. Patras.
19.00	*Crown M*	Igoumenitsa. Patras.
20.00	*Erotokritos*	Patras.

③
13.00	Marlines	Igoumenitsa. Patras.
13.00	Strintzis Lines	Corfu. Igoumenitsa. Patras.
14.00	*El. Venizelos*	Corfu. Igoumenitsa. Patras.

④
13.00	*Carlo R*	Igoumenitsa.
21.00	*Erotokritos*	Igoumenitsa.
21.00	Strintzis Lines	Igoumenitsa. Corfu. Patras.

⑤
17.00	*Kydon*	Igoumenitsa. Patras.
19.00	*Crown M*	Igoumenitsa. Patras. Crete (Iraklion).
21.00	Strintzis Lines	Igoumenitsa. Patras.

⑥
14.00	*Erotokritos*	Patras.
16.00	*Carlo R*	Patras. Çeşme.
20.00	Marlines	Corfu. Igoumenitsa. Patras.
21.00	Strintzis Lines	Igoumenitsa. Corfu. Patras.
23.00	*El. Venizelos*	Igoumenitsa. Corfu. Patras.

⑦
21.00	*Lato*	Igoumenitsa. Corfu. Patras.

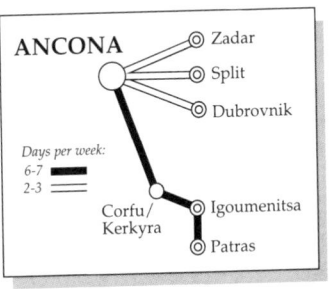

Andros

Cyclades North
p. 176

①
09.55	*Penelope A*	Tinos. Mykonos.
11.00	*Super Ferry*	Rafina.
14.55	*Bari Express*	Tinos. Mykonos.
17.00	*Penelope A*	Rafina.
21.00	*Bari Express*	Rafina.

②
09.55	*Penelope A*	Tinos. Mykonos.
11.00	*Super Ferry*	Rafina.
14.55	*Bari Express*	Tinos. Mykonos.
17.00	*Penelope A*	Rafina.
21.00	*Bari Express*	Rafina.

③
09.55	*Penelope A*	Tinos. Mykonos.
11.00	*Super Ferry*	Rafina.
14.55	*Bari Express*	Tinos. Mykonos.
17.00	*Penelope A*	Rafina.

④
09.55	*Super Ferry*	Tinos. Mykonos.
11.00	*Bari Express*	Rafina.
15.30	*Super Ferry*	Rafina.
19.00	*Penelope A*	Tinos. Mykonos.
20.30	*Super Ferry*	Tinos. Mykonos. Rafina.

⑤
09.55	*Super Ferry*	Tinos. Mykonos.
10.00	*Bari Express*	Rafina.
13.30	*Penelope A*	Rafina.
19.00	*Bari Express*	Rafina.

⑥
09.00	*Bari Express*	Tinos.
09.25	*Penelope A*	Tinos.
09.55	*Super Ferry*	Tinos. Mykonos.
13.30	*Penelope A*	Rafina.
17.00	*Super Ferry*	Rafina.
19.00	*Bari Express*	Rafina.
19.00	*Penelope A*	Tinos. Mykonos.

⑦
09.30	*Bari Express*	Tinos.
09.55	*Super Ferry*	Tinos. Mykonos.
15.00	*Bari Express*	Rafina.
16.30	*Super Ferry*	Rafina.
17.30	*Penelope A*	Rafina.
19.30	*Penelope A*	Tinos. Mykonos.
21.30	*Super Ferry*	Rafina.
22.15	*Penelope A*	Rafina.

```
Rafina ◎━━━━━○ ANDROS
                 │
                 ○ Tinos
Days per week:   │
6-7 ▬▬▬         ○ Mykonos
```

Andros (Batsi)

Cyclades North
p. 178

①
07.00	*Catamaran II*	Tinos. Mykonos.
09.10	ILIO H/F	Tinos. Mykonos.
10.30	*Catamaran II*	Rafina.
11.55	ILIO H/F	Tinos. Mykonos.
17.50	*Catamaran II*	Tinos. Mykonos.
17.55	ILIO H/F	Tinos. Mykonos. Paros. Naxos.
18.00	ILIO H/F	Rafina.
21.00	*Catamaran II*	Rafina.

②
09.10	*Catamaran II*	Tinos. Mykonos.
09.10	ILIO H/F	Tinos. Mykonos. Paros. Naxos.
12.20	*Catamaran II*	Rafina.
17.50	*Catamaran II*	Tinos. Mykonos.
18.00	ILIO H/F	Rafina.
21.00	*Catamaran II*	Rafina.

③
09.10	*Catamaran II*	Tinos. Mykonos. Syros. Paros. Naxos. Iraklia. Schinoussa. Koufonissia. Amorgos (Katapola).
09.10	ILIO H/F	Tinos. Mykonos.
12.05	ILIO H/F	Tinos. Mykonos.
17.55	ILIO H/F	Tinos. Mykonos. Paros. Naxos.
18.00	ILIO H/F	Rafina.
21.00	*Catamaran II*	Rafina.

④
09.10	*Catamaran II*	Tinos. Mykonos.
09.10	ILIO H/F	Tinos. Mykonos. Paros. Naxos. Iraklia. Schinoussa. Koufonissia. Amorgos (Egiali).
10.30	ILIO H/F	Rafina.
12.20	*Catamaran II*	Rafina.
17.50	*Catamaran II*	Tinos. Mykonos.
19.00	ILIO H/F	Rafina.
21.00	*Catamaran II*	Rafina.

⑤
09.10	*Catamaran II*	Tinos. Mykonos.
09.10	ILIO H/F	Tinos. Mykonos. Paros. Naxos.
11.55	ILIO H/F	Tinos. Mykonos.
12.20	*Catamaran II*	Rafina.
17.50	*Catamaran II*	Tinos. Mykonos.
21.00	*Catamaran II*	Rafina.

⑥
09.10	*Catamaran II*	Tinos. Mykonos.
09.10	ILIO H/F	Tinos. Mykonos. Paros. Naxos.
12.20	*Catamaran II*	Rafina.
12.25	ILIO H/F	Rafina.
17.50	*Catamaran II*	Tinos. Mykonos.
19.25	ILIO H/F	Tinos (Isternia). Tinos. Mykonos. Rafina.
21.00	*Catamaran II*	Rafina.

⑦
09.10	*Catamaran II*	Tinos. Mykonos.
09.10	ILIO H/F	Tinos. Mykonos. Paros. Naxos.
12.20	*Catamaran II*	Rafina.
14.50	ILIO H/F	Rafina.
17.50	*Catamaran II*	Tinos. Mykonos.
18.00	ILIO H/F	Rafina.
21.00	*Catamaran II*	Rafina.
22.10	ILIO H/F	Syros.

Angistri

Argo-Saronic   p. 369

Ⓓ
07.00	*Moschos Express*	Aegina.
07.15	*Keravnos*	Aegina. Piraeus.
10.00	*Moschos Express*	Aegina.
11.20	*Keravnos*	Aegina. Piraeus.
13.00	*Moschos Express*	Aegina.
15.00	*Moschos Express*	Aegina.
18.00	*Moschos Express*	Aegina.

①
05.55	*Manaras Express*	Piraeus.
07.10	*Kitsolakis Express*	Piraeus.
09.45	*Manaras Express*	Piraeus.
14.30	Poseidon Co.	Epidavros.
16.10	*Manaras Express*	Piraeus.
17.15	Poseidon Co.	Aegina. Piraeus.

②
| 07.10 | *Kitsolakis Express* | Piraeus. |

② ③ ④
| 06.10 | *Manaras Express* | Piraeus. |
| 16.40 | *Manaras Express* | Piraeus. |

③
07.10	*Kitsolakis Express*	Piraeus.
14.30	Poseidon Co.	Epidavros.
17.15	Poseidon Co.	Aegina. Piraeus.

④
| 07.10 | *Kitsolakis Express* | Piraeus. |

⑤
09.45	*Manaras Express*	Piraeus.
12.40	*Kitsolakis Express*	Piraeus.
14.30	Poseidon Co.	Epidavros.
15.30	*Manaras Express*	Piraeus.

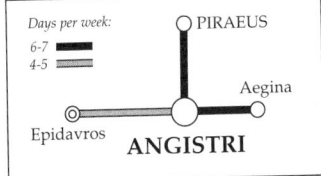

Days per week:
6-7 ▰▰▰
4-5 ▨▨▨

ANGISTRI

PIRAEUS
Aegina
Epidavros

| 17.15 | Poseidon Co. | Aegina. Piraeus. |
| 20.15 | *Manaras Express* | Piraeus. |

⑥
06.15	*Kitsolakis Express*	Piraeus.
09.00	*Manaras Express*	Piraeus.
11.45	Poseidon Co.	Epidavros.
12.10	*Kitsolakis Express*	Piraeus.
15.45	Poseidon Co.	Aegina. Piraeus.
17.00	*Manaras Express*	Piraeus.

⑦
12.00	Poseidon Co.	Epidavros.
15.00	*Manaras Express*	Piraeus.
16.00	*Kitsolakis Express*	Piraeus.
19.10	*Manaras Express*	Piraeus.
19.45	Poseidon Co.	Aegina. Piraeus.

Antikithera

Argo-Saronic   p. 369

②
| 04.00 | *Theseus* | Crete (Kasteli). |

④
| 01.50 | *Theseus* | Kalamata. |
| 21.20 | *Theseus* | Kithera (Kapsali). Neapoli. Monemvassia. Kiparissi. Piraeus. |

⑥
| 11.50 | *Theseus* | Crete (Kasteli). |

⑦
| 11.00 | *Theseus* | Kithera (Kapsali). Neapoli. Monemvassia. Gerakas. Kiparissi. Piraeus. |

Antiparos

Cyclades Central   p. 140

Ⓓ Ⓗ
| 07.00–10.00, 21.00–24.00; ev. 30 min 10.30–20.30 | *Agioi Anargiri* | Antiparos. |
| 08.00–18.00 | Antiparos TBs | Paros. |

Ⓓ
| x 4 | *Kasos Express* | Paros. |

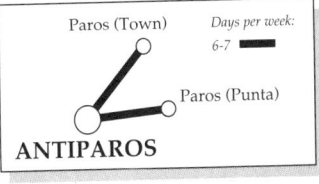

Paros (Town)
Days per week:
6-7 ▰▰▰
Paros (Punta)

ANTIPAROS

Arki

Dodecanese p. 263

④
09.30 *Chioni*   Lipsi. Patmos.
13.00 *Chioni*   Agathonisi. Samos (Pithagorio).
                   Chios.

Ashdod

Israel p. 68

②
18.00 *Princesa Amorosa*   Limassol. Port Said.

Astakos

Ionian Line p. 391

Ⓓ
14.00 *Thiaki*   Ithaca. Kefalonia (Agia Efimia).

① ③ ④ ⑥
20.30 *Thiaki*   Kefalonia (Agia Efimia).

⑤
20.30 *Thiaki*   Ithaca. Kefalonia (Agia Efimia).

⑥
17.40 *Europe 1*   Ithaca.

⑦
21.30 *Thiaki*   Kefalonia (Agia Efimia).

Astipalea

Eastern Cyclades
p. 234

①
05.30 *Ergina*   Amorgos (Egiali). Amorgos
                   (Katapola). Koufonissia.
                   Schinoussa. Iraklia. Naxos.
                   Paros. Syros. Piraeus.

②
03.00 *Dimitra*   Amorgos (Egiali). Amorgos
                    (Katapola). Mykonos. Syros.
                    Piraeus.
22.30 *Nissos Kalimnos*   Kalimnos.

④
10.00 *Nissos Kalimnos*   Kalimnos.
11.00 *Dimitra*   Amorgos (Egiali). Amorgos
                    (Katapola). Koufonissia.
                    Donoussa. Mykonos. Syros.
                    Piraeus.

PIRAEUS
Days per week:
4-5
2-3
Syros
Tinos
Naxos
Mykonos
Amorgos
Kalimnos
ASTIPALEA Kos
Rhodes

⑤
05.00 *Express Santorini*   Amorgos (Egiali).
                             Amorgos (Katapola).
                             Naxos. Paros. Piraeus.
15.00 ILIO H/F   Kalimnos. Kos. Rhodes.

⑥
02.20 *Ionian Sea*   Kalimnos. Kos. Nissiros.
                       Tilos. Rhodes.
22.15 *Ionian Sea*   Paros. Syros. Piraeus.

Avşa

Turkey p. 416

Ⓓ
00.00 TML   Marmara. İstanbul.

Ⓓ ex ⑦
00.00 TML   Marmara.
00.00 TML   Erdek.

Ⓓ x ④
00.00 Deniz Otobusleri   Marmara. İstanbul.

Ayvalık

Turkey p. 416

Ⓓ
08.00 *Jale*   Lesbos (Mytilini).
17.00 *Aeolis/Eresos II*   Lesbos (Mytilini).

Bandırma

Turkey p. 417

Ⓓ
01.15 TML   İstanbul.
14.30 TML   İstanbul.

Bari

Italy   p. 82

Ⓓ
20.30	*Dimitrios Express/*	
	Silver Paloma	Igoumenitsa.
20.30	Marlines	Corfu. Igoumenitsa.
		Patras.
20.30	*Pegasus/Vega*	Corfu. Igoumenitsa.
20.30	*Polaris/Saturnus*	Patras.

Ⓐ
20.30	*Athens Express*	Kefalonia (Sami).
		Patras.

①
19.00	*Sea Serenade*	Igoumenitsa. Patras.

③
12.00	*Baroness M*	Patras. Çeşme.
19.00	*Sea Serenade*	Igoumenitsa.
22.00	Adriatica	Dürres.

⑤
10.00	*Sea Serenade*	Igoumenitsa.

⑥
19.00	*Sea Serenade*	Igoumenitsa. Patras.
20.00	*Baroness M*	Igoumenitsa. Patras.
		Çeşme.
22.00	Adriatica	Dürres.

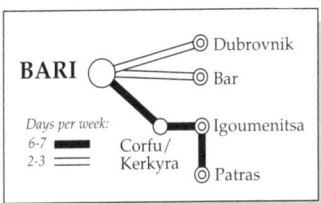

Bodrum

Turkey   p. 417

Ⓓ
09.00	*Fari Kaptain I*	Kos.
09.30	*Bodrum Express*	Datca (Körmen).
11.00	Bodrum T/Bs	Orak Is.
11.00	Bodrum T/Bs	Korada Is. Ada Is. Orak Is.
16.00	*Hermes*	Kos.
17.00	*Bodrum Express*	Datca (Körmen).

Bozcaada

Turkey   p. 417

Ⓓ x 2   TML   Odum Iskalesi.

Brindisi

Italy   p. 82

Ⓓ
00.00	*Misano*	Corfu. Igoumenitsa.
09.00	*Apollonia II*	Corfu. Igoumenitsa.
10.00	*Ionian Sun*	Corfu. Igoumenitsa.
20.30	AK Ventouris	Igoumenitsa.
		Patras.
20.30	*Raffaello/Valentino*	[○ Igoumentisa].
		Patras.
21.00	*Eolos/Ouranos*	Corfu. Igoumenitsa.
		Patras.
21.45	*Kapetan Alexandros*	Corfu. Igoumenitsa.
22.00	Adriatica	Igoumenitsa.
		Corfu.
22.30	Adriatica	Corfu. Igoumenitsa.
		Patras.
23.00	*European Glory*	Corfu. Valona.

Ⓐ
15.00	*Afrodite II*	Igoumenitsa.
		Kefalonia (Sami).
		Patras.
20.00	Adriatica	Patras.
20.00	HML Ferries	Paxi. Kefalonia (Sami).
		Patras.
20.00	*Poseidonia*	Kefalonia (Sami).
		Patras.
22.00	*Egnatia*	Corfu.
		Kefalonia (Sami).
		Patras.
22.00	HML Ferries	Kefalonia (Sami).
		Patras.

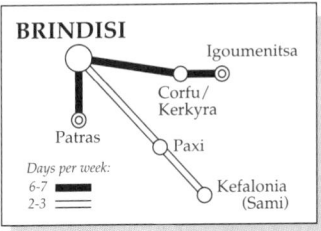

Çanakkale

Turkey   p. 417

Ⓓ x 6
00.00	TML	Kilitbahir.

Ⓓ ev 2 Ⓗ 07.30–02.00   Eceabat.

Ⓦ x 5
00.00	TML	Gökçeada.

Çeşme

Turkey   p. 418

ⓓ
| 08.00 | *Erturk I* | Chios. |
| 18.00 | *Capetan Stamatis* | Chios. |

①
| 15.00 | *Baroness M* | Patras. Igoumenitsa. Bari. |

②
| 01.00 | *Carlo R* | Patras. Ancona. |

③
| 08.30 | *Festos* | Crete (Iraklion). Patras. Kefalonia (Sami). |
| 14.00 | *Samsum* | Venice. |

⑤
| 01.00 | *Baroness M* | Patras. Bari. |

Chalki

Dodecanese   p. 264

ⓓ
| 06.00 | *Chalki* | Rhodes (Kamiros). |

③
| 10.30 | Ventouris SL | Symi. Rhodes. |
| 17.40 | Ventouris SL | Karpathos (Diafani). Karpathos (Town). Kassos. Crete (Sitia). Crete (Agios Nikolaos). Santorini. Sikinos. Folegandros. Milos. Sifnos. Piraeus. |

⑦
11.15	ILIO H/F	Tilos.
12.15	*Ialyssos*	Karpathos (Town). Crete (Iraklion).
16.00	ILIO H/F	Rhodes. Symi.

Chios

Eastern Line
p. 304

ⓓ
| 08.00 | *Capetan Stamatis* | Çeşme. |
| 14.00 | *Oinousses* | Oinousses. |

ⓓ ex①
| 08.00 | *Chios I* H/F | Samos (Vathi). Ikaria (Agios Kyrikos). Fourni. Patmos. |

①
07.00	*Capetan Stamatis*	Samos (Karlovassi). Samos (Vathi). Fourni. Ikaria (Agios Kyrikos).
09.00	Miniotis	Oinousses.
09.00	*Sappho*	Lesbos (Mytilini).
21.30	*Sappho*	Piraeus.

②
03.00	*Mytilene*	Lesbos (Mytilini). Limnos. Kavala.
07.00	*Psara*	Psara.
08.45	ILIO H/F	Samos (Vathi). Patmos.
20.10	ILIO H/F	Lesbos (Mytilini).
20.30	*Alcaeos*	Piraeus.

③
04.00	*Sappho*	Lesbos (Mytilini). Limnos. Thessalonika.
06.00	*Nissos Chios*	Lesbos (Mytilini).
09.00	Miniotis	Oinousses.
10.30	*Mytilene*	Piraeus.
11.00	*Nissos Chios*	Piraeus.
19.30	*Chioni*	Samos (Pithagorio). Agathonisi. Arki. Lipsi. Patmos.

④
04.00	*Mytilene*	Lesbos (Mytilini). Piraeus.
07.00	*Capetan Stamatis*	Samos (Karlovassi). Samos (Vathi). Fourni. Ikaria (Agios Kyrikos).
07.00	*Psara*	Psara.
08.45	ILIO H/F	Samos (Vathi). Samos (Karlovassi). Ikaria (Agios Kyrikos). Patmos.
20.10	ILIO H/F	Lesbos (Mytilini).
21.30	*Sappho*	Piraeus.

⑤
04.30	*Nissos Chios*	Lesbos (Mytilini). Limnos. Kavala.
09.00	Miniotis	Oinousses.
11.00	*Mytilene*	Piraeus.

⑥		
02.00	*Sappho*	Lesbos (Mytilini).
05.00	*Mytilene*	Lesbos (Mytilini). Limnos. Thessalonika.
07.00	*Psara*	Psara.
08.45	ILIO H/F	Samos (Vathi). Patmos.
10.30	*Sappho*	Piraeus.
12.00	*Nissos Chios*	Rafina.
20.10	ILIO H/F	Lesbos (Mytilini).

⑦		
04.00	*Alcaeos*	Samos (Vathi). Patmos.
06.00	*Sappho*	Lesbos (Mytilini).
08.15	ILIO H/F	Samos (Pithagorio). Patmos.
09.00	Miniotis	Oinousses.
14.00	*Sappho*	Piraeus.
19.30	*Alcaeos*	Lesbos (Mytilini). Limnos. Thessalonika.
19.45	ILIO H/F	Lesbos (Mytilini).
21.30	*Mytilene*	Piraeus.

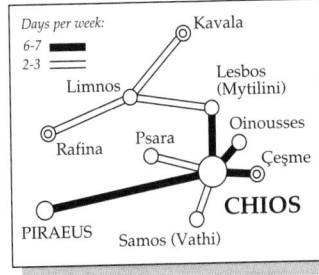

Days per week:
6-7 ▬▬▬
2-3 ═══

Kavala
Lesbos (Mytilini)
Limnos
Oinousses
Rafina
Psara
Çeşme
CHIOS
PIRAEUS
Samos (Vathi)

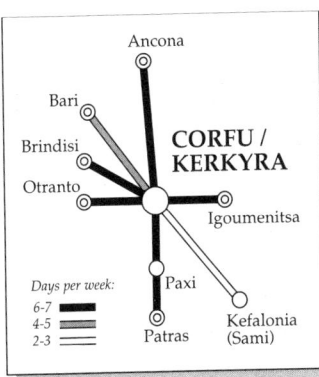

Ancona
Bari
Brindisi
Otranto
CORFU / KERKYRA
Igoumenitsa
Paxi
Kefalonia (Sami)
Patras

Days per week:
6-7 ▬▬▬
4-5 ▬▬▬
2-3 ═══

Corfu / Kerkyra

Ionian Line   p. 82

International Services:

Ⓓ		
00.00	*Misano*	Brindisi.
01.00	*Ionian Sun*	Brindisi.
06.00	*European Glory*	Valona. Brindisi.
06.30	*Eolos/Ouranos*	Igoumenitsa. Patras.
07.00	Adriatica	Igoumenitsa. Patras.
07.00	*Kapetan Alexandros*	Igoumenitsa. Brindisi.
08.00	Adriatica	Brindisi.
08.00	Marlines	Igoumenitsa. Patras.
08.00	Minoan Lines	Igoumenitsa. Ancona.
08.30	*Eolos/Ouranos*	Brindisi.
09.00	Adriatica	Brindisi.
09.00	Marlines	Bari.
09.00	*Pegasus/Vega*	Igoumenitsa.
18.00	*Apollonia II*	Igoumenitsa.
22.30	Minoan Lines	Patras.
22.30	*Pegasus/Vega*	Bari.
23.30	*Apollonia II*	Brindisi.

Ⓐ		
06.30	*Egnatia*	Brindisi.
07.00	*Egnatia*	Kefalonia (Sami). Patras.

①		
23.00	*Lato*	Patras.

②		
08.00	*El. Venizelos*	Igoumenitsa. Ancona.
08.45	Strintzis Lines	Igoumenitsa. Ancona.
09.00	*Petrakis/Sotirakis*	Sarandë.
11.30	Strintzis Lines	Igoumenitsa. Patras.

③		
07.30	*Lato*	Igoumenitsa. Trieste.
08.45	Strintzis Lines	Igoumenitsa. Ancona.

④		
11.30	Strintzis Lines	Igoumenitsa. Patras.
12.00	*El. Venizelos*	Igoumenitsa. Patras.

⑤		
07.30	*El. Venizelos*	Igoumenitsa. Trieste.
08.45	Strintzis Lines	Igoumenitsa. Ancona.
12.00	Marlines	Ancona.
22.00	Strintzis Lines	Patras.

⑥		
08.00	*Lato*	Igoumenitsa. Ancona.
09.00	*Petrakis/Sotirakis*	Sarandë.

⑦		
08.45	Strintzis Lines	Igoumenitsa. Ancona.
09.00	*Petrakis/Sotirakis*	Sarandë.
19.15	*Zephyros*	Igoumenitsa. Paxi.
21.00	Marlines	Igoumenitsa. Patras.
22.00	Strintzis Lines	Patras.
23.00	*El. Venizelos*	Patras.

② ④ ⑤ ⑦		
11.00	*Anna Maria Lauro*	Otranto.

Domestic Services:

Ⓗ
06.00–22.00   Local   Igoumenitsa.

Ⓓ
09.30   *Kamelia*   Paxi.
15.00   *Paxos Star*   Paxi.

Ⓓ ex ⑦
14.00   *Pegasus*   Paxi (Old Port).

①
10.00   *Zephyros*   Igoumenitsa. Paxi.
19.00   *Zephyros*   Paxi.

① ③ ⑤
14.00   Corfu-Paxi Line   Paxi.

① ④
13.00   *Kamelia*   Paxi.

② ⑥
06.30   Othoni Line   Erikoussa. Mathraki.
                         Orthoni.
14.30   *Zephyros*   Igoumenitsa. Paxi.

④
13.00   *Zephyros*   Paxi.

⑤
17.00   *Zephyros*   Paxi.

⑤ ⑥ ⑦
16.00   *Kamelia*   Paxi.

⑦
19.15   *Zephyros*   Igoumenitsa. Paxi.

Corfu (Lefkimi)

Ⓓ
06.00   09.00   12.00   16.00   18.00
           Local   Igoumenitsa.

Corfu (Sidari)

① ④
11.00   Othoni Line   Erikoussa.
                         Mathraki. Orthoni.

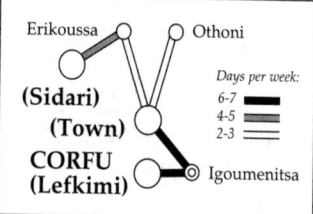

Days per week:
6-7
4-5
2-3

(Sidari)
(Town)
CORFU
(Lefkimi)
Erikoussa   Othoni
Igoumenitsa

Crete
(Agia Roumeli)

Crete   p. 251

Ⓓ
09.30   14.00   15.45   17.00
           South Crete Line   Lutro. Sfakia.
18.00   South Crete Line   Sfakia.
16.30   South Crete Line   Sougia. Paleochora.

Crete
(Agios Nikolaos)

Crete
p. 241

◯
00.00   *Vitsentzos*
          Kornaros   Crete (Sitia). Kassos.
                         Karpathos.

00.00   *Vitsentzos*
          Kornaros   Milos. Piraeus.

②
07.00   *Kriti*   Crete (Sitia).
19.30   *Kriti*   Milos. Piraeus.
24.00   Ventouris SL   Crete (Sitia). Kassos.
                         Karpathos (Town).
                         Karpathos (Diafani).
                         Chalki. Symi. Rhodes.

④
03.40   Ventouris SL   Santorini. Sikinos.
                         Folegandros. Milos.
                         Sifnos. Piraeus.
07.00   *Kriti*   Crete (Sitia).
19.30   *Kriti*   Milos. Piraeus.

⑥
08.00   *Kriti*   Crete (Sitia).
19.30   *Kriti*   Milos. Piraeus.

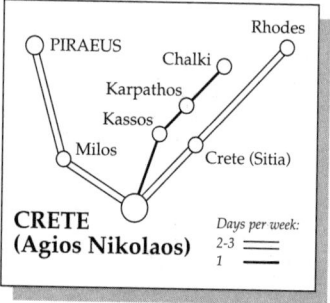

Rhodes
PIRAEUS   Chalki
          Karpathos
          Kassos
       Milos   Crete (Sitia)

CRETE   Days per week:
(Agios Nikolaos)   2-3
                   1

Crete (Chania)

Crete   p. 243

Ⓓ
18.30   *Aptera/Lissos*   Piraeus.

② ⑤ ⑥
07.00   *Knossos*   Piraeus.

③
19.45   *Knossos*   Piraeus.

⑦
19.45   *Knossos*   Piraeus.

Crete (Iraklion)

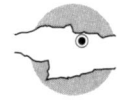

Crete   p. 244

International Services:

①
24.00   *Festos*   Çeşme.

③
22.00   *Festos*   Patras. Kefalonia (Sami).

Domestic Services:

Ⓓ
19.15   *King Minos/*
         N. Kazantzakis   Piraeus.
19.30   *Kantia/Rethimno*   Piraeus.

①
08.00   *Nearchos*   Santorini. Ios. Paros. Naxos.
16.00   *Daliana*   Santorini. Naxos. Paros.
                              Piraeus.

②
08.00   *Nearchos*   Santorini. Ios. Paros. Syros.
19.30   *Anemos*   Santorini. Paros.
                              Mykonos. Tinos. Skiathos.
                              Thessalonika.

③
07.00   *Daliana*   Karpathos (Town). Rhodes.
08.00   *Nearchos*   Santorini. Ios. Paros.
                              Mykonos.

④
08.00   *Nearchos*   Santorini. Ios. Naxos. Paros.
09.00   *Daliana*   Santorini. Naxos. Paros.
                              Piraeus.
21.30   *Anemos*   Santorini. Paros. Syros.
                              Thessalonika.

⑤
08.00   *Nearchos*   Santorini. Ios. Paros.
                              Mykonos.

Days per week:
6-7 ▰▰▰▰
4-5 ▭▭▭▭
2-3 ▱▱▱▱

◎ Thessalonika
○ Skiathos
◎ Ancona
○ Tinos
○ Mykonos
○ PIRAEUS
Paros
Ios
Karpathos
Santorini
Rhodes
Limassol
Haifa

CRETE (Iraklion)

⑥
06.00   *Daliana*   Karpathos (Town). Rhodes.
21.30   *Anemos*   Santorini. Paros. Mykonos.
                              Tinos. Skiathos.
                              Thessalonika.

⑦
08.00   *Nearchos*   Santorini. Ios.
08.30   *Daliana*   Santorini. Paros. Piraeus.
21.00   *Crown M*   Igoumenitsa. Ancona.
23.00   *Ialyssos*   Karpathos (Town).
                              Rhodes. Kos. Kalimnos.
                              Leros. Patmos. Piraeus.

Crete (Kasteli)

Crete   p. 249

②
09.30   *Theseus*   Kalamata.

③
08.00   *Theseus*   Gythio.
23.50   *Theseus*   Antikithera. Kalamata.

④
19.00   *Theseus*   Antikithera. Kithera (Kapsali).
                              Neapoli. Monemvassia.
                              Kiparissi. Piraeus.

⑥
14.30   *Theseus*   Kalamata.

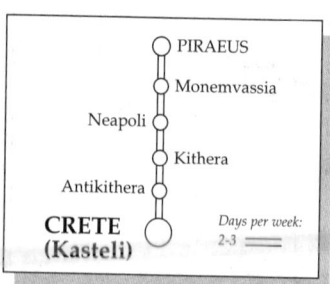

CRETE (Kasteli)

PIRAEUS
Monemvassia
Neapoli
Kithera
Antikithera

Days per week:
2-3

⑦
09.00   *Theseus*   Antikithera. Kithera (Kapsali).
Neapoli. Monemvassia.
Gerakas. Kiparissi. Piraeus.

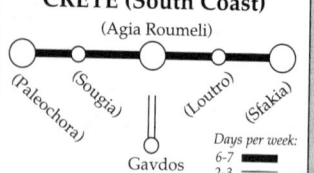

CRETE (South Coast)

(Agia Roumeli)

(Paleochora) (Sougia) (Loutro) (Sfakia)

Gavdos

Days per week:
6-7
2-3

⑤
18.00   South Crete Line   Gavdos.

⑥ ⑦
09.00   South Crete Line   Gavdos.

Crete (Paleochora)

Crete p. 251

Ⓓ
08.15   South Crete Line   Sougia.
10.00   South Crete Line   Agia Roumeli.
Elafonisi.

Crete (Rethimno)

Crete p. 250

② ④ ⑥ ⑦
19.30   *Arkadi/Preveli*   Piraeus.

PIRAEUS

CRETE
(Rethimno)

Days per week:
4-5

Crete (Sfakia)

Crete p. 251

Ⓓ
10.30   11.45   13.45
15.45   17.00   18.00
South Crete Line   Lutro. Agia Roumeli.

Crete (Sitia)

Crete p. 250

○
00.00   *Vitsentzos Kornaros*   Crete (Agios Nikolaos).
Milos. Piraeus.
00.00   *Vitsentzos Kornaros*   Kassos. Karpathos.

②⑥
17.00   *Kriti*   Crete (Agios Nikolaos).
Milos. Piraeus.

③
02.30   Ventouris SL   Kassos. Karpathos (Town).
Karpathos (Diafani). Chalki.
Symi. Rhodes.

④
02.05   Ventouris SL   Crete (Agios Nikolaos).
Santorini. Sikinos. Folegand-
ros. Milos. Sifnos. Piraeus.
17.00   *Kriti*   Crete (Agios Nikolaos).
Milos. Piraeus.

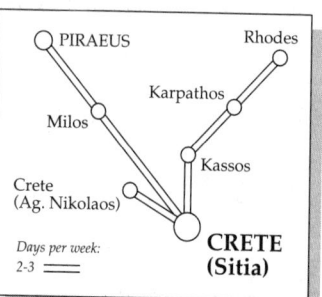

PIRAEUS   Rhodes

Karpathos

Milos   Kassos

Crete
(Ag. Nikolaos)

Days per week:
2-3

CRETE
(Sitia)

Tables   Donoussa • **439**

Cyprus (Larnaca)

Cyprus p. 68

○
Service Suspended   Jounieh.

Cyprus (Limassol)

Cyprus
p. 68

①
12.00   Sea Wave   Rhodes. Piraeus.
13.00   Nissos Kypros   Rhodes. Piraeus.
15.00   Princesa Marissa   Port Said.

③
15.00   Princesa Amorosa   Port Said.
19.30   Princesa Marissa   Haifa. Port Said.
20.00   Sea Harmony   Haifa.

④
20.00   Princessa Cypria   Haifa.

⑤
11.00   Sea Harmony   Rhodes. Piraeus.
17.00   Princesa Amorosa   Port Said.

⑥
15.00   Princessa Cypria   Rhodes.
                           Lesbos (Mytilini).
                           Tinos. Piraeus.
19.00   Sea Wave   Haifa.
19.30   Princesa Marissa   Haifa.
20.00   Nissos Kypros   Haifa.

⑦
17.00   Princesa Amorosa   Port Said. Ashdod.
18.00   Rodos   Rhodes.
21.00   Vergina Sky   Haifa. Port Said.
                           Rhodes. Mykonos.
                           Thessalonika.

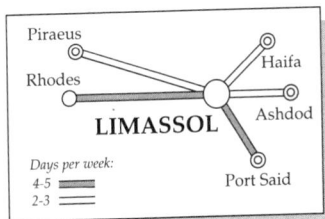

Piraeus
Haifa
Rhodes
LIMASSOL
Ashdod
Days per week:
4-5
2-3
Port Said

Turkish Occupied Ports:

Famagusta / Magosa

② ④ ⑦
22.00   Yeşilada   Mersin.

Kyrenia / Girne

Ⓓ
13.00   Hydrofoil   Taşucu.

② ③ ④
13.00   Liberty/Ertürk   Taşucu.

Datça (Körmen)

Turkey p. 418

Ⓓ
09.00   Bodrum Express   Bodrum.
17.00   Bodrum Express   Bodrum.

Delos

Cyclades North p. 179

Ⓓ
10.15   Hera   Mykonos.
12.30   Niki   Mykonos.
13.45   Hera   Mykonos.
14.00   Delos Express   Mykonos.
14.15   Niki   Mykonos.

Donoussa

Eastern Cyclades
p. 237

①
08.30   Skopelitis   Koufonissia. Schinoussa.
                           Iraklia. Naxos.
18.30   Skopelitis   Amorgos (Egiali).
                           Amorgos (Katapola).

③
08.30   Skopelitis   Koufonissia. Schinoussa.
                           Iraklia. Naxos.
18.30   Skopelitis   Amorgos (Egiali).
                           Amorgos (Katapola).

④
01.40   Express Olympia   Amorgos (Egiali).
                           Amorgos (Katapola).
                           Naxos. Paros.
                           Syros.
                           Piraeus.

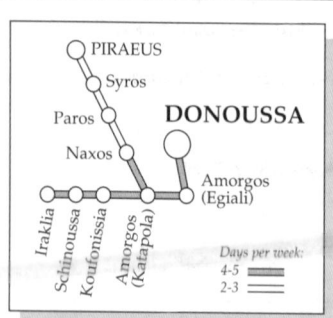

PIRAEUS
Syros
Paros
DONOUSSA
Naxos
Amorgos
(Egiali)
Iraklia
Schinoussa
Koufonissia
Amorgos
(Katapola)

Days per week:
4-5
2-3

| 03.00 | Dimitra | Koufonissia. Amorgos (Katapola). Amorgos (Egiali). Astipalea. |
| 16.30 | Dimitra | Mykonos. Syros. Piraeus. |

⑥
| 17.30 | Ventouris SL | Naxos. Paros. Piraeus. |
| 22.15 | Ergina | Amorgos (Egiali). Amorgos (Katapola). |

⑦
02.00	Ergina	Naxos. Mykonos. Piraeus.
08.30	Skopelitis	Koufonissia. Schinoussa. Iraklia. Naxos.
18.30	Skopelitis	Amorgos (Egiali). Amorgos (Katapola).

Dürres

Albania   p. 86

②
| 22.00 | Adriatica | Bari. |

③ ⑥
| 19.00 | Adriatica | Trieste. |

④
| 12.00 | Adriatica | Bari. |

⑦
| 12.00 | Adriatica | Ancona. |

Eceabat

Turkey   p. 418

Ⓓ ev 2Ⓗ 08.00–03.00   Çanakkale.

Egion

Ionian   p. 391

Ⓓ
07.30   10.30   13.30   17.00   19.00
        Panagia T. II   Agios Nikolaos.

Elafonissos

Argo-Saronic   p. 370

Ⓓ
| 07.00 | Martha | Neapoli. Kithera (Agia Pelagia). Gythio. |

⑥
| 01.40 | Theseus | Kithera (Kapsali). Gythio. Antikithera. Crete (Kasteli). |

Epidavros

Argo-Saronic   p. 370

①
| 16.00 | Poseidon Co. | Angistri. Aegina. Piraeus. |

③
| 17.15 | Poseidon Co. | Angistri. Aegina. Piraeus. |

⑤
| 16.00 | Poseidon Co. | Angistri. Aegina. Piraeus. |

⑥
| 14.00 | Poseidon Co. | Angistri. Aegina. Piraeus. |

⑦
| 14.00 | Poseidon Co. | Aegina. Piraeus. |
| 18.30 | Poseidon Co. | Angistri. Aegina. Piraeus. |

Erdek

Turkey   p. 418

Ⓓ ex ⑦
00.00   TML   Avşa. Marmara.

① ⑥
00.00   TML   Paşalimanı.

⑤ ⑦
00.00   TML   Avşa. Marmara. Tekirdağ.

Ermioni

Argo-Saronic   p. 370

Ⓓ
12.30   *Eftichia*   Spetses.
14.30   *Eftichia*   Hydra. Poros.
                       Methana.
                       Aegina. Piraeus.

③ ⑥
12.40   *Georgios*   Spetses. Porto Helio.
15.30   *Georgios*   Poros. Methana. Aegina.
                       Piraeus.

🐬 *Flying Dolphins* include:
Ⓓ
x 6   Hydra. Piraeus (Zea).
x 4   Poros.

Evia (Kimi)

Northern Aegean   p. 182

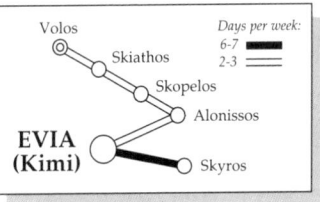

Ⓓ ex ⑦
11.00   *Lykomides*   Skyros.
17.00   *Lykomides*   Skyros.

③
17.00   *Skopelos*   Alonissos. Skopelos.
                        Skopelos (Glossa). Skiathos.
                        Volos.
⑥
22.30   *Skopelos*   Limnos.

⑦
13.00   *Lykomides*   Skyros.
13.30   *Skopelos*   Alonissos. Skopelos.
                        Skiathos. Volos.
19.00   *Lykomides*   Skyros.

```
Volos                    Days per week:
  ◎                        6-7  ▰▰▰
     Skiathos              2-3  ══
        ○
           Skopelos
              ○
                 ○ Alonissos
EVIA     ○
(Kimi)       ○ Skyros
```

Evia (Marmari)

Cyclades North   p. 182

①
06.00   *Marmari I*   Rafina.
10.30   *Marmari I*   Rafina.
16.45   *Marmari I*   Rafina.
20.05   ILIO H/F   Evia (Karystos).
                        Rafina.

② ③ ④
06.00   *Marmari I*   Rafina.
10.30   *Marmari I*   Rafina.
16.45   *Marmari I*   Rafina.

⑤
06.00   *Marmari I*   Rafina.
10.00   *Marmari I*   Rafina.
16.15   *Marmari I*   Evia (Karystos).
                        Rafina.

⑥
07.00   *Marmari I*   Rafina.
07.05   ILIO H/F   Rafina.
10.00   *Marmari I*   Evia (Karystos).
                        Rafina.
16.30   *Marmari I*   Rafina.
19.05   ILIO H/F   Evia (Karystos).

⑦
07.00   *Marmari I*   Rafina.
14.00   *Marmari I*   Rafina.
17.15   *Marmari I*   Rafina.
20.45   *Marmari I*   Rafina.

Folegandros

Cyclades West   p. 204

○
17.00   *Delfini Express*   Sikinos. Ios.

①
24.00   *Milos Express*   Sikinos. Ios. Santorini.

②
09.45   *Milos Express*   Kimolos. Milos. Sifnos.
                              Serifos. Kythnos.
                              Piraeus.
16.40   Ventouris SL   Sikinos. Santorini.
                              Crete (Agios Nikolaos).
                              Crete (Sitia). Kassos.
                              Karpathos (Town).
                              Karpathos (Diafani).
                              Chalki. Symi. Rhodes.
19.00   *Express Paros*   Sifnos. Serifos. Syros.

③
18.30   *Express Paros*   Sifnos. Paros. Mykonos.

④
11.15   Ventouris SL   Milos. Sifnos. Piraeus.
17.00   *Milos Express*   Sikinos. Ios. Santorini.
21.00   *Milos Express*   Kimolos. Milos. Sifnos.
                              Serifos. Kythnos. Piraeus.

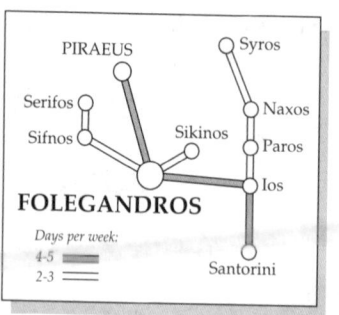

②
| 04.30 | *Milena* | Samos (Karlovassi). Samos (Vathi). |
| 18.15 | *Milena* | Ikaria (Agios Kyrikos). Naxos. Paros. Piraeus. |

③
| 04.30 | *Dimitra* | Samos (Karlovassi). Samos (Vathi). |
| 08.15 | *Dimitra* | Ikaria (Agios Kyrikos). Mykonos. Syros. Piraeus. |

④
05.20	*Golden Vergina*	Samos (Karlovassi). Samos (Vathi).
14.00	*Capetan Stamatis*	Ikaria (Agios Kyrikos).
18.30	*Capetan Stamatis*	Samos (Vathi). Samos (Karlovassi). Chios.
18.30	*Golden Vergina*	Ikaria (Agios Kyrikos). Paros. Piraeus.

⑥
| 04.30 | *Milena* | Samos (Karlovassi). Samos (Vathi). |
| 09.30 | *Milena* | Ikaria (Agios Kyrikos). Naxos. Piraeus. |

⑦
| 18.45 | *Milena* | Ikaria (Agios Kyrikos). Naxos. Paros. Piraeus. |

⑤
| 06.15 | *Apollo Express 2* | Santorini. Ios. Naxos. Paros. Syros. Piraeus. |

⑥
| 18.00 | *Milos Express* | Sikinos. Milos. Piraeus. |

⑦
| 05.30 | *Apollo Express 1* | Santorini. Ios. Naxos. Paros. Piraeus. |
| 19.15 | *Romilda* | Sikinos. Naxos. Paros. Piraeus. |

Fourni

Eastern Line
p. 307

ⒹⒹ
| 07.00 | *Maria Express* | Ikaria (Agios Kyrikos). |

Ⓓ ex①
| 11.00 | *Chios I* | Patmos. |
| 16.30 | *Chios I* | Ikaria (Agios Kyrikos). Samos (Vathi). Chios. |

①
| 14.00 | *Capetan Stamatis* | Ikaria (Agios Kyrikos). |
| 18.30 | *Capetan Stamatis* | Samos (Vathi). Samos (Karlovassi). Chios. |

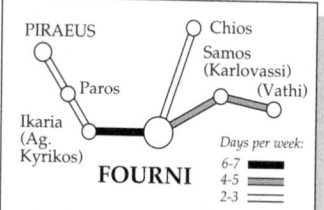

Gavdos

Crete p. 251

⑥ ⑦
| 16.00 | South Crete Line | Sfakia. |

Gelibolu

Turkey p. 418

Ⓓ x 7 06.00–23.00 Lâpseki.

Gerakas

Argo-Saronic p. 370

⑤
| 21.00 | *Theseus* | Monemvassia. Neapoli. Elafonissos. Kithera (Kapsali). Gythio. Antikithera. Crete (Kasteli). |

⑦
| 17.30 | *Theseus* | Kiparissi. Piraeus. |

Gökçeada

Turkey p. 418

Ⓦ x 5 TML Çanakkale.

Gythio

Argo-Saronic
p. 371

Ⓓ ex ⑦
| 13.40 | *Martha* | Kithera (Agia Pelagia).
Neapoli.
Elafonissos. |

③
| 15.30 | *Theseus* | Kithera (Kapsali).
Crete (Kasteli). |

⑥
| 07.00 | *Theseus* | Antikithera.
Crete (Kasteli). |

⑦
| 17.45 | *Martha* | Kithera (Agia Pelagia).
Neapoli.
Elafonissos. |

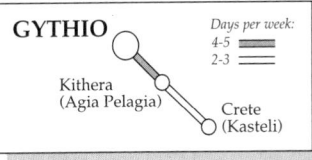

GYTHIO

Days per week:
4-5
2-3

Kithera
(Agia Pelagia)

Crete
(Kasteli)

Haifa

Israel   p. 69

①
| 19.00 | *Vergina Sky* | Port Said.
Rhodes.
Mykonos.
Thessalonika. |

④
| 19.00 | *Princesa Marissa* | Port Said.
Limassol. |
| 20.00 | *Sea Harmony* | Limassol. Rhodes.
Piraeus. |

⑤
| 20.00 | *Princessa Cypria* | Limassol. Rhodes.
Lesbos (Mytilini).
Tinos. Piraeus. |

⑦
19.00	*Sea Wave*	Limassol. Rhodes. Piraeus.
20.00	*Nissos Kypros*	Limassol. Rhodes. Piraeus.
20.00	*Princesa Marissa*	Limassol. Port Said.

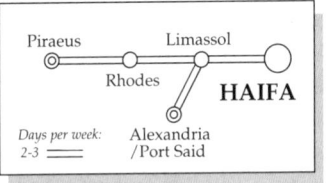

Piraeus   Limassol

Rhodes   HAIFA

Days per week: Alexandria
2-3   /Port Said

Hydra

Argo-Saronic
p. 371

Ⓓ
12.00	*Eftichia*	Ermioni. Spetses.
12.00	*Methodia*	Spetses. Porto Helio.
15.00	*Methodia*	Poros. Methana. Aegina. Piraeus.
15.15	*Eftichia*	Poros. Methana. Aegina. Piraeus.

⑥ ⑦
| 12.30 | *Agios Nektarios* | Spetses. Porto Helio. |
| 16.30 | *Agios Nektarios* | Poros. Methana.
Aegina. Piraeus. |

🚢 *Flying Dolphins* include:
| Ⓓ x 10 | Piraeus. |
| x 7 | Poros. / Spetses. Porto Helio. |

Igoumenitsa

Ionian Line   p. 86

International Services:

Ⓓ
00.00	*Misano*	Brindisi.
06.00	Adriatica	Corfu. Brindisi.
06.30	*Eolos/Ouranos*	Corfu. Brindisi.
07.00	Adriatica	Corfu. Brindisi.
07.00	AK Ventouris	Brindisi.
07.00	Marlines	Corfu. Bari.
08.00	AK Ventouris	Patras.
08.15	*Eolos/Ouranos*	Patras.
09.00	Adriatica	Patras.
09.30	Marlines	Patras.
10.00	*Kapetan Alexandros*	Brindisi.
11.00	Minoan Lines	Ancona.
20.30	Minoan Lines	Corfu. Patras.
20.30	*Pegasus/Vega*	Corfu. Bari.
21.00	*Dimitrios Express/* *Silver Paloma*	Bari.
21.30	*Apollonia II*	Corfu. Brindisi.
23.30	*Ionian Sun*	Corfu. Brindisi.

Ⓐ
23.00	*Afrodite II*	Kefalonia (Sami).
		Patras.
23.00	*Afrodite II*	Brindisi.

①
11.30	*Zephyros*	Paxi.
16.00	*Zephyros*	Corfu. Paxi.
17.00	*Crown M*	Ancona.
20.30	*Lato*	Corfu.
		Patras.

②
06.00	*Sea Serenade*	Patras.
08.00	Marlines	Ancona.
09.30	*Zephyros*	Corfu.
10.30	*El. Venizelos*	Ancona.
10.30	Strintzis Lines	Ancona.
13.00	Strintzis Lines	Patras.
15.00	*Kydon*	Patras.
16.00	*Zephyros*	Paxi.
19.00	*Baroness M*	Bari.
24.00	*Sea Serenade*	Bari.

③
09.30	*Lato*	Trieste.
10.30	Strintzis Lines	Ancona.
11.00	Strintzis Lines	Patras.
17.00	*Crown M*	Patras.
17.00	*Zephyros*	Paxi.

④
10.30	*Kydon*	Ancona.
10.30	Strintzis Lines	Ancona.
12.00	*Crown M*	Ancona.
13.00	Strintzis Lines	Patras.
14.00	*El. Venizelos*	Patras.
15.00	Marlines	Patras.
18.30	*Zephyros*	Paxi.
22.00	*Sea Serenade*	Bari.

⑤
07.40	*Zephyros*	Paxi.
09.30	*El. Venizelos*	Trieste.
10.00	Marlines	Corfu. Ancona.
10.30	Strintzis Lines	Ancona.
14.00	*Carlo R*	Ancona.
15.30	*Lato*	Patras.
20.00	*Erotokritos*	Ancona.
20.30	Strintzis Lines	Corfu. Patras.
24.00	*Sea Serenade*	Bari.

⑥
09.30	*Zephyros*	Corfu.
10.30	*Lato*	Ancona.
15.00	*Kydon*	Patras.
16.00	*Zephyros*	Paxi.
17.00	*Crown M*	Patras.
		Crete (Iraklion).
19.00	Strintzis Lines	Patras.

⑦
06.00	*Sea Serenade*	Patras.
09.00	*Baroness M*	Patras. Cesme.
10.30	*Kydon*	Ancona.
10.30	Strintzis Lines	Ancona.
20.30	Strintzis Lines	Corfu. Patras.
21.15	*Zephyros*	Paxi.
21.30	*El. Venizelos*	Corfu. Patras.
23.00	Marlines	Patras.
24.00	*Sea Serenade*	Bari.

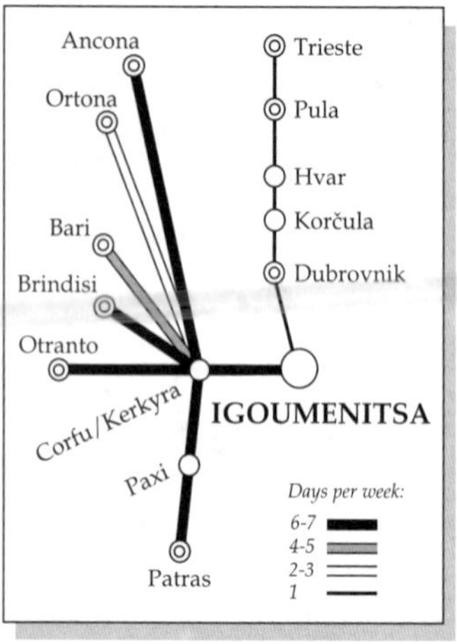

② ④ ⑤ ⑦
| 08.30 | *Anna Maria Lauro* |

Ⓓ Ⓗ

Ⓓ

①
| | *Zephyros* |
| | *Zephyros* |

②
| | *Zephyros* |
| | *Zephyros* |

③
| | *Zephyros* |

④
| | *Zephyros* |

⑤
| | *Zephyros* |

⑥
| | *Zephyros* |
| | *Zephyros* |

⑦
| | *Zephyros* |

Ikaria
(Agios Kyrikos)

Eastern Line   p. 308

○
| 13.00 | *Maria Express* | Fourni. |

Ⓓ ex①
| 10.30 | *Chios I* | Fourni. Patmos. |
| 17.00 | *Chios I* | Samos (Vathi). Chios. |

①
05.20	*Samaina*	Samos (Karlovassi). Samos (Vathi).
08.30	ILIO H/F	Patmos. Lipsi. Leros. Kalimnos. Kos.
12.15	*Samaina*	Ikaria (Evdilos). Piraeus.
16.00	*Capetan Stamatis*	Fourni. Samos (Vathi). Samos (Karlovassi). Chios.
17.00	ILIO H/F	Samos (Karlovassi). Samos (Vathi).

②
03.15	*Milena*	Fourni. Samos (Karlovassi). Samos (Vathi).
18.15	*Samaina*	Samos (Karlovassi). Samos (Vathi).
19.00	*Milena*	Naxos. Paros. Piraeus.

③
01.10	*Golden Vergina*	Samos (Karlovassi). Samos (Vathi).
04.00	*Dimitra*	Fourni. Samos (Karlovassi). Samos (Vathi).
08.35	*Golden Vergina*	Paros. Piraeus.
10.30	*Dimitra*	Mykonos. Syros. Piraeus.
21.00	*Samaina*	Ikaria (Evdilos). Piraeus.

④
03.15	*Milena*	Samos (Karlovassi). Samos (Vathi).
04.30	*Golden Vergina*	Fourni. Samos (Karlovassi). Samos (Vathi).
12.10	ILIO H/F	Patmos.
16.00	*Capetan Stamatis*	Fourni. Samos (Vathi). Samos (Karlovassi). Chios.
16.30	ILIO H/F	Samos (Karlovassi). Samos (Vathi). Chios. Lesbos (Mytilini).
18.15	*Samaina*	Samos (Karlovassi). Samos (Vathi).
19.00	*Milena*	Naxos. Paros. Piraeus.
19.20	*Golden Vergina*	Paros. Piraeus.
22.45	*Samaina*	Piraeus.

⑤
08.30	ILIO H/F	Patmos. Lipsi. Leros. Kalimnos. Kos.
17.00	ILIO H/F	Samos (Karlovassi). Samos (Vathi).
17.15	*Samaina*	Samos (Karlovassi).
21.00	*Samaina*	Piraeus.

⑥
03.00	*Milena*	Fourni. Samos (Karlovassi). Samos (Vathi).
10.00	*Milena*	Naxos. Piraeus.
18.15	*Samaina*	Samos (Karlovassi). Samos (Vathi).

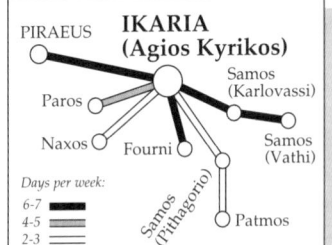

PIRAEUS   **IKARIA**
(Agios Kyrikos)
Paros   Samos (Karlovassi)
Naxos   Fourni   Samos (Vathi)
Days per week:
6-7
4-5
2-3
Samos (Pithagorio)   Patmos

⑦
09.50	*Samaina*	Ikaria (Karkinagri). Piraeus.
10.00	*Milena*	Samos (Karlovassi). Samos (Vathi).
19.15	*Milena*	Naxos. Paros. Piraeus.

Ikaria (Evdilos)

Eastern Line   p. 310

①
06.40	*Golden Vergina*	Samos (Karlovassi). Samos (Vathi).
13.15	*Samaina*	Piraeus.
18.45	*Golden Vergina*	Paros. Piraeus.

②
| 18.15 | *Samaina* | Ikaria (Agios Kyrikos). Samos (Karlovassi). Samos (Vathi). |

③
| 21.00 | *Samaina* | Piraeus. |

⑥
| 02.10 | *Golden Vergina* | Samos (Karlovassi). Samos (Vathi). |
| 09.15 | *Golden Vergina* | Paros. Piraeus. |

⑦
| 04.40 | *Golden Vergina* | Samos (Karlovassi). Samos (Vathi). |
| 10.40 | *Golden Vergina* | Paros. Piraeus. |

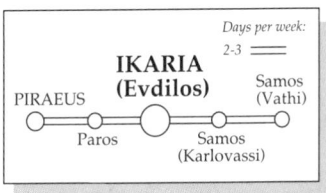

Days per week:
2-3
IKARIA
(Evdilos)
PIRAEUS
Paros   Samos (Karlovassi)   Samos (Vathi)

Ikaria (Karkinagri)

Eastern Line   p. 310

⑥
16.30   *Samaina*   Ikaria (Agios Kyrikos).
                      Samos (Karlovassi).
                      Samos (Vathi).
⑦
10.30   *Samaina*   Piraeus.

Ios

Cyclades Central
p. 144

PIRAEUS

Syros

Mykonos

Serifos

Naxos

Paros

Sifnos

Folegandros   **IOS**

Sikinos

Santorini

Days per week:
6-7
4-5
2-3

Crete (Iraklion)

Ⓓ
11.00   *Mykonos Express*   Naxos. Paros. Mykonos.
20.00   *Mykonos Express*   Santorini.

①
01.30   *Poseidon Express*   Santorini.
03.45   *Apollo Express 1*   Santorini.
05.45   *Express Santorini*   Santorini.
08.45   *Poseidon Express*   Naxos. Paros. Piraeus.
09.15   *Apollo Express 1*   Naxos. Paros. Piraeus.
10.35   ILIO H/F   Santorini.
11.30   *Express Santorini*   Naxos. Paros. Piraeus.
12.00   *Nearchos*   Paros. Naxos.
13.30   *Express Paros*   Santorini.
15.30   *Apollo Express 2*   Santorini.
15.45   *Express Olympia*   Santorini.
17.00   *Express Paros*   Naxos. Paros. Mykonos.
17.00   *Nearchos*   Santorini.
                              Crete (Iraklion).
17.40   ILIO H/F   Naxos. Paros. Mykonos.
                              Tinos. Syros.
20.15   *Express Olympia*   Naxos. Paros. Piraeus.
20.30   *Apollo Express 2*   Naxos. Paros. Piraeus.

②
01.30   *Poseidon Express*   Santorini.
02.00   *Milos Express*   Santorini.
06.45   *Express Santorini*   Santorini. Anafi.
08.30   *Milos Express*   Sikinos. Folegandros.
                              Kimolos. Milos. Sifnos.
                              Serifos. Kythnos.
                              Piraeus.
08.45   *Poseidon Express*   Naxos. Paros. Piraeus.
10.35   ILIO H/F   Santorini. Anafi.
11.30   *Express Santorini*   Naxos. Paros. Syros.
                              Piraeus.
12.00   *Nearchos*   Paros. Syros.
13.30   *Express Paros*   Sikinos. Folegandros.
                              Sifnos. Serifos. Syros.
15.30   *Apollo Express 1*   Santorini.
16.00   *Express Olympia*   Santorini.
17.30   *Nearchos*   Santorini.
                              Crete (Iraklion).
17.40   ILIO H/F   Naxos. Paros. Mykonos.
                              Tinos. Syros.

20.15   *Express Olympia*   Naxos. Paros. Piraeus.
20.30   *Apollo Express 1*   Naxos. Paros. Piraeus.

③
01.30   *Poseidon Express*   Santorini.
03.40   *Apollo Express 2*   Santorini.
08.00   ILIO H/F   Kuşadası.
08.45   *Poseidon Express*   Naxos. Paros. Piraeus.
09.15   *Apollo Express 2*   Naxos. Paros. Piraeus.
10.35   ILIO H/F   Santorini. Iraklia.
                              Schinoussa.
                              Koufonissia.
                              Amorgos (Egiali).
                              Amorgos (Katapola).
12.00   *Nearchos*   Paros. Mykonos.
13.30   *Express Paros*   Santorini.
15.30   *Apollo Express 1*   Santorini.
15.45   *Express Santorini*   Santorini. Anafi.
17.00   *Express Paros*   Sikinos. Folegandros.
                              Sifnos. Paros.
                              Mykonos.
17.00   *Nearchos*   Santorini.
                              Crete (Iraklion).
17.40   ILIO H/F   Naxos. Paros.
                              Mykonos.
                              Tinos. Syros.
20.30   *Apollo Express 1*   Naxos. Paros. Piraeus.
20.30   *Express Santorini*   Naxos. Paros. Piraeus.

④
03.40   *Apollo Express 2*   Santorini.
09.15   *Apollo Express 2*   Naxos. Paros. Piraeus.
10.35   ILIO H/F   Santorini.
12.00   *Nearchos*   Naxos. Paros.
13.30   *Express Paros*   Santorini.
15.30   *Apollo Express 1*   Santorini.
15.30   *Nearchos*   Santorini.
                              Crete (Iraklion).
17.00   *Express Paros*   Naxos. Paros.
                              Mykonos. Syros.
17.40   ILIO H/F   Naxos. Paros.
                              Mykonos.
                              Tinos. Syros.

19.00	*Milos Express*	Santorini. Folegandros. Kimolos. Milos. Sifnos. Serifos. Kythnos. Piraeus.
20.30	*Apollo Express 1*	Naxos. Paros. Piraeus.

⑤

01.30	*Poseidon Express*	Santorini.
04.45	*Apollo Express 2*	Sikinos. Folegandros. Santorini.
08.45	*Poseidon Express*	Naxos. Paros. Piraeus.
09.15	*Apollo Express 2*	Naxos. Paros. Syros. Piraeus.
10.35	ILIO H/F	Santorini.
12.00	*Nearchos*	Paros. Mykonos.
13.30	*Express Paros*	Santorini.
16.00	*Express Olympia*	Santorini.
17.00	*Express Paros*	Naxos. Paros. Mykonos.
17.00	*Nearchos*	Santorini. Crete (Iraklion).
17.40	ILIO H/F	Naxos. Paros. Mykonos. Tinos. Syros.
20.15	*Express Olympia*	Naxos. Paros. Piraeus.

⑥

01.30	*Apollo Express 1*	Santorini. Anafi.
02.50	*Poseidon Express*	Santorini.
05.45	*Express Santorini*	Santorini.
08.00	ILIO H/F	Kuşadası.
08.45	*Poseidon Express*	Naxos. Paros. Piraeus.
09.15	*Apollo Express 1*	Naxos. Paros. Piraeus.
11.30	*Express Santorini*	Naxos. Paros. Piraeus.
13.30	*Express Paros*	Santorini.
15.30	*Apollo Express 2*	Santorini.
16.00	*Express Olympia*	Santorini.
17.00	*Express Paros*	Naxos. Paros. Mykonos. Syros.
20.15	*Express Olympia*	Naxos. Paros. Piraeus.
20.30	*Apollo Express 2*	Naxos. Paros. Piraeus.

⑦

01.30	*Poseidon Express*	Santorini.
03.00	*Apollo Express 1*	Sikinos. Folegandros. Santorini.
05.45	*Express Santorini*	Santorini.
08.00	ILIO H/F	Kuşadası.
08.35	*Poseidon Express*	Naxos. Paros. Piraeus.
09.15	*Apollo Express 1*	Naxos. Paros. Piraeus.
11.30	*Express Santorini*	Naxos. Paros. Piraeus.
13.30	*Express Paros*	Santorini.
15.30	*Apollo Express 2*	Santorini.
15.40	*Nearchos*	Santorini. Crete (Iraklion).
16.00	*Express Olympia*	Santorini.
17.00	*Express Paros*	Naxos. Paros. Mykonos. Syros.
20.15	*Express Olympia*	Naxos. Paros. Piraeus.
20.30	*Apollo Express 2*	Naxos. Paros. Piraeus.

○

10.00	*Delfini Express*	Sikinos. Folegandros.

Iraklia

Eastern Cyclades p. 238

Ⓓ
Ferries and Catamarans as **Schinoussa**

Times for boats to:

Naxos & Piraeus:
Schinoussa departure time +30 minutes.

Amorgos:
Schinoussa departure time −30 minutes.

İstanbul

Turkey p. 419

Ⓓ Ⓗ 06.45–21.00		Princes' Islands. [x 5 steaming on to Yalova or Çinarcik.]
Ⓓ 09.30 20.00		Bandırma.
10.30 13.30		Bosphorus 'Tour'.
08.00		Armutlu. Mudanya.
08.00		Marmara. Avşa.
x 4	Deniz Otobusleri	Marmara. Avşa.
① ③ ⑤ 14.00	TML	İzmir. [③ August only]

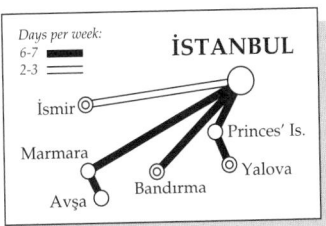

İSTANBUL

Days per week:
6-7
2-3

İsmir
Princes' Is.
Marmara
Yalova
Avşa
Bandırma

Ithaca (Frikes)

Ionian Line p. 392

Ⓓ 11.00	*Meganisi*	Kefalonia (Fiskardo). Lefkada (Nidri).
13.00	*Capt. Aristidis*	Lefkada (Nidri).
17.45	*Capt. Aristidis*	Kefalonia (Fiskardo). Lefkada (Nidri).

Ithaca (Pisaetos)

Ionian Line   p. 392

Ⓓ

06.30	Aphrodite L	Kefalonia (Sami).
08.10	Aphrodite L	Kefalonia (Fiskardo). Lefkada (Vassiliki).
13.00	Aphrodite L	Kefalonia (Sami).
14.50	Aphrodite L	Kefalonia (Fiskardo). Lefkada (Vassiliki).
20.00	Aphrodite L	Kefalonia (Sami).
21.30	Aphrodite L	Kefalonia (Sami).

Ο

| 09.00 | HML Ferries | Patras. |
| 21.00 | HML Ferries | Kefalonia (Sami). Brindisi. |

Ithaca (Vathi)

Ionian Line   p. 392

Ⓓ

07.00	Eptanisos	Kefalonia (Sami). Patras.
11.00	Thiaki	Astakos.
16.00	Thiaki	Kefalonia (Agia Efimia).
18.30	Eptanisos	Patras.

① ② ④ ⑥

| 09.00 | Europe 1 | Kefalonia (Sami). Patras. |

②

| 09.00 | Europe 1 | Kefalonia (Sami). Patras. |
| 15.55 | Europe 1 | Kefalonia (Sami). Kefalonia (Poros). Zakinthos. |

③ ⑤ ⑦

| 09.00 | Europe 1 | Kefalonia (Poros). Patras. |

⑤

| 15.55 | Europe 1 | Kefalonia (Sami). Kefalonia (Poros). Patras. |
| 22.20 | Thiaki | Kefalonia (Agia Efimia). |

⑥

| 16.40 | Europe 1 | Astakos. |

⑦

| 15.55 | Europe 1 | Kefalonia (Sami). Kefalonia (Poros). Patras. |
| 19.30 | Thiaki | Astakos. Kefalonia (Ag. Efimia). |

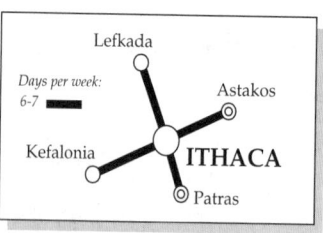

Lefkada

Days per week:
6-7

Astakos

Kefalonia   **ITHACA**

Patras

İzmir

Turkey   p. 420

② ⑦

| 14.00 | TML | İstanbul. |

Kabatepe

Turkey   p. 420

③ ⑦

| 13.00 | TML | Gökçeada. |

Kalamata

Argo-Saronic   p. 373

②

| 21.30 | Theseus | Crete (Kasteli). |

④

| 10.00 | Theseus | Crete (Kasteli). |

⑥

| 23.50 | Theseus | Crete (Kasteli). |

Kalimnos

Dodecanese   p. 265

Ⓓ
07.00 16.00 19.00

| | Olympios Apollon | Kos (Mastihari). |

①

06.00	Nissos Kalimnos	Kos. Nissiros. Tilos. Symi. Rhodes. Kastelorizo.
07.00	ILIO H/F	Kos. Rhodes. Symi.
10.40	Marina	Kos. Rhodes.
14.10	ILIO H/F	Leros. Lipsi. Patmos. Ikaria (Agios Kyrikos). Samos (Karlovassi). Samos (Vathi).
18.35	Ialyssos	Leros. Patmos. Piraeus.
22.30	Marina	Leros. Patmos. Piraeus.

②

02.00	Kamiros	Kos. Rhodes.
04.30	Romilda	Kos. Nissiros. Tilos. Symi. Rhodes. Kastelorizo.
07.00	ILIO H/F	Kos. Nissiros. Symi. Tilos. Rhodes.
14.10	ILIO H/F	Leros. Lipsi. Patmos. Samos (Pithagorio). Samos (Vathi).

17.30	*Kamiros*	Leros. Patmos. Piraeus.
20.00	*Nissos Kalimnos*	Astipalea.
③		
02.00	*Ialyssos*	Kos. Rhodes.
03.00	*Marina*	Kos. Rhodes.
07.00	ILIO H/F	Kos. Rhodes.
07.00	*Nissos Kalimnos*	Leros. Lipsi. Patmos. Agathonisi. Samos (Pithagorio).
09.00	*Romilda*	Leros. Lipsi. Patmos. Naxos. Paros. Syros. Piraeus.
09.40	ILIO H/F	Leros. Patmos.
17.30	*Ialyssos*	Leros. Patmos. Piraeus.
17.30	ILIO H/F	Kos. Agathonisi. Samos (Pithagorio).
20.30	*Marina*	Piraeus.
④		
00.30	*Nissos Kalimnos*	Kos.
02.00	*Kamiros*	Kos. Rhodes.
07.00	ILIO H/F	Kos. Rhodes. Symi.
07.00	*Nissos Kalimnos*	Astipalea.
10.30	ILIO H/F	Kos.
16.40	ILIO H/F	Leros. Lipsi. Patmos. Samos (Pithagorio).
17.30	*Kamiros*	Leros. Patmos. Piraeus.
20.30	*Rodanthi*	Piraeus.
⑤		
02.00	*Ialyssos*	Kos. Rhodes.
03.00	*Marina*	Kos. Rhodes.
06.00	*Nissos Kalimnos*	Kos. Nissiros. Tilos. Symi. Rhodes. Kastelorizo.
07.00	ILIO H/F	Kos. Rhodes. Nissiros.
11.20	ILIO H/F	Kos.
14.10	ILIO H/F	Leros. Lipsi. Patmos. Ikaria (Agios Kyrikos). Samos (Vathi).
17.30	*Ialyssos*	Leros. Patmos. Piraeus.
20.30	*Marina*	Piraeus.
⑥		
02.00	*Kamiros*	Kos. Rhodes.
04.45	*Ionian Sea*	Kos. Nissiros. Tilos. Rhodes.
07.00	ILIO H/F	Kos. Rhodes. Symi. Tilos. Nissiros.
17.30	ILIO H/F	Kos. Patmos. Samos (Pithagorio).
17.30	*Kamiros*	Leros. Patmos. Piraeus.
19.45	*Ionian Sea*	Astipalea. Paros. Syros. Piraeus.
⑦		
01.00	*Marina*	Kos. Leros. Patmos. Naxos. Paros. Piraeus.
02.20	*Ialyssos*	Kos. Rhodes. Chalki. Karpathos (Town). Crete (Iraklion).
07.00	ILIO H/F	Kos. Rhodes. Chalki. Tilos.
07.00	*Nissos Kalimnos*	Leros. Lipsi. Patmos. Agathonisi. Samos (Pithagorio).
09.30	ILIO H/F	Leros. Patmos.
17.30	ILIO H/F	Kos. Samos (Pithagorio). Samos (Vathi).
22.45	*Nissos Kalimnos*	Kos.

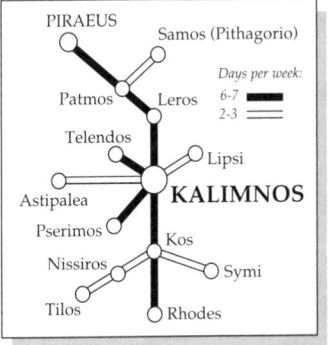

PIRAEUS   Samos (Pithagorio)

Days per week:
6-7
2-3

Patmos   Leros

Telendos

Lipsi

Astipalea   **KALIMNOS**

Pserimos

Nissiros   Kos

Symi

Tilos

Rhodes

Karpathos (Diafani)

Dodecanese
p. 268

③		
08.15	*Georgios Express*	Chalki. Symi. Rhodes.
19.55	*Georgios Express*	Karpathos (Town). Kassos. Crete (Sitia). Crete (Agios Nikolaos). Santorini. Sikinos. Folegandros. Milos. Sifnos. Kythnos. Piraeus.

Karpathos (Town)

Dodecanese   p. 267

①		
06.00	*Ialyssos*	Rhodes. Kos. Kalimnos. Leros. Patmos. Piraeus.
③		
07.00	Ventouris SL	Karpathos (Diafani). Chalki. Symi. Rhodes.
08.15	Ventouris SL	Chalki. Symi. Rhodes.
13.30	*Daliana*	Rhodes.
19.55	Ventouris SL	Karpathos (Town). Kassos. Crete (Sitia). Crete (Agios Nikolaos). Santorini. Sikinos. Folegandros. Milos. Sifnos. Piraeus.

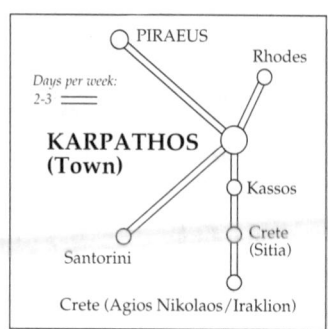

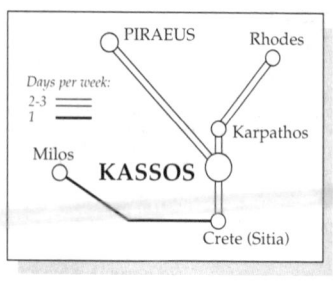

21.05	Ventouris SL	Kassos. Crete (Sitia). Crete (Agios Nikolaos). Santorini. Sikinos. Folegandros. Milos. Sifnos. Piraeus.
④ 01.30	*Daliana*	Crete (Iraklion). Santorini. Naxos. Paros. Piraeus.
⑥ 12.30	*Daliana*	Rhodes.
⑦ 01.30	*Daliana*	Crete (Iraklion). Santorini. Paros. Piraeus.
15.00	*Ialyssos*	Crete (Iraklion).
○ 00.00	*Vitsentzos Kornaros*	Kassos. Crete (Sitia). Crete (Agios Nikolaos). Milos. Piraeus.

Kassos

Dodecanese p. 270

○ 00.00	*Vitsentzos Kornaros*	Crete (Sitia). Crete (Agios Nikolaos). Milos. Piraeus.
00.00	*Vitsentzos Kornaros*	Karpathos.
③ 05.20	Ventouris SL	Karpathos (Town). Karpathos (Diafani). Chalki. Symi. Rhodes.
22.40	Ventouris SL	Crete (Sitia). Crete (Agios Nikolaos). Santorini. Sikinos. Folegandros. Milos. Sifnos. Piraeus.

Kastelorizo / Meganisi

Dodecanese p. 271

① ⑤ 21.10	*Nissos Kalimnos*	Rhodes. Symi. Tilos. Nissiros. Kos. Kalimnos.
② 16.30	*Romilda*	Rhodes. Symi. Tilos. Nissiros. Kos. Kalimnos. Leros. Lipsi. Patmos. Naxos. Paros. Syros. Piraeus.

Kavala

Northern Aegean p. 333

⑩ 07.50	09.30 12.00 14.00 16.00 18.00 19.30 ANET Line	Thassos (Skala Prinos).
07.00	12.30 14.00 18.30 Santa H/F	Thassos (Town).
08.30	15.30 Santa H/F	Thassos (Limenaria).
① 14.00	09.00 ILIO H/F	*Arsinoe* Samothrace. Alexandroupolis. Lesbos (Mytilini).
② 17.30 20.00	*Arsinoe* *Mytilene*	Samothrace. Limnos. Lesbos (Mytilini). Chios. Piraeus.
③ 14.00	*Arsinoe*	Samothrace.

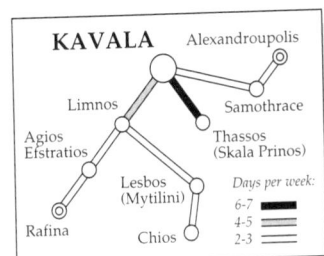

KAVALA Alexandroupolis

Limnos

Samothrace

Agios Efstratios

Thassos (Skala Prinos)

Lesbos (Mytilini)

Days per week:

Rafina

Chios

6-7 ▬▬▬
4-5 ▬▬▬
2-3 ═══

④
| 15.00 | Alcaeos | Limnos. Agios Efstratios. Skyros. Rafina. |

⑤
15.00	ILIO H/F	Lesbos (Mytilini).
17.00	Arsinoe	Samothrace.
21.00	Nissos Chios	Limnos. Lesbos (Mytilini). Chios. Rafina.

⑥
| 12.00 | Alcaeos | Limnos. Agios Efstratios. Lesbos (Mytilini). Chios. Samos (Vathi). Patmos. |
| 15.00 | Arsinoe | Samothrace. |

⑦
| 15.30 | Santa Lines | Thassos (Skala Marion). |
| 19.00 | Nissos Chios | Limnos. Agios Efstratios. Rafina. |

Kea

Cyclades West p. 207

ⓓ
| 10.40 | Flying Dolphin | Kythnos. |
| 12.50 | Flying Dolphin | Piraeus (Zea). |

①
06.00	Mirina Express	Lavrion.
08.55	ILIO H/F	Kythnos. Serifos. Sifnos. Kimolos. Milos.
17.00	ILIO H/F	Rafina.
17.00	Mirina Express	Lavrion.

②
07.00	Mirina Express	Lavrion.
10.30	Mirina Express	Kythnos.
17.00	Mirina Express	Lavrion.

③
| 07.00 | Mirina Express | Lavrion. |

④
| 07.00 | Mirina Express | Lavrion. |
| 17.00 | Mirina Express | Lavrion. |

⑤
07.00	Mirina Express	Lavrion.
11.00	Mirina Express	Lavrion.
16.30	Mirina Express	Lavrion.
19.45	Mirina Express	Lavrion.

⑥
07.00	Mirina Express	Lavrion.
10.30	Mirina Express	Lavrion.
16.00	Mirina Express	Lavrion.
19.30	Mirina Express	Lavrion.

⑦
12.00	Mirina Express	Lavrion.
15.30	Mirina Express	Lavrion.
19.00	Mirina Express	Lavrion.
22.15	Mirina Express	Lavrion.

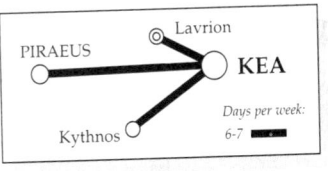

Lavrion

PIRAEUS

KEA

Days per week:

Kythnos

6-7 ▬▬▬

Kefalonia (Agia Efimia)

Ionian Line
p. 394

ⓓ
| 09.15 | Thiaki | Ithaca. Astakos. |

① ② ③ ④ ⑥
| 18.00 | Thiaki | Astakos. [⑤ ⑦ Ithaca]. |

Kefalonia (Argostoli)

Ionian Line
p. 394

ⓓ
07.15	Myrtos	Kilini.
09.00	Europe 2	Patras.
16.00	Europe 2	Zakinthos.
19.30	Myrtos	Kefalonia (Lixouri). Kilini.

Kefalonia (Fiskardo)

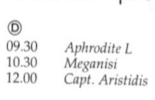

Ionian Line   p. 394

Ⓓ
09.30	Aphrodite L	Lefkada (Vassiliki).
10.30	Meganisi	Lefkada (Nidri).
12.00	Capt. Aristidis	Ithaca (Frikes). Lefkada (Nidri).
12.20	Aphrodite L	Ithaca (Pisaetos). Kefalonia (Sami).
15.45	Aphrodite L	Lefkada (Vassiliki).
17.00	Meganisi	Lefkada (Vathi).
19.00	Capt. Aristidis	Lefkada (Nidri).
20.40	Aphrodite L	Ithaca (Pisaetos). Kefalonia (Sami).

Kefalonia (Lixouri)

Ionian Line   p. 394

Ⓓ
06.30	Myrtos	Kefalonia (Argostoli). Kilini.
17.45	Myrtos	Kefalonia (Argostoli).
19.45	Myrtos	Kilini.

Kefalonia (Pessada)

Ionian Line   p. 394

Ⓓ
| 07.45 | Ionion Pelagos | Zakinthos (Skinaria). |
| 17.30 | Ionion Pelagos | Zakinthos (Skinaria). |

Kefalonia (Poros)

Ionian Line   p. 394

Ⓓ
09.15	Delos	Kilini.
13.00	Myrtos	Kilini.
15.00	Delos	Kilini.
19.30	Delos	Kilini.

②
17.15	Europe 1	Zakinthos.
19.25	Europe 1	Kefalonia (Sami). Ithaca.
20.00	Europe 1	Ithaca.

③ ⑤ ⑦
| 09.50 | Europe 1 | Patras. |
| 15.40 | Europe 1 | Kefalonia (Sami). Ithaca. |

⑤ ⑦
| 20.55 | Europe 1 | Kefalonia (Sami). |

Kefalonia (Sami)

Ionian Line   p. 394

International Services:

Ⓐ
01.00	Athens Express	Bari.
06.00	Afrodite II	Patras.
09.30	HML Ferries	Patras.
13.00	HML Ferries	Patras.
14.00	Athens Express	Patras.
17.00	Afrodite II	Igoumenitsa. Brindisi.
20.30	HML Ferries	Paxi. Brindisi.
24.00	HML Ferries	Corfu. Brindisi.

⑦
| 20.00 | Festos | Patras. Crete (Iraklion). Çeşme. |

Domestic Services:

Ⓓ
01.00	Eptanisos	Ithaca.
06.00	Aphrodite L	Ithaca (Pisaetos).
08.00	Aphrodite L	Ithaca (Pisaetos). Kefalonia (Fiskardo). Lefkada (Vassiliki).
08.45	Eptanisos	Patras.
14.00	Aphrodite L	Ithaca (Pisaetos). Kefalonia (Fiskardo). Lefkada (Vassiliki).
16.15	Eptanisos	Ithaca.

① ② ④ ⑥
| 09.45 | Europe 1 | Patras. |

⑤ ⑦
| 16.40 | Europe 1 | Patras. |
| 21.30 | Europe 1 | Ithaca. |

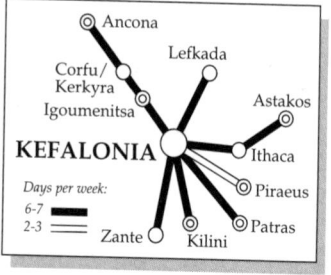

Keramoti

Northern Aegean   p. 334

Ⓓ
07.15 09.15 11.15 13.15 15.15 16.45
17.45 18.45 19.45 20.45 21.45 22.30
        ANET Line   Thassos (Town).

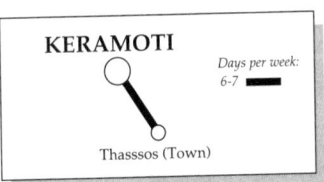

KERAMOTI

Days per week:
6-7 ▬▬

Thasssos (Town)

Kimolos

Cyclades West   p. 209

①
00.30   *Georgios Express*   Milos. Piraeus.
11.30   ILIO H/F   Milos.
14.30   *Georgios Express*   Milos. Sifnos. Serifos.
                             Kythnos. Piraeus.
14.30   ILIO H/F   Sifnos. Serifos. Kythnos.
                             Kea. Rafina.
23.10   *Milos Express*   Folegandros. Sikinos.
                             Ios. Santorini.

②
11.25   *Milos Express*   Milos. Sifnos. Serifos.
                             Kythnos. Piraeus.
19.45   *Georgios Express*   Milos. Sifnos. Serifos.
                             Kythnos. Piraeus.

③
14.20   *Milos Express*   Milos. Sifnos. Serifos.
                             Kythnos. Piraeus.

④
22.00   *Milos Express*   Milos. Sifnos. Serifos.
                             Kythnos. Piraeus.

⑤
03.30   *Georgios Express*   Milos. Piraeus.
21.45   *Georgios Express*   Milos. Piraeus.

⑥
16.15   *Milos Express*   Folegandros. Sikinos.
                             Milos. Piraeus.

⑦
03.30   *Georgios Express*   Milos.
10.00   *Georgios Express*   Sifnos. Serifos. Kythnos.
                             Piraeus.

Kilini

Ionian Line   p. 396

Ⓓ
10.15   *Dimitirus Miras/*
        Proteos/Zakinthos I   Zakinthos.
10.30   *Myrtos*   Kefalonia (Poros).
12.00   *Delos*   Kefalonia (Poros).
14.30   *Dimitirus Miras/*
        Proteos/Zakinthos I   Zakinthos.
15.30   *Myrtos*   Kefalonia (Lixouri).
                                Kefalonia (Argostoli).
17.30   *Delos*   Kefalonia (Poros).
17.30   *Dimitirus Miras/*
        Proteos/Zakinthos I   Zakinthos.
20.15   *Dimitirus Miras/*
        Proteos/Zakinthos I   Zakinthos.
21.30   *Delos*   Kefalonia (Poros).
22.30   *Myrtos*   Kefalonia (Lixouri).

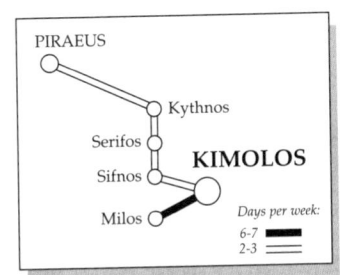

PIRAEUS

Kythnos

Serifos

Sifnos

Milos

KIMOLOS

Days per week:
6-7 ▬▬
2-3 ═══

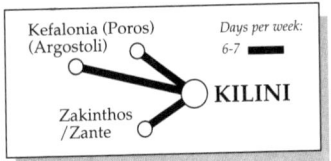

Kefalonia (Poros)
(Argostoli)

Days per week:
6-7 ▬▬

KILINI

Zakinthos
/Zante

Kilitbahir

Turkey   p. 421

Ⓓ x 6
00.00   TML   Çanakkale.

Kiparissi

Argo-Saronic   p. 373

①
20.00   *Theseus*   Monemvassia. Neapoli.
                    Kithera (Kapsali).
                    Antikithera. Crete (Kasteli).

⑤
04.50	*Theseus*	Piraeus.
20.00	*Theseus*	Gerakas. Monemvassia. Neapoli. Elafonissos. Kithera (Kapsali). Gythio. Antikithera. Crete (Kasteli).

⑦
18.15	*Theseus*	Piraeus.

⛴ *Flying Dolphins* include:
ⅅ x 1   Piraeus.

Kithera (Agia Pelagia)

Argo-Saronic p. 374

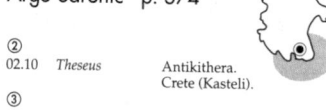

ⅅ
10.00	*Martha*	Gythio.
17.00	*Martha*	Neapoli. Elafonissos.

⛴ *Flying Dolphins*
② ③ ⑥
14.05	Monemvassia. Gerakas. Kiparissi. Spetses. Hydra. Piraeus (Zea).

Kithera (Kapsali)

Argo-Saronic p. 374

②
02.10	*Theseus*	Antikithera. Crete (Kasteli).

③
18.00	*Theseus*	Crete (Kasteli).

④
23.20	*Theseus*	Neapoli. Monemvassia. Kiparissi. Piraeus.

⑥
02.10	*Theseus*	Gythio. Antikithera. Crete (Kasteli).

⑦
13.20	*Theseus*	Neapoli. Monemvassia. Gerakas. Kiparissi. Piraeus.

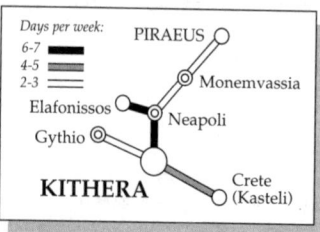

Days per week:
6-7
4-5
2-3

PIRAEUS
Monemvassia
Elafonissos
Neapoli
Gythio
KITHERA
Crete (Kasteli)

Kos

Dodecanese
p. 272

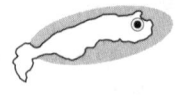

ⅅ
08.00	Hydrofoil	Rhodes.
10.00	Tour Boat	Kalimnos.
10.00	Tour Boat	Pserimos.
10.00	Tour Boat	Nissiros.
18.00	Hydrofoil	Rhodes.

①
00.25	*Nissos Kalimnos*	Kalimnos.
07.25	*Nissos Kalimnos*	Nissiros. Tilos. Symi. Rhodes. Kastelorizo.
07.50	ILIO H/F	Rhodes. Symi.
12.00	*Marina*	Rhodes.
13.30	ILIO H/F	Kalimnos. Leros. Lipsi. Patmos. Ikaria (Agios Kyrikos). Samos (Karlovassi). (Vathi).
15.15	ILIO H/F	Symi. Rhodes.
17.15	*Ialyssos*	Kalimnos. Leros. Patmos. Piraeus.
20.00	ILIO H/F	Kalimnos.
21.30	*Marina*	Kalimnos. Leros. Patmos. Piraeus.

②
03.00	*Rodanthi*	Rhodes.
03.30	*Kamiros*	Rhodes.
03.45	*Ionian Sea*	Rhodes.
04.00	*Patmos*	Rhodes.
05.30	*Romilda*	Nissiros. Tilos. Symi. Rhodes. Kastelorizo.
07.50	ILIO H/F	Nissiros. Symi. Tilos. Rhodes.
15.30	*Kamiros*	Kalimnos. Leros. Patmos. Piraeus.
18.15	*Nissos Kalimnos*	Kalimnos.
19.15	*Ionian Sea*	Paros. Piraeus.
19.30	*Rodanthi*	Piraeus.
20.00	ILIO H/F	Kalimnos.
20.30	*Patmos*	Piraeus.

③
03.30	*Ialyssos*	Rhodes.
04.00	*Marina*	Rhodes.
07.30	*Romilda*	Kalimnos. Leros. Lipsi. Patmos. Naxos. Paros. Syros. Piraeus.
07.50	ILIO H/F	Rhodes. Symi. Nissiros.
09.00	ILIO H/F	Kalimnos. Leros. Patmos.
10.00	Hydrofoil	Tilos.
14.30	ILIO H/F	Nissiros. Symi. Rhodes.
15.30	*Ialyssos*	Kalimnos. Leros. Patmos. Piraeus.
18.10	ILIO H/F	Samos (Pithagorio).
19.30	*Marina*	Kalimnos. Piraeus.

④
01.30	*Nissos Kalimnos*	Kalimnos.
03.00	*Rodanthi*	Rhodes.
03.30	*Kamiros*	Rhodes.
03.45	*Ionian Sea*	Rhodes.
04.00	*Patmos*	Rhodes.
07.50	ILIO H/F	Rhodes. Symi.

15.30	*Kamiros*	Kalimnos. Leros. Patmos. Piraeus.
16.00	ILIO H/F	Kalimnos. Lipsi. Patmos. Samos (Pithagorio).
19.15	*Ionian Sea*	Paros. Piraeus.
19.30	*Rodanthi*	Kalimnos. Piraeus.
20.25	ILIO H/F	Kalimnos.
20.30	*Patmos*	Piraeus.

⑤
03.30	*Ialyssos*	Rhodes.
04.00	*Marina*	Rhodes.
07.25	*Nissos Kalimnos*	Nissiros. Tilos. Symi. Rhodes. Kastelorizo.
07.50	ILIO H/F	Rhodes. Nissiros.
15.00	*Patmos*	Thessalonika.
15.15	ILIO H/F	Nissiros. Rhodes.
15.30	*Ialyssos*	Kalimnos. Leros. Patmos. Piraeus.
19.30	*Marina*	Kalimnos. Piraeus.
20.00	ILIO H/F	Kalimnos.

⑥
03.30	*Kamiros*	Rhodes.
04.00	*Rodanthi*	Rhodes.
06.00	*Ionian Sea*	Nissiros. Tilos. Rhodes.
07.50	ILIO H/F	Rhodes. Symi. Tilos. Nissiros.
10.00	ILIO H/F	Kalimnos. Leros. Patmos.
13.00	*Rodanthi*	Paros. Piraeus.
14.00	ILIO H/F	Nissiros. Tilos. Symi. Rhodes.
15.30	*Kamiros*	Kalimnos. Leros. Patmos. Piraeus.
18.15	ILIO H/F	Patmos. Samos (Pithagorio).
18.15	*Nissos Kalimnos*	Kalimnos.
18.30	*Ionian Sea*	Kalimnos. Astipalea. Paros. Syros. Piraeus.
20.00	ILIO H/F	Kalimnos.

⑦
| 04.00 | *Patmos* | Rhodes. |
| 04.10 | *Ialyssos* | Rhodes. Chalki. Karpathos (Town). Crete (Iraklion). |

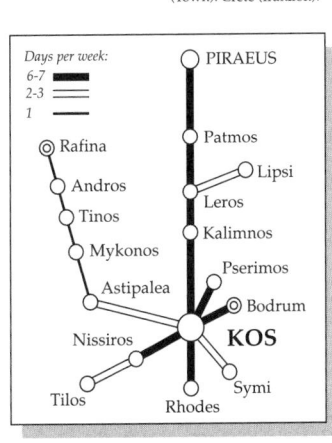

Days per week:
6-7 ▬▬▬
2-3 ═══
1 ───

PIRAEUS

◎ Rafina
Patmos
Andros
Lipsi
Tinos
Leros
Mykonos
Kalimnos
Astipalea
Pserimos
Nissiros
◎ Bodrum
KOS
Tilos
Symi
Rhodes

06.15	*Marina*	Leros. Patmos. Naxos. Paros. Piraeus.
08.30	Hydrofoil	Leros. Samos (Pithagorio).
08.50	ILIO H/F	Kalimnos. Leros. Patmos.
12.00	*Rodanthi*	Rhodes.
18.15	ILIO H/F	Samos (Pithagorio). (Vathi).
20.30	*Patmos*	Piraeus.
21.15	ILIO H/F	Kalimnos.
21.30	*Rodanthi*	Patmos. Piraeus.

Kos (Kardamena)

Dodecanese
p. 272

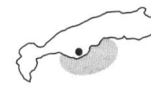

ⓓ
| 09.00 | *Nissiros Express* | Nissiros. |

Kos (Mastihari)

Dodecanese
p. 272

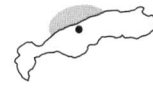

ⓓ
09.00 17.30 23.15
| | *Olympios Apollon* | Kalimnos. |

Kosta

Argo-Saronic   p. 379

ⓓ
10.30 13.30 17.00   *Alexandros M*   Spetses.

① ② ③ ④ ⑤
06.50 08.00 18.30   *Alexandros M*   Spetses.

Koufonissia

Eastern Cyclades   p. 239

ⓓ
Ferries and Catamarans as **Schinoussa**

Times for boats to:

Naxos & Piraeus:
Schinoussa departure time –35 minutes.

Amorgos:
Schinoussa departure time +35 minutes.

Kuşadası

Turkey   p. 421

ⓓ
| 08.00 | *Fari Kaptain/Sultan I* | Samos (Vathi). |
| 17.00 | *Kapetan Giorgis* | Samos (Vathi). |

③ ⑥ ⑦
| 14.30 | ILIO H/F | Ios. Santorini. |

Kythnos

Cyclades West
p. 210

ⓓ
| 12.00 | Flying Dolphin | Kea. Piraeus (Zea). |

①
09.45	ILIO H/F	Serifos. Sifnos. Kimolos. Milos.
11.00	*Georgios Express*	Serifos. Sifnos. Kimolos. Milos.
16.10	ILIO H/F	Kea. Rafina.
18.00	*Milos Express*	Serifos. Sifnos. Milos. Kimolos. Folegandros. Sikinos. Ios. Santorini.
19.15	*Georgios Express*	Piraeus.

②
15.00	*Mirina Express*	Kea. Lavrion.
17.00	*Georgios Express*	Serifos. Sifnos. Kimolos. Milos.
17.00	*Milos Express*	Piraeus.

③
00.30	*Georgios Express*	Piraeus.
11.00	*Georgios Express*	Serifos. Sifnos. Milos.
11.00	*Milos Express*	Serifos. Sifnos. Kimolos. Milos.
19.20	*Milos Express*	Piraeus.
20.00	*Georgios Express*	Piraeus.

④
11.00	*Georgios Express*	Serifos. Sifnos.
11.00	*Milos Express*	Serifos. Sifnos. Milos. Folegandros. Sikinos. Ios. Santorini.
16.30	*Georgios Express*	Piraeus.
24.00	*Georgios Express*	Serifos. Sifnos. Kimolos. Milos. Piraeus.

⑤
03.50	*Milos Express*	Piraeus.
18.50	*Georgios Express*	Serifos. Sifnos. Kimolos. Milos. Piraeus.
20.00	*Milos Express*	Serifos. Sifnos. Milos. Piraeus.

⑥
11.00	*Milos Express*	Serifos. Sifnos. Milos. Kimolos. Folegandros. Sikinos.
12.00	*Georgios Express*	Serifos. Sifnos.
15.45	*Georgios Express*	Piraeus.
24.00	*Georgios Express*	Serifos. Sifnos. Kimolos. Milos.

⑦
10.45	*Milos Express*	Serifos. Sifnos. Milos.
11.30	Ventouris SL	Serifos. Sifnos. Milos.
13.30	*Georgios Express*	Piraeus.
19.00	*Milos Express*	Piraeus.
19.55	Ventouris SL	Piraeus.
21.00	*Georgios Express*	Serifos. Sifnos. Kimolos. Milos. Piraeus.

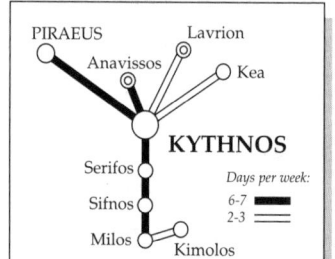

Lâpseki

Turkey   p. 421

ⓓ x 7   07.30–24.00   Gelibolu.

Lavrion

Athens & Piraeus   p. 125

①
| 09.00 | *Mirina Express* | Kea. |
| 19.00 | *Mirina Express* | Kea. |

②
| 09.00 | *Mirina Express* | Kea. Kythnos. |
| 19.00 | *Mirina Express* | Kea. |

③
| 19.00 | *Mirina Express* | Kea. |

④
| 09.00 | *Mirina Express* | Kea. |
| 19.00 | *Mirina Express* | Kea. |

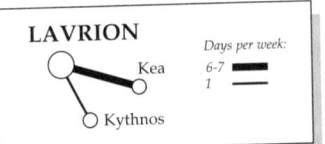

LAVRION

Kea

Days per week:
6-7
1

Kythnos

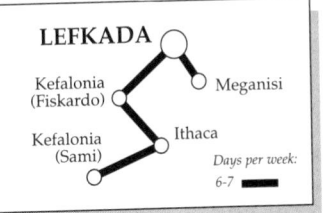

LEFKADA

Kefalonia (Fiskardo)

Meganisi

Kefalonia (Sami)

Ithaca

Days per week:
6-7

⑤
09.00	Mirina Express	Kea.
15.00	Mirina Express	Kea.
18.15	Mirina Express	Kea.
21.30	Mirina Express	Kea.

⑥
09.00	Mirina Express	Kea.
12.30	Mirina Express	Kea.
16.00	Mirina Express	Kea.

⑦
09.00	Mirina Express	Kea.
13.30	Mirina Express	Kea.
17.00	Mirina Express	Kea.
20.30	Mirina Express	Kea.
23.45	Mirina Express	Kea.

Leonidio

Argo-Saronic   p. 375

 *Flying Dolphins* include:
② ③ ④ ⑥ ⑦
| 11.40 | Monemvassia. Gerakas. Kiparissi. |
| 15.50 | Spetses. Hydra. Piraeus (Zea). |

Lefkada (Nidri)

Ionian Line   p. 396

Ⓓ
07.15	Meganisi	Meganisi (Vathi). Meganisi (Spartohori).
08.30	Meganisi	Kefalonia (Fiskardo).
10.00	Capt. Aristidis	Kefalonia (Fiskardo). Ithaca (Frikes).
13.15	Meganisi	Meganisi (Vathi). Meganisi (Spartohori).
15.30	Meganisi	Kefalonia (Fiskardo).
16.30	Capt. Aristidis	Ithaca (Frikes). Kefalonia (Fiskardo).

Leros (Agia Marina)

Dodecanese   p. 280

○
Agia Marina is used as an alternative hydrofoil port in certain wind and sea conditions.

Leros (Lakki)

Dodecanese   p. 280

Lefkada (Vassiliki)

Ionian Line   p. 396

Ⓓ
| 11.10 | Aphrodite L | Kefalonia (Fiskardo). Ithaca (Pisaetos). Kefalonia (Sami). |
| 17.00 | Aphrodite L | Kefalonia (Fiskardo). Ithaca (Pisaetos). Kefalonia (Sami). |

①
09.40	Marina	Kalimnos. Kos. Rhodes.
10.40	ILIO H/F	Kalimnos. Kos.
14.55	ILIO H/F	Lipsi. Patmos. Ikaria (Agios Kyrikos). Samos (Karlovassi). Samos (Vathi).
19.30	Ialyssos	Patmos. Piraeus.
24.00	Kamiros	Kalimnos. Kos. Rhodes.

②
00.10	Marina	Patmos. Piraeus.
03.00	Romilda	Kalimnos. Kos. Nissiros. Tilos. Symi. Rhodes. Kastelorizo.
09.50	ILIO H/F	Kalimnos. Kos.
14.55	ILIO H/F	Lipsi. Patmos. Samos (Pithagorio). (Vathi).

| 18.30 | *Kamiros* | Patmos. Piraeus. |
| 24.00 | *Ialyssos* | Kalimnos. Kos. Rhodes. |

③
08.35	*Nissos Kalimnos*	Lipsi. Patmos.
		Agathonisi.
		Samos (Pithagorio).
10.25	ILIO H/F	Patmos.
10.45	*Romilda*	Lipsi. Patmos. Naxos.
		Paros. Syros. Piraeus.
16.45	ILIO H/F	Kalimnos. Kos.
		Agathonisi.
		Samos (Pithagorio).
18.30	*Ialyssos*	Patmos. Piraeus.
23.10	*Nissos Kalimnos*	Kalimnos. Kos.
24.00	*Kamiros*	Kalimnos. Kos.
		Rhodes.

④
09.45	ILIO H/F	Kalimnos. Kos.
17.25	ILIO H/F	Lipsi. Patmos.
		Samos (Pithagorio).
18.30	*Kamiros*	Patmos. Piraeus.
24.00	*Ialyssos*	Kalimnos. Kos. Rhodes.

⑤
10.40	ILIO H/F	Kalimnos. Kos.
14.55	ILIO H/F	Lipsi. Patmos.
		Ikaria (Agios Kyrikos).
		Samos (Karlovassi).
		Samos (Vathi).
18.30	*Ialyssos*	Patmos. Piraeus.
24.00	*Kamiros*	Kalimnos. Kos. Rhodes.

⑥
11.25	ILIO H/F	Patmos.
16.45	ILIO H/F	Kalimnos. Kos. Patmos.
		Samos (Pithagorio).
18.30	*Kamiros*	Patmos. Piraeus.
24.00	*Ialyssos*	Kalimnos. Kos. Rhodes.
		Chalki.
		Karpathos (Town).
		Crete (Iraklion).
24.00	*Marina*	Kalimnos. Kos.

⑦
07.10	*Marina*	Patmos. Naxos. Paros.
		Piraeus.
08.35	*Nissos Kalimnos*	Lipsi. Patmos.
		Agathonisi.
		Samos (Pithagorio).
16.45	ILIO H/F	Kalimnos. Kos.
		Samos (Pithagorio).
		Samos (Vathi).
21.10	*Nissos Kalimnos*	Kalimnos. Kos.
23.10	*Nissos Kalimnos*	Kalimnos. Kos.

Lesbos (Mytilini)

Eastern Line
p. 310

Ⓓ
| 08.00 | *Aeolis/Eresos II* | Ayvalık. |
| 17.00 | *Jale* | Ayvalık. |

①
07.00	ILIO H/F	Kavala.
		Alexandroupolis.
18.00	*Sappho*	Chios. Piraeus.

②
07.00	ILIO H/F	Chios. Samos (Vathi).
		Patmos.
08.00	*Mytilene*	Limnos. Kavala.
16.00	*Agios Rafail*	Piraeus.
16.30	*Alcaeos*	Chios. Piraeus.

③
07.00	ILIO H/F	Limnos.
		Alexandroupolis.
07.00	*Mytilene*	Chios. Piraeus.
08.30	*Nissos Chios*	Chios. Piraeus.
09.00	*Sappho*	Limnos. Thessalonika.
24.00	*Agios Rafail*	Piraeus.

④
07.00	ILIO H/F	Chios. Samos (Vathi).
		Samos (Karlovassi).
		Ikaria (Agios Kyrikos).
		Patmos.
09.00	*Mytilene*	Piraeus.
18.00	*Sappho*	Chios. Piraeus.

⑤
06.00	*Agios Rafail*	Piraeus.
07.00	ILIO H/F	Alexandroupolis.
		Kavala.
08.00	*Mytilene*	Chios. Piraeus.
08.30	*Nissos Chios*	Limnos.
		Kavala.

⑥
07.00	ILIO H/F	Chios. Samos (Vathi).
		Patmos.
07.00	*Sappho*	Chios. Piraeus.
08.00	*Nissos Chios*	Chios. Rafina.
10.00	*Mytilene*	Limnos. Thessalonika.
24.00	*Alcaeos*	Chios. Samos (Vathi).
		Patmos.

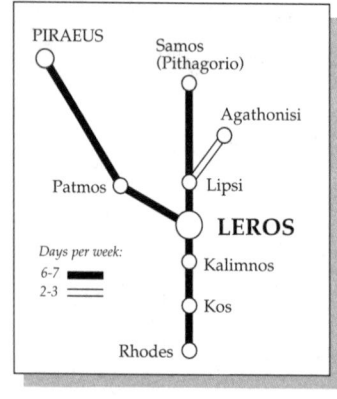

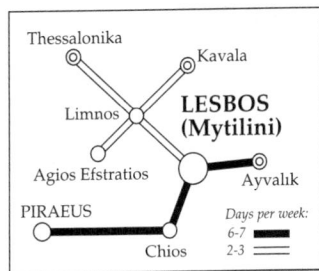

④		
08.00	*Sappho*	Lesbos (Mytilini). Chios. Piraeus.
08.30	*Alcaeos*	Kavala.
20.10	*Alcaeos*	Agios Efstratios. Skyros. Rafina.
⑤		
12.00	*Nissos Chios*	Kavala.
⑥		
02.00	*Nissos Chios*	Lesbos (Mytilini). Chios. Rafina.
06.00	*Alcaeos*	Kavala.
15.30	*Mytilene*	Thessalonika.
17.00	*Alcaeos*	Agios Efstratios. Lesbos (Mytilini). Chios. Samos (Vathi). Patmos.
⑦		
06.00	*Skopelos*	Evia (Kimi). Alonissos. Skopelos. Skiathos. Volos.
07.30	*Mytilene*	Lesbos (Mytilini). Chios. Piraeus.
13.30	*Nissos Chios*	Kavala.
24.00	*Nissos Chios*	Agios Efstratios. Rafina.

⑦		
06.30	ILIO H/F	Chios. Samos (Pithagorio). Patmos.
10.30	*Sappho*	Chios. Piraeus.
17.00	*Agios Rafail*	Piraeus.
18.00	*Mytilene*	Chios. Piraeus.
24.00	*Alcaeos*	Limnos. Thessalonika.

Limnos

Northern Aegean
p. 335

①		
06.30	*Alcaeos*	Thessalonika.
②		
05.00	*Alcaeos*	Lesbos (Mytilini). Chios. Piraeus.
08.00	*Nissos Chios*	Agios Efstratios. Piraeus.
13.00	*Mytilene*	Kavala.
15.00	*Saos*	Samothrace. Alexandroupolis.
24.00	*Mytilene*	Lesbos (Mytilini). Chios. Piraeus.
③		
10.00	ILIO H/F	Alexandroupolis.
14.30	*Sappho*	Thessalonika.
17.00	ILIO H/F	Lesbos (Mytilini).

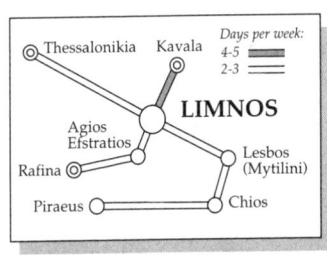

Lipsi

Dodecanese   p. 282

Ⓓ		
16.00	*Megalohori/ Patmos Express*	Patmos.
①		
10.00	ILIO H/F	Leros. Kalimnos. Kos.
15.35	ILIO H/F	Patmos. Ikaria (Agios Kyrikos). Samos (Karlovassi). (Vathi).
②		
02.00	*Romilda*	Leros. Kalimnos. Kos. Nissiros. Tilos. Symi. Rhodes. Kastelorizo.
09.10	ILIO H/F	Leros. Kalimnos. Kos.
15.35	ILIO H/F	Patmos. Samos (Pithagorio). (Vathi).

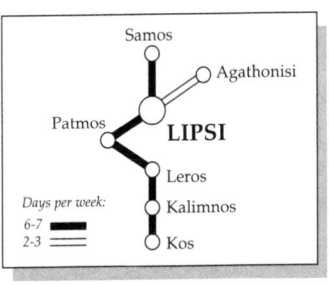

③		
10.05	*Nissos Kalimnos*	Patmos. Agathonisi. Samos (Pithagorio).
11.45	*Romilda*	Patmos. Naxos. Paros. Syros. Piraeus.
21.45	*Nissos Kalimnos*	Leros. Kalimnos. Kos.
④		
09.05	ILIO H/F	Leros. Kalimnos. Kos.
10.00	*Chioni*	Patmos.
12.30	*Chioni*	Arki. Agathonisi. Samos (Pithagorio). Chios.
18.05	ILIO H/F	Patmos. Samos (Pithagorio).
⑤		
10.00	ILIO H/F	Leros. Kalimnos. Kos.
15.35	ILIO H/F	Patmos. Ikaria (Agios Kyrikos). Samos (Karlovassi). (Vathi).
⑦		
03.00	*Dimitra*	Patmos. Mykonos. Syros. Tinos. Piraeus.
10.05	*Nissos Kalimnos*	Patmos. Agathonisi. Samos (Pithagorio).
19.45	*Nissos Kalimnos*	Leros. Kalimnos. Kos.

Marmara

Turkey p. 421

Ⓓ		
00.00	TML	Istanbul.
00.00	TML	Avşa.

Ⓓ x ④		
00.00	Deniz Otobusleri	Avşa.
00.00	Deniz Otobusleri	İstanbul.

⑤ ⑦		
00.00	TML	Avşa. Erdek.
00.00	TML	Tekirdağ.

Marmaras

Northern Aegean p. 336

Ⓓ		
08.00	Taxi boat	Mt. Athos boat tour.

Flying Dolphins:

② ④ ⑤ ⑦	
20.15	Nea Moudania.

② ④	
20.15	Alonissos. Skopelos. Skopelos (Glossa). Skiathos. Volos.

⑤ ⑦	
20.15	Alonissos. Skopelos. Skiathos. Agios Konstantinos.

Marmaris

Turkey p. 422

Ⓓ		
09.00 16.00	*Yesil Marmaris*	Rhodes.

Meganisi (Spartochori)

Ionian Line p. 398

Ⓓ		
08.00 14.00	*Meganisi*	Lefkada (Nidri).

Meganisi (Vathi)

Ionian Line p. 398

Ⓓ		
07.45	*Meganisi*	Meganisi (Spartochori). Lefkada (Nidri).
13.45	*Meganisi*	Meganisi (Spartochori). Lefkada (Nidri).
17.00	*Meganisi*	Lefkada (Vathi).

Mersin

Turkey p. 415

① ③ ⑤		
22.00	*Yeşilada*	Famagusta.

Methana

Argo-Saronic p. 375

Ⓓ		
06.30	Poseidon Co.	Aegina. Piraeus.
09.40	*Agios Nektarios*	Poros.
09.55	*Methodia*	Poros. Hydra. Spetses. Porto Helio.
10.00	*Eftichia*	Poros. Hydra. Ermioni. Spetses.
10.25	*Georgios*	Poros. Spetses. Porto Helio.
11.20	*Agios Nektarios*	Aegina. Piraeus.
11.20	Poseidon Co.	Aegina. Piraeus.

14.00	Poseidon Co.	Aegina. Piraeus.
16.45	*Methodia*	Aegina. Piraeus.
17.10	*Eftichia*	Aegina. Piraeus.
17.25	*Georgios*	Aegina. Piraeus.
18.20	*Agios Nektarios*	Poros.
19.30	*Agios Nektarios*	Aegina. Piraeus.
⑤		
18.55	Poseidon Co.	Aegina. Piraeus.
⑦		
18.00	Poseidon Co.	Aegina. Piraeus.

Milos

Cyclades West p. 211

○		
01.30	*Vitsentzos Kornaros*	Piraeus.
24.00	*Vitsentzos Kornaros*	Crete (Agios Nikolaos). Crete (Sitia).
24.00	*Vitsentzos Kornaros*	Crete (Agios Nikolaos). Crete (Sitia). Kassos. Karpathos.
①		
01.00	*Georgios Express*	Piraeus.
14.00	ILIO H/F	Kimolos. Sifnos. Serifos. Kythnos. Kea. Rafina.
15.30	*Georgios Express*	Sifnos. Serifos. Kythnos. Piraeus.
22.00	*Milos Express*	Kimolos. Folegandros. Sikinos. Ios. Santorini.
23.00	*Kriti*	Crete (Agios Nikolaos). Crete (Sitia).
②		
13.00	*Milos Express*	Sifnos. Serifos. Kythnos. Piraeus.
14.25	Ventouris SL	Folegandros. Sikinos. Santorini. Crete (Agios Nikolaos). (Sitia). Kassos. Karpathos (Tn).(Diafani). Chalki. Symi. Rhodes.
20.30	*Georgios Express*	Sifnos. Serifos. Kythnos. Piraeus.
③		
01.30	*Kriti*	Piraeus.
15.30	*Milos Express*	Sifnos. Serifos. Kythnos. Piraeus.
16.15	*Georgios Express*	Sifnos. Serifos. Kythnos. Piraeus.
23.00	*Kriti*	Crete (Agios Nikolaos). Crete (Sitia).
④		
13.30	Ventouris SL	Sifnos. Piraeus.
15.00	*Milos Express*	Folegandros. Sikinos. Ios. Santorini.
23.30	*Milos Express*	Sifnos. Serifos. Kythnos. Piraeus.
⑤		
01.30	*Kriti*	Piraeus.
06.30	*Ergina*	Nafplio.
07.00	*Georgios Express*	Piraeus.
18.10	*Ergina*	Santorini. Amorgos (Katapola). (Egiali). Naxos. Piraeus.

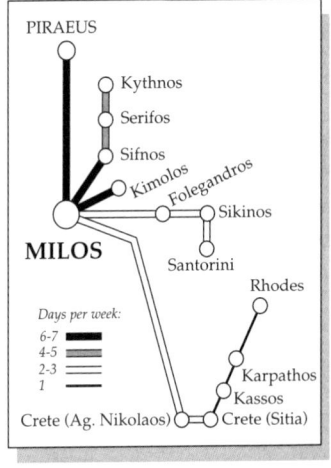

PIRAEUS

Kythnos

Serifos

Sifnos

Kimolos

Folegandros

Sikinos

MILOS

Santorini

Rhodes

Days per week:
6-7
4-5
2-3
1

Karpathos

Kassos

Crete (Ag. Nikolaos)

Crete (Sitia)

22.25	*Georgios Express*	Piraeus.
24.00	*Kriti*	Crete (Agios Nikolaos). Crete (Sitia).
24.00	*Milos Express*	Piraeus.
⑥		
15.00	*Milos Express*	Kimolos. Folegandros. Sikinos.
21.00	*Milos Express*	Piraeus.
⑦		
01.30	*Kriti*	Piraeus.
09.00	*Georgios Express*	Kimolos. Sifnos. Serifos. Kythnos. Piraeus.
14.30	*Milos Express*	Sifnos. Serifos. Kythnos. Piraeus.
16.00	Ventouris SL	Sifnos. Serifos. Kythnos. Piraeus.

Monemvassia

Argo-Saronic p. 375

①		
22.50	*Theseus*	Neapoli. Kithera (Kapsali). Antikithera. Crete (Kasteli).
⑤		
03.20	*Theseus*	Kiparissi. Piraeus.
22.50	*Theseus*	Neapoli. Elafonissos. Kithera (Kapsali). Gythio. Antikithera. Crete (Kasteli).
⑦		
16.50	*Theseus*	Gerakas. Kiparissi. Piraeus.

MONEMVASSIA   PIRAEUS

Gythio

Neapoli

Days per week:
4-5
2-3

Kithera   Crete
(Kasteli)

Mykonos

Cyclades North
p. 185

Ⓓ		
09.00	*Hera*	Delos.
09.30	*Niki*	Delos.
10.15	*Delos Express*	Delos.
10.45	*Niki*	Delos.
12.30	*Hera*	Delos.
14.45	*Panagia Tinou 2*	Tinos. Syros. Piraeus.
16.00	*Mykonos Express*	Paros. Ios. Santorini.
①		
01.30	*Panagia Tinou 2*	Syros. Piraeus.
07.50	ILIO H/F	Tinos. Tinos (Isternia). Andros (Batsi). Rafina.
08.00	*Dimitra*	Syros. Piraeus.
08.00	ILIO H/F	Paros. Naxos. Ios. Santorini.
08.00	*Super Ferry*	Tinos. Andros. Rafina.
09.00	*Catamaran II*	Andros (Batsi). Rafina.
09.00	*Express Paros*	Paros. Naxos. Ios. Santorini.
10.45	ILIO H/F	Tinos.
13.45	ILIO H/F	Tinos. Rafina.
14.00	*Penelope A*	Tinos. Andros. Rafina.
15.05	*Naias II*	Tinos. Syros. Piraeus.
16.30	ILIO H/F	Tinos. Andros (Batsi). Rafina.
18.00	*Bari Express*	Tinos. Andros. Rafina.
19.15	*Catamaran II*	Tinos. Andros (Batsi). Rafina.
19.25	ILIO H/F	Paros. Naxos.
20.20	ILIO H/F	Tinos. Syros.
21.30	*Dimitra*	Amorgos (Katapola). Amorgos (Egiali). Astipalea.
②		
01.30	*Panagia Tinou 2*	Syros. Piraeus.
08.00	*Anemos*	Paros. Santorini. Crete (Iraklion).
08.00	*Dimitra*	Syros. Piraeus.
08.00	ILIO H/F	Paros. Naxos. Ios. Santorini. Anafi.
08.00	*Super Ferry*	Tinos. Andros. Rafina.
09.00	*Express Paros*	Paros. Naxos. Ios. Sikinos. Folegandros. Sifnos. Serifos. Syros.
09.00	ILIO H/F	Tinos. Andros (Batsi). Rafina.
10.45	*Catamaran II*	Tinos. Andros (Batsi). Rafina.

10.45	ILIO H/F	Paros. Naxos.
14.00	*Naias II*	Tinos. Syros. Piraeus.
14.00	*Penelope A*	Tinos. Andros. Rafina.
14.00	*Skopelitis*	Naxos. Paros (Piso Livadi). Iraklia. Schinoussa. Koufonissia. Amorgos (Katapola).
16.30	ILIO H/F	Tinos. Andros (Batsi). Rafina.
18.00	*Bari Express*	Tinos. Andros. Rafina.
19.15	*Catamaran II*	Tinos. Andros (Batsi). Rafina.
20.00	*Ergina*	Amorgos (Egiali). Amorgos (Katapola). Naxos. Paros. Sifnos. Nafplio.
20.20	ILIO H/F	Tinos. Syros.
23.00	*Dimitra*	Ikaria (Ágios Kyrikos). Fourni. Samos (Karlovassi). Samos (Vathi).
③		
04.20	*Anemos*	Tinos. Skiathos. Thessalonika.
08.00	ILIO H/F	Paros. Naxos. Ios. Santorini. Iraklia. Schinoussa. Koufonissia. Amorgos (Egiali). (Katapola).
08.00	*Super Ferry*	Tinos. Andros. Rafina.
09.00	*Express Paros*	Paros. Naxos. Ios. Santorini.
10.45	ILIO H/F	Tinos.
10.50	*Catamaran II*	Syros. Paros. Naxos. Iraklia. Schinoussa. Koufonissia. Amorgos (Katapola).
12.00	*Dimitra*	Syros. Piraeus.
13.15	*Naias II*	Tinos. Piraeus.
13.45	ILIO H/F	Tinos. Rafina.
14.00	*Penelope A*	Tinos. Andros. Rafina.
14.45	*Nearchos*	Paros. Ios. Santorini. Crete (Iraklion).
16.30	ILIO H/F	Tinos. Andros (Batsi). Rafina.
19.20	*Catamaran II*	Tinos. Andros (Batsi). Rafina.
19.25	ILIO H/F	Paros. Naxos.
20.20	ILIO H/F	Tinos. Syros.
21.45	*Super Ferry*	Rafina.
④		
00.30	*Naias II*	Piraeus.
01.15	*Dimitra*	Donoussa. Koufonissia. Amorgos (Katapola). Amorgos (Egiali). Astipalea.
02.30	*Ergina*	Piraeus.
08.00	*Bari Express*	Tinos. Andros. Rafina.
08.00	ILIO H/F	Paros. Naxos. Ios. Santorini.
09.00	*Express Paros*	Paros. Naxos. Ios. Santorini.
09.00	ILIO H/F	Tinos. Andros (Batsi). Rafina.
10.35	*Anemos*	Paros. Santorini. Crete (Iraklion).
10.45	*Catamaran II*	Tinos. Andros (Batsi). Rafina.
10.45	ILIO H/F	Paros. Naxos. Iraklia. Schinoussa. Koufonissia. Amorgos (Egiali).
12.45	*Super Ferry*	Tinos. Andros. Rafina.
14.00	*Skopelitis*	Naxos. Paros (Piso Livadi). Iraklia. Schinoussa. Koufonissia. Amorgos (Katapola).
15.05	*Naias II*	Tinos. Syros. Piraeus.

10.45	ILIO H/F	Paros. Naxos.
14.00	*Naias II*	Tinos. Syros. Piraeus.
14.00	*Penelope A*	Tinos. Andros. Rafina.
14.00	*Skopelitis*	Naxos. Paros (Piso Livadi). Iraklia. Schinoussa. Koufonissia. Amorgos (Katapola).
16.30	ILIO H/F	Tinos. Andros (Batsi). Rafina.

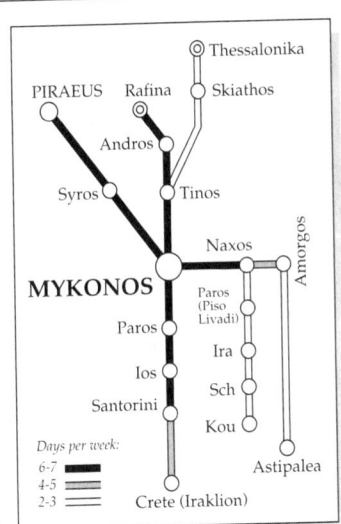

PIRAEUS   Rafina   Skiathos
            Andros
Syros   Tinos
              Naxos
MYKONOS
            Paros
            (Piso
   Paros   Livadi)
            Ira
   Ios   Sch
 Santorini   Kou

Thessalonika

Amorgos

Astipalea

Crete (Iraklion)

Days per week:
6-7
4-5
2-3

17.30	ILIO H/F	Tinos. Andros (Batsi). Rafina.
18.30	Dimitra	Syros. Piraeus.
19.15	Catamaran II	Tinos. Andros (Batsi). Rafina.
20.20	ILIO H/F	Tinos. Syros.
22.30	Express Paros	Syros.
23.15	Super Ferry	Rafina.

⑤
01.30	Panagia Tinou 2	Syros. Piraeus.
08.00	ILIO H/F	Paros. Naxos. Ios. Santorini.
09.00	Express Paros	Paros. Naxos. Ios. Santorini.
10.45	Catamaran II	Tinos. Andros (Batsi). Rafina.
10.45	ILIO H/F	Paros. Naxos.
10.45	Penelope A	Tinos. Andros. Rafina.
13.15	Naias II	Tinos. Piraeus.
14.45	Nearchos	Paros. Ios. Santorini. Crete (Iraklion).
15.00	ILIO H/F	Tinos. Syros.
19.15	Catamaran II	Tinos. Andros (Batsi). Rafina.
19.30	ILIO H/F	Tinos. Skala Oropou. Evia (Chalcis).
20.20	ILIO H/F	Tinos. Syros.
22.15	Penelope A	Rafina.
22.30	Dimitra	Piraeus.

⑥
00.30	Naias II	Piraeus.
09.00	Express Paros	Paros. Naxos. Ios. Santorini.
10.15	Anemos	Paros. Santorini. Crete (Iraklion).
10.45	Catamaran II	Tinos. Andros (Batsi). Rafina.

10.45	ILIO H/F	Paros. Naxos.
11.00	ILIO H/F	Tinos. Andros (Batsi). Rafina.
11.50	ILIO H/F	Tinos.
13.15	ILIO H/F	Tinos. Andros (Batsi). Rafina.
14.00	Naias II	Tinos. Syros. Piraeus.
14.00	Skopelitis	Naxos. Paros (Piso Livadi). Iraklia. Schinoussa. Koufonissia. Amorgos (Katapola).
14.00	Super Ferry	Tinos. Andros. Rafina.
16.30	ILIO H/F	Tinos. Evia (Karystos). Rafina.
19.00	ILIO H/F	Tinos. Evia (Karystos). Rafina.
19.15	Catamaran II	Tinos. Andros (Batsi). Rafina.
19.50	Ergina	Naxos. Donoussa. Amorgos (Egiali). Amorgos (Katapola).
21.00	ILIO H/F	Rafina.
22.30	Express Paros	Syros.

⑦
01.00	Dimitra	Lipsi. Patmos.
01.45	Panagia Tinou 2	Piraeus.
04.00	Ergina	Piraeus.
06.25	Anemos	Tinos. Skiathos. Thessalonika.
09.00	Express Paros	Paros. Naxos. Ios. Santorini.
10.45	Catamaran II	Tinos. Andros (Batsi). Rafina.
10.45	ILIO H/F	Paros. Naxos.
11.00	Dimitra	Syros. Tinos. Piraeus.
13.15	ILIO H/F	Tinos. Tinos (Isternia). Andros (Batsi). Rafina.
13.15	Naias II	Tinos. Piraeus.
13.30	Super Ferry	Tinos. Andros. Rafina.
14.30	Penelope A	Tinos. Andros. Rafina.
16.30	ILIO H/F	Tinos. Andros (Batsi). Rafina.
19.00	ILIO H/F	Tinos. Rafina.
19.15	Catamaran II	Tinos. Andros (Batsi). Rafina.
21.30	Bari Express	Tinos. Rafina.
22.30	Express Paros	Syros.

Nafplio

Argo-Saronic p. 375

③
11.15	Ergina	Sifnos. Paros. Naxos. Amorgos (Katapola). Amorgos (Egiali). Mykonos. Piraeus.

⑤
12.15	Ergina	Milos. Santorini. Amorgos (Katapola). Amorgos (Egiali). Naxos. Piraeus.

Flying Dolphins
② ③ ④ ⑤ ⑥ ⑦
07.15	Tolo. Porto Helio. Spetses. Ermioni. Hydra. Poros. Aegina. Piraeus (Zea).

Naxos

Cyclades Central
p. 148

Ⓓ

| 13.00 | *Mykonos Express* | Paros. Mykonos. |

①

00.05	*Poseidon Express*	Ios. Santorini.
02.25	*Apollo Express 1*	Ios. Santorini.
04.00	*Express Santorini*	Ios. Santorini.
06.40	*Daliana*	Santorini. Crete (Iraklion).
09.15	*Daphne II*	Iraklia. Koufonissia.
09.40	ILIO H/F	Ios. Santorini.
10.20	*Poseidon Express*	Paros. Piraeus.
11.10	*Apollo Express 1*	Paros. Piraeus.
11.30	*Ergina*	Paros. Syros. Piraeus.
12.00	*Express Paros*	Ios. Santorini.
13.00	*Express Santorini*	Paros. Piraeus.
14.00	*Express Olympia*	Ios. Santorini.
14.05	*Apollo Express 2*	Ios. Santorini.
14.45	*Nearchos*	Paros. Ios. Santorini. Crete (Iraklion).
15.00	*Skopelitis*	Iraklia. Schinoussa. Koufonissia. Donoussa. Amorgos (Egiali). Amorgos (Katapola).
18.40	*Express Paros*	Paros. Mykonos.
18.40	ILIO H/F	Paros. Mykonos. Tinos. Syros.
21.00	*Romilda*	Patmos. Lipsi. Leros. Kalimnos. Kos. Nissiros. Tilos. Symi. Rhodes. Kastelorizo.
21.50	*Express Olympia*	Paros. Piraeus.
22.10	*Apollo Express 2*	Paros. Piraeus.
23.00	*Daliana*	Paros. Piraeus.
23.00	*Ventouris SL*	Paros. Piraeus.
23.50	*Milena*	Ikaria (Agios Kyrikos). Fourni. Samos (Karlovassi). Samos (Vathi).

②

00.05	*Poseidon Express*	Ios. Santorini.
05.00	*Express Santorini*	Ios. Santorini. Anafi.
09.15	*Daphne II*	Delos. Mykonos.
09.40	ILIO H/F	Ios. Santorini. Anafi.
10.20	*Poseidon Express*	Paros. Piraeus.
11.00	*Skopelitis*	Mykonos.
12.00	*Express Paros*	Ios. Sikinos. Folegandros. Sifnos. Serifos. Syros.
13.00	*Express Santorini*	Paros. Syros. Piraeus.
14.00	*Express Olympia*	Ios. Santorini.
14.05	*Apollo Express 1*	Ios. Santorini.
14.40	ILIO H/F	Paros. Mykonos. Tinos. Andros (Batsi). Rafina.
15.30	*Skopelitis*	Paros (Piso Livadi). Iraklia. Schinoussa. Koufonissia. Amorgos (Katapola).
18.40	ILIO H/F	Paros. Mykonos. Tinos.
21.50	*Express Olympia*	Paros. Piraeus.
22.10	*Apollo Express 1*	Paros. Piraeus.
22.40	*Daliana*	Santorini. Crete (Iraklion). Karpathos (Town). Rhodes.
23.00	*Milena*	Paros. Piraeus.

③

00.05	*Poseidon Express*	Ios. Santorini.
02.15	*Ergina*	Paros. Sifnos. Nafplio.
02.25	*Apollo Express 2*	Ios. Santorini.
08.00	*Daphne II*	Santorini.
09.40	ILIO H/F	Ios. Santorini. Iraklia. Schinoussa. Koufonissia. Amorgos (Egiali). Amorgos (Katapola).
10.20	*Poseidon Express*	Paros. Piraeus.
11.10	*Apollo Express 2*	Paros. Piraeus.
12.00	*Express Paros*	Ios. Santorini.
12.45	*Catamaran II*	Iraklia. Schinoussa. Koufonissia. Amorgos (Katapola).
14.00	*Express Santorini*	Ios. Santorini. Anafi.
14.05	*Apollo Express 1*	Ios. Santorini.
15.00	*Skopelitis*	Iraklia. Schinoussa. Koufonissia. Donoussa. Amorgos (Egiali). Amorgos (Katapola).
16.15	*Romilda*	Paros. Syros. Piraeus.
17.15	*Catamaran II*	Paros. Syros. Mykonos. Tinos. Andros. Rafina.
18.40	ILIO H/F	Paros. Mykonos. Syros.
20.25	*Ergina*	Amorgos (Katapola). Amorgos (Egiali). Mykonos. Piraeus.
22.00	*Express Santorini*	Paros. Piraeus.
22.10	*Apollo Express 1*	Paros. Piraeus.
23.30	*Milena*	Ikaria (Agios Kyrikos). Samos (Karlovassi). Samos (Vathi).
23.45	*Express Olympia*	Donoussa. Amorgos (Egiali). (Katapola).

④

02.25	*Apollo Express 2*	Ios. Santorini.
07.15	ILIO H/F	Paros. Mykonos. Tinos. Andros (Batsi). Rafina.
09.15	*Daphne II*	Delos. Mykonos.
09.30	*Express Olympia*	Paros. Syros. Piraeus.
09.40	ILIO H/F	Ios. Santorini.
11.00	*Skopelitis*	Mykonos.
11.10	*Apollo Express 2*	Paros. Piraeus.
12.00	*Express Paros*	Ios. Santorini.
12.25	ILIO H/F	Iraklia. Schinoussa. Koufonissia. Amorgos (Egiali).
12.30	*Nearchos*	Paros.
13.30	*Romilda*	Santorini.
14.05	*Apollo Express 1*	Ios. Santorini.
14.15	*Nearchos*	Ios. Santorini. Crete (Iraklion).
15.30	*Skopelitis*	Paros (Piso Livadi). Iraklia. Schinoussa. Koufonissia. Amorgos (Katapola).
15.50	ILIO H/F	Paros. Mykonos. Tinos. Andros (Batsi). Rafina.
16.30	*Daliana*	Paros. Piraeus.
18.40	ILIO H/F	Mykonos. Tinos. Syros.
19.00	*Express Paros*	Paros. Mykonos. Syros.
20.30	*Ergina*	Amorgos (Egiali). Amorgos (Katapola). Santorini. Milos. Nafplio.
20.45	*Romilda*	Paros. Piraeus.
22.10	*Apollo Express 1*	Paros. Piraeus.
23.00	*Express Santorini*	Amorgos (Katapola). Amorgos (Egiali). Astipalea.
23.00	*Milena*	Paros. Piraeus.

Tables

⑤

00.05	*Poseidon Express*	Ios. Santorini.
03.10	*Apollo Express 2*	Ios. Sikinos. Folegandros. Santorini.
09.15	*Daphne II*	Delos. Mykonos.
09.40	ILIO H/F	Ios. Santorini.
10.00	*Express Santorini*	Paros. Piraeus.
10.20	*Poseidon Express*	Paros. Piraeus.
10.45	*Apollo Express 2*	Paros. Syros. Piraeus.
12.00	*Express Paros*	Ios. Santorini.
12.25	ILIO H/F	Paros. Syros. Andros (Batsi). Rafina.
13.30	*Romilda*	Santorini.
14.00	*Express Olympia*	Ios. Santorini.
15.00	Ventouris SL	Santorini.
18.40	*Express Paros*	Paros. Mykonos.
18.40	ILIO H/F	Paros. Mykonos. Tinos. Syros.
20.45	*Romilda*	Paros. Piraeus.
21.50	*Express Olympia*	Paros. Piraeus.
22.30	Ventouris SL	Paros. Piraeus.
23.00	*Milena*	Ikaria (Agios Kyrikos). Fourni. Samos (Karlovassi). Samos (Vathi).
23.45	*Apollo Express 1*	Ios. Santorini. Anafi.

⑥

01.30	*Poseidon Express*	Ios. Santorini.
03.20	*Ergina*	Piraeus.
04.00	*Express Santorini*	Ios. Santorini.
09.15	*Daphne II*	Delos. Mykonos.
10.20	*Poseidon Express*	Paros. Piraeus.
11.00	*Apollo Express 1*	Paros. Piraeus.
11.00	*Skopelitis*	Mykonos.
12.00	*Express Paros*	Ios. Santorini.
12.25	ILIO H/F	Mykonos. Tinos. Andros (Batsi). Rafina.
13.00	*Express Santorini*	Paros. Piraeus.
13.30	*Romilda*	Santorini.
14.00	*Express Olympia*	Ios. Santorini.
14.00	*Milena*	Piraeus.
14.05	*Apollo Express 2*	Ios. Santorini.
15.30	*Skopelitis*	Paros (Piso Livadi). Iraklia. Schinoussa. Koufonissia. Amorgos (Katapola). Donoussa.
16.00	Ventouris SL	Patmos. Leros. Kalimnos. Kos.
18.30	*Marina*	
19.00	*Express Paros*	Paros. Mykonos. Syros.
20.45	*Romilda*	Paros. Piraeus.
21.15	*Ergina*	Donoussa. Amorgos (Egiali). Amorgos (Katapola).
21.50	*Express Olympia*	Paros. Piraeus.
22.10	*Apollo Express 2*	Paros. Piraeus.
23.00	Ventouris SL	Paros. Piraeus.

⑦

00.05	*Poseidon Express*	Ios. Santorini.
02.25	*Apollo Express 1*	Ios. Sikinos. Folegandros. Santorini.
02.30	*Ergina*	Mykonos. Piraeus.
04.00	*Express Santorini*	Ios. Santorini.
06.15	*Milena*	Ikaria (Agios Kyrikos). Samos (Karlovassi). Samos (Vathi).
09.15	*Daphne II*	Delos. Mykonos.
10.05	*Poseidon Express*	Paros. Piraeus.
11.10	*Apollo Express 1*	Paros. Piraeus.
12.00	*Express Paros*	Ios. Santorini.

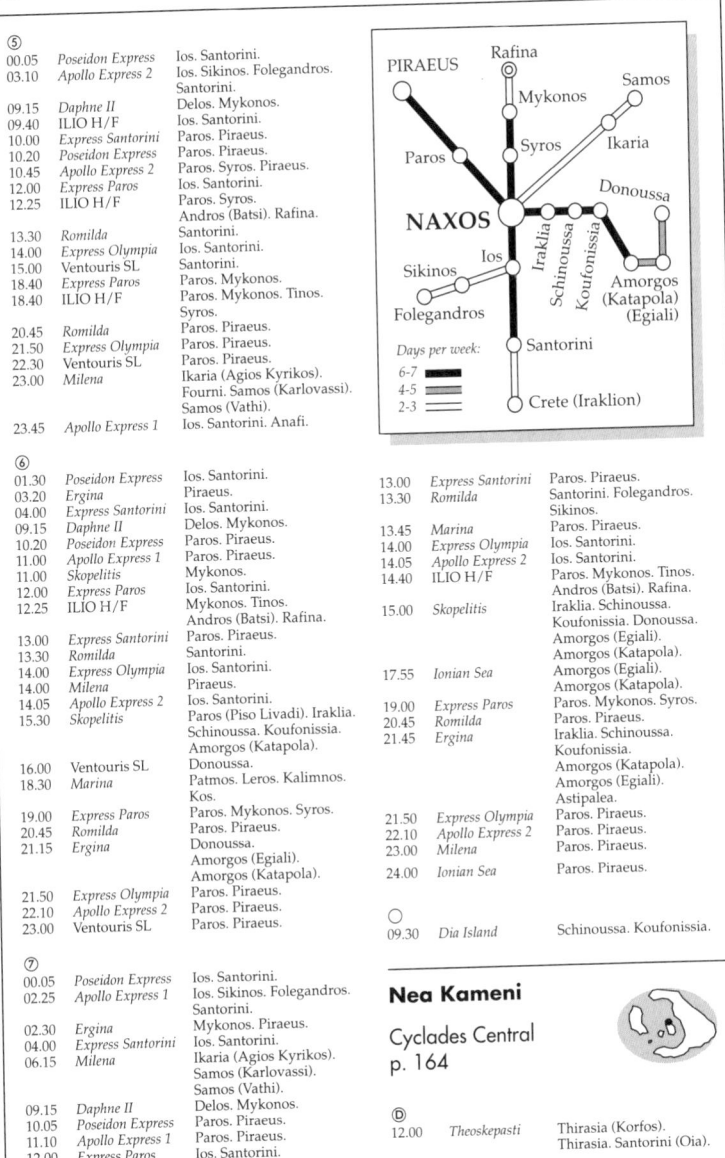

13.00	*Express Santorini*	Paros. Piraeus.
13.30	*Romilda*	Santorini. Folegandros. Sikinos.
13.45	*Marina*	Paros. Piraeus.
14.00	*Express Olympia*	Ios. Santorini.
14.05	*Apollo Express 2*	Ios. Santorini.
14.40	ILIO H/F	Paros. Mykonos. Tinos. Andros (Batsi). Rafina.
15.00	*Skopelitis*	Iraklia. Schinoussa. Koufonissia. Donoussa. Amorgos (Egiali). Amorgos (Katapola).
17.55	*Ionian Sea*	Amorgos (Egiali). Amorgos (Katapola).
19.00	*Express Paros*	Paros. Mykonos. Syros.
20.45	*Romilda*	Paros. Piraeus.
21.45	*Ergina*	Iraklia. Schinoussa. Koufonissia. Amorgos (Katapola). Amorgos (Egiali). Astipalea.
21.50	*Express Olympia*	Paros. Piraeus.
22.10	*Apollo Express 2*	Paros. Piraeus.
23.00	*Milena*	Paros. Piraeus.
24.00	*Ionian Sea*	Paros. Piraeus.

○

09.30	*Dia Island*	Schinoussa. Koufonissia.

Nea Kameni

Cyclades Central
p. 164

Ⓓ

12.00	*Theoskepasti*	Thirasia (Korfos). Thirasia. Santorini (Oia).

Nea Moudania

Northern Aegean p. 336

🐬 *Flying Dolphins*

① ③ ⑥
08.00   Alonissos. Skopelos. Skopelos (Glossa).
           Skiathos.

② ④ ⑤ ⑦
07.30   Marmaras. Alonissos. Skopelos.
           Skopelos (Glossa). Skiathos.

① ③ ⑤ ⑦
10.10   Thessalonikia.
17.20   Skiathos. Glossa. Skopelos. Alonissos.

Nea Peramos

Northern Aegean p. 336

ⓓ 08.30   12.30   16.30   20.45
           ANET Line   Thassos (Skala Prinos).

Neapoli

Argo-Saronic p. 376

ⓓ
08.15   *Martha*   Kithera (Agia Pelagia). Gythio.
18.00   *Martha*   Elafonissos.

②
01.10   *Theseus*   Kithera (Kapsali). Antikithera.
                     Crete (Kasteli).

⑤
01.00   *Theseus*   Monemvassia. Kiparissi. Piraeus.

⑥
01.10   *Theseus*   Elafonissos. Kithera (Kapsali).
                     Gythio. Antikithera. Crete (Kasteli).

⑦
14.20   *Theseus*   Monemvassia. Gerakas. Kiparissi.
                     Piraeus.

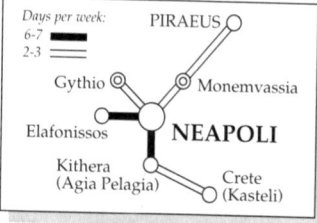

Days per week:
6-7 ▬▬▬
2-3 ════

PIRAEUS
Gythio   Monemvassia
Elafonissos   **NEAPOLI**
Kithera
(Agia Pelagia)   Crete
                  (Kasteli)

Nissiros

Dodecanese p. 283

ⓓ
07.00   Taxi boat   Kos (Kardamena).
16.00   *Nissiros Express* Kos (Kardamena).

①
09.25   *Nissos Kalimnos*   Tilos. Symi. Rhodes.
                               Kastelorizo.

②
07.00   *Romilda*   Tilos. Symi. Rhodes.
                               Kastelorizo.
08.40   ILIO H/F   Symi. Tilos. Rhodes.
16.10   *Nissos Kalimnos*   Kos. Kalimnos.
19.00   ILIO H/F   Kos. Kalimnos.

③
04.45   *Romilda*   Kos. Kalimnos. Leros.
                               Lipsi. Patmos. Naxos.
                               Paros. Syros. Piraeus.
12.10   ILIO H/F   Kos.
15.25   ILIO H/F   Symi. Rhodes. Kos.
                               Kalimnos.

⑤
09.25   *Nissos Kalimnos*   Tilos. Symi. Rhodes.
                               Kastelorizo.
11.40   ILIO H/F   Kos.
16.10   ILIO H/F   Rhodes. Kos. Kalimnos.

⑥
07.30   *Ionian Sea*   Tilos. Rhodes.
12.40   ILIO H/F   Kos.
14.55   ILIO H/F   Tilos. Symi. Rhodes.
16.10   *Nissos Kalimnos*   Kos. Kalimnos.
16.50   *Ionian Sea*   Kos. Kalimnos. Astipalea.
                               Paros. Syros. Piraeus.

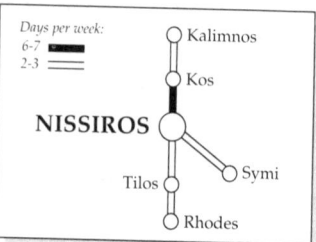

Days per week:
6-7 ▬▬▬
2-3 ════

Kalimnos
Kos
NISSIROS
Symi
Tilos
Rhodes

Odum Iskalesi

Turkey p. 422

ⓓ x ②
00.00   TML   Bozcaada.

Tables

Oinousses

Eastern Line p. 314

Ⓓ
| 08.00 | Oinousses | Chios. |

① ③ ⑤ ⑦
| 16.00 | Miniotis | Chios. |

Otranto

Italy p. 86

① ③ ④ ⑥
| 22.30 | Anna Maria Lauro | Igoumenitsa. Corfu. |

Paros

Cyclades Central p. 152

Ⓓ
11.30	Kasos Express	Antiparos.
14.30	Mykonos Express	Mykonos.
15.30	Kasos Express	Antiparos.
16.00	Margarita	Sifnos.
19.00	Kasos Express	Antiparos.
19.15	Mykonos Express	Ios. Santorini.

09.45 10.30 11.30		
12.30 13.30 14.30		
16.00 17.30 19.00		
Antiparos T/Bs		Antiparos.

①
00.45	Apollo Express 1	Naxos. Ios. Santorini.
01.15	Ionian Sea	Piraeus.
03.00	Express Santorini	Naxos. Ios. Santorini.
03.00	Golden Vergina	Ikaria (Evdilos). Samos (Karlovassi). Samos (Vathi).
05.30	Daliana	Naxos. Santorini. Crete (Iraklion).
06.55	ILIO H/F	Mykonos. Tinos. Tinos (Isternia). Andros (Batsi). Rafina.
09.00	ILIO H/F	Naxos. Ios. Santorini.
11.00	Express Paros	Naxos. Ios. Santorini.
11.45	Poseidon Express	Piraeus.
12.00	Ergina	Syros. Piraeus.
12.15	Apollo Express 1	Piraeus.
12.45	Apollo Express 2	Naxos. Ios. Santorini.
13.00	Express Olympia	Naxos. Ios. Santorini.
13.00	Nearchos	Naxos.
14.00	Express Santorini	Piraeus.
16.10	Nearchos	Ios. Santorini. Crete (Iraklion).
19.20	ILIO H/F	Mykonos. Tinos. Syros.
19.45	Ventouris SL	Naxos.

20.00	Romilda	Naxos. Patmos. Lipsi. Leros. Kalimnos. Kos. Nissiros. Tilos. Symi. Rhodes. Kastelorizo.
20.25	ILIO H/F	Naxos.
20.45	Express Paros	Mykonos.
21.30	Ionian Sea	Kos. Rhodes.
22.30	Golden Vergina	Piraeus.
22.30	Milena	Naxos. Ikaria (Agios Kyrikos). Fourni. Samos (Karlovassi). (Vathi).
22.55	Express Olympia	Piraeus.
23.00	Poseidon Express	Naxos. Ios. Santorini.
23.15	Apollo Express 2	Piraeus.

②
00.10	Daliana	Piraeus.
00.20	Ventouris SL	Piraeus.
04.00	Express Santorini	Naxos. Ios. Santorini. Anafi.
07.55	ILIO H/F	Mykonos. Tinos. Andros (Batsi). Rafina.
09.00	ILIO H/F	Naxos. Ios. Santorini. Anafi.
09.45	Anemos	Santorini. Crete (Iraklion).
11.00	Express Paros	Naxos. Ios. Sikinos. Folegandros. Sifnos. Serifos. Syros.
11.45	ILIO H/F	Naxos.
11.45	Poseidon Express	Piraeus.
12.45	Apollo Express 1	Naxos. Ios. Santorini.
13.00	Express Olympia	Naxos. Ios. Santorini.
13.30	Nearchos	Syros.
14.00	Express Santorini	Syros. Piraeus.
15.20	ILIO H/F	Mykonos. Tinos. Andros (Batsi). Rafina.
16.30	Nearchos	Ios. Santorini. Crete (Iraklion).
19.20	ILIO H/F	Mykonos. Tinos. Syros.
21.20	Golden Vergina	Ikaria (Agios Kyrikos). Samos (Karlovassi). Samos (Vathi).
21.30	Daliana	Naxos. Santorini. Crete (Iraklion). Karpathos (Town). Rhodes.
22.55	Express Olympia	Piraeus.
23.00	Poseidon Express	Naxos. Ios. Santorini.
23.15	Apollo Express 1	Piraeus.
24.00	Milena	Piraeus.

③
01.00	Apollo Express 2	Naxos. Ios. Santorini.
01.30	Ionian Sea	Piraeus.
02.30	Anemos	Mykonos. Tinos. Skiathos. Thessalonika.
03.20	Ergina	Sifnos. Nafplio.
09.00	ILIO H/F	Naxos. Ios. Santorini. Iraklia. Schinoussa. Koufonissia. Amorgos (Egiali). (Katapola).
11.00	Express Paros	Naxos. Ios. Santorini.
11.45	Poseidon Express	Piraeus.
12.10	Catamaran II	Naxos. Iraklia. Schinoussa. Koufonissia. Amorgos (Katapola).
12.15	Apollo Express 2	Piraeus.
12.15	Golden Vergina	Piraeus.
12.45	Apollo Express 1	Naxos. Ios. Santorini.
13.00	Express Santorini	Naxos. Ios. Santorini. Anafi.

13.00	*Nearchos*	Mykonos.
16.00	*Nearchos*	Ios. Santorini. Crete (Iraklion).
17.30	*Romilda*	Syros. Piraeus.
18.00	*Catamaran II*	Syros. Mykonos. Tinos. Andros (Batsi). Rafina.
19.15	*Ergina*	Naxos. Amorgos (Katapola). (Egiali). Mykonos. Piraeus.
19.20	ILIO H/F	Mykonos. Tinos. Syros.
20.25	ILIO H/F	Naxos.
21.30	*Ionian Sea*	Kos. Rhodes.
22.00	*Express Paros*	Mykonos.
22.30	*Milena*	Naxos. Ikaria (Agios Kyrikos). Samos (Karlovassi). (Vathi).
22.45	*Express Olympia*	Naxos. Donoussa. Amorgos (Egiali). Amorgos (Katapola).
23.00	*Express Santorini*	Piraeus.
23.15	*Apollo Express 1*	Piraeus.

④

00.30	*Golden Vergina*	Ikaria (Agios Kyrikos). Fourni. Samos (Karlovassi). Samos (Vathi).
01.00	*Apollo Express 2*	Naxos. Ios. Santorini.
07.55	ILIO H/F	Mykonos. Tinos. Andros (Batsi). Rafina.
09.00	ILIO H/F	Naxos. Ios. Santorini.
10.30	*Express Olympia*	Syros. Piraeus.
11.00	*Express Paros*	Naxos. Ios. Santorini.
11.35	ILIO H/F	Naxos. Iraklia. Schinoussa. Koufonissia. Amorgos (Egiali).

12.15	*Apollo Express 2*	Piraeus.
12.20	*Anemos*	Santorini. Crete (Iraklion).
12.30	*Romilda*	Naxos. Santorini.
12.45	*Apollo Express 1*	Naxos. Ios. Santorini.
13.00	*Nearchos*	Naxos. Ios. Santorini. Crete (Iraklion).
16.30	ILIO H/F	Mykonos. Tinos. Andros (Batsi). Rafina.
18.00	*Daliana*	Piraeus.
19.20	ILIO H/F	Mykonos. Tinos. Syros.
20.45	*Express Paros*	Mykonos. Syros.
22.00	*Express Santorini*	Naxos. Amorgos (Katapola). (Egiali). Astipalea.
22.30	*Romilda*	Piraeus.
23.00	*Golden Vergina*	Piraeus.
23.00	*Poseidon Express*	Naxos. Ios. Santorini.
23.15	*Apollo Express 1*	Piraeus.
24.00	*Milena*	Piraeus.

⑤

01.30	*Ionian Sea*	Piraeus.
02.00	*Apollo Express 2*	Naxos. Ios. Sikinos. Folegandros. Santorini.
04.30	*Anemos*	Syros. Thessalonika.
09.00	ILIO H/F	Naxos. Ios. Santorini.
11.00	*Express Paros*	Naxos. Ios. Santorini.
11.00	*Express Santorini*	Piraeus.
11.45	ILIO H/F	Naxos.
11.45	*Poseidon Express*	Piraeus.
12.00	*Apollo Express 2*	Syros. Piraeus.
12.30	*Romilda*	Naxos. Santorini.
13.00	*Express Olympia*	Naxos. Ios. Santorini.
13.00	*Nearchos*	Mykonos.
14.00	*Ventouris SL*	Naxos. Santorini.
16.00	*Nearchos*	Ios. Santorini. Crete (Iraklion).
19.20	ILIO H/F	Mykonos. Tinos. Syros.
20.45	*Express Paros*	Mykonos.
21.15	*Rodanthi*	Kos. Rhodes.
21.30	*Daliana*	Santorini. Crete (Iraklion). Karpathos (Town). Rhodes.
21.30	*Ionian Sea*	Astipalea. Kalimnos. Kos. Nissiros. Tilos. Rhodes.
22.15	*Golden Vergina*	Ikaria (Evdilos). Samos (Karlovassi). Samos (Vathi).
22.30	*Romilda*	Piraeus.
22.45	*Apollo Express 1*	Naxos. Ios. Santorini. Anafi.
22.55	*Express Olympia*	Piraeus.
23.30	*Ventouris SL*	Piraeus.

⑥

00.15	*Poseidon Express*	Naxos. Ios. Santorini.
03.00	*Express Santorini*	Naxos. Ios. Santorini.
11.00	*Express Paros*	Naxos. Ios. Santorini.
11.45	ILIO H/F	Naxos. Mykonos. Tinos. Andros (Batsi). Rafina.
11.45	*Poseidon Express*	Piraeus.
12.00	*Apollo Express 1*	Piraeus.
12.10	*Anemos*	Santorini. Crete (Iraklion).
12.30	*Romilda*	Naxos. Santorini.
12.45	*Apollo Express 2*	Naxos. Ios. Santorini.
13.00	*Express Olympia*	Naxos. Ios. Santorini.
13.00	*Golden Vergina*	Piraeus.

PIRAEUS
Thessalonika
Rafina
Skiathos
Tinos
Samos
Syros
Mykonos
Naxos
Ikaria
PAROS
Kou.
Don.
Antiparos
Amorgos
Sifnos
Ira.
Schinoussa
Foleg.
Sikinos
Ios
Santorini
Rhodes
Karpathos
Crete (Iraklion)

Days per week:
6-7
4-5
2-3

14.00	*Express Santorini*	Piraeus.
14.30	Ventouris SL	Naxos. Donoussa.
17.00	*Marina*	Naxos. Patmos. Leros. Kalimnos. Kos.
18.30	*Rodanthi*	Piraeus.
20.45	*Express Paros*	Mykonos. Syros.
22.30	*Romilda*	Piraeus.
22.55	*Express Olympia*	Piraeus.
23.00	*Poseidon Express*	Naxos. Ios. Santorini.
23.15	*Apollo Express 2*	Piraeus.

⑦

00.15	Ventouris SL	Piraeus.
00.30	*Golden Vergina*	Ikaria (Evdilos). Samos (Karlovassi). (Vathi).
01.00	*Apollo Express 1*	Naxos. Ios. Sikinos. Folegandros. Santorini.
03.00	*Express Santorini*	Naxos. Ios. Santorini.
03.00	*Ionian Sea*	Syros. Piraeus.
04.40	*Anemos*	Mykonos. Tinos. Skiathos. Thessalonika.
05.15	*Milena*	Naxos. Ikaria (Agios Kyrikos). Samos (Karlovassi). (Vathi).
11.00	*Express Paros*	Naxos. Ios. Santorini.
11.20	*Poseidon Express*	Piraeus.
11.45	ILIO H/F	Naxos.
12.15	*Apollo Express 1*	Piraeus.
12.30	*Romilda*	Naxos. Santorini. Folegandros. Sikinos.
12.45	*Apollo Express 2*	Naxos. Ios. Santorini.
13.00	*Express Olympia*	Naxos. Ios. Santorini.
14.00	*Express Santorini*	Piraeus.
14.30	*Golden Vergina*	Piraeus.
14.45	*Marina*	Piraeus.
15.20	ILIO H/F	Mykonos. Tinos. Andros (Batsi). Rafina.
16.30	*Daliana*	Piraeus.
16.45	*Ionian Sea*	Naxos.
20.30	*Ergina*	Amorgos (Egiali). Amorgos (Katapola). Naxos. Iraklia. Schinoussa. Koufonissia. Amorgos (Katapola). Amorgos (Egiali). Astipalea.
20.45	*Express Paros*	Mykonos. Syros.
22.55	*Express Olympia*	Piraeus.
23.00	*Poseidon Express*	Naxos. Ios. Santorini.
23.15	*Apollo Express 2*	Piraeus.
23.45	*Romilda*	Piraeus.
24.00	*Milena*	Piraeus.

Paros (Piso Livadi)

Cyclades Central
p. 156

② ④ ⑥
| 10.00 | *Skopelitis* | Naxos. Mykonos. |
| 16.45 | *Skopelitis* | Iraklia. Schinoussa. Koufonissia. Amorgos (Katapola). |

Paros (Punta)

Cyclades Central   p. 156

Ⓗ
07.00–10.00,
21.00–24.00;
ev. 30 min
10.30–20.30   *Agioi Anargiri*   Antiparos.

Paşalmanı

Turkey   p. 422

① ⑥
| 00.00 | TML | Erdek. |

Patmos

Dodecanese   p. 284

Ⓓ Tourist boats:
10.00	*Anna Express*	Lipsi. / Arki.
10.00	*Megalohori/ Patmos Express*	Lipsi.
16.00	*Cassandra* or	Samos (Pithagorio).
	Hydrofoil	Samos (Pithagorio).

Ⓓ ex①
| 16.00 | *Chios I* | Fourni. Ikaria (Agios Kyrikos). Samos (Vathi). Chios. |

①
09.00	*Marina*	Leros. Kalimnos. Kos. Rhodes.
09.30	ILIO H/F	Lipsi. Leros. Kalimnos. Kos.
16.00	ILIO H/F	Ikaria (Agios Kyrikos). Samos (Karlovassi). Samos (Vathi).
21.25	*Ialyssos*	Piraeus.
22.30	*Kamiros*	Leros. Kalimnos. Kos. Rhodes.
24.00	*Romilda*	Lipsi. Leros. Kalimnos. Kos. Nissiros. Tilos. Symi. Rhodes. Kastelorizo.

②
01.00	*Marina*	Piraeus.
08.40	ILIO H/F	Lipsi. Leros. Kalimnos. Kos.
11.00	*Sea Harmony*	Rhodes. Limassol. Haifa.
16.00	ILIO H/F	Samos (Pithagorio). Samos (Vathi).
16.30	ILIO H/F	Samos (Vathi). Chios. Lesbos (Mytilini).
19.30	*Kamiros*	Piraeus.
22.30	*Ialyssos*	Leros. Kalimnos. Kos. Rhodes.

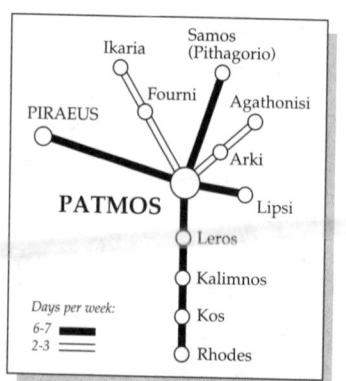

Days per week:
6-7 ▬▬▬
2-3 ══

③
11.10	Nissos Kalimnos	Agathonisi. Samos (Pithagorio).
12.00	Princessa Cypria	Limassol. Haifa.
12.00	Romilda	Naxos. Paros. Syros. Piraeus.
16.00	ILIO H/F	Leros. Kalimnos. Kos. Agathonisi. Samos (Pithagorio).
20.20	Nissos Kalimnos	Lipsi. Leros. Kalimnos. Kos.
20.30	Ialyssos	Piraeus.
22.30	Kamiros	Leros. Kalimnos. Kos. Rhodes.

④
08.35	ILIO H/F	Lipsi. Leros. Kalimnos. Kos.
11.30	Chioni	Lipsi. Arki. Agathonisi. Samos (Pithagorio). Chios.
19.30	Kamiros	Piraeus.
22.30	Ialyssos	Leros. Kalimnos. Kos. Rhodes.

⑤
09.30	ILIO H/F	Lipsi. Leros. Kalimnos. Kos.
16.00	ILIO H/F	Ikaria (Agios Kyrikos). Samos (Karlovassi). Samos (Vathi).
20.30	Ialyssos	Piraeus.
22.30	Kamiros	Leros. Kalimnos. Kos. Rhodes.

⑥
08.10	ILIO H/F	Kos. Kalimnos. Leros.
16.00	ILIO H/F	Leros. Kalimnos. Kos.
16.30	ILIO H/F	Samos (Vathi). Chios. Lesbos (Mytilini).
19.30	Kamiros	Piraeus.
19.55	ILIO H/F	Samos (Pithagorio).
22.00	Marina	Leros. Kalimnos. Kos.
23.00	Ialyssos	Leros. Kalimnos. Kos. Rhodes. Chalki. Karpathos (Town). Crete (Iraklion).

⑦
04.15	Dimitra	Mykonos. Syros. Tinos. Piraeus.
09.00	Marina	Naxos. Paros. Piraeus.
09.30	Rodanthi	Kos. Rhodes.
11.10	Nissos Kalimnos	Agathonisi. Samos (Pithagorio).
12.00	Alcaeos	Samos (Vathi). Chios. Lesbos (Mytilini). Limnos. Thessalonika.
16.00	ILIO H/F	Leros. Kalimnos. Kos. Samos (Pithagorio). Samos (Vathi).
16.30	ILIO H/F	Samos (Pithagorio). Chios. Lesbos (Mytilini).
18.40	Nissos Kalimnos	Lipsi. Leros. Kalimnos. Kos.
24.00	Rodanthi	Piraeus.

Patras

Adriatic Line p. 87

International Services:

Ⓓ
21.00	AK Ventouris	Igoumenitsa. Brindisi.
21.00	Marlines	Igoumenitsa. Corfu. Bari.
21.00	Raffaello/Valentino	[Ⓞ Igoumenitsa]. Brindisi.
21.30	Eolos/Ouranos	Igoumenitsa. Corfu. Brindisi.
21.30	Polaris/Saturnus	Bari.
22.00	Adriatica	Igoumenitsa. Corfu. Brindisi.
22.00	Minoan Lines	Corfu. Igoumenitsa. Ancona.

Ⓐ
14.00	Afrodite II	Kefalonia (Sami). Igoumenitsa. Brindisi.
17.00	HML Ferries	Kefalonia (Sami). Paxi. Brindisi.
17.00	Poseidonia	Kefalonia (Sami). Brindisi.
19.00	Adriatica	Brindisi.

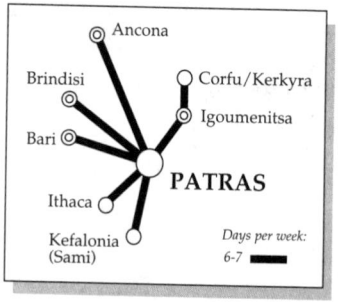

Days per week:
6-7 ▬▬▬

21.00	*Egnatia*	Kefalonia (Sami). Corfu. Brindisi.
21.00	HML Ferries	Kefalonia (Sami). Brindisi.
21.30	*Athens Express*	Kefalonia (Sami). Bari.
21.30	*Venus*	Bari.

①

13.00	*Ionian Sun*	Igoumenitsa. Corfu. Ancona.
22.00	Marlines	Igoumenitsa. Ancona.
22.00	Strintzis Lines	Corfu. Igoumenitsa. Ancona.
23.00	*El. Venizelos*	Corfu. Igoumenitsa. Ancona.

②

10.00	*Baroness M*	Igoumenitsa. Bari.
17.00	*Sea Serenade*	Igoumenitsa. Bari.
23.00	*Lato*	Corfu. Igoumenitsa. Trieste.
23.50	Strintzis Lines	Corfu. Igoumenitsa. Ancona.

③

01.00	*Carlo R*	Ancona.
23.00	*Kydon*	Igoumenitsa. Ancona.
23.50	Strintzis Lines	Igoumenitsa. Ancona.
24.00	*Crown M*	Igoumenitsa. Ancona.

④

08.00	*Baroness M*	Cesme.
20.00	*Erotokritos*	Ancona.
21.30	*Festos*	Kefalonia (Sami).
23.00	*El. Venizelos*	Corfu. Igoumenitsa. Trieste.
23.50	Strintzis Lines	Corfu. Igoumenitsa. Ancona.
24.00	Marlines	Igoumenitsa. Corfu. Ancona.

⑤

20.00	*Baroness M*	Bari.
24.00	*Lato*	Corfu. Igoumenitsa. Ancona.

⑥

22.00	Strintzis Lines	Corfu. Igoumenitsa. Ancona.
24.00	*Crown M*	Crete (Iraklion).
24.00	*Kydon*	Igoumenitsa. Ancona.

⑦

13.00	Strintzis Lines	Igoumenitsa. Ancona.
17.00	*Sea Serenade*	Igoumenitsa. Bari.
20.00	*Baroness M*	Çeşme.
20.00	*Erotokritos*	Ancona.
23.00	*Carlo R*	Çeşme.
24.00	*Festos*	Crete (Iraklion). Çeşme.

Domestic Services:

Ⓓ

13.00	*Eptanisos*	Kefalonia (Sami). Ithaca.
13.00	*Europe 2*	Kefalonia (Argostoli). Zakinthos.
22.00	*Eptanisos*	Kefalonia (Sami). Ithaca.

① ⑥

14.00	*Europe 1*	Kefalonia (Sami). Ithaca.

②

14.50	*Europe 1*	Ithaca.

③

14.00	*Europe 1*	Kefalonia (Poros). Kefalonia (Sami). Ithaca.

④

14.00	*Europe 1*	Kefalonia (Sami). Ithaca.
21.30	*Festos*	Kefalonia (Sami).

⑤ ⑦

14.00	*Europe 1*	Ithaca.
19.15	*Europe 1*	Kefalonia (Poros). Kefalonia (Sami). Ithaca.

Paxi / Paxos

Ionian Line p. 399

Ⓓ

11.00	Corfu—Paxi Line	Corfu.

Ⓓ ex ⑦

07.00	*Pegasus*	Corfu.

Ⓐ

05.30	HML Ferries	Kefalonia (Sami). Patras.
24.00	HML Ferries	Brindisi.

①

07.00	*Zephyros*	Corfu. Igoumenitsa.
14.30	*Zephyros*	Igoumenitsa. Corfu.

① ③ ⑤

16.30	Corfu—Paxi Line	Corfu.

② ⑥

07.00	*Zephyros*	Igoumenitsa. Corfu.

③

07.00	*Zephyros*	Igoumenitsa.

④

07.00	*Zephyros*	Corfu.

④

16.00	*Zephyros*	Igoumenitsa.

⑤

06.30	*Zephyros*	Igoumenitsa.
10.30	*Zephyros*	Corfu.

⑦

17.00	*Zephyros*	Corfu. Igoumenitsa.

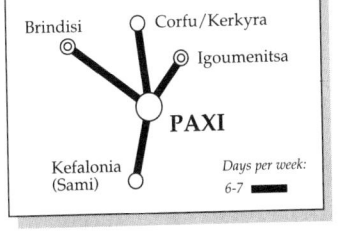

Brindisi   Corfu/Kerkyra

Igoumenitsa

PAXI

Kefalonia (Sami)

Days per week:
6-7

Piraeus (Great Harbour)

Athens & Piraeus   p. 122

Note:
Current weekly domestic schedules (running Thursday to Wednesday) are available from the Syntagma
Square National Bank NTOG/EOT. A 48-hour Saronic Gulf ferry schedule (in Greek) is posted up on the
Port Police kiosk on the Saronic Gulf ferry quay. Full Saronic Gulf hydrofoil timetables are available from
the Zea Marina ticket kiosk. International ferry information is obtained from respective agents.

International Services:

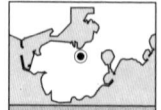

①		
19.00	*Sea Harmony*	Patmos. Rhodes. Limassol. Haifa.

②		
20.00	*Princessa Cypria*	Patmos. Limassol. Haifa.

④		
17.00	*Sea Wave*	Rhodes. Limassol. Haifa.
19.00	*Nissos Kypros*	Rhodes. Limassol. Haifa.

⑥		
20.00	*Sea Harmony*	Lesbos (Mytilini). Mykonos.

Domestic Services:

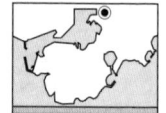

1. Cyclades, Crete, Dodecanese,
Eastern & Northern Aegean

Ⓓ		
08.00	*Panagia Tinou 2*	Syros. Tinos. Mykonos.
19.30	*Kantia/Rethimno*	Crete (Iraklion).
20.00	*Aptera/Lissos*	Crete (Chania).
20.15	*King Minos/*	
	N. Kazantzakis	Crete (Iraklion).

①		
00.45	*Dimitra*	Syros. Mykonos.
01.00	*Daliana*	Paros. Naxos. Santorini. Crete (Iraklion).
08.00	*Apollo Express 2*	Paros. Naxos. Ios. Santorini.
08.00	*Georgios Express*	Kythnos. Serifos. Sifnos. Kimolos. Milos.
08.15	*Express Olympia*	Paros. Naxos. Ios. Santorini.
08.30	*Naias II*	Syros. Tinos. Mykonos.
13.00	*Kamiros*	Patmos. Leros. Kalimnos. Kos. Rhodes.
14.00	*Romilda*	Syros. Paros. Naxos. Patmos. Lipsi. Leros. Kalimnos. Kos. Nissiros. Tilos. Symi. Rhodes. Kastelorizo.
14.00	*Ventouris SL*	Paros. Naxos.
15.00	*Milos Express*	Kythnos. Serifos. Sifnos. Milos. Kimolos. Folegandros. Sikinos. Ios. Santorini.
15.30	*Ionian Sea*	Syros. Paros. Kos. Rhodes.
16.00	*Dimitra*	Syros. Mykonos. Amorgos (Katapola). Amorgos (Egiali). Astipalea.
16.00	*Rodanthi*	Kos. Rhodes.
16.30	*Theseus*	Kiparissi. Monemvassia. Neapoli. Kithera (Kapsali). Antikithera. Crete (Kasteli).
17.00	*Patmos*	Kos. Rhodes.
17.15	*Milena*	Paros. Naxos. Ikaria (Agios Kyrikos). Fourni. Samos (Karlovassi). Samos (Vathi).
18.00	*Agios Rafail*	Lesbos (Mytilini).
18.15	*Poseidon Express*	Paros. Naxos. Ios. Santorini.
18.30	*Kriti*	Milos. Crete (Agios Nikolaos). Crete (Sitia).
19.00	*Mytilene*	Chios. Lesbos (Mytilini). Limnos. Kavala.

19.45	*Knossos*	Crete (Chania).
20.30	*Arkadi/Preveli*	Crete (Rethimno).
21.00	*Panagia Tinou 2*	Mykonos. Syros.
22.00	*Express Santorini*	Syros. Paros. Naxos. Ios. Santorini. Anafi.

②

08.00	*Apollo Express 1*	Paros. Naxos. Ios. Santorini.
08.00	*Naias II*	Syros. Tinos. Mykonos.
08.00	*Ventouris SL*	Sifnos. Milos. Folegandros. Sikinos. Santorini. Crete (Agios Nikolaos). Crete (Sitia). Kassos. Karpathos (Town). Karpathos (Diafani). Chalki. Symi. Rhodes.
08.15	*Express Olympia*	Paros. Naxos. Ios. Santorini.
09.00	*Samaina*	Ikaria (Evdilos). Ikaria (Agios Kyrikos). Samos (Karlovassi). Samos (Vathi).
13.00	*Ialyssos*	Patmos. Leros. Kalimnos. Kos. Rhodes.
14.00	*Ergina*	Mykonos. Amorgos (Egiali). Amorgos (Katapola). Naxos. Paros. Sifnos. Nafplio.
14.00	*Georgios Express*	Kythnos. Serifos. Sifnos. Kimolos. Milos.
16.00	*Daliana*	Paros. Naxos. Santorini. Crete (Iraklion). Karpathos (Town). Rhodes.
16.00	*Golden Vergina*	Paros. Ikaria (Agios Kyrikos). Samos (Karlovassi). Samos (Vathi).
16.00	*Marina*	Kalimnos. Kos. Rhodes.
17.00	*Rodos*	Rhodes.
18.15	*Poseidon Express*	Paros. Naxos. Ios. Santorini.
19.00	*Dimitra*	Syros. Mykonos. Ikaria (Agios Kyrikos). Fourni. Samos (Karlovassi). Samos (Vathi).
19.00	*Sappho*	Chios. Lesbos (Mytilini). Limnos. Thessalonika.
19.30	*Nissos Chios*	Chios. Lesbos (Mytilini).
19.45	*Knossos*	Crete (Chania).
20.00	*Apollo Express 2*	Paros. Naxos. Ios. Santorini.

③

08.00	*Apollo Express 1*	Paros. Naxos. Ios. Santorini.
08.00	*Milos Express*	Kythnos. Serifos. Sifnos. Kimolos. Milos.
08.00	*Naias II*	Tinos. Mykonos.
08.15	*Express Santorini*	Paros. Naxos. Ios. Santorini. Anafi.
08.45	*Georgios Express*	Kythnos. Serifos. Sifnos. Milos.
11.00	*Agios Rafail*	Lesbos (Mytilini).
13.00	*Kamiros*	Patmos. Leros. Kalimnos. Kos. Rhodes.
15.30	*Ionian Sea*	Syros. Paros. Kos. Rhodes.
16.00	*Rodanthi*	Kos. Rhodes.
17.00	*Alcaeos*	Skyros. Agios Efstratios. Limnos. Kavala.
17.00	*Express Olympia*	Syros. Paros. Naxos. Donoussa. Amorgos (Egiali). Amorgos (Katapola).
17.00	*Patmos*	Kos. Rhodes.
17.15	*Milena*	Paros. Naxos. Ikaria (Agios Kyrikos). Samos (Karlovassi). Samos (Vathi).
18.30	*Kriti*	Milos. Crete (Agios Nikolaos). Crete (Sitia).
19.15	*Naias II*	Syros. Mykonos.
19.30	*Golden Vergina*	Paros. Ikaria (Agios Kyrikos). Fourni. Samos (Karlovassi). Samos (Vathi).
20.00	*Apollo Express 2*	Paros. Naxos. Ios. Santorini.
20.00	*Mytilene*	Chios. Lesbos (Mytilini).
20.30	*Arkadi/Preveli*	Crete (Rethimno).
22.00	*Dimitra*	Syros. Mykonos. Donoussa. Koufonissia. Amorgos (Katapola). Amorgos (Egiali). Astipalea.

④

07.30	*Romilda*	Paros. Naxos. Santorini.
08.00	*Apollo Express 1*	Paros. Naxos. Ios. Santorini.
08.00	*Milos Express*	Kythnos. Serifos. Sifnos. Milos. Folegandros. Sikinos. Ios. Santorini.
08.30	*Naias II*	Syros. Tinos. Mykonos.
08.45	*Georgios Express*	Kythnos. Serifos. Sifnos.
09.00	*Samaina*	Ikaria (Agios Kyrikos). Samos (Karlovassi). Samos (Vathi).
13.00	*Ialyssos*	Patmos. Leros. Kalimnos. Kos. Rhodes.
14.00	*Ergina*	Naxos. Amorgos (Egiali). Amorgos (Katapola). Santorini. Milos. Nafplio.
16.00	*Agios Rafail*	Lesbos (Mytilini).
16.00	*Marina*	Kalimnos. Kos. Rhodes.
17.00	*Express Santorini*	Paros. Naxos. Amorgos (Katapola). Amorgos (Egiali). Astipalea.
17.00	*Nissos Chios*	Chios. Lesbos (Mytilini). Limnos. Kavala.
18.15	*Poseidon Express*	Paros. Naxos. Ios. Santorini.
19.45	*Knossos*	Crete (Chania).
20.00	*Apollo Express 2*	Syros. Paros. Naxos. Ios. Sikinos. Folegandros. Santorini.
21.00	*Georgios Express*	Kythnos. Serifos. Sifnos. Kimolos. Milos.
21.00	*Mytilene*	Lesbos (Mytilini). Chios.
21.00	*Panagia Tinou 2*	Mykonos. Syros.

⑤
07.30	Romilda	Paros. Naxos. Santorini.
08.00	Naias II	Tinos. Mykonos.
08.00	Ventouris SL	Paros. Naxos. Santorini.
08.15	Express Olympia	Paros. Naxos. Ios. Santorini.
09.00	Samaina	Ikaria (Agios Kyrikos). Samos (Vathi).
13.00	Kamiros	Patmos. Leros. Kalimnos. Kos. Rhodes.
15.00	Daliana	Paros. Santorini. Crete (Iraklion). Karpathos (Town). Rhodes.
15.30	Ionian Sea	Syros. Paros. Astipalea. Kalimnos. Kos. Nissiros. Tilos. Rhodes.
16.00	Dimitra	Syros. Tinos. Mykonos.
16.00	Georgios Express	Kythnos. Serifos. Sifnos. Kimolos. Milos.
16.00	Rodanthi	Paros. Kos. Rhodes.
16.30	Theseus	Kiparissi. Gerakas. Monemvassia. Neapoli. Elafonissos. Kithera (Kapsali). Gythio. Antikithera. Crete (Kasteli).
16.45	Milos Express	Kythnos. Serifos. Sifnos. Milos.
17.00	Apollo Express 1	Syros. Paros. Naxos. Ios. Santorini. Anafi.
17.00	Golden Vergina	Paros. Ikaria (Evdilos). Samos (Karlovassi). Samos (Vathi).
17.00	Rodos	Rhodes.
17.00	Sappho	Chios. Lesbos (Mytilini).
17.15	Milena	Naxos. Ikaria (Agios Kyrikos). Fourni. Samos (Karlovassi). Samos (Vathi).
19.15	Naias II	Syros. Mykonos.
19.30	Kriti	Milos. Crete (Agios Nikolaos). Crete (Sitia).
19.30	Poseidon Express	Paros. Naxos. Ios. Santorini.
19.45	Knossos	Crete (Chania).
20.30	Arkadi/Preveli	Crete (Rethimno).
21.00	Agios Rafail	Lesbos (Mytilini).
21.00	Mytilene	Chios. Lesbos (Mytilini). Limnos. Thessalonika.
22.00	Express Santorini	Paros. Naxos. Ios. Santorini.

⑥
07.30	Romilda	Paros. Naxos. Santorini.
07.45	Dimitra	Tinos. Mykonos. Lipsi. Patmos.
08.00	Apollo Express 2	Paros. Naxos. Ios. Santorini.
08.00	Milos Express	Kythnos. Serifos. Sifnos. Milos. Kimolos. Folegandros. Sikinos.
08.00	Naias II	Syros. Tinos. Mykonos.
08.15	Express Olympia	Paros. Naxos. Ios. Santorini.
08.25	Georgios Express	Kythnos. Serifos. Sifnos.
08.30	Ventouris SL	Paros. Naxos. Donoussa.
09.00	Samaina	Ikaria (Karkinagri). Ikaria (Agios Kyrikos). Samos (Karlovassi). Samos (Vathi).
12.00	Marina	Paros. Naxos. Patmos. Leros. Kalimnos. Kos.
13.00	Ialyssos	Patmos. Leros. Kalimnos. Kos. Rhodes. Chalki. Karpathos. Crete (Iraklion).
14.00	Ergina	Mykonos. Naxos. Donoussa. Amorgos (Egiali). Amorgos (Katapola).
18.15	Poseidon Express	Paros. Naxos. Ios. Santorini.
19.30	Golden Vergina	Paros. Ikaria (Evdilos). Samos (Karlovassi). Samos (Vathi).
19.45	Knossos	Crete (Chania).
20.00	Apollo Express 1	Paros. Naxos. Ios. Sikinos. Folegandros. Santorini.
21.00	Georgios Express	Kythnos. Serifos. Sifnos. Kimolos. Milos.
21.00	Panagia Tinou 2	Syros. Mykonos.
21.00	Sappho	Chios. Lesbos (Mytilini).
22.00	Express Santorini	Paros. Naxos. Ios. Santorini.
23.00	Milena	Paros. Naxos. Ikaria (Agios Kyrikos). Samos (Karlovassi). Samos (Vathi).

⑦
01.00	Rodanthi	Patmos. Kos. Rhodes.
07.30	Arkadi/Preveli	Crete (Rethimno).
07.30	Milos Express	Kythnos. Serifos. Sifnos. Milos.
07.30	Romilda	Paros. Naxos. Santorini. Folegandros. Sikinos.
08.00	Apollo Express 2	Paros. Naxos. Ios. Santorini.
08.00	Naias II	Tinos. Mykonos.
08.00	Ventouris SL	Kythnos. Serifos. Sifnos. Milos.
08.15	Express Olympia	Paros. Naxos. Ios. Santorini.
11.00	Ionian Sea	Syros. Paros. Naxos. Amorgos (Egiali). Amorgos (Katapola).
14.00	Ergina	Syros. Paros. Naxos. Iraklia. Schinoussa. Koufonissia. Amorgos (Katapola). Amorgos (Egiali). Astipalea.
18.00	Georgios Express	Kythnos. Serifos. Sifnos. Kimolos. Milos.
18.15	Poseidon Express	Paros. Naxos. Ios. Santorini.
20.00	Apollo Express 1	Paros. Naxos. Ios. Santorini.
20.00	Samaina	Ikaria (Agios Kyrikos). Samos (Karlovassi). Samos (Vathi).
21.00	Panagia Tinou 2	Mykonos. Syros.
22.00	Express Santorini	Paros. Naxos. Ios. Santorini.
22.00	Golden Vergina	Paros. Ikaria (Evdilos). Samos (Karlovassi). Samos (Vathi).
23.45	Marina	Patmos. Leros. Kalimnos. Kos. Rhodes.
24.00	Sappho	Chios. Lesbos (Mytilini).

Piraeus (Great Harbour):

2. Saronic Gulf

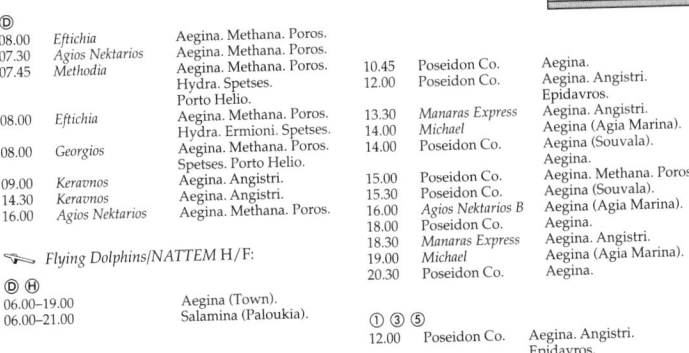

Ⓓ

08.00	*Eftichia*	Aegina. Methana. Poros.
07.30	*Agios Nektarios*	Aegina. Methana. Poros.
07.45	*Methodia*	Aegina. Methana. Poros. Hydra. Spetses. Porto Helio.
08.00	*Eftichia*	Aegina. Methana. Poros. Hydra. Ermioni. Spetses.
08.00	*Georgios*	Aegina. Methana. Poros. Spetses. Porto Helio.
09.00	*Keravnos*	Aegina. Angistri.
14.30	*Keravnos*	Aegina. Angistri.
16.00	*Agios Nektarios*	Aegina. Methana. Poros.

🜚 *Flying Dolphins/NATTEM H/F:*

Ⓓ Ⓗ

06.00–19.00	Aegina (Town).
06.00–21.00	Salamina (Paloukia).

○ Typical daily ferry departures:

06.30	Poseidon Co.	Aegina (Souvala).
06.30	Poseidon Co.	Aegina (Souvala).
07.30	Poseidon Co.	Aegina. Methana. Poros.
08.00	Manaras Express	Aegina. Angistri.
08.00	*Elvira*	Aegina (Agia Marina).
09.15	Poseidon Co.	Aegina (Souvala). Aegina.
09.30	*Agios Nektarios B*	Aegina (Agia Marina).
10.30	Poseidon Co.	Aegina. Methana. Poros.

10.45	Poseidon Co.	Aegina.
12.00	Poseidon Co.	Aegina. Angistri. Epidavros.
13.30	*Manaras Express*	Aegina. Angistri.
14.00	*Michael*	Aegina (Agia Marina).
14.00	Poseidon Co.	Aegina (Souvala).
15.00	Poseidon Co.	Aegina. Methana. Poros.
15.30	Poseidon Co.	Aegina (Souvala).
16.00	*Agios Nektarios B*	Aegina (Agia Marina).
18.00	Poseidon Co.	Aegina.
18.30	*Manaras Express*	Aegina. Angistri.
19.00	*Michael*	Aegina (Agia Marina).
20.30	Poseidon Co.	Aegina.

① ③ ⑤

12.00	Poseidon Co.	Aegina. Angistri. Epidavros.

Weekends sees additional services including:

⑥

09.15	Poseidon Co.	Aegina. Angistri. Epidavros.

⑦

09.30	Poseidon Co.	Aegina. Angistri. Epidavros.
14.30	Poseidon Co.	Aegina. Angistri. Epidavros.

Piraeus (Zea Marina)

Athens & Piraeus   p. 124

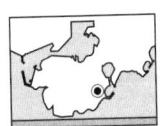

🜚 *Flying Dolphins* include:

Ⓓ

x 12	Hydra.
x 12	Poros.
x 12	Spetses.
08.00	Poros. Hydra. Ermioni.
08.25	Hydra. Spetses. Porto Helio.
09.00	Aegina (Town). Methana. Poros. Hydra. Ermioni. Spetses. Porto Helio. [① ② ③ ④ Leonidio].
09.00	Kea. Kythnos.
10.00	Poros. Hydra. Spetses. Porto Helio.
12.00	Poros. Hydra.
13.45	Poros. Hydra. Ermioni.
14.30	Hydra. Spetses. Porto Helio.
16.00	Aegina (Town). Methana. Poros. Hydra. Ermioni. Spetses. Porto Helio. Tolo. Nafplio [ex ⑦].

① ④ ⑥ ⑦

08.15	Spetses. Monemvassia. Kithera (Agia Pelagia).

③

08.15	Aegina. Methana. Poros. Ermioni. Leonidio. Kiparissi. Monemvassia. Kithera (Agia Pelagia).

Poros

Argo-Saronic p. 376

Ⓓ ev 20 min:
06.00–22.00 *Elpis I* Galatas.

Ⓓ
10.30 *Eftichia* Hydra. Ermioni. Spetses.
10.45 Poseidon Co. Methana. Aegina. Piraeus.
10.50 *Agios Nektarios* Methana. Aegina. Piraeus.
10.50 *Georgios* Spetses. Porto Helio.
11.00 *Methodia* Hydra. Spetses. Porto Helio.
14.00 Poseidon Co. Methana. Aegina. Piraeus.
16.00 *Methodia* Methana. Aegina. Piraeus.
16.40 *Eftichia* Methana. Aegina. Piraeus.
17.00 *Georgios* Methana. Aegina. Piraeus.
18.00 Poseidon Co. [⑦ 16.20] Methana. Aegina. Piraeus.
19.00 *Agios Nektarios* Methana. Aegina. Piraeus.

① ② ③ ④ ⑤
06.30 *Poros Express* Methana. Aegina. Piraeus.

⑥ ⑦
07.00 Poseidon Co. Methana. Aegina. Piraeus.
10.00 *Poros Express* Methana. Aegina. Piraeus.
19.00 *Poros Express* Methana. Aegina. Piraeus.

⌁ *Flying Dolphins* include:
Ⓓ
x 6 Hydra
x 7 Piraeus (Zea).
x 4 Spetses.

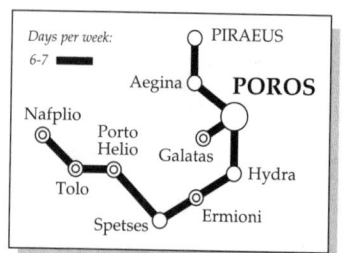

Days per week:
6-7 ▬▬

PIRAEUS
Aegina
POROS
Nafplio
Porto Helio
Galatas
Tolo
Hydra
Spetses
Ermioni

Port Said

Egypt p. 69

①
20.30 *Princesa Amorosa* Ashdod. Limassol.

②
19.30 *Vergina Sky* Rhodes. Mykonos. Thessalonika.
20.00 *Princesa Marissa* Limassol. Haifa.

④
20.00 *Princesa Amorosa* Limassol.

⑤
20.00 *Princesa Marissa* Limassol. Haifa.

⑥
20.00 *Princesa Amorosa* Limassol.

Porto Helio

Argo-Saronic
p. 379

Ⓓ
13.30 *Methodia* Spetses. Hydra. Poros. Methana. Aegina. Piraeus.

⌁ *Flying Dolphins* include:

Ⓓ x 6 Hydra. Spetses. Piraeus (Zea).

Princes' Islands

Turkey p. 422

Ⓓ x 6
06.45–21.00 TML İstanbul.
00.00–00.00 TML Yalova.

Psara

Eastern Line p. 315

② ④ ⑥
12.00 *Psara* Chios.

○
00.00 *Nissos Chios* Chios. Piraeus.

Rafina

Athens & Piraeus   p. 126

Ⓓ
| 07.45 | ILIO H/F | Evia (Nea Styra). |

①
05.50	Catamaran II	Andros (Batsi). Tinos. Mykonos.
06.10	ILIO H/F	Syros. Tinos. Mykonos. Paros. Naxos. Ios. Santorini.
08.00	ILIO H/F	Kea. Kythnos. Serifos. Sifnos. Kimolos. Milos.
08.00	ILIO H/F	Andros (Batsi). Tinos. Mykonos.
08.00	Penelope A	Andros. Tinos. Mykonos.
08.30	Marmari I	Evia (Marmari).
10.00	Karistos	Evia (Karystos).
10.45	ILIO H/F	Andros (Batsi). Tinos. Mykonos.
13.00	Bari Express	Andros. Tinos. Mykonos.
15.00	Marmari I	Evia (Marmari).
15.45	ILIO H/F	Evia (Nea Styra). (Aliveri). Skala Oropou.
16.45	Catamaran II	Andros (Batsi). Tinos. Mykonos.
16.45	ILIO H/F	Andros (Batsi). Tinos. Mykonos. Paros. Naxos.
17.00	Super Ferry	Andros. Tinos. Mykonos.
17.15	Karistos	Evia (Karystos).
18.30	Marmari I	Evia (Marmari).
19.00	Nissos Chios	Agios Efstratios. Limnos.
19.30	ILIO H/F	Evia (Marmari). (Karystos).

②
| 08.00 | ILIO H/F | Andros (Batsi). Tinos. Mykonos. Paros. Naxos. |
| 08.00 | Penelope A | Andros. Tinos. Mykonos. |

Kavala
Limnos
Ag. Efstratios
RAFINA
Evia (Marmari)
Evia (Karystos)
Syros
Andros
Paros
Tinos
Naxos
Mykonos
Little Cyclades
Amorgos

Days per week:
6-7
2-3

08.05	Catamaran II	Andros (Batsi). Tinos. Mykonos.
08.30	Marmari I	Evia (Marmari).
10.00	Karistos	Evia (Karystos).
13.00	Bari Express	Andros. Tinos. Mykonos.
15.00	Marmari I	Evia (Marmari).
16.45	Catamaran II	Andros (Batsi). Tinos. Mykonos.
17.00	Super Ferry	Andros. Tinos. Mykonos.
17.30	Karistos	Evia (Karystos).
18.15	ILIO H/F	Evia (Nea Styra).
18.30	Marmari I	Evia (Marmari).
19.15	ILIO H/F	Evia (Nea Styra). Evia (Aliveri).
19.30	ILIO H/F	Evia (Karystos).

③
08.00	ILIO H/F	Andros (Batsi). Tinos. Mykonos.
08.00	Penelope A	Andros. Tinos. Mykonos.
08.05	Catamaran II	Andros (Batsi). Tinos. Mykonos. Syros. Paros. Naxos. Iraklia. Schinoussa. Koufonissia. Amorgos (Katapola).
08.30	Marmari I	Evia (Marmari).
10.00	Karistos	Evia (Karystos).
10.45	ILIO H/F	Evia (Karystos). Andros (Batsi). Tinos. Mykonos.
13.00	Bari Express	Andros. Tinos. Mykonos.
15.00	Marmari I	Evia (Marmari).
16.45	ILIO H/F	Andros (Batsi). Tinos. Mykonos. Paros. Naxos.
17.00	Super Ferry	Andros. Mykonos.
17.15	Karistos	Evia (Karystos).
18.30	Marmari I	Evia (Marmari).
19.15	ILIO H/F	Evia (Nea Styra). Skala Oropou. Evia (Chalcis).
19.30	ILIO H/F	Evia (Karystos).

④
08.00	ILIO H/F	Andros (Batsi). Tinos. Mykonos. Paros. Naxos. Iraklia. Schinoussa. Koufonissia. Amorgos (Egiali).
08.00	Super Ferry	Andros. Tinos. Mykonos.
08.05	Catamaran II	Andros (Batsi). Tinos. Mykonos.
08.30	Marmari I	Evia (Marmari).
10.00	Karistos	Evia (Karystos).
15.00	Marmari I	Evia (Marmari).
16.45	Catamaran II	Andros (Batsi). Tinos. Mykonos.
17.00	Penelope A	Andros. Tinos. Mykonos.
17.15	Karistos	Evia (Karystos).
18.15	ILIO H/F	Evia (Nea Styra).
18.30	Marmari I	Evia (Marmari).
18.30	Super Ferry	Andros. Tinos. Mykonos.
19.30	ILIO H/F	Evia (Karystos).
20.15	ILIO H/F	Skala Oropou. Evia (Chalcis).

⑤
07.30	Bari Express	Andros.
08.00	ILIO H/F	Andros (Batsi). Tinos. Mykonos. Paros. Naxos.
08.00	Super Ferry	Andros. Tinos. Mykonos.
08.05	Catamaran II	Andros (Batsi). Tinos. Mykonos.
08.30	Marmari I	Evia (Marmari).

09.15	*Karistos*	Evia (Karystos).
10.45	ILIO H/F	Andros (Batsi). Tinos. Mykonos.
14.30	*Marmari I*	Evia (Karystos). (Marmari).
16.30	*Bari Express*	Andros.
16.45	*Catamaran II*	Andros (Batsi). Tinos. Mykonos.
16.45	ILIO H/F	Evia (Karystos).
17.15	ILIO H/F	Mykonos. Tinos. Skala Oropou. Evia (Chalcis).
18.30	*Karistos*	Evia (Karystos).
19.00	*Alcaeos*	Agios. Efstratios. Limnos. Kavala.
19.30	*Marmari I*	Evia (Marmari).

⑥
07.00	*Bari Express*	Andros. Tinos.
07.30	*Penelope A*	Andros. Tinos.
08.00	ILIO H/F	Andros (Batsi). Tinos. Mykonos. Paros. Naxos.
08.00	*Super Ferry*	Andros. Tinos. Mykonos.
08.05	*Catamaran II*	Andros (Batsi). Tinos. Mykonos.
08.15	*Marmari I*	Evia (Karystos). Evia (Marmari).
09.00	ILIO H/F	Evia (Karystos). Tinos. Mykonos.
11.30	*Karistos*	Evia (Karystos).
15.00	*Marmari I*	Evia (Marmari).
16.30	ILIO H/F	Tinos. Mykonos.
16.45	*Catamaran II*	Andros (Batsi). Tinos. Mykonos.
17.00	*Karistos*	Evia (Karystos).
17.00	*Penelope A*	Andros. Tinos. Mykonos.

18.15	ILIO H/F	Andros (Batsi). Tinos (Isternia). Tinos. Mykonos.
18.30	ILIO H/F	Evia (Marmari). Evia (Karystos). Rafina.
18.30	*Marmari I*	Evia (Marmari).
22.00	*Nissos Chios*	Agios Efstratios. Limnos. Kavala.

⑦
07.30	*Bari Express*	Andros. Tinos.
08.00	ILIO H/F	Andros (Batsi). Tinos. Mykonos. Paros. Naxos.
08.00	*Super Ferry*	Andros. Tinos. Mykonos.
08.05	*Catamaran II*	Andros (Batsi). Tinos. Mykonos.
08.30	*Marmari I*	Evia (Marmari).
09.00	ILIO H/F	Tinos. Mykonos.
09.30	*Karistos*	Evia (Karystos).
15.30	*Marmari I*	Evia (Marmari).
16.15	ILIO H/F	Syros. Mykonos. Tinos.
16.45	*Catamaran II*	Andros (Batsi). Tinos. Mykonos.
16.45	*Karistos*	Evia (Karystos).
17.30	*Bari Express*	Mykonos. Tinos.
17.30	*Penelope A*	Andros. Tinos. Mykonos.
19.00	*Marmari I*	Evia (Marmari).
19.00	*Super Ferry*	Andros.
20.00	*Penelope A*	Andros.
21.05	ILIO H/F	Andros (Batsi). Syros.
21.30	*Karistos*	Evia (Karystos).
22.00	*Marmari I*	Evia (Marmari).
24.00	*Super Ferry*	Mykonos.

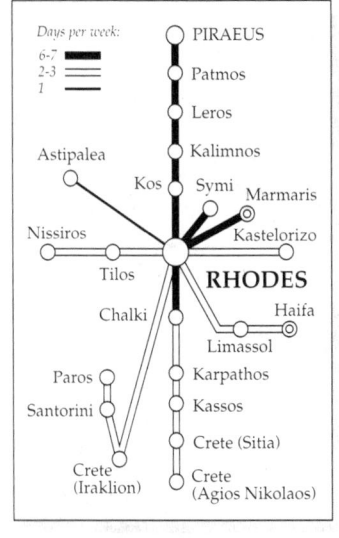

Days per week:
6-7
2-3
1

PIRAEUS
Patmos
Leros
Kalimnos
Astipalea
Kos
Symi
Marmaris
Nissiros
Kastelorizo
Tilos
RHODES
Chalki
Haifa
Limassol
Paros
Karpathos
Santorini
Kassos
Crete (Sitia)
Crete (Iraklion)
Crete (Agios Nikolaos)

Rhodes

Dodecanese   p. 287

International Services:

Ⓓ
| 08.00 | Hydrofoil | Marmaris. |
| 17.00 | *Deniz Turk* | Marmaris. |

②
12.00	*Sea Wave*	Piraeus.
14.00	*Nissos Kypros*	Piraeus.
22.00	*Sea Harmony*	Limassol. Haifa.

⑤
| 14.00 | *Sea Wave* | Limassol. Haifa. |
| 16.00 | *Nissos Kypros* | Limassol. Haifa. |

⑥
| 03.00 | *Sea Harmony* | Piraeus. |
| 17.00 | *Rodos* | Cyprus (Limassol). |

⑦
| 15.00 | *Princessa Cypria* | Lesbos (Mytilini). Tinos. Piraeus. |

Domestic Services:

Ⓓ
08.00	Hydrofoil	Kos.
09.00	*Symi II*	Symi.
18.00	Hydrofoil	Kos.

①		
10.00	ILIO H/F	Symi. Kos.
13.00	*Ialyssos*	Kos. Kalimnos. Leros. Patmos. Piraeus.
15.30	*Nissos Kalimnos*	Kastelorizo.
17.00	*Rodos*	Piraeus.
18.00	*Marina*	Kos. Kalimnos. Leros. Patmos. Piraeus.
②		
10.00	*Nissos Kalimnos*	Symi. Tilos. Nissiros. Kos. Kalimnos.
12.00	*Kamiros*	Kos. Kalimnos. Leros. Patmos. Piraeus.
12.00	*Romilda*	Kastelorizo.
15.15	ILIO H/F	Tilos. Symi. Nissiros. Kos. Kalimnos.
15.30	*Ionian Sea*	Kos. Paros. Piraeus.
16.00	*Rodanthi*	Kos. Piraeus.
17.00	*Patmos*	Kos. Piraeus.
18.00	*Symi I*	Symi.
23.45	*Romilda*	Symi. Tilos. Nissiros. Kos. Kalimnos. Leros. Lipsi. Patmos. Naxos. Paros. Syros. Piraeus.
③		
10.00	ILIO H/F	Symi. Nissiros. Kos.
12.00	*Ialyssos*	Kos. Kalimnos. Leros. Patmos. Piraeus.
15.00	Ventouris SL	Chalki. Karpathos (Diafani). Karpathos (Town). Kassos. Crete (Sitia). Crete (Agios Nikolaos). Santorini. Sikinos. Folegandros. Milos. Sifnos. Piraeus.
16.00	*Marina*	Kos. Kalimnos. Piraeus.
18.00	ILIO H/F	Kos. Kalimnos.
18.00	*Symi I*	Symi.
20.00	*Daliana*	Karpathos (Town). Crete (Iraklion). Santorini. Naxos. Paros. Piraeus.
④		
10.00	ILIO H/F	Symi. Kos.
12.00	*Kamiros*	Kos. Kalimnos. Leros. Patmos. Piraeus.
15.30	*Ionian Sea*	Kos. Paros. Piraeus.
16.00	*Rodanthi*	Kos. Kalimnos. Piraeus.
17.00	*Patmos*	Kos. Piraeus
17.00	*Rodos*	Piraeus.
18.00	ILIO H/F	Symi. Kos. Kalimnos.
⑤		
10.00	ILIO H/F	Nissiros. Kos.
11.30	*Patmos*	Kos. Thessalonika.
12.00	*Ialyssos*	Kos. Kalimnos. Leros. Patmos. Piraeus.
15.30	*Nissos Kalimnos*	Kastelorizo.
16.00	*Marina*	Kos. Kalimnos. Piraeus.
17.00	*Symi I*	Symi.
⑥		
08.00	*Rodanthi*	Kos. Paros. Piraeus.
10.00	*Nissos Kalimnos*	Symi. Tilos. Nissiros. Kos. Kalimnos.
12.00	*Kamiros*	Kos. Kalimnos. Leros. Patmos. Piraeus.
13.00	*Ionian Sea*	Tilos. Nissiros. Kos. Kalimnos. Astipalea. Paros. Syros. Piraeus.
18.00	*Symi I*	Symi.
20.00	*Daliana*	Karpathos (Town). Crete (Iraklion). Santorini. Paros. Piraeus.
⑦		
10.00	*Ialyssos*	Chalki. Karpathos (Town). Crete (Iraklion).
10.00	ILIO H/F	Chalki. Tilos.
17.00	*Patmos*	Kos. Piraeus.
17.20	ILIO H/F	Symi.
18.00	*Rodanthi*	Kos. Patmos. Piraeus.
18.00	*Symi I*	Symi.
19.15	ILIO H/F	Kos. Kalimnos.

Rhodes (Kamiros)

Dodecanese p. 288

⑩		
14.30	*Chalki*	Chalki.

Salamina / Salamis (Paloukia)

Athens & Piraeus p. 127

⑩ ⑪		
06.30–21.30	NATTEM H/F	Piraeus.

Samos (Karlovassi)

Eastern Line p. 317

①		
07.00	*Samaina*	Samos (Vathi).
07.40	ILIO H/F	Ikaria (Agios Kyrikos). Patmos. Lipsi. Leros. Kalimnos. Kos.
08.05	*Golden Vergina*	Samos (Vathi).
10.25	*Samaina*	Ikaria (Agios Kyrikos). Ikaria (Evdilos). Piraeus.
11.30	*Capetan Stamatis*	Samos (Vathi). Fourni. Ikaria (Agios Kyrikos).
17.10	*Golden Vergina*	Ikaria (Evdilos). Paros. Piraeus.
18.00	ILIO H/F	Samos (Vathi).
21.00	*Capetan Stamatis*	Chios.
②		
06.30	*Milena*	Samos (Vathi).
17.00	*Milena*	Fourni. Ikaria (Agios Kyrikos). Naxos. Paros. Piraeus.
20.00	*Samaina*	Samos (Vathi).

③
02.45	Golden Vergina	Samos (Vathi).
05.15	Dimitra	Samos (Vathi).
07.15	Dimitra	Fourni. Ikaria (Agios Kyrikos). Mykonos. Syros. Piraeus.
07.15	Golden Vergina	Ikaria (Agios Kyrikos). Paros. Piraeus.
19.20	Samaina	Ikaria (Agios Kyrikos). Ikaria (Evdilos). Piraeus.

④
05.30	Milena	Samos (Vathi).
06.40	Golden Vergina	Samos (Vathi).
11.30	Capetan Stamatis	Samos (Vathi). Fourni. Ikaria (Agios Kyrikos).
17.00	Milena	Ikaria (Agios Kyrikos). Naxos. Paros. Piraeus.
17.10	Golden Vergina	Fourni. Ikaria (Agios Kyrikos). Paros. Piraeus.
17.30	ILIO H/F	Samos (Vathi). Chios. Lesbos (Mytilini).
20.00	Samaina	Samos (Vathi).

⑤
07.40	ILIO H/F	Ikaria (Agios Kyrikos). Patmos. Lipsi. Leros. Kalimnos. Kos.
18.00	ILIO H/F	Samos (Vathi).
19.20	Samaina	Ikaria (Agios Kyrikos). Piraeus.

⑥
03.45	Golden Vergina	Samos (Vathi).
05.00	Milena	Samos (Vathi).
07.40	Golden Vergina	Ikaria (Evdilos). Paros. Piraeus.
08.00	Milena	Fourni. Ikaria (Agios Kyrikos). Naxos. Piraeus.
20.00	Samaina	Samos (Vathi).

⑦
06.15	Golden Vergina	Samos (Vathi).
08.15	Samaina	Ikaria (Agios Kyrikos). Ikaira (Karkinagri). Piraeus.
09.10	Golden Vergina	Ikaria (Evdilos). Paros. Piraeus.
12.00	Milena	Samos (Vathi).
17.00	Milena	Fourni. Ikaria (Agios Kyrikos). Naxos. Paros. Piraeus.

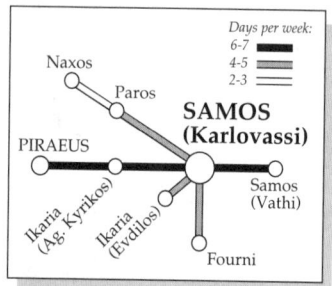

SAMOS
(Karlovassi)

Days per week:
6-7
4-5
2-3

Naxos
Paros
PIRAEUS
Ikaria (Ag. Kyrikos)
Ikaria (Evdilos)
Samos (Vathi)
Fourni

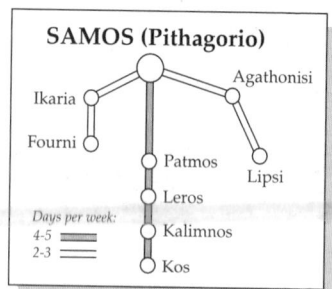

SAMOS (Pithagorio)

Ikaria
Fourni
Agathonisi
Patmos
Lipsi
Leros
Kalimnos
Kos

Days per week:
4-5
2-3

Samos (Pithagorio)

Eastern Line   p. 317

○
| 09.00 | Cassandra | Patmos. |

②
| 07.30 | ILIO H/F | Patmos. Lipsi. Leros (Agia Marina). Kalimnos. Kos. |
| 17.10 | ILIO H/F | Samos (Vathi). |

③
| 07.00 | ILIO H/F | Agathonisi. Kos. Kalimnos. Leros (Agia Marina). Patmos. |
| 17.00 | Nissos Kalimnos | Agathonisi. Patmos. Lipsi. Leros. Kalimnos. Kos. |

④
07.30	ILIO H/F	Patmos. Lipsi. Leros (Agia Marina). Kalimnos. Kos.
08.00	Chioni	Agathonisi. Arki. Lipsi. Patmos.
16.00	Chioni	Chios.

⑥
| 07.00 | ILIO H/F | Patmos. Kos. Kalimnos. Leros (Agia Marina). |

⑦
07.00	ILIO H/F	Kos. Kalimnos. Leros (Agia Marina). Patmos.
10.25	ILIO H/F	Patmos.
14.35	Nissos Kalimnos	Agathonisi. Patmos. Lipsi. Leros. Kalimnos. Kos.
17.00	Hydrofoil	Patmos. Leros. Kos.
17.35	ILIO H/F	Chios. Lesbos (Mytilini).
20.00	ILIO H/F	Samos (Vathi).

Samos
(Vathi)

Eastern Line p. 316

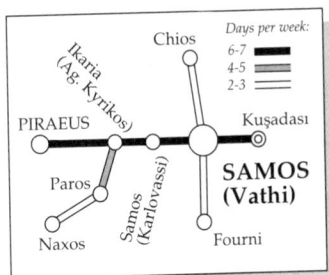

Ⓓ
08.00	*Kapetan Giorgis*	Kuşadası.
17.00	*Fari Kaptain/Sultan I*	Kuşadası.

①
07.00	ILIO H/F	Samos (Karlovassi). Ikaria (Agios Kyrikos). Patmos. Lipsi. Leros. Kalimnos. Kos.
09.00	*Samaina*	Samos (Karlovassi). Ikaria (Agios Kyrikos). Ikaria (Evdilos). Piraeus.
12.30	*Capetan Stamatis*	Fourni. Ikaria (Agios Kyrikos).
16.00	*Golden Vergina*	Samos (Karlovassi). Ikaria (Evdilos). Paros. Piraeus.
20.00	*Capetan Stamatis*	Samos (Karlovassi). Chios.

②
10.40	ILIO H/F	Patmos.
16.00	*Milena*	Samos (Karlovassi). Fourni. Ikaria (Agios Kyrikos). Naxos. Paros. Piraeus.
18.15	ILIO H/F	Chios. Lesbos (Mytilini).

③
06.00	*Dimitra*	Samos (Karlovassi). Fourni. Ikaria (Agios Kyrikos). Mykonos. Syros. Piraeus.
06.00	*Golden Vergina*	Samos (Karlovassi). Ikaria (Agios Kyrikos). Paros. Piraeus.
18.00	*Samaina*	Samos (Karlovassi). Ikaria (Agios Kyrikos). Ikaria (Evdilos). Piraeus.

④
06.15	ILIO H/F	Samos (Pithagorio). Patmos. Lipsi. Leros. Kalimnos. Kos.
10.40	ILIO H/F	Samos (Karlovassi). Ikaria (Agios Kyrikos). Patmos.
12.30	*Capetan Stamatis*	Fourni. Ikaria (Agios Kyrikos).
15.30	*Golden Vergina*	Samos (Karlovassi). Fourni. Ikaria (Agios Kyrikos). Paros. Piraeus.
16.00	*Milena*	Samos (Karlovassi). Ikaria (Agios Kyrikos). Naxos. Paros. Piraeus.
18.15	ILIO H/F	Chios. Lesbos (Mytilini).
20.00	*Capetan Stamatis*	Samos (Karlovassi). Chios.
21.00	*Samaina*	Ikaria (Agios Kyrikos). Piraeus.

⑤
07.00	ILIO H/F	Samos (Karlovassi). Ikaria (Agios Kyrikos). Patmos. Lipsi. Leros. Kalimnos. Kos.
18.00	*Samaina*	Samos (Karlovassi). Ikaria (Agios Kyrikos). Piraeus.

⑥
06.20	ILIO H/F	Samos (Pithagorio). Patmos. Kos. Kalimnos. Leros.
06.30	*Golden Vergina*	Samos (Karlovassi). Ikaria (Evdilos). Paros. Piraeus.
07.00	*Milena*	Samos (Karlovassi). Fourni. Ikaria (Agios Kyrikos). Naxos. Piraeus.
10.40	ILIO H/F	Patmos.
18.00	ILIO H/F	Chios. Lesbos (Mytilini).

⑦
07.00	*Samaina*	Samos (Karlovassi). Ikaria (Agios Kyrikos). Ikaira (Karkinagri). Piraeus.
07.30	*Alcaeos*	Patmos.
08.00	*Golden Vergina*	Samos (Karlovassi). Ikaria (Evdilos). Paros. Piraeus.
15.30	*Alcaeos*	Chios. Lesbos (Mytilini). Limnos. Thessalonika.
16.00	*Milena*	Samos (Karlovassi). Fourni. Ikaria (Agios Kyrikos). Naxos. Paros. Piraeus.

Samothrace

Northern Aegean
p. 337

①
11.30	*Saos*	Alexandroupolis.
15.00	*Arsinoe*	Alexandroupolis.
19.00	*Saos*	Alexandroupolis.

②
10.00	*Saos*	Limnos.
12.30	*Arsinoe*	Kavala.
20.00	*Saos*	Alexandroupolis.

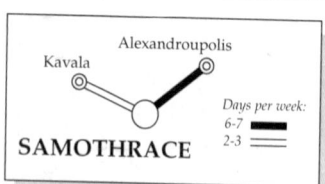

SAMOTHRACE

Kavala — Alexandroupolis

Days per week:
6-7 ▬
2-3 ═

③
08.00	Arsinoe	Kavala.
13.00	Saos	Alexandroupolis.
19.30	Arsinoe	Alexandroupolis.

④
09.00	Saos	Alexandroupolis.
15.00	Arsinoe	Alexandroupolis.
19.00	Saos	Alexandroupolis.

⑤
11.30	Arsinoe	Kavala.
13.30	Saos	Alexandroupolis.
20.30	Saos	Alexandroupolis.

⑥
09.00	Arsinoe	Kavala.
11.30	Saos	Alexandroupolis.
19.00	Saos	Alexandroupolis.

⑦
08.30	Arsinoe	Alexandroupolis.
14.00	Saos	Alexandroupolis.
16.00	Arsinoe	Kavala.
20.00	Saos	Alexandroupolis.

Santorini / Thira (Athinios)

Cyclades Central
p. 158

Ⓓ
| 09.00 | Mykonos Express | Ios. Naxos. Paros. Mykonos. |
| 10.00 | Theoskepasti | Santorini (Old Port). Nea Kameni. Thirasia (Korfos). Thirasia. Santorini (Oia). |

①
07.30	Poseidon Express	Ios. Naxos. Paros. Piraeus.
08.00	Apollo Express 1	Ios. Naxos. Paros. Piraeus.
09.40	Daliana	Crete (Iraklion).
10.00	Express Santorini	Ios. Naxos. Paros. Piraeus.
11.15	Nearchos	Ios. Paros. Naxos.
15.30	Express Paros	Ios. Naxos. Paros. Mykonos.
17.00	ILIO H/F	Ios. Naxos. Paros. Mykonos. Tinos. Syros.
18.30	Nearchos	Crete (Iraklion).
19.00	Express Olympia	Ios. Naxos. Paros. Piraeus.
19.15	Apollo Express 2	Ios. Naxos. Paros. Piraeus.
20.15	Daliana	Naxos. Paros. Piraeus.

②
07.30	Milos Express	Ios. Sikinos. Folegandros. Kimolos. Milos. Sifnos. Serifos. Kythnos. Piraeus.
07.30	Poseidon Express	Ios. Naxos. Paros. Piraeus.
08.00	Express Santorini	Anafi.
10.00	Express Santorini	Ios. Naxos. Paros. Syros. Piraeus.
11.15	Nearchos	Ios. Paros. Syros.
11.30	ILIO H/F	Anafi.
13.00	Anemos	Crete (Iraklion).
17.00	ILIO H/F	Ios. Naxos. Paros. Mykonos. Tinos. Syros.
18.45	Nearchos	Crete (Iraklion).
19.00	Express Olympia	Ios. Naxos. Paros. Piraeus.
19.15	Apollo Express 1	Ios. Naxos. Paros. Piraeus.
19.30	Ventouris SL	Crete (Agios Nikolaos). Crete (Sitia). Kassos. Karpathos (Town). Karpathos (Diafani). Chalki. Symi. Rhodes.
23.25	Anemos	Paros. Mykonos. Tinos. Skiathos. Thessalonika.

③
01.30	Daliana	Crete (Iraklion). Karpathos (Town). Rhodes.
07.30	ILIO H/F	Ios. Kuşadası.
07.30	Poseidon Express	Ios. Naxos. Paros. Piraeus.
08.00	Apollo Express 2	Ios. Naxos. Paros. Piraeus.
11.15	Nearchos	Ios. Paros. Mykonos.
11.30	ILIO H/F	Iraklia. Schinoussa. Koufonissia. Amorgos (Egiali). Amorgos (Katapola).
15.30	Express Paros	Ios. Sikinos. Folegandros. Sifnos. Paros. Mykonos.
17.00	Express Santorini	Anafi.
17.00	ILIO H/F	Ios. Naxos. Paros. Mykonos. Tinos. Syros.
18.30	Nearchos	Crete (Iraklion).
19.00	Express Santorini	Ios. Naxos. Paros. Piraeus.
19.15	Apollo Express 1	Ios. Naxos. Paros. Piraeus.

④
| 08.00 | Apollo Express 2 | Ios. Naxos. Paros. Piraeus. |
| 08.30 | Ventouris SL | Sikinos. Folegandros. Milos. Sifnos. Piraeus. |

11.15	*Nearchos*	Ios. Naxos. Paros.
13.00	*Daliana*	Naxos. Paros. Piraeus.
15.30	*Express Paros*	Ios. Naxos. Paros. Mykonos. Syros.
15.35	*Anemos*	Crete (Iraklion).
17.00	ILIO H/F	Ios. Naxos. Paros. Mykonos. Tinos. Syros.
17.30	*Nearchos*	Crete (Iraklion).
18.00	*Romilda*	Naxos. Paros. Piraeus.
19.15	*Apollo Express 1*	Ios. Naxos. Paros. Piraeus.
20.00	*Milos Express*	Folegandros. Kimolos. Milos. Sifnos. Serifos. Kythnos. Piraeus.

⑤

01.25	*Anemos*	Paros. Syros. Thessalonika.
02.15	*Ergina*	Milos. Nafplio.
07.30	*Poseidon Express*	Ios. Naxos. Paros. Piraeus.
08.00	*Apollo Express 2*	Ios. Naxos. Paros. Syros. Piraeus.
11.15	*Nearchos*	Ios. Paros. Mykonos.
15.30	*Express Paros*	Ios. Naxos. Paros. Mykonos.
17.00	ILIO H/F	Ios. Naxos. Paros. Mykonos. Tinos. Syros.
18.00	*Romilda*	Naxos. Paros. Piraeus.
18.30	*Nearchos*	Crete (Iraklion).
19.00	*Express Olympia*	Ios. Naxos. Paros. Piraeus.
19.15	*Ventouris SL*	Naxos. Paros. Piraeus.
21.55	*Ergina*	Amorgos (Katapola). Amorgos (Egiali). Naxos. Piraeus.

⑥

01.00	*Daliana*	Crete (Iraklion). Karpathos (Town). Rhodes.
03.15	*Apollo Express 1*	Anafi.
07.30	ILIO H/F	Ios. Kuşadası.
07.30	*Poseidon Express*	Ios. Naxos. Paros. Piraeus.
08.00	*Apollo Express 1*	Ios. Naxos. Paros. Piraeus.
10.00	*Express Santorini*	Ios. Naxos. Paros. Piraeus.
15.25	*Anemos*	Crete (Iraklion).
15.30	*Express Paros*	Ios. Naxos. Paros. Mykonos. Syros.
18.00	*Romilda*	Naxos. Paros. Piraeus.
19.00	*Express Olympia*	Ios. Naxos. Paros. Piraeus.
19.15	*Apollo Express 2*	Ios. Naxos. Paros. Piraeus.

⑦

01.25	*Anemos*	Paros. Mykonos. Tinos. Skiathos. Thessalonika.
07.15	*Poseidon Express*	Ios. Naxos. Paros. Piraeus.
07.30	ILIO H/F	Ios. Kuşadası.
08.00	*Apollo Express 1*	Ios. Naxos. Paros. Piraeus.
10.00	*Express Santorini*	Ios. Naxos. Paros. Piraeus.
11.15	*Nearchos*	Ios.
12.45	*Daliana*	Paros. Piraeus.
15.30	*Express Paros*	Ios. Naxos. Paros. Mykonos. Syros.
16.30	*Nearchos*	Crete (Iraklion).
18.00	*Romilda*	Folegandros. Sikinos. Naxos. Paros. Piraeus.
19.00	*Express Olympia*	Ios. Naxos. Paros. Piraeus.
19.15	*Apollo Express 2*	Ios. Naxos. Paros. Piraeus.

PIRAEUS — Thessalonika — Skiathos — Tinos — Syros — Mykonos — Serifos — Naxos — Sifnos — Paros — Foleg. — Ios — Sikinos — SANTORINI — Milos — Anafi — Thirasia — Rhodes — Karpathos — Crete (Iraklion).

Days per week:
6-7 ▬▬
4-5 ══
2-3 ═══

Santorini (Fira / Old Port)

Cyclades Central p. 159

Ⓓ

| 10.30 | *Theoskepasti* | Nea Kameni. Thirasia (Korfos). Thirasia (Riva). Santorini (Oia). |
| 16.50 | *Theoskepasti* | Santorini. |

Sarandë

Albania p. 89

② ⑥ ⑦

| 18.00 | *Patrakis/Sotirakis* | Corfu. |

Schinoussa

Eastern Cyclades p. 240

①
09.40	Ergina	Iraklia. Naxos. Paros. Syros. Piraeus.
10.15	Skopelitis	Iraklia. Naxos.
17.00	Skopelitis	Koufonissia. Donoussa. Amorgos (Egiali). Amorgos (Katapola).

②
| 07.45 | Skopelitis | Iraklia. Paros (Piso Livadi). Naxos. Mykonos. |
| 18.30 | Skopelitis | Koufonissia. Amorgos (Katapola). |

③
10.15	Skopelitis	Iraklia. Naxos.
12.30	ILIO H/F	Koufonissia. Amorgos (Egiali). Amorgos (Katapola).
13.10	Catamaran II	Koufonissia. Amorgos (Katapola).
15.10	ILIO H/F	Iraklia. Santorini. Ios. Naxos. Paros. Mykonos. Tinos. Syros.
16.20	Catamaran II	Iraklia. Naxos. Paros. Syros. Mykonos. Tinos. Andros. Rafina.
17.00	Skopelitis	Koufonissia. Donoussa. Amorgos (Egiali). Amorgos (Katapola).

④
07.45	Skopelitis	Iraklia. Paros (Piso Livadi). Naxos. Mykonos.
13.15	ILIO H/F	Koufonissia. Amorgos (Egiali). Koufonissia. Naxos. Paros. Mykonos. Tinos. Andros (Batsi). Rafina.
18.30	Skopelitis	Koufonissia. Amorgos (Katapola).

⑥
| 07.45 | Skopelitis | Iraklia. Paros (Piso Livadi). Naxos. Mykonos. |
| 18.30 | Skopelitis | Koufonissia. Amorgos (Katapola). |

```
        ○ PIRAEUS
                        Days per week:
              ● Mykonos    6-7  ▬▬▬
Paros                      4-5  ▭▭▭
       ○   ● Syros
                        ○ Donoussa
Naxos  ○  ○  ○
IRAKLIA
SCHINOUSSA      ○  Amorgos
KOUFONISSIA     (Katapola) (Egiali)
```

⑦
10.15	Skopelitis	Iraklia. Naxos.
17.00	Skopelitis	Koufonissia. Donoussa. Amorgos (Egiali). Amorgos (Katapola).
23.30	Ergina	Koufonissia. Amorgos (Katapola). Amorgos (Egiali). Astipalea.

Serifos

Cyclades West
p. 216

①
10.25	ILIO H/F	Sifnos. Kimolos. Milos.
12.20	Georgios Express	Sifnos. Kimolos. Milos.
15.30	ILIO H/F	Kythnos. Kea. Rafina.
18.15	Georgios Express	Kythnos. Piraeus.
19.40	Milos Express	Sifnos. Milos. Kimolos. Folegandros. Sikinos. Ios. Santorini.

②
15.20	Milos Express	Kythnos. Piraeus.
18.15	Georgios Express	Sifnos. Kimolos. Milos.
21.30	Express Paros	Syros.
23.00	Georgios Express	Kythnos. Piraeus.

③
12.30	Georgios Express	Sifnos. Milos.
12.40	Milos Express	Sifnos. Kimolos. Milos.
17.20	Milos Express	Kythnos. Piraeus.
19.00	Georgios Express	Kythnos. Piraeus.

④
12.30	Georgios Express	Sifnos.
12.40	Milos Express	Sifnos. Milos. Folegandros. Sikinos. Ios. Santorini.
15.00	Georgios Express	Kythnos. Piraeus.

⑤
01.30	Georgios Express	Sifnos. Kimolos. Milos. Piraeus.
01.40	Milos Express	Kythnos. Piraeus.
20.20	Georgios Express	Sifnos. Kimolos. Milos. Piraeus.
22.00	Milos Express	Sifnos. Milos. Piraeus.

⑥
12.40	Milos Express	Sifnos. Milos. Kimolos. Folegandros. Sikinos.
13.00	Georgios Express	Sifnos.
14.45	Georgios Express	Kythnos. Piraeus.

⑦
| 01.30 | Georgios Express | Sifnos. Kimolos. Milos. |
| 11.45 | Georgios Express | Kythnos. Piraeus. |

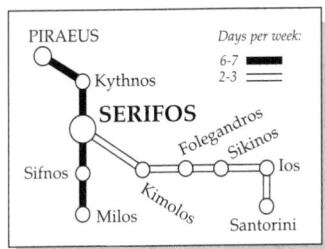

12.30	*Milos Express*	Sifnos. Milos.
12.55	Ventouris SL	Sifnos. Milos.
17.15	*Milos Express*	Kythnos. Piraeus.
18.30	Ventouris SL	Kythnos. Piraeus.
22.00	*Georgios Express*	Sifnos. Kimolos. Milos. Piraeus.

Sifnos

Cyclades West
p. 217

Ⓓ [① ③ ⑤ Out of July and August]
| 11.30 | *Margarita* | Paros. |

①
11.00	ILIO H/F	Kimolos. Milos.
13.30	*Georgios Express*	Kimolos. Milos.
15.00	ILIO H/F	Serifos. Kythnos. Kea. Rafina.
17.30	*Georgios Express*	Serifos. Kythnos. Piraeus.
20.35	*Milos Express*	Milos. Kimolos. Folegandros. Sikinos. Ios. Santorini.

②
12.45	Ventouris SL	Milos. Folegandros. Sikinos. Santorini. Crete (Agios Nikolaos). Crete (Sitia). Kassos. Karpathos (Town). Karpathos (Diafani). Chalki. Symi. Rhodes.
14.30	*Milos Express*	Serifos. Kythnos. Piraeus.
19.00	*Georgios Express*	Kimolos. Milos.
20.30	*Express Paros*	Serifos. Syros.
22.00	*Georgios Express*	Serifos. Kythnos. Piraeus.

③
05.10	*Ergina*	Nafplio.
13.30	*Milos Express*	Kimolos. Milos.
14.00	*Georgios Express*	Milos.
16.30	*Milos Express*	Serifos. Kythnos. Piraeus.

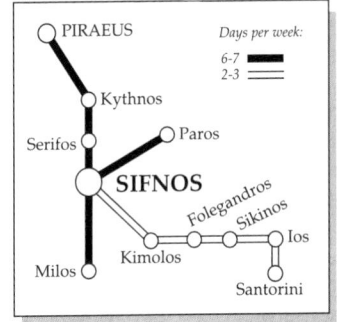

17.30	*Ergina*	Paros. Naxos. Amorgos (Katapola). Amorgos (Egiali). Mykonos. Piraeus.
18.00	*Georgios Express*	Serifos. Kythnos. Piraeus.
21.00	*Express Paros*	Paros. Mykonos.

④
13.55	*Milos Express*	Milos. Folegandros. Sikinos. Ios. Santorini.
14.15	*Georgios Express*	Serifos. Kythnos. Piraeus.
15.30	Ventouris SL	Piraeus.

⑤
00.55	*Milos Express*	Serifos. Kythnos. Piraeus.
02.30	*Georgios Express*	Kimolos. Milos. Piraeus.
21.00	*Georgios Express*	Kimolos. Milos. Piraeus.
22.50	*Milos Express*	Milos. Piraeus.

⑥
| 13.35 | *Milos Express* | Milos. Kimolos. Folegandros. Sikinos. |
| 13.40 | *Georgios Express* | Serifos. Kythnos. Piraeus. |

⑦
02.30	*Georgios Express*	Kimolos. Milos.
11.00	*Georgios Express*	Serifos. Kythnos. Piraeus.
13.15	*Milos Express*	Milos.
14.05	Ventouris SL	Milos.
16.00	*Milos Express*	Serifos. Kythnos. Piraeus.
17.30	Ventouris SL	Serifos. Kythnos. Piraeus.
23.30	*Georgios Express*	Kimolos. Milos. Piraeus.

Sikinos

Cyclades West
p. 220

Ⓓ
| 11.30 | *Delfini Express* | Folegandros. |
| 18.00 | *Delfini Express* | Ios. |

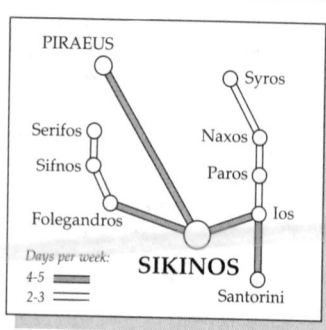

PIRAEUS

Syros

Serifos

Naxos

Sifnos

Paros

Folegandros

Ios

Days per week:
4-5
2-3

SIKINOS

Santorini

②		
01.15	*Milos Express*	Ios. Santorini.
09.15	*Milos Express*	Folegandros. Kimolos. Milos. Sifnos. Serifos. Kythnos. Piraeus.
18.00	*Express Paros*	Folegandros. Sifnos. Serifos. Syros.
18.00	*Ventouris SL*	Santorini. Crete (Agios Nikolaos). Crete (Sitia). Kassos. Karpathos (Town). Karpathos (Diafani). Chalki. Symi. Rhodes.
③		
18.00	*Express Paros*	Folegandros. Sifnos. Paros. Mykonos.
④		
10.25	*Ventouris SL*	Folegandros. Milos. Sifnos. Piraeus.

Thessalonikia

Volos

SKIATHOS

(Glossa)
Skopelos
Alonissos

Agios
Konstantinos

Skyros

Evia (Kimi)

Tinos

Mykonos

Days per week:
6-7
4-5
2-3

Paros

Santorini

Crete (Iraklion)

18.30	*Milos Express*	Ios. Santorini. Folegandros. Kimolos. Milos. Sifnos. Serifos. Kythnos. Piraeus.
⑤		
05.25	*Apollo Express 2*	Folegandros. Santorini. Ios. Naxos. Paros. Syros. Piraeus.
⑥		
18.30	*Milos Express*	Milos. Piraeus.
⑦		
04.40	*Apollo Express 1*	Folegandros. Santorini. Ios. Naxos. Paros. Piraeus.
20.15	*Romilda*	Naxos. Paros. Piraeus.

Skiathos

Northern Aegean p. 340

①		
08.30	*Lemnos*	Volos.
11.50	*Skopelos*	Skopelos (Glossa). Skopelos. Alonissos.
12.30	*Macedon*	Skopelos. Alonissos.
14.50	*Lemnos*	Skopelos (Glossa).
16.00	*Papadia. II*	Skopelos (Glossa).
16.15	*Lemnos*	Volos.
17.00	*Macedon*	Ag. Konstantinos.
17.30	*Papadia. II*	Volos.
18.50	*Skopelos*	Nisi. Volos.
22.20	*Lemnos*	Skopelos. Alonissos.
22.50	*Anemos*	Skyros. Tinos. Mykonos. Paros. Santorini. Crete (Iraklion).
②		
00.40	*Macedon*	Skopelos. Thessalonika.
10.45	*Lemnos*	Agios Konstantinos.
11.00	*Papadia. II*	Skopelos.
11.10	*Skopelos*	Skopelos.
14.15	*Papadia. II*	Volos.
14.40	*Skopelos*	Volos.
16.30	*Lemnos*	Skopelos (Glossa). Skopelos. Alonissos.
19.00	*Macedon*	Evia (Orei). Ag. Konstantinos.
20.20	*Papadia. II*	Skopelos (Glossa). Skopelos. Alonissos.
21.10	*Skopelos*	Skopelos. Alonissos.
③		
01.30	*Skopelos*	Volos.
08.00	*Papadia. II*	Volos.
08.20	*Lemnos*	Volos.
11.10	*Skopelos*	Skopelos (Glossa). Skopelos. Alonissos. Evia (Kimi).
12.35	*Anemos*	Thessalonika.
13.30	*Macedon*	Skopelos. Alonissos.
15.10	*Lemnos*	Skopelos.
15.30	*Papadia. II*	Skopelos (Glossa).
17.00	*Macedon*	Ag. Konstantinos.
17.10	*Papadia. II*	Volos.
17.30	*Lemnos*	Volos.
22.30	*Skopelos*	Volos.
23.20	*Lemnos*	Skopelos. Thessalonika.

Skopelos

Northern Aegean
p. 343

④

00.30	*Macedon*	Skopelos (Glossa). Skopelos.
08.00	*Macedon*	Ag. Konstantinos.
11.00	*Papadia. II*	Skopelos.
11.10	*Skopelos*	Skopelos.
14.00	*Skopelos*	Volos.
14.15	*Papadia. II*	Volos.
15.30	*Macedon*	Skopelos. Alonissos.
16.30	*Lemnos*	Volos.
20.20	*Papadia. II*	Skopelos (Glossa). Skopelos. Alonissos.
20.30	*Macedon*	Ag. Konstantinos.
20.30	*Skopelos*	Skopelos (Glossa). Skopelos. Alonissos.
22.10	*Lemnos*	Skopelos. Alonissos.

⑤

00.50	*Skopelos*	Volos.
08.00	*Papadia. II*	Volos.
08.30	*Lemnos*	Volos.
12.10	*Skopelos*	Skopelos (Glossa).
12.30	*Macedon*	Skopelos. Alonissos.
13.40	*Skopelos*	Volos.
14.50	*Lemnos*	Skopelos (Glossa).
15.30	*Papadia. II*	Skopelos (Glossa).
16.15	*Lemnos*	Volos.
17.00	*Macedon*	Ag. Konstantinos.
17.10	*Papadia. II*	Volos.
20.55	*Skopelos*	Skopelos (Glossa). Skopelos. Alonissos.
22.10	*Lemnos*	Skopelos. Thessalonika.

⑥

00.30	*Macedon*	Skopelos (Glossa). Skopelos.
07.00	*Macedon*	Ag. Konstantinos.
08.30	*Skopelos*	Volos.
14.30	*Macedon*	Skopelos.
16.00	*Lemnos*	Volos.
16.00	*Papadia. II*	Skopelos (Glossa). Skopelos. Alonissos.
16.10	*Skopelos*	Skopelos (Glossa). Skopelos. Alonissos. Evia (Kimi). Limnos.
17.40	*Macedon*	Ag. Konstantinos.
22.10	*Lemnos*	Skopelos. Alonissos.
00.00	*Anemos*	Tinos. Mykonos. Paros. Santorini. Crete (Iraklion).

⑦

01.00	*Macedon*	Skopelos. Alonissos.
08.00	*Macedon*	Ag. Konstantinos.
08.30	*Lemnos*	Volos.
12.35	*Anemos*	Thessalonika.
14.35	*Lemnos*	Skopelos (Glossa).
15.30	*Macedon*	Skopelos. Alonissos.
15.55	*Lemnos*	Nesi. Volos.
16.15	*Papadia. II*	Volos.
18.30	*Skopelos*	Volos.
20.30	*Macedon*	Ag. Konstantinos.
22.20	*Lemnos*	Skopelos. Alonissos.

⌁ *Flying Dolphins* include:

Ⓓ

07.50	Thessalonikia.
x 8	Volos / Agios Konstantinos.
x 8	Skopelos (Glossa). Skopelos. Alonissos.

Ⓓ ex ③ (High Season only)

09.40	Skopelos (Glossa). Skopelos. Alonissos. Skyros.

①

07.15	*Lemnos*	Skiathos. Volos.
13.30	*Macedon*	Alonissos.
14.00	*Skopelos*	Alonissos.
15.30	*Macedon*	Skiathos. Ag. Konstantinos.
15.45	*Skopelos*	Skopelos (Glossa). Skiathos. Nesi. Volos.
23.35	*Lemnos*	Alonissos.

②

02.00	*Macedon*	Thessalonika.
06.45	*Lemnos*	Skopelos (Glossa). Skiathos. Agios Konstantinos.
12.15	*Papadia. II*	Skopelos (Glossa). Skiathos. Volos.
12.30	*Skopelos*	Skopelos (Glossa). Skiathos. Volos.
17.20	*Macedon*	Skiathos. Evia (Orei). Ag. Konstantinos.
18.30	*Lemnos*	Alonissos.
22.30	*Papadia. II*	Alonissos.
22.30	*Skopelos*	Alonissos.

③

06.00	*Papadia. II*	Skopelos (Glossa). Skiathos. Volos.
07.00	*Lemnos*	Skiathos. Volos.
13.05	*Skopelos*	Alonissos. Evia (Kimi).
13.30	*Macedon*	Alonissos.
15.30	*Macedon*	Skiathos. Ag. Konstantinos.
16.20	*Lemnos*	Skiathos. Volos.
20.30	*Skopelos*	Skopelos (Glossa). Skiathos. Volos.

④

00.40	*Lemnos*	Thessalonika.
05.45	*Macedon*	Skopelos (Glossa). Skiathos. Ag. Konstantinos.
12.15	*Papadia. II*	Skopelos (Glossa). Skiathos. Volos.
12.30	*Skopelos*	Skiathos. Volos.
14.40	*Lemnos*	Skopelos (Glossa). Skiathos. Volos.
16.50	*Macedon*	Alonissos.

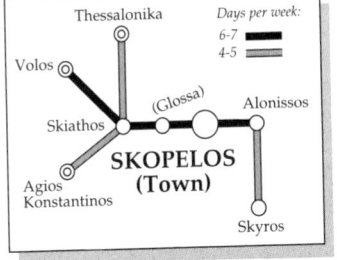

Thessalonika — Days per week:
6-7
4-5
Volos
Skiathos
(Glossa)
Alonissos
Agios Konstantinos
SKOPELOS (Town)
Skyros

18.50	*Macedon*	Skiathos. Ag. Konstantinos.
22.30	*Papadia. II*	Alonissos.
22.30	*Skopelos*	Alonissos. Skiathos. Volos.
23.20	*Lemnos*	Alonissos.

⑤
06.00	*Papadia. II*	Skopelos (Glossa). Skiathos. Volos.
07.15	*Lemnos*	Skiathos. Volos.
13.30	*Macedon*	Alonissos.
15.30	*Macedon*	Skiathos. Ag. Konstantinos.
22.50	*Skopelos*	Alonissos.
23.30	*Lemnos*	Thessalonika.

⑥
05.20	*Macedon*	Skiathos. Ag. Konstantinos.
06.15	*Skopelos*	Skopelos (Glossa). Skiathos. Volos.
14.40	*Lemnos*	Skiathos. Volos.
16.00	*Macedon*	Skiathos. Ag. Konstantinos.
18.00	*Papadia. II*	Alonissos.
18.20	*Skopelos*	Alonissos. Evia (Kimi). Limnos.
23.20	*Lemnos*	Alonissos.

⑦
02.30	*Macedon*	Alonissos.
05.40	*Macedon*	Skopelos (Glossa). Skiathos. Ag. Konstantinos.
07.15	*Lemnos*	Skiathos. Volos.
14.00	*Papadia. II*	Skopelos (Glossa). Skiathos. Volos.
16.50	*Macedon*	Alonissos.
17.00	*Skopelos*	Skiathos. Volos.
18.50	*Macedon*	Skiathos. Ag. Konstantinos.
23.35	*Lemnos*	Alonissos.

🐬 *Flying Dolphins* include:
ⓓ
06.55	Thessalonikia.
x 8	Volos. / Agios Konstantinos.
x 8	Alonissos.
x 4	Skopelos (Glossa).

ⓓ ex ③ (High Season only)
| 10.30 | Alonissos. Skyros. |

Skopelos (Glossa)

Northern Aegean
p. 344

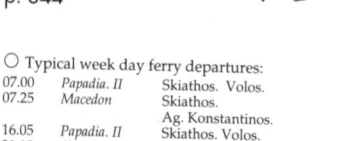

○ Typical week day ferry departures:
07.00	*Papadia. II*	Skiathos. Volos.
07.25	*Macedon*	Skiathos. Ag. Konstantinos.
16.05	*Papadia. II*	Skiathos. Volos.
21.10	*Skopelos*	Skopelos. Alonissos. Skiathos. Volos.

③
| 11.50 | *Skopelos* | Skopelos. Alonissos. Evia (Kimi). |

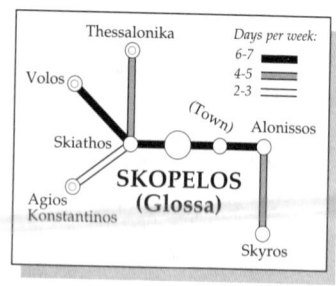

Thessalonika

Days per week:
6-7
4-5
2-3

Volos

(Town)

Alonissos

Skiathos

**SKOPELOS
(Glossa)**

Agios
Konstantinos

Skyros

⑥
07.00	*Papadia. II*	Skiathos. Volos.
07.30	*Macedon*	Skiathos. Volos.
16.00	*Skopelos*	Skopelos. Alonissos.
17.00	*Skopelos*	Skopelos. Alonissos. Evia (Kimi). Limnos.

⑦
00.20	*Macedon*	Skopelos. Alonissos.
07.25	*Macedon*	Skopelos. Agios Konstantinos.
11.30	*Papadia. II*	Skopelos.
15.25	*Lemnos*	Skopelos. Volos.
21.35	*Papadia. II*	Skopelos. Alonissos. Skopelos (Glossa).

🐬 *Flying Dolphins* include:
ⓓ
| 07.30 | Skiathos. Thessalonika. |
| x 6 | Volos. / Skopelos. Alonissos. |

Skyros

Northern Aegean
p. 345

ⓓ ex ⑦
| 08.00 | *Lykomides* | Evia (Kimi). |
| 14.00 | *Lykomides* | Evia (Kimi). |

②
| 01.50 | *Anemos* | Tinos. Mykonos. Paros. Santorini. Crete (Iraklion). |

④
| 03.30 | *Alcaeos* | Agios Efstratios. Limnos. Kavala. |
| 09.20 | *Anemos* | Mykonos. Paros. Santorini. Crete (Iraklion). |

⑤
| 00.30 | *Alcaeos* | Rafina. |

⑦
| 10.00 | *Lykomides* | Evia (Kimi). |
| 16.00 | *Lykomides* | Evia (Kimi). |

🐬 *Flying Dolphins:*
② ③ ⑤ ⑥ ⑦
| 17.00 | Alonissos. Skopelos. Skopelos (Glossa). Skiathos. Volos. |

SKYROS

Volos — Thessalonika
Alonissos
Skiathos (Glossa) — Skopelos (Town)

Evia (Kimi)

Tinos
Mykonos
Paros
Santorini
Crete (Iraklion)

Days per week:
6-7
4-5
1

Spetses

Argo-Saronic p. 379

ⓓ
10.00 *Alexandros M* Kosta.
13.00 *Alexandros M* Kosta.
13.00 *Methodia* Porto Helio.
13.30 *Eftichia* Ermioni. Hydra. Poros. Methana. Aegina. Piraeus.
14.00 *Methodia* Hydra. Poros. Methana. Aegina. Piraeus.
14.45 *Georgios* Poros. Methana. Aegina. Piraeus.
16.30 *Alexandros M* Kosta.

① ② ③ ④ ⑤
06.20 *Alexandros M* Kosta.
07.20 *Alexandros M* Kosta.
18.00 *Alexandros M* Kosta.

 Flying Dolphins:
ⓓ x 6 Poros. Piraeus (Zea).

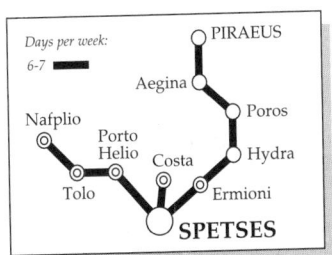

SPETSES

Symi

Dodecanese p. 292

ⓓ
06.00 *Symi I* Rhodes.

①
10.55 ILIO H/F Kos.
13.25 *Nissos Kalimnos* Rhodes. Kastelorizo.
16.40 ILIO H/F Rhodes. Kos. Kalimnos.

②
09.55 ILIO H/F Tilos. Rhodes.
10.00 *Romilda* Rhodes. Kastelorizo.
12.00 *Nissos Kalimnos* Tilos. Nissiros. Kos. Kalimnos.
17.45 ILIO H/F Nissiros. Kos. Kalimnos.

③
01.15 *Romilda* Tilos. Nissiros. Kos. Kalimnos. Leros. Lipsi. Patmos. Naxos. Paros. Syros. Piraeus.
10.55 ILIO H/F Nissiros. Kos.
13.00 Ventouris SL Rhodes. Chalki. Karpathos (Diafani). Karpathos (Town). Kassos. Crete (Sitia). Crete (Agios Nikolaos). Santorini. Sikinos. Folegandros. Milos. Sifnos. Piraeus.
16.45 ILIO H/F Rhodes. Kos. Kalimnos.

④
10.55 ILIO H/F Kos.
16.40 ILIO H/F Rhodes.
18.55 ILIO H/F Kos. Kalimnos.

⑤
13.25 *Nissos Kalimnos* Rhodes. Kastelorizo.

⑥
10.55 ILIO H/F Tilos. Nissiros. Kos.
12.00 *Nissos Kalimnos* Tilos. Nissiros. Kos. Kalimnos.
16.40 ILIO H/F Rhodes.

⑦
18.20 ILIO H/F Rhodes. Kos. Kalimnos.
20.00 *Symi II* Rhodes.

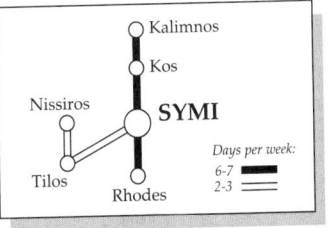

SYMI

Syros

Cyclades North
p. 189

①
| 12.10 | *Panagia Tinou 2* | Tinos. Mykonos. |
| 16.30 | *Panagia Tinou 2* | Piraeus. |

①
02.20	*Panagia Tinou 2*	Piraeus.
05.15	*Dimitra*	Mykonos.
06.00	ILIO H/F	Paros. Mykonos. Tinos. Tinos (Isternia). Andros (Batsi). Rafina.
07.00	ILIO H/F	Tinos. Mykonos. Paros. Naxos. Ios. Santorini.
07.15	*Express Paros*	Mykonos. Paros. Naxos. Ios. Santorini.
09.00	*Dimitra*	Piraeus.
12.50	*Naias II*	Tinos. Mykonos.
13.30	*Ergina*	Piraeus.
16.50	*Naias II*	Piraeus.
18.30	*Romilda*	Paros. Naxos. Patmos. Lipsi. Leros. Kalimnos. Kos. Nissiros. Tilos. Symi. Rhodes. Kastelorizo.
19.50	*Ionian Sea*	Paros. Kos. Rhodes.
20.30	*Dimitra*	Mykonos. Amorgos (Katapola). Amorgos (Egiali). Astipalea.

②
02.20	*Panagia Tinou 2*	Piraeus.
03.00	*Express Santorini*	Paros. Naxos. Ios. Santorini. Anafi.
07.20	ILIO H/F	Mykonos. Paros. Naxos. Ios. Santorini. Anafi.
09.00	*Dimitra*	Piraeus.
12.20	*Naias II*	Tinos. Mykonos.
15.00	*Express Santorini*	Piraeus.
15.00	*Nearchos*	Paros. Ios. Santorini. Crete (Iraklion).
15.45	*Naias II*	Piraeus.
22.00	*Dimitra*	Mykonos. Ikaria (Agios Kyrikos). Fourni. Samos (Karlovassi). Samos (Vathi).

③
07.00	ILIO H/F	Tinos. Mykonos. Paros. Naxos. Ios. Santorini. Iraklia. Schinoussa. Koufonissia. Amorgos (Egiali). Amorgos (Katapola).
07.15	*Express Paros*	Mykonos. Paros. Naxos. Ios. Santorini.
11.30	*Catamaran II*	Paros. Naxos. Iraklia. Schinoussa. Koufonissia. Amorgos (Katapola).
13.00	*Dimitra*	Piraeus.
18.50	*Catamaran II*	Mykonos. Tinos. Andros. Rafina.

19.30	*Romilda*	Piraeus.
19.50	*Ionian Sea*	Paros. Kos. Rhodes.
21.55	*Express Olympia*	Paros. Naxos. Donoussa. Amorgos (Egiali). Amorgos (Katapola).
23.25	*Naias II*	Mykonos. Piraeus.

④
00.30	*Dimitra*	Mykonos. Donoussa. Koufonissia. Amorgos (Katapola). Amorgos (Egiali). Astipalea.
07.20	ILIO H/F	Mykonos. Paros. Naxos. Ios. Santorini.
12.30	*Express Olympia*	Piraeus.
12.50	*Naias II*	Tinos. Mykonos.
16.50	*Naias II*	Piraeus.
19.30	*Dimitra*	Piraeus.

⑤
00.30	*Apollo Express 2*	Paros. Naxos. Ios. Sikinos. Folegandros. Santorini.
02.20	*Panagia Tinou 2*	Piraeus.
06.15	*Anemos*	Thessalonika.
07.15	*Express Paros*	Mykonos. Paros. Naxos. Ios. Santorini.
07.20	ILIO H/F	Mykonos. Paros. Naxos. Ios. Santorini.
13.30	*Apollo Express 2*	Piraeus.
19.30	*Ionian Sea*	Paros. Astipalea. Kalimnos. Kos. Nissiros. Tilos. Rhodes.
20.30	*Dimitra*	Tinos. Mykonos. Piraeus.
21.20	*Apollo Express 1*	Paros. Naxos. Ios. Santorini. Anafi.
23.25	*Naias II*	Mykonos. Piraeus.

⑥
| 12.20 | *Naias II* | Tinos. Mykonos. |
| 15.45 | *Naias II* | Piraeus. |

PIRAEUS Rafina

Days per week:
6-7
4-5
2-3

Tinos

SYROS Mykonos

Naxos

Amorgos

Paros

Ira

Ios Sch

Sikinos Kou

Folegandros

Santorini

Astipalea

⑦
00.45	*Panagia Tinou 2*	Mykonos. Piraeus.
04.45	*Ionian Sea*	Piraeus.
07.15	*Express Paros*	Mykonos. Paros. Naxos. Ios. Santorini.
12.00	*Dimitra*	Tinos. Piraeus.
15.20	*Ionian Sea*	Paros. Naxos. Amorgos (Egiali). Amorgos (Katapola).
18.00	ILIO H/F	Mykonos. Tinos. Rafina.
19.00	*Ergina*	Paros. Naxos. Iraklia. Schinoussa. Koufonissia. Amorgos (Katapola). Amorgos (Egiali). Astipalea.

Tekirdağ

Turkey p. 423

⑤ ⑦
14.00	TML	Marmara. Avşa. Erdek.

Thassos (Skala Prinos)

Northern Aegean p. 351

Ⓓ
06.00 07.20 12.00
14.15 16.00 18.00 19.00
ANET Line   Kavala.

10.30 14.30 19.00
ANET Line   Nea Peramos.

Thassos (Town)

Ⓓ
05.45 08.15 10.15 12.15
14.00 15.30 16.30 17.30
18.30 19.30 20.30 21.30
ANET Line   Keramoti.

07.50 13.20 14.50 19.20
Santa Line   Kavala.

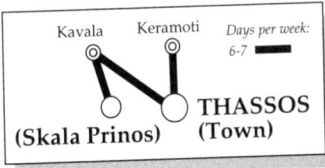

Kavala   Keramoti   *Days per week:*
6-7 ▬

THASSOS
(Skala Prinos)   (Town)

Thessalonika

Northern Aegean p. 352

①
17.00	*Anemos*	Skiathos. Skyros. Tinos. Mykonos. Paros. Santorini. Crete (Iraklion).
20.30	*Alcaeos*	Limnos. Lesbos (Mytilini). Chios. Piraeus.

②
08.00	*Macedon*	Skopelos. Skiathos. Evia (Orei). Ag. Konstantinos.

③
21.00	*Anemos*	Skyros. Mykonos. Paros. Santorini. Crete (Iraklion).
24.00	*Sappho*	Limnos. Lesbos (Mytilini). Chios. Piraeus.

④
06.00	*Lemnos*	Skopelos. Skopelos (Glossa). Skiathos. Volos.

⑤
17.00	*Vergina Sky*	Tinos. Limassol. Haifa. Port Said.
21.00	*Anemos*	Tinos. Mykonos. Paros. Santorini. Crete (Iraklion).

⑥
07.45	*Lemnos*	Skopelos. Skiathos. Volos.
15.00	*Patmos*	Kos. Rhodes.
24.00	*Mytilene*	Limnos. Lesbos (Mytilini). Chios. Piraeus.

Flying Dolphins:
Ⓓ
16.00   Skiathos. Skopelos. Glossa. Alonissos.

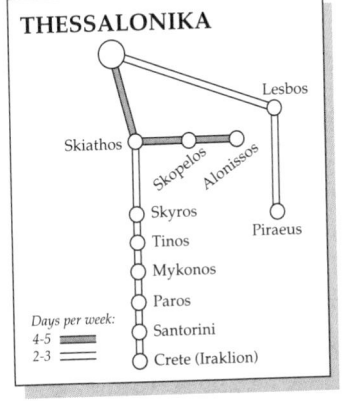

THESSALONIKA

Lesbos

Skiathos

Skopelos   Alonissos

Skyros

Piraeus

Tinos

Mykonos

Paros

Days per week:
4-5 ▬▬
2-3 ═══

Santorini

Crete (Iraklion)

Thirasia

Cyclades Central p. 165

ⓓ
| 16.00 | Theoskepasti | Santorini (Oia). Santorini (Old Port). Santorini. |

ⓖ
| 07.45 | Poseidon Ex. | Ios. Naxos. Paros. Piraeus. |

Tilos

Dodecanese p. 293

①
| 11.05 | Nissos Kalimnos | Symi. Rhodes. Kastelorizo. |

②
08.15	Romilda	Symi. Rhodes. Kastelorizo.
10.55	ILIO H/F	Rhodes.
14.25	Nissos Kalimnos	Nissiros. Kos. Kalimnos.
16.45	ILIO H/F	Symi. Nissiros. Kos. Kalimnos.

③
| 03.10 | Romilda | Nissiros. Kos. Kalimnos. Leros. Lipsi. Patmos. Naxos. Paros. Syros. Piraeus. |
| 16.20 | Hydrofoil | Kos. |

⑤
| 11.05 | Nissos Kalimnos | Symi. Rhodes. Kastelorizo. |

⑥
08.45	Ionian Sea	Rhodes.
11.55	ILIO H/F	Nissiros. Kos.
14.25	Nissos Kalimnos	Nissiros. Kos. Kalimnos.
15.40	ILIO H/F	Symi. Rhodes.
15.45	Ionian Sea	Nissiros. Kos. Kalimnos. Astipalea. Paros. Syros. Piraeus.

⑦
| 15.20 | ILIO H/F | Chalki. Rhodes. Symi. |

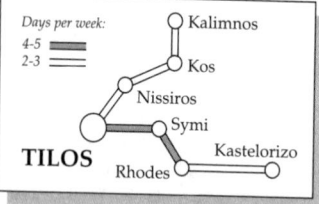

Days per week:
4-5 ═══
2-3 ═══

TILOS

Kalimnos
Kos
Nissiros
Symi
Kastelorizo
Rhodes

Tinos

Cyclades North p. 192

ⓓ
09.00	Megalochori	Mykonos. Delos.
13.05	Panagia Tinou 2	Mykonos.
15.35	Panagia Tinou 2	Syros. Piraeus.

①
07.30	ILIO H/F	Mykonos. Paros. Naxos. Ios. Santorini.
08.00	Catamaran II	Mykonos. Andros (Batsi). Rafina.
08.20	ILIO H/F	Tinos (Isternia). Andros (Batsi). Rafina.
09.00	Super Ferry	Andros. Rafina.
10.35	ILIO H/F	Mykonos.
11.45	Penelope A	Mykonos.
13.00	ILIO H/F	Mykonos.
13.45	Naias II	Mykonos.
14.15	ILIO H/F	Rafina.
15.00	Penelope A	Andros. Rafina.
15.15	ILIO H/F	Mykonos.
15.55	Naias II	Syros. Piraeus.
16.45	Bari Express	Mykonos.
17.00	ILIO H/F	Andros (Batsi). Rafina.
18.50	Catamaran II	Mykonos.
19.00	Bari Express	Andros. Rafina.
19.00	ILIO H/F	Mykonos. Paros. Naxos.
20.00	Catamaran II	Andros (Batsi). Rafina.
20.50	ILIO H/F	Syros.

②
06.55	Anemos	Mykonos. Paros. Santorini. Crete (Iraklion).
09.00	Super Ferry	Andros. Rafina.
09.30	ILIO H/F	Andros (Batsi). Rafina.
10.10	Catamaran II	Mykonos.
10.15	ILIO H/F	Mykonos. Paros. Naxos.
11.20	Catamaran II	Andros (Batsi). Rafina.
11.45	Penelope A	Mykonos.
13.15	Naias II	Mykonos.
14.50	Naias II	Syros. Piraeus.
15.00	Penelope A	Andros. Rafina.
16.45	Bari Express	Mykonos.
17.00	ILIO H/F	Andros (Batsi). Rafina.
18.50	Catamaran II	Mykonos.
19.00	Bari Express	Andros. Rafina.
20.00	Catamaran II	Andros (Batsi). Rafina.
20.50	ILIO H/F	Syros.

③
05.20	Anemos	Skiathos. Thessalonika.
07.30	ILIO H/F	Mykonos. Paros. Naxos. Ios. Santorini. Iraklia. Schinoussa. Koufonissia. Amorgos (Egiali). Amorgos (Katapola).
09.00	Super Ferry	Andros. Rafina.
10.10	Catamaran II	Mykonos. Syros. Paros. Naxos. Iraklia. Schinoussa.Koufonissia. Amorgos (Katapola).
10.35	ILIO H/F	Mykonos.
11.45	Penelope A	Mykonos.
12.30	Naias II	Mykonos.
13.10	ILIO H/F	Mykonos.

14.00	*Naias II*	Piraeus.
14.15	ILIO H/F	Rafina.
15.00	*Penelope A*	Andros. Rafina.
15.15	ILIO H/F	Mykonos.
16.45	*Bari Express*	Mykonos.
17.00	ILIO H/F	Andros (Batsi). Rafina.
20.00	*Catamaran II*	Andros (Batsi). Rafina.
20.50	ILIO H/F	Syros.

④

09.00	*Bari Express*	Andros. Rafina.
09.30	ILIO H/F	Andros (Batsi). Rafina.
10.10	*Catamaran II*	Mykonos.
10.15	ILIO H/F	Mykonos. Paros. Naxos. Iraklia. Schinoussa. Koufonissia. Amorgos (Egiali).
11.20	*Catamaran II*	Andros (Batsi). Rafina.
11.45	*Super Ferry*	Mykonos.
13.30	*Super Ferry*	Andros. Rafina.
13.45	*Naias II*	Mykonos.
15.55	*Naias II*	Syros. Piraeus.
18.00	ILIO H/F	Andros (Batsi). Rafina.
18.50	*Catamaran II*	Mykonos.
20.00	*Catamaran II*	Andros (Batsi). Rafina.
20.45	*Penelope A*	Mykonos.
20.50	ILIO H/F	Syros.
22.15	*Super Ferry*	Mykonos. Rafina.

⑤

10.10	*Catamaran II*	Mykonos.
10.15	ILIO H/F	Mykonos. Paros. Naxos.
11.20	*Catamaran II*	Andros (Batsi). Rafina.
11.30	*Penelope A*	Andros. Rafina.
11.45	*Super Ferry*	Mykonos.
12.30	*Naias II*	Mykonos.
13.00	ILIO H/F	Mykonos.
14.00	*Naias II*	Piraeus.
15.30	ILIO H/F	Syros.
18.50	*Catamaran II*	Mykonos.
20.00	*Catamaran II*	Andros (Batsi). Rafina.
20.00	ILIO H/F	Skala Oropou. Evia (Chalcis).
20.50	ILIO H/F	Syros.
21.30	*Dimitra*	Mykonos. Piraeus.

⑥

09.15	*Anemos*	Mykonos. Paros. Santorini. Crete (Iraklion).
09.20	ILIO H/F	Mykonos.
10.10	*Catamaran II*	Mykonos.
10.15	ILIO H/F	Mykonos. Paros. Naxos.
11.20	*Catamaran II*	Andros (Batsi). Rafina.
11.20	ILIO H/F	Mykonos.
11.25	ILIO H/F	Andros (Batsi). Rafina.
11.30	*Penelope A*	Andros. Rafina.
11.45	*Super Ferry*	Mykonos.
12.00	*Vergina Sky*	Limassol. Haifa. Port Said.
13.15	*Naias II*	Mykonos.
13.45	ILIO H/F	Andros (Batsi). Rafina.
14.50	*Naias II*	Syros. Piraeus.
15.00	*Super Ferry*	Andros. Rafina.
15.15	ILIO H/F	Mykonos.
17.00	*Bari Express*	Andros. Rafina.
17.00	ILIO H/F	Evia (Karystos). Rafina.
18.30	ILIO H/F	Mykonos.
18.50	*Catamaran II*	Mykonos.
19.30	ILIO H/F	Evia (Karystos). Rafina.
20.00	*Catamaran II*	Andros (Batsi). Rafina.
20.35	ILIO H/F	Mykonos. Rafina.
20.45	*Penelope A*	Mykonos.
24.00	*Dimitra*	Mykonos. Lipsi. Patmos.

⑦

07.25	*Anemos*	Skiathos. Thessalonika.
10.10	*Catamaran II*	Mykonos.
10.15	ILIO H/F	Mykonos. Paros. Naxos.
11.00	ILIO H/F	Mykonos.
11.20	*Catamaran II*	Andros (Batsi). Rafina.
11.45	*Super Ferry*	Mykonos.
12.30	*Naias II*	Mykonos.
13.00	*Bari Express*	Andros. Rafina.
13.00	*Dimitra*	Piraeus.
13.45	ILIO H/F	Tinos (Isternia). Andros (Batsi). Rafina.
14.00	*Naias II*	Piraeus.
14.30	*Super Ferry*	Andros. Rafina.
15.30	*Penelope A*	Andros. Rafina.
17.00	ILIO H/F	Andros (Batsi). Rafina.
18.50	*Catamaran II*	Mykonos.
19.30	ILIO H/F	Rafina.
20.00	*Catamaran II*	Andros (Batsi). Rafina.
21.15	*Penelope A*	Mykonos.
22.15	*Bari Express*	Rafina.

Tinos (Isternia)

①

08.40	ILIO H/F	Andros (Batsi). Rafina.

⑥

20.10	ILIO H/F	Tinos. Mykonos. Rafina.

⑦

14.05	ILIO H/F	Andros (Batsi). Rafina.

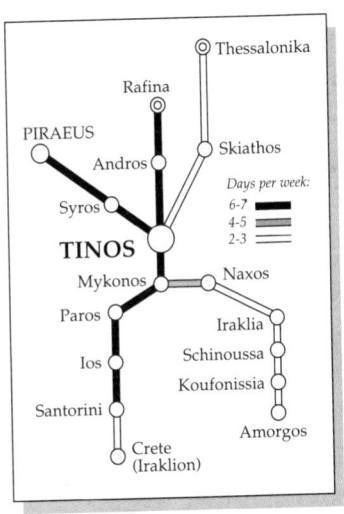

Thessalonika

Rafina

PIRAEUS

Andros

Skiathos

Syros

Days per week:
6-7
4-5
2-3

TINOS

Mykonos

Naxos

Paros

Iraklia

Ios

Schinoussa

Koufonissia

Santorini

Amorgos

Crete (Iraklion)

Trieste

Italy p. 89

②
13.00 Adriatica Durres.

④
13.00 *Lato* Igoumenitsa. Patras.

⑤
13.00 Adriatica Durres.

⑥
13.30 *El. Venizelos* Ancona. Igoumenitsa.
Corfu. Patras.

Valona

Albania p. 89

Ⓓ
14.00 *European Glory* Brindisi. Corfu.

Venice

Italy p. 89

⑥
19.00 *Samsum* Çeşme.
21.00 *Ankara* Izmir.

Volos

Northern Aegean p. 355

🐟 *Flying Dolphins* include:

Ⓓ x 4
Skiathos. Skopelos (Glossa).
Skopelos. Alonissos.

Ⓓ Typical (ex ⑦):
08.00 *Papadia. II* Skiathos. Skopelos.
08.00 *Skopelos* Skiathos. Skopelos.
17.30 *Papadia. II* Skiathos. Skopelos (Glossa).
Skopelos. Alonissos.
18.00 *Skopelos* Skiathos. Skopelos.
Alonissos.

②
08.00 *Papadia. II* Skiathos. Skopelos.
08.00 *Skopelos* Skiathos. Skopelos.
17.30 *Papadia. II* Skiathos. Skopelos (Glossa).
Skopelos. Alonissos.
18.00 *Skopelos* Skiathos. Skopelos. Alonissos.

③
08.00 *Skopelos* Skiathos. Skopelos (Glossa).
Skopelos. Alonissos.
Evia (Kimi).

20.30 *Lemnos* Skiathos. Skopelos.
Thessalonika.

⑤
19.30 *Lemnos* Skiathos. Skopelos.
Thessalonika.

⑥
13.00 *Skopelos* Skiathos. Skopelos (Glossa).
Skopelos. Alonissos.
Evia (Kimi). Limnos.

⑦
12.00 *Lemnos* Skiathos. Skopelos (Glossa).
19.00 *Alcaeos* Lesbos (Mytilini).
19.00 *Lemnos* Skiathos. Skopelos. Alonissos.

Zakinthos / Zante (Town)

Ionian Line p. 400

Ⓓ
05.30 08.00 09.00
10.45 13.00 14.30
18.00 19.45
Dimitrius Miras
Proteos
Zakinthos I Kilini.

Ⓓ
07.55 *Europe 2* Kefalonia (Argostoli). Patras.

②
18.20 *Europe 1* Kefalonia (Poros).
Kefalonia (Sami). Ithaca.

○
00.00 *Europe H/F* Katakolon.

Zakinthos / Zante (Skinari)

Ionian Line p. 402

Ⓓ
09.15 *Ionion Pelagos* Kefalonia (Pessada).
18.30 *Ionion Pelagos* Kefalonia (Pessada).

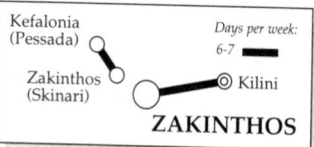

Kefalonia
(Pessada)

Zakinthos
(Skinari)

Days per week:
6-7 ▬▬

Kilini

ZAKINTHOS

Ferry Companies: UK Agents

Agent	Line
Amathus (UK) Ltd. 51 Tottenham Court Road, London. W1 0HS ☎ 071 636 6158	Hellenic Mediterranean Lines Co. Ltd.
Golden Sun Holidays 15 Kentish Town Road, London. NW1 8NH ☎ 071 267 2657 Fax 071 267 6138	Arkadia Lines
Hellenic MacTravel Ltd. 36 King Street, London. WC2 8JS ☎ 071 836 8216	G.A. Ferries
Magnum Travel 729 Green Lane, Winchmore Hill, London. N21 3RZ ☎ 081 360 5353	Minoan Lines
Serena Holidays 40 Kenway Rd, London. SW5 0RA ☎ 071 244 8422	Adriatica
Sunquest Holiday Ltd. 9 Grand Parade, Green Lanes, London. N4 1JX ☎ 071 499 9991	Turkish Maritime Lines
Viamare Travel Ltd. Graphic House, 2 Sumatra House, London. NW6 1PU ☎ 071 431 4560 Fax 071 431 5456	AK Ventouris, Arkadia Lines, ANEK, European Seaways, Fragline, Louis Shipping, Marlines, Poseidon Lines, Stability Lines, Strintzis Lines, Ventouris Ferries

Main Ferry Companies

Company   **Logo**

ADRIATICA de Navigazione S.p.A. **1**
30123 Venezia, ITALY.
Zattere 1411. P.O.B. 705
☎ (041) 781611
Tlx 410045 ADRNAV I

Egitto Express, Laurana, Palladio, Sansovino, Tiepolo, Tiziano.

AGAPITOS EXPRESS FERRIES **16**
99, Kolokotroni Street
185 35 PIRAEUS (2nd floor)
☎ (01) 4130566, 4123159
Tlx 24-1679

Aegeon, Express Olympia, Express Santorini.

AGAPITOS LINES **15**
99, Kolokotroni Street
185 35 PIRAEUS (1st floor)
☎ (01) 4136246, 4134931
Tlx 21-3230

Golden Vergina, Naias II.

A.K. VENTOURIS **8**
73 Possidonos Av.
175 62 P. Faliro, Greece.
☎ (01) 9389280
Fax (01) 9389289

Agia Methodia, Anna V, Igoumenitsa Express.

ANEK LINES **27**
N. Plastira-Apokoronou
CHANIA
☎ (0821) 51915-18, 53394-97
Tlx 291-106
Fax (0821) 44911

Aptera, El. Venizelos, Kantia, Kriti, Kydon, Lato, Lissos, Rethimno.

ARKADIA LINES **18**
Akti Miaouli 93, PIRAEUS
☎ (01) 4186583-89
Tlx 241077
Fax 4516945

Dimitrios Express, Ioannis Express, Paloma, Poseidon Express, Samaina.

DANE **19**
(DODEKANISSIAKI SHIPPING Co)
Parodos Amerikis, 851 00 RODOS
☎ (0241) 30930

Iylassos, Kamiros, Patmos, Rodos.

G.A. FERRIES **22**
Akti Kondili & 2, Aitolikou
PIRAEUS
☎ (01) 4110007, 4110254
Tlx 241986
Fax 4232383

Daliana, Dimitra, Marina, Milena, Rodanthi, Romilda.

GOUTOS G. **24**
43, Konitsis Street,
152 35 ATHENS
☎ 8028334
Tlx 21-3507

Karistos, Marmari I, Myrina Express, Papadiamantis II.

**HELLENIC MEDITERRANEAN
LINES Co. Ltd.** **7**
Electric Railway Station Building,
P.O. Box 80057, 18510 Piraeus, Greece.
☎ (01) 4174341-5
Tlx 21 2517

Apollonia II, Egnatia, Lydia, Media II, Poseidonia.

Company	Logo

LINDOS SHIPPING Co.   **20**
4, Akti Tzelepi,
185 31 PIRAEUS
☎ (01) 4121679, 4113956
Tlx 21-3565

Laburnum, Milos Express.

LOUCAS NOMIKOS SONS   **29**
120, Karaiskou Street,
185 35 PIRAEUS
☎ (01) 4172415, 4178080
Tlx 21-2446

Anemos, Lemnos, Macedon, Skopelos.

LOUIS CRUISE LINES   **14**
54-58 Evagoras Avenue,
P.O. Box 1301
Nicosia, Cyprus.
☎ (02) 442114 Tlx 2341

*Princesa Amorosa, Princesa Cypria,
Princesa Marissa.*

MARITIME Co. of LESVOS S.A.   **23**
47, Kountouriotou Street,
811 00 Mytilini, LESBOS
☎ (0251) 23097, 29087 Tlx 297-152

Agios Rafail, Alcaeos, Mytilene, Sappho.

MARLINES   **6**
38 Akti Possidonas
185 31 Piraeus, Greece.
☎ (01) 411 0777 Tlx 241691

*Baroness M, Countess M, Crown M, Dame M,
Duchess M, Grace M, Vicountess M.*

MEDITERRANEAN LINES   **10**
Alkiviadou 271, 185 36
Piraeus, Greece.
☎ (01) 4531882
Tlx 211888 DEK GR

Raffaello, Valentino.

MINOAN LINES S.A.   **28**
28, Akti Possidonos, PIRAEUS
☎ (01) 4118211-6 Tlx 21-3265
Passenger Office and Bus Terminal:
2, Leoforos Vassileos Konstantinou (Stadion)
116 35 Athens, Greece.
☎ 7512356 Tlx 215582 Fax (01) 7520540

*Aretousa, Ariadne, Daedalus, El Greco, Erotokritos,
Fedra, Festos, King Minos, Knossos, N. Kazantzakis.*

POSEIDON LINES   **3**
166 73 Voula, Athens, Greece.
☎ 8958923 Tlx 215926

Sea Harmony, Sea Serenade, Sea Wave.

RETHIMNIAKI S.A.   **26**
2 Akti Possidonos, Piraeus, Greece.
☎ (01) 4177770 Fax 4178980

Arkadi, Preveli.

STRINTZIS LINES   **4**
26 Akti Possidonos, 185 31 Piraeus, Greece.
☎ (01) 4129815 Tlx 241401

*Delos, Eptanisos, Ionian Galaxy, Ionian Island,
Ionian Sea, Ionian Star, Ionian Sun, Super Ferry II.*

VENTOURIS FERRIES   **2**
91 Pireos Av. & Kithiron 2
185 41 Piraeus, Greece.
☎ (01) 4825815 Tlx 212564 KOVE GR

*Agios Nektarios, Athens Express, Bari Express,
Methodia, Pegasus, Pollux, Poros Express,
Saturnus, Vega, Venus.*

VENTOURIS SEA LINES   **17**
Address: see VENTOURIS FERRIES
☎ (01) 4828001-7, 4825815-9
Tlx 21-2564 Fax 4813701

*Apollo Express 1, Apollo Express 2, Artemis,
Ergina, Georgios Express, Panagia Tinou 2.*

Ferry Company Colours

International Ferry Liveries:

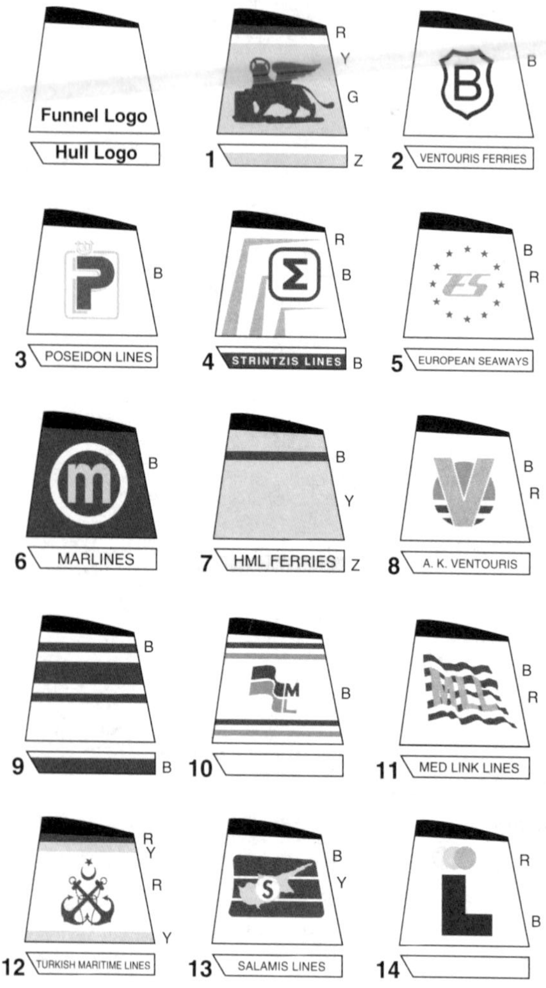
Funnel Logo
Hull Logo
1 R Y G Z
2 B VENTOURIS FERRIES
3 B POSEIDON LINES
4 R B STRINTZIS LINES B
5 B R EUROPEAN SEAWAYS
6 B MARLINES
7 B Y HML FERRIES Z
8 B R A. K. VENTOURIS
9 B B
10 B
11 B R MED LINK LINES
12 R Y R Y TURKISH MARITIME LINES
13 B Y SALAMIS LINES
14 R B

Ferry	Logo
Agia Methodia	8
Agios Nektarios	2
Agios Rafail	23
Alcaeos	23
Anemos	29
Ankara	12
Anna V	8
Aphrodite II	11
Apollo Express 1	17
Apollo Express 2	17
Apollonia II	7
Aptera	27
Aretousa	28
Ariadne	28
Arkadi	26
Artemis	17
Athens Express	2
Bari Express	2
Baroness M	6
Countess M	6
Crown M	6
Daedalus	28
Daliana	22
Delos	4
Dimitra	22
Dimitrios Ex.	18
Duchess M	6
Egitto Express	1
Egnatia	7
El Greco	28
El. Venizelos	27
Eolos	9
Eptanisos	4
Ergina	17
Erotokritos	28
Espresso Grecia	1
Espresso Venezia	1
European Glory	5
European Pride	5
European Spirit	5
Express Olympia	16
Express Santorini	16
Fedra	28
Festos (Phestos)	28
Georgios Express	17
Golden Vergina	15
Grace M	6
Ialyssos	19
Igoumenitsa Ex.	8
Ionian Galaxy	4
Ionian Island	4
Ionian Sea/Star	4
Kamiros	19
Kantia (Candia)	27
Kapetan Alexand.	21
King Minos	28

COLOUR KEY: B – BLUE   G – GREEN   O – ORANGE   R – RED   Y – YELLOW   Z – GREY

Greek Domestic/International Ferry Liveries:

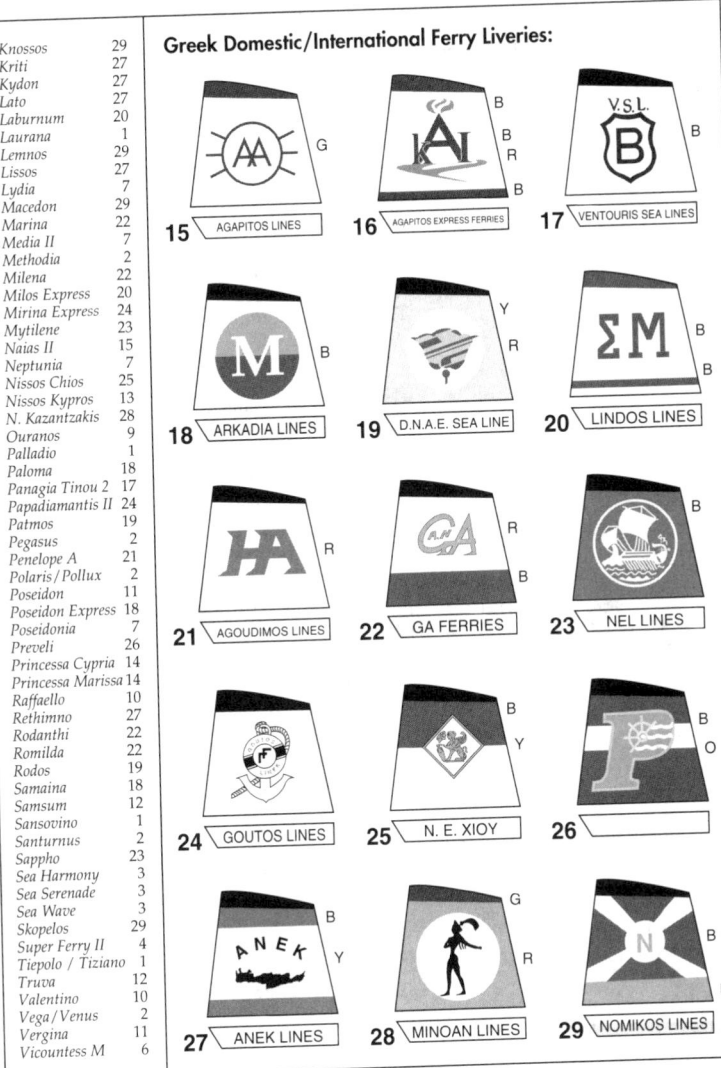

15 AGAPITOS LINES — G

16 AGAPITOS EXPRESS FERRIES — B, R, B

17 VENTOURIS SEA LINES — B (V.S.L.)

18 ARKADIA LINES — B

19 D.N.A.E. SEA LINE — Y, R

20 LINDOS LINES — B, B (ΣΜ)

21 AGOUDIMOS LINES — R

22 GA FERRIES — R, B

23 NEL LINES — B

24 GOUTOS LINES

25 N. E. XIOY — B, Y

26 — B, O (P)

27 ANEK LINES — B, Y

28 MINOAN LINES — G, R

29 NOMIKOS LINES — B, R, Z

Useful Greek

The Greek Alphabet — Transliteration

Greek Capital	Small	English Equivalent	Name	Pronounced like
Α	α	A	Alpha	cat
Β	β	B/V	Beta	van
Γ	γ	G	Gamma	sugar/yes
Δ	δ	D	Delta	this
Ε	ε	E	Epsilon	egg
Ζ	ζ	Z	Zeta	zoo
Η	η	E	Eta	feet
Θ	θ	TH	Theta	thick
Ι	ι	I	Iota	feet
Κ	κ	K	Kappa	king
Λ	λ	L	Lamtha	long
Μ	μ	M	Mu	man
Ν	ν	N	Nu	not
Ξ	ξ	TS/KS	Tsi/Xi	box
Ο	ο	O	O-mikron	dot
Π	π	P	Pi	pick
Ρ	ρ	R	Rho	red
Σ	σ, ς	S	Sigma	sit (ς only at the end of a word)
Τ	τ	T	Tau	tap
Υ	υ	U	Upsilon	meet
Φ	φ	PH/F	Phi	fat
Χ	χ	CH/H	Chi	loch
Ψ	ψ	PS	Psi	lapse
Ω / Ω	ω	O	O-mega	dot

Combinations & Dipthongs

ΑΙ	αι	AI		egg
ΑΥ	αυ	AV/AF		have
ΕΙ	ει	I		seen
ΕΥ	ευ	EV/EF		ever/effort
ΟΙ	οι	I		seen
ΟΥ	ευ	OU		moon
ΓΓ	γγ	NG		go/ring
ΓΚ	γκ	G/NG		go/ring
ΜΠ	μπ	B		boat
ΝΤ	ντ	D/ND		dog/send
ΤΖ	τζ	TS		deeds
ΤΣ	τσ	TS		deeds
ΥΙ	υι	I		seen

Greek Pronunciation English

Basics:

Greek	Pronunciation	English
Ναι	Ne	Yes
Οχι	ochi	No
Παρακαλω	parakalo	Please
Ευχαριστω	efcharisto	Thank You
Με σογχωρειτε	me sinkhorite	Excuse Me
Φυγετε	fiyete	Hop It!
Βοηθεια	voithia	Help!
Γεια σας	yassas (pl.)	Hello/
Γεια σου	yassoo (s.)	Goodbye
Καλησπερα	Kalimera	Good morning
Καληνυχτα	Kalinihta	Good night
Συγνωμη	signomi	Sorry
Ποτε;	pote	When?
Ποσο;	posso	How much?
Που;	pu	Where?

Signs:

Greek	Pronunciation	English
ΑΦΙΤΕΙΣ	Afitese	Arrivals
ΑΝΔΡΩΝ	Andron	Gentlemen
ΑΝΑΧΩΡΗΣΕΙΣ	Anachoresis	Departures
ΓΥΝΑΙΚΩΝ	Ginekon	Ladies
ΕΙΣΟΔΟΣ	Eisodos	Entrance
ΕΞΟΔΟΣ	Exodos	Exit
ΣΤΑΣΙΣ	Stasis	Bus Stop
ΤΟΥΑΛΕΤΕΣ	Toualetes	Toilets
ΦΑΡΜΑΚΕΙΟΝ	Farmakion	Pharmacy
ΖΕΝΟΔΟΧΕΙΟ	zenodokhio	Hotel

Miscellaneous:

Greek	Pronunciation	English
Αγια	Agia	Saint
Αστυνομια	Astinomia	Police Stn.
Εισιτηρια	Isitiria	Tickets
Λεωφορειο	Leoforio	Bus
Λιμανι	Limani	Port
Νησι / Νισι	Nissi	Island
Οδος	Odhos	Street
Πλατεια	Platia	Square
Πλοιο	Plio	Boat/Ferry
Σπηλιο	Spileo	Cave
Τραινο	Treno	Train
Χωριο	Chorio/Chora	Village

Numbers:

Greek	Pronunciation	
Ενας	enas	1
Δυο	deo	2
Τρεις	tris	3
Τεσσεπεις	teseres	4
Πεντε	pende	5
Εξι	exi	6
Επτα	epta	7
Οκτω	okto	8
Εννεα	ennea	9
Δεκα	deka	10
Ενδεκα	andeka	11
Δωδεκα	dodeka	12
Δεκατρια	deka tria	13
Δεκατεσσερα	deka tessera	14
Εικοσι	ikosi	20
Πενηντα	peninda	50
Εκατο	ekato	100
Χιλια	chilia	1000

Days:

Greek	Pronunciation	English
Δευτερα	deftera	Monday
Τριτη	triti	Tuesday
Τεταρτη	tetarti	Wednesday
Πεμπτη	pempti	Thursday
Παρασχευη	paraskevi	Friday
Ζαββατο	savato	Saturday
Κυριακη	kiriaki	Sunday
Σημερα	simera	Today
Αυριω	avrio	Tomorrow
Χθες	hthes	Yesterday

Accommodation:

Greek	Pronunciation	English
Εχετε δωματια	ehete domatia	Do you have rooms?
Θελω ενα	thelo enna	I want a...
μονο	mono	single...
διπλο	thiplo	double...
δωματιο	domatio	room
για	yia	for...
δυο μερεζ	deo meres	two days
τρειζ μερεζ	tris meres	three days

Index

The Thomas Cook Guide to
Greek Island Hopping
Reader's Questionnaire

This guide is intended to be of maximum use to both new and regular island hoppers. We are therefore interested in your views on how it could be improved. Please take a few minutes to fill in this form and let us know how you fared with this publication. A free Thomas Cook book will be sent to you in return for your completed questionnaire. Please send this page to:

The Editor, Greek Island Hopping, Thomas Cook Publishing, PO Box 227, PETERBOROUGH, PE3 8BQ, UK.

1. What exactly did you use this guide to try and find out?

2. Did you use this guide more for pre-planning or for on the spot reference?

3. What would you like to see more of in the guide? (Please number in order of preference)

Sightseeing Information ☐   Expanded Island Descriptions ☐   Hotel / Rooms Descriptions ☐

Port Street Maps ☐   Other _____ ☐

4. Are there any other changes you would like to see made to the guide?

5. Did you take any other guide books with you to the Greek Islands?

(Please specify) _____

6. How many Greek Islands have you visited? [   ]

7. At what time of the year did you visit the Greek Islands with this guide?

From: [   ]   To: [   ]

From: [   ]   To: [   ]

8. Which islands and mainland ports did you visit and how many days did you spend at each?

Island/Port: Days: [   ] [ ]   [   ] [ ]

[   ] [ ]   [   ] [ ]   [   ] [ ]

[   ] [ ]   [   ] [ ]   [   ] [ ]

[   ] [ ]   [   ] [ ]   [   ] [ ]

[   ] [ ]   [   ] [ ]   [   ] [ ]

9. How far in advance would you buy a guidebook to the Greek Islands?

[   ]

10. Which of the following age categories do you fall in to?

Under 21 [ ]   21-30 [ ]   30-40 [ ]   40-55 [ ]   55+ [ ]

Name: [   ]

Address: [   ]

[   ]

[   ]   Post Code: [   ]

Telephone: [   ]   Date: [   ]